THE

COMPLETE POETICAL WORKS

OF

WILLIAM WORDSWORTH

WITH AN INTRODUCTION

BY

JOHN MORLEY

NEW YORK: 46 EAST 14TH STREET.

THOMAS Y. CROWELL & CO.

BOSTON: 100 PURCHASE STREET.

Part 1

Printing Statement:

Due to the very old age and scarcity of this book,
many of the pages may be hard to read due to the
blurring of the original text, possible missing pages,
missing text and other issues beyond our control.

Because this is such an important and rare work, we
believe it is best to reproduce this book regardless of
its original condition.

Thank you for your understanding.

2

WILLIAM WORDSWORTH.

INTRODUCTION.

THE poet whose works are contained in the present volume was born in the little town of Cockermouth, in Cumberland, on April 7, 1770. He died at Rydal Mount in the neighboring county of Westmoreland, on April 23, 1850. In this long span of mortal years, events of vast and enduring moment shook the world. A handful of scattered and dependent colonies in the northern continent of America made themselves into one of the most powerful and beneficent of states. The ancient monarchy of France, and all the old ordering of which the monarchy had been the keystone, was overthrown, and it was not until after many a violent shock of arms, after terrible slaughter of men, after strange diplomatic combinations, after many social convulsions, after many portentous mutations of Empire, that Europe once more settled down for a season into established order and system. In England almost alone, after the loss of her great possessions across the Atlantic Ocean, the fabric of the State stood fast and firm. Yet here, too in these eighty years, an old order slowly gave place to new. The restoration of peace, after a war conducted with extraordinary tenacity and fortitude, led to a still more wonderful display of ingenuity, industry, and enterprise, in the more fruitful field of commerce and of manufactures. Wealth, in spite of occasional vicissitudes, increased with amazing rapidity. The population of England and Wales grew from being seven and a half millions in 1770, to nearly eighteen millions in 1850. Political power was partially transferred from a territorial aristocracy to the middle and trading classes. Laws were made at once more equal and more humane. During all the tumult of the great war which for so many years bathed Europe in fire, through all the throes and agitations in which peace brought forth the new time, Wordsworth for half a century (1799–1850) dwelt sequestered in unbroken composure and steadfastness in his chosen home amid the mountains and lakes of his native region, working out his own ideal of the poet's high office.

The interpretation of life in books and the development of imagination underwent changes of its own. Most of the great lights of the eighteenth century were still burning, though burning low, when Wordsworth came into the world. Pope, indeed, had been dead for six and twenty years, and all the rest of the Queen Anne men had gone. But Gray only died in 1771, and Goldsmith in 1774. Ten years later Johnson's pious and manly heart ceased to beat. Voltaire and Rousseau, those two diverse oracles of their age, both died in 1778. Hume had passed away two years before. Cowper was forty years older than Wordsworth, but Cowper's most delightful work was not produced until 1783. Crabbe, who anticipated Wordsworth's choice of themes from rural life, while treating them with a sterner realism, was virtually his contemporary, having been born in 1754, and dying in 1832. The

wo great names of his own date were Scott and Coleridge, the first born in 1771,
ind the second a year afterwards. Then a generation later came another new
ind illustrious group. Byron was born in 1788, Shelley in 1792, and Keats in
795. Wordsworth was destined to see one more orb of the first purity and
orilliance rise to its place in the poetic firmament. Tennyson's earliest volume of
ooems was published in 1830, and "In Memoriam," one of his two masterpieces,
n 1850. Any one who realizes for how much these famous names will always stand
n the history of human genius, may measure the great transition that Wordsworth's
iighty years witnessed in some of men's deepest feelings about art and life and
'the speaking face of earth and heaven."

Here, too, Wordsworth stood isolated and apart. "Scott and Southey were
valued friends, but he thought little of Scott's poetry, and less of Southey's. Byron
ind Shelley he seems scarcely to have read; and he failed altogether to appreciate
Keats. (*Myers.*) Of Blake's "Songs of Innocence and Experience" he said,
'There is something in the madness of this man which interests me more than the
anity of Lord Byron and Walter Scott." Coleridge was the only man of the shin-
ng company with whom he ever had any real intimacy of mind, for whom he ever
iourished real deference and admiration, as one "unrelentingly possessed by thirst
if greatness, love, and beauty," and in whose intellectual power, as the noble lines
n the Sixth Book of the "Prelude" so gorgeously attest, he took the passionate interest
if a man at once master, disciple, and friend. It is true to say, as Emerson says,
hat Wordsworth's genius was the great exceptional fact of the literature of his
ieriod ; but he had no teachers nor inspirers save nature and solitude.

Wordsworth was the son of a solicitor, and all his early circumstances were
omely, unpretentious, and rather straitened. His mother died when he was
ight years old, and when his father followed her five years later, two of his uncles
orovided means for continuing at Cambridge the education which had been begun
n the rural grammar school of Hawkshead. It was in 1787 that he went up to
it. John's College. He took his Bachelor's degree at the beginning of 1791, and
here his connection with the university ended.

For some years after leaving Cambridge, Wordsworth let himself drift. He did
iot feel good enough for the Church; he shrank from the law; fancying that he
iad talents for command, he thought of being a soldier. Meanwhile, he passed a
bort time desultorily in London. Towards the end of 1791, through Paris, he
oassed on to Orleans and Blois, where he made some friends and spent most of a
'ear. He returned to Paris in October, 1792. France was no longer standing
n the top of golden hours. The September massacres filled the sky with a lurid
lame. Wordsworth still retained his ardent faith in the Revolution, and was even
eady, though no better than "a landsman on the deck of a ship struggling with a
iideous storm," to make common cause with the Girondists. But the prudence of
riends at home forced him back to England before the beginning of the terrible
ear of '93. With his return closed that first survey of its inheritance, which most
erious souls are wont to make in the fervid prime of early manhood.

It would be idle to attempt any commentary on the bare facts that we have just
ecapitulated; for Wordsworth himself has clothed them with their full force and
neaning in the "Prelude." This record of the growth of a poet's mind, told by the
ooet himself with all the sincerity of which he was capable, is never likely to be
oopular. Of that, as of so much more of his poetry, we must say that, as a whole,
: has not the musical, harmonious, sympathetic quality which seizes us in even the
orose of such a book as Rousseau's "Confessions." Macaulay thought the "Prelude"
poorer and more tiresome "Excursion," with the old flimsy philosophy about the
ffect of scenery on the mind, the old crazy mystical metaphysics, and the endless

wildernesses of twaddle; still he admits that there are some fine descriptions and energetic declamations. All Macaulay's tastes and habits of mind made him a poo judge of such a poet as Wordsworth. He valued spirit, energy, pomp, stateli ness of form and diction, and actually thought Dryden's fine lines about to-morrow being falser than the former day, as fine as any eight lines in Lucretius. But hi words truly express the effect of the " Prelude "on more vulgar minds than his own George Eliot, on the other hand, who had the inward eye that was not among Macaulay's gifts, found the " Prelude " full of material for a daily liturgy, and it i: easy to imagine how she lingered as she did, over such a thought as this —

> " There is
> One great society alone on earth:
> The noble Living and the noble Dead."

There is, too, as may be found imbedded even in Wordsworth's dullest work, man a line of the truest poetical quality, such as that on Newton's statue in the silen Chapel of Trinity College —

> "The marble index of a mind forever
> Voyaging through strange seas of Thought alone."

Apart, however, from beautiful lines like this, and from many noble passages c high reflection set to sonorous verse, this remarkable poem is in its whole effec unique in impressive power, as a picture of the advance of an elect and seriou spirit from childhood and school-time, through the ordeal of adolescence, throug close contact with stirring and enormous events, to the stage when it has foun the sources of its strength, and is fully and finally prepared to put its temper to th proof.

The three Books that describe the poet's residence in France have a specia and a striking value of their own. Their presentation of the phases of good men' minds as the successive scenes of the Revolution unfolded themselves, has re: historic interest. More than this, it is an abiding lesson to brave men how to bea themselves in hours of public stress. It portrays exactly that mixture of perseverin faith and hope with firm and reasoned judgment, with which I like to think tha Turgot, if he had lived, would have confronted the workings of the Revolutionar power. Great masters in many kinds have been inspired by the French Revolutior Human genius might seem to have exhausted itself in the burning political passio of Burke, in the glowing melodrama of fire and tears of Carlyle, Michelet, Hugo; bt the ninth, tenth, and eleventh Books of the " Prelude," by their strenuous simplicit; their deep truthfulness, their slowfooted and inexorable transition from ardent hoլ to dark imaginations, sense of woes to come, sorrow for human kind, and pai of heart, breathe the very spirit of the great catastrophe. There is none of th ephemeral glow of the political exhortation, none of the tiresome falsity of th dithyramb in history. Wordsworth might well wish that some dramatic tale, endue with livelier shapes and flinging out less guarded words, might set forth the lessor of his experience. The material was fitting. The story of these three Books h: something of the severity, the self-control, the inexorable necessity of classic traged\ and like classic tragedy it has a noble end. The dregs and sour sediment tha reaction from exaggerated hope is so apt to stir in poor natures, had no place her: The French Revolution made the one crisis in Wordsworth's mental history, the or heavy assault on his continence of soul, and when he emerged from it all his grea less remained to him.   After a long spell of depression, bewilderment, mortification, and sore disappointment, the old faith in new shapes was given back.

> "Nature's self,
> By all varieties of human love
> Assisted, led me back through opening day
> To those sweet counsels between head and heart
> Whence grew that genuine knowledge, fraught with peace,
> Which, through the later sinkings of this cause,
> Hath still upheld me and upholds me now."

It was six years after his return from France before Wordsworth finally settled down in the scenes with which his name and the power of his genius were to be forever associated.   During this interval it was that two great sources of personal influence were opened to him.   He entered upon that close and beloved companionship with his sister, which remained unbroken to the end of their days; and he first made the acquaintance of Coleridge.   The character of Dorothy Wordsworth has long taken its place in the gallery of admirable and devoted women who have inspired the work and the thoughts of great men.   "She is a woman, indeed," said Coleridge, "in mind, I mean, and heart; for her person is such that if you expected to see a pretty woman, you would think her rather ordinary; if you expected to see an ordinary woman, you would think her pretty."   To the solidity, sense, and strong intelligence of the Wordsworth stock, she added a grace, a warmth, and liveliness peculiarly her own.   Her nature shines transparent in her letters, her truly admirable journal, and in every report that we have of her.   Wordsworth's own feelings for her, and his sense of the debt that he owed to her faithful affection and eager mind, he has placed on lasting record.

The intimacy with Coleridge was, as has been said, Wordsworth's one strong friendship, and must be counted among the highest examples of that generous relation between great writers.   Unlike in the quality of their genius, and unlike in force of character and the fortunes of life, they remained bound to one another by sympathies that neither time nor harsh trial ever extinguished.   Coleridge had left Cambridge in 1794, had married, had started various unsuccessful projects for combining the improvement of mankind with the earning of an income, and was now settled in a small cottage at Nether Stowey in Somersetshire, with an acre and a half of land, from which he hoped to raise corn and vegetables enough to support himself and his wife, as well as to feed a couple of pigs on the refuse.   Wordsworth and his sister were settled at Racedown, near Crewkerne, in Dorsetshire.   In 1797 they moved to Alfoxden in Somersetshire, their principal inducement to the change being Coleridge's society.   The friendship bore fruit in the production of "Lyrical Ballads" in 1798, mainly the work of Wordsworth, but containing no less notable a contribution from Coleridge than the "Ancient Mariner."   The two poets only received thirty guineas for their work, and the publisher lost his money.   The taste of the country was not yet ripe for Wordsworth's poetic experiment.

Immediately after the publication of the "Lyrical Ballads," the two Wordsworths and Coleridge started from Yarmouth for Hamburg.   Coleridge's account in Satyrane's Letters, published in the "Biographia Literaria," of the voyage and of the conversations between the two English poets and Klopstock, is worth turning to.   The pastor told them that Klopstock was the German Milton.   "A very German Milton indeed," they thought.   The Wordsworths remained for four wintry months at Goslar in Saxony, while Coleridge went on to Ratzeburg, Göttingen, and other places, mastering German, and "delving in the unwholesome quicksilver mines of metaphysic depths." Wordsworth made little way with the language, but worked diligently at his own verse.

When they came back to England, Wordsworth and his sister found their hearts turning with irresistible attraction to their own familiar countryside. They at last made their way to Grasmere. The opening book of the "Recluse," which is published for the first time in the present volume, describes in fine verse the emotions and the scene. The face of this delicious vale is not quite what it was when

> " Cottages of mountain stone
> Clustered like stars some few, but single most,
> And lurking dimly in their shy retreats,
> Or glancing at each other cheerful looks
> Like separated stars with clouds between."

But it is foolish to let ourselves be fretted by the villa, the hotel, and the tourist. We may well be above all this in a scene that is haunted by a great poetic shade. The substantial features and elements of beauty still remain, the crags and woody steeps, the lake, " its one green island and its winding shores ; the multitude of little rocky hills." Wordsworth was not the first poet to feel its fascination. Gray visited the Lakes in the autumn of 1769, and coming into the vale of Grasmere from the north-west, declared it to be one of the sweetest landscapes that art ever attempted to imitate, an unsuspected paradise of peace and rusticity. We cannot indeed compare the little crystal mere, set like a gem in the verdant circle of the hills, with the grandeur and glory of Lucerne, or the radiant gladness and expanse of Como: yet it has an inspiration of its own, to delight, to soothe, to fortify, and to refresh.

> " What want we ? have we not perpetual streams,
>   Warm woods, and sunny hills, and fresh green fields,
>   And mountains not less green, and flocks and herds,
>   And thickets full of songsters, and the voice
>   Of lordly birds, an unexpected sound
>   Heard now and then from morn to latest eve,
>   Admonishing the man who walks below
>   Of solitude and silence in the sky.
>   These have we, and a thousand nooks of earth
>   Have also these, but nowhere else is found,
>   Nowhere (or is it fancy?) can be found
>   The one sensation that is here; . . .
>   'tis the sense
>   Of majesty, of beauty, and repose,
>   A blended holiness of earth and sky,
>   Something that makes this individual spot,
>   This small abiding-place of many men,
>   A termination, and a last retreat,
>   A centre, come from wheresoe'er you will,
>   A whole without dependence or defect,
>   Made for itself, and happy in itself,
>   Perfect contentment, Unity entire."

In the Grasmere vale Wordsworth lived for half a century, first in a little cottage at the northern corner of the lake, and then (1813) in a more commodious house at Rydal Mount at the southern end, on the road to Ambleside. In 1802 he married Mary Hutchinson, of Penrith, and this completed the circle of his felicity. Mary, he once said, was to his ear the most musical and most truly English in sound of all the names we have. The name was of harmonious omen. The two beautiful sonnets that he wrote on his wife's portrait long years after, when "morning into noon had passed, noon into eve," show how much her large heart and humble mind had done for the blessedness of his home.

Their life was almost more simple than that of the dalesmen their neighbors. "It is my opinion," ran one of his oracular sayings to Sir George Beaumont, "that a man of letters, and indeed all public men of every pursuit, should be severely frugal." Means were found for supporting the modest home out of two or three small windfalls bequeathed by friends or relatives, and by the time that children had begun to come Wordsworth was raised to affluence by obtaining the post of distributor of stamps for Westmoreland and part of Cumberland. His life was happily devoid of striking external incident. Its essential part lay in meditation and composition.

He was surrounded by friends. Southey had made a home for himself and his beloved library a few miles over the hills at Keswick. De Quincey, with his clever brains and shallow character, took up his abode in the cottage which Wordsworth had first lived in at Grasmere. Coleridge, born the most golden genius of them all, came to and fro in those fruitless unhappy wanderings which consumed a life that once promised to be so rich in blessing and in glory. In later years Dr. Arnold built a house at Fox How, attracted by the Wordsworths and the scenery; and other lesser lights came into the neighborhood. "Our intercourse with the Wordsworths," Arnold wrote on the occasion of his first visit in 1832, "was one of the brightest spots of all; nothing could exceed their friendliness, and my almost daily walks with him were things not to be forgotten. Once and once only we had a good fight about the Reform Bill during a walk up Greenhead Ghyll to see the unfinished sheepfold, recorded in "Michael." But I am sure that our political disagreement did not at all interfere with our enjoyment of each other's society; for I think that in the great principles of things we agreed very entirely." It ought to be possible, for that matter, for magnanimous men, even if they do not agree in the great principles of things, to keep pleasant terms with one another for more than one afternoon's walk. Many pilgrims came, and the poet seems to have received them with cheerful equanimity. Emerson called upon him in 1833, and found him plain, elderly, white-haired, not prepossessing. "He led me out into his garden, and showed me the gravel walk in which thousands of his lines were composed. He had just returned from Staffa, and within three days had made three sonnets on Fingal's Cave, and was composing a fourth when he was called in to see me. He said, ' If you are interested in my verses, perhaps you will like to hear these lines.' I gladly assented, and he recollected himself for a few moments, and then stood forth and repeated, one after another, the three entire sonnets with great animation. This recitation was so unlooked for and surprising — he, the old Wordsworth, standing apart, and reciting to me in a garden-walk like a schoolboy declaiming — that I was at first near to laugh; but recollecting myself, that I had come thus far to see a poet, and he was chanting poems to me, I saw that he was right, and I was wrong, and gladly gave myself up to him. He never was in haste to publish; partly because he corrected a good deal. . . . He preferred such of his poems as touched the affections to any others ; for whatever is didactic — what theories of society and so on — might perish quickly, but whatever combined a truth with an affection was good to-day and good forever." (*English Traits*, ch. i.)

Wordsworth was far too wise to encourage the pilgrims to turn into abiding sojourners in his chosen land. Clough has described how, when he was a lad of eighteen (1837), with a mild surprise he heard the venerable poet correct the tendency to exaggerate the importance of flowers and fields, lakes, waterfalls, and scenery. " People come to the Lakes,'' said Wordsworth, "and are charmed with a particular spot, and build a house, and find themselves discontented, forgetting that these things are only the sauce and garnish of life.''

In spite of a certain hardness and stiffness, Wordsworth must have been an admirable companion for anybody capable of true elevation of mind. The unfortunate Haydon says, with his usual accent of enthusiasm, after a saunter at Hampstead, "Never did any man so beguile the time as Wordsworth. His purity of heart, his kindness, his soundness of principle, his information, his knowledge, and the intense and eager feelings with which he pours forth all he knows, affect, interest, and enchant one.'' (*Autobiog.* i. 298, 384.) The diary of Crabb Robinson, the correspondence of Charles Lamb, the delightful autobiography of Mrs. Fletcher, and much less delightfully the autobiography of Harriet Martineau, all help us to realize by many a trait Wordsworth's daily walk and conversation. Of all the glimpses that we get, from these and many other sources, none are more pleasing than those of the intercourse between Wordsworth and Scott. They were the two manliest and most wholesome men of genius of their time. They held different theories of poetic art, but their affection and esteem for one another never varied, from the early days when Scott and his young wife visited Wordsworth in his cottage at Grasmere, down to that sorrowful autumn evening (1831) when Wordsworth and his daughter went to Abbotsford to bid farewell to the wondrous potentate, then just about to start on his vain search for new life, followed by "the might of the whole earth's good wishes.''

Of Wordsworth's demeanor and physical presence, De Quincey's account, silly, coxcombical, and vulgar, is the worst; Carlyle's, as might be expected from his magical gift of portraiture, is the best. Carlyle cared little for Wordsworth's poetry, had a real respect for the antique greatness of his devotion to Poverty and Peasanthood, recognized his strong intellectual powers and strong character, but thought him rather dull, bad-tempered, unproductive, and almost wearisome, and found his divine reflections and unfathomabilities stinted, scanty, uncertain, palish. From these and many other disparagements, one gladly passes to the picture of the poet as he was in the flesh at a breakfast party given by Henry Taylor, at a tavern in St. James's Street, in 1840. The subject of the talk was Literature, its laws, practices, and observances: — "He talked well in his way; with veracity, easy brevity, and force ; as a wise tradesman would of his tools and workshop, and as no unwise one could. His voice was good, frank, and sonorous, though practically clear, distinct, and forcible, rather than melodious ; the tone of him business-like, sedately confident, no discourtesy, yet no anxiety about being courteous: a fine wholesome rusticity, fresh as his mountain breezes, sat well on the stalwart veteran, and on all he said and did. You would have said he was a usually taciturn man, glad to unlock himself, to audience sympathetic and intelligent, when such offered itself. His face bore marks of much, not always peaceful, meditation; the look of it not bland or benevolent, so much as close, impregnable, and hard; a man *multa tacere loquive paratus*, in a world where he had experienced no lack of contradictions as he strode along ! The eyes were not very brilliant, but they had a quiet clearness; there was enough of brow, and well shaped; rather too much of cheek (' horse-face,' I have heard satirists say), face of squarish shape and decidedly longish, as I think the head itself was (*its* 'length' going *horizontal*): he was large-boned, lean, but still firm-knit, tall, and strong-looking when he stood; a right good old steel-gray figure, with a fine rustic simplicity and dignity about him, and a veracious *strength* looking through him which might have suited one of those old steel-gray *Markgrafs* (Graf = Grau, 'Steel-gray') whom Henry the Fowler set up to ward the marches, and do battle with the intrusive heathen, in a stalwart and judicious manner.''

Whoever might be his friends within an easy walk, or dwelling afar, the poet knew how to live his own life. The three fine sonnets headed " Personal Talk '' so well known, so warmly accepted in our better hours, so easily forgotten in hours not so good between pleasant levities and grinding preoccupations, show us how little his neighbors had to do with the poet's genial seasons of "smooth passions, smooth discourse, and joyous thought."

For those days Wordsworth was a considerable traveller. Between 1820 and 1837 he made long tours abroad, to Switzerland, to Holland, to Belgium, to Italy. In other years he visited Wales, Scotland, and Ireland. He was no mechanical tourist, admiring to order and marvelling by regulation; and he confessed to Mrs. Fletcher that he fell asleep before the Venus de Medici at Florence. But the product of these wanderings is to be seen in some of his best sonnets, such as the first on Calais Beach, the famous one on Westminster Bridge, the second of the two on Bruges, where "the Spirit of Antiquity mounts to the seat of grace within the mind — a deeper peace than that in deserts found" — and in some other fine pieces.

In weightier matters than mere travel, Wordsworth showed himself no mere recluse: He watched the great affairs then being transacted in Europe with the ardent interest of his youth, and his sonnets to Liberty, commemorating the attack by France upon the Swiss, the fate of Venice, the struggle of Hofer, the resistance of Spain, give no unworthy expression to the best of the varied motives that animated England in her long struggle with Bonaparte. The sonnet to Toussaint l'Ouverture concludes with some of the noblest lines in the English language. The strong verses on the expected death of Mr. Fox are alive with a magnanimous public spirit that goes deeper than political opinion. In his young days he had sent Fox a copy of the "Lyrical Ballads," with a long letter indicating his sense of Fox's great and generous qualities. Pitt, he admits that he could never regard with complacency. "I believe him, however," he said, "to have been as disinterested a man, and as true a lover of his country, as it was possible for so ambitious a man to be. His first wish (though probably unknown to himself) was that his country should prosper under his administration; his next that it should prosper. Could the order of these wishes have been reversed, Mr. Pitt would have avoided many of the grievous mistakes into which, I think, he fell." "You always went away from Burke," he once told Haydon, "with your mind filled; from Fox with your feelings excited; and from Pitt with wonder at his having had the power to make the worse appear the better reason."

Of the poems composed under the influence of that best kind of patriotism which ennobles local attachments by associating them with the lasting elements of moral grandeur and heroism, it is needless to speak. They have long taken their place as something higher even than literary classics. As years began to dull the old penetration of a mind which had once approached, like other youths, the shield of human nature from the golden side, and had been eager to "clear a passage for just government," Wordsworth lost his interest in progress. Waterloo may be taken for the date at which his social grasp began to fail, and with it his poetic glow. He opposed Catholic emancipation as stubbornly as Eldon, and the Reform Bill as bitterly as Croker. For the practical reforms of his day, even in education, for which he had always spoken up, Wordsworth was not a force. His heart clung to England as he found it. "This concrete attachment to the scenes about him," says Mr. Myers, "had always formed an important element in his character. Ideal politics, whether in Church or State, had never occupied his mind, which sought rather to find its informing principles embodied in the England of his own day." This flowed, we may suppose, from Burke. In a passage in the seventh Book of the "Prelude," he describes, in lines a little prosaic but quite true, how he sat, saw, and heard, not unthankful nor uninspired, the great orator.

> "While he forewarns, denounces, launches forth,
> Against all systems, built on abstract rights."

The Church, as conceived by the spirit of Laud, and described by Hooker's voice, was the great symbol of the union of high and stable institution with thought, faith, right living, and "sacred religion, mother of form and fear." As might be expected from such a point of view, the church pieces, to which Wordsworth gave so much thought, are, with few exceptions, such as the sonnet on "Seathwaite Chapel," formal, hard, and but thinly enriched with spiritual grace or unction. They are ecclesiastical, not religious. In religious poetry, the Church of England finds her most affecting voice, not in Wordsworth, but in the "Lyra Innocentium," and the "Christian Year." Wordsworth abounds in the true devotional cast of mind, but less than anywhere else in his properly ecclesiastical verse.

It was perhaps natural that when events no longer inspired him, Wordsworth should have turned with new feelings towards the classic, and discovered a virtue in classic form to which his own method had hitherto made him a little blind. Towards the date of Waterloo, he read over again some of the Latin writers, in attempting to prepare his son for college. He even at a later date set about a translation of the "Æneid" of Virgil, but the one permanent result of the classic movement in his mind is "Laodamia." Earlier in life he had translated some books of Ariosto at the rate of a hundred lines a day, and he even attempted fifteen of the sonnets of Michael Angelo, but so much meaning is compressed into so little room in those pieces that he found the difficulty insurmountable. He had a high opinion of the resources of the Italian language. The poetry of Dante and of Michael Angelo, he said, proves that if there be little majesty and strength in Italian verse, the fault is in the authors and not in the tongue.

Our last glimpse of Wordsworth in the full and peculiar power of his genius is the Ode "Composed on an Evening of Extraordinary Splendor and Beauty." It is the one exception to the critical dictum that all his good work was done in the decade between 1798 and 1808. He lived for more than thirty years after this fine composition. But he added nothing more of value to the work that he had already done. The public appreciation of it was very slow. The most influential among the critics were for long hostile and contemptuous. Never at any time did Wordsworth come near to such popularity as that of Scott or of Byron. Nor was that all. For many years most readers of poetry thought more even of "Lalla Rookh" than of the "Excursion." While Scott, Byron, and Moore were receiving thousands of pounds, Wordsworth received nothing. Between 1830 and 1840 the current turned in Wordsworth's direction, and when he received the honor of a doctor's degree at the Oxford Commemoration in 1839, the Sheldonian theatre made him the hero of the day. In the spring of 1843 Southey died, and Sir Robert Peel pressed Wordsworth to succeed him in the office of Poet Laureate. "It is a tribute of respect," said the Minister, "justly due to the first of living poets." But almost immediately the light of his common popularity was eclipsed by Tennyson, as it had earlier been eclipsed by Scott, by Byron, and in some degree by Shelley. Yet his fame among those who know, among competent critics with a right to judge, to-day stands higher than it ever stood. Only two writers have contributed so many lines of daily popularity and application. In the handbooks of familiar quotations Wordsworth fills more space than anybody save Shakespeare and Pope. He exerted commanding influence over great minds that have powerfully affected our generation. "I never before," said George Eliot in the days when her character was forming itself (1839), "met with so many of my own feelings expressed just as I should like them," and her reverence for Wordsworth remained to the end. J. S. Mill has described how important an event in his life was his first reading of Wordsworth. "What made his poems a medicine for my state of mind was that they expressed not mere outward beauty, but states of feeling and of thought colored by feeling, under the excitement of beauty. I needed to be made to feel that there was real permanent happiness in tranquil contemplation. Wordsworth taught me this, not only without turning away from, but with greatly increased interest in the common feelings and common destiny of human beings.'' (*Autobiog.*, 148.) This effect of Wordsworth on Mill is the very illustration of the phrase of a later poet of our own day, one of the most eminent and by his friends best beloved of all those whom Wordsworth had known, and on whom he poured out a generous portion of his own best spirit : —

> "Time may restore us in his course
> Goethe's sage mind and Byron's force:
> But where will Europe's latter hour
> Again find Wordsworth's healing power?"

It is the power for which Matthew Arnold found this happy designation, that compensates us for that absence of excitement of which the heedless complain in Wordsworth's verse — excitement so often meaning mental fever, hysterics, distorted passion, or other fitful agitation of the soul.

Pretensions are sometimes advanced as to Wordsworth's historic position, which involve a mistaken view of literary history. Thus, we are gravely told by the too zealous Wordsworthian that the so-called poets of the eighteenth century were simply men of letters; they had various accomplishments and great general ability, but their thoughts were expressed in prose, or in mere metrical diction, which passed current as poetry without being so. Yet Burns belonged wholly to the eighteenth century (1759–96), and no verse writer is so little literary as Burns, so little prosaic; no writer more truly poetic in melody, diction, thought, feeling, and spontaneous song. It was Burns who showed Wordsworth's own youth "How verse may build a princely throne on humble truth." Nor can we understand how Cowper is to be set down as simply a man of letters. We may, too, if we please, deny the name of poetry to Collins's tender and pensive "Ode to Evening;" but we can only do this on critical principles, which would end in classing the author of "Lycidas" and "Comus," of the "Allegro" and "Penseroso," as a writer of various accomplishments and great general ability, but at bottom simply a man of letters and by no means a poet. It is to Gray, however, that we must turn for the distinctive character of the best poetry of the eighteenth century. With reluctance we will surrender the Pindaric Odes, though not without risking the observation that some of Wordsworth's own criticism on Gray is as narrow and as much beside the mark as Jeffrey's on the "Excursion." But the "Ode on Eton College" is not to have grudged to it the noble name and true quality of poetry, merely because, as one of Johnson's most unfortunate criticisms expresses it, the ode suggests nothing to Gray which every beholder does not equally think and feel. To find beautiful and pathetic language, set to harmonious numbers, for the common impressions of meditative minds, is no small part of the poet's task. That part has never been achieved by any poet in any tongue, with more complete perfection and success than in the immortal "Elegy," of which we may truly say that it has for nearly a century and a half given to greater multitudes of men more of the exquisite pleasure of poetry than any other single piece in all the glorious treasury of English verse. It abounds, as Johnson says, "with images which find a mirror in every mind, and with sentiments to which every bosom returns an echo." These moving commonplaces of the human lot, Gray approached through books and studious contemplation; not as Wordsworth approached them, by daily contact with the lives and habit of men and the forces and magical apparitions of external nature. But it is a narrow view to suppose that the men of the eighteenth century did not look through the literary conventions of the day to the truths of life and nature behind them. The conventions have gone, or are changed, and we are all glad of it. Wordsworth effected a wholesome

deliverance when he attacked the artificial diction, the personifications, the alle-
gories, the antitheses, the barren rhymes and monotonous metres, which the reigning
taste had approved.   But while welcoming the new freshness, sincerity, and direct
and fertile return on nature, that is a very bad reason why we should disparage
poetry so genial, so simple, so humane, and so perpetually pleasing as the best
verse of the rationalistic century.

What Wordsworth did was to deal with themes that had been partially handled
by precursors and contemporaries, in a larger and more devoted spirit, with wider
amplitude of illustration, and with the steadfastness and persistency of a religious
teacher. "Every great poet is a teacher," he said ; "I wish to be considered as a
teacher or as nothing."   It may be doubted whether his general proposition is at
all true, and whether it is any more the essential business of a poet to be a teacher
than it was the business of Händel, Beethoven, or Mozart.   They attune the soul
to high states of feeling; the direct lesson is often as naught.   But of himself no
view could be more sound.   He is a teacher, or he is nothing.   "To console the
afflicted; to add sunshine to daylight by making the happy happier; to teach the
young and the gracious of every age to see, to think, and feel, and therefore
to become more actively and sincerely virtuous " — that was his vocation; to
show that the mutual adaptation of the external world and the inner mind is able
to shape a paradise from the "simple produce of the common day" — that was
his high argument.

Simplification was, as I have said elsewhere, the keynote of the revolutionary
time.   Wordsworth was its purest exponent, but he had one remarkable peculiarity,
which made him, in England at least, not only its purest but its greatest.   While
leading men to pierce below the artificial and conventional to the natural man and
natural life, as Rousseau did, Wordsworth still cherished the symbols, the traditions,
and the great institutes of social order.   Simplification of life and thought and
feeling was to be accomplished without summoning up the dangerous spirit of
destruction and revolt.   Wordsworth lived with nature, yet waged no angry railing
war against society.   The chief opposing force to Wordsworth in literature was
Byron.   Whatever he was in his heart, Byron in his work was drawn by all the forces
of his character, genius, and circumstances to the side of violent social change, and
hence the extraordinary popularity of Byron in the continental camp of emancipa-
tion.   Communion with nature is in Wordsworth's doctrine the school of duty.
With Byron nature is the mighty consoler and the vindicator of the rebel.

A curious thing, which we may note in passing, is that Wordsworth, who clung
fervently to the historic foundations of society as it stands, was wholly indifferent to
history ; while Byron, on the contrary, as the fourth canto of "Childe Harold" is
enough to show, had at least the sentiment of history in as great a degree as any
poet that ever lived, and has given to it by far the most magnificent expression.
No doubt, it was history on its romantic, and not its philosophic or its political
side.

On Wordsworth's exact position in the hierarchy of sovereign poets, a deep
difference of estimate still divides even the most excellent judges.   Nobody now
dreams of placing him so low as the *Edinburgh Reviewers* did, nor so high as Southey
placed him when he wrote to the author of "Philip van Artevelde" in 1829, that a
greater poet than Wordsworth there never has been nor ever will be.   An extrava-
gance of this kind was only the outburst of generous friendship.   Coleridge deliber-
ately placed Wordsworth "nearest of all modern writers to Shakespeare and Milton,
yet in a kind perfectly unborrowed and his own."   Arnold, himself a poet of rare
and memorable quality, declares his firm belief that the poetical performance of
Wordsworth is, after that of Shakespeare and Milton, undoubtedly the most con-
siderable in our language from the Elizabethan age to the present time.   Dryden,

Pope, Gray, Cowper, Goldsmith, Burns, Coleridge, Byron, Shelley, Keats—
"Wordsworth's name deserves to stand, and will finally stand, above them all."
Mr. Myers, also a poet, and the author of a volume on Wordsworth as much dis-
tinguished by insight as by admirable literary grace and power, talks of "a Plato,
a Dante, a Wordsworth," all three in a breath, as stars of equal magnitude in the
great spiritual firmament.   To Mr. Swinburne, on the contrary, all these panegyrical
estimates savor of monstrous and intolerable exaggeration.   Amid these contentions
of celestial minds it will be safest to content ourselves with one or two plain observa-
tions in the humble positive degree, without hurrying into high and final compara-
tives and superlatives.

One admission is generally made at the outset.   Whatever definition of poetry
we fix upon, whether it is the language of passion or imagination formed into regular
numbers; or, with Milton, that it should be "simple, sensuous, passionate;" in any
case there are great tracts in Wordsworth which, by no definition and on no terms,
can be called poetry.   If we say with Shelley, that poetry is what redeems from
decay the visitations of the divinity in man, and is the record of the best and hap-
piest moments of the best and happiest minds, then are we bound to agree that
Wordsworth records too many moments that are not specially good or happy, that he
redeems from decay frequent visitations that are not from any particular divinity in
man, and treats them all as very much on a level.   Mr. Arnold is undoubtedly right
in his view that, to be receivable as a classic, Wordsworth must be relieved of a
great deal of the poetical baggage that now encumbers him.

The faults and hindrances in Wordsworth's poetry are obvious to every reader.
For one thing, the intention to instruct, to improve the occasion, is too deliberate
and too hardly pressed.   "We hate poetry," said Keats, "that has a palpable
design upon us.   Poetry should be great and unobtrusive."   Charles Lamb's friendly
remonstrance on one of Wordsworth's poems is applicable to more of them.   "The
instructions conveyed in it are too direct; they don't slide into the mind of the
reader while he is imagining no such matter."

Then, except the sonnets and half a score of the pieces where he reaches his top-
most height, there are few of his poems that are not too long, and it often happens
even that no degree of reverence for the teacher prevents one from finding passages
of almost unbearable prolixity.   A defence was once made by a great artist for what,
to the unregenerate mind, seemed the merciless tardiness of movement in one of
Goethe's romances, that it was meant to impress on his readers the slow march and
the tedium of events in human life.   The lenient reader may give Wordsworth the
advantage of the same ingenious explanation.   We may venture on a counsel which
is more to the point, in warning the student that not seldom in these blocks of
afflicting prose, suddenly we come upon some of the profoundest and most beautiful
passages that the poet ever wrote.   In deserts of preaching we find, almost within
sight of one another, delightful oases of purest poetry.   Besides being prolix,
Wordsworth is often cumbrous; has often no flight; is not liquid, is not musical.
He is heavy and self-conscious with the burden of his message.   How much at his
best he is, when, as in the admirable and truly Wordsworthian poem of "Michael," he
spares us a sermon and leaves us the story.   Then, he is apt to wear a somewhat
stiff-cut garment of solemnity, when not solemnity, but either sternness or sadness,
which are so different things, would seem the fitter mood.   In truth Wordsworth
hardly knows how to be stern, as Dante or Milton was stern; nor has he the note of
plangent sadness which strikes the ear in men as morally inferior to him as Rousseau,
Keats, Shelley, or Coleridge; nor has he the Olympian air with which Goethe
delivered sage oracles.   This mere solemnity is specially oppressive in some parts of
the "Excursion"—the performance where we best see the whole poet, and where the
poet most absolutely identifies himself with his subject.   Yet, even in the midst of

these solemn discoursings, he suddenly introduces an episode in which his peculiar power is at its height. There is no better instance of this than the passage in the Second Book of the " Excursion," where he describes with a fidelity, at once realistic and poetic, the worn-out almsman, his patient life and sorry death, and then the unimaginable vision in the skies, as they brought the ancient man down through dull mists from the mountain ridge to die. These hundred and seventy lines are like the landscape in which they were composed; you can no more appreciate the beauty of the one by a single or a second perusal, than you can the other in a scamper through the vale on the box of the coach. But any lover of poetry who will submit himself with leisure and meditation to the impressions of the story, the pity of it, the naturalness of it, the glory and the mystic splendors of the indifferent heavens, will feel that here indeed is the true strength which out of the trivial raises expression for the pathetic and the sublime.

Apart, however, from excess of prolixity and of solemnity, can it be really contended that in purely poetic quality — in aerial freedom and space, in radiant purity of light or depth and variety of color, in penetrating and subtle sweetness of music, in supple mastery of the instrument, in vivid spontaneity of imagination, in clean-cut sureness of touch — Wordsworth is not surpassed by men who were below him in weight and greatness? Even in his own field of the simple and the pastoral has he touched so sweet and spontaneous a note as Burns's " Daisy," or the " Mouse "? When men seek immersion or absorption in the atmosphere of pure poesy, without lesson or moral, or anything but delight of fancy and stir of imagination, they will find him less congenial to their mood than poets not worthy to loose the latchet of his shoe in the greater elements of his art. In all these comparisons, it is not merely Wordsworth's theme and motive and dominant note that are different; the skill of hand is different, and the musical ear and the imaginative eye.

To maintain or to admit so much as this, however, is not to say the last word. The question is whether Wordsworth, however unequal to Shelley in lyric quality, to Coleridge or to Keats in imaginative quality, to Burns in tenderness, warmth, and that humor which is so nearly akin to pathos, to Byron in vividness and energy, yet possesses excellences of his own which place him in other respects above these master-spirits of his time. If the question is to be answered affirmatively, it is clear that only in one direction must we look. The trait that really places Wordsworth on an eminence above his poetic contemporaries, and ranks him, as the ages are likely to rank him, on a line just short of the greatest of all time, is his direct appeal to will and conduct. " There is volition and self-government in every line of his poetry, and his best thoughts come from his steady resistance to the ebb and flow of ordinary desires and regrets. He contests the ground inch by inch with all despondent and indolent humors, and often, too, with movements of inconsiderate and wasteful joy." (*R. H. Hutton.*) That would seem to be his true distinction and superiority over men to whom more had been given of fire, passion, and ravishing music. Those who deem the end of poetry to be intoxication, fever, or rainbow dreams, can care little for Wordsworth. If its end be not intoxication, but on the contrary a search from the wide regions of imagination and feeling for elements of composure deep and pure, and of self-government in a far loftier sense than the merely prudential, then Wordsworth has a gift of his own in which he was approached by no poet of his time. Scott's sane and humane genius, with much the same aims, yet worked with different methods. He once remonstrated with Lockhart for being too apt to measure things by some reference to literature. " I have read books enough," said Scott, " and observed and conversed with enough of eminent and splendidly cultivated minds; but I assure you, I have heard higher sentiments from the lips of poor uneducated men and women, when exerting the spirit of severe yet gentle heroism under difficulties and afflictions, or speaking their simple thoughts as to circumstances in the lot of friends and neighbors, than I ever yet met with out of the pages of the Bible. We shall never learn to respect our real calling and destiny, unless we have taught ourselves to consider everything as moonshine compared with the education of the heart.'' This admirable deliverance of Scott's is, so far as it goes, eminently Wordsworthian; but Wordsworth went higher and further, striving not only to move the sympathies of the heart, but to enlarge the understanding, and exalt and widen the spiritual vision, all with the aim of leading us towards firmer and austerer self-control.

Certain favorers of Wordsworth answer our question with a triumphant affirmative, on the strength of some ethical, or metaphysical, or theological system which they believe themselves to find in him. But is it creditable that poets can permanently live by systems? Or is not system, whether ethical, theological, or philosophical, the heavy lead of poetry? Lucretius is indisputably one of the mighty poets of the world, but Epicureanism is not the soul of that majestic muse. So with Wordsworth. Thought is, on the whole, predominant over feeling in his verse, but a prevailing atmosphere of deep and solemn reflection does not make a system. His theology and his ethics, and his so-called Platonical metaphysics, have as little to do with the power of his poetry over us, as the imputed Arianism or any other aspect of the theology of '' Paradise Lost '' has to do with the strength and the sublimity of Milton, and his claim to a high perpetual place in the hearts of men. It is best to be entirely sceptical as to the existence of system and ordered philosophy in Wordsworth. When he tells us that '' one impulse from a vernal wood may teach you more of man, of moral evil and of good, than all the sages can,'' such a proposition cannot be seriously taken as more than a half-playful sally for the benefit of some too bookish friend. No impulse from a vernal wood can teach us anything at all of moral evil and of good. When he says that it is his faith, '' that every flower enjoys the air it breathes,'' and that when the budding twigs spread out their fan to catch the air, he is compelled to think '' that there was pleasure there,'' he expresses a charming poetic fancy and no more, and it is idle to pretend to see in it the fountain of a system of philosophy. In the famous '' Ode on Intimations of Immortality,'' the poet doubtless does point to a set of philosophic ideas, more or less complete; but the thought from which he sets out, that our birth is but a sleep and a forgetting, and that we are less and less able to perceive the visionary gleam, less and less alive to the glory and the dream of external nature, as infancy recedes farther from us, is, with all respect for the declaration of Mr. Ruskin to the contrary, contrary to notorious fact, experience, and truth. It is a beggarly conception, no doubt, to judge as if poetry should always be capable of a prose rendering; but it is at least fatal to the philosophic pretension of a line or a stanza if, when it is fairly reduced to prose, the prose discloses that it is nonsense, and there is at least one stanza of the great '' Ode '' that this doom would assuredly await. Wordsworth's claim, his special gift, his lasting contribution, lies in the extraordinary strenuousness, sincerity, and insight with which he first idealizes and glorifies the vast universe around us, and then makes of it, not a theatre on which men play their parts, but an animate presence, intermingling with our works, pouring its companionable spirit about us, and '' breathing grandeur upon the very humblest face of human life.'' This twofold and conjoint performance, consciously and expressly — perhaps only too consciously — undertaken by a man of strong inborn sensibility to natural impressions, and systematically carried out in a lifetime of brooding meditation and active composition, is Wordsworth's distinguishing title to fame and gratitude. In '' words that speak of nothing more than what we are,'' he revealed new faces of nature; he dwelt on men as they are men themselves, he strove to do that which has been declared to be the true secret of force in art, to make the trivial serve the expression of the sublime. '' Wordsworth's distinctive work,'' Mr. Ruskin has justly said

("Modern Painters," iii. 293), "was a war with pomp and pretence, and a display of the majesty of simple feelings and humble hearts, together with high reflective truths in his analysis of the courses of policies and ways of men; without these his love of nature would have been comparatively worthless."

Yet let us not forget that he possessed the gift which to an artist is the very root of the matter. He saw nature truly, he saw her as she is, and with his own eyes. The critic whom I have just quoted boldly pronounces him "the keenest eyed of all modern poets for what is deep and essential in nature." When he describes the daisy, casting the beauty of the star-shaped shadow on the smooth stone, or the boundless depth of the abysses of the sky, or the clouds made vivid as fire by the rays of light, every touch is true, not the copying of a literary phrase, but the result of direct observation.

It is true that Nature has sides to which Wordsworth was not energetically alive —Nature "red in tooth and claw." He was not energetically alive to the blind and remorseless cruelties of life and the world. When in early spring he heard the blended notes of the birds, and saw the budding twigs and primrose tufts, it grieved him amid such fair works of nature, to think "what man has made of man." As if nature itself, excluding the conscious doings of that portion of nature which is the human race, and excluding also nature's own share in the making of poor Man, did not abound in raking cruelties and horrors of her own. "*Edel sei der Mensch*," sang Goethe in a noble psalm. "*Hülfreich und gut, denn das allein unterscheidet ihn, von allen Wesen die wir kennen.*" "*Let man be noble, helpful, and good, for that alone distinguishes him from all beings that we know. No feeling has nature : to good and bad gives the sun his light, and for the evildoer as for the best shine moon and stars.*" That the laws which nature has fixed for our lives are mighty and eternal, Wordsworth comprehended as fully as Goethe, but not that they are laws pitiless as iron. Wordsworth had not rooted in him the sense of Fate—of the inexorable sequences of things, of the terrible chain that so often binds an awful end to some slight and trivial beginning.

This optimism or complacency in Wordsworth will be understood if we compare his spirit and treatment with that of the illustrious French painter whose subjects and whose life were in some ways akin to his own. Millet, like Wordsworth, went to the realities of humble life for his inspiration. The peasant of the great French plains and the forest was to him what the Cumbrian dalesman was to Wordsworth. But he saw the peasant differently. "You watch figures in the fields," said Millet, "digging and delving with spade or pick. You see one of them from time to time straightening his loins, and wiping his face with the back of his hand. Thou shalt eat thy bread in the sweat of thy brow. Is that the gay lively labor in which some people would have you believe? Yet it is there that for me you must seek true humanity and great poetry. They say that I deny the charm of the country; I find in it far more than charms, I find infinite splendors. I see in it, just as they do, the little flowers of which Christ said that Solomon in all his glory was not arrayed like one of them. I see clearly enough the sun as he spreads his splendor amid the clouds. None the less do I see on the plain, all smoking, the horses at the plough. I see in some stony corner a man all worn out, whose *han han* have been heard ever since daybreak—trying to straighten himself a moment to get breath." The hardness, the weariness, the sadness, the ugliness, out of which Millet's consummate skill made pictures that affect us like strange music, were to Wordsworth not the real part of the thing. They were all absorbed in the thought of nature as a whole, wonderful, mighty, harmonious, and benign.

We are not called upon to place great men of his stamp as if they were collegians in a class-list. It is best to take with thankfulness and admiration from each man what he has to give. What Wordsworth does is to assuage, to reconcile, to fortify.   He has not Shakespeare's richness and vast compass, nor Milton's sublime and unflagging strength, nor Dante's severe, vivid, ardent force of vision.   Probably he is too deficient in clear beauty of form and in concentrated power to be classed by the ages among these great giants.   We cannot be sure.   We may leave it to the ages to decide.   But Wordsworth, at any rate, by his secret of bringing the infinite into common life, as he evokes it out of common life, has the skill to lead us, so long as we yield ourselves to his influence, into inner moods of settled peace, to touch "the depth and not the tumult of the soul," to give us quietness, strength, steadfast-ness, and purpose, whether to do or to endure.   All art or poetry that has the effect of breathing into men's hearts, even if it be only for a space, these moods of settled peace, and strongly confirming their judgment and their will for good, — whatever limitations may be found besides, however prosaic may be some or much of the detail, — is great art and noble poetry, and the creator of it will always hold, as Wordsworth holds, a sovereign title to the reverence and gratitude of mankind.

J. M.

October, 1888.

NOTE.

In this edition the Poems of WORDSWORTH are arranged in the order of their composition, in accordance with Mr. Knight's chronology printed in the Transactions of the Wordsworth Society.   The date at the left hand, after each poem, is that of its composition; the date at the right gives the time of its first publication.   The text and notes are taken from the edition of 1857.

WORDSWORTH'S POETICAL WORKS.

LINES

WRITTEN AS A SCHOOL EXERCISE AT HAWKSHEAD, ANNO ÆTATIS 14.

"AND has the Sun his flaming chariot driven
Two hundred times around the ring of heaven,
Since Science first, with all her sacred train,
Beneath yon roof began her heavenly reign?
While thus I mused, methought, before mine eyes,
The Power of EDUCATION seemed to rise;
Not she whose rigid precepts trained the boy
Dead to the sense of every finer joy;
Nor that vile wretch who bade the tender age
Spurn Reason's law and humor Passion's rage;
But she who trains the generous British youth
In the bright paths of fair majestic Truth:
Emerging slow from Academus' grove
In heavenly majesty she seemed to move.
Stern was her forehead, but a smile serene
'Softened the terrors of her awful mien.'
Close at her side were all the powers, designed
To curb, exalt, reform the tender mind:
With panting breast, now pale as winter snows,
Now flushed as Hebe, Emulation rose;
Shame followed after with reverted eye,
And hue far deeper than the Tyrian dye;

Last Industry appeared with steady pace,
A smile sat beaming on her pensive face.
I gazed upon the visionary train,
Threw back my eyes, returned, and gazed again.
When lo! the heavenly goddess thus began,
Through all my frame the pleasing accents ran:

"'When Superstition left the golden light
And fled indignant to the shades of night;
When pure Religion reared the peaceful breast
And lulled the warring passions into rest,
Drove far away the savage thoughts that roll
In the dark mansions of the bigot's soul,
Enlivening Hope displayed her cheerful ray,
And beamed on Britain's sons a brighter day;
So when on Ocean's face the storm subsides,
Hushed are the winds and silent are the tides;
The God of day, in all the pomp of light,
Moves through the vault of heaven, and dissipates the night;
Wide o'er the main a trembling lustre plays,
The glittering waves reflect the dazzling blaze;
Science with joy saw Superstition fly
Before the lustre of Religion's eye;
With rapture she beheld Britannia smile,

Clapped her strong wings, and sought
the cheerful isle,
The shades of night no more the soul in-
volve,
She sheds her beam, and, lo! the shades
dissolve;
No jarring monks, to gloomy cell con-
fined,
With mazy rules perplex the weary mind;
No shadowy forms entice the soul aside,
Secure she walks, Philosophy her guide.
Britain, who long her warriors had
adored,
And deemed all merit centred in the
sword;
Britain, who thought to stain the field
was fame,
Now honored Edward's less than Bacon's
name.
Her sons no more in listed fields advance
To ride the ring, or toss the beamy lance;
No longer steel their indurated hearts
To the mild influence of the finer arts;
Quick to the secret grotto they retire
To court majestic truth, or wake the
golden lyre;
By generous Emulation taught to rise,
The seats of learning brave the distant
skies.
Then noble Sandys, inspired with great
design,
Reared Hawkshead's happy roof, and
called it mine.
There have I loved to show the tender
age
The golden precepts of the classic page;
To lead the mind to those Elysian plains
Where, throned in gold, immortal Science
reigns;
Fair to the view is sacred Truth displayed,
In all the majesty of light arrayed,
To teach, on rapid wings, the curious soul
To roam from heaven to heaven, from
pole to pole,
From thence to search the mystic cause
of things
And follow Nature to her secret springs;
Nor less to guide the fluctuating youth
Firm in the sacred paths of moral truth,
To regulate the mind's disordered frame,
And quench the passions kindling into
flame;
The glimmering fires of Virtue to enlarge,

And purge from Vice's dross my tender
charge.
Oft have I said, the paths of Fame pursue,
And all that Virtue dictates, dare to do;
Go to the world, peruse the book of man,
And learn from thence thy own defects
to scan;
Severely honest, break no plighted trust,
But coldly rest not here — be more than
just;
Join to the rigors of the sires of Rome
The gentler manners of the private dome;
When Virtue weeps in agony of woe,
Teach from the heart the tender tear to
flow;
If Pleasure's soothing song thy soul en-
tice,
Or all the gaudy pomp of splendid Vice,
Arise superior to the Siren's power,
The wretch, the short-lived vision of an
hour;
Soon fades her cheek, her blushing
beauties fly,
As fades the checkered bow that paints
the sky,
So shall thy sire, whilst hope his
breast inspires,
And wakes anew life's glimmering trem-
bling fires,
Hear Britain's sons rehearse thy praise
with joy,
Look up to heaven, and bless his darling
boy.
If e'er these precepts quelled the pas-
sions' strife,
If e'er they smoothed the rugged walks
of life,
If e'er they pointed forth the blissful
way
That guides the spirit to eternal day,
Do thou, if gratitude inspire thy breast,
Spurn the soft fetters of lethargic rest.
Awake, awake! and snatch the slumber-
ing lyre,
Let this bright morn and Sandys the
song inspire.'

" I looked obedience: the celestial
Fair
Smiled like the morn, and vanished
into air."

1785.   1850.

EXTRACT

FROM THE CONCLUSION OF A POEM, COMPOSED IN ANTICIPATION OF LEAVING SCHOOL.

Written at Hawkshead. The beautiful image with which this poem concludes, suggested itself to me while I was resting in a boat along with my companions under the shade of a magnificent row of sycamores, which then extended their branches from the shore of the promontory upon which stands the ancient, and at that time the more picturesque, Hall of Coniston, the seat of the Le Flemings from very early times. The poem of which it was the conclusion was of many hundred lines, and contained thoughts and images most of which have been dispersed through my other writings.

DEAR native regions, I foretell,
From what I feel at this farewell,
That, whereso'er my steps may tend,
And whensoe'er my course shall end,
If in that hour a single tie
Survive of local sympathy,
My soul will cast the backward view,
The longing look alone on you.

Thus, while the Sun sinks down to rest
Far in the regions of the west,
Though to the vale no parting beam
Be given, not one memorial gleam,
A lingering light he fondly throws
On the dear hills where first he rose.
 1786.   1815.

WRITTEN IN VERY EARLY YOUTH.

CALM is all nature as a resting wheel.
The kine are couched upon the dewy
 grass;
The horse alone, seen dimly as I pass,
Is cropping audibly his later meal:
Dark is the ground; a slumber seems
 to steal
O'er vale, and mountain, and the starless
 sky.
Now, in this blank of things, a harmony,
Home-felt, and home-created, comes to
 heal
That grief for which the senses still sup-
 ply
Fresh food; for only then, when mem-
 ory

Is hushed, am I at rest. My Friends!
 restrain
Those busy cares that would allay my
 pain;
Oh! leave me to myself, nor let me feel
The officious touch that makes me droop
 again.
 1786?   1807.

AN EVENING WALK.

ADDRESSED TO A YOUNG LADY.

The young Lady to whom this was addressed was my sister. It was composed at school, and during my two first college vacations. There is not an image in it which I have not observed; and now, in my seventy-third year, I recollect the time and place where most of them were noticed. I will confine myself to one instance:

" Waving his hat, the shepherd, from the vale,
 Directs his winding dog the cliffs to scale, —
 The dog, loud barking, 'mid the glittering rocks,
 Hunts, where his master points, the intercepted
  flocks."

I was an eye-witness of this for the first time while crossing the Pass of Dunmail Raise. Upon second thought, I will mention another image:

" And, fronting the bright west, yon oak entwines
 Its darkening boughs and leaves, in stronger
  lines."

This is feebly and imperfectly expressed, but I recollect distinctly the very spot where this first struck me. It was in the way between Hawkshead and Ambleside, and gave me extreme pleasure. The moment was important in my poetical history; for I date from it my consciousness of the infinite variety of natural appearances which had been unnoticed by the poets of any age or country, so far as I was acquainted with them; and I made a resolution to supply, in some degree, the deficiency. I could not have been at that time above fourteen years of age. The description of the swans, that follows, was taken from the daily opportunities I had of observing their habits, not as confined to the gentleman's park, but in a state of nature. There were two pairs of them that divided the lake of Esthwaite and its in-and-out-flowing streams between them, never trespassing a single yard upon each other's separate domain. They were of the old magnificent species, bearing in beauty and majesty about the same relation to the Thames swan which that does to the goose. It was from the remembrance of those noble creatures I took, thirty years after, the picture of the swan which I have discarded from the poem of Dion. While I was a schoolboy, the late Mr. Curwen introduced a little fleet of those birds, but of the inferior species, to the lake of Windermere. Their principal home was about his own island; but they sailed about into remote parts of the lake, and, either from real or imagined injury done to the adjoining fields, they were got rid of at the request of the farmers and proprietors, but to the great regret of all who had become attached to them, from noticing their beauty and quiet habits. I will conclude my notice of this poem by observing that the plan of it has not been confined to a particular walk or an individual place, — a proof (of which I was unconscious at the time) of my unwillingness to submit the poetic spirit to the chains of fact and real circumstance. The country is idealized rather than described in any one of its local aspects.

General Sketch of the Lakes — Author's regret of his youth which was passed among them — Short description of Noon — Cascade — Noontide Retreat — Precipice and sloping Lights — Face of Nature as the Sun declines — Mountain-farm, and the Cock — Slate-quarry — Sunset — Superstition of the Country connected with that moment — Swans — Female Beggar — Twilight-sounds — Western Lights — Spirits — Night — Moonlight — Hope — Night-sounds — Conclusion.

FAR from my dearest Friend, 'tis mine to rove
Through bare gray dell, high wood, and pastoral cove;
Where Derwent rests, and listens to the roar
That stuns the tremulous cliffs of high Lodore;
Where peace to Grasmere's lonely island leads,
To willowy hedge-rows, and to emerald meads;
Leads to her bridge, rude church, and cottaged grounds,
Her rocky sheepwalks, and her woodland bounds;
Where, undisturbed by winds, Winander[1] sleeps
'Mid clustering isles, and holly-sprinkled steeps;

[1] These lines are only applicable to the middle part of that lake.

Where twilight glens endear my Esthwaite's shore,
And memory of departed pleasures, more.
Fair scenes, erewhile, I taught, a happy child,
The echoes of your rocks my carols wild:
The spirit sought not then, in cherished sadness,
A cloudy substitute for failing gladness.
In youth's keen eye the livelong day was bright,
The sun at morning, and the stars at night,
Alike, when first the bittern's hollow bill
Was heard, or woodcocks[2] roamed the moonlight hill.
In thoughtless gayety I coursed the plain,
And hope itself was all I knew of pain;
For then, the inexperienced heart would beat
At times, while young Content forsook her seat,
And wild Impatience, pointing upward, showed,
Through passes yet unreached, a brighter road.
Alas! the idle tale of man is found
Depicted in the dial's moral round;
Hope with reflection blends her social rays
To gild the total tablet of his days;
Yet still, the sport of some malignant power,
He knows but from its shade the present hour.
But why, ungrateful, dwell on idle pain?
To show what pleasures yet to me remain,
Say, will my Friend, with unreluctant ear,
The history of a poet's evening hear?
When, in the south, the wan noon, brooding still,
Breathed a pale steam around the glaring hill,
And shades of deep-embattled clouds were seen,
Spotting the northern cliffs with lights between;
When crowding cattle, checked by rails that make

[2] In the beginning of winter, these mountains are frequented by woodcocks, which in dark nights retire into the woods.

A fence far stretched into the shallow
  lake,
Lashed the cool water with their restless
  tails,
Or from high points of rock looked out
  for fanning gales:
When school-boys stretched their length
  upon the green;
And round the broad-spread oak, a glim-
  mering scene,
In the rough fern-clad park, the herded
  deer
Shook the still-twinkling tail and glan-
  cing ear;
When horses in the sunburnt intake [1]
  stood,
And vainly eyed below the tempting flood,
Or tracked the passenger, in mute dis-
  tress,
With forward neck the closing gate to
  press —
Then, while I wandered where the hud-
  dling rill
Brightens with water-breaks the hollow
  ghyll [2]
As by enchantment, an obscure retreat
Opened at once, and stayed my devious
  feet.
While thick above the rill the branches
  close,
In rocky basin its wild waves repose,
Inverted shrubs, and moss of gloomy
  green,
Cling from the rocks, with pale wood-
  weeds between;
And its own twilight softens the whole
  scene,
Save where aloft the subtle sunbeams
  shine
On withered briars that o'er the crags
  recline;
Save where, with sparkling foam, a small
  cascade
Illumines, from within, the leafy shade;
Beyond, along the vista of the brook,
Where antique roots its bustling course
  o'erlook,

The eye reposes on a secret bridge [3]
Half gray, half shagged with ivy to its
  ridge;
There, bending o'er the stream, the list-
  less swain
Lingers behind his disappearing wain.
— Did Sabine grace adorn my living line,
Blandusia's praise, wild stream, should
  yield to thine !
Never shall ruthless minister of death
'Mid thy soft glooms the glittering steel
  unsheath;
No goblets shall, for thee, be crowned
  with flowers,
No kid with piteous outcry thrill thy
  bowers;
The mystic shapes that by thy margin
  rove
A more benignant sacrifice approve —
A mind, that, in a calm angelic mood
Of happy wisdom, meditating good,
Beholds, of all from her high powers re-
  quired,
Much done, and much designed, and more
  desired, —
Harmonious thoughts, a soul by truth
  refined,
Entire affection for all human kind.
  Dear Brook, farewell ! To-morrow's
  noon again
Shall hide me, wooing long thy wild-
  wood strain;
But now the sun has gained his western
  road,
And eve's mild hour invites my steps
  abroad.
  While, near the midway cliff, the sil-
  vered kite
In many a whistling circle wheels her
  flight;
Slant watery lights, from parting clouds,
  apace
Travel along the precipice's base;
Cheering its naked waste of scattered
  stone,
By lichens gray and scanty moss o'er-
  grown;
Where scarce the foxglove peeps, or
  thistle's beard;

[1] The word *intake* is local, and signifies a
mountain enclosure.
  [2] Ghyll is also, I believe, a term confined to
this country: ghyll, and dingle, have the same
meaning.

[3] The reader who has made the tour of this
country, will recognize, in this description, the
features which characterize the lower waterfall in
the grounds of Rydal.

And restless stone-chat, all day long, is
  heard.
  How pleasant, as the sun declines, to
    view
The spacious landscape change in form
  and hue!
Here, vanish, as in mist, before a flood
Of bright obscurity, hill, lawn, and
  wood;
There, objects, by the searching beams
  betrayed, .
Come forth, and here retire in purple
  shade;
Even the white stems of birch, the cot-
  tage white,
Soften their glare before the mellow
  light;
The skiffs, at anchor where with umbrage
  wide
Yon chestnuts half the latticed boat-
  house hide,
Shed from their sides, that face the sun's
  slant beam,
Strong flakes of radiance on the tremu-
  lous stream:
Raised by yon travelling flock, a dusty
  cloud
Mounts from the road, and spreads its
  moving shroud;
The shepherd, all involved in wreaths of
  fire,
Now shows a shadowy speck, and now
  is lost entire.
  Into a gradual calm the breezes sink,
A blue rim borders all the lake's still
  brink;
There doth the twinkling aspen's foliage
  sleep,
And insects clothe, like dust, the glassy
  deep:
And now, on every side, the surface
  breaks
Into blue spots, and slowly lengthening
  streaks;
Here, plots of sparkling water tremble
  bright
With thousand thousand twinkling points
  of light;
There, waves that, hardly weltering, die
  away,
Tip their smooth ridges with a softer ray;
And now the whole wide lake in deep
  repose

Is hushed, and like a burnished mirror
  glows,
Save where, along the shady western
  marge,
Coasts, with industrious oar, the char-
  coal barge.
  Their panniered train a group of pot-
  ters goad,
Winding from side to side up the steep
  road;
The peasant, from yon cliff of fearful
  edge
Shot, down the headlong path darts with
  his sledge;
Bright beams the lonely mountain-horse
  illume
Feeding 'mid purple heath, "green
  rings," [1] and broom;
While the sharp slope the slackened
  team confounds,
Downward the ponderous timber-wain
  resounds;
In foamy breaks the rill, with merry
  song,
Dashed o'er the rough rock, lightly leaps
  along;
From lonesome chapel at the mountain's
  feet,
Three humble bells their rustic chime
  repeat;
Sounds from the water-side the ham-
  mered boat;
And *blasted* · quarry thunders, heard
  remote!
Even here, amid the sweep of endless
  woods,
Blue pomp of lakes, high cliffs, and fall-
  ing floods,
Not undelightful are the simplest charms,
Found by the grassy door of mountain-
  farms.
  Sweetly ferocious,[2] round his native
  walks,
Pride of his sister-wives, the monarch
  stalks;
Spur-clad his nervous feet, and firm his
  tread;

[1] "Vivid rings of green." — GREENWOOD'S
POEM ON SHOOTING.
[2] "Dolcemente feroce."—TASSO. In this de-
scription of the cock, I remembered a spirited
one of the same animal in *L'Agriculture, ou
Les Géorgiques François*, of M. Rossuet.

A crest of purple tops the warrior's head.
Bright sparks his black and rolling eye-
　　ball hurls
Afar, his tail he closes and unfurls;
On tiptoe reared, he strains his clarion
　　throat,
Threatened by faintly-answering farms
　　remote:
Again with his shrill voice the mountain
　　rings,
While, flapped with conscious pride, re-
　　sound his wings.
　　Where, mixed with graceful birch, the
　　　sombrous pine
And yew-tree o'er the silver rocks re-
　　cline;
I love to mark the quarry's moving
　　trains,
Dwarf panniered steeds, and men, and
　　numerous wains;
How busy all the enormous hive within,
While Echo dallies with its various din!
Some (hear you not their chisels' clink-
　　ing sound?)
Toil, small as pygmies in the gulf pro-
　　found;
Some, dim between the lofty cliffs de-
　　scried,
O'erwalk the slender plank from side to
　　side;
These, by the pale-blue rocks that cease-
　　less ring,
In airy baskets hanging, work and sing.
　　Just where a cloud above the mountain
　　　rears
An edge all flame, the broadening sun
　　appears;
A long blue bar its ægis orb divides,
And breaks the spreading of its golden
　　tides;
And now that orb has touched the pur-
　　ple steep
Whose softened image penetrates the
　　deep.
'Cross the calm lake's blue shades the
　　cliffs aspire,
With towers and woods, a "prospect all
　　on fire;"
While coves and secret hollows, through
　　a ray
Of fainter gold, a purple gleam betray.
Each slip of lawn the broken rocks be-
　　tween

Shines in the light with more than earthly
　　green:
Deep yellow beams the scattered stems
　　illume,
Far in the level forest's central gloom:
Waving his hat, the shepherd, from the
　　vale,
Directs his winding dog the cliffs to scale,—
The dog, loud barking, 'mid the glitter-
　　ing rocks,
Hunts, where his master points, the inter-
　　cepted flocks.
Where oaks o'erhang the road the ra-
　　diance shoots
On tawny earth, wild weeds, and twisted
　　roots;
The druid-stones a brightened ring un-
　　fold;
And all the babbling brooks are liquid
　　gold;
Sunk to a curve, the day-star lessens still,
Gives one bright glance, and drops
　　behind the hill.[1]
　　In these secluded vales, if village fame,
Confirmed by hoary hairs, belief may
　　claim;
When up the hills, as now, retired the
　　light,
Strange apparitions mocked the shep-
　　herd's sight.
　　The form appears of one that spurs his
　　　steed
Midway along the hill with desperate
　　speed;
Unhurt pursues his lengthened flight,
　　while all
Attend, at every stretch, his headlong fall.
Anon, appears a brave, a gorgeous show
Of horsemen-shadows moving to and fro;
At intervals imperial banners stream,
And now the van reflects the solar beam;
The rear through iron brown betrays a
　　sullen gleam.
While silent stands the admiring crowd
　　below,
Silent the visionary warriors go,
Winding in ordered pomp their upward
　　way.[2]

[1] From Thomson.
[2] See a description of an appearance of this kind
in Clark's Survey of the Lakes, accompanied by
vouchers of its veracity, that may amuse the
reader.

Till the last banner of the long array
Has disappeared, and every trace is fled
Of splendor — save the beacon's spiry
        head
Tipt with eve's latest gleam of burning
        red.
  Now, while the solemn evening shad-
        ows sail,
On slowly-waving pinions, down the vale;
And, fronting the bright west, yon oak
        entwines
Its darkening boughs and leaves, in
        stronger lines;
'Tis pleasant near the tranquil lake to
        stray
Where, winding on along some secret
        bay,
The swan uplifts his chest, and backward
        flings
His neck, a varying arch, between his
        towering wings:
The eye that marks the gliding creature
        sees
How graceful, pride can be, and how
        majestic, ease.
While tender cares and mild domestic
        loves
With furtive watch pursue her as she
        moves,
The female with a meeker charm suc-
        ceeds,
And her brown little-ones around her
        leads,
Nibbling the water lilies as they pass,
Or playing wanton with the floating grass.
She, in a mother's care, her beauty's
        pride
Forgetting, calls the wearied to her side;
Alternately they mount her back, and rest
Close by her mantling wings' embraces
        prest.
  Long may they float upon this flood
        serene;
Theirs be these holms untrodden, still,
        and green,
Where leafy shades fence off the bluster-
        ing gale,
And breathes in peace the lily of the
        vale !
Yon isle, which feels not even the milk-
        maid's feet,
Yet hears her song, " by distance made
        more sweet,"

Yon isle conceals their home, their hut·
        like bower;
Green water-rushes overspread the floor;
Long grass and willows form the woven
        wall,
And swings above the roof the poplar tall.
Thence issuing often with unwieldy stalk,
They crush with broad black feet their
        flowery walk;
Or, from the neighboring water, hear at
        morn
The hound, the horse's tread, and mellow
        horn;
Involve their serpent-necks in changeful
        rings,
Rolled wantonly between their slippery
        wings,
Or, starting up with noise and rude
        delight,
Force half upon the wave their cumbrous
        flight.
  Fair Swan ! by all a mother's joys
        caressed,
Haply some wretch has eyed, and called
        thee blessed;
When with her infants, from some shady
        seat
By the lake's edge, she rose — to face
        the noontide heat;
Or taught their limbs along the dusty road
A few short steps to totter with their load.
  I see her now, denied to lay her head,
On cold blue nights, in hut or straw-built
        shed,
Turn to a silent smile their sleepy cry,
By pointing to the gliding moon on high.
— When low-hung clouds each star of
        summer hide,
And fireless are the valleys far and wide,
Where the brook brawls along the public
        road
Dark with bat-haunted ashes stretching
        broad,
Oft has she taught them on her lap to lay
The shining glow-worm; or, in heedless
        play,
Toss it from hand to hand, disquieted;
While others, not unseen, are free to
        shed
Green unmolested light upon their mossy
        bed.
  Oh ! when the sleety showers her path
        assail,

And like a torrent roars the headstrong
    gale;
No more her breath can thaw their fingers
    cold,
Their frozen arms her neck no more can
    fold;
Weak roof a cowering form two babes to
    shield,
And faint the fire a dying heart can yield!
Press the sad kiss, fond mother! vainly
    fears
Thy flooded cheek to wet them with its
    tears;
No tears can chill them, and no bosom
    warms,
Thy breast their death-bed, coffined in
    thine arms!
    Sweet are the sounds that mingle from
    afar,
Heard by calm lakes, as peeps the fold-
    ing star,
Where the duck dabbles 'mid the rustling
    sedge,
And feeding pike starts from the water's
    edge,
Or the swan stirs the reeds, his neck and
    bill
Wetting, that drip upon the water still;
And heron, as resounds the trodden
    shore,
Shoots upward, darting his long neck
    before.
    Now, with religious awe, the farewell
    light
Blends with the solemn coloring of night;
'Mid groves of clouds that crest the
    mountain's brow,
And round the west's proud lodge their
    shadows throw,
Like Una shining on her gloomy way,
The half-seen form of Twilight roams
    astray;
Shedding, through paly loop-holes mild
    and small,
Gleams that upon the lake's still bosom
    fall;
Soft o'er the surface creep those lustres
    pale
Tracking the motions of the fitful gale.
With restless interchange at once the
    bright
Wins on the shade, the shade upon the
    light.

No favored eye was e'er allowed to gaze
On lovelier spectacle in faery days;
When gentle Spirits urged a sportive
    chase,
Brushing with lucid wands the water's
    face:
While music, stealing round the glimmer-
    ing deeps,
Charmed the tall circle of the enchanted
    steeps.
—The lights are vanished from the
    watery plains;
No wreck of all the pageantry remains.
Unheeded night has overcome the vales:
On the dark earth the wearied vision
    fails;
The latest lingerer of the forest train,
The lone black fir, forsakes the faded
    plain;
Last evening sight, the cottage smoke, no
    more,
Lost in the thickened darkness, glimmers
    hoar;
And, towering from the sullen dark-
    brown mere,
Like a black wall, the mountain-steeps
    appear.
—Now o'er the soothed accordant heart
    we feel
A sympathetic twilight slowly steal,
And ever, as we fondly muse, we find
The soft gloom deepening on the tran-
    quil mind.
Stay! pensive, sadly-pleasing visions,
    stay!
Ah no! as fades the vale, they fade
    away:
Yet still the tender, vacant gloom remains;
Still the cold cheek its shuddering tear
    retains.
    The bird, who ceased, with fading light,
    to thread
Silent the hedge or steamy rivulet's bed,
From his gray reappearing tower shall
    soon
Salute with gladsome note the rising
    moon,
While with a hoary light she frosts the
    ground,
And pours a deeper blue to Æther's
    bound;
Pleased, as she moves, her pomp of
    clouds to fold

In robes of azure, fleecy-white, and gold.
　　Above yon eastern hill, where darkness
　　　broods
O'er all its vanished dells, and lawns,
　　and woods;
Where but a mass of shade the sight can
　　trace,
Even now she shows, half-veiled, her
　　lovely face:
Across the gloomy valley flings her light,
Far to the western slopes with hamlets
　　white;
And gives, where woods the checkered
　　upland strew,
To the green corn of summer, autumn's
　　hue.
　　Thus Hope, first pouring from her
　　　blessed horn
Her dawn, far lovelier than the moon's
　　own morn,
Till higher mounted, strives in vain to
　　cheer
The weary hills, impervious, blackening
　　near;
Yet does she still, undaunted, throw the
　　while
On darling spots remote her tempting
　　smile.
　　Even now she decks for me a distant
　　　scene,
(For dark and broad the gulf of time
　　between)
Gilding that cottage with her fondest ray,
(Sole bourn, sole wish, sole object of my
　　way;
How fair its lawns and sheltering woods
　　appear!
How sweet its streamlet murmurs in
　　mine ear!)
Where we, my Friend, to happy days
　　shall rise,
Till our small share of hardly-paining
　　sighs
(For sighs will ever trouble human
　　breath)
Creep hushed into the tranquil breast of
　　death.
　　But now the clear bright Moon her
　　　zenith gains,
And, rimy without speck, extend the
　　plains:
The deepest cleft the mountain's front
　　displays

Scarce hides a shadow from her search·
　　ing rays;
From the dark-blue faint silvery threads
　　divide
The hills, while gleams below the azure
　　tide;
Time softly treads; throughout the land-
　　scape breathes
A peace enlivened, not disturbed, by
　　wreaths
Of charcoal-smoke, that o'er the fallen
　　wood,
Steal down the hill, and spread along the
　　flood.
　　The song of mountain-streams, un-
　　　heard by day,
Now hardly heard, beguiles my home-
　　ward way.
Air listens, like the sleeping water, still,
To catch the spiritual music of the hill,
Broke only by the slow clock tolling deep,
Or shout that wakes the ferry-man from
　　sleep,
The echoed hoof nearing the distant
　　shore,
The boat's first motion — made with
　　dashing oar;
Sound of closed gate, across the water
　　borne,
Hurrying the timid hare through rustling
　　corn;
The sportive outcry of the mocking owl;
And at long intervals the mill-dog's howl;
The distant forge's swinging thump pro-
　　found;
Or yell, in the deep woods, of lonely
　　hound.
1787–89.　　　　　　　　　　　1793.

LINES

WRITTEN WHILE SAILING IN A BOAT
AT EVENING.

This title is scarcely correct. It was during a
solitary walk on the banks of the Cam that I was
first struck with this appearance, and applied
it to my own feelings in the manner here
expressed, changing the scene to the Thames,
near Windsor. This, and the three stanzas of
the following poem, " Remembrance of Collins,"
formed one piece; but, upon the recommendation
of Coleridge, the three last stanzas were separated
from the other.

How richly glows the water's breast
Before us, tinged with evening hues,
While, facing thus the crimson west,
The boat her silent course pursues!
And see how dark the backward stream!
A little moment past so smiling!
And still, perhaps, with faithless gleam,
Some other loiterers beguiling.

Such views the youthful Bard allure;
But, heedless of the following gloom,
He deems their colors shall endure
Till peace go with him to the tomb.
— And let him nurse his fond deceit,
And what if he must die in sorrow!
Who would not cherish dreams so sweet,
Though grief and pain may come to-mor-
   row?
1789   1798

REMEMBRANCE OF COLLINS.

COMPOSED UPON THE THAMES NEAR RICHMOND.

GLIDE gently, thus for ever glide,
O Thames! that other bards may see
As lovely visions by thy side
As now, fair river! come to me.
O glide, fair stream! for ever so,
Thy quiet soul on all bestowing,
Till all our minds for ever flow
As thy deep waters now are flowing.

Vain thought! — Yet be as now thou art,
That in thy waters may be seen
The image of a poet's heart,
How bright, how solemn, how serene!
Such as did once the Poet bless,
Who murmuring here a later [1] ditty,
Could find no refuge from distress
But in the milder grief of pity.

Now let us, as we float along,
For *him* suspend the dashing oar;
And pray that never child of song
May know that Poet's sorrows more.

[1] Collins's Ode on the death of Thomson, the last written, I believe, of the poems which were published during his lifetime. This Ode is also alluded to in the next stanza.

How calm! how still! the only sound,
The dripping of the oar suspended!
— The evening darkness gathers round
By virtue's holiest Powers attended.
1789   1798

DESCRIPTIVE SKETCHES.

TAKEN DURING A PEDESTRIAN TOUR AMONG THE ALPS.

Much the greatest part of this poem was composed during my walks upon the banks of the Loire in the years 1791, 1792. I will only notice that the description of the valley filled with mist, beginning — " In solemn shapes," was taken from that beautiful region of which the principal features are Lungarn and Sarnen. Nothing that I ever saw in nature left a more delightful impression on my mind than that which I have attempted, alas! how feebly, to convey to others in these lines. Those two lakes have always interested me especially, from bearing, in their size and other features, a resemblance to those of the North of England. It is much to be deplored that a district so beautiful should be so unhealthy as it is.

TO
THE REV. ROBERT JONES,

FELLOW OF ST. JOHN'S COLLEGE, CAMBRIDGE.

DEAR SIR,

However desirous I might have been of giving you proofs of the high place you hold in my esteem, I should have been cautious of wounding your delicacy by thus publicly addressing you, had not the circumstance of our having been companions among the Alps, seemed to give this dedication a propriety sufficient to do away any scruples which your modesty might otherwise have suggested.

In inscribing this little work to you, I consult my heart. You know well how great is the difference between two companions lolling in a postchaise, and two travellers plodding slowly along the road, side by side, each with his little knapsack of necessaries upon his shoulders. How much more of heart between the two latter!

I am happy in being conscious that I shall have one reader who will approach the conclusion of these few pages with regret. You they must certainly interest, in reminding you of moments to which you can hardly look back without a pleasure not the less dear from a shade of melancholy. You will meet with few images without recollecting the spot where we observed them together; consequently, whatever is feeble in my design, or spiritless in my coloring, will be amply supplied by your own memory.

With still greater propriety I might have inscribed to you a description of some of the features of your native mountains, through which we have wandered together, in the same manner, with so much pleasure. But the sea-sunsets, which give such splendor to the vale of Clwyd, Snowdon, the chair of Idris, the quiet village of Bethgelert, Menai and her Druids, the Alpine steeps of the Conway, and the still more interesting windings of the wizard stream of the Dee, remain yet untouched. Apprehensive that my pencil may never be exercised on these subjects, I cannot let slip this opportunity of thus publicly assuring you with how much affection and esteem

I am, dear Sir,

Most sincerely yours,

London, 1793.   W. WORDSWORTH.

Happiness (if she had been to be found on earth) among the charms of Nature — Pleasures of the pedestrian Traveller — Author crosses France to the Alps — Present state of the Grande Chartreuse — Lake of Como — Time, Sunset — Same Scene, Twilight—Same Scene, Morning ; its voluptuous Character ; Old man and forest-cottage music — River Tusa — Via Mala and Grison Gipsy — Sckellenen-thal — Lake of Uri — Stormy sunset — Chapel of William Tell — Force of local emotion — Chamois-chaser — View of the higher Alps — Manner of life of a Swiss mountaineer, interspersed with views of the higher Alps — Golden age of the Alps — Life and views continued — Ranz des Vaches, famous Swiss Air — Abbey of Einsiedlen and its pilgrims — Valley of Chamouny — Mont Blanc — Slavery of Savoy — Influence of liberty on cottage-happiness — France — Wish for the Extirpation of slavery — Conclusion.

WERE there, below, a spot of holy ground
Where from distress a refuge might be found,
And solitude prepare the soul for heaven;
Sure, nature's God that spot to man had given
Where falls the purple morning far and wide
In flakes of light upon the mountain side;
Where with loud voice the power of water shakes
The leafy wood, or sleeps in quiet lakes.
   Yet not unrecompensed the man shall roam,
Who at the call of summer quits his home,
And plods through some wide realm o'er vale and height,
Though seeking only holiday delight;
At least, not owning to himself an aim
To which the sage would give a prouder name.
No gains too cheaply earned his fancy cloy,
Though every passing zephyr whispers joy;
Brisk toil, alternating with ready ease,
Feeds the clear current of his sympathies.
For him sod-seats the cottage-door adorn;
And peeps the far-off spire, his evening bourn !
Dear is the forest frowning o'er his head,
And dear the velvet green-sward to his tread:
Moves there a cloud o'er mid-day's flaming eye?
Upward he looks —" and calls it luxury:"
Kind Nature's charities his steps attend;
In every babbling brook he finds a friend;
While chastening thoughts of sweetest use, bestowed
By wisdom, moralize his pensive road.
Host of his welcome inn, the noon-tide bower,
To his spare meal he calls the passing poor;
He views the sun uplift his golden fire,
Or sink, with heart alive like Memnon's lyre;[1]
Blesses the moon that comes with kindly ray,
To light him shaken by his rugged way.
Back from his sight no bashful children steal;
He sits a brother at the cottage-meal;
His humble looks no shy restraint impart;
Around him plays at will the virgin heart.
While unsuspended wheels the village dance,
The maidens eye him with inquiring glance,
Much wondering by what fit of crazing care,
Or desperate love, bewildered, he came there.

[1] The lyre of Memnon is reported to have emitted melancholy or cheerful tones, as it was touched by the sun's evening or morning rays.

A hope, that prudence could not then
approve,
That clung to Nature with a truant's love,
O'er Gallia's wastes of corn my footsteps
led;
Her files of road-elms, high above my
head
In long-drawn vista, rustling in the
breeze;
Or where her pathways straggle as they
please
By lonely farms and secret villages.
But lo! the Alps ascending white in air,
Toy with the sun and glitter from afar.
　And now, emerging from the forest's
gloom,
I greet thee, Chartreuse, while I mourn
thy doom.
Whither is fled that Power whose frown
severe
Awed sober Reason till she crouched in
fear?
That Silence, once in deathlike fetters
bound,
Chains that were loosened only by the
sound
Of holy rites chanted in measured round?
—The voice of blasphemy the fane
alarms,
The cloister startles at the gleam of arms.
The thundering tube the aged angler
hears,
Bent o'er the groaning flood that sweeps
away his tears.
Cloud-piercing pine-trees nod their trou-
bled heads,
Spires, rocks, and lawns a browner night
o'erspreads;
Strong terror checks the female peasant's
sighs,
And start the astonished shades at female
eyes.
From Bruno's forests screams the affright-
ed jay,
And slow the insulted eagle wheels away.
A viewless flight of laughing Demons
mock
The Cross, by angels planted[1] on the
aërial rock.

The " parting Genius " sighs with hollow
breath
Along the mystic streams of Life and
Death.[2]
Swelling the outcry dull, that long re-
sounds
Portentous through her old woods' track-
less bounds,
Vallombre,[3] 'mid her falling fanes, de-
plores,
For ever broke, the sabbath of her
bowers.
　More pleased, my foot the hidden
margin roves
Of Como, bosomed deep in chestnut
groves.
No meadows thrown between, the giddy
steeps
Tower, bare of sylvan, from the narrow
deeps.
— To towns, whose shades of no rude
noise complain,
From ringing team apart and grating
wain —
To flat-roofed towns, that touch the
water's bound,
Or lurk in woody sunless glens profound,
Or, from the bending rocks, obtrusive
cling,
And o'er the whitened wave their shadows
fling —
The pathway leads, as round the steeps
it twines;
And Silence loves its purple roof of vines.
The loitering traveller hence, at evening,
sees
From rock-hewn steps the sail between
the trees;
Or marks, 'mid opening cliffs, fair dark-
eyed maids
Tend the small harvest of their garden
glades;
Or stops the solemn mountain-shades to
view
Stretch o'er the pictured mirror broad
and blue,
And track the yellow lights from steep to
steep,
As up the opposing hills they slowly
creep.

[1] Alluding to crosses seen on the tops of the
spiry rocks of Chartreuse, which have every ap-
pearance of being inaccessible.

[2] Names of rivers of the Chartreuse.
[3] Names of one of the valleys of the Char-
treuse.

Aloft, here, half a village shines, arrayed
In golden light; half hides itself in shade:
While, from amid the darkened roofs, the spire,
Restlessly flashing, seems to mount like fire:
There, all unshaded, blazing forests throw
Rich golden verdure on the lake below.
Slow glides the sail along the illumined shore,
And steals into the shade the lazy oar;
Soft bosoms breathe around contagious sighs,
And amorous music on the water dies.
    How blest, delicious scene! the eye that greets
Thy open beauties, or thy lone retreats;
Beholds the unwearied sweep of wood that scales
Thy cliffs; the endless waters of thy vales;
Thy lowly cots that sprinkle all the shore,
Each with its household boat beside the door;
Thy torrents shooting from the clear-blue sky;
Thy towns, that cleave, like swallows' nests, on high;
That glimmer hoar in eve's last light, descried
Dim from the twilight water's shaggy side,
Whence lutes and voices down the enchanted woods
Steal, and compose the oar-forgotten floods;
Thy lake, that, streaked or dappled, blue or gray,
'Mid smoking woods gleams hid from morning's ray
Slow-travelling down the western hills, to enfold
Its green-tinged margin in a blaze of gold;
Thy glittering steeples, whence the matin bell
Calls forth the woodman from his desert cell,
And quickens the blithe sound of oars that pass
Along the steaming lake, to early mass,
But now farewell to each and all — adieu
To every charm, and last and chief to you,
Ye lovely maidens that in noontide shade

Rest near your little plots of wheaten glade;
To all that binds the soul in powerless trance,
Lip-dewing song, and ringlet-tossing dance;
Where sparkling eyes and breaking smiles illume
The sylvan cabin's lute-enlivened gloom.
— Alas! the very murmur of the streams
Breathes o'er the failing soul voluptuous dreams,
While Slavery, forcing the sunk mind to dwell
On joys that might disgrace the captive's cell,
Her shameless timbrel shakes on Como's marge,
And lures from bay to bay the vocal barge.
    Yet are thy softer arts with power indued
To soothe and cheer the poor man's solitude.
By silent cottage-doors, the peasant's home
Left vacant for the day, I loved to roam.
But once I pierced the mazes of a wood
In which a cabin deserted stood;
There an old man an olden measure scanned
On a rude viol touched with withered hand.
As lambs or fawns in April clustering lie
Under a hoary oak's thin canopy,
Stretched at his feet, with steadfast upward eye,
His children's children listened to the sound;
—A Hermit with his family around!
    But let us hence; for fair Locarno smiles
Embowered in walnut slopes and citron isles:
Or seek at eve the banks of Tusca's stream,
Where, 'mid dim towers and woods, her [1] waters gleam.
From the bright wave, in solemn gloom, retire
The dull-red steeps, and, darkening still, aspire

[1] The river along whose banks you descend in crossing the Alps by the Simplon Pass.

To where afar rich orange lustres glow
Round undistinguished clouds, and rocks,
    and snow:
Or, led where Via Mala's chasms confine
The indignant waters of the infant Rhine,
Hang o'er the abyss, whose else impervi-
    ous gloom
His burning eyes with fearful light illume.
    The mind condemned, without re-
      prieve, to go
O'er life's long deserts with its charge of
    woe,
With sad congratulation joins the train
Where beasts and men together o'er the
    plain
Move on — a mighty caravan of pain:
Hope, strength, and courage, social suf-
    fering brings,
Freshening the wilderness with shades
    and springs.
— There be whose lot far otherwise is
    cast:
Sole human tenant of the piny waste,
By choice or doom a gypsy wanders here,
A nursling babe her only comforter;
Lo, where she sits beneath yon shaggy
    rock,
A cowering shape half hid in curling
    smoke!
    When lightning among clouds and
      mountain-snows
Predominates, and darkness comes and
    goes,
And the fierce torrent, at the flashes
    broad
Starts, like a horse, beside the glaring
    road —
She seeks a covert from the battering
    shower
In the roofed bridge; [1] the bridge, in that
    dread hour,
Itself all trembling at the torrent's power.
    Nor is she more at ease on some *still*
      night,
When not a star supplies the comfort of
    its light;
Only the waning moon hangs dull and
    red
Above a melancholy mountain's head,

[1] Most of the bridges among the Alps are of
wood, and covered: these bridges have a heavy
appearance, and rather injure the effect of the
scenery in some places.

Then sets. In total gloom the Vagrant
    , sighs,
Stoops her sick head, and shuts her weary
    eyes;
Or on her fingers counts the distant clock,
Or, to the drowsy crow of midnight cock,
Listens, or quakes while from the forest's
    gulf
Howls near and nearer yet the famished
    wolf.
    From the green vale of Urseren smooth
      and wide
Descend we now, the maddened Reuss
    our guide;
By rocks that, shutting out the blessed
    day,
Cling tremblingly to rocks as loose as
    they;
By cells [2] upon whose image, while he
    prays,
The kneeling peasant scarcely dares to
    gaze;
By many a votive death-cross [3] planted
    near,
And watered duly with the pious tear,
That faded silent from the upward eye
Unmoved with each rude form of peril
    nigh;
Fixed on the anchor left by Him who
    saves
Alike in whelming snows, and roaring
    waves.
    But soon a peopled region on the sight
Opens — a little world of calm delight ;
Where mists, suspended on the expiring
    gale,
Spread rooflike o'er the deep secluded
    vale,
And beams of evening slipping in
    between,
Gently illuminate a sober scene: —
Here, on the brown wood-cottages [4] they
    sleep,
There, over rock or sloping pasture creep.

[2] The Catholic religion prevails here: these
cells are, as is well known, very common in the
Catholic countries, planted, like the Roman
tombs, along the road side.

[3] Crosses, commemorative of the deaths of
travellers by the fall of snow, and other accidents,
are very common along this dreadful road.

[4] The houses in the more retired Swiss valleys
are all built of wood.

On as we journey, in clear view dis-
    played,
The still vale lengthens underneath its
    shade
Of low-hung vapor: on the freshened
    mead
The green light sparkles ; — the dim
    bowers recede.
While pastoral pipes and streams the
    landscape lull,
And bells of passing mules that tinkle dull,
In solemn shapes before the admiring eye
Dilated hang the misty pines on high,
Huge convent domes with pinnacles and
    towers,
And antique castles seen through gleamy
    showers.

From such romantic dreams, my soul,
    awake !
To sterner pleasure, where, by Uri's lake
In Nature's pristine majesty outspread,
Winds neither road nor path for foot to
    tread :
The rocks rise naked as a wall, or stretch
Far o'er the water, hung with groves of
    beech;
Aërial pines from loftier steeps ascend,
Nor stop but where creation seems to end.
Yet here and there, if 'mid the savage
    scene
Appears a scanty plot of smiling green,
Up from the lake a zigzag path will creep
To reach a small wood-hut hung boldly
    on the steep,
— Before those thresholds (never can
    they know
The face of traveller passing to and fro,)
No peasant leans upon his pole, to tell
For whom at morning tolled the funeral
    bell;
Their watch-dog ne'er his angry bark
    foregoes,
Touched by the beggar's moan of human
    woes;
The shady porch ne'er offered a cool seat
To pilgrims overcome by summer's heat,
Yet thither the world's business finds its
    way
At times, and tales unsought beguile the
    day,
And *there* are those fond thoughts which
    Solitude,
However stern, is powerless to exclude.

There doth the maiden watch her lover's
    sail
Approaching, and upbraid the tardy gale;
At midnight listens till his parting oar,
And its last echo, can be heard no more.
    And what if ospreys, cormorants,
      herons, cry
Amid tempestuous vapors driving by,
Or hovering over wastes too bleak to rear
That common growth of earth, the food-
    ful ear;
Where the green apple shrivels on the
    spray,
And pines the unripened pear in sum-
    mer's kindliest ray;
Contentment shares the desolate domain
With Independence, child of high Dis-
    dain.
Exulting 'mid the winter of the skies,
Shy as the jealous chamois, Freedom flies,
And grasps by fits her sword, and often
    eyes;
And sometimes, as from rock to rock she
    bounds
The Patriot nymph starts at imagined
    sounds,
And, wildly pausing, oft she hangs
    aghast,
Whether some old Swiss air hath checked
    her haste
Or thrill of Spartan fife is caught be-
    tween the blast.
Swoln with incessant rains from hour
    to hour,
All day the floods a deepening murmur
    pour :
The sky is veiled, and every cheerful
    sight :
Dark is the region as with coming night;
But what a sudden burst of overpower-
    ing light !
Triumphant on the bosom of the storm,
Glances the wheeling eagle's glorious
    form !
Eastward, in long perspective glittering,
    shine
The wood-crowned cliffs that o'er the
    lake recline;
Those lofty cliffs a hundred streams un-
    fold,
At once to pillars turned that flame with
    gold :
Behind his sail the peasant shrinks, to shun

The *west*, that burns like one dilated sun,
A crucible of mighty compass, felt
By mountains, glowing till they seem to
    melt.
    But, lo! the boatman, overawed, be-
    fore
The pictured fane of Tell suspends his
    oar;
Confused the Marathonian tale appears,
While his eyes sparkle with heroic tears.
And who, that walks where men of an-
    cient days
Have wrought with godlike arm the
    deeds of praise,
Feels not the spirit of the place control,
Or rouse and agitate his laboring soul?
Say, who, by thinking on Canadian hills,
Or wild Aosta lulled by Alpine rills,
On Zutphen's plain; or on that highland
    dell,
Through which rough Garry cleaves his
    way, can tell
What high resolves exalt the tenderest
    thought
Of him who passion rivets to the spot,
Where breathed the gale that caught
    Wolfe's happiest sigh,
And the last sunbeam fell on Bayard's
    eye;
Where bleeding Sidney from the cup re-
    tired,
And glad Dundee in "faint huzzas"
    expired?
But now with other mind I stand alone
Upon the summit of this naked cone,
And watch the fearless chamois-hunter
    chase
His prey, through tracts abrupt of deso-
    late space,
[1] Through vacant worlds where Nature
    never gave
A brook to murmur or a bough to wave,
Which unsubstantial Phantoms sacred
    keep;
Thro' worlds where Life and Voice and
    Motion sleep;
Where silent Hours their death like sway
    extend,

Save when the avalanche breaks loose,
    to rend
Its way with uproar, till the ruin,
    drowned
In some dense wood or gulf of snow
    profound,
Mocks the dull ear of Time with deaf
    abortive sound.
— 'Tis his, while wandering on from
    height to height,
To see a planet's pomp and steady light
In the least star of scarce-appearing
    night;
While the pale moon moves near him,
    on the bound
Of ether, shining with diminished round,
And far and wide the icy summits blaze,
Rejoicing in the glory of her rays:
To him the day-star glitters small and
    bright,
Shorn of its beams, insufferably white,
And he can look beyond the sun, and
    view
Those fast-receding depths of sable blue
Flying till vision can no more pursue!
— At once bewildering mists around him
    close,
And cold and hunger are his least of
    woes;
The Demon of the snow, with angry roar
Descending, shuts for aye his prison door.
Soon with despair's whole weight his
    spirits sink;
Bread has he none, the snow must be his
    drink;
And, ere his eyes can close upon the day,
The eagle of the Alps o'ershades her prey.
    Now couch thyself where, heard with
    fear afar,
Thunders through echoing pines the
    headlong Aar;
Or rather stay to taste the mild delights
Of pensive Underwalden's [2] pastoral
    heights.
— Is there who 'mid these awful wilds
    has seen
The native Genii walk the mountain
    green?

[1] For most of the images in the next sixteen verses, I am indebted to M. Raymond's interesting observations annexed to his translation of Coxe's tour in Switzerland.

[2] The people of this Canton are supposed to be of a more melancholy disposition than the other inhabitants of the Alps; this, if true, may proceed from their living more secluded.

Or heard, while other worlds their charms
    reveal,
Soft music o'er the aerial summit steal?
While o'er the desert, answering every
    close,
Rich steam of sweetest perfume comes
    and goes.
— And sure there is a secret Power that
    reigns
Here, where no trace of man the spot
    profanes,
Nought but the *châlets*,[1] flat and bare, on
    high
Suspended 'mid the quiet of the sky;
Or distant herds that pasturing upward
    creep,
And, not untended, climb the dangerous
    steep.
How still! no irreligious sound or sight
Rouses the soul from her severe delight.
An idle voice the sabbath region fills
Of Deep that calls to Deep across the
    hills,
And with that voice accords the soothing
    sound
Of drowsy bells, for ever tinkling round;
Faint wail of eagle melting into blue
Beneath the cliffs, and pine-woods'
    steady *sugh;*[2]
The solitary heifer's deepened low;
Or rumbling, heard remote, of falling
    snow.
All motions, sounds, and voices, far and
    nigh,
Blend in a music of tranquillity;
Save when, a stranger seen below, the
    boy
Shouts from the echoing hills with sav-
    age joy.
    When, from the sunny breast of open
    seas,
And bays with myrtle fringed, the south-
    ern breeze
Comes on to gladden April with the sight
Of green isles widening on each snow-
    clad height;
When shouts and lowing herds the valley
    fill,

[1] This picture is from the middle region of
the Alps. *Châlets* are summer huts for the
Swiss herdsmen.

[2] Sugh, a Scotch word expressive of the
sound of the wind through the trees.

And louder torrents stun the noon-tide
    hill,
The pastoral Swiss begin the cliffs to
    scale,
Leaving to silence the deserted vale;
And like the Patriarchs in their simple
    age
Move, as the verdure leads, from stage
    to stage:
High and more high in summer's heat
    they go,
And hear the rattling thunder far below;
Or steal beneath the mountains, half-de-
    terred,
Where huge rocks tremble to the bellow-
    ing herd.
    One I behold who, 'cross the foaming
    flood,
Leaps with a bound of graceful hardi-
    hood;
Another, high on that green ledge; — he
    gained
The tempting spot with every sinew
    strained;
And downward thence a knot of grass he
    throws,
Food for his beasts in time of winter
    snows.
— Far different life from what Tradition
    hoar
Transmits of happier lot in times of yore!
Then Summer lingered long; and honey
    flowed
From out the rocks, the wild bees' safe
    abode:
Continual waters welling cheered the
    waste,
And plants were wholesome, now of
    deadly taste:
Nor Winter yet his frozen stores had
    piled,
Usurping where the fairest herbage
    smiled:
Nor Hunger driven the herds from pas-
    tures bare,
To climb the treacherous cliffs for scanty
    fare.
Then the milk-thistle flourished through
    the land,
And forced the full-swoln udder to de-
    mand,
Thrice every day, the pail and welcome
    hand.

Thus does the father to his children tell
Of banished bliss, by fancy loved too
    well.
Alas! that human guilt provoked the rod
Of angry Nature to avenge her God.
Still, Nature, ever just, to him imparts
Joys only given to uncorrupted hearts.
   'Tis morn: with gold the verdant
    mountain glows
More high, the snowy peaks with hues of
    rose.
Far-stretched beneath the many-tinted
    hills,
A mighty waste of mist the valley fills,
A solemn sea! whose billows wide
    around
Stand motionless, to awful silence bound:
Pines, on the coast, through mist their
    tops uprear,
That like to leaning masts of stranded
    ships appear.
A single chasm, a gulf of gloomy blue,
Gapes in the centre of the sea — and,
    through
That dark mysterious gulf ascending,
    sound
Innumerable streams with roar profound.
Mount through the nearer vapors notes
    of birds,
And merry flageolet; the low of herds,
The bark of dogs, the heifer's tinkling bell,
Talk, laughter, and perchance a church-
    tower knell:
Think not, the peasant from aloft has
    gazed
And heard with heart unmoved, with soul
    unraised:
Nor is his spirit less enrapt, nor less
Alive to independent happiness,
Then, when he lies, outstretched, at even-
    tide
Upon the fragrant mountain's purple side:
For as the pleasures of his simple day
Beyond his native valley seldom stray,
Nought round its darling precincts can he
    find
But brings some past enjoyment to his
    mind;
While Hope, reclining upon Pleasure's
    urn,
Binds her wild wreaths, and whispers his
    return.
   Once, Man entirely free, alone and wild,

Was blest as free — for he was Nature's
.   child.
He, all superior but his God disdained,
Walked, none restraining and by none
    restrained,
Confessed no law but what his reason
    taught,
Did all he wished, and wished but what
    he ought.
As man in his primeval dower arrayed
The image of his glorious Sire displayed,
Even so, by faithful Nature guarded, here
The traces of primeval Man appear;
The simple dignity no forms debase;
The eye sublime, and surly lion-grace:
The slave of none, of beasts alone the
    lord,
His book he prizes, nor neglects his
    sword;
Well taught by that to feel his rights, pre-
    pared
With this "the blessings he enjoys to
    guard."
   And, as his native hills encircle ground
For many a marvellous victory renowned,
The work of Freedom daring to oppose,
With few in arms,[1] innumerable foes,
When to those famous fields his steps are
    led,
An unknown power connects him with
    the dead:
For images of other worlds are there;
Awful the light, and holy is the air.
Fitfully, and in flashes, through his soul,
Like sun-lit tempests, troubled trans-
    ports roll;
His bosom heaves, his Spirit towers
    amain,
Beyond the senses and their little reign.
   And oft, when that dread vision hath
    past by,

---

[1] Alluding to several battles which the Swiss in very small numbers have gained over their oppressors, the house of Austria; and in particular, to one fought at Naeffels near Glarus, where three hundred and thirty men are said to have defeated an army of between fifteen and twenty thousand Austrians. Scattered over the valley are to be found eleven stones, with this inscription, 1388, the year the battle was fought, marking out, as I was told upon the spot, the several places where the Austrians, attempting to make a stand, were repulsed anew.

He holds with God himself communion
  high,
There where the peal of swelling torrents
  fills
The sky-roofed temple of the eternal
  hills;
Or when, upon the mountain's silent
  brow
Reclined, he sees, above him and below,
Bright stars of ice and azure fields of
  snow;
While needle peaks of granite shooting
  bare
Tremble in ever-varying tints of air.
And when a gathering weight of shadows
  brown
Falls on the valleys as the sun goes down;
And Pikes, of darkness named and fear
  and storms,[1]
Uplift in quiet their illumined forms,
In sea-like reach of prospect round him
  spread,
Tinged like an angel's smile all rosy
  red —
Awe in his breast with holiest love unites,
And the near heavens impart their own
  delights.
  When downward to his winter hut he
  goes,
Dear and more dear the lessening circle
  grows;
That hut which on the hill so oft em-
  ploys
His thoughts, the central point of all i..s
  joys.
And as a swallow, at the hour of rest,
Peeps often ere she darts into her nest,
So to the homestead, where the grand-
  sire tends
A little prattling child, he oft descends,
To glance a look upon the well-matched
  pair;
Till storm and driving ice blockade him
  there.
There, safely guarded by the woods be-
  hind,
He hears the chiding of the baffled wind,
Hears Winter calling all his terrors round,
And, blest within himself, he shrinks not
  from the sound.

  [1] As Schreck-Horn, the pike of terror; Wet-
ter-Horn, the pike of storms, etc., etc.

Through Nature's vale his homely
  pleasures glide,
Unstained by envy, discontent, and pride;
The bound of all his vanity, to deck,
With one bright bell, a favorite heifer's
  neck;
Well pleased upon some simple annual
  feast,
Remembered half the year and hoped the
  rest,
If dairy-produce, from his inner hoard,
Of thrice ten summers dignify the board.
— Alas! in every clime a flying ray
Is all we have to cheer our wintry way;
And here the unwilling mind may more
  than trace
The general sorrows of the human race;
The churlish gales of penury, that blow
Cold as the north-wind o'er a waste of
  snow,
To them the gentle groups of bliss deny
That on the noon-day bank of leisure lie.
Yet more; — compelled by Powers which
  only deign
That *solitary* man disturb their reign,
Powers that support an unremitting strife
With all the tender charities of life,
Full oft the father, when his sons have
  grown
To manhood, seems their title to disown;
And from his nest amid the storms of
  heaven
Drives, eagle-like, those sons as he was
  driven;
With stern composure watches to the
  plain —
And never, eagle-like, beholds again!
  When long-familiar joys are all re-
  signed,
Why does their sad remembrance haunt
  the mind?
Lo! where through flat Batavia's willowy
  groves,
Or by the lazy Seine, the exile roves;
O'er the curled waters Alpine measures
  swell,
And search the affections to their inmost
  cell;
Sweet poison spreads along the listener's
  veins,
Turning past pleasures into mortal pains;
Poison, which not a frame of steel can
  brave,

Bows his young head with sorrow to the grave.[1]
  Gay lark of hope, thy silent song resume!
Ye flattering eastern lights, once more the hills illume!
Fresh gales and dews of life's delicious morn,
And thou, lost fragrance of the heart, return!
Alas! the little joy to man allowed
Fades like the lustre of an evening cloud;
Or like the beauty in a flower installed,
Whose season was, and cannot be recalled.
Yet, when opprest by sickness, grief, or care,
And taught that pain is pleasure's natural heir,
We still confide in more than we can know;
Death would be else the favorite friend of woe.
  'Mid savage rocks, and seas of snow that shine,
Between interminable tracts of pine,
Within a temple stands an awful shrine,
By an uncertain light revealed, that falls
On the mute Image and the troubled walls.
Oh! give not me that eye of hard disdain
That views, undimmed, Einsiedlen's[2] wretched fane.
While ghastly faces through the gloom appear,
Abortive joy, and hope that works in fear;
While prayer contends with silenced agony,
Surely in other thoughts contempt may die.
If the sad grave of human ignorance bear
One flower of hope — oh, pass and leave it there!
  The tall sun, pausing on an Alpine spire,
Flings o'er the wilderness a stream of fire:
Now meet we other pilgrims ere the day

Close on the remnant of their weary way;
While they are drawing toward the sacred floor
Where, so they fondly think, the worm shall gnaw no more.
How gayly murmur and how sweetly taste
The fountains[3] reared for them amid the waste!
Their thirst they slake: — they wash their toil-worn feet
And some with tears of joy each other greet.
Yes, I must see you when ye first behold
Those holy turrets tipped with evening gold,
In that glad moment will for you a sigh
Be heaved, of charitable sympathy;
In that glad moment when your hands are prest
In mute devotion on the thankful breast!
  Last, let us turn to Chamouny that shields
With rocks and gloomy woods her fertile fields:
Five streams of ice amid her cots descend,
And with wild flowers and blooming orchards blend; —
A scene more fair than what the Grecian feigns
Of purple lights and ever-vernal plains;
Here all the seasons revel hand in hand:
'Mid lawns and shades by breezy rivulets fanned,
They sport beneath that mountain's matchless height
That holds no commerce with the summer night.
From age to age, throughout his lonely bounds
The crash of ruin fitfully resounds;
Appalling havoc! but serene his brow,
Where daylight lingers on perpetual snow;
Glitter the stars above, and all is black below.
  What marvel then if many a Wanderer sigh,
While roars the sullen Arve in anger by,
That not for thy reward, unrivalled Vale!

[1] The well-known effect of the famous air, called in French Ranz des Vaches, upon the Swiss troops.

[2] This shrine is resorted to, from a hope of relief, by multitudes, from every corner of the Catholic world, laboring under mental or bodily afflictions.

[3] Rude fountains built and covered with sheds for the accommodation of the Pilgrims, in their ascent of the mountain

Waves the ripe harvest in the autumnal
gale;
That thou, the slaves of slaves, art
doomed to pine
And droop, while no Italian arts are thine,
To soothe or cheer, to soften or refine.
Hail Freedom! whether it was mine to
stray,
With shrill winds whistling round my
lonely way,
On the bleak sides of Cumbria's heath-
clad moors,
Or where dank sea-weed lashes Scot-
land's shores;
To scent the sweets of Piedmont's breath-
ing rose,
And orange gale that o'er Lugano blows;
Still have I found, where Tyranny pre-
vails,
That virtue languishes and pleasure fails,
While the remotest hamlets blessings
share
In thy loved presence known, and only
there;
Heart-blessings — outward treasures too
which the eye
Of the sun peeping through the clouds
can spy,
And every passing breeze will testify.
There, to the porch, belike with jasmine
bound
Or woodbine wreaths, a smoother path is
wound;
The housewife there a brighter garden
sees,
Where hum on busier wing her happy
bees;
On infant cheeks there fresher roses blow;
And gray-haired men look up with live-
lier brow, —
To greet the traveller needing food and
rest;
Housed for the night, or but a half-hour's
guest.
And oh, fair France! though now the
traveller sees
Thy three-striped banner fluctuate on the
breeze;
Though martial songs have banished
songs of love,
And nightingales desert the village grove,
Scared by the fife and rumbling drum's
alarms,

And the short thunder, and the flash of
arms;
That cease not till night falls, when far
and nigh,
Sole sound, the Sourd [1] prolongs his
mournful cry!
— Yet, hast thou found that Freedom
spreads her power
Beyond the cottage-hearth, the cottage-
door:
All nature smiles, and owns beneath her
eyes
Her fields peculiar, and peculiar skies.
Yes, as I roamed where Loiret's waters
glide
Through rustling aspens heard from side to
side,
When from October clouds a milder light
Fell where the blue flood rippled into
white;
Methought from every cot the watchful
bird
Crowed with ear-piercing power till then
unheard;
Each clacking mill, that broke the mur-
muring streams,
Rocked the charmed thought in more
delightful dreams;
Chasing those pleasant dreams, the falling
leaf
Awoke a fainter sense of moral grief;
The measured echo of the distant flail
Wound in more welcome cadence down
the vale;
With more majestic course [2] the water
rolled,
And ripening foliage shone with richer
gold.
— But foes are gathering — Liberty must
raise
Red on the hills her beacon's far-seen
blaze;
Must bid the tocsin ring from tower to
tower! —
Nearer and nearer comes the trying hour!

[1] An insect so called, which emits a short,
melancholy cry, heard at the close of the summer
evenings, on the banks of the Loire.
[2] The duties upon many parts of the French
rivers were so exorbitant, that the poorer people,
deprived of the benefit of water carriage, were
obliged to transport their goods by land.

Rejoice, brave Land, though pride's per-
verted ire
Rouse hell's own aid, and wrap thy fields
in fire:
Lo, from the flames a great and glorious
birth;
As if a new-made heaven were hailing a
new earth!
— All cannot be: the promise is too fair
For creatures doomed to breathe terres-
trial air:
Yet not for this will sober reason frown
Upon that promise, nor the hope disown;
She knows that only from high aims en-
sue·
Rich guerdons, and to them alone are
due.
Great God! by whom the strifes of
men are weighed
In an impartial balance, give thine aid
To the just cause; and, oh! do thou pre-
side
Over the mighty stream now spreading
wide:
So shall its waters, from the heavens
supplied
In copious showers, from earth by whole-
some springs,
Brood o'er the long-parched lands with
Nile-like wings!
And grant that every sceptred child of
clay
Who cries presumptuous, " Here the flood
shall stay,"
May in its progress see thy guiding hand,
And cease the acknowledged purpose to
withstand;
Or, swept in anger from the insulted
shore,
Sink with his servile bands, to rise no
more!
To-night, my Friend, within this hum-
ble cot
Be scorn and fear and hope alike forgot
In timely sleep; and when, at break of
day,
On the tall peaks the glistening sunbeams
play,
With a light heart our course we may
renew,
The first whose footsteps print the moun-
tain dew.

1793.   1793.

GUILT AND SORROW;
OR,
INCIDENTS UPON SALISBURY PLAIN.

Unwilling to be unnecessarily particular, I
have assigned this poem to the dates 1793 and
'94; but in fact much of the " Female Vagrant's "
story was composed at least two years before.
All that relates to her sufferings as a sailor's wife
in America, and her condition of mind during her
voyage home, were faithfully taken from the
report made to me of her own case by a friend
who had been subjected to the same trials and
affected in the same way. Mr. Coleridge, when
I first became acquainted with him, was so much
impressed with this poem, that it would have
encouraged me to publish the whole as it then
stood; but the mariner's fate appeared to me so
tragical as to require a treatment more subdued
and yet more strictly applicable in expression than
I had at first given to it. This fault was corrected
nearly fifty years afterwards, when I determined
to publish the whole. It may be worth while to
remark, that, though the incidents of this attempt
do only in a small degree produce each other, and
it deviates accordingly from the general rule by
which narrative pieces ought to be governed, it
is not therefore wanting in continuous hold upon
the mind, or in unity, which is effected by the
identity of moral interest that places the two
personages upon the same footing in the reader's
sympathies. My rambles over many parts of
Salisbury Plain put me, as mentioned in the pref-
ace, upon writing this poem, and left on my
mind imaginative impressions the force of which
I have felt to this day. From that district I pro-
ceeded to Bath, Bristol, and so on to the banks
of the Wye, where I took again to travelling on
foot. In remembrance of that part of my jour-
ney, which was in '93, I began the verses—
" Five years have passed."

ADVERTISEMENT
PREFIXED TO THE FIRST EDITION OF THIS POEM,
PUBLISHED IN 1842.

Not less than one-third of the following poem,
though it has from time to time been altered in
the expression, was published so far back as the
year 1798, under the title of "The Female Va-
grant." The extract is of such length that an
apology seems to be required for reprinting it
here: but it was necessary to restore it to its
original position, or the rest would have been
unintelligible. The whole was written before the
close of the year 1794, and I will detail, rather
as a matter of literary biography than for any

other reason, the circumstances under which it was produced.

During the latter part of the summer of 1793, having passed a month in the Isle of Wight, in view of the fleet which was then preparing for sea off Portsmouth at the commencement of the war, I left the place with melancholy forebodings. The American war was still fresh in memory. The struggle which was beginning, and which many thought would be brought to a speedy close by the irresistible arms of Great Britain being added to those of the allies, I was assured in my own mind would be of long continuance, and productive of distress and misery beyond all possible calculation. This conviction was pressed upon me by having been a witness, during a long residence in revolutionary France, of the spirit which prevailed in that country. After leaving the Isle of Wight, I spent two days in wandering on foot over Salisbury Plain, which, though cultivation was then widely spread through parts of it, had upon the whole a still more impressive appearance than it now retains.

The monuments and traces of antiquity, scattered in abundance over that region, led me unavoidably to compare what we know or guess of those remote times with certain aspects of modern society, and with calamities, principally those consequent upon war, to which, more than other classes of men, the poor are subject. In those reflections, joined with particular facts that had come to my knowledge, the following stanzas originated.

In conclusion, to obviate some distraction in the minds of those who are well acquainted with Salisbury Plain, it may be proper to say, that of the features described as belonging to it, one or two are taken from other desolate parts of England.

I.

A TRAVELLER on the skirt of Sarum's Plain
Pursued his vagrant way, with feet half bare;
Stooping his gait, but not as if to gain
Help from the staff he bore; for mien and air
Were hardy, though his cheek seemed worn with care
Both of the time to come, and time long fled:
Down fell in straggling locks his thin gray hair;
A coat he wore of military red
But faded, and stuck o'er with many a patch and shred.

II.

While thus he journeyed, step by step led on,
He saw and passed a stately inn, full sure
That welcome in such house for him was none.
No board inscribed the needy to allure
Hung there, no bush proclaimed to old and poor
And desolate, "Here you will find a friend!"
The pendent grapes glittered above the door; —
On he must pace, perchance 'till night descend,
Where'er the dreary roads their bare white lines extend.

III.

The gathering clouds grow red with stormy fire,
In streaks diverging wide and mounting high;
That inn he long had passed; the distant spire,
Which oft as he looked back had fixed his eye,
Was lost, though still he looked, in the blank sky.
Perplexed and comfortless he gazed around,
And scarce could any trace of man descry,
Save cornfields stretched and stretching without bound;
But where the sower dwelt was nowhere to be found.

IV.

No tree was there, no meadow's pleasant green,
No brook to wet his lip or soothe his ear;
Long files of corn-stacks here and there were seen,
But not one dwelling-place his heart to cheer.
Some laborer, thought he, may perchance be near;
And so he sent a feeble shout — in vain;
No voice made answer, he could only hear

Winds rustling over plots of unripe grain,
Or whistling thro' thin grass along the
unfurrowed plain.

v.

Long had he fancied each successive slope
Concealed some cottage, whither he
might turn
And rest; but now along heaven's dark-
ening cope
The crows rushed by in eddies, home-
ward borne.
Thus warned he sought some shepherd's
spreading thorn
Or hovel from the storm to shield his
head,
But sought in vain; for now, all wild,
forlorn,
And vacant, a huge waste around him
spread;
The wet cold ground, he feared, must be
his only bed.

vi.

And be it so — for to the chill night
shower
And the sharp wind his head he oft hath
bared;
A Sailor he, who many a wretched hour
Hath told; for, landing after labor hard,
Full long endured in hope of just reward,
He to an armèd fleet was forced away
By seamen, who perhaps themselves had
shared
Like fate; was hurried off, a helpless
prey,
'Gainst all that in *his* heart, or theirs
perhaps, said nay.

vii.

For years the work of carnage did not
cease,
And death's dire aspect daily he surveyed,
Death's minister; then came his glad
release,
And hope returned, and pleasure fondly
made
Her dwelling in his dreams.   By Fancy's
aid
The happy husband flies, his arms to
throw
Round his wife's neck; the prize of vic-
tory laid

In her full lap, he sees such sweet tears
flow
As if thenceforth nor pain nor trouble
she could know.

viii

Vain hope! for fraud took all that he had
earned.
The lion roars and gluts his tawny brood
Even in the desert's heart; but he, re-
turned,
Bears not to those he loves their needful
food.
His home approaching, but in such a
mood
That from his sight his children might
have run.
He met a traveller, robbed him, shed his
blood;
And when the miserable work was done
He fled, a vagrant since, the murderer's
fate to shun.

ix.

From that day forth no place to him
could be
So lonely, but that thence might come a
pang
Brought from without to inward misery.
Now, as he plodded on, with sullen clang
A sound of chains along the desert rang;
He looked, and saw upon a gibbet high
A human body that in irons swang,
Uplifted by the tempest whirling by;
And, hovering, round it often did a raven
fly.[1]

x.

It was a spectacle which none might
view,
In spot so savage, but with shuddering
pain;
Nor only did for him at once renew
All he had feared from man, but roused a
train
Of the mind's phantoms, horrible as vain.
The stones, as if to cover him from day,
Rolled at his back along the living plain;
He fell, and without sense or motion lay;
But, when the trance was gone, feebly
pursued his way.

[1] See Note.

XI.

As one whose brain habitual frensy fires
Owes to the fit in which his soul hath
  tossed
Profounder quiet, when the fit retires,
Even so the dire phantasma which had
  crossed
His sense, in sudden vacancy quite lost,
Left his mind still as a deep evening
  stream.
Nor, if accosted now, in thought en-
  grossed,
Moody, or inly troubled, would he seem
To traveller who might talk of any casual
  theme.

XII.

Hurtle the clouds in deeper darkness
  piled,
Gone is the raven timely rest to seek;
He seemed the only creature in the wild
On whom the elements their rage might
  wreak;
Save that the bustard, of those regions
  bleak
Shy tenant, seeing by the uncertain light
A man there wandering, gave a mournful
  shriek,
And half upon the ground, with strange
  affright,
Forced hard against the wind a thick
  unwieldy flight.

XIII.

All, all was cheerless to the horizon's
  bound;
The weary eye — which, whereso'er it
  strays,
Marks nothing but the red sun's setting
  round,
Or on the earth strange lines, in former
  days
Left by gigantic arms — at length sur-
  veys
What seems an antique castle spreading
  wide;
Hoary and naked are its walls, and raise
Their brow sublime : in shelter there to
  bide
He turned, while rain poured down
  smoking on every side.

XIV.

Pile of Stone-henge ! so proud to hint yet
  keep
Thy secrets, thou that lov'st to stand and
  hear
The Plain resounding to the whirlwind's
  sweep,
Inmate of lonesome Nature's endless
  year;
Even if thou saw'st the giant wicker
  rear
For sacrifice its throngs of living men,
Before thy face did ever wretch appear,
Who in his heart had groaned with dead-
  lier pain
Than he who, tempest-driven, thy shelter
  now would gain.

XV.

Within that fabric of mysterious form,
Winds met in conflict, each by turns
  supreme;
And, from the perilous ground dislodged,
  through storm
And rain he wildered on, no moon to
  stream
From gulf of parting clouds one friendly
  beam,
Nor any friendly sound his footsteps led;
Once did the lightning's faint disastrous
  gleam
Disclose a naked guide-post's double
  head,
Sight which tho' lost at once a gleam of
  pleasure shed.

XVI.

No swinging sign-board creaked from
  cottage elm
To stay his steps with faintness overcome;
'Twas dark and void as ocean's watery
  realm
Roaring with storms beneath night's star-
  less gloom;
No gypsy cowered o'er fire of furze or
  broom;
No laborer watched his red kiln glaring
  bright,
Nor taper glimmered dim from sick man's
  room;
Along the waste no line of mournful light
From lamp of lonely toll-gate streamed
  athwart the night.

XVII.

At length, though hid in clouds, the
    moon arose;
The downs were visible — and now re-
    vealed
A structure stands, which two bare slopes
    enclose.
It was a spot, where, ancient vows ful-
    filled,
Kind pious hands did to the Virgin build
A lonely Spital, the belated swain
From the night terrors of that waste to
    shield:
But there no human being could remain,
And now the walls are named the "Dead
    House" of the plain.

XVIII.

Though he had little cause to love the
    abode
Of man, or covet sight of mortal face,
Yet when faint beams of light that ruin
    showed,
How glad he was at length to find some
    trace
Of human shelter in that dreary place.
Till to his flock the early shepherd goes,
Here shall much-needed sleep his frame
    embrace.
In a dry nook where fern the floor be-
    strows
He lays his stiffened limbs, — his eyes
    begin to close;

XIX.

When hearing a deep sigh, that seemed
    to come
From one who mourned in sleep, he
    raised his head,
And saw a woman in the naked room
Outstretched, and turning on a restless
    bed:
The moon a wan dead light around her
    shed.
He waked her — spake in tone that
    would not fail,
He hoped to calm her mind; but ill he
    sped,
For of that ruin she had heard a tale
Which now with freezing thoughts did all
    her powers assail;

XX.

Had heard of one who, forced from
    storms to shroud,
Felt the loose walls of this decayed Re-
    treat
Rock to incessant neighings shrill and
    loud,
While his horse pawed the floor with
    furious heat;
Till on a stone, that sparkled to his feet,
Struck, and still struck again, the troubled
    horse:
The man half raised the stone with pain
    and sweat,
Half raised, for well his arm might lose
    its force
Disclosing the grim head of a late mur-
    dered corse.

XXI.

Such tale of this lone mansion she had
    learned,
And, when that shape, with eyes in sleep
    half drowned,
By the moon's sullen lamp she first dis-
    cerned,
Cold stony horror all her senses bound.
Her he addressed in words of cheering
    sound;
Recovering heart, like answer did she
    make;
And well it was that, of the corse there
    found,
In converse that ensued she nothing
    spake;
She knew not what dire pangs in him
    such tale could wake.

XXII.

But soon his voice and words of kind in-
    tent
Banished that dismal thought; and now
    the wind
In fainter howlings told its *rage* was
    spent:
Meanwhile discourse ensued of various
    kind,
Which by degrees a confidence of mind
And mutual interest failed not to create.
And, to a natural sympathy resigned,
In that forsaken building where they sate
The Woman thus retraced her own unto-
    ward fate.

XXIII.

"By Derwent's side my father dwelt —
    a man
Of virtuous life, by pious parents bred;
And I believe that, soon as I began
To lisp, he made me kneel beside my bed,
And in his hearing there my prayers I
    said:
And afterwards, by my good father
    taught,
I read, and loved the books in which I
    read;
For books in every neighboring house I
    sought,
And nothing to my mind a sweeter pleas-
    ure brought.

XXIV.

"A little croft we owned — a plot of
    corn,
A garden stored with peas, and mint, and
    thyme,
And flowers for posies, oft on Sunday
    morn
Plucked while the church bells rang their
    earliest chime.
Can I forget our freaks at shearing time!
My hen's rich nest through long grass
    scarce espied;
The cowslip-gathering in June's dewy
    prime;
The swans that with white chests up-
    reared in pride
Rushing and racing came to meet me at
    the water-side.

XXV.

"The staff I well remember which up-
    bore
The bending body of my active sire;
His seat beneath the honied sycamore
Where the bees hummed, and chair by
    winter fire;
When market-morning came, the neat
    attire
With which, though bent on haste, my-
    self I decked;
Our watchful house-dog, that would tease
    and tire
The stranger till its barking-fit I checked;
The red-breast, known for years, which
    at my casement pecked.

XXVI.

"The suns of twenty summers danced
    along, —
Too little marked how fast they rolled
    away:
But, through severe mischance and cruel
    wrong,
My father's substance fell into decay:
We toiled and struggled, hoping for a
    day
When Fortune might put on a kinder
    look;
But vain were wishes, efforts vain as they;
He from his old hereditary nook
Must part; the summons came; — our
    final leave we took.

XXVII.

"It was indeed a miserable hour
When, from the last hill-top, my sire sur-
    veyed,
Peering above the trees, the steeple tower
That on his marriage day sweet music
    made!
Till then, he hoped his bones might there
    be laid
Close by my mother in their native bow-
    ers:
Bidding me trust in God, he stood and
    prayed; —
I could not pray: — through tears that fell
    in showers
Glimmered our dear-loved home, alas!
    no longer ours!

XXVIII.

"There was a Youth whom I had loved
    so long,
That when I loved him not I cannot say:
'Mid the green mountains many a thought-
    less song
We two had sung, like gladsome birds in
    May;
When we began to tire of childish play,
We seemed still more and more to prize
    each other;
We talked of marriage and our marriage
    day;
And I in truth did love him like a brother,
For never could I hope to meet with such
    another.

XXIX.

"Two years were passed since to a dis-
      tant town
He had repaired to ply a gainful trade:
What tears of bitter grief, till then un-
      known!
What tender vows, our last sad kiss de-
      layed!
To him we turned: — we had no other
      aid:
Like one revived, upon his neck I wept;
And her whom he had loved in joy, he
      said,
He well could love in grief; his faith he
      kept;
And in a quiet home once more my
      father slept.

XXX.

"We lived in peace and comfort; and
      were blest
With daily bread, by constant toil sup-
      plied.
Three lovely babes had lain upon my
      breast;
And often, viewing their sweet smiles, I
      sighed,
And knew not why. My happy father
      died,
When threatened war reduced the chil-
      dren's meal:
Thrice happy! that for him the grave
      could hide
The empty loom, cold hearth, and silent
      wheel,
And tears that flowed for ills which
      patience might not heal.

XXXI.

"'T was a hard change; an evil time was
      come;
We had no hope, and no relief could
      gain;
But soon, with proud parade, the noisy
      drum
Beat round to clear the streets of want
      and pain.
My husband's arms now only served to
      strain
Me and his children hungering in his
      view;
In such dismay my prayers and tears
      were vain:

To join those miserable men he flew,
And now to the sea coast, with numbers
      more, we drew.

XXXII.

"There were we long neglected, and we
      bore
Much sorrow ere the fleet its anchor
      weighed;
Green fields before us, and our native
      shore,
We breathed a pestilential air, that made
Ravage for which no knell was heard.
      We prayed
For our departure; wished and wished
      — nor knew,
'Mid that long sickness and those hopes
      delayed,
That happier days we never more must
      view.
The parting signal streamed — at last
      the land withdrew.

XXXIII.

"But the calm summer season now was
      past.
On as we drove, the equinoctial deep
Ran mountains high before the howling
      blast,
And many perished in the whirlwind's
      sweep.
We gazed with terror on their gloomy
      sleep,
Untaught that soon such anguish must
      ensue,
Our hopes such harvest of affliction reap,
That we the mercy of the waves should
      rue:
We reached the western world, a poor
      devoted crew.

XXXIV.

"The pains and plagues that on our
      heads came down,
Disease and famine, agony and fear,
In wood or wilderness, in camp or town,
It would unman the firmest heart to hear.
All perished — all in one remorseless year,
Husband and children! one by one, by
      sword
And ravenous plague, all perished: every
      tear

Dried up, despairing, desolate, on board
A British ship I waked, as from a trance
   restored.''

XXXV.

Here paused she of all present thought
   forlorn,
Nor voice nor sound, that moment's pain
   expressed,
Yet Nature, with excess of grief o'er-
   borne,
From her full eyes their watery load re-
   leased.
He too was mute; and, ere her weeping
   ceased,
He rose, and to the ruin's portal went,
And saw the dawn opening the silvery
   east
With rays of promise, north and south-
   ward sent;
And soon with crimson fire kindled the
   firmament.

XXXVI.

'O come,'' he cried, ''come, after
   weary night
Of such rough storm, this happy change
   to view.''
So forth she came, and eastward looked;
   the sight
Over her brow like dawn of gladness
   threw;
Upon her cheek, to which its youthful hue
Seemed to return, dried the last linger-
   ing tear,
And from her grateful heart a fresh one
   drew:
The whilst her comrade to her pensive
   cheer
Tempered fit words of hope; and the
   lark warbled near.

XXXVII.

They looked and saw a lengthening road,
   and wain
That rang down a bare slope not far re-
   mote:
The barrows glistered bright with drops
   of rain,
Whistled the wagoner with merry note,
The cock far off sounded his clarion
   throat;

But town, or farm, or hamlet, none they
   viewed,
Only were told there stood a lonely cot
A long mile thence.   While thither they
   pursued
Their way, the Woman thus her mourn-
   ful tale renewed.

XXXVIII.

'' Peaceful as this immeasurable plain
Is now, by beams of dawning light im-
   prest,
In the calm sunshine slept the glittering
   main;
The very ocean hath its hour of rest.
I too forgot the heavings of my breast.
How quiet 'round me ship and ocean
   were !
As quiet all within me.   I was blest,
And looked, and fed upon the silent air
Until it seemed to bring a joy to my
   despair.

XXXIX.

'' Ah ! how unlike those late terrific sleeps,
And groans that rage of racking famine
   spoke;
The unburied dead that lay in festering
   heaps,
The breathing pestilence that rose like
   smoke,
The shriek that from the distant battle
   broke,
The mine's dire earthquake, and the pal-
   lid host
Driven by the bomb's incessant thunder-
   stroke
To loathsome vaults, where heart-sick
   anguish tossed,
Hope died, and fear itself in agony was
   lost !

XL.

'' Some mighty gulf of separation past,
I seemed transported to another world;
A thought resigned with pain, when from
   the mast
The impatient mariner the sail unfurled,
And, whistling, called the wind that
   hardly curled
The silent sea.   From the sweet thoughts
   of home
And from all hope I was forever hurled.

For me — farthest from earthly port to
 roam
Was best, could I but shun the spot
 where man might come.

XLI.

"And oft I thought (my fancy was so
 strong)
That I, at last, a resting-place had found;
'Here will I dwell,' said I, 'my whole
 life long,
Roaming the illimitable waters round;
Here will I live, of all but heaven dis-
 owned,
And end my days upon the peaceful
 flood.' —
To break my dream the vessel reached
 its bound;
And homeless near a thousand homes I
 stood,
And near a thousand tables pined and
 wanted food.

XLII.

"No help I sought; in sorrow turned
 adrift,
Was hopeless, as if cast on some bare
 rock;
Nor morsel to my mouth that day did lift,
Nor raised my hand at any door to knock.
I lay where, with his drowsy mates, the
 cock
From the cross-timber of an out-house
 hung:
Dismally tolled, that night, the city clock!
At morn my sick heart hunger scarcely
 stung, .
Nor to the beggar's language could I fit
 my tongue.

XLIII.

"So passed a second day; and, when
 the third
Was come, I tried in vain the crowd's
 resort.
— In deep despair, by frightful wishes
 - stirred,
Near the seaside I reached a ruined fort;
There, pains which nature could no more
 support,
With blindness linked, did on my vitals
 fall;
And, after many interruptions short

Of hideous sense, I sank, nor step could
 crawl:
Unsought for was the help that did my
 life recall.

XLIV.

"Borne to a hospital, I lay with brain
Drowsy and weak, and shattered memory;
I heard my neighbors in their beds com-
 plain
Of many things which never troubled me—
Of feet still bustling round with busy
 glee,
Of looks where common kindness had
 no part,
Of service done with cold.formality,
Fretting the fever round the languid heart,
And groans which, as they said, might
 make a dead man start.

XLV.

"These things just served to stir the
 slumbering sense,
Nor pain nor pity in my bosom raised.
With strength did memory return; and,
 thence
Dismissed, again on open day I gazed,
At houses, men, and common light,
 amazed.
The lanes I sought, and, as the sun re-
 tired,
Came where beneath the trees a fagot
 blazed,
The travellers saw me weep, my fate in-
 quired,
And gave me food — and rest, more wel-
 come, more desired.

XLVI.

"Rough potters seemed they, trading
 soberly
With panniered asses driven from door
 to door;
But life of happier sort set forth to me,
And other joys my fancy to allure —
The bagpipe dinning on the midnight
 moor
In barn uplighted; and companions boon,
Well met from far with revelry secure
Among the forest glades, while jocund
 June
Rolled fast along the sky his warm and
 genial moon.

XLVII.

"But ill they suited me — those journeys
    dark
O'er moor and mountain, midnight theft
    to hatch !
To charm the surly house-dog's faithful
    bark,
Or hang on tiptoe at the lifted latch.
The gloomy lantern, and the dim blue
    match,
The black disguise, the warning whistle
    shrill,
And ear still busy on its nightly watch,
Were not for me, brought up in nothing
    ill :
Besides, on griefs so fresh my thoughts
    were brooding still.

XLVIII.

"What could I do, unaided and unblest ?
My father ! gone was every friend of
    thine :
And kindred of dead husband are at best
Small help ; and, after marriage such as
    mine,
With little kindness would to me incline.
Nor was I then for toil or service fit ;
My deep-drawn sighs no effort could con-
    fine ;
In open air forgetful would I sit
Whole hours, with idle arms in moping
    sorrow knit.

XLIX.

"The roads I paced, I loitered through
    the fields ;
Contentedly, yet sometimes self-accused.
Trusted my life to what chance bounty
    yields,
Now coldly given, now utterly refused.
The ground I for my bed have often used :
But what afflicts my peace with keenest
    ruth,
Is that I have my inner self abused,
Foregone the home delight of constant
    truth,
And clear and open soul, so prized in
    fearless youth.

L.

"Through tears the rising sun I oft have
    viewed,
Through tears have seen him towards
    that world descend

Where my poor heart lost all its fortitude :
Three years a wanderer now my course I
    bend —
Oh ! tell me whither — for no earthly
    friend
Have I." — She ceased, and weeping
    turned away ;
As if because her tale was at an end,
She wept ; because she had no more to
    say
Of that perpetual weight which on her
    spirit lay.

LI.

True sympathy the Sailor's looks ex-
    pressed,
His looks — for pondering he was mute
    the while.
Of social Order's care for wretchedness,
Of Time's sure help to calm and reconcile,
Joy's second spring and Hope's long-
    treasured smile,
'T was not for *him* to speak — a man so
    tried.
Yet, to relieve her heart, in friendly style
Proverbial words of comfort he applied,
And not in vain, while they went pacing
    side by side.

LII.

Ere long, from heaps of turf, before
    their sight,
Together smoking in the sun's slant
    beam,
Rise various wreaths that into one unite
Which high and higher mounts with sil-
    ver gleam :
Fair spectacle, — but instantly a scream
Thence bursting shrill did all remark pre-
    vent ;
They paused, and heard a hoarser voice
    blaspheme,
And female cries. Their course they
    thither bent,
And met a man who foamed with anger
    vehement.

LIII.

A woman stood with quivering lips and
    pale,
And, pointing to a little child that lay
Stretched on the ground, began a piteous
    tale ;
How in a simple freak of thoughtless play

He had provoked his father, who straight-
way,
As if each blow were deadlier than the last,
Struck the poor innocent. Pallid with
dismay
The Soldier's Widow heard and stood
aghast;
And stern looks on the man her gray-
haired comrade cast.

LIV.

His voice with indignation rising high
Such further deed in manhood's name
forbade;
The peasant, wild in passion, made reply
With bitter insult and revilings sad;
Asked him in scorn what business there
he had;
What kind of plunder he was hunting
now;
The gallows would one day of him be
glad; —
Though inward anguish damped the
Sailor's brow,
Yet calm he seemed as thoughts so poi-
gnant would allow.

LV.

Softly he stroked the child, who lay out-
stretched
With face to earth; and, as the boy
turned round
His battered head, a groan the Sailor
fetched
As if he saw — there and upon that
ground —
Strange repetition of the deadly wound
He had himself inflicted. Through his
brain
At once the griding iron passage found;
Deluge of tender thoughts then rushed
amain,
Nor could his sunken eyes the starting
tear restrain.

LVI.

Within himself he said — What hearts
have we!
The blessing this a father gives his child!
Yet happy thou, poor boy! compared
with me,
Suffering not doing ill — fate far more
mild.

The stranger's looks and tears of wrath
beguiled
The father, and relenting thoughts awoke;
He kissed his son — so all was reconciled.
Then, with a voice which inward trouble
broke
Ere to his lips it came, the Sailor them
bespoke.

LVII.

" Bad is the world, and hard is the
world's law
Even for the man who wears the warm-
est fleece;
Much need have ye that time more
closely draw
The bond of nature, all unkindness cease,
And that among so few there still be peace:
Else can ye hope but with such numerous
foes
Your pains shall ever with your years
increase? " —
While from his heart the appropriate les-
son flows,
A correspondent calm stole gently o'er
his woes.

LVIII.

Forthwith the pair passed on; and down
they look
Into a narrow valley's pleasant scene
Where wreaths of vapor tracked a wind-
ing brook,
That babbled on through groves and
meadows green;
A low-roofed house peeped out the trees
between;
The dripping groves resound with cheer-
ful lays,
And melancholy lowings intervene
Of scattered herds, that in the meadow
graze,
Some amid lingering shade, some touched
by the sun's rays.

LIX.

They saw and heard, and, winding with
the road,
Down a thick wood, they dropt into the
vale;
Comfort, by prouder mansions unbe-
stowed,
Their wearied frames, she hoped, would
soon regale.

Erelong they reached that cottage in the dale:
It was a rustic inn;— the board was spread,
The milk-maid followed with her brimming pail,
And lustily the master carved the bread,
Kindly the housewife pressed, and they in comfort fed.

LX.

Their breakfast done, the pair, though loth, must part ;
Wanderers whose course no longer now agrees.
She rose and bade farewell! and, while her heart
Struggled with tears nor could its sorrow ease,
She left him there; for, clustering round his knees,
With his oak-staff the cottage children played.
And soon she reached a spot o'erhung with trees
And banks of ragged earth; beneath the shade
Across the pebbly road a little runnel strayed.

LXI.

A cart and horse beside the rivulet stood;
Checkering the canvas roof the sunbeams shone.
She saw the carman bend to scoop the flood
As the wain fronted her, — wherein lay one,
A pale-faced Woman; in disease far gone.
The carman wet her lips as well behoved;
Bed under her lean body there was none,
Though even to die near one she most had loved
She could not of herself those wasted limbs have moved.

LXII.

The Soldier's Widow learned with honest pain
And homefelt force of sympathy sincere,
Why thus that worn-out wretch must there sustain
The jolting road and morning air severe.

The wain pursued its way; and following near
In pure compassion she her steps retraced
Far as the cottage. "A sad sight is here,"
She cried aloud; and forth ran out in haste
The friends whom she had left but a few minutes past.

LXIII.

While to the door with eager speed they ran,
From her bare straw the Woman half up-raised
Her bony visage — gaunt and deadly wan;
No pity asking, on the group she gazed
With a dim eye, distracted and amazed;
Then sank upon her straw with feeble moan.
Fervently cried the housewife — "God be praised,
I have a house that I can call my own;
Nor shall she perish there, untended and alone !"

LXIV.

So in they bear her to the chimney seat,
And busily, though yet with fear, untie
Her garments, and, to warm her icy feet
And chafe her temples, careful hands apply.
Nature reviving, with a deep-drawn sigh
She strove, and not in vain, her head to rear ;
Then said — "I thank you all ; if I must die,
The God in heaven my prayers for you will hear ;
Till now I did not think my end had been so near.

LXV.

"Barred every comfort labor could procure,
Suffering what no endurance could assuage,
I was compelled to seek my father's door,
Though loath to be a burthen on his age.

But sickness stopped me in an early stage
Of my sad journey ; and within the wain
They placed me — there to end life's
    pilgrimage,
Unless beneath your roof I may remain ;
For I shall never see my father's door
    again.

LXVI.
" My life, Heaven knows, hath long been
    burthensome ;
But, if I have not meekly suffered, meek
May my end be ! Soon will this voice
    be dumb:
Should child of mine e'er wander hither,
    speak
Of me, say that the worm is on my
    cheek. —
Torn from our hut, that stood beside the
    sea
Near Portland lighthouse in a lonesome
    creek,
My husband served in sad captivity
On shipboard, bound till peace or death
    should set him free.

LXVII.
" A sailor's wife I knew a widow's cares,
Yet two sweet little ones partook my
    bed ;
Hope cheered my dreams, and to my
    daily prayers
Our heavenly Father granted each day's
    bread ;
Till one was found by stroke of violence
    dead,
Whose body near our cottage chanced to
    lie ;
A dire suspicion drove us from our shed ;
In vain to find a friendly face we try,
Nor could we live together those poor
    boys and I ;

LXVIII.
" For evil tongues made oath how on
    that day
My husband lurked about the neighbor-
    hood ;
Now he had fled, and whither none could
    say,
And _he_ had done the deed in the dark
    wood —

Near his own home ! — but he was mild
    and good ;
Never on earth was gentler creature seen;
He'd not have robbed the raven of its
    food.
My husband's loving kindness stood be-
    tween
Me and all worldly harms and wrongs
    however keen."

LXIX.
Alas ! the thing she told with laboring
    breath
The Sailor knew too well. That wick-
    edness
His hand had wrought; and when, in the
    hour of death,
He saw his Wife's lips move his name to
    bless
With her last words, unable to suppress
His anguish, with his heart he ceased to
    strive;
And, weeping loud in this extreme dis-
    tress,
He cried — " Do pity me ! That thou
    shouldst live
I neither ask nor wish — forgive me, but
    forgive ! "

LXX.
To tell the change that Voice within her
    wrought
Nature by sign or sound made no essay;
A sudden joy surprised expiring thought,
And every mortal pang dissolved away.
Borne gently to a bed, in death she lay;
Yet still while over her the husband bent,
A look was in her face which seemed to
    say,
" Be blest; by sight of thee from heaven
    was sent
Peace to my parting soul, the fulness of
    content."

LXXI.
She slept in peace, — his pulses throbbed
    and stopped,
Breathless he gazed upon her face, —
    then took
Her hand in his, and raised it, but both
    dropped,
When on his own he cast a rueful look.

His ears were never silent; sleep forsook
His burning eyelids stretched and stiff as
　　lead;
All night from time to time under him
　　shook
The floor as he lay shuddering on his
　　bed;
And oft he groaned aloud, " O God, that
　　I were dead ! "

LXXII.

The Soldier's Widow lingered in the cot,
And, when he rose, he thanked her pious
　　care
Through which his Wife, to that kind
　　shelter brought,
Died in his arms; and with those thanks
　　a prayer
He breathed for her, and for that merci-
　　ful pair.
The corse interred, not one hour he re-
　　mained
Beneath their roof, but to the open air
A burthen, now with fortitude sustained,
He bore within a breast where dreadful
　　quiet reigned.

LXXIII.

Confirmed of purpose, fearlessly prepared
For act and suffering, to the city straight
He journeyed, and forthwith his crime
　　declared:
" And from your doom," he added,
　　" now I wait,
Nor let it linger long, the murderer's
　　fate."
Not ineffectual was that piteous claim:
" O welcome sentence which will end
　　though late,"
He said, " the pangs that to my con-
　　science came
Out of that deed.　My trust, Saviour ! is
　　in thy name ! "

LXXIV.

His fate was pitied.　Him in iron case
(Reader, forgive the intolerable thought)
They hung not:— no one on *his* form or
　　face
Could gaze, as on a show by idlers
　　sought;

No kindred sufferer, to his death-place
　　brought
By lawless curiosity or chance,
When into storm the evening sky is
　　wrought,
Upon his swinging corse an eye can
　　glance,
And drop, as he once dropped, in miser-
　　able trance.
1793–94.　　　　　　　　　　　　1842.

LINES

Left upon a Seat in a Yew-tree, which stands
near the lake of Esthwaite, on a desolate part
of the shore, commanding a beautiful prospect.

Composed in part at school at Hawkshead.
The tree has disappeared, and the slip of Common
on which it stood, that ran parallel to the lake,
and lay open to it, has long been enclosed; so
that the road has lost much of its attraction.
This spot was my favorite walk in the evenings
during the latter part of my school-time.　The in-
dividual whose habits and character are here given,
was a gentleman of the neighborhood, a man of
talent and learning, who had been educated at one
of our Universities, and returned to pass his time
in seclusion on his own estate.　He died a bachelor
in middle age.　Induced by the beauty of the
prospect, he built a small summer-house on the
rocks above the peninsula on which the ferry-house
stands.　This property afterwards passed into the
hands of the late Mr. Curwen.　The site was long
ago pointed out by Mr. West in his "Guide," as the
pride of the lakes, and now goes by the name of
" The Station."　So much used I to be delighted
with the view from it, while a little boy, that some
years before the first pleasure-house was built, I
led thither from Hawkshead a youngster about
my own age, an Irish boy, who was a servant to
an itinerant conjurer.　My motive was to witness
the pleasure I expected the boy would receive
from the prospect of the islands below and the
intermingling water.　I was not disappointed ;
and I hope the fact, insignificant as it may appear
to some, may be thought worthy of note by others
who may cast their eye over these notes.

NAY, Traveller ! rest.　This lonely Yew-
　　tree stands
Far from all human dwelling: what if here
No sparkling rivulet spread the verdant
　　herb?
What if the bee love not these barren
　　boughs?

Yet, if the wind breathe soft, the curling
    waves,
That break against the shore, shall lull thy
    mind
By one soft impulse saved from vacancy.
——————————————Who he was
That piled these stones and with the mossy
    sod
First covered, and here taught this aged
    Tree
With its dark arms to form a circling
    bower,
I well remember. — He was one who
    owned
No common soul. In youth by science
    nursed,
And led by nature into a wild scene
Of lofty hopes, he to the world went forth
A favored Being, knowing no desire
Which genius did not hallow; 'gainst the
    taint
Of dissolute tongues, and jealousy, and
    hate,
And scorn, — against all enemies pre-
    pared,
All but neglect. The world, for so it
    thought,
Owed him no service; wherefore he at
    once
With indignation turned himself away,
And with the food of pride sustained his
    soul
In solitude. — Stranger! these gloomy
    boughs
Had charms for him; and here he loved
    to sit,
His only visitants a straggling sheep,
The stone-chat, or the glancing sand-
    piper:
And on these barren rocks, with fern and
    heath,
And juniper and thistle, sprinkled o'er,
Fixing his downcast eye, he many an hour
A morbid pleasure nourished, tracing here
An emblem of his own unfruitful life:
And, lifting up his head, he then would
    gaze
On the more distant scene,— how lovely
    't is
Thou seest,— and he would gaze till it
    became
Far lovelier, and his heart could not sus-
    tain

The beauty, still more beauteous! Nor,
    that time,
When nature had subdued him to herself,
Would he forget those Beings to whose
    minds,
Warm from the labors of benevolence,
The world, and human life, appeared a
    scene
Of kindred loveliness: then he would sigh,
Inly disturbed, to think that others felt
What he must never feel: and so, lost
    Man!
On visionary views would fancy feed,
Till his eye streamed with tears. In this
    deep vale   ·
He died, — this seat his only monument.
  If Thou be one whose heart the holy
    forms
Of young imagination have kept pure,
Stranger! henceforth be warned; and
    know that pride,
Howe'er disguised in its own majesty,
Is littleness; that he, who feels contempt
For any living thing, hath faculties
Which he has never used; that thought
    with him
Is in its infancy. The man whose eye
Is ever on himself doth look on one,
The least of Nature's works, one who
    might move
The wise man to that scorn which wis-
    dom holds
Unlawful, ever. O be wiser, Thou!
Instructed that true knowledge leads to
    love;
True dignity abides with him alone
Who, in the silent hour of inward thought,
Can still suspect, and still revere himself,
In lowliness of heart.

1795.   1798.

THE BORDERERS.[1]

A Tragedy.

Of this dramatic work I have little to say in
addition to the short note which will be found at
the end of the volume. It was composed at
Racedown in Dorsetshire during the latter part
of the year 1795, and in the course of the follow-
ing year. Had it been the work of a later period
of life, it would have been different in some re-
spects from what it is now. The plot would have
been something more complex, and a greater

[1] See Note.

variety of characters introduced to relieve the mind from the pressure of incidents so mournful. The manners also would have been more attended to. My care was almost exclusively given to the passions and the characters, and the position in which the persons in the Drama stood relatively to each other, that the reader (for I had then no thought of the Stage) might be moved, and to a degree instructed, by lights penetrating somewhat into the depths of our nature. In this endeavor, I cannot think, upon a very late review, that I have failed. As to the scene and period of action, little more was required for my purpose than the absence of established law and government; so that the agents might be at liberty to act on their own impulses. Nevertheless, I do remember that, having a wish to color the manners in some degree from local history more than my knowledge enabled me to do, I read Redpath's "History of the Borders," but found there nothing to my purpose. I once made an observation to Sir Walter Scott, in which he concurred, that it was difficult to conceive how so dull a book could be written on such a subject. Much about the same time, but a little after, Coleridge was employed in writing his tragedy of "Remorse;" and it happened that soon after, through one of the Mr. Pooles, Mr. Knight the actor heard that we had been engaged in writing Plays, and upon his suggestion mine was curtailed, and I believe Coleridge's also was offered to Mr. Harris, manager of Covent Garden. For myself, I had no hope nor even a wish (though a successful play would, in the then state of my finances, have been a most welcome piece of good fortune) that he should accept my performance; so that I incurred no disappointment when the piece was *judiciously* returned as not calculated for the Stage. In this judgment I entirely concurred, and had it been otherwise, it was so natural for me to shrink from public notice, that any hope I might have had of success would not have reconciled me altogether to such an exhibition. Mr. C.'s play was, as is well known, brought forward several years after through the kindness of Mr. Sheridan. In conclusion I may observe that while I was composing this Play I wrote a short essay illustrative of that constitution and those tendencies of human nature which make the apparently *motiveless* actions of bad men intelligible to careful observers. This was partly done with reference to the character of Oswald, and his persevering endeavor to lead the man he disliked into so heinous a crime; but still more to preserve in my distinct remembrance what I had observed of transition in character, and the reflections I had been led to make during the time I was a witness of the changes through which the French Revolution passed.

DRAMATIS PERSONÆ.

MARMADUKE. }
OSWALD.
WALLACE. } Of the Band of Borderers.
LACY.
LENNOX. }
HERBERT.
WILFRED, Servant to MARMADUKE.
Host.
Forester.
ELDRED, a Peasant.
Peasant, Pilgrims, etc.
IDONEA.
Female Beggar.
ELEANOR, Wife to ELDRED.

SCENE. — *Borders of England and Scotland.*

TIME. — *The Reign of Henry III.*

Readers already acquainted with my Poems will recognize, in the following composition, some eight or ten lines which I have not scrupled to retain in the places where they originally stood. It is proper, however, to add, that they would not have been used elsewhere, if I had foreseen the time when I might be induced to publish this Tragedy.

February 28, 1842.

ACT I.

SCENE. — *Road in a Wood.*

WALLACE *and* LACY.

Lacy. The troop will be impatient; let us hie
Back to our post, and strip the Scottish Foray
Of their rich Spoil, ere they recross the Border.
— Pity that our young Chief will have no part
In this good service.
Wal.   Rather let us grieve
That, in the undertaking which has caused
His absence, he hath sought, whate'er his aim,
Companionship with One of crooked ways,
From whose perverted soul can come no good
To our confiding, open-hearted, Leader.
Lacy. True; and, remembering how the Band have proved
That Oswald finds small favor in our sight,
Well may we wonder he has gained such power
Over our much-loved Captain.

Wal.   I have heard
Of some dark deed to which in early life
His passion drove him — then a Voyager
Upon the midland Sea. You knew his
          bearing
In Palestine?
    Lacy.   Where he despised alike
Mahommedan and Christian.   But
          enough;
Let us begone — the Band may else be
          foiled.   [*Exeunt.*
Enter MARMADUKE *and* WILFRED.
    Wil. Be cautious, my dear Master.
    Mar.   I perceive
That fear is like a cloak which old men
          huddle
About their love, as if to keep it warm.
    Wil. Nay, but I grieve that we should
          part. This Stranger,
For such he is —
    Mar.   Your busy fancies, Wilfred,
Might tempt me to a smile; but what of
          him?
    Wil. You know that you have saved
          his life.
    Mar. I know it.
    Wil. And that he hates you! — Pardon
          me, perhaps
That word was hasty.
    Mar.   Fy! no more of it.
    Wil. Dear Master! gratitude's a heavy
          burden
To a proud Soul. — Nobody loves this
          Oswald —
Yourself, you do not love him.
    Mar.   I do more,
I honor him.   Strong feelings to his heart
Are natural; and from no one can be
          learnt   .
More of man's thoughts and ways than
          his experience
Has given him power to teach: and then
          for courage
And enterprise — what perils hath he
          shunned?
What obstacles hath he failed to over-
          come?
Answer these questions, from our common
          knowledge,
And be at rest.
    Wil.   Oh, Sir!
    Mar.   Peace, my good Wilfred;
Repair to Liddesdale, and tell the Band

I shall be with them in two days, at far-
      thest.
    Wil. May He whose eye is over all
          protect you!   [*Exit.*

Enter OSWALD (*a bunch of plants in his
          hand*).
    Osw. This wood is rich in plants and
          curious simples.
    Mar. (*looking at them*). The wild
          rose, and the poppy, and the night-
          shade:
Which is your favorite, Oswald?
    Osw.   That which, while it is
Strong to destroy, is also strong to heal—
                    [*Looking forward.*
Not yet in sight! — We'll saunter here
          awhile;
They cannot mount the hill, by us unseen.
    Mar. (*a letter in his hand*). It is no
          common thing when one like you
Peforms these delicate services, and
          therefore
I feel myself much bounden to you,
          Oswald;
'Tis a strange letter this! — You saw her
          write it?
    Osw. And saw the tears with which
          she blotted it.
    Mar. And nothing less would satisfy
          him?
    Osw.   No less;
For that another in his Child's affection
Should hold a place, as if 'twere robbery,
He seemed to quarrel with the very
          thought.
Besides, I know not what strange prejudice
Is rooted in his mind; this Band of ours,
Which you've collected for the noblest
          ends,
Along the confines of the Esk and Tweed
To guard the Innocent — he calls us
          "Outlaws";
And, for yourself, in plain terms he asserts
This garb was taken up that indolence
Might want no cover, and rapacity
Be better fed.
    Mar.   . Ne'er may I own the heart
That cannot feel for one, helpless as he is.
    Osw. Thou know'st me for a Man not
          easily moved,
Yet was I grievously provoked to think
Of what I witnessed.

Mar.　　　　　This day will suffice
To end her wrongs.
　　Osw.　　　　But if the blind Man's tale
Should *yet* be true?
　　Mar.　　　　Would it were possible!
Did not the soldier tell thee that himself,
And others who survived the wreck, be-
　　　　held
The Baron Herbert perish in the waves
Upon the coast of Cyprus?
　• *Osw.*　　　　　Yes, even so,
And I had heard the like before: in sooth
The tale of this his quondam Barony
Is cunningly devised; and, on the back
Of his forlorn appearance, could not fail
To make the proud and vain his tributar-
　　　　ies,
And stir the pulse of lazy charity.
The seignories of Herbert are in Devon;
We, neighbors of the Esk and Tweed:
　　　　'tis much
The Arch-Impostor —
　　Mar.　　　　Treat him gently, Oswald;
Though I have never seen his face, me-
　　　　thinks,
There cannot come a day when I shall
　　　　cease
To love him.　I remember, when a Boy
Of scarcely seven years' growth, beneath
　　　　the Elm
That casts its shade over our village school,
'Twas my delight to sit and hear Idonea
Repeat her Father's terrible adventures,
Till all the band of playmates wept to-
　　　　gether;
And that was the beginning of my love.
And, through all converse of our later
　　　　years,
An image of this old Man still was present,
When I had been most happy.　Pardon
　　　　me
If this be idly spoken.
　　Osw.　　　　　See, they come,
Two Travellers!
　　Mar. (*points*).　The woman is Idonea.
　　Osw.　And leading Herbert.
　　Mar.　　　　We must let them pass—
This thicket will conceal us.　·
　　　　　　　　[*They step aside.*
Enter IDONEA, *leading* HERBERT *blind.*
　　Idon.　Dear Father, you sigh deeply;
　　　　ever since
We left the willow shade by the brookside,

Your natural breathing has been troubled.
　　Her.　　　　　　　　Nay,
You are too fearful; yet must I confess,
Our march of yesterday had better suited
A firmer step than mine.
　　Idon.　　　　That dismal Moor—
In spite of all the larks that cheered our
　　　　path,
I never can forgive it: but how steadily
You paced along, when the bewildering
　　　　moonlight
Mocked me with many a strange fantastic
　　　　shape! —
I thought the Convent never would ap-
　　　　pear;
It seemed to move away from us: and yet,
That you are thus the fault is mine; for
　　　　the air
Was soft and warm, no dew lay on the
　　　　grass,
And midway on the waste ere night had
　　　　fallen
I spied a Covert walled and roofed with
　　　　sods —
A miniature; belike some Shepherd-boy,
Who might have found a nothing-doing
　　　　hour
Heavier than work, raised it: within that
　　　　hut
We might have made a kindly bed of
　　　　heath,
And thankfully there rested side by side
Wrapped in our cloaks, and, with recruited
　　　　strength,
Have hailed the morning sun.　But cheer-
　　　　ily, Father, —
That staff of yours, I could almost have
　　　　heart
·To fling't away from you: you make no use
Of me, or of my strength; — come, let me
　　　　feel
That you do press upon me.　There —
　　　　indeed
You are quite exhausted.　Let us rest
　　　　awhile
On this green bank.　　　[*He sits down.*
　　Her. (*after some time*).　Idonea, you
　　　　are silent,
And I divine the cause.
　　Idon.　　　　　Do not reproach me :·
I pondered patiently your wish and will
When I gave way to your request; and
　　　　now,

When I behold the ruins of that face,
Those eyeballs dark — dark beyond hope
    of light,
And think that they were blasted for my
    sake,
The name of Marmaduke is blown away:
Father, I would not change that sacred
    feeling
For all this world can give.
  Her.   Nay, be composed:
Few minutes gone a faintness overspread
My frame, and I bethought me of two
    things
I ne'er had heart to separate—my grave,
And thee, my Child!
  Idon.   Believe me, honored Sire!
'T is weariness that breeds these gloomy
    fancies,
And you mistake the cause: you hear the
    woods
Resound with music, could you see the sun,
And look upon the pleasant face of
    Nature —
  Her. I comprehend thee — I should be
    as cheerful
As if we two were twins; two songsters
    bred
In the same nest, my springtime one with
    thine.
My fancies, fancies if they be, are such
As come, dear Child! from a far deeper
    source
Than bodily weariness. While here we sit
I feel my strength returning. — The be-
    quest
Of thy kind Patroness, which to receive
We have thus far adventured, will suffice
To save thee from the extreme of penury;
But when thy Father must lie down and
    die,
How wilt thou stand alone?
  Idon.   Is he not strong?
Is he not valiant?
  Her.   Am I then so soon
Forgotten? have my warnings passed so
    quickly
Out of thy mind? My dear, my only,
    Child;
Thou wouldst be leaning on a broken
    reed —
This Marmaduke —
  Idon.   O could you hear his voice:
Alas! you do not know him. He is one

(I wot not what ill tongue has wronged
    him with you)
All gentleness and love. His face be-
    speaks
A deep and simple meekness: and that
    Soul,
Which with the motion of a virtuous act
Flashes a look of terror upon guilt,
Is, after conflict, quiet as the ocean,
By a miraculous finger, stilled at once.
  Her. Unhappy Woman!
  Idon.   Nay, it was my duty
Thus much to speak; but think not I for-
    get —
Dear Father! how *could* I forget and
    live —
You and the story of that doleful night
When, Antioch blazing to her topmost
    towers,
You rushed into the murderous flames,
    returned
Blind as the grave, but, as you oft have
    told me,
Clasping your infant Daughter to your
    heart.
  Her. Thy Mother too! — scarce had I
    gained the door,
I caught her voice; she threw herself upon
    me,
I felt my infant brother in her arms;
She saw my blasted face — a tide of sol-
    diers
That instant rushed between us, and I
    heard
Her last death-shriek, distinct among a
    thousand.
  Idon. Nay, Father, stop not; let me
    hear it all.
  Her. Dear Daughter! precious relic of
    that time —
For my old age it doth remain with thee
To make it what thou wilt. Thou hast
    been told,
That when, on our return from Palestine,
I found how my domains had been usurped,
I took thee in my arms, and we began
Our wanderings together. Providence
At length conducted us to Rossland, —
    there,
Our melancholy story moved a Stranger
To take thee to her home, and for myself,
Soon after, the good Abbot of St. Cuth-
    bert's

Supplied my helplessness with food and
   raiment,
And, as thou know'st, gave me that hum-
   ble Cot
Where now we dwell. — For many years
   I bore
Thy absence, till old age and fresh infirmi-
   ties
Exacted thy return, and our reunion.
I did not think that, during that long
   absence,
My Child, forgetful of the name of Herbert,
Had given her love to a wild Freebooter,
Who here, upon the borders of the Tweed,
Doth prey alike on two distracted Coun-
   tries,
Traitor to both.
   Idon.   Oh, could you hear his voice !
I will not call on Heaven to vouch for me,
But let this kiss speak what is in my heart.

          Enter a Peasant.

   Pea. Good morrow, Strangers ! If you
   want a Guide,
Let me have leave to serve you !
   Idon.   My Companion
Hath need of rest; the sight of Hut or
   Hostel
Would be most welcome.
   Pea.   Yon white Hawthorn gained,
You will look down into a dell, and there
Will see an ash from which a sign-board
   hangs;
The house is hidden by the shade. Old
   Man,
You seem worn out with travel — shall I
   support you? ·
   Her. I thank you; but, a resting-place
   so near,
'T were wrong to trouble you.
   Pea.   God speed you both.
            [*Exit* Peasant.
   Her. Idonea, we must part. Be not
   alarmed —
'T is but for a few days — a thought has
   struck me.
   Idon.   That I should leave you at this
   house, and thence
Proceed alone. It shall be so; for strength
Would fail you ere our journey's end be
   reached.

   [*Exit* HERBERT *supported by* IDONEA.
   Re-enter MARMADUKE *and* OSWALD.

   Mar.   This instant we will stop him —
   Osw.   Be not hasty,
For, sometimes, in despite of my convic-
   tion,
He tempted me to think the Story true;
'T is plain he loves the Maid, and what
   he said
That savored of aversion to thy name
Appeared the genuine color of his soul —
Anxiety lest mischief should befall her
After his death.
   Mar.   I have been much deceived.
   Osw.   But sure he loves the Maiden,
   and never love
Could find delight to nurse itself so
   strangely,
Thus to torment her with *inventions !* —
   death —
There must be truth in this.
   Mar.   Truth in his story !
He must have felt it then, known what
   it was,
And in such wise to rack her gentle heart
Had been a tenfold cruelty.
   Osw.   Strange pleasures
Do we poor mortals cater for ourselves !
To see him thus provoke her tenderness
With tales of weakness and infirmity !
I'd wager on his life for twenty years.
   Mar.   We will not waste an hour in
   such a cause.
   Osw.   Why, this is noble ! shake her
   off at once.
   Mar.   Her virtues are his instru-
   ments. — A Man
Who has so practised on the world's cold
   sense,
May well deceive his Child — what ! leave
   her thus,
A prey to a deceiver? — no — no — no —
'Tis but a word and then —
   Osw.   Something is here
More than we see, or whence this strong
   aversion?
Marmaduke ! I suspect unworthy tales
Have reached his ear — you have had
   enemies.
   Mar.   Enemies ! — of his own coinage.
   Osw.   That may be,
But wherefore slight protection such as you
Have power to yield? perhaps he looks
   elsewhere. —
I am perplexed.

Mar. What hast thou heard or seen?
Osw. No — no — the thing stands clear
    of mystery;
(As you have said) he coins himself the
    slander
With which he taints her ear ; — for a
    plain reason;
He dreads the presence of a virtuous
    man
Like you; he knows your eye would
    search his heart,
Your justice stamp upon his evil deeds
The punishment they merit. All is plain:
It cannot be —
    Mar. What cannot be?
    Osw. Yet that a Father
Should in his love admit no rivalship,
And torture thus the heart of his own
    Child —
Mar. Nay, you abuse my friendship!
Osw. Heaven forbid! —
There was a circumstance, trifling in-
    deed —
It struck me at the time — yet I believe
I never should have thought of it again
But for the scene which we by chance
    have witnessed.
Mar. What is your meaning?
Osw. Two days gone I saw,
Though at a distance and he was dis-
    guised,
Hovering round Herbert's door, a man
    whose figure
Resembled much that cold voluptuary,
The villain, Clifford. He hates you, and
    he knows
Where he can stab you deepest.
Mar. Clifford never
Would stoop to skulk about a Cottage
    door —
It could not be.
Osw. And yet I now remember,
That, when your praise was warm upon
    my tongue,
And the blind Man was told how you had
    rescued
A maiden from the ruffian violence
Of this same Clifford, he became impa-
    tient
And would not hear me.
Mar. No — if cannot be —
I dare not trust myself with such a
    thought —

Yet whence this strange aversion? You
    are a man
Not used to rash conjectures —
    Osw. If you deem it
A thing worth further notice, we must act
With caution, sift the matter artfully.
    [*Exeunt* MARMADUKE *and* OSWALD.

SCENE. — *The door of the Hostel.*
HERBERT, IDONEA, *and* Host.
Her. (*seated*). As I am dear to you,
    remember, Child!
This last request.
    Idon. You know me, Sire; farewell!
    Her. And are you going then?
    Come, come, Idonea.
We must not part, — I have measured
    many a league
When these old limbs had need of rest, —
    and now
I will not play the sluggard.
    Idon. Nay, sit down.
    [*Turning to* Host.
Good Host, such tendance as you would
    expect
From your own Children, if yourself
    were sick,
Let this old Man find at your hands;
    poor Leader,
    [*Looking at the dog.*
We soon shall meet again. If thou ne-
    glect
This charge of thine, then ill befall thee!
    — Look,
The little fool is loath to stay behind.
Sir Host! by all the love you bear to
    courtesy,
Take care of him, and feed the truant
    well.
    Host. Fear not, I will obey you; —
    but One so young,
And One so fair, it goes against my heart
That you should travel unattended,
    Lady! —
I have a palfrey and a groom: the lad
Shall squire you, (would it not be better,
    Sir?)
And for less fee than I would let him run
For any lady I have seen this twelvemonth.
    Idon. You know, Sir, I have been
    too long your guard
Not to have learnt to laugh at little
    fears.

Why, if a wolf should leap from out a
    thicket,
A look of mine would send him scouring
    back,
Unless I differ from the thing I am
When you are by my side.

Her.   Idonea, wolves
Are not the enemies that move my fears.

Idon.   No more, I pray, of this.
    Three days at farthest
Will bring me back — protect him,
.   Saints — farewell ! [*Exit* IDONEA.

Host. 'Tis never drought with us —
    St. Cuthbert and his Pilgrims,
Thanks to them, are to us a stream of
    comfort :
Pity the Maiden did not wait a while;
She could not, Sir, have failed of com-
    pany.

Her. Now she is gone, I fain would
    call her back.

Host (*calling*). Holla !

Her.   No, no, the business
    must be done. —
What means this riotous noise?

Host.   The villagers
Are flocking in — a wedding festival —
That's all — God save you, Sir.

    Enter OSWALD.

Osw.   Ha ! as I live,
The Baron Herbert.

Host.   Mercy, the Baron Herbert !

Osw. So far into your journey ! on my
    life,
You are a lusty Traveller. But how fare
    you?

Her. Well as the wreck I am per-
    mits. And you, Sir?

Osw. I do not see Idonea.

Her.   Dutiful Girl,
She is gone before, to spare my weari-
    ness.
But what has brought you hither?

Osw.   A slight affair,
That will be soon despatched.

Her.   Did Marmaduke
Receive that letter?

Osw.   Be at peace. — The tie
Is broken, you will hear no more of *him*.

Her. This is true comfort, thanks a
    thousand times ! —
That noise ! — would I had gone with
    her as far

As the Lord Clifford's Castle : I have
    heard
That, in his milder moods, he has ex-
    pressed
Compassion for me. His influence is
    great
With Henry, our good King; — the Baron
    might
Have heard my suit, and urged my plea
    at Court.
No matter — he's a dangerous Man. —
    That noise !—
'T is too disorderly for sleep or rest.
Idonea would have fears for me, — the
    Convent
Will give me quiet lodging. You have a
    boy, good Host,
And he must lead me back.

Osw.   You are most lucky;
I have been waiting in the wood hard by
For a companion — here he comes; our
    journey

    Enter MARMADUKE.

Lies on your way; accept us as your
    Guides.

Her. Alas ! I creep so slowly.

Osw.   Never fear;
We'll not complain of that.

Her.   My limbs are stiff
And need repose. Could you but wait
    an hour?

Osw. Most willingly !— Come, let me
    lead you in,
And, while you take your rest, think not
    of us;
We'll stroll into the wood; lean on my
    arm.
    [*Conducts* HERBERT *into the house.*

    Exit MARMADUKE.

    Enter Villagers.

Osw. (*to himself coming out of the Hostel*).
    I have prepared a most apt instru-
    ment —
The Vagrant must, no doubt, be loitering
    somewhere
About this ground; she hath a tongue
    well skilled,
By mingling natural matter of her own
With all the daring fictions I have taught
    her,
To win belief, such as my plot requires.
    [*Exit* OSWALD.

Enter more Villagers, *a* Musician *among them.*

Host (*to them*). Into the court, my
Friend, and perch yourself
Aloft upon the elm-tree.   Pretty maids,
Garlands and flowers, and cakes and
merry thoughts,
Are here, to send the sun into the west
More speedily than you belike would wish.

SCENE *changes to the Wood adjoining the
Hostel.* — MARMADUKE *and* OSWALD
entering.

Mar.   I would fain hope that we de-
ceive ourselves:
When first I saw him sitting there, alone,
It struck upon my heart I know not how.

Osw.   To-day will clear up all. — You
marked a Cottage,
That ragged Dwelling, close beneath a
rock
By the brookside: it is the abode of One,
A Maiden innocent till ensnared by Clif-
ford,
Who soon grew weary of her; but, alas!
What she had seen and suffered turned
her brain.
Cast off by her Betrayer, she dwells alone,
Nor moves her hands to any needful work:
She eats her food which every day the
peasants
Bring to her hut; and so the Wretch has
lived
Ten years; and no one ever heard her
voice;
But every night at the first stroke of twelve
She quits her house, and, in the neigh-
boring Churchyard
Upon the self-same spot, in rain or storm,
She paces out the hour 'twixt twelve and
one —
She paces round and round an Infant's
grave,
And in the churchyard sod her feet have
worn
A hollow ring; they say it is knee-deep —
Ah! what is here?

[*A female Beggar rises up, rubbing
her eyes as if in sleep — a Child
in her arms.*

Beg.   Oh! Gentlemen, I thank you;
I've had the saddest dream that ever
troubled

The heart of living creature. — My poor
Babe
Was crying, as I thought, crying for bread
When I had none to give him; whereupon,
I put a slip of foxglove in his hand,
Which pleased him so, that he was hushed
at once:
When, into one of those same spotted bells
A bee came darting, which the Child with
joy
Imprisoned there, and held it to his ear,
And suddenly grew black, as he would
die.

Mar.   We have no time for this, my
babbling Gossip;
Here's what will comfort you.
[*Gives her money.*

Beg.   The Saints reward you
For this good deed! — Well, Sirs, this
passed away;
And afterwards I fancied, a strange dog,
Trotting alone along the beaten road,
Came to my child as by my side he slept,
And, fondling, licked his face, then on a
sudden
Snapped fierce to make a morsel of his
head:
But here he is, [*kissing the Child*] it must
have been a dream.

Osw.   When next inclined to sleep, take
my advice,
And put your head, good Woman, under
cover.

Beg.   Oh, sir, you would not talk thus,
if you knew .
What life is this of ours, how sleep will
master
The weary-worn. — You gentlefolk have
got
Warm chambers to your wish.   I'd rather
be
A stone than what I am. — But two nights
gone,
The darkness overtook me — wind and
rain
Beat hard upon my head — and yet I saw
A glow-worm, through the covert of the
furze,
Shine calmly as if nothing ailed the sky:
At which I half accused the God in
Heaven. —
You must forgive me.

Osw.   Ay, and if you think

The Fairies are to blame, and you should
 chide
Your favorite saint — no matter — this
 good day
Has made amends.
 Beg. Thanks to you both; but, O sir!
How would you like to travel on whole
 hours
As I have done, my eyes upon the ground,
Expecting still, I knew not how, to find
A piece of money glittering through the
 dust.
 Mar. This woman is a prater. Pray,
 good Lady!
Do you tell fortunes?
 Beg. Oh Sir, you are like the rest.
This Little-one — it cuts me to the heart—
Well! they might turn a beggar from
 their doors,
But there are Mothers who can see the
 Babe
Here at my breast, and ask me where I
 bought it:
This they can do, and look upon my
 face —
But you, Sir, should be kinder.
 Mar.   Come hither, Fathers,
And learn what nature is from this poor
 Wretch!
 Beg. Ay, Sir, there's nobody that feels
 for us.
Why now — but yesterday I overtook
A blind old Graybeard and accosted him,
I' th' name of all the Saints, and by the
 Mass
He should have used me better! — Char-
 ity!
If you can melt a rock, he is your man;
But I'll be even with him — here again
Have I been waiting for him.
 Osw.   Well, but softly,
Who is it that hath wronged you?
 Beg.   Mark you me;
I'll point him out;—a Maiden is his
 guide,
Lovely as Spring's first rose; a little dog,
Tied by a woollen cord, moves on before
With look as sad as he were dumb; the
 cur,
I owe him no ill will, but in good sooth
He does his Master credit.
 Mar.   As I live,
'T is Herbert and no other!

 Beg.   'T is a feast to see him,
Lank as a ghost and tall, his shoulders
 bent,
And long beard white with age — yet
 evermore,
As if he were the only Saint on earth,
He turns his face to heaven.
 Osw.   But why so violent
Against this venerable Man?
 Beg.   I'll tell you:
He has the very hardest heart on earth;
I had as lief turn to the Friar's school
And knock for entrance, in mid holiday.
 Mar. But to your story.
 Beg.   I was saying, Sir —
Well! he has often spurned me like a
 toad,
But yesterday was worse than all;— at last
I overtook him, Sirs, my Babe and I,
And begged a little aid for charity:
But he was snappish as a cottage cur.
Well then, says I — I'll out with it; at
 which
I cast a look upon the Girl, and felt
As if my heart would burst; and so I left
 him.
 Osw. I think, good Woman, you are
 the very person
Whom, but some few days past, I saw
 in Eskdale,
At Herbert's door.
 Beg. Ay; and if truth were known
I have good business there.
 Osw.   I met you at the threshold,
And he seemed angry.
 Beg.   Angry! well he might;
And long as I can stir I'll dog him. —
 Yesterday,
To serve me so, and knowing that he owes
The best of all he has to me and mine.
But 't is all over now. — That good old
 Lady
Has left a power of riches; and, I say it,
If there's a lawyer in the land, the knave
Shall give me half.
 Osw. What's this? — I fear, good
 Woman,
You have been insolent.
 Beg.   And there's the Baron,
I spied him skulking in his peasant's dress.
 Osw. How say you? in disguise? —
 Mar.   But what's your business
With Herbert or his Daughter?

Beg.   Daughter! truly —
But how's the day? — I fear, my little
    Boy,
We've overslept ourselves. — Sirs, have
    you seen him?   [*Offers to go.*
Mar. I must have more of this; —
    you shall not stir
An inch, till I am answered. Know you
    aught
That doth concern this Herbert?
Beg.   You are provoked,
And will misuse me, Sir?
Mar.   No trifling, Woman!
Osw. You are safe as in a sanctuary;
Speak.
Mar.   Speak!
Beg. He is a most hard-hearted Man.
Mar. Your life is at my mercy.
Beg.   Do not harm me,
And I will tell you all! — You know not,
    Sir,
What strong temptations press upon the
    Poor.
Osw. Speak out.
Beg.   Oh Sir, I've been a wicked
    Woman.
Osw. Nay, but speak out!
Beg.   He flattered me, and said
What harvest it would bring us both; and
    so,
I parted with the Child.
Mar.   Parted with whom?
Beg. Idonea, as he calls her; but the
    Girl is mine.
Mar. Yours, Woman! are you Her-
    bert's wife?
Beg. Wife, Sir! his wife — not I; my
    husband, Sir,
Was of Kirkoswald — many a snowy
    winter
We've weathered out together. My poor
    Gilfred!
He has been two years in his grave.
Mar.   Enough.
Osw. We've solved the riddle — Mis-
    creant!
Mar.   Do you,
Good Dame, repair to Liddesdale and
    wait
For my return; be sure you shall have
    justice.
Osw. A lucky woman! go, you have
    done good service.   [*Aside.*

Mar. (*to himself*). Eternal praises on
    the power that saved her! —
Osw. (*gives her money*). Here's for
    your little boy — and when you
    christen him
I'll be his Godfather.
Beg. Oh Sir, you are merry with me.
In grange or farm this Hundred scarcely
    owns
A dog that does not know me. — These
    good Folks,
For love of God, I must not pass their
    doors;
But I'll be back with my best speed: for
    you —
God bless and thank you both, my gentle
    Masters.   [*Exit* Beggar.
Mar. (*to himself*). The cruel Viper! —
    Poor devoted Maid,
Now I *do* love thee.
Osw.   I am thunderstruck.
Mar. Where is she — holla!
[*Calling to the* Beggar, *who returns;
    he looks at her steadfastly.*
                     You are Idonea's mother? —
Nay, be not terrified — it does me good
To look upon you.
Osw. (*interrupting*). In a peasant's
    dress
You saw, who was it?
Beg.   Nay, I dare not speak;
He is a man, if it should come to his ears
I never shall be heard of more.
Osw.   Lord Clifford?
Beg. What can I do? believe me, gentle
    Sirs,
I love her, though I dare not call her
    daughter.
Osw. Lord Clifford — did you see him
    talk with Herbert?
Beg. Yes, to my sorrow — under the
    great oak
At Herbert's door — and when he stood
    beside
The blind Man — at the silent Girl he
    looked
With such a look — it makes me tremble,
    Sir,
To think of it.
Osw.   Enough! you may depart.
Mar. (*to himself*). Father! — to God
    himself we cannot give
A holier name; and, under such a mask,

To lead a Spirit, spotless as the blessed,
To that abhorrèd den of brutish vice! —
Oswald, the firm foundation of my life
Is going from under me; these strange
    discoveries —
Looked at from every point of fear or hope,
Duty, or love — involve, I feel, my ruin.

ACT II.

SCENE. — *A Chamber in the Hostel —*
  OSWALD *alone, rising from a Table*
  on which he had been writing.
  Osw. They chose *him* for their Chief!
  — what covert part
He, in the preference, modest Youth,
  might take,
I neither know nor care. The insult bred
More of contempt than hatred; both are
  flown;
That either e'er existed is my shame:
'T was a dull spark — a most unnatural
  fire
That died the moment the air breathed
  upon it.
— These fools of feeling are mere birds
  of winter
That haunt some barren island of the
  north,
Where, if a famishing man stretch forth
  his hand,
They think it is to feed them. I have
  left him
To solitary meditation; — now
For a few swelling phrases, and a flash
Of truth, enough to dazzle and to blind,
And he is mine forever — here he comes.
    Enter MARMADUKE.
  Mar. These ten years she has moved
  her lips all day
And never speaks!
  Osw.   Who is it?
  Mar.   I have seen her.
  Osw. Oh! the poor tenant of that
  ragged homestead,
Her whom the Monster, Clifford, drove
  to madness.
  Mar. I met a peasant near the spot;
  he told me,
These ten years she had sate all day alone
Within those empty walls.
  Osw.   I too have seen her;
Chancing to pass this way some six
  months gone,

At midnight, I betook me to the Church
  yard:
The moon shone clear, the air was still,
  so still
The trees were silent as the graves be-
  neath them.
Long did I watch, and saw her pacing
  round
Upon the self-same spot, still round and
  round,
Her lips forever moving.
  Mar.   At her door
Rooted I stood; for, looking at the
  woman,
I thought I saw the skeleton of Idonea.
  Osw. But the pretended Father —
  Mar.   Earthly law
Measures not crimes like his.
  Osw.   *We* rank not, happily,
With those who take the spirit of their
  rule
From that soft class of devotees who feel
Reverence for life so deeply, that they
  spare
The verminous brood, and cherish what
  they spare
While feeding on their bodies. Would
  that Idonea
Were present, to the end that we might
  hear
What she can urge in his defence; she
  loves him.
  Mar. Yes, loves him; 't is a truth that
  multiplies
His guilt a thousand-fold.
  Osw.   'T is most perplexing:
What must be done?
  Mar.   We will conduct her hither;
These walls shall witness it — from first
  to last
He shall reveal himself.
  Osw.   Happy are we,
Who live in these disputed tracts, that own
No law but what each man makes for
  himself;
Here justice has indeed a field of triumph.
  Mar. Let us be gone and bring her
  hither; — here
The truth shall be laid open, his guilt
  proved
Before her face. The rest be left to me.
  Osw. You will be firm: but though we
  well may trust

The issue to the justice of the cause,
Caution must not be flung aside; remember,
Yours is no common life. Self-stationed here
Upon these savage confines, we have seen you
Stand like an isthmus 'twixt two stormy seas
That oft have checked their fury at your bidding.
'Mid the deep holds of Solway's mossy waste,
Your single virtue has transformed a Band
Of fierce barbarians into Ministers
Of peace and order. Aged men with tears
Have blessed their steps, the fatherless retire
For shelter to their banners. But it is,
As you must needs have deeply felt, it is
In darkness and in tempest that we seek
The majesty of Him who rules the world.
Benevolence, that has not heart to use
The wholesome ministry of pain and evil,
Becomes at last weak and contemptible.
Your generous qualities have won due praise,
But vigorous Spirits look for something more
Than Youth's spontaneous products; and to-day
You will not disappoint them; and hereafter —
Mar. You are wasting words; hear me then, once for all:
You are a Man — and therefore, if compassion,
Which to our kind is natural as life,
Be known unto you, you will love this Woman,
Even as I do; but I should loathe the light,
If I could think one weak or partial feeling —
Osw. You will forgive me —
Mar.   If I ever knew
My heart, could penetrate its inmost core,
'T is at this moment. — Oswald, I have loved
To be the friend and father of the oppressed,
A comforter of sorrow; — there is something
Which looks like a transition in my soul,
And yet it is not. — Let us lead him hither.
Osw. Stoop for a moment; 't is an act of justice;
And where's the triumph if the delegate
Must fall in the execution of his office?
The deed is done — if you will have it so —
Here where we stand — that tribe of vulgar wretches
(You saw them gathering for the festival)
Rush in — the villains seize us —
Mar.   Seize!
Osw.   Yes, they —
Men who are little given to sift and weigh —
Would wreak on us the passion of the moment.
Mar. The cloud will soon disperse — farewell — but stay,
Thou wilt relate the story.
Osw.   Am I neither
To bear a part in this Man's punishment,
Nor be its witness?
Mar.   I had many hopes
That were most dear to me, and some will bear
To be transferred to thee.
Osw.   When I'm dishonored!
Mar. I would preserve thee. How may this be done?
Osw. By showing that you look beyond the instant.
A few leagues hence we shall have open ground,
And nowhere upon earth is place so fit
To look upon the deed. Before we enter
The barren Moor, hangs from a beetling rock
The shattered Castle in which Clifford oft
Has held infernal orgies — with the gloom,
And very superstition of the place,
Seasoning his wickedness. The Debauchee
Would there perhaps have gathered the first fruits
Of this mock Father's guilt.·

Enter Host *conducting* HERBERT.

Host.   The Baron Herbert
Attends your pleasure.
Osw. (*to* Host). We are ready —
(*to* HERBERT) Sir!

I hope you are refreshed. — I have just
written
A notice for your Daughter, that she may
know
What is become of you. — You'll sit down
and sign it;
'Twill glad her heart to see her father's
signature.
   [*Gives the letter he had written.*
Her. Thanks for your care.
   [*Sits down and writes. Exit* Host.
Osw. (*aside to* MARMADUKE). Perhaps
it would be useful
That you too should subscribe your name.
   [MARMADUKE *overlooks* HERBERT —
   then writes — examines the letter
   eagerly.
Mar. I cannot leave this paper.
   [*He puts it up, agitated.*
Osw. (*aside*).   Dastard! Come.
   [MARMADUKE *goes towards* HERBERT
   and supports him — MARMADUKE
   tremblingly beckons OSWALD to take
   his place.
Mar. (*as he quits* HERBERT). There is
a palsy in his limbs — he shakes.
   [*Exeunt* OSWALD *and* HERBERT
   — MARMADUKE *following.*

SCENE *changes to a Wood* — *a Group of*
Pilgrims *and* IDONEA *with them.*

First Pil. A grove of darker and more
lofty shade I never saw.
Sec. Pil.   The music of the birds
Drops deadened from a roof so thick with
leaves.
Old Pil. This news! It made my heart
leap up with joy.
Idon. I scarcely can believe it.
Old Pil.   Myself, I heard
The Sheriff read, in open Court, a letter
Which purported it was the royal pleas-
ure
The Baron Herbert, who, as was sup-
posed,
Had taken refuge in this neighborhood,
Should be forthwith restored. The hear-
ing, Lady,
Filled my dim eyes with tears. — When I
returned
From Palestine, and brought with me a
heart,

Though rich in heavenly, poor in earthly,
comfort,
I met your Father, then a wandering Out-
cast :
He had a Guide, a Shepherd's boy; but
grieved
He was that One so young should pass
his youth
In such sad service; and he parted with
him.
We joined our tales of wretchedness to-
gether,
And begged our daily bread from door to
door.
I talk familiarly to you, sweet Lady!
For once you loved me.
Idon.   You shall back with me
And see your Friend again. The good
old Man
Will be rejoiced to greet you.
Old Pil.   It seems but yesterday
That a fierce storm o'ertook us, worn with
travel,
In a deep wood remote from any town.
A cave that opened to the road presented
A friendly shelter, and we entered in.
Idon. And I was with you?
Old Pil.   If indeed 't was you —
But you were then a tottering Little-one —
We sate us down. The sky grew dark and
darker :
I struck my flint, and built up a small fire
With rotten boughs and leaves, such as
the winds
Of many autumns in the cave had piled.
Meanwhile the storm fell heavy on the
woods;
Our little fire sent forth a cheering warmth
And we were comforted, and talked of
comfort;
But 't was an angry night, and o'er our
heads
The thunder rolled in peals that would
have made
A sleeping man uneasy in his bed.
O Lady, you have need to love your
Father.
His voice — methinks I hear it now, his
voice
When, after a broad flash that filled the
cave,
He said to me, that he had seen his
Child,

A face (no cherub's face more beautiful)
Revealed by lustre brought with it from
    Heaven;
And it was you, dear Lady!
    Idon.   God be praised,
That I have been his comforter till now!
And will be so through every change of
    fortune
And every sacrifice his peace requires. —
Let us be gone with speed, that he may
    hear
These joyful tidings from no lips but mine.
    [*Exeunt* IDONEA *and* Pilgrims.

SCENE. — *The Area of a half-ruined
Castle — on one side the entrance to a
dungeon —* OSWALD *and* MARMADUKE
pacing backwards and forwards.
    Mar. 'T is a wild night.
    Osw.   I'd give my cloak and bonnet
For sight of a warm fire.
    Mar.   The wind blows keen;
My hands are numb.
    Osw.   Ha! ha! 't is nipping cold.
             [*Blowing his fingers.*
I long for news of our brave Comrades;
    Lacy
Would drive those Scottish Rovers to their
    dens
If once they blew a horn this side the
    Tweed.
    Mar. I think I see a second range of
    Towers;
This castle has another Area — come,
Let us examine it.
    Osw.   'Tis a bitter night;
I hope Idonea is well housed. That
    horseman,
Who at full speed swept by us where the
    wood
Roared in the tempest, was within an ace
Of sending to his grave our precious
    Charge:
That would have been a vile mischance.
    Mar.   It would.
    Osw. Justice had been most cruelly
    defrauded.
    Mar. Most cruelly.
    Osw.   As up the steep we clomb,
I saw a distant fire in the north-east;
I took it for the blaze of Cheviot Beacon:
With proper speed our quarters may be
    gained

To-morrow evening.
    [*Looks restlessly towards the mouth of
    the dungeon.*
    Mar.   When, upon the plank,
I had led him 'cross the torrent, his voice
    blessed me:
You could not hear, for the foam beat
    the rocks
With deafening noise, — the benediction
    fell
Back on himself; but changed into a curse.
    Osw. As well indeed it might.
    Mar.   And this you deem
The fittest place?
    Osw. (*aside*). He is growing pitiful.
    Mar. (*listening*). What an odd moan-
    ing that is! —
    Osw.   Mighty odd
The wind should pipe a little, while we
    stand
Cooling our heels in this way! — I'll be-
    gin
And count the stars.
    Mar. (*still listening*). That dog of his,
    you are sure,
Could not come after us — he *must* have
    perished;
The torrent would have dashed an oak to
    splinters.
You said you did not like his looks —
    that he
Would trouble us; if he were here again,
I swear the sight of him would quail me
    more
Than twenty armies.
    Osw.   How?
    Mar.   The old blind Man,
When you had told him the mischance,
    was troubled
Even to the shedding of some natural
    tears
Into the torrent over which he hung,
Listening in vain.
    Osw.   He has a tender heart!
    [OSWALD *offers to go down into the
    dungeon.*
    Mar. How now, what mean you?
    Osw.   Truly, I was going
To waken our stray Baron. Were there
    not
A farm or dwelling-house within five
    leagues,
We should deserve to wear a cap and bells,

Three good round years, for playing the
    fool here
In such a night as this.
    Mar.   Stop, stop.
    Osw.   Perhaps,
You'd better like we should descend
    together,
And lie down by his side — what say you
    to it?
Three of us — we should keep each other
    warm :
I'll answer for it that our four-legged
    friend
Shall not disturb us; further I'll not en-
    gage;
Come, come, for manhood's sake !
    Mar.   These drowsy shiverings,
This mortal stupor which is creeping over
    me,
What do they mean? were this my single
    body
Opposed to armies, not a nerve would
    tremble :
Why do I tremble now? — Is not the
    depth
Of this Man's crimes beyond the reach
    of thought?
And yet, in plumbing the abyss for judg-
    ment,
Something I strike upon which turns my
    mind
Back on herself, I think, again — my
    breast
Concentres all the terrors of the Universe :
I look at him and tremble like a child.
    Osw. Is it possible?
    Mar.   One thing you noticed not :
Just as we left the glen a clap of thunder
Burst on the mountains with hell-rousing
    force.
This is a time, said he, when guilt may
    shudder;
But there's a Providence for them who
    walk
In helplessness, when innocence is with
    them.
At this audacious blasphemy, I thought
The spirit of vengeance seemed to ride
    the air.
    Osw. Why are you not the man you
        were that moment?
    [He *draws* MARMADUKE *to the dun-
    geon.*

    Mar. You say he was asleep, — look
        at this arm,
And tell me if 'tis fit for such a work.
Oswald, Oswald !
                [*Leans upon* OSWALD.
    Osw. This is some sudden seizure !
    Mar. A most strange faintness, — will
        you hunt me out
A draught of water?
    Osw.   Nay, to see you thus
Moves me beyond my bearing. — I will try
To gain the torrent's brink.
                [*Exit* OSWALD.
    Mar. (*after a pause*). It seems an age
Since that Man left me. — No, I am not
    lost.
    Her. (*at the mouth of the dungeon*). Give
        me your hand; where are you,
        Friends? and tell me
How goes the night.
    Mar.   'Tis hard to measure time.
In such a weary night, and such a place.
    Her. I do not hear the voice of my
        friend Oswald.
    Mar. A minute past, he went to fetch
        a draught
Of water from the torrent. 'Tis, you'll say,
A cheerless beverage.
    Her.   How good it was in you
To stay behind ! — Hearing at first no
    answer,
I was alarmed.
    Mar.   No wonder; this is a place
That well may put some fears into *your*
    heart.
    Her. Why so? a roofless rock had
        been a comfort,
Storm-beaten and bewildered as we were;
And in a night like this, to lend your
    cloaks
To make a bed for me ! — My Girl will
    weep
When she is told of it.
    Mar.   This Daughter of yours
Is very dear to you.
    Her.   Oh ! but you are young;
Over your head twice twenty years must
    roll,
With all their natural weight of sorrow
    and pain,
Ere can be known to you how much a
    Father
May love his Child.

Mar.   Thank you, old Man. for this!   [*Aside,*

Her. Fallen am I, and worn out, a useless Man;
Kindly have you protected me to-night,
And no return have I to make but prayers;
May you in age be blest with such a daughter! —
When from the Holy Land I had returned
Sightless, and from my heritage was driven,
A wretched Outcast — but this strain of thought
Would lead me to talk fondly.

Mar.   Do not fear;
Your words are precious to my ears; go on.

Her. You will forgive me, but my heart runs over.
When my old Leader slipped into the flood
And perished, what a piercing outcry you
Sent after him. I have loved you ever since.
You start — where are we?

Mar.   Oh, there is no danger;
The cold blast struck me.

Her.   'T was a foolish question.

Mar. But when you were an Outcast?— Heaven is just;
Your piety would not miss its due reward;
The little Orphan then would be your succor,
And do good service, though she knew it not.

Her. I turned me from the dwellings of my Fathers,
Where none but those who trampled on my rights
Seemed to remember me. To the wide world
I bore her, in my arms; her looks won pity;
She was my Raven in the wilderness,
And brought me food. Have I not cause to love her?

Mar. Yes.

Her.   More than ever Parent loved a Child?

Mar. Yes, yes.

Her. I will not murmur, merciful God!
I will not murmur; blasted as I have been,
Thou hast left me ears to hear my Daughter's voice,
And arms to fold her to my heart. Submissively
Thee I adore, and find my rest in faith.

Enter OSWALD.

Osw. Herbert! — confusion! (*aside*).
Here it is, my Friend,
          [*Presents the Horn.*
A charming beverage for you to carouse,
This bitter night.

Her. Ha! Oswald! ten bright crosses
I would have given, not many minutes gone,
To have heard your voice.

Osw. Your couch, I fear, good Baron,
Has been but comfortless; and yet that place,
When the tempestuous wind first drove us hither,
Felt warm as a wren's nest. You'd better turn
And under covert rest till break of day,
Or till the storm abate.
(*To* MARMADUKE *aside*). He has restored you.
No doubt you have been nobly entertained?
But soft! — how came he forth? The Night-mare Conscience
Has driven him out of harbor?

Mar.   I believe
You have guessed right.

Her. The trees renew their murmur:
Come, let us house together.
[OSWALD *conducts him to the dungeon.*

Osw. (*returns*).   Had I not
Esteemed you worthy to conduct the affair
To its most fit conclusion, do you think
I would so long have struggled with my Nature,
And smothered all that's man in me? — away! —
       [*Looking towards the dungeon.*
This man's the property of him who best
Can feel his crimes. I have resigned a privilege;
It now becomes my duty to resume it.

Mar. Touch not a finger —

Osw.   What then must be done?

Mar. Which way soe'er I turn, I am perplexed.

Osw. Now, on my life, I grieve for you.
The misery
Of doubt is insupportable. Pity, the facts
Did not admit of stronger evidence;
Twelve honest men, plain men, would set
us right;
Their verdict would abolish these weak
scruples.
Mar. Weak! I am weak — there does
my torment lie,
Feeding itself.
Osw. Verily, when he said
How his old heart would leap to hear her
steps,
You thought his voice the echo of Idonea's.
Mar. And never heard a sound so
terrible.
Osw. Perchance you think so now?
Mar. I cannot do it:
Twice did I spring to grasp his withered
throat,
When such a sudden weakness fell upon
me,
I could have dropped asleep upon his
breast.
Osw. Justice — is there not thunder in
the word?
Shall it be law to stab the petty robber
Who aims but at our purse; and shall this
Parricide —
Worse is he far, far worse (if foul dis-
honor
Be worse than death) to that confiding
Creature
Whom he to more than filial love and duty
Hath falsely trained — shall he fulfil his
purpose?
But you are fallen.
Mar. Fallen should I be indeed —
Murder — perhaps asleep, blind, old,
alone,
Betrayed, in darkness! Here to strike
the blow —
Away! away! —
[*Flings away his sword.*
Osw. Nay, I have done with you:
We'll lead him to the Convent. He shall
live,
And she shall love him. With unques-
tioned title
He shall be seated in his Barony,
And we too chant the praise of his good
deeds.

I now perceive we do mistake our
masters,
And most despise the men who best can
teach us:
Henceforth it shall be said that bad men
only
Are brave: Clifford is brave; and that
old Man
Is brave.
[*Taking* MARMADUKE'S *sword and
giving it to him.*
To Clifford's arms he would have led
His Victim — haply to this desolate house.
Mar. (*advancing to the dungeon*). It
must be ended! —
Osw. Softly; do not rouse him;
He will deny it to the last. He lies
Within the Vault, a spear's length to the
left.
[MARMADUKE *descends to the dungeon.*
(*Alone.*) The Villains rose in mutiny to
destroy me;
I could have quelled the Cowards, but this
Stripling
Must needs step in, and save my life. The
look
With which he gave the boon — I see it
now!
The same that tempted me to loathe the
gift. —
For this old venerable Graybeard — faith
'T is his own fault if he hath got a face
Which doth play tricks with them that look
on it;
'Twas that that put it in my thoughts —
that countenance —
His staff — his figure — Murder! — what,
of whom?
We kill a worn-out horse, and who but
women
Sigh at the deed? Hew down a withered
tree,
And none look grave but dotards. He
may live
To thank me for this service. Rainbow
arches,
Highways of dreaming passion, have too
long,
Young as he is, diverted wish and hope
From the unpretending ground we mortals
tread; —
Then shatter the delusion, break it
up

And set him free. What follows? I
  have learned
That things will work to ends the slaves o'
  the world
Do never dream of. I *have* been what
  he —
This Boy — when he comes forth with
  bloody hands —
Might envy, and am now, — but he shall
  know
What I am now —
    [*Goes and listens at the dungeon.*
      Praying or parleying? — tut !
Is he not eyeless? He has been half-dead
These fifteen years —
Enter female Beggar *with two or three of
    her Companions.*
(*Turning abruptly.*) *Ha! speak* — what
  Thing art thou?
(*Recognizes her.*) Heavens! my good
  Friend !   [*To her.*
  Beg.   Forgive me, gracious Sir ! —
  Osw. (*to her companions*). Begone, ye
    Slaves, or I will raise a whirlwind
And send ye dancing to the clouds, like
  leaves.   [*They retire affrighted.*
  Beg.   Indeed we meant no harm; we
    lodge sometimes
In this deserted Castle — *I repent me.*
  [Oswald *goes to the dungeon — listens
    — returns to the* Beggar.
  Osw. Woman, thou hast a helpless
    Infant — keep
Thy secret for its sake, or verily
That wretched life of thine shall be the
  forfeit.
  Beg. I *do* repent me, Sir; I fear the
    curse
Of that blind Man. 'T was not your
  money, sir —
  Osw. Begone !
  Beg. (*going*). There is some wicked
    deed in hand: [*Aside.*
Would I could find the old Man and his
  Daughter.   [*Exit* Beggar.
MARMADUKE *re-enters from the dungeon.*
  Osw. It is all over then; — your fool-
    ish fears
Are hushed to sleep, by your own act and
  deed,
Made quiet as he is.
  Mar.   Why came you down?
And when I felt your hand upon my arm

And spake to you, why did you give no
  answer?
Feared you to waken him? he must have
  been
In a deep sleep. I whispered to him thrice.
There are the strangest echoes in that
  place !
  Osw. Tut ! let them gabble till the day
  of doom.
  Mar. Scarcely, by groping, had I
  reached the Spot,
When round my wrist I felt a cord drawn
  tight,
As if the blind Man's dog were pulling
  at it.
  Osw. But after that?
  Mar.   The features of Idonea
Lurked in his face —
  Osw.   Psha ! Never to these eyes
Will retribution show itself again
With aspect so inviting. Why forbid me
To share your triumph?
  Mar.   Yes, her very look,
Smiling in sleep —
  Osw.   A pretty feat of Fancy !
  Mar. Though but a glimpse, it sent
    me to my prayers.
  Osw. Is he alive?
  Mar.   What mean you? who alive?
  Osw. Herbert ! since you will have it,
    Baron Herbert;
He who will gain his Seignory when
  Idonea
Hath become Clifford's harlot — is *he*
  living?
  Mar. The old Man in that dungeon
  is alive.
  Osw. Henceforth, then, will I never
  in camp or field
Obey you more. Your weakness, to the
  Band,
Shall be proclaimed: brave Men, they all
  shall hear it.
You a protector of humanity !
Avenger you of outraged innocence !
  Mar. 'T was dark — dark as the grave;
    yet did I see,
Saw him — his face turned toward me;
    and I tell thee
Idonea's filial countenance was there
To baffle me — it put me to my prayers.
Upwards I cast my eyes, and, through a
  crevice,

Beheld a star twinkling above my head,
And, by the living God, I could not do it.
[*Sinks exhausted.*
Osw. (*to himself*). Now may I perish
   if this turn do more
Than make me change my course.
(*To* MARMADUKE.) Dear Marmaduke,
My words were rashly spoken; I recall
   them:
I feel my error; shedding human blood
Is a most serious thing.
Mar.   Not I alone,
Thou too art deep in guilt.
Osw.   We have indeed
Been most presumptuous. There *is* guilt
   in this,
Else could so strong a mind have ever
   known
These trepidations? Plain it is that
   Heaven
Has marked out this foul Wretch as one
   whose crimes
Must never come before a mortal judg-
   ment-seat,
Or be chastised by mortal instruments.
Mar. A thought that's worth a thou-
   sand worlds!
[*Goes towards the dungeon.*
Osw.   I grieve
That, in my zeal, I have caused you so
   much pain.
Mar. Think not of that! 't is over —
   we are safe.
Osw. (*as if to himself, yet speaking
   aloud*). The truth is hideous, but
   how stifle it?
[*Turning to* MARMADUKE.
Give me your sword — nay, here are
   stones and fragments,
The least of which would beat out a
   man's brains;
Or you might drive your head against that
   wall.
No! this is not the place to hear the tale:
It should be told you pinioned in your bed,
Or on some vast and solitary plain
Blown to you from a trumpet.
Mar.   Why talk thus?
Whate'er the monster brooding in your
   breast
I care not: fear I have none, and cannot
   fear —
[*The sound of a horn is heard.*

That horn again — 'T is some one of our
   Troop;
What do they here? Listen!
Osw.   What! dogged like thieves!
Enter WALLACE *and* LACY, etc.
Lacy. You are found at last, thanks
   to the vagrant Troop
For not misleading us.
Osw. (*looking at* WALLACE). That
   subtle Graybeard —
I'd rather see my father's ghost.
Lacy (*to* MARMADUKE). My Captain,
We come by order of the Band. Belike
You have not heard that Henry has at
   last
Dissolved the Barons' League, and sent
   abroad
His Sheriffs with fit force to reinstate
The genuine owners of such Lands and
   Baronies
As, in these long commotions, have been
   seized.
His Power is this way tending. It befits
   us
To stand upon our guard, and with our
   swords
Defend the innocent.
Mar.   Lacy! we look
But at the surfaces of things; we hear
Of towns in flames, fields ravaged, young
   and old
Driven out in troops to want and naked-
   ness;
Then grasp our swords and rush upon a
   cure
That flatters us, because it asks not
   thought:
The deeper malady is better hid;
The world is poisoned at the heart.
Lacy.   What mean you?
Wal. (*whose eye has been fixed suspi-
   ciously upon* OSWALD). Ay, what
   is it you mean?
Mar.   Hark'e, my Friends; —
[*Appearing gay.*
Were there a Man who, being weak and
   helpless
And most forlorn, should bribe a Mother,
   pressed
By penury, to yield him up her Daughter,
A little Infant, and instruct the Babe,
Prattling upon his knee, to call him
   Father —

Lacy. Why, if his heart be tender, that offence
I could forgive him.

Mar. (*going on*). And should he make the Child
An instrument of falsehood, should he teach her
To stretch her arms, and dim the gladsome light
Of infant playfulness with piteous looks
Of misery that was not —

Lacy. Troth, 't is hard —
But in a world like ours —

Mar. (*changing his tone*). This selfsame Man —
Even while he printed kisses on the cheek
Of this poor babe, and taught its innocent tongue
To lisp the name of Father — could he look
To the unnatural harvest of that time
When he should give her up, a Woman grown,
To him who bid the highest in the market
Of foul pollution —

Lacy. The whole visible world
Contains not such a Monster!

Mar. For this purpose
Should he resolve to taint her Soul by means
Which bathe the limbs in sweat to think of them;
Should he, by tales which would draw tears from iron,
Work on her nature, and so turn compassion
And gratitude to ministers of vice,
And make the spotless spirit of filial love
Prime mover in a plot to damn his Victim
Both soul and body —

Wal. 'T is too horrible;
Oswald, what say you to it?

Lacy. Hew him down,
And fling him to the ravens.

Mar. But his aspect
It is so meek, his countenance so venerable.

Wal. (*with an appearance of mistrust*). But how, what say you, Oswald?

Lacy (*at the same moment*). Stab him, were it
Before the Altar.

Mar. What, if he were sick,
Tottering upon the very verge of life,
And old, and blind —

Lacy. Blind, say you?

Osw. (*coming forward*). Are we Men,
Or own we baby Spirits? Genuine courage
Is not an accidental quality,
A thing dependent for its casual birth
On opposition and impediment.
Wisdom, if Justice speak the word, beats down
The giant's strength; and, at the voice of Justice,
Spares not the worm. The giant and the worm —
She weighs them in one scale. The wiles of woman,
And craft of age, seducing reason, first
Made weakness a protection, and obscured
The moral shapes of things. His tender cries
And helpless innocence — do they protect
The infant lamb? and shall the infirmities,
Which have enabled this enormous Culprit
To perpetrate his crimes, serve as a Sanctuary
To cover him from punishment? Shame!
— Justice,
Admitting no resistance, bends alike
The feeble and the strong. She needs not here
Her bonds and chains, which make the mighty feeble.
— We recognize in this old Man a victim
Prepared already for the sacrifice.

Lacy. By heaven, his words are reason!

Osw. Yes, my Friends,
His countenance is meek and venerable;
And, by the Mass, to see him at his prayers! —
I am of flesh and blood, and may I perish
When my heart does not ache to think of it! —
Poor Victim! not a virtue under heaven
But what was made an engine to ensnare thee;
But yet I trust, Idonea, thou art safe.

Lacy. Idonea!

Wal. How! what? your Idonea?
To MARMADUKE.

Mar. Mine;

But now no longer mine. You know
    Lord Clifford;
He is the Man to whom the Maiden —
    pure
As beautiful, and gentle and benign,
And in her ample heart loving even me —
Was to be yielded up.
    Lacy.   Now, by the head
Of my own child, this Man must die; my
    hand,
A worthier wanting, shall itself entwine
In his gray hairs ! —
    Mar. (*to* LACY). I love the Father in
    thee.
You know me, Friends; I have a heart to
    feel,
And I have felt, more than perhaps be-
    comes me
Or duty sanctions.
    Lacy.   We will have ample justice.
Who are we, Friends? Do we not live
    on ground
Where Souls are self-defended, free to
    grow
Like mountain oaks rocked by the stormy
    wind.
Mark the Almighty Wisdom, which de-
    creed
This monstrous crime to be laid open —
    here,
Where Reason has an eye that she can
    use,
And Men alone are Umpires. To the
    Camp
He shall be led, and there, the Country
    round
All gathered to the spot, in open day
Shall Nature be avenged.
    Osw.   'T is nobly thought;
His death will be a monument for ages.
    Mar. (*to* LACY). I thank you for that
    hint. He shall be brought
Before the Camp, and would that best and
    wisest
Of every country might be present.
    There,
His crime shall be proclaimed; and for
    the rest
It shall be done as Wisdom shall decide:
Meanwhile, do you two hasten back and
    see
That all is well prepared.
    Wal.   We will obey you.

(*Aside.*) But softly ! we must look a little
    nearer.
    Mar. Tell where you found us. At
    some future time
I will explain the cause.   [*Exeunt.*

ACT III.

SCENE — *The door of the Hostel, a group
of* Pilgrims *as before;* IDONEA *and the*
HOST *among them.*

    Host. Lady, you'll find your Father at
    the Convent
As I have told you: He left us yesterday
With two Companions; one of them, as
    seemed,
His most familiar Friend. (*Going.*) There
    was a letter
Of which I heard them speak, but that I
    fancy
Has been forgotten.
    Idon. (*to* Host). Farewell !
    Host.   Gentle pilgrims,
St. Cuthbert speed you on your holy er-
    rand.
    [*Exeunt* IDONEA *and* Pilgrims.

SCENE. — *A desolate Moor.*
OSWALD (*alone*).

    Osw. Carry him to the Camp ! Yes,
    to the Camp.
Oh, Wisdom ! a most wise resolve ! and
    then,
That half a word should blow it to the
    winds !
This last device must end my work. —
    Methinks
It were a pleasant pastime to construct
A scale and table of belief — as thus —
Two columns, one for passion, one for
    proof;
Each rises as the other falls: and first,
Passion a unit and *against* us — proof —
Nay, we must travel in another path,
Or we're stuck fast forever; — passion,
    then,
Shall be a unit *for* us ; proof — no, pas-
    sion !
We'll not insult thy majesty by time,
Person, and place — the where, the when,
    the how,
And all particulars that dull brains require
To constitute the spiritless shape of Fact,

They bow to, calling the idol, Demonstra-
tion.
A whipping to the Moralists who preach
That misery is a sacred thing: for me,
I know no cheaper engine to degrade a
man,
Nor any half so sure. This Stripling's
mind
Is shaken till the dregs float on the sur-
face;
And, in the storm and anguish of the
heart,
He talks of a transition in his Soul,
And dreams that he is happy. We dis-
sect
The senseless body, and why not the
mind? —
These are strange sights — the mind of
man, upturned,
Is in all natures a strange spectacle;
In some a hideous one — hem! shall I
stop?
No. — Thoughts and feelings will sink
deep, but then
They have no substance. Pass but a few
minutes,
And something shall be done which
Memory
May touch, whene'er her Vassals are at
work.
Enter MARMADUKE, *from behind.*
Osw. (*turning to meet him*). But
listen, for my peace —
Mar.   Why, I *believe* you.
Osw. But hear the proofs —
Mar. Ay, prove that when two peas
Lie snugly in a pod, the pod must then
Be larger than the peas — prove this —
'twere matter
Worthy the hearing. Fool was I to
dream
It ever could be otherwise!
Osw.   Last night
When I returned with water from the
brook,
I overheard the Villains — every word
Like red-hot iron burnt into my heart.
Said one, " It is agreed on. The blind
Man
Shall feign a sudden illness, and the Girl,
Who on her journey must proceed alone,
Under pretence of violence, be seized.
She is," continued the detested Slave,

" She is right willing — strange if she
were not! —
They say, Lord Clifford is a savage man;
But, faith, to see him in his silken tunic,
Fitting his low voice to the minstrel's harp,
There's witchery in't. I never knew a
maid
That could withstand it. True," con-
tinued he,
" When we arranged the affair, she wept
a little
(Not the less welcome to my Lord for
that)
And said,' My Father he will have it so.' "
Mar. I am your hearer.
Osw.   This I caught, and more
That may not be retold to any ear,
The obstinate bolt of a small iron door
Detained them near the gateway of the
Castle.
By a dim lantern's light I saw that wreaths
Of flowers were in their hands, as if
designed
For festive decoration; and they said,
With brutal laughter and most foul allu-
sion,
That they should share the banquet with
their Lord
And his new Favorite.
Mar.   Misery! —
Osw.   I knew
How you would be disturbed by this dire
news,
And therefore chose this solitary Moor,
Here to impart the tale, of which, last
night,
I strove to ease my mind, when our two
Comrades,
Commissioned by the Band, burst in upon
us.
Mar. Last night, when moved to lift
the avenging steel,
I did believe all things were shadows —
yea,
Living or dead all things were bodiless,
Or but the mutual mockeries of body,
Till that same star summoned me back
again.
Now I could laugh till my ribs ached.
Oh Fool!
To let a creed, built in the heart of things,
Dissolve before a twinkling atom! —
Oswald,

I could fetch lessons out of wiser schools
Than you have entered, were it worth the
pains.
Young as I am, I might go forth a teacher,
And you should see how deeply I could
reason
Of love in all its shapes, beginnings, ends;
Of moral qualities in their diverse aspects;
Of actions, and their laws and tendencies.

Osw. You take it as it merits —

Mar. One a King,
General or Cham, Sultan or Emperor,
Strews twenty acres of good meadow-
ground
With carcasses, in lineament and shape
And substance, nothing differing from his
own,
But that they cannot stand up of them-
selves;
Another sits i' th' sun, and by the hour
Floats kingcups in the brook—a Hero one
We call, and scorn the other as Time's
spendthrift;
But have they not a world of common
ground
To occupy — both fools, or wise alike,
Each in his way?

Osw. Troth, I begin to think so.

Mar. Now for the corner-stone of my
philosophy:
I would not give a denier for the man
Who, on such provocation as this earth
Yields, could not chuck his babe beneath
the chin,
And send it with a fillip to its grave.

Osw. Nay, you leave me behind.

Mar. That such a One,
So pious in demeanor! in his look
So saintly and so pure! — Hark'e, my
Friend,
I'll plant myself before Lord Clifford's
Castle,
A surly mastiff kennels at the gate,
And he shall howl and I will laugh, a
medley
Most tunable.

Osw. In faith, a pleasant scheme;
But take your sword along with you, for
that
Might in such neighborhood find seemly
use. —
But first, how wash our hands of this old
Man?

Mar. Oh yes, that mole, that viper in
the path;
Plague on my memory, him I had for-
gotten.

Osw. You know we left him sitting —
see him yonder.

Mar. Ha! ha! —

Osw. As 't will be but a moment's work,
I will stroll on; you follow when 'tis done.
[*Exeunt.*

SCENE *changes to another part of the
Moor at a short distance.* — HER-
BERT *is discovered seated on a stone.*

Her. A sound of laughter, too! — 'tis
well — I feared,
The Stranger had some pitiable sorrow
Pressing upon his solitary heart.
Hush! — 'tis the feeble and earth-loving
wind
That creeps along the bells of the crisp
heather.
Alas! 't is cold—I shiver in the sunshine—
What can this mean? There is a psalm
that speaks
Of God's parental mercies — with Idonea
I used to sing it. — Listen! — what foot
is there?

Enter MARMADUKE.

Mar. (*aside — looking at* HERBERT).
And I have loved this Man! and
she hath loved him!
And I loved her, and she loves the Lord
Clifford!
And there it ends; — if this be not enough
To make mankind merry for evermore,
Then plain it is as day, that eyes were
made
For a wise purpose —verily to weep with!
[*Looking round.*
A pretty prospect this, a masterpiece
Of Nature, finished with most curious
skill!
(*To* HERBERT.) Good Baron, have you
ever practised tillage?
Pray tell me what this land is worth by
the acre?

Her. How glad I am to hear your voice!
I know not
Wherein I have offended you; — last night
I found in you the kindest of Protectors;
This morning, when I spoke of weariness,

You from my shoulder took my scrip and
    threw it
About your own; but for these two hours
    past
Once only have you spoken, when the lark
Whirred from among the fern beneath our
    feet,
And I, no coward in my better days,
Was almost terrified.
  Mar.   That's excellent! —
So, you bethought you of the many ways
In which a man may come to his end,
    whose crimes
Have roused all Nature up against him —
    pshaw! —
  Her. For mercy's sake, is nobody in
    sight?
No traveller, peasant, herdsman?
  Mar. .   Not a soul:
Here is a tree, raggèd, and bent, and
    bare,
That turns its goat's-beard flakes of pea-
    green moss
From the stern breathing of the rough sea-
    wind;
This have we, but no other company:
Commend me to the place. If a man
    should die
And leave his body here, it were all one
As he were twenty fathoms under ground.
  Her. Where is our common Friend?
  Mar.   A ghost, methinks —
The Spirit of a murdered man, for in-
    stance —
Might have fine room to ramble about
    here,
A grand domain to squeak and gibber in.
  Her. Lost Man! if thou have any close-
    pent guilt
Pressing upon thy heart, and this the hour
Of visitation —
  Mar.   A bold word from *you!*
  Her. Restore him, Heaven!
  Mar. The desperate Wretch! — A
    Flower,
Fairest of all flowers, was she once, but
    now
They have snapped her from the stem —
    Poh! let her lie
Besoiled with mire, and let the houseless
    snail
Feed on her leaves. You knew her
    well — ay, there,

Old Man! you were a very Lynx, you
    knew
The worm was in her —
  Her.   Mercy! Sir, what mean you?
  Mar. You have a Daughter!
  Her.   Oh that she were here! —
She hath an eye that sinks into all hearts,
And if I have in aught offended you,
Soon would her gentle voice make peace
    between us.
  Mar. (*aside*). I do believe he weeps—
    I could weep too —
There is a vein of her voice that runs
    through his:
Even such a Man my fancy bodied forth
From the first moment that I loved the
    Maid;
And for his sake I loved her more: these
    tears —
I did not think that aught was left in me
Of what I have been — yes, I thank thee,
    Heaven!
One happy thought has passed across my
    mind.
— It may not be — I am cut off from man;
No more shall I be man — no more shall I
Have human feelings! — (*To* HER-
    BERT) —
    Now, for a little more
About your Daughter!
  Her.   Troops of armed men,
Met in the roads, would bless us; little
    children,
Rushing along in the full tide of play,
Stood silent as we passed them! I have
    heard
The boisterous carman, in the miry road,
Check his loud whip and hail us with mild
    voice,
And speak with milder voice to his poor
    beasts.
  Mar. And whither were you going?
  Her.   Learn, young Man,
To fear the virtuous, and reverence misery,
Whether too much for patience, or, like
    mine,
Softened till it becomes a gift of mercy.
  Mar. Now, this is as it should be!
  Her.   I am weak! —
My Daughter does not know how weak
    I am;
And, as thou see'st, under the arch of
    heaven

Here do I stand, alone, to helplessness,
By the good God, our common Father,
   doomed! —
But I had once a spirit and an arm —
  Mar. Now, for a word about your
   Barony:
I fancy when you left the Holy Land,
And came to — what's your title — eh?
   your claims
Were undisputed!
  Her.   Like a mendicant,
Whom no one comes to meet, I stood
   alone; —
I murmured — but, remembering Him
   who feeds
The pelican and ostrich of the desert,
From my own threshold I looked up to
   Heaven
And did not want glimmerings of quiet
   hope.
So, from the court I passed, and down the
   brook,
Led by its murmur, to the ancient oak
I came; and when I felt its cooling shade,
I sate me down, and cannot but believe —
While in my lap I held my little Babe
And clasped her to my heart, my heart
   that ached
More with delight than grief — I heard a
   voice
Such as by Cherith on Elijah called;
It said, "I will be with thee." A little
   boy,
A shepherd-lad, ere yet my trance was
   gone,
Hailed us as if he had been sent from
   heaven,
And said, with tears, that he would be our
   guide:
I had a better guide — that innocent
   Babe —
Her, who hath saved me, to this hour,
   from harm,
From cold, from hunger, penury, and
   death;
To whom I owe the best of all the good
I have, or wish for, upon earth — and
   more
And higher far than lies within earth's
   bounds:
Therefore I bless her: when I think of
   Man,
I bless her with sad spirit, — when of God,

I bless her in the fulness of my joy!
  Mar. The name of daughter in his
   mouth, he prays!
With nerves so steady, that the very flies
Sit unmolested on his staff. — Inno-
   cent! —
If he were innocent — then he would
   tremble
And be disturbed, as I am. (*Turning
   aside.*) I have read
In Story, what men now alive have wit-
   nessed,
How, when the People's mind was racked
   with doubt,
Appeal was made to the great Judge: the
   Accused
With naked feet walked over burning
   ploughshares.
Here is a Man by Nature's hand prepared
For a like trial, but more merciful.
Why else have I been led to this bleak
   Waste?
Bare is it, without house or track, and
   destitute
Of obvious shelter, as a shipless sea.
Here will I leave him — here — All-seeing
   God!
Such as *he* is, and sore perplexed as I
   am,
I will commit him to this final *Ordeal!* —
He heard a voice — a shepherd-lad came
   to him
And was his guide; if once, why not again,
And in this desert? If never — then the
   whole
Of what he says, and looks, and does, and
   is,
Makes up one damning falsehood. Leave
   him here
To cold and hunger! — Pain is of the
   heart,
And what are a few throes of bodily suf-
   fering
If they can waken one pang of remorse?
           [*Goes up to* HERBERT.
Old Man! my wrath is as a flame burnt
   out,
It cannot be rekindled. Thou art here
Led by my hand to save thee from perdi-
   tion;
Thou wilt have time to breathe and
   think —
  Her.   Oh, Mercy!

Mar. I know the need that all men have of mercy,
And therefore leave thee to a righteous judgment.
Her. My Child, my blessèd Child!
Mar.   No more of that;
Thou wilt have many guides if thou art innocent;
Yea, from the utmost corners of the earth,
That Woman will come o'er this Waste to save thee.
[*He pauses and looks at* HERBERT'S *staff*.
Ha! what is here? and carved by her own hand! (*Reads upon the staff.*)
" I am eyes to the blind, saith the Lord.
He that puts his trust in me shall not fail ! "
Yes, be it so; — repent and be forgiven —
God and that staff are now thy only guides.
[*He leaves* HERBERT *on the Moor.*

SCENE. — *An eminence, a Beacon on the summit.*
LACY, WALLACE, LENNOX, etc. etc.
Several of the Band (*confusedly*). But patience!
One of the Band. Curses on that Traitor, Oswald ! —
Our Captain made a prey to foul device ! —
Len. (*to* WAL.) His tool, the wandering Beggar, made last night
A plain confession, such as leaves no doubt,
Knowing what otherwise we know too well,
That she revealed the truth.   Stand by me now;
For rather would I have a nest of vipers
Between my breast-plate and my skin, than make
Oswald my special enemy, if you
Deny me your support.
Lacy.   We have been fooled —
But for the motive?
Wal.   Natures such as his
Spin motives out of their own bowels, Lacy!
I learned this when I was a Confessor.
I know him well; there needs no other motive
Than that most strange incontinence in crime

Which haunts this Oswald.   Power is life to him
And breath and being; where he cannot govern,
He will destroy.
Lacy.   To have been trapped like moles ! —
Yes, you are right, we need not hunt for motives:
There is no crime from which this man would shrink;
He recks not human law; and I have noticed
That often when the name of God is uttered,
A sudden blankness overspreads his face.
Len.   Yet, reasoner as he is, his pride has built
Some uncouth superstition of its own.
Wal. I have seen traces of it.
Len.   Once he headed
A band of Pirates in the Norway seas;
And when the King of Denmark summoned him
To the oath of fealty, I well remember,
'Twas a strange answer that he made; he said,
" I hold of Spirits, and the Sun in heaven."
Lacy. He is no madman.
Wal.   A most subtle doctor
Were that man, who could draw the line that parts
Pride and her daughter, Cruelty, from Madness,
That should be scourged, not pitied.   Restless Minds,
Such Minds as find amid their fellow-men
No heart that loves them, none that they can love,
Will turn perforce and seek for sympathy
In dim relation to imagined Beings.
One of the Band.   What if he mean to offer up our Captain
An expiation and a sacrifice
To those infernal fiends !
Wal.   Now, if the event
Should be as Lennox has foretold, then swear,
My Friends, his heart shall have as many wounds
As there are daggers here.

Lacy.   What need of swearing!
One of the Band. Let us away!
Another.   Away!
A third.   Hark! how the horns
Of those Scotch Rovers echo through the
          vale.
Lacy. Stay you behind; and when the
          sun is down,
Light up this beacon.
One of the Band. You shall be obeyed.
                    [*They go out together.*

SCENE. — *The Wood on the edge of the
      Moor.* MARMADUKE (*alone*).
Mar. Deep, deep and vast, vast be-
      yond human thought,
Yet calm. — I could believe, that there
      was here
The only quiet heart on earth. In terror,
Remembered terror, there is peace and
      rest.
            Enter OSWALD.
Osw. Ha! my dear Captain.
Mar.   A later meeting, Oswald,
Would have been better timed.
Osw.   Alone, I see;
You have done your duty. I had hopes,
      which now
I feel that you will justify.
Mar.   I had fears,
From which I have freed myself — but
      't is my wish
To be alone, and therefore we must part.
Osw. Nay, then — I am mistaken.
      There's a weakness
About you still; you talk of solitude —
I am your friend.
Mar.   What need of this assurance
At any time? and why given now?
Osw.   Because
You are now in truth my Master; you
      have taught me
What there is not another living man
Had strength to teach; — and therefore
      gratitude
Is bold, and would relieve itself by praise.
Mar. Wherefore press this on me?
Osw.   Because I feel
That you have shown, and by a signal
      instance,
How they who would be just must seek
      the rule
By diving for it into their own bosoms.

To-day you have thrown off a tyranny
That lives but in the torpid acquiescence
Of our emasculated souls, the tyranny
Of the world's masters, with the musty
      rules
By which they uphold their craft from
      age to age:
You have obeyed the only law that sense
Submits to recognize; the immediate law,
From the clear light of circumstances,
      flashed
Upon an independent Intellect.
Henceforth new prospects open on your
      path;
Your faculties should grow with the
      demand;
I still will be your friend, will cleave to
      you
Through good and evil, obloquy and
      scorn,
Oft as they dare to follow on your steps.
Mar. I would be left alone.
Osw. (*exultingly*). I know your
      motives!
I am not of the world's presumptuous
      judges,
Who damn where they can neither see nor
      feel,
With a hard-hearted ignorance; your
      struggles
I witnessed, and now hail your victory.
Mar. Spare me awhile that greeting.
Osw.   It may be,
That some there are, squeamish half-
      thinking cowards,
Who will turn pale upon you, call you
      murderer,
And you will walk in solitude among them.
A mighty evil for a strong-built mind! —
Join twenty tapers of unequal height
And light them joined, and you will see
      the less
How 'twill burn down the taller; and
      they all
Shall prey upon the tallest. Solitude! —
The Eagle lives in Solitude.
Mar.   Even so,
The Sparrow so on the housetop, and I,
The weakest of God's creatures, stand
      resolved
To abide the issue of my act, alone.
Osw. *Now* would you? — and for-
      ever? —

My young Friend,
As time advances either we become
The prey or masters of our own past deeds.
Fellowship we *must* have, willing or no;
And if good Angels fail, slack in their
  duty,
Substitutes, turn our faces where we may,
Are still forthcoming; some which,
  though they bear
Ill names, can render no ill services,
In recompense for what themselves re-
  quired.
So meet extremes in this mysterious world,
And opposites thus melt into each other.
  Mar. Time, since Man first drew
    breath, has never moved
With such a weight upon his wings as
  now;
But they will soon be lightened.
  Osw. Ay, look up —
Cast round you your mind's eye, and you
  will learn
Fortitude is the child of Enterprise:
Great actions move our admiration, chiefly
Because they carry in themselves an
  earnest
That we can suffer greatly.
  Mar. Very true.
  Osw. Action is transitory — a step, a
    blow,
The motion of a muscle — this way or
  that —
'T is done, and in the after-vacancy
We wonder at ourselves like men be-
  trayed:
Suffering is permanent, obscure and dark,
And shares the nature of infinity.
  Mar. Truth — and I feel it.
  Osw. What! if you had bid
Eternal farewell to unmingled joy
And the light dancing of the thoughtless
  heart;
It is the toy of fools, and little fit
For such a world as this. The wise abjure
All thoughts whose idle composition lives
In the entire forgetfulness of pain.
— I see I have disturbed you.
  Mar. By no means.
  Osw. Compassion! — pity! — pride
    can do without them;
And what if you should never know them
  more? —
He is a puny soul who, feeling pain,

Finds ease because another feels it too.
If e'er I open out this heart of mine
It shall be for a nobler end — to teach
And not to purchase puling sympathy.
— Nay, you are pale.
  Mar. It may be so.
  Osw. Remorse —
It cannot live with thought; think on,
  think on,
And it will die. What! in this universe,
Where the least things control the great-
  est, where
The faintest breath that breathes can
  move a world;
What! feel remorse, where, if a cat had
  sneezed,
A leaf had fallen, the thing had never been
Whose very shadow gnaws us to the vitals.
  Mar. Now, whither are you wandering?
    That a man
So used to suit his language to the time,
Should thus so widely differ from him-
  self —
It is most strange.
  Osw. Murder! — what's in the word! —
I have no cases by me ready made
To fit all deeds. Carry him to the
  Camp! —
A shallow project; — you of late have seen
More deeply, taught us that the institutes
Of Nature, by a cunning usurpation
Banished from human intercourse, exist
Only in our relations to the brutes
That make the fields their dwelling. If
  a snake
Crawl from beneath our feet we do not ask
A license to destroy him: our good
  governors
Hedge in the life of every pest and plague
That bears the shape of man; and for
  'what purpose,
But to protect themselves from extirpa-
  tion? —
This flimsy barrier you have overleaped.
  Mar. My Office is fulfilled — the Man
    is now
Delivered to the Judge of all things.
  Osw. Dead!
  Mar. I have borne my burthen to its
    destined end.
  Osw. This instant we'll return to our
    companions —
Oh how I long to see their faces again!

Enter IDONEA, *with* Pilgrims, *who continue their journey.*

Idon. (*after some time*). What, Marmaduke! now thou art mine for ever.
And Oswald, too! (*To* MARMADUKE).
On will we to my Father
With the glad tidings which this day hath brought;
We'll go together, and, such proof received
Of his own rights restored, his gratitude
To God above will make him feel for ours.

Osw. I interrupt you?

Idon.   Think not so.

Mar.   Idonea,
That I should ever live to see this moment!

Idon. Forgive me. — Oswald knows it all — he knows,
Each word of that unhappy letter fell
As a blood drop from my heart.

Osw.   'T was even so.

Mar. I have much to say, but for whose ear? — not thine.

Idon. Ill can I bear that look — Plead for me, Oswald!
You are my Father's Friend.
(*To* MARMADUKE). Alas, you know not,
And never *can* you know, how much he loved me.
Twice had he been to me a father, twice
Had given me breath, and was I not to be
His daughter, once his daughter? could I withstand
His pleading face, and feel his clasping arms,
And hear his prayer that I would not forsake him
In his old age —   [*Hides her face.*

Mar.   Patience — Heaven grant me patience! —
She weeps, she weeps — *my* brain shall burn for hours
Ere *I* can shed a tear.

Idon.   I was a woman;
And, balancing the hopes that are the dearest
To womankind with duty to my Father,
I yielded up those precious hopes, which nought
On earth could else have wrested from me; — if erring,
Oh, let me be forgiven!

Mar.   I *do* forgive thee.

Idon. But take me to your arms — this breast, alas!
It throbs, and you have a heart that does not feel it.

Mar. (*exultingly*). She is innocent.
                    [*He embraces her.*

Osw. (*aside*).   Were I a Moralist,
I should make wondrous revolution here;
It were a quaint experiment to show
The beauty of truth —[*Addressing them.*
                    I see I interrupt you;
I shall have business with you, Marmaduke;
Follow me to the hostel. [*Exit* OSWALD.

Idon.   Marmaduke,
This is a happy day. My Father soon
Shall sun himself before his native doors;
The lame, the hungry, will be welcome there.
No more shall he complain of wasted strength,
Of thoughts that fail, and a decaying heart;
His good works will be balm and life to him.

Mar.   This is most strange!—I know not what it was,
But there was something which most plainly said,
That thou wert innocent.

Idon.   How innocent! —
Oh heavens! you've been deceived.

Mar.   Thou art a Woman,
To bring perdition on the universe.

Idon. Already I've been punished to the height
Of my offence. [*Smiling affectionately.*
             I see you love me still,
The labors of my hand are still your joy;
Bethink you of the hour when on your shoulder
I hung this belt.
    [*Pointing to the belt on which was suspended* HERBERT'S *scrip.*

Mar.   Mercy of Heaven!   [*Sinks.*

Idon. What ails you! [*Distractedly.*

Mar.   The scrip that held his food, and I forgot
To give it back again!

Idon.   What mean your words?

Mar. I know not what I said — all may be well.

Idon. That smile hath life in it!
Mar. This road is perilous;
I will attend you to a Hut that stands
Near the wood's edge — rest there to-
night, I pray you:
For me, I have business, as you heard,
with Oswald,
But will return to you by break of day.
[*Exeunt.*

ACT IV.

SCENE.— *A desolate prospect — a ridge of
rocks — a Chapel on the summit of one
— Moon behind the rocks — night
stormy — irregular sound of a Bell —*
HERBERT *enters exhausted.*

Her. That Chapel-bell in mercy
seemed to guide me,
But now it mocks my steps; its fitful stroke
Can scarcely be the work of human hands.
Hear me, ye Men, upon the cliffs, if such
There be who pray nightly before the
Altar.
Oh that I had but strength to reach the
place!
My Child — my child — dark — dark — I
faint — this wind —
These stifling blasts — God help me!
Enter ELDRED.
Eld. Better this bare rock,
Though it were tottering over a man's
head,
Than a tight case of dungeon walls for
shelter
From such rough dealing.
[*A moaning voice is heard.*
Ha! what sound is that?
Trees creaking in the wind (but none are
here)
Send forth such noises — and that weary
bell!
Surely some evil Spirit abroad to-night
Is ringing it — 't would stop a Saint in
prayer,
And that — what is it? never was sound
so like
A human groan. Ha! what is here?
Poor Man —
Murdered! alas! speak — speak, I am
your friend:
No answer — hush — lost wretch, he lifts
his hand

And lays it to his heart—(*Kneels to him*).
I pray you speak!
What has befallen you?
Her. (*feebly*). A stranger has done
this,
And in the arms of a stranger I must die.
Eld. Nay, think not so: come, let
me raise you up: [*Raises him.*
This is a dismal place — well — that is
well —
I was too fearful — take me for your guide
And your support — my hut is not far off.
[*Draws him gently off the stage.*

SCENE. — *A room in the Hostel.* —MAR-
MADUKE *and* OSWALD.
Mar. But for Idonea! — I have cause
to think
That she is innocent.
Osw. Leave that thought awhile,
As one of those beliefs, which in their
hearts
Lovers lock up as pearls, though oft no
better
Than feathers clinging to their points of
passion.
This day's event has laid on me the duty
Of opening out my story; you must hear
it,
And without further preface. — In my
youth,
Except for that abatement which is paid
By envy as a tribute to desert,
I was the pleasure of all hearts, the darling
Of every tongue — as you are now.
You've heard
That I embarked for Syria. On our
voyage
Was hatched among the crew a foul
Conspiracy
Against my honor, in the which our
Captain
Was, I believed, prime Agent. The
wind fell;
We lay becalmed week after week, until
The water of the vessel was exhausted;
I felt a double fever in my veins,
Yet rage suppressed itself;— to a deep
stillness
Did my pride tame my pride;— for many
days,
On a dead sea under a burning sky,
I brooded o'er my injuries, deserted

By man and nature; — if a breeze had
 blown,
It might have found its way into my
 heart,
And I had been — no matter — do you
 mark me?
 Mar. Quick — to the point — if any
 untold crime
Doth haunt your memory.
 Osw. Patience, hear me further! —
One day in silence did we drift at noon
By a bare rock, narrow, and white, and
 bare;
No food was there, no drink, no grass,
 no shade,
No tree, nor jutting eminence, nor form
Inanimate large as the body of man,
Nor any living thing whose lot of life
Might stretch beyond the measure of one
 moon.
To dig for water on the spot, the Captain
Landed with a small troop, myself being
 one:
There I reproached him with his treachery.
Imperious at all times, his temper rose;
He struck me; and that instant had I
 killed him,
And put an end to his insolence, but my
 Comrades
Rushed in between us: then did I insist
(All hated him, and I was stung to mad-
 ness)
That we should leave him there, alive! —
 we did so.
 Mar. And he was famished?
 Osw. Naked was the spot;
Methinks I see it now — how in the sun
Its stony surface glittered like a shield;
And in that miserable place we left him,
Alone but for a swarm of minute creatures
Not one of which could help him while
 alive,
Or mourn him dead.
 Mar. A man by men cast off,
Left without burial! nay, not dead nor
 dying,
But standing, walking, stretching forth
 his arms,
In all things like ourselves, but in the
 agony
With which he called for mercy; and —
 even so —
He was forsaken?

 Osw. There is a power in sounds:
The cries he uttered might have stopped
 the boat
That bore us through the water —
 Mar. You returned
Upon that dismal hearing — did you not?
 Osw. Some scoffed at him with hellish
 mockery,
And laughed so loud it seemed that the
 smooth sea
Did from some distant region echo us.
 Mar. We all are of one blood, our
 veins are filled
At the same poisonous fountain!
 Osw. 'T was an island
Only by sufferance of the winds and waves,
Which with their foam could cover it at
 will.
I know not how he perished; but the calm,
The same dead calm, continued many days.
 Mar. But his own crime had brought
 on him this doom,
His wickedness prepared it; these expe-
 dients
Are terrible, yet ours is not the fault.
 Osw. The man was famished, and was
 innocent!
 Mar. Impossible!
 Osw. The man had never wronged me.
 Mar. Banish the thought, crush it, and
 be at peace.
His guilt was marked — these things
 · could never be
Were there not eyes that see, and for
 good ends,
Where ours are baffled.
 Osw. I had been deceived.
 Mar. And from that hour the misera-
 ble man
No more was heard of?
 Osw. I had been betrayed.
 Mar. And he found no deliverance!
 Osw. The Crew
Gave me a hearty welcome; they had laid
The plot to rid themselves, at any cost,
Of a tyrannic Master whom they loathed.
So we pursued our voyage: when we
 landed,
The tale was spread abroad; my power
 at once
Shrunk from me; plans and schemes,
 and lofty hopes —
All vanished. I gave way—do you attend?

Mar. The Crew deceived you?
Osw.   Nay, command yourself.
Mar. It is a dismal night — how the wind howls!
Osw. I hid my head within a Convent, there
Lay passive as a dormouse in mid-winter.
That was no life for me — I was o'erthrown,
But not destroyed.
   Mar. The proofs — you ought to have seen
The guilt — have touched it — felt it at your heart —
As I have done.
   Osw.   A fresh tide of Crusaders
Drove by the place of my retreat: three nights
Did constant meditation dry my blood;
Three sleepless nights I passed in sounding on,
Through words and things, a dim and perilous way;
And, wheresoe'er I turned me, I beheld
A slavery compared to which the dungeon
And clanking chains are perfect liberty.
You understand me — I was comforted;
I saw that every possible shape of action
Might lead to good — I saw it and burst forth
Thirsting for some of those exploits that fill
The earth for sure redemption of lost peace.
[*Marking* MARMADUKE'S *countenance.*]
Nay, you have had the worst. Ferocity
Subsided in a moment, like a wind
That drops down dead out of a sky it vexed.
And yet I had within me evermore
A salient spring of energy; I mounted
From action up to action with a mind
That never rested — without meat or drink
Have I lived many days — my sleep was bound
To purposes of reason — not a dream
But had a continuity and substance
That waking life had never power to give.
   Mar. O wretched Human-kind! —
Until the mystery
Of all this world is solved, well may we envy

The worm, that, underneath a stone whose weight
Would crush the lion's paw with mortal anguish,
Doth lodge, and feed, and coil, and sleep, in safety.
Fell not the wrath of Heaven upon those traitors?
   Osw. Give not to them a thought.
From Palestine
We marched to Syria: oft I left the Camp,
When all that multitude of hearts was still,
And followed on, through woods of gloomy cedar,
Into deep chasms troubled by roaring streams;
Or from the top of Lebanon surveyed
The moonlight desert, and the moonlight sea:
In these my lonely wanderings I perceived
What mighty objects do impress their forms
To elevate our intellectual being;
And felt, if aught on earth deserves a curse,
'Tis that worst principle of ill which dooms
A thing so great to perish self-consumed.
— So much for my remorse!
   Mar.   Unhappy Man!
   Osw. When from these forms I turned to contemplate
The World's opinions and her usages,
I seemed a Being who had passed alone
Into a region of futurity,
Whose natural element was freedom —
   Mar.   Stop —
I may not, cannot, follow thee.
   Osw.   You must.
I had been nourished by the sickly food
Of popular applause. I now perceived
That we are praised, only as men in us
Do recognize some image of themselves,
An abject counterpart of what they are,
Or the empty thing that they would wish to be.
I felt that merit has no surer test
Than obloquy; that, if we wish to serve
The world in substance, not deceive by show,
We must become obnoxious to its hate,
Or fear disguised in simulated scorn.

Mar. I pity, can forgive, you; but those wretches —
That monstrous perfidy!
Osw.   Keep down your wrath.
False Shame discarded, spurious Fame despised,
Twin sisters both of Ignorance, I found
Life stretched before me smooth as some broad way
Cleared for a monarch's progress. Priests might spin
Their veil, but not for me — 't was in fit place
Among its kindred cobwebs. I had been,
And in that dream had left my native land,
One of Love's simple bondsmen — the soft chain
Was off forever; and the men, from whom
This liberation came, you would destroy:
Join me in thanks for their blind services.
Mar. 'T is a strange aching that, when we would curse
And cannot. — You have betrayed me — I have done —
I am content — I know that he is guiltless —
That both are guiltless, without spot or stain,
Mutually consecrated. Poor old Man!
And I had heart for this, because thou lovedst
Her who from very infancy had been
Light to thy path, warmth to thy blood! —
     Together [*Turning to* OSWALD.
We propped his steps, he leaned upon us both.
Osw. Ay, we are coupled by a chain of adamant;
Let us be fellow-laborers, then, to enlarge
Man's intellectual empire. We subsist
In slavery; all is slavery; we receive
Laws, but we ask not whence those laws have come;
We need an inward sting to goad us on.
Mar. Have you betrayed me? Speak to that.
Osw.   The mask,
Which for a season I have stooped to wear,
Must be cast off. — Know then that I was urged,
(For other impulse let it pass) was driven,
To seek for sympathy, because I saw
In you a mirror of my youthful self;

I would have made us equal once again,
But that was a vain hope. You have struck home,
With a few drops of blood cut short the business;
Therein forever you must yield to me.
But what is done will save you from the blank
Of living without knowledge that you live:
Now you are suffering — for the future day,
'T is his who will command it. — Think of my story —
Herbert is *innocent.*
Mar. (*in a faint voice, and doubtingly*).
          You do but echo
My own wild words?
Osw.   Young Man, the seed must lie
Hid in the earth, or there can be no harvest;
'T is Nature's law. What I have done in darkness
I will avow before the face of day.
Herbert *is* innocent.
Mar.   What fiend could prompt
This action? Innocent! — oh, breaking heart! —
Alive or dead, I'll find him.   [*Exit.*
Osw.   Alive — perdition!   [*Exit.*

SCENE. — *The inside of a poor Cottage.*
     ELEANOR *and* IDONEA *seated.*
Idon. The storm beats hard — Mercy for poor or rich,
Whose heads are shelterless in such a night!
A Voice without. Holla! to bed, good Folks, within!
Elea.   O save us!
Idon. What can this mean?
Elea. Alas, for my poor husband! —
We'll have a counting of our flocks tomorrow;
The wolf keeps festival these stormy nights:
Be calm, sweet Lady, they are wassailers
     [*The voices die away in the distance.*
Returning from their Feast — my heart beats so —
A noise at midnight does *so* frighten me.
Idon. Hush!   [*Listening.*
Elea. They are gone. On such a night
Dragged from his bed, was cast into a dungeon,
Where, hid from me, he counted many years,

A criminal in no one's eyes but theirs —
Not even in theirs—whose brutal violence
So dealt with him.

Idon.   I have a noble Friend
First among youths of knightly breeding,
    One
Who lives but to protect the weak or
    injured.
There again !   [*Listening.*

Elea.   'T is my husband's foot. Good
    Eldred
Has a kind heart; but his imprisonment
Has made him fearful, and he'll never be
The man he was.

Idon.   I will retire; — good night !
                [*She goes within.*

Enter ELDRED (*hides a bundle*).

Eld. Not yet in bed, Eleanor ! — there
are stains in that frock which must be
washed out.

Elea.   What has befallen you?

Eld. I am belated, and you must know
the cause—(*speaking low*) that is the blood
of an unhappy Man.

Elea.   Oh! we are undone forever.

Eld. Heaven forbid that I should lift my
hand against any man. Eleanor, I have
shed tears to-night, and it comforts me to
think of it.

Elea.   Where, where is he?

Eld. I have done him no harm, but —
it will be forgiven me; it would not have
been so once.

Elea.   You have not *buried* anything?
You are no richer than when you left me?

Eld.   Be at peace; I am innocent.

Elea.   Then God be thanked —
            [*A short pause; she falls
                upon his neck.*

Eld.   To-night I met with an old Man
lying stretched upon the ground — a sad
spectacle: I raised him up with a hope
that we might shelter and restore him.

Elea. (*as if ready to run*). Where is he?
You were not able to bring him *all* the way
with you; let us return, I can help you.
                [ELDRED *shakes his head.*

Eld. He did not seem to wish for life:
as I was struggling on, by the light of the
moon I saw the stains of blood upon my
clothes—he waved his hand, as if it were
all useless; and I let him sink again to the
ground.

Elea.   Oh that I had been by your
side !

Eld.   I tell you his hands and his body
were cold — how could I disturb his last
moments? he strove to turn from me as if
he wished to settle into sleep.

Elea.   But, for the stains of blood —

Eld. He must have fallen, I fancy, for
his head was cut; but I think his malady
was cold and hunger.

Elea. Oh, Eldred, I shall never be able
to look up at this roof in storm or fair but
I shall tremble.

Eld.   Is it not enough that my ill stars
have kept me abroad to-night till this hour?
I come home, and this is my comfort !

Elea.   But did he say nothing which
might have set you at ease?

Eld.   I thought he grasped my hand
while he was muttering something about
his Child—his Daughter—(*starting as if
he heard a noise*). What is that?

Elea.   Eldred, you are a father.

Eld. God knows what was in my heart,
and will not curse my son for my sake.

Elea.   But you prayed by him? you
waited the hour of his release?

Eld. The night was wasting fast; I have
no friend; I am spited by the world — his
wound terrified me — if I had brought him
along with me, and he had died in my
arms ! — I am sure I heard something
breathing — and this chair !

Elea.   Oh, Eldred, you will die alone.
You will have nobody to close your eyes —
no hand to grasp your dying hand—I shall
be in my grave. A curse will attend us
all.

Eld. Have you forgot your own troubles
when I was in the dungeon?

Elea.   And you left him alive?

Eld Alive !—the damps of death were
upon him — he could not have survived
an hour.

Elea.   In the cold, cold night.

Eld. (*in a savage tone*). Ay, and his head
was bare; I suppose you would have had
me lend my bonnet to cover it. — You will
never rest till I am brought to a felon's end.

Elea.   Is there nothing to be done?
cannot we go to the Convent?

Eld. Ay, and say at once that I murdered
him !

Elea. Eldred, I know that ours is the only house upon the Waste; let us take heart; this Man may be rich; and could he be saved by our means, his gratitude may reward us.

Eld. 'T is all in vain.

Elea. But let us make the attempt. This old Man may have a wife, and he may have children — let us return to the spot; we may restore him, and his eyes may yet open upon those that love him.

Eld. He will never open them more; even when he spoke to me, he kept them firmly sealed as if he had been blind.

Idon. (*rushing out*). It is, it is, my Father —

Eld. We are betrayed (*looking at* IDONEA).

Elea. His Daughter !—God have mercy ! (*turning to* IDONEA).

Idon. (*sinking down*). Oh ! lift me up and carry me to the place. You are safe; the whole world shall not harm you.

Elea. This Lady is his Daughter.

Eld. (*moved*). I'll lead you to the spot.

Idon. (*springing up*). Alive ! — you heard him breathe? quick, quick — [*Exeunt.*

ACT V.

SCENE. — *A wood on the edge of the Waste.*
Enter OSWALD *and a* Forester.

For. He leaned upon the bridge that spans the glen,
And down into the bottom cast his eye,
That fastened there, as it would check the current.

Osw. He listened too; did you not say he listened?

For. As if there came such moaning from the flood
As is heard often after stormy nights.

Osw. But did he utter nothing?

For. See him there !
MARMADUKE *appearing.*

Mar. Buzz, buzz, ye black and winged freebooters;
That is no substance which ye settle on !

For. His senses play him false; and see, his arms

Outspread, as if to save himself from falling ! —
Some terrible phantom I believe is now
Passing before him, such as God will not
Permit to visit any but a man
Who has been guilty of some horrid crime.
[MARMADUKE *disappears.*

Osw. The game is up ! —

For. If it be needful, Sir,
I will assist you to lay hands upon him.

Osw. No, no, my Friend, you may pursue your business —
'T is a poor wretch of an unsettled mind,
Who has a trick of straying from his keepers;
We must be gentle. Leave him to my care.
[*Exit* Forester.

If his own eyes play false with him, these freaks
Of fancy shall be quickly tamed by mine;
The goal is reached. My Master shall become
A shadow of myself — made by myself.

SCENE. — *The edge of the Moor.*
MARMADUKE *and* ELDRED *enter from opposite sides.*

Mar. (*raising his eyes and perceiving* ELDRED). In any corner of this savage Waste,
Have you, good Peasant, seen a blind old Man?

Eld. I heard —

Mar. You heard him, where? when heard him?

Eld. As you know,
The first hours of last night were rough with storm:
I had been out in search of a stray heifer;
Returning late, I heard a moaning sound;
Then, thinking that my fancy had deceived me,
I hurried on, when straight a second moan,
A human voice distinct, struck on my ear,
So guided, distant a few steps, I found
An aged Man, and such as you describe.

Mar. You heard ! — he called you to him? Of all men
The best and kindest ! — but where is he? guide me,
That I may see him.

Eld. On a ridge of rocks
A lonesome Chapel stands, deserted now:
The bell is left, which no one dares remove;
And, when the stormy wind blows o'er the peak,
It rings, as if a human hand were there
To pull the cord. I guess he must have heard it;
And it had led him towards the precipice,
To climb up to the spot whence the sound came;
But he had failed through weakness.
From his hand
His staff had dropped, and close upon the brink .
Of a small pool of water he was laid,
As if he had stooped to drink, and so remained
Without the strength to rise.
Mar. Well, well, he lives,
And all is safe: what said he?
Eld. But few words:
He only spake to me of a dear Daughter,
Who, so he feared, would never see him more;
And of a Stranger to him, One by whom
He had been sore misused; but he forgave
The wrong and the wrong-doer. You are troubled —
Perhaps you are his son?
Mar. The All-seeing knows,
I did not think he had a living Child. —
But whither did you carry him? |
Eld. He was torn,
His head was bruised, and there was blood about him —
Mar. That was no work of mine.
Eld. Nor was it mine.
Mar. But had he strength to walk? I could have borne him
A thousand miles.
Eld. I am in poverty,
And know how busy are the tongues of men;
My heart was willing, Sir, but I am one
Whose good deeds will not stand by their own light;
And, though it smote me more than words can tell,
I left him.
Mar. I believe that there are phantoms,

That in the shape of man do cross our path
On evil instigation, to make sport
Of our distress — and thou art one of them!
But things substantial have so pressed on me —
Eld. My wife and children came into my mind.
Mar. Oh Monster! Monster! there are three of us,
And we shall howl together.
[*After a pause and in a feeble voice.*
I am deserted
At my worst need, my crimes have in a net
(*Pointing to* ELDRED) Entangled this poor man. — Where was it? where?
[*Dragging him along.*
Eld. 'T is needless; spare your violence.
His Daughter —
Mar. Ay, in the word a thousand scorpions lodge.
This old man *had* a Daughter.
Eld. To the spot
I hurried back with her. — O save me, Sir,
From such a journey! — there was a black tree, .
A single tree; she thought it was her Father. —
Oh Sir, I would not see that hour again
For twenty lives. The daylight dawned, and now —
Nay; hear my tale, 't is fit that you should hear it —
As we approached, a solitary crow
Rose from the spot; — the Daughter clapped her hands,
And then I heard a shriek so terrible
[MARMADUKE *shrinks back.*
The startled bird quivered upon the wing.
Mar. Dead, dead! —
Eld. (*after a pause*). A dismal matter, Sir, for me,
And seems the like for you; if 't is your wish,
I'll lead you to his Daughter; but 't were best
That she should be prepared; I'll go before.
Mar. There will be need of preparation.

[ELDRED *goes off*.

Elea. (*enters*).   Master!
Your limbs sink under you, shall I sup-
　port you?
　Mar. (*taking her arm*). Woman, I've
lent my body to the service
Which now thou tak'st upon thee.　God
　forbid
That thou shouldst ever meet a like occa-
　sion
With such a purpose in thine heart as
　mine was.
　Elea. Oh, why have I to do with
　things like these?　　　[*Exeunt*.

SCENE *changes to the door of* ELDRED'S
cottage — IDONEA *seated* — *enter* ELDRED.
　Eld. Your Father, Lady, from a wilful
　hand
Has met unkindness; so indeed he told
　me,
And you remember such was my report:
From what has just befallen me I have
　cause
To fear the very worst.
　Idon.　　　　My Father is dead;
Why dost thou come to me with words
　like these?
　Eld. A wicked Man should answer for
　his crimes.
　Idon. Thou seest me what I am.
　Eld.　　　　It was most heinous,
And doth call out for vengeance.
　Idon.　　　　Do not add,
I prithee, to the harm thou'st done al-
　ready;
　Eld. Hereafter you will thank me for
　this service.
Hard by, a Man I met, who, from plain
　proofs
Of interfering Heaven, I have no doubt,
Laid hands upon your Father.　Fit it were
You should prepare to meet him.
　Idon.　　　　I have nothing
To do with others; help me to my Father—
　[*She turns and sees* MARMADUKE *lean-
　　ing on* ELEANOR — *throws herself
　　upon his neck, and after some time*,
In joy I met thee, but a few hours past;
And thus we meet again; one human stay
Is left me still in thee.　Nay, shake not so.
　Mar. In such a wilderness — to see no
　thing,

No, not the pitying moon!
　Idon.　　　　And perish so.
　Mar. Without a dog to moan for him.
　Idon.　　　　Think not of it,
But enter there and see him how he sleeps,
Tranquil as he had died in his own bed.
　Mar. Tranquil — why not?
　Idon.　　　　Oh, peace!
　Mar.　　　　He is at peace;
His body is at rest: there was a plot,
A hideous plot, against the soul of man:
It took effect — and yet I baffled it,
In *some* degree.
　Idon.　　Between us stood, I thought,
A cup of consolation, filled from Heaven
For both our needs;. must I, and in thy
　presence,
Alone partake of it? — Belovèd Marma-
　duke!
　Mar. Give me a reason why the wisest
　thing
That the earth owns shall never choose
　to die,
But some one must be near to count his
　groans.
The wounded deer retires to solitude,
And dies in solitude: all things but man,
All die in solitude.
　　[*Moving towards the cottage door*.
　　　　　Mysterious God,
If she had never lived I had not done it!—
　Idon. Alas, the thought of such a cruel
　death
Has overwhelmed him. — I must follow.
　Eld.　　　　Lady!
You will do well; (*she goes*) unjust sus-
　picion may
Cleave to this Stranger: if, upon his
　entering,
The dead Man heave a groan, or from his
　side
Uplift his hand—that would be evidence.
　Elea. Shame! Eldred, shame!
　Mar. (*both returning*).　The dead
　　have but one face (*to himself*).
And such a Man — so meek and unoffend-
　ing —
Helpless and harmless as a babe: a Man,
By obvious signal to the world's protec-
　tion,
Solemnly dedicated — to decoy him! —
　Idon. Oh, had you seen him living! —
　Mar.　　　　I (so filled

With horror in this world) am unto thee
The thing most precious, that it now
    contains:
Therefore through me alone must be
    revealed
By whom thy Parent was destroyed,
    Idonea!
I have the proofs! —
    Idon.   O miserable Father!
Thou didst command me to bless all man-
    kind;
Nor to this moment, have I ever wished
Evil to any living thing; but hear me,
Hear me, ye Heavens! — (*kneeling*) —
    may vengeance haunt the fiend
For this most cruel murder: let him live
And move in terror of the elements;
The thunder send him on his knees to
    prayer
In the open streets, and let him think he
    sees,
If e'er he entereth the house of God,
The roof, self-moved, unsettling o'er his
    head;
And let him, when he would lie down at
    night,
Point to his wife the blood-stains on his
    pillow!
    Mar. My voice was silent, but my
    heart hath joined thee.
    Idon. (*leaning on* MARMADUKE). Left
to the mercy of that savage Man!
How could he call upon his Child! — O
    Friend! [*Turns to* MARMADUKE.
My faithful true and only Comforter.
    Mar. Ay, come to me and weep.
    (*He kisses her.*) (*To* ELDRED.)
Yes, Varlet, look,
The devils at such sights do clap their
    hands.
        [ELDRED *retires alarmed.*
    Idon. Thy vest is torn, thy cheek is
    deadly pale;
Hast thou pursued the monster?
    Mar.   I have found him. —
Oh! would that thou hadst perished in
    the flames!
    Idon. Here art thou, then can I be
    desolate? —
    Mar. There was a time, when this pro-
    tecting hand
Availed against the mighty; never more
Shall blessings wait upon a deed of mine.

    Idon. Wild words for me to hear, for
    me, an orphan
Committed to thy guardianship by
    Heaven;
And, if thou hast forgiven me, let me
    hope,
In this deep sorrow, trust, that I am thine
For closer care; — here, is no malady.
        [*Taking his arm.*
    Mar. There, *is* a malady —
(*Striking his heart and forehead*). And
    here, and here,
A mortal malady. — I am accurst:
All nature curses me, and in my heart
Thy curse is fixed; the truth must be
    laid bare.
It must be told, and borne. I am the man,
(Abused, betrayed, but how it matters
    not)
Presumptuous above all that ever
    breathed,
Who, casting as I thought a guilty Person
Upon Heaven's righteous judgment, did
    become
An instrument of Fiends. Through me,
    through me
Thy Father perished.
    Idon. Perished — by what mischance?
    Mar. Beloved! — if I dared, so would
    I call thee —
Conflict must cease, and, in thy frozen
    heart,
The extremes of suffering meet in absolute
    peace.   [*He gives her a letter.*
    Idon. (*reads*). "Be not surprised if
you hear that some signal judgment has
befallen the man who calls himself your
father; he is now with me, as his signa-
ture will show: abstain from conjecture
till you see me.   "HERBERT.
            "MARMADUKE."
The writing Oswald's; the signature my
    Father's:
(*Looks steadily at the paper*). And here is
    yours, — or do my eyes deceive
    me?
You have then seen my Father?
    Mar.   He has leaned
Upon this arm.
    Idon. You led him towards the Con-
    vent?
    Mar. That Convent was Stone-Arthur
    Castle. Thither

We were his guides. I on that night
    resolved
That he should wait thy coming till the day
Of resurrection.
    Idon.   Miserable Woman,
Too quickly moved, too easily giving way,
I put denial on thy suit, and hence,
With the disastrous issue of last night,
Thy perturbation, and these frantic words.
Be calm, I pray thee!
    Mar.   Oswald —
    Idon.   Name him not.
       Enter female Beggar.
    Beg. And he is dead! — that Moor —
    how shall I cross it?
By night, by day, never shall I be able
To travel half a mile alone. — Good Lady!
Forgive me! — Saints forgive me. Had
    I thought
It would have come to this! —
    Idon. What brings you hither? speak!
    Beg. (*pointing to* MARMADUKE). This
    innocent Gentleman.   Sweet
    heavens! I told him
Such tales of your dead Father! — God
    is my judge.
I thought there was no harm: but that
    bad Man,
He bribed me with his gold, and looked
    so fierce.
Mercy! I said I know not what — oh
    pity me —
I said, sweet Lady, you were not his
    Daughter —
Pity me, I am haunted; — thrice this day
My conscience made me wish to be
    struck blind;
And then I would have prayed, and had
    no voice.
    Idon. (*to* MARMADUKE). Was it my
    Father? — no, no, no, for he
Was-meek and patient, feeble, old and
    blind,
Helpless, and loved me dearer than his
    life.
— But hear me. For *one* question, I have
    a heart
That will sustain me. Did you murder
    him?
    Mar. No, not by stroke of arm. But
learn the process:
Proof after proof was pressed upon me;
    guilt

Made evident, as seemed, by blacker
    guilt,
Whose impious folds enwrapped even
    thee; and truth
And innocence, embodied in his looks,
His words and tones and gestures, did but
    serve
With me to aggravate his crimes, and
    heaped
Ruin upon the cause for which they
    pleaded.
Then pity crossed the path of my resolve:
Confounded, I looked up to Heaven, and
    cast,
Idonea! thy blind Father, on the Ordeal
Of the bleak Waste — left him — and so
    he died! —
    [IDONEA *sinks senseless;* Beggar,
    ELEANOR, *etc., crowd round, and
    bear her off.*
Why may we speak these things, and do
    no more;
Why should a thrust of the arm have such
    a power,
And words that tell these things be heard
    in vain?
She is not dead. Why! — if I loved
    this Woman,
I would take care she never woke again;
But she WILL wake, and she will weep
    for me,
And say, no blame was mine — and so,
    poor fool,
Will waste her curses on another name.
    [*He walks about distractedly.*
        Enter OSWALD.
    Osw. (*to himself*). Strong to o'erturn,
    strong also to build up.
            [*To* MARMADUKE.
The starts and sallies of our last encounter
Were natural enough; but that, I trust,
Is all gone by. You have cast off the
    chains
That fettered your nobility of mind —
Delivered heart and head!
            Let us to Palestine;
This is a paltry field for enterprise.
    Mar. Ay, what shall we encounter
    next? This issue —
'T was nothing more than darkness deep-
    ening darkness,
And weakness crowned with the impo-
    tence of death! —

Your pupil is, you see, an apt proficient
(*ironically*).
Start not! — here is another face hard by;
Come, let us take a peep at both to-
gether,
And, with a voice at which the dead will
quake,
Resound the praise of your morality —
Of this too much.
[*Drawing* OSWALD *towards the Cottage
— stops short at the door.*
Men are there, millions, Oswald,
Who with bare hands would have plucked
out thy heart
And flung it to the dogs: but I am
raised
Above, or sunk below, all further sense
Of provocation. Leave me, with the
weight
Of that old Man's forgiveness on thy
heart,
Pressing as heavily as it doth on mine.
Coward I have been; know, there lies
not now
Within the compass of a mortal thought,
A deed that I would shrink from; — but
to endure,
That is my destiny. May it be thine:
Thy office, thy ambition, be henceforth
To feed remorse, to welcome every sting
Of penitential anguish, yea with tears.
When seas and continents shall lie be-
tween us —
The wider space the better — we may
find
In such a course fit links of sympathy,
An incommunicable rivalship
Maintained, for peaceful ends beyond our
view.
[*Confused voices — several of the band
enter — rush upon* OSWALD, *and
seize him.*
One of them. I would have dogged him
to the jaws of hell —
Osw. Ha! is it so? — That vagrant
Hag! — this comes
Of having left a thing like her alive!
[*Aside.*
Several voices. Despatch him!
Osw. If I pass beneath a rock
And shout, and, with the echo of my voice,
Bring down a heap of rubbish, and it
crush me,

I die without dishonor. Famished,
starved,
A Fool and Coward blended to my wish!
[*Smiles scornfully and exultingly at*
MARMADUKE.
Wal. 'T is done! (*Stabs him*).
Another of the band. The ruthless
Traitor!
Mar. A rash deed! —
With that reproof I do resign a station
Of which I have been proud.
Wil. (*approaching* MARMADUKE). O
my poor Master!
Mar. Discerning Monitor, my faithful
Wilfred,
Why art thou here?
[*Turning to* WALLACE.
Wallace, upon these Borders,
Many there be whose eyes will not want
cause
To weep that I am gone. Brothers in
arms!
Raise on that dreary Waste a monument
That may record my story: nor let
words —
Few must they be, and delicate in their
touch
As light itself — be there withheld from
Her
Who, through most wicked arts, was
made an orphan
By One who would have died a thousand
times,
To shield her from a moment's harm. To
you,
Wallace and Wilfred, I commend the
Lady,
By lowly nature reared, as if to make
her
In all things worthier of that noble birth,
Whose long-suspended rights are now on
the eve
Of restoration: with your tenderest care
Watch over her, I pray — sustain her —
Several of the band (*eagerly*). Captain!
Mar. No more of that; in silence hear
my doom:
A hermitage has furnished fit relief
To some offenders: other penitents,
Less patient in their wretchedness, have
fallen,
Like the old Roman, on their own sword's
point.

They had their choice: a wanderer *must*
      I go,
The Spectre of that innocent Man, my
      guide.
No human ear shall ever hear me speak;
No human dwelling ever give me food,
Or sleep, or rest: but, over waste and
      wild,
In search of nothing, that this earth can
      give,
But expiation, will I wander on —
A Man by pain and thought compelled to
      live,
Yet loathing life — till anger is appeased
In Heaven, and Mercy gives me leave to
      die.
      1795-96.   1842.

THE REVERIE OF POOR SUSAN.

This arose out of my observation of the affect-
ing music of these birds hanging in this way in
the London streets during the freshness and still-
ness of the Spring morning.

AT the corner of Wood Street, when
      daylight appears,
Hangs a Thrush that sings loud, it has
      sung for three years:
Poor Susan has passed by the spot, and
      has heard
In the silence of morning the song of the
      Bird.

'Tis a note of enchantment; what ails her?
      She sees
A mountain ascending, a vision of trees;
Bright volumes of vapor through Loth-
      bury glide,
And a river flows on through the vale of
      Cheapside.

Green pastures she views in the midst of
      the dale,
Down which she so often has tripped
      with her pail;
And a single small cottage, a nest like a
      dove's,
The one only dwelling on earth that she
      loves.

She looks, and her heart is in heaven:
      but they fade,

The mist and the river, the hill and the
      shade:
The stream will not flow, .and the hill
      will not rise,
And the colors have all passed away
      from her eyes!
      1797.   1800.

THE BIRTH OF LOVE.

Translated from some French stanzas by
Francis Wrangham, and printed in "Poems by
Francis Wrangham, M.A."

WHEN Love was born of heavenly line,
      What dire intrigues disturbed Cythera's
            joy!
Till Venus cried, "A mother's heart is
            mine;
      None but myself shall nurse my boy."

But, infant as he was, the child
      In that divine embrace enchanted lay;
And, by the beauty of the vase beguiled,
      Forgot the beverage — and pined away.

" And must my offspring languish in my
            sight?"
      (Alive to all a mother's pain,
The Queen of Beauty thus her court
            addressed)
" No: Let the most discreet of all my
            train
Receive him to her breast:
Think all, he is the God of young delight."

Then TENDERNESS with CANDOR joined,
      And GAIETY the charming office
            sought;
Nor even DELICACY stayed behind:
      But none of those fair Graces brought
Wherewith to nurse the child — and still
      he pined.
Some fond hearts to COMPLIANCE seemed
      inclined;
      But she had surely spoiled the boy:
      And sad experience forbade a thought
On the wild Goddess of VOLUPTUOUS JOY.

Long undecided lay th' important choice,
Till of the beauteous court, at length, a
      voice

Pronounced the name of HOPE: — The
    conscious child
Stretched forth his little arms, and smiled.

'T is said ENJOYMENT (who averred
    The charge belonged to her alone)
Jealous that HOPE had been preferred
    Laid snares to make the babe her own.

Of INNOCENCE the garb she took,
The blushing mien and downcast look;
    And came her services to proffer:
And HOPE (what has not Hope believed!)
By that seducing air deceived,
    Accepted of the offer.

It happened that, to sleep inclined,
Deluded HOPE for one short hour
    To that false INNOCENCE'S power
Her little charge consigned.

The Goddess then her lap with sweet-
    meats filled
    And gave, in handfuls gave, the treach-
    erous store:
A wild delirium first the infant thrilled;
    But soon upon her breast he sunk —
    to wake no more.
1795.   1842.

A NIGHT-PIECE.

Composed on the road between Nether Stowey
and Alfoxden, extempore. I distinctly recollect
the very moment when I was struck, as described,
— " He looks up — the clouds are split," etc.

      — THE sky is overcast
With a continuous cloud of texture close,
Heavy and wan, all whitened by the
    Moon,
Which through that veil is indistinctly
    seen,
A dull, contracted circle, yielding light
So feebly spread, that not a shadow falls,
Checkering the ground — from rock,
    plant, tree, or tower.
At length a pleasant instantaneous gleam
Startles the pensive traveller while he
    treads
His lonesome path, with unobserving eye
Bent earthwards; he looks up — the
    clouds are split

Asunder, — and above his head he sees
The clear Moon, and the glory of the
    heavens.
There, in a black-blue vault she sails
    along,
Followed by multitudes of stars, that,
    small
And sharp, and bright, along the dark
    abyss
Drives as she drives: how fast they wheel
    away,
Yet vanish not! — the wind is in the tree,
But they are silent; — still they roll along
Immeasurably distant; and the vault,
Built round by those white clouds, enor-
    mous clouds,
Still deepens its unfathomable depth.
At length the Vision closes; and the
    mind,
Not undisturbed by the delight it feels,
Which slowly settles into peaceful calm,
Is left to muse upon the solemn scene.
    1798.   1815.

WE ARE SEVEN.

    Written at Alfoxden in the spring of 1798,
under circumstances somewhat remarkable. The
little girl who is the heroine I met within the area
of Goodrich Castle in the year 1793. Having left
the Isle of Wight and crossed Salisbury Plain, as
mentioned in the preface to " Guilt and Sorrow,"
I proceeded by Bristol up the Wye, and so on to
North Wales, to the Vale of Clwydd, where I
spent my summer under the roof of the father of
my friend, Robert Jones. In reference to this
Poem I will here mention one of the most re-
markable facts in my own poetic history and that
of Mr. Coleridge. In the spring of the year 1798,
he, my sister, and myself, started from Alfoxden,
pretty late in the afternoon, with a view to visit
Lenton and the valley of Stones near it; and as
our united funds were very small, we agreed to
defray the expenses of the tour by writing a poem,
to be sent to the New Monthly Magazine set up
by Phillips the Bookseller, and edited by Dr.
Aikin. Accordingly we set off and proceeded
along the Quantock Hills towards Watchet, and
in the course of this walk was planned the poem
of the " Ancient Mariner," founded on a dream,
as Mr. Coleridge said, of his friend, Mr. Cruik-
shank. Much the greatest part of the story was
Mr. Coleridge's invention; but certain parts I
myself suggested: — for example, some crime was
to be committed which should bring upon the old

Navigator, as Coleridge afterwards delighted to call him, the spectral persecution, as a consequence of that crime, and his own wanderings. I had been reading in Shelvock's Voyages a day or two before that while doubling Cape Horn they frequently saw Albatrosses in that latitude, the largest sort of sea-fowl, some extending their wings twelve or fifteen feet. "Suppose," said I, "you represent him as having killed one of these birds on entering the South Sea, and that the tutelary Spirits of those regions take upon them to avenge the crime." The incident was thought fit for the purpose and adopted accordingly. I also suggested the navigation of the ship by the dead men, but do not recollect that I had anything more to do with the scheme of the poem. The Gloss with which it was subsequently accompanied was not thought of by either of us at the time; at least, not a hint of it was given to me, and I have no doubt it was a gratuitous afterthought. We began the composition together on that, to me, memorable evening. I furnished two or three lines at the beginning of the poem, in particular : —

> "And listened like a three years' child ;
> The Mariner had his will."

These trifling contributions, all but one (which Mr. C. has with unnecessary scrupulosity recorded) slipt out of his mind as they well might. As we endeavored to proceed conjointly (I speak of the same evening) our respective manners proved so widely different that it would have been quite presumptuous in me to do anything but separate from an undertaking upon which I could only have been a clog. We returned after a few days from a delightful tour, of which I have many pleasant, and some of them droll-enough, recollections. We returned by Dulverton to Alfoxden. The "Ancient Mariner" grew and grew till it became too important for our first object, which was limited to our expectation of five pounds, and we began to talk of a Volume, which was to consist, as Mr. Coleridge has told the world, of poems chiefly on supernatural subjects taken from common life, but looked at, as much as might be, through an imaginative medium. Accordingly I wrote "The Idiot Boy," "Her Eyes are wild," etc., "We are Seven," "The Thorn," and some others. To return to "We are Seven," the piece that called forth this note, I composed it while walking in the grove at Alfoxden. My friends will not deem it too trifling to relate that while walking to and fro I composed the last stanza first, having begun with the last line. When it was all but finished, I came in and recited it to Mr. Coleridge and my sister, and said, "A prefatory stanza must be added, and I should sit down to our little tea-meal with

greater pleasure if my task were finished." I mentioned in substance what I wished to be expressed, and Coleridge immediately threw off the stanza thus : —

> "A little child, dear brother Jem," —

I objected to the rhyme, "dear brother Jem," as being ludicrous, but we all enjoyed the joke of hitching in our friend, James T——'s name, who was familiarly called Jem. He was the brother of the dramatist, and this reminds me of an anecdote which it may be worth while here to notice. The said Jem got a sight of the Lyrical Ballads as it was going through the press at Bristol, during which time I was residing in that city. One evening he came to me with a grave face, and said, "Wordsworth, I have seen the volume that Coleridge and you are about to publish. There is one poem in it which I earnestly entreat you will cancel, for, if published, it will make you everlastingly ridiculous." I answered that I felt much obliged by the interest he took in my good name as a writer, and begged to know what was the unfortunate piece he alluded to. He said, "It is called ' We are Seven.' " Nay! said I, that shall take its chance, however, and he left me in despair. I have only to add that in the spring of 1841 I revisited Goodrich Castle, not having seen that part of the Wye since I met the little Girl there in 1793. It would have given me greater pleasure to have found in the neighboring hamlet traces of one who had interested me so much; but that was impossible, as unfortunately I did not even know her name. The ruin, from its position and features, is a most impressive object. I could not but deeply regret that its solemnity was impaired by a fantastic new Castle set up on a projection of the same ridge, as if to show how far modern art can go in surpassing all that could be done by antiquity and nature with their united graces, remembrances, and associations.

    — A SIMPLE Child,
That lightly draws its breath,
And feels its life in every limb,
What should it know of death?

I met a little cottage Girl:
She was eight years old, she said;
Her hair was thick with many a curl
That clustered round her head.

She had a rustic, woodland air,
And she was wildly clad:
Her eyes were fair, and very fair;
— Her beauty made me glad.

"Sisters and brothers, little Maid,
How many may you be?"
"How many? Seven in all," she said,
And wondering looked at me.

"And where are they? I pray you tell."
She answered, "Seven are we;
And two of us at Conway dwell,
And two are gone to sea.

"Two of us in the church-yard lie,
My sister and my brother;
And, in the church-yard cottage, I
Dwell near them with my mother."

"You say that two at Conway dwell,
And two are gone to sea,
Yet ye are seven! — I pray you tell,
Sweet Maid, how this may be."

Then did the little Maid reply,
"Seven boys and girls are we;
Two of us in the church-yard lie,
Beneath the church-yard tree."

"You run about, my little Maid,
Your limbs they are alive;
If two are in the church-yard laid,
Then ye are only five."

"Their graves are green, they may be
    seen,"
The little Maid replied,
"Twelve steps or more from my mother's
    door,
And they are side by side.

"My stockings there I often knit,
My kerchief there I hem;
And there upon the ground I sit,
And sing a song to them.

"And often after sunset, Sir,
When it is light and fair,
I take my little porringer,
And eat my supper there.

"The first that died was sister Jane;
In bed she moaning lay,
Till God released her of her pain;
And then she went away.

"So in the church-yard she was laid;
And, when the grass was dry,
Together round her grave we played,
My brother John and I.

"And when the ground was white with
    snow,
And I could run and slide,
My brother John was forced to go,
And he lies by her side."

"How many are you, then," said I,
"If they two are in heaven?"
Quick was the little Maid's reply,
"O Master! we are seven."

"But they are dead; those two are dead!
Their spirits are in heaven!"
'T was throwing words away; for still
The little Maid would have her will,
And said, "Nay, we are seven!"
1798.   1798.

ANECDOTE FOR FATHERS.

"Retine vim istam, falsa enim dicam, si coges."
— EUSEBIUS.

This was suggested in front of Alfoxden. The Boy was a son of my friend, Basil Montagu, who had been two or three years under our care. The name of Kilve is from a village on the Bristol Channel, about a mile from Alfoxden; and the name of Liswyn Farm was taken from a beautiful spot on the Wye. When Mr. Coleridge, my sister, and I, had been visiting the famous John Thelwall, who had taken refuge from politics, after a trial for high treason, with a view to bring up his family by the profits of agriculture, which proved as unfortunate a speculation as that he had fled from, Coleridge and he had both been public lecturers; Coleridge mingling, with his politics, Theology, from which the other elocutionist abstained, unless it were for the sake of a sneer. This quondam community of public employment induced Thelwall to visit Coleridge at Nether Stowey, where he fell in my way. He really was a man of extraordinary talent, an affectionate husband, and a good father. Though brought up in the City, he was truly sensible of the beauty of natural objects. I remember once, when Coleridge, he, and I were seated together upon the turf on the brink of a stream in the most beautiful part of the most beautiful glen of Alfoxden, Coleridge exclaimed, "This is a place to reconcile one to all the jarrings and conflicts of the wide world." — " Nay," said Thelwall, " to make one forget them altogether." The visit of this man to Coleridge was, as I believe Coleridge has related, the occasion of a spy being sent by Government to watch our proceedings, which were, I can say with truth, such as the world at large would have thought ludicrously harmless.

I HAVE a boy of five years old;
His face is fair and fresh to see;
His limbs are cast in beauty's mould,
And dearly he loves me.

One morn we strolled on our dry walk,
Our quiet home all full in view,
And held such intermitted talk
As we are wont to do.

My thoughts on former pleasures ran;
I thought of Kilve's delightful shore,
Our pleasant home when spring began,
A long, long year before.

A day it was when I could bear
Some fond regrets to entertain;
With so much happiness to spare,
I could not feel a pain.

The green earth echoed to the feet
Of lambs that bounded through the glade,
From shade to sunshine, and as fleet
From sunshine back to shade.

Birds warbled round me — and each trace
·Of inward sadness had its charm;
Kilve, thought I, was a favored place,
And so is Liswyn farm.

My boy beside me tripped, so slim
And graceful in his rustic dress!
And, as we talked, I questioned him,
In very idleness.

" Now tell me, had you rather be,"
I said, and took him by the arm,
" On Kilve's smooth shore, by the green sea,
Or here at Liswyn farm ? "

In careless mood he looked at me,
While still I held him by the arm,
And said, " At Kilve I'd rather be
Than here at Liswyn farm."

" Now, little Edward, say why so:
My little Edward, tell me why." —
" I cannot tell, I do not know." —
" Why, this is strange," said I;

" For, here are woods, hills smooth and
  warm :
There surely must some reason be
Why you would change sweet Liswyn
  farm
For Kilve by the green sea."

At this, my boy hung down his head,
He blushed with shame, nor made reply:
And three times to the child I said,
" Why, Edward, tell me why?"

His head he raised — there was in sight,
It caught his eye, he saw it plain —
Upon the house-top, glittering bright,
A broad and gilded vane.

Then did the boy his tongue unlock,
And eased his mind with this reply:
" At Kilve there was no weather-cock;
And that's the reason why."

O dearest, dearest boy ! my heart
For better lore would seldom yearn,
Could I but teach the hundredth part
Of what from thee I learn.

1798.   1798.

THE THORN.

Written at Alfoxden. Arose out of my observing, on the ridge of Quantock Hill, on a stormy day, a thorn which I had often passed, in calm and bright weather, without noticing it. I said to myself, " Cannot I by some invention do as much to make this Thorn permanently an impressive object as the storm has made it to my eyes at this moment?" I began the poem accordingly, and composed it with great rapidity. Sir George Beaumont painted a picture from it which Wilkie thought his best. He gave it me ; though when he saw it several times at Rydal Mount afterwards, he said, "I could make a better, and would like to paint the same subject over again." The sky in this picture is nobly done, but it reminds one too much of Wilson. The only fault, however, of any consequence is the female figure,

which is too old and decrepit for one likely to
frequent an eminence on such a call.

I.

"THERE is a Thorn — it looks so old,
In truth, you'd find it hard to say
How it could ever have been young,
It looks so old and gray.
Not higher than a two years' child
It stands erect, this aged Thorn;
No leaves it has, no prickly points;
It is a mass of knotted joints,
A wretched thing forlorn.
It stands erect, and like a stone
With lichens is it overgrown.

II.

"Like rock or stone, it is o'ergrown,
With lichens to the very top,
And hung with heavy tufts of moss,
A melancholy crop:
Up from the earth these mosses creep,
And this poor Thorn they clasp it round
So close, you'd say that they are bent
With plain and manifest intent
To drag it to the ground;
And all have joined in one endeavor
To bury this poor Thorn forever.

III.

"High on a mountain's highest ridge,
Where oft the stormy winter gale
Cuts like a scythe, while through the
        clouds
It sweeps from vale to vale;
Not five yards from the mountain path,
This Thorn you on your left espy;
And to the left, three yards beyond,
You see a little muddy pond
Of water — never dry,
Though but of compass small, and bare
To thirsty suns and parching air.

IV.

"And, close beside this aged Thorn,
There is a fresh and lovely sight,
A beauteous heap, a hill of moss,
Just half a foot in height.
All lovely colors there you see,
All colors that were ever seen;
And mossy network too is there,
As if by hand of lady fair
The work had woven been;

And cups, the darlings of the eye,
So deep is their vermilion dye.

V.

"Ah me! what lovely tints are there
Of olive green and scarlet bright,
In spikes, in branches, and in stars,
Green, red, and pearly white!
This heap of earth o'ergrown with moss,
Which close beside the Thorn you see,
So fresh in all its beauteous dyes,
Is like an infant's grave in size,
As like as like can be:
But never, never anywhere,
An infant's grave was half so fair.

VI.

"Now would you see this aged Thorn,
This pond, and beauteous hill of moss,
You must take care and choose your time
The mountain when to cross.
For oft there sits between the heap
So like an infant's grave in size,
And that same pond of which I spoke,
A Woman in a scarlet cloak,
And to herself she cries,
'Oh misery! oh misery!
Oh woe is me! oh misery!'

VII.

"At all times of the day and night
This wretched Woman thither goes;
And she is known to every star,
And every wind that blows;
And there, beside the Thorn, she sits
When the blue daylight's in the skies,
And when the whirlwind's on the hill,
Or frosty air is keen and still,
And to herself she cries,
'Oh misery! oh misery!
Oh woe is me! oh misery!'"

VIII.

"Now wherefore, thus, by day and night,
In rain, in tempest, and in snow,
Thus to the dreary mountain-top
Does this poor Woman go?
And why sits she beside the Thorn
When the blue daylight's in the sky,
Or when the whirlwind's on the hill,
Or frosty air is keen and still,
And wherefore does she cry? —
O wherefore? wherefore? tell me why
Does she repeat that doleful cry?"

IX.

"I cannot tell; I wish I could;
For the true reason no one knows:
But would you gladly view the spot,
The spot to which she goes;
The hillock like an infant's grave,
The pond — and Thorn, so old and gray;
Pass by her door — 't is seldom shut —
And, if you see her in her hut —
Then to the spot away!
I never heard of such as dare
Approach the spot when she is there."

X.

"But wherefore to the mountain-top
Can this unhappy Woman go?
Whatever star is in the skies,
Whatever wind may blow?"
"Full twenty years are past and gone
Since she (her name is Martha Ray)
Gave with a maiden's true good-will
Her company to Stephen Hill;
And she was blithe and gay,
While friends and kindred all approved
Of him whom tenderly she loved.

XI.

"And they had fixed the wedding day,
The morning that must wed them both;
But Stephen to another Maid
Had sworn another oath;
And, with this other Maid, to church
Unthinking Stephen went —
Poor Martha! on that woful day
A pang of pitiless dismay
Into her soul was sent;
A fire was kindled in her breast,
Which might not burn itself to rest.

XII.

"They say, full six months after this,
While yet the summer leaves were green,
She to the mountain-top would go,
And there was often seen.
What could she seek? — or wish to hide?
Her state to any eye was plain;
She was with child, and she was mad;
Yet often was she sober sad
From her exceeding pain.
O guilty Father — would that death
Had saved him from that breach of faith!

XIII.

"Sad case for such a brain to hold
Communion with a stirring child!
Sad case, as you may think, for one
Who had a brain so wild!
Last Christmas-eve we talked of this,
And gray-haired Wilfred of the glen
Held that the unborn infant wrought
About its mother's heart, and brought
Her senses back again:
And, when at last her time drew near,
Her looks were calm, her senses clear.

XIV.

"More know I not, I wish I did,
And it should all be told to you;
For what became of this poor child
No mortal ever knew;
Nay — if a child to her was born
No earthly tongue could ever tell;
And if 't was born alive or dead,
Far less could this with proof be said;
But some remember well,
That Martha Ray about this time
Would up the mountain often climb.

XV.

"And all that winter, when at night
The wind blew from the mountain-peak,
'T was worth your while, though in the
  dark,
The churchyard path to seek:
For many a time and oft were heard
Cries coming from the mountain head:
Some plainly living voices were
And others, I've heard many swear,
Were voices of the dead:
I cannot think, whate'er they say,
They had to do with Martha Ray.

XVI.

"But that she goes to this old Thorn,
The Thorn which I described to you,
And there sits in a scarlet cloak
I will be sworn is true.
For one day with my telescope,
To view the ocean wide and bright,
When to this country first I came,
Ere I had heard of Martha's name,
I climbed the mountain's height: —
A storm came on, and I could see
No object higher than my knee.

XVII.

" 'T was mist and rain, and storm and rain:
No screen, no fence could I discover;
And then the wind! in sooth, it was
A wind full ten times over.
I looked around, I thought I saw
A jutting crag, — and off I ran,
Head-foremost, through the driving rain,
The shelter of the crag to gain;
And, as I am a man,
Instead of jutting crag, I found
A Woman seated on the ground.

XVIII.

" I did not speak — I saw her face;
Her face! — it was enough for me;
I turned about and heard her cry,
'Oh misery! oh misery!'
And there she sits, until the moon
Through half the clear blue sky will go;
And, when the little breezes make
The waters of the pond to shake,
As all the country know,
She shudders, and you hear her cry,
'Oh misery! oh misery!'"

XIX.

" But what 's the Thorn? and what the
    pond?
And what the hill of moss to her?
And what the creeping breeze that comes
The little pond to stir?"
" I cannot tell; but some will say
She hanged her baby on the tree;
Some say she drowned it in the pond,
Which is a little step beyond:
But all and each agree,
The little Babe was buried there,
Beneath that hill of moss so fair.

XX.

" I 've heard, the moss is spotted red
With drops of that poor infant's blood;
But kill a new-born infant thus,
I do not think she could!
Some say, if to the pond you go,
And fix on it a steady view,
The shadow of a babe you trace,
A baby and a baby's face,
And that it looks at you;
Whene'er you look on it, 't is plain
The baby looks at you again.

XXI.

" And some had sworn an oath that she
Should be to public justice brought;
And for the little infant's bones
With spades they would have sought.
But instantly the hill of moss
Before their eyes began to stir!
And, for full fifty yards around,
The grass — it shook upon the ground!
Yet all do still aver
The little Babe lies buried there,
Beneath that hill of moss so fair.

XXII.

" I cannot tell how this may be,
But plain it is the Thorn is bound
With heavy tufts of moss that strive
To drag it to the ground;
And this I know, full many a time,
When she was on the mountain high,
By day, and in the silent night,
When all the stars shone clear and bright,
That I have heard her cry,
'Oh misery! oh misery!
Oh woe is me! oh misery!'"
1798.   1798.

GOODY BLAKE AND HARRY GILL.

A TRUE STORY.

Written at Alfoxden. The incident from Dr.
Darwin's Zoönomia.

OH! what's the matter? what's the matter?
What is 't that ails young Harry Gill?
That evermore his teeth they chatter,
Chatter, chatter, chatter still!
Of waistcoats Harry has no lack,
Good duffle gray, and flannel fine;
He has a blanket on his back,
And coats enough to smother nine.

In March, December, and in July,
'T is all the same with Harry Gill;
The neighbors tell, and tell you truly,
His teeth they chatter, chatter still.
At night, at morning, and at noon,
'T is all the same with Harry Gill;
Beneath the sun, beneath the moon,
His teeth they chatter, chatter still!

Young Harry was a lusty drover,
And who so stout of limb as he?

His cheeks were red as ruddy clover;
His voice was like the voice of three.
Old Goody Blake was old and poor;
Ill fed she was, and thinly clad;
And any man who passed her door
Might see how poor a hut she had.

All day she spun in her poor dwelling:
And then her three hours' work at night,
Alas! 't was hardly worth the telling,
It would not pay for candle-light.
Remote from sheltered village-green,
On a hill's northern side she dwelt,
Where from sea-blasts the hawthorns lean,
And hoary dews are slow to melt.

By the same fire to boil their pottage,
Two poor old Dames, as I have known,
Will often live in one small cottage;
But she, poor Woman! housed alone.
'T was well enough when summer came,
The long, warm, lightsome summer-day,
Then at her door the *canty* Dame
Would sit, as any linnet, gay.

But when the ice our streams did fetter,
Oh then how her old bones would shake!
You would have said, if you had met her,
'T was a hard time for Goody Blake.
Her evenings then were dull and dead:
Sad case it was, as you may think,
For very cold to go to bed;
And then for cold not sleep a wink.

O joy for her! whene'er in winter
The winds at night had made a rout;
And scattered many a lusty splinter
And many a rotten bough about.
Yet never had she, well or sick,
As every man who knew her says,
A pile beforehand, turf or stick,
Enough to warm her for three days.

Now, when the frost was past enduring,
And made her poor old bones to ache,
Could anything be more alluring
Than an old hedge to Goody Blake?
And, now and then, it must be said,
When her old bones were cold and chill,
She left her fire, or left her bed,
To seek the hedge of Harry Gill.

Now Harry he had long suspected
This trespass of old Goody Blake;

And vowed that she should be detected —
That he on her would vengeance take.
And oft from his warm fire he 'd go,
And to the fields his road would take;
And there, at night, in frost and snow,
He watched to seize old Goody Blake.

And once, behind a rick of barley,
Thus looking out did Harry stand:
The moon was full and shining clearly,
And crisp with frost the stubble land.
— He hears a noise — he 's all awake —
Again? — on tip-toe down the hill
He softly creeps — 't is Goody Blake;
She 's at the hedge of Harry Gill!

Right glad was he when he beheld her:
Stick after stick did Goody pull:
He stood behind a bush of elder,
Till she had filled her apron full.
When with her load she turned about,
The by-way back again to take;
He started forward, with a shout,
And sprang upon poor Goody Blake.

And fiercely by the arm he took her,
And by the arm he held her fast,
And fiercely by the arm he shook her,
And cried, "I 've caught you then at
        last!" —
Then Goody, who had nothing said,
Her bundle from her lap let fall;
And, kneeling on the sticks, she prayed
To God that is the judge of all.

She prayed, her withered hand uprearing,
While Harry held her by the arm —
"God! who art never out of hearing,
O may he never more be warm!"
The cold, cold moon above her head,
Thus on her knees did Goody pray;
Young Harry heard what she had said:
And icy cold he turned away.

He went complaining all the morrow
That he was cold and very chill:
His face was gloom, his heart was sorrow,
Alas! that day for Harry Gill!
That day he wore a riding-coat,
But not a whit the warmer he:
Another was on Thursday brought,
And ere the Sabbath he had three.

'T was all in vain, a useless matter,
And blankets were about him pinned;
Yet still his jaws and teeth they clatter;
Like a loose casement in the wind.
And Harry's flesh it fell away;
And all who see him say, 't is plain,
That, live as long as live he may,
He never will be warm again.

No word to any man he utters,
A-bed or up, to young or old;
But ever to himself he mutters,
"Poor Harry Gill is very cold."
A-bed or up, by night or day;
His teeth they chatter, chatter still.
Now think, ye farmers all, I pray,
Of Goody Blake and Harry Gill!
1798.   1798.

HER EYES ARE WILD.

Written at Alfoxden. The subject was reported
to me by a lady of Bristol, who had seen the poor
creature.

I.

HER eyes are wild, her head is bare,
The sun has burnt her coal-black hair;
Her eyebrows have a rusty stain,
And she came far from over the main.
She has a baby on her arm,
Or else she were alone:
And underneath the haystack warm,
And on the greenwood stone,
She talked and sung the woods among,
And it was in the English tongue.

II.

"Sweet babe! they say that I am mad,
But nay, my heart is far too glad;
And I am happy when I sing
Full many a sad and doleful thing:
Then, lovely baby, do not fear!
I pray thee have no fear of me;
But safe as in a cradle, here,
My lovely baby! thou shalt be:
To thee I know too much I owe,
I cannot work thee any woe.

III.

"A fire was once within my brain;
And in my head a dull, dull pain;
And fiendish faces, one, two, three,
Hung at my breast, and pulled at me;

But then there came a sight of joy;
It came at once to do me good;
I waked, and saw my little boy,
My little boy of flesh and blood;
Oh joy for me that sight to see!
For he was here, and only he.

IV.

"Suck, little babe, oh suck again!
It cools my blood; it cools my brain;
Thy lips I feel them, baby! they
Draw from my heart the pain away.
Oh! press me with thy little hand;
It loosens something at my chest; ·
About that tight and deadly band
I feel thy little fingers prest.
The breeze I see is in the tree:
It comes to cool my babe and me.

V.

"Oh! love me, love me, little boy!
Thou art thy mother's only joy;
And do not dread the waves below,
When o'er the sea-rock's edge we go;
The high crag cannot work me harm,
Nor leaping torrents when they howl;
The babe I carry on my arm,
He saves for me my precious soul;
Then happy lie; for blest am I;
Without me my sweet babe would die.

VI.

"Then do not fear, my boy! for thee
Bold as a lion will I be;
And I will always be thy guide,
Through hollow snows and rivers wide.
I 'll build an Indian bower; I know
The leaves that make the softest bed:
And, if from me thou wilt not go,
But still be true till I am dead,
My pretty thing! then thou shalt sing
As merry as the birds in spring.

VII.

"Thy father cares not for my breast,
'T is thine, sweet baby, there to rest;
'T is all thine own!—and, if its hue
Be changed, that was so fair to view,
'T is fair enough for thee, my dove!
My beauty, little child, is flown,
But thou wilt live with me in love,
And what if my poor cheek be brown?
'T is well for me, thou canst not see
How pale and wan it else would be.

VIII.

" Dread not their taunts, my little Life;
I am thy father's wedded wife;
And underneath the spreading tree
We two will live in honesty.
If his sweet boy he could forsake,
With me he never would have stayed:
From him no harm my babe can take;
But he, poor man! is wretched made;
And every day we two will pray
For him that 's gone and far away.

IX.

" I 'll teach my boy the sweetest things:
I'll teach him how the owlet sings.
My little babe! thy lips are still,
And thou hast almost sucked thy fill.
— Where art thou gone, my own dear
      child?
What wicked looks are those I see?
Alas! alas! that look so wild,
It never, never came from me:
If thou art mad, my pretty lad,
Then I must be forever sad.

X.

" Oh! smile on me, my little lamb!
For I thy own dear mother am:
My love for thee has well been tried:
I 've sought thy father far and wide.
I know the poisons of the shade;
I know the earth-nuts fit for food:
Then, pretty dear, be not afraid:
We 'll find thy father in the wood.
Now laugh and be gay, to the woods
      away!
And there, my babe, we 'll live for aye."
1798.   1798.

SIMON LEE,

THE OLD HUNTSMAN;

WITH AN INCIDENT IN WHICH HE WAS
CONCERNED.

This old man had been huntsman to the squires
of Alfoxden, which, at the time we occupied it,
belonged to a minor. The old man's cottage
stood upon the common, a little way from the
entrance to Alfoxden Park. But it had disap-
peared. Many other changes had taken place in
the adjoining village, which I could not but notice
with a regret more natural than well-considered.
Improvements but rarely appear such to those
who, after long intervals of time, revisit places
they have had much pleasure in. It is unneces-
sary to add, the fact was as mentioned in the
poem; and I have, after an interval of forty-five
years, the image of the old man as fresh before my
eyes as if I had seen him yesterday. The expres-
sion when the hounds were out, " I dearly love
their voice," was word for word from his own
lips.

IN the sweet shire of Cardigan,
Not far from pleasant Ivor-hall,
An old Man dwells, a little man, —
'T is said he once was tall.
Full five and thirty years he lived
A running huntsman merry;
And still the centre of his cheek
Is red as a ripe cherry.

No man like him the horn could sound,
And hill and valley rang with glee
When Echo bandied, round and round,
The halloo of Simon Lee.
In those proud days, he little cared
For husbandry or tillage;
To blither tasks did Simon rouse
The sleepers of the village.

He all the country could outrun,
Could leave both man and horse behind;
And often, ere the chase was done,
He reeled, and was stone-blind.
And still there 's something in the world
At which his heart rejoices;
For when the chiming hounds are out,
He dearly loves their voices!

But, oh the heavy change! — bereft
Of health, strength, friends, and kindred,
      see!
Old Simon to the world is left
In liveried poverty.
His Master 's dead, — and no one now
Dwells in the Hall of Ivor;
Men, dogs, and horses, all are dead;
He is the sole survivor.

And he is lean and he is sick;
His body, dwindled and awry,
Rests upon ankles swoln and thick;
His legs are thin and dry.
One prop he has, and only one,
His wife, an aged woman,
Lives with him, near the waterfall,
Upon the village Common.

Beside their moss-grown hut of clay,
Not twenty paces from the door,
A scrap of land they have, but they
Are poorest of the poor.
This scrap of land he from the heath
Enclosed when he was stronger;
But what to them avails the land
Which he can till no longer?

Oft, working by her Husband's side,
Ruth does what Simon cannot do;
For she, with scanty cause for pride,
Is stouter of the two.
And, though you with your utmost skill
From labor could not wean them,
'T is little, very little — all
That they can do between them.

Few months of life has he in store,
As he to you will tell,
For still, the more he works, the more
Do his weak ankles swell.
My gentle Reader, I perceive
How patiently you 've waited,
And now I fear that you expect
Some tale will be related.

O Reader! had you in your mind
Such stores as silent thought can bring,
O gentle Reader! you would find
A tale in everything.
What more I have to say is short,
And you must kindly take it:
It is no tale; but, should you think,
Perhaps a tale you 'll make it.

One summer day I chanced to see
This old Man doing all he could
To unearth the root of an old tree,
A stump of rotten wood.
The mattock tottered in his hand;
So vain was his endeavor,
That at the root of the old tree
He might have worked forever.

" You 're overtasked, good Simon Lee,
Give me your tool," to him I said;
And at the word right gladly he
Received my proffered aid.
I struck, and with a single blow
The tangled root I severed,
At which the poor old Man so long
And vainly had endeavored.

The tears into his eyes were brought,
And thanks and praises seemed to run
So fast out of his heart, I thought
They never would have done.
— I've heard of hearts unkind, kind deeds
With coldness still returning;
Alas! the gratitude of men
Hath oftener left me mourning.
        1798.   1798.

LINES WRITTEN IN EARLY SPRING.

Actually composed while I was sitting by the
side of the brook that runs down from the Comb,
in which stands the village of Alford, through the
grounds of Alfoxden. It was a chosen resort of
mine. The brook fell down a sloping rock so as
to make a waterfall considerable for that country,
and across the pool below had fallen a tree, an
ash if I rightly remember, from which rose per-
pendicularly, boughs in search of the light inter-
cepted by the deep shade above. The boughs
bore leaves of green that for want of sunshine
had faded into almost lily-white; and from the
underside of this natural sylvan bridge depended
long and beautiful tresses of ivy which waved
gently in the breeze that might poetically speaking
be called the breath of the waterfall. This motion
varied of course in proportion to the power of
water in the brook. When, with dear friends, I
revisited this spot, after an interval of more than
forty years, this interesting feature of the scene
was gone. To the owner of the place I could not
but regret that the beauty of this retired part of
the grounds had not tempted him to make it more
accessible by a path, not broad or obtrusive, but
sufficient for persons who love such scenes to
creep along without difficulty.

I HEARD a thousand blended notes,
While in a grove I sate reclined,
In that sweet mood when pleasant thoughts
Bring sad thoughts to the mind.

To her fair works did Nature link
The human soul that through me ran;
And much it grieved my heart to think
What man has made of man.

Through primrose tufts, in that green
        bower,
The periwinkle trailed its wreaths;
And 't is my faith that every flower
Enjoys the air it breathes.

The birds around me hopped and played,
Their thoughts I cannot measure : —
But the least motion which they made
It seemed a thrill of pleasure.

The budding twigs spread out their fan,
To catch the breezy air;
And I must think, do all I can,
That there was pleasure there.

If this belief from heaven be sent,
If such be Nature's holy plan,
Have I not reason to lament
What man has made of man?

1798.   1798.

TO MY SISTER.

Composed in front of Alfoxden House. My lit-
tle boy-messenger on this occasion was the son of
Basil Montagu. The larch mentioned in the first
stanza was standing when I revisited the place in
May, 1841, more than forty years after. I was
disappointed that it had not improved in appear-
ance as to size, nor had it acquired anything of
the majesty of age, which, even though less per-
haps than any other tree, the larch sometimes
does. A few score yards from this tree, grew,
when we inhabited Alfoxden, one of the most re-
markable beech-trees ever seen. The ground
sloped both towards and from it. It was of im-
mense size, and threw out arms that struck into
the soil, like those of the banyan-tree, and rose
again from it. Two of the branches thus inserted
themselves twice, which gave to each the appear-
ance of a serpent moving along by gathering itself
up in folds. One of the large boughs of this tree
had been torn off by the wind before we left
Alfoxden, but five remained. In 1841 we could
barely find the spot where the tree had stood. So
remarkable a production of nature could not have
been wilfully destroyed.

IT is the first mild day of March :
Each minute sweeter than before
The redbreast sings from the tall larch
That stands beside our door.

There is a blessing in the air,
Which seems a sense of joy to yield
To the bare trees, and mountains bare,
And grass in the green field.

My sister ! ('t is a wish of mine)
Now that our morning meal is done,
Make haste, your morning task resign;
Come forth and feel the sun.

Edward will come with you; — and, pray,
Put on with speed your woodland dress;
And bring no book : for this one day
We 'll give to idleness.

No joyless forms shall regulate
Our living calendar :
We from to-day, my Friend, will date
The opening of the year.

Love, now a universal birth,
From heart to heart is stealing,
From earth to man, from man to earth :
— It is the hour of feeling.

One moment now may give us more
Than years of toiling reason :
Our minds shall drink at every pore
The spirit of the season.

Some silent laws our hearts will make,
Which they shall long obey :
We for the year to come may take
Our temper from to-day.

And from the blessed power that rolls
About, below, above,
We 'll frame the measure of our souls :
They shall be tuned to love.

Then come, my Sister ! come, I pray,
With speed put on your woodland dress;
And bring no book : for this one day
We 'll give to idleness.

1798.   1798.

Observed in the holly-grove at Alfoxden, where
these verses were written in the spring of 1799. I
had the pleasure of again seeing, with dear friends,
this grove in unimpaired beauty forty-one years
after.

A WHIRL-BLAST from behind the hill
Rushed o'er the wood with startling
          sound;
Then — all at once the air was still,
And showers of hailstones pattered round.
Where leafless oaks towered high above,
I sat within an undergrove

Of tallest hollies, tall and green;
A fairer bower was never seen.
From year to year the spacious floor
With withered leaves is covered o'er,
And all the year the bower is green.
But see! where'er the hailstones drop
The withered leaves all skip and hop;
There's not a breeze — no breath of air —
Yet here, and there, and everywhere
Along the floor, beneath the shade
By those embowering hollies made,
The leaves in myriads jump and spring,
As if with pipes and music rare
Some Robin Good-fellow were there,
And all those leaves, in festive glee,
Were dancing to the minstrelsy.

1799.   1800.

EXPOSTULATION AND REPLY.

*This poem is a favorite among the Quakers, as
I have learnt on many occasions. It was com-
posed in front of the house at Alfoxden, in the
spring of 1798.*

"Why, William, on that old gray stone,
Thus for the length of half a day,
Why, William, sit you thus alone,
And dream your time away?

"Where are your books? — that light
    bequeathed
To Beings else forlorn and blind!
Up! up! and drink the spirit breathed
From dead men to their kind.

"You look round on your Mother Earth,
As if she for no purpose bore you;
As if you were her first-born birth,
And none had lived before you!"

One morning thus, by Esthwaite lake,
When life was sweet, I knew not why,
To me my good friend Matthew spake,
And thus I made reply:

"The eye — it cannot choose but see;
We cannot bid the ear be still;
Our bodies feel, where'er they be,
Against or with our will.

"Nor less I deem that there are Powers
Which of themselves our minds impress;
That we can feed this mind of ours
In a wise passiveness.

"Think you, 'mid all this mighty sum
Of things forever speaking,
That nothing of itself will come,
But we must still be seeking?

" — Then ask not wherefore, here, alone,
Conversing as I may,
I sit upon this old gray stone,
And dream my time away."

1798.   1798.

THE TABLES TURNED.

AN EVENING SCENE ON THE SAME SUBJECT.

Up! up! my Friend, and quit your books;
Or surely you 'll grow double:
Up! up! my Friend, and clear your looks;
Why all this toil and trouble?

The sun, above the mountain's head,
A freshening lustre mellow
Through all the long green fields has
    spread,
His first sweet evening yellow.

Books! 't is a dull and endless strife:
Come, hear the woodland linnet,
How sweet his music! on my life,
There 's more of wisdom in it.

And hark! how blithe the throstle sings!
He, too, is no mean preacher:
Come forth into the light of things,
Let Nature be your teacher.

She has a world of ready wealth,
Our minds and hearts to bless —
Spontaneous wisdom breathed by health,
Truth breathed by cheerfulness.

One impulse from a vernal wood
May teach you more of man,
Of moral evil and of good,
Than all the sages can.

Sweet is the lore which Nature brings;
Our meddling intellect
Mis-shapes · the beauteous forms of
        things: —
We murder to dissect.

Enough of Science and of Art;
Close up those barren leaves;
Come forth, and bring with you a heart
That watches and receives.
  1798.   ·   1798.

THE COMPLAINT

OF A FORSAKEN INDIAN WOMAN.

Written at Alfoxden, where I read Hearne's
Journey with deep interest. It was composed for
the volume of Lyrical Ballads.

When a Northern Indian, from sickness, is un-
able to continue his journey with his companions,
he is left behind, covered over with deer-skins,
and is supplied with water, food, and fuel, if the
situation of the place will afford it. He is in-
formed of the track which his companions intend
to pursue, and if he be unable to follow, or over-
take them, he perishes alone in the desert ; unless
he should have the good fortune to fall in with
some other tribes of Indians. The females are
equally, or still more, exposed to the same fate.
See that very interesting work HEARNE's *Jour-
ney from Hudson's Bay to the Northern Ocean.*
In the high northern latitudes, as the same writer
informs us, when the northern lights vary their
position in the air, they make a rustling and a
crackling noise, as alluded to in the following
poem.

I.

BEFORE I see another day,
Oh let my body die away!
In sleep I heard the northern gleams;
The stars, they were among my dreams;
In rustling conflict through the skies,
I heard, I saw the flashes drive,
And yet they are upon my eyes,
And yet I am alive;
Before I see another day,
Oh let my body die away!

II.

My fire is dead: it knew no pain;
Yet is it dead, and I remain:
All stiff with ice the ashes lie;
And they are dead, and I will die.

When I was well, I wished to live,
For clothes, for warmth, for food, and
        fire;
But they to me no joy can give,
No pleasure now, and no desire.
Then here contented will I lie!
Alone, I cannot fear to die.

III.

Alas! ye might have dragged me on
Another day, a single one!
Too soon I yielded to despair;
Why did ye listen to my prayer?
When ye were gone my limbs were
        stronger;
And oh, how grievously I rue,
That, afterwards, a little longer,
My friends, I did not follow you!
For strong and without pain I lay,
Dear friends, when ye were gone away.

IV.

My Child! they gave thee to another,
A woman who was not thy mother.
When from my arms my Babe they took,
On me how strangely did he look!
Through his whole body something ran,
A most strange working did I see;
— As if he strove to be a man,
That he might pull the sledge for me:
And then he stretched his arms, how wild!
Oh mercy! like a helpless child.

V.

My little joy! my little pride!
In two days more I must have died.
Then do not weep and grieve for me;
I feel I must have died with thee.
O wind, that o'er my head art flying
The way my friends their course did bend,
I should not feel the pain of dying,
Could I with thee a message send;
Too soon, my friends, ye went away;
For I had many things to say.

VI.

I 'll follow you across the snow;
Ye travel heavily and slow;
In spite of all my weary pain
I 'll look upon your tents again.
— My fire is dead, and snowy white
The water which beside it stood:

The wolf has come to me to-night,
And he has stolen away my food.
For ever left alone am I;
Then wherefore should I fear to die?

VII.

Young as I am, my course is run,
I shall not see another sun;
I cannot lift my limbs to know
If they have any life or no.
My poor forsaken Child, if I
For once could have thee close to me,
With happy heart I then would die,
And my last thought would happy be;
But thou, dear Babe, art far away,
Nor shall I see another day.

1798.   1798.

THE LAST OF THE FLOCK.

Produced at the same time and for the same
purpose. The incident occurred in the village of
Holford, close by Alfoxden.

I.

In distant countries have I been,
And yet I have not often seen
A healthy man, a man full grown,
Weep in the public roads, alone.
But such a one, on English ground,
And in the broad highway, I met;
Along the broad highway he came,
His cheeks with tears were wet:
Sturdy he seemed, though he was sad;
And in his arms a Lamb he had.

II.

He saw me, and he turned aside,
As if he wished himself to hide:
And with his coat did then essay
To wipe those briny tears away.
I followed him, and said, " My friend,
What ails you? wherefore weep you so? "
— " Shame on me, Sir! this lusty Lamb,
He makes my tears to flow.
To-day I fetched him from the rock;
He is the last of all my flock.

III.

" When I was young, a single man,
And after youthful follies ran,

Though little given to care and thought,
Yet, so it was, an ewe I bought;
And other sheep from her I raised,
As healthy sheep as you might see;
And then I married, and was rich
As I could wish to be;
Of sheep I numbered a full score,
And every year increased my store.

IV.

" Year after year my stock it grew;
And from this one, this single ewe,
Full fifty comely sheep I raised,
As fine a flock as ever grazed!
Upon the Quantock hills they fed;
They throve, and we at home did thrive:
— This lusty Lamb of all my store
Is all that is alive;
And now I care not if we die,
And perish all of poverty.

V.

" Six Children, Sir! had I to feed;
Hard labor in a time of need!
My pride was tamed, and in our grief
I of the Parish asked relief.
They said, I was a wealthy man;
My sheep upon the uplands fed,
And it was fit that thence I took
Whereof to buy us bread.
' Do this: how can we give to you,'
They cried, ' what to the poor is due?'

VI.

" I sold a sheep, as they had said,
And bought my little children bread,
And they were healthy with their food
For me — it never did me good.
A woful time it was for me,
To see the end of all my gains,
The pretty flock which I had reared
With all my care and pains,
To see it melt like snow away —
For me it was a woful day.

VII.

" Another still! and still another!
A little lamb, and then its mother!
It was a vein that never stopped —
Like blood-drops from my heart they
                    dropped.

'Till thirty were not left alive
They dwindled, dwindled, one by one;
And I may say, that many a time
I wished they all were gone —
Reckless of what might come at last
Were but the bitter struggle past.

VIII.

"To wicked deeds I was inclined,
And wicked fancies crossed my mind;
And every man I chanced to see,
I thought he knew some ill of me:
No peace, no comfort could I find,
No ease, within doors or without;
And, crazily and wearily
I went my work about;
And oft was moved to flee from home,
And hide my head where wild beasts
        roam.

IX.

"Sir! 't was a precious flock to me
As dear as my own children be;
For daily with my growing store
I loved my children more and more.
Alas! it was an evil time;
God cursed me in my sore distress;
I prayed, yet every day I thought
I loved my children less;
And every week, and every day,
My flock it seemed to melt away.

X.

"They dwindled, Sir, sad sight to see!
From ten to five, from five to three,
A lamb, a wether, and a ewe;—
And then at last from three to two;
And, of my fifty, yesterday
I had but only one:
And here it lies upon my arm,
Alas! and I have none; —
To-day I fetched it from the rock;
It is the last of all my flock."
1798.

THE IDIOT BOY.

The last stanza — "The Cocks did crow to-
whoo, to-whoo, And the sun did shine so cold" —
was the foundation of the whole. The words
were reported to me by my dear friend, Thomas
Poole; but I have since heard the same repeated
of other Idiots. Let me add that this long poem
was composed in the groves of Alfoxden, almost
extempore; not a word, I believe, being corrected,
though one stanza was omitted. I mention this
in gratitude to those happy moments, for, in
truth, I never wrote anything with so much glee.

'T is eight o'clock, — a clear March night,
The moon is up, — the sky is blue,
The owlet, in the moonlight air,
Shouts from nobody knows where;
He lengthens out his lonely shout,
Halloo! halloo! a long halloo!

— Why bustle thus about your door,
What means this bustle, Betty Foy?
Why are you in this mighty fret?
And why on horseback have you set
Him whom you love, your Idiot Boy?

Scarcely a soul is out of bed;
Good Betty, put him down again;
His lips with joy they burr at you;
But, Betty! what has he to do
With stirrup, saddle, or with rein?

But Betty 's bent on her intent;
For her good neighbor, Susan Gale,
Old Susan, she who dwells alone,
Is sick, and makes a piteous moan
As if her very life would fail.

There 's not a house within a mile,
No hand to help them in distress;
Old Susan lies a-bed in pain,
And sorely puzzled are the twain,
For what she ails they cannot guess.

And Betty's husband 's at the wood,
Where by the week he doth abide,
A woodman in the distant vale;
There 's none to help poor Susan Gale;
What must be done? what will betide?

And Betty from the lane has fetched
Her Pony, that is mild and good;
Whether he be in joy or pain,
Feeding at will along the lane,
Or bringing fagots from the wood.

And he is all in travelling trim, —
And, by the moonlight, Betty Foy
Has on the well-girt saddle set
(The like was never heard of yet)
Him whom she loves, her Idiot Boy.

1798.

And he must post without delay
Across the bridge and through the dale,
And by the church, and o'er the down,
To bring a Doctor from the town,
Or she will die, old Susan Gale.

There is no need of boot or spur,
There is no need of whip or wand;
For Johnny has his holly-bough,
And with a *hurly-burly* now
He shakes the green bough in his hand.

And Betty o'er and o'er has told
The Boy, who is her best delight,
Both what to follow, what to shun,
What do, and what to leave undone,
How turn to left, and how to right.

And Betty's most especial charge,
Was, "Johnny! Johnny! mind that you
Come home again, nor stop at all, —
Come home again, whate'er befall,
My Johnny, do, I pray you do."

To this did Johnny answer make,
Both with his head and with his hand,
And proudly shook the bridle too;
And then! his words were not a few,
Which Betty well could understand.

And now that Johnny is just going,
Though Betty 's in a mighty flurry,
She gently pats the Pony's side,
On which her Idiot Boy must ride,
And seems no longer in a hurry.

But when the Pony moved his legs,
Oh! then for the poor Idiot Boy!
For joy he cannot hold the bridle,
For joy his head and heels are idle,
He 's idle all for very joy.

And while the Pony moves his legs,
In Johnny's left hand you may see
The green bough motionless and dead:
The Moon that shines above his head
Is not more still and mute than he.

His heart it was so full of glee,
That till full fifty yards were gone,
He quite forgot his holly whip,
And all his skill in horsemanship:
Oh! happy, happy, happy John.

And while the Mother, at the door,
Stands fixed, her face with joy o'erflows,
Proud of herself, and proud of him,
She sees him in his travelling trim,
How quietly her Johnny goes.

The silence of her Idiot Boy,
What hopes it sends to Betty's heart!
He 's at the guide-post — he turns right;
She watches till he 's out of sight,
And Betty will not then depart.

Burr, burr — now Johnny's lips they burr,
As loud as any mill, or near it;
Meek as a lamb the Pony moves,
And Johnny makes the noise he loves,
And Betty listens, glad to hear it.

Away she hies to Susan Gale:
Her Messenger 's in merry tune;
The owlets hoot, the owlets curr,
And Johnny's lips they burr, burr, burr,
As on he goes beneath the moon.

His steed and he right well agree;
For of this Pony there 's a rumor,
That, should he lose his eyes and ears,
And should he live a thousand years,
He never will be out of humor.

But then he is a horse that thinks!
And when he thinks, his pace is slack;
Now, though he knows poor Johnny well,
Yet, for his life, he cannot tell
What he has got upon his back.

So through the moonlight lanes they go,
And far into the moonlight dale,
And by the church, and o'er the down,
To bring a Doctor from the town,
To comfort poor old Susan Gale.

And Betty, now at Susan's side,
Is in the middle of her story,
What speedy help her Boy will bring,
With many a most diverting thing,
Of Johnny's wit, and Johnny's glory.

And Betty, still at Susan's side,
By this time is not quite so flurried:
Demure with porringer and plate
She sits, as if in Susan's fate
Her life and soul were buried.

But Betty, poor good woman! she,
You plainly in her face may read it,
Could lend out of that moment's store
Five years of happiness or more
To any that might need it.

But yet I guess that now and then
With Betty all was not so well;
And to the road she turns her ears,
And thence full many a sound she hears,
Which she to Susan will not tell.

Poor Susan moans, poor Susan groans;
" As sure as there 's a moon in heaven,"
Cries Betty, " he 'll be back again;
They 'll both be here — 't is almost ten —
Both will be here before eleven."

Poor Susan moans, poor Susan groans;
The clock gives warning for eleven;
'T is on the stroke — " He must be near,"
Quoth Betty, " and will soon be here,
As sure as there 's a moon in heaven."

The clock is on the stroke of twelve,
And Johnny is not yet in sight:
— The Moon 's in heaven, as Betty sees,
But Betty is not quite at ease;
And Susan has a dreadful night.

And Betty, half an hour ago,
On Johnny vile reflections cast:
" A little idle sauntering Thing ! "
With other names, an endless string;
But now that time is gone and past.

And Betty 's drooping at the heart,
That happy time all past and gone,
" How can it be he is so late?
The Doctor, he has made him wait;
Susan ! they 'll both be here anon."

And Susan 's growing worse and worse,
And Betty 's in a sad *quandary;*
And then there 's nobody to say
If she must go, or she must stay !
— She 's in a sad *quandary.*

The clock is on the stroke of one;
But neither Doctor nor his Guide
Appears along the moonlight road;
There 's neither horse nor man abroad,
And Betty 's still at Susan's side.

And Susan now begins to fear
Of sad mischances not a few,
That Johnny may perhaps be drowned;
Or lost, perhaps, and never found;
Which they must both forever rue.

She prefaced half a hint of this
With, " God forbid it should be true ! "
At the first word that Susan said
Cried Betty, rising from the bed,
" Susan, I 'd gladly stay with you.

" I must be gone, I must away:
Consider, Johnny 's but half-wise;
Susan, we must take care of him,
If he is hurt in life or limb " —
" Oh God forbid ! " poor Susan cries.

" What can I do? " says Betty, going,
" What can I do to ease your pain?
Good Susan tell me, and I 'll stay;
I fear you 're in a dreadful way,
But I shall soon be back again."

" Nay, Betty, go ! good Betty, go !
There 's nothing that can ease my pain."
Then off she hies; but with a prayer
That God poor Susan's life would spare,
Till she comes back again.

So, through the moonlight lane she goes,
And far into the moonlight dale;
And how she ran, and how she walked,
And all that to herself she talked,
Would surely be a tedious tale.

In high and low, above, below,
In great and small, in round and square,
In tree and tower was Johnny seen,
In bush and brake, in black and green;
'T was Johnny, Johnny, everywhere.

And while she crossed the bridge, there
    came
A thought with which her heart is sore —
Johnny perhaps his horse forsook,
To hunt the moon within the brook,
And never will be heard of more.

Now is she high upon the down,
Alone amid a prospect wide;
There 's neither Johnny nor his Horse
Among the fern or in the gorse;
There 's neither Doctor nor his Guide.

"O saints! what is become of him?
Perhaps he 's climbed into an oak,
Where he will stay till he is dead;
Or, sadly he has been misled, ·
And joined the wandering gypsy-folk.

"Or him that wicked Pony 's carried
To the dark cave, the goblin's hall;
Or in the castle he 's pursuing
Among the ghosts his own undoing;
Or playing with the waterfall."

At poor old Susan then she railed,
While to the town she posts away;
"If Susan had not been so ill,
Alas! I should have had him still,
My Johnny, till my dying day."

Poor Betty, in this sad distemper,
The Doctor's self could hardly spare:
Unworthy things she talked, and wild;
Even he, of cattle the most mild,
The Pony had his share.

But now she 's fairly in the town,
And to the Doctor's door she hies;
'T is silence all on every side;
The town so long, the town so wide,
Is silent as the skies.

And now she 's at the Doctor's door,
She lifts the knocker, rap, rap, rap;
The Doctor at the casement shows
His glimmering eyes that peep and doze!
And one hand rubs his old night-cap.

"O Doctor! Doctor! where 's my John-
ny?"
"I 'm here, what is 't you want with me?"
"O Sir! you know I 'm Betty Foy,
And I have lost my poor dear Boy,
You know him — him you often see;

"He 's not so wise as some folks be:"
"The devil take his wisdom!" said
The Doctor, looking somewhat grim,
"What, Woman! should I know of him?"
And, grumbling, he went back to bed!

"O woe is me! O woe is me!
Here will I die; here will I die;
I thought to find my lost one here,
But he is neither far nor near,
Oh! what a wretched Mother I!"

She stops, she stands, she looks about;
Which way to turn she cannot tell.
Poor Betty! it would ease her pain
If she had heart to knock again;
— The clock strikes three — a disma
knell!

Then up along the town she hies,
No wonder if her senses fail,
This piteous news so much it shocked her
She quite forgot to send the Doctor,
To comfort poor old Susan Gale.

And now she 's high upon the down,
And she can see a mile of road:
"O cruel! I 'm almost threescore;
Such night as this was ne'er before,
There 's not a single soul abroad."

She listens, but she cannot hear
The foot of horse, the voice of man;
The streams with softest sound are flowing
The grass you almost hear it growing,
You hear it now, if e'er you can.

The owlets through the long blue night
Are shouting to each other still:
Fond lovers! yet not quite hob nob,
They lengthen out the tremulous sob,
That echoes far from hill to hill.

Poor Betty now has lost all hope,
Her thoughts are bent on deadly sin,
A green-grown pond she just has past,
And from the brink she hurries fast,
Lest she should drown herself therein.

And now she sits her down and weeps;
Such tears she never shed before;
"Oh dear, dear Pony! my sweet joy!
Oh carry back my Idiot Boy!
And we will ne'er o'erload thee more."

A thought is come into her head:
The Pony he is mild and good,
And we have always used him well;
Perhaps he 's gone along the dell,
And carried Johnny to the wood.

Then up she springs as if on wings;
She thinks no more of deadly sin;
If Betty fifty ponds should see,
The last of all her thoughts would be
To drown herself therein.

) Reader! now that I might tell
Nhat Johnny and his Horse are doing
Nhat they 've been doing all this time,
)h could I put it into rhyme,
\ most delightful tale pursuing!

'erhaps, and no unlikely thought!
Ie with his Pony now doth roam
he cliffs and peaks so high that are,
o lay his hands upon a star,
ind in his pocket bring it home.

'erhaps he 's turned himself about,
Iis face unto his horse's tail,
ind, still and mute, in wonder lost,
ill silent as a horseman-ghost,
Ie travels slowly down the vale.

ind now, perhaps, is hunting sheep,
ι fierce and dreadful hunter he;
'on valley, now so trim and green,
n five months' time, should he be seen,
ι desert wilderness will be!

'erhaps, with head and heels on fire,
ind like the very soul of evil,
Ie 's galloping away, away,
ind so will gallop on for aye,
he bane of all that dread the devil!

to the Muses have been bound
hese fourteen years, by strong indent-
    ures:
ι gentle Muses! let me tell
ut half of what to him befell;
Ie surely met with strange adventures.

ι gentle Muses! is this kind?
Vhy will ye thus my suit repel?
Vhy of your further aid bereave me?
ind can ye thus unfriended leave me
'e Muses! whom I love so well?

Vho 's yon, that, near the waterfall,
Vhich thunders down with headlong
    force,
eneath the moon, yet shining fair,
s careless as if nothing were,
its upright on a feeding horse?

Unto his horse — there feeding free,
He seems, I think, the rein to give;
Of moon or stars he takes no heed;
Of such we in romances read:
— 'T is Johnny! Johnny! as I live.

And that 's the very Pony, too!
Where is she, where is Betty Foy?
She hardly can sustain her fears;
The roaring waterfall she hears,
And cannot find her Idiot Boy.

Your Pony 's worth his weight in gold:
Then calm your terrors, Betty Foy!
She 's coming from among the trees,
And now all full in view she sees
Him whom she loves, her Idiot Boy.

And Betty sees the Pony too:
Why stand you thus, good Betty Foy?
It is no goblin, 't is no ghost,
'T is he whom you so long have lost,
He whom you love, your Idiot Boy.

She looks again — her arms are up —
She screams — she cannot move for joy;
She darts, as with a torrent 's force,
She almost has o'erturned the Horse,
And fast she holds her Idiot Boy.

And Johnny burrs, and laughs aloud
Whether in cunning or in joy
I cannot tell; but while he laughs,
Betty a drunken pleasure quaffs
To hear again her Idiot Boy.

And now she 's at the Pony's tail,
And now is at the Pony's head, —
On that side now, and now on this;
And, almost stifled with her bliss,
A few sad tears does Betty shed.

She kisses o'er and o'er again
Him whom she loves, her Idiot Boy;
She 's happy here, is happy there,
She is uneasy everywhere;
Her limbs are all alive with joy.

She pats the Pony, where or when
She knows not, happy Betty Foy!
The little Pony glad may be,
But he is milder far than she,
You hardly can perceive his joy.

"Oh! Johnny, never mind the Doctor;
You 've done your best, and that is all:"
She took the reins, when this was said,
And gently turned the Pony's head
From the loud waterfall.

By this the stars were almost gone,
The moon was setting on the hill,
So pale you scarcely looked at her:
The little birds began to stir,
Though yet their tongues were still.

The Pony, Betty, and her Boy,
Wind slowly through the woody dale;
And who is she, betimes abroad,
That hobbles up the steep rough road?
Who is it, but old Susan Gale?

Long time lay Susan lost in thought;
And many dreadful fears beset her,
Both for her Messenger and Nurse;
And, as her mind grew worse and worse,
Her body — it grew better.

She turned, she tossed herself in bed,
On all sides doubts and terrors met her;
Point after point did she discuss;
And, while her mind was fighting thus,
Her body still grew better.

"Alas! what is become of them?
These fears can never be endured;
I 'll to the wood." — The word scarce
　　　said,
Did Susan rise up from her bed,
As if by magic cured.

Away she goes up hill and down,
And to the wood at length is come;
She spies her Friends, she shouts a greet-
　　　ing;
Oh me! it is a merry meeting
As ever was in Christendom.

The owls have hardly sung their last,
While our four travellers homeward
　　　wend;
The owls have hooted all night long,
And with the owls began my song,
And with the owls must end.

For while they all were travelling hom
Cried Betty, "Tell us, Johnny, do,
Where all this long night you have bee
What you have heard, what you hav
　　　seen:
And, Johnny, mind you tell us true."

Now Johnny all night long had heard
The owls in tuneful concert strive;
No doubt too he the moon had seen;
For in the moonlight he had been
From eight o'clock till five.

And thus, to Betty's question, he
Made answer, like a traveller bold,
(His very words I give to you,)
"The cocks did crow to-whoo, to-whoo
And the sun did shine so cold!"
—Thus answered Johnny in his glory,
And that was all his travel's story.
　1798.　　　　　　　　　　　1798.

LINES.

COMPOSED A FEW MILES ABOVE TINTER
　ABBEY, ON REVISITING THE BANKS C
　THE WYE DURING A TOUR. JULY 1:
　1798.

No poem of mine was composed under circur
stances more pleasant for me to remember tha
this. I began it upon leaving Tintern, aft
crossing the Wye, and concluded it just as I w
entering Bristol in the evening, after a ramble
four or five days, with my Sister. Not a line
it was altered, and not any part of it written dov
till I reached Bristol. It was published almo
immediately after in the little volume of which
much has been said in these Notes. — (The Ly
cal Ballads, as first published at Bristol 1
Cottle.)

FIVE years have passed; five summer
　　　with the length
Of five long winters! and again I hear
These waters, rolling from their mountair
　　　springs
With a soft inland murmur.[1] — One
　　　again
Do I behold these steep and lofty cliff
That on a wild secluded scene impress

[1] The river is not affected by the tides a fe
miles above Tintern.

Thoughts of more deep seclusion; and
connect
The landscape with the quiet of the sky.
The day is come when I again repose
Here, under this dark sycamore, and view
These plots of cottage-ground, these
orchard-tufts,
Which at this season, with their unripe
fruits,
Are clad in one green hue, and lose them-
selves
'Mid groves and copses.   Once again I
see
These hedge-rows, hardly hedge-rows,
little lines
Of sportive wood run wild: these pastoral
farms,
Green to the very door; and wreaths of
smoke
Sent up, in silence, from among the trees!
With some uncertain notice, as might
seem
Of vagrant dwellers in the houseless
woods,
Or of some Hermit's cave, where by his
fire
The Hermit sits alone.
                    These beauteous forms,
Through a long absence, have not been
to me
As is a landscape to a blind man's eye:
But oft, in lonely rooms, and 'mid the din
Of towns and cities, I have owed to them
In hours of weariness, sensations sweet,
Felt in the blood, and felt along the heart;
And passing even into my purer mind,
With tranquil restoration:— feelings too
Of unremembered pleasure: such, per-
haps,
As have no slight or trivial influence
On that best portion of a good man's life,
His little, nameless, unremembered acts
Of kindness and of love.   Nor less, I trust,
To them I may have owed another gift,
Of aspect more sublime; that blessèd
mood,
In which the burthen of the mystery,
In which the heavy and the weary weight
Of all this unintelligible world,
Is lightened:— that serene and blessed
mood,
In which the affections gently lead us
on, —

Until, the breath of this corporeal frame
And even the motion of our human blood
Almost suspended, we are laid asleep
In body, and become a living soul:
While with an eye made quiet by the
power
Of harmony, and the deep power of joy,
We see into the life of things.
                                    If this
Be but a vain belief, yet, oh! how oft —
In darkness and amid the many shapes
Of joyless daylight; when the fretful stir
Unprofitable, and the fever of the world,
Have hung upon the beatings of my
heart — ·
How oft, in spirit, have I turned to thee,
O sylvan Wye! thou wanderer thro' the
woods,
How often has my spirit turned to thee!
    And now, with gleams of half-extin-
guished thought,
With many recognitions dim and faint,
And somewhat of a sad perplexity,
The picture of the mind revives again:
While here I stand, not only with the
sense
Of present pleasure, but with pleasing
thoughts
That in this moment there is life and food
For future years.   And so I dare to hope,
Though changed, no doubt, from what I
was when first
I came among these hills; when like a roe
I bounded o'er the mountains, by the sides
Of the deep rivers, and the lonely
streams,
Wherever nature led: more like a man
Flying from something that he dreads,
than one
Who sought the thing he loved.   For
nature then
(The coarser pleasures of my boyish days,
And their glad animal movements all
gone by)
To me was all in all. — I cannot paint
What then I was.   The sounding cataract
Haunted me like a passion; the tall rock,
The mountain, and the deep and gloomy
wood,
Their colors and their forms, were then
to me
An appetite; a feeling and a love,
That had no need of a remoter charm,

By thought supplied, nor any interest
Unborrowed from the eye. — That time
    is past,
And all its aching joys are now no more,
And all its dizzy raptures.   Not for this
Faint I, nor mourn nor murmur; other
    gifts
Have followed; for such loss, I would
    believe,
Abundant   recompence.   For I have
    learned
To look on nature, not as in the hour
Of thoughtless youth; but hearing often-
    times
The still, sad music of humanity,
Nor harsh, nor grating, though of ample
    power
To chasten and subdue.   And I have felt
A presence that disturbs me with the joy
Of elevated thoughts; a sense sublime
Of something far more deeply interfused,
Whose dwelling is the light of setting suns,
And the round ocean and the living air,
And the blue sky, and in the mind of
    man;
A motion and a spirit, that impels
All thinking things, all objects of all
    thought,
And rolls through all things.   Therefore
    am I still
A lover of the meadows and the woods,
And mountains; and of all that we be-
    hold
From this green earth; of all the mighty
    world
Of eye, and ear, — both what they half
    create,[1]
And   what perceive; well pleased to
    recognize
In nature and the language of the sense,
The anchor of my purest thoughts, the
    nurse,
The guide, the guardian of my heart, and
    soul
Of all my moral being.
                 Nor perchance,
If I were not thus taught, should I the
    more
Suffer my genial spirits to decay:

[1] This line has a close resemblance to an admirable line of Young's, the exact expression of which I do not recollect.

For thou art with me here upon the banks
Of this fair river; thou my dearest Friend,
My dear, dear Friend; and in thy voice
    I catch
The language of my former heart, and
    read
My former pleasures in the shooting lights
Of thy wild eyes.   Oh! yet a little while
May I behold in thee what I was once,
My dear, dear Sister! and this prayer I
    make,
Knowing that Nature never did betray
The heart that loved her; 't is her privi-
    lege,
Through all the years of this our life, to
    lead
From joy to joy: for she can so inform
The mind that is within us, so impress
With quietness and beauty, and so feed
With lofty thoughts, that neither evil
    tongues,
Rash judgments, nor the sneers of selfish
    men,
Nor greetings where no kindness is, nor
    all
The dreary intercourse of daily life,
Shall e'er prevail against us or disturb
Our cheerful faith, that all which we be-
    hold
Is full of blessings.   Therefore let the
    moon
Shine on thee in thy solitary walk;
And let the misty mountain-winds be free
To blow against thee: and, in after years,
When these wild ecstasies shall be
    matured
Into a sober pleasure; when thy mind
Shall be a mansion for all lovely forms,
Thy memory be as a dwelling-place
For all sweet sounds and harmonies; oh!
    then,
If solitude, or fear, or pain, or grief,
Should be thy portion, with what healing
    thoughts
Of tender joy wilt thou remember me,
And these my exhortations! Nor, per-
    chance —
If I should be where I no more can hear
Thy voice, nor catch from thy wild eyes
    these gleams
Of past existence — wilt thou then forget
That on the banks of this delightful stream
We stood together; and that I, so long

A worshipper of Nature, hither came
Unwearied in that service: rather say
With warmer love — oh! with far deeper
      zeal
Of holier love. Nor wilt thou then forget,
That after many wanderings, many years
Of absence, these steep woods and lofty
      cliffs,
And this green pastoral landscape, were
      to me
More dear, both for themselves and for
      thy sake!
      July 13, 1798.   1798.

THE OLD CUMBERLAND BEGGAR.

Observed, and with great benefit to my own heart, when I was a child: written at Racedown and Alfoxden in my twenty-third year. The political economists were about that time beginning their war upon mendicity in all its forms, and by implication, if not directly, on alms-giving also. This heartless process has been carried as far as it can go by the AMENDED poor-law bill, though the inhumanity that prevails in this measure is somewhat disguised by the profession that one of its objects is to throw the poor upon the voluntary donations of their neighbors; that is, if rightly interpreted, to force them into a condition between relief in the Union poorhouse, and alms robbed of their Christian grace and spirit, as being *forced* rather from the benevolent than given by them; while the avaricious and selfish, and all in fact but the humane and charitable, are at liberty to keep all they possess from their distressed brethren.

The class of Beggars to which the Old Man here described belongs, will probably soon be extinct. It consisted of poor, and, mostly, old and infirm persons, who confined themselves to a stated round in their neighborhood, and had certain fixed days, on which, at different houses, they regularly received alms, sometimes in money, but mostly in provisions.

I SAW an aged Beggar in my walk;
And he was seated, by the highway side,
On a low structure of rude masonry
Built at the foot of a huge hill, that they
Who lead their horses down the steep
      rough road
May thence remount with ease. The
      aged Man

Had placed his staff across the broad
      smooth stone
That overlays the pile; and, from a bag
All white with flour, the dole of village
      dames,
He drew his scraps and fragments, one
      by one;
And scanned them with a fixed and serious
      look
Of idle computation. In the sun,
Upon the second step of that small pile,
Surrounded by those wild unpeopled hills,
He sat, and ate his food in solitude:
And ever, scattered from his palsied hand,
That, still attempting to prevent the
      waste,
Was baffled still, the crumbs in little
      showers
Fell on the ground; and the small moun-
      tain birds
Not venturing yet to peck their destined
      meal,
Approached within the length of half his
      staff.
    Him from my childhood have I known;
      and then
He was so old, he seems not older now;
He travels on, a solitary Man,
So helpless in appearance, that for him
The sauntering Horseman throws not
      with a slack
And careless hand his alms upon the
      ground,
But stops, — that he may safely lodge the
      coin
Within the old Man's hat; nor quits him
      so,
But still, when he has given his horse
      the rein,
Watches the aged Beggar with a look
Sidelong and half-reverted. She who
      tends
The toll-gate, when in summer at her door
She turns her wheel, if on the road she
      sees
The aged beggar coming, quits her work,
And lifts the latch for him that he may
      pass.
The post-boy, when his rattling wheels
      o'ertake
The aged Beggar in the woody lane,
Shouts to him from behind; and if, thus
      warned,

The old man does not change his course,
the boy
Turns with less noisy wheels to the road-
side,
And passes gently by, without a curse
Upon his lips, or anger at his heart.
He travels on, a solitary Man;
His age has no companion. On the
ground
His eyes are turned, and, as he moves
along,
They move along the ground; and, ever-
more,
Instead of common and habitual sight
Of fields with rural works, of hill and
dale,
And the blue sky, one little span of earth
Is all his prospect. Thus, from day to
day,
Bow-bent, his eyes forever on the ground,
He plies his weary journey; seeing still,
And seldom knowing that he sees, some
straw,
Some scattered leaf, or marks which, in
one track,
The nails of cart or chariot-wheel have left
Impressed on the white road, — in the
same line,
At distance still the same. Poor Traveller!
His staff trails with him; scarcely do his
feet
Disturb the summer dust; he is so still
In look and motion, that the cottage curs,
Ere he has passed the door, will turn
away,
Weary of barking at him. Boys and girls,
The vacant and the busy, maids and
youths,
And urchins newly breeched — all pass
him by:
Him even the slow-paced wagon leaves
behind.
But deem not this Man useless. —
Statesmen! ye
Who are so restless in your wisdom, ye
Who have a broom still ready in your
hands
To rid the world of nuisances; ye proud,
Heart-swoln, while in your pride ye con-
template
Your talents, power, or wisdom, deem
him not
A burthen of the earth! 'T is Nature's law

That none, the meanest of created things,
Or forms created the most vile and brute,
The dullest or most noxious, should exist
Divorced from good — a spirit and pulse
of good,
A life and soul, to every mode of being
Inseparably linked. Then be assured
That least of all can aught — that ever
owned
The heaven-regarding eye and front sub-
lime
Which man is born to — sink, howe'er
depressed,
So low as to be scorned without a sin;
Without offence to God cast out of view;
Like the dry remnant of a garden-flower
Whose seeds are shed, or as an implement
Worn out and worthless. While from
door to door,
This old Man creeps, the villagers in him
Behold a record which together binds
Past deeds and offices of charity,
Else unremembered, and so keeps alive
The kindly mood in hearts which lapse
of years,
And that half-wisdom, half-experience
gives,
Make slow to feel, and by sure steps
resign
To selfishness and cold oblivious cares.
Among the farms and solitary huts,
Hamlets and thinly-scattered villages,
Where'er the aged Beggar takes his
rounds,
The mild necessity of use compels
To acts of love; and habit does the work
Of reason; yet prepares that after-joy
Which reason cherishes. And thus the
soul,
By that sweet taste of pleasure unpursued,
Doth find herself insensibly disposed
To virtue and true goodness.
Some there are,
By their good works exalted, lofty minds
And meditative, authors of delight
And happiness, which to the end of time
Will live, and spread, and kindle: even
such minds
In childhood, from this solitary Being,
Or from like wanderer, haply have re-
ceived
(A thing more precious far than all that
books

Or the solicitudes of love can do!)
That first mild touch of sympathy and
    thought,
In which they found their kindred with
    a world
Where want and sorrow were.   The easy
    man
Who sits at his own door, — and, like
    the pear
That overhangs his head from the green
    wall,
Feeds in the sunshine; the robust and
    young,
The prosperous and unthinking, they
    who live
Sheltered, and flourish in a little grove
Of their own kindred; — all behold in him
A silent monitor, which on their minds
Must needs impress a transitory thought
Of self-congratulation, to the heart
Of each recalling his peculiar boons,
His charters and exemptions; and, per-
    chance,
Though he to no one give the fortitude
And circumspection needful to preserve
His present blessings, and to husband up
The respite of the season, he, at least,
And 't is no vulgar service, makes them
    felt.
    Yet further. — Many, I believe, there
    are
Who live a life of virtuous decency,
Men who can hear the Decalogue and feel
No self-reproach; who of the moral law
Established in the land where they abide
Are strict observers; and not negligent
In acts of love to those with whom they
    dwell,
Their kindred, and the children of their
    blood.
Praise be to such, and to their slumbers
    peace!
— But of the poor man ask, the abject
    poor;
Go, and demand of him, if there be here
In this cold abstinence from evil deeds,
And these inevitable charities,
Wherewith to satisfy the human soul?
No — man is dear to man; the poorest
    poor
Long for some moments in a weary life
When they can know and feel that they
    have been,

Themselves, the fathers and the dealers-
    out
Of some small blessings; have been
    kind to such
As needed kindness, for this single cause,
That we have all of us one human heart.
— Such pleasure is to one kind Being
    known,
My neighbor, when with punctual care,
    each week
Duly as Friday comes, though pressed
    herself
By her own wants, she from her store of
    meal
Takes one unsparing handful for the
    scrip
Of this old Mendicant, and, from her door
Returning with exhilarated heart,
Sits by her fire, and builds her hope in
    heaven.
    Then let him pass, a blessing on his
    head!
And while in that vast solitude to which
The tide of things has borne him, he
    appears
To breathe and live but for himself alone,
Unblamed, uninjured, let him bear about
The good which the benignant law of
    Heaven
Has hung around him: and, while life is
    his,
Still let him prompt the unlettered vil-
    lagers
To tender offices and pensive thoughts.
— Then let him pass, a blessing on his
    head!
And, long as he can wander, let him
    breathe
The freshness of the valleys; let his blood
Struggle with frosty air and winter snows;
And let the chartered wind that sweeps
    the heath
Beat his gray locks against his withered
    face.
Reverence the hope whose vital anxious-
    ness
Gives the last human interest to his heart.
May never HOUSE, misnamed of IN-
    DUSTRY,
Make him a captive! — for that pent-up
    din,
Those life-consuming sounds that clog
    the air,

Be his the natural silence of old age !
Let him be free of mountain solitudes;
And have around him, whether heard or
    not,
The pleasant melody of woodland birds.
Few are his pleasures: if his eyes have
    now
Been doomed so long to settle upon
    earth
That not without some effort they behold
The countenance of the horizontal sun,
Rising or setting, let the light at least
Find a free entrance to their languid
    orbs.
And let him, *where* and *when* he will, sit
    down
Beneath the trees, or on a grassy bank
Of highway side, and with the little
    birds
Share his chance-gathered meal; and,
    finally,
As in the eye of Nature he has lived,
So in the eye of Nature let him die !
1798.   1800.

ANIMAL TRANQUILLITY AND
DECAY.

THE little hedgerow birds,
That peck along the roads, regard him
    not.
He travels on, and in his face, his step,
His gait, is one expression: every limb,
His look and bending figure, all bespeak
A man who does not move with pain,
    but moves
With thought. — He is insensibly sub-
    dued
To settled quiet: he is one by whom
All effort seems forgotten ; one to whom
Long patience hath such mild compo-
    sure given,
That patience now doth seem a thing of
    which
He hath no need.   He is by nature led
To peace so perfect that the young be-
    hold
With envy, what the old Man hardly
    feels.
1798.   1798.

PETER BELL.
A TALE.

What 's in a *Name* ?

. . . . . .

Brutus will start a Spirit as soon as Cæsar !

Written at Alfoxden. Founded upon an anec-
dote, which I read in a newspaper, of an ass being
found hanging his head over a canal in a wretched
posture. Upon examination a dead body was
found in the water and proved to be the body of
its master. The countenance, gait, and figure of
Peter, were taken from a wild rover with whom
I walked from Builth, on the river Wye, down-
wards nearly as far as the town of Hay. He
told me strange stories. It has always been a
pleasure to me through life to catch at every
opportunity that has occurred in my rambles of
becoming acquainted with this class of people.
The number of Peter's wives was taken from the
trespasses in this way of a lawless creature who
lived in the county of Durham, and used to be
attended by many women, sometimes not less
than half a dozen, as disorderly as himself.
Benoni, or the child of sorrow, I knew when I
was a school-boy. His mother had been deserted
by a gentleman in the neighborhood, she herself
being a gentlewoman by birth. The circum-
stances of her story were told me by my dear old
Dame, Anne Tyson, who was her confidante.
The Lady died broken-hearted. — In the woods of
Alfoxden I used to take great delight in noticing
the habits, tricks, and physiognomy of asses;
and I have no doubt that I was thus put upon
writing the poem out of liking for the creature
that is so often dreadfully abused. — The crescent-
moon, which makes such a figure in the prologue,
assumed this character one evening while I was
watching its beauty in front of Alfoxden House.
I intended this poem for the volume before
spoken of, but it was not published for more than
twenty years afterwards. — The worship of the
Methodists or Ranters is often heard during the
stillness of the summer evening in the country
with affecting accompaniments of rural beauty.
In both the psalmody and the voice of the
preacher there is, not unfrequently, much solem-
nity likely to impress the feelings of the rudest
characters under favorable circumstances.

TO

ROBERT SOUTHEY, ESQ., P.L.,
    ETC., ETC.

MY DEAR FRIEND,

The Tale of Peter Bell, which I now introduce
to your notice, and to that of the Public, has, in

its Manuscript state, nearly survived its *mi-nority*: — for it first saw the light in the summer of 1798. During this long interval, pains have been taken at different times to make the production less unworthy of a favorable reception; or, rather, to fit it for filling *permanently* a station, however humble, in the Literature of our Country. This has, indeed, been the aim of all my endeavors in Poetry, which, you know, have been sufficiently laborious to prove that I deem the Art not lightly to be approached; and that the attainment of excellence in it may laudably be made the principal object of intellectual pursuit by any man, who, with reasonable consideration of circumstances, has faith in his own impulses.

The poem of Peter Bell, as the Prologue will show, was composed under a belief that the Imagination not only does not require for its exercise the intervention of supernatural agency, but that, though such agency be excluded, the faculty may be called forth as imperiously and for kindred results of pleasure, by incidents, within the compass of poetic probability, in the humblest departments of daily life. Since that Prologue was written, *you* have exhibited most splendid effects of judicious daring, in the opposite and usual course. Let this acknowledgment make my peace with the lovers of the supernatural; and I am persuaded it will be admitted, that to you, as a Master in that province of the Art, the following Tale, whether from contrast or congruity, is not an unappropriate offering. Accept it, then, as a public testimony of affectionate admiration from one with whose name yours has been often coupled (to use your own words) for evil and for good; and believe me to be, with earnest wishes that life and health may be granted you to complete the many important works in which you are engaged, and with high respect,

Most faithfully yours,
WILLIAM WORDSWORTH.
Rydal Mount, April 7, 1819.

PROLOGUE.

THERE 's something in a flying horse,
There 's something in a huge balloon;
But through the clouds I 'll never float
Until I have a little Boat,
Shaped like the crescent-moon.

And now I *have* a little Boat,
In shape a very crescent-moon.
Fast through the clouds my boat can sail;
But if perchance your faith should fail,
Look up — and you 'shall see me soon!

The woods, my Friends, are round you roaring,
Rocking and roaring like a sea;
The noise of danger 's in your ears,
And ye have all a thousand fears
Both for my little Boat and me!

Meanwhile untroubled I admire
The pointed horns of my canoe;
And, did not pity touch my breast,
To see how ye are all distrest,
Till my ribs ached, I 'd laugh at you!

Away we go, my Boat and I —
Frail man ne'er sate in such another;
Whether among the winds we strive,
Or deep into the clouds we dive,
Each is contented with the other.

Away we go — and what care we
For treasons, tumults, and for wars?
We are as calm in our delight
As is the crescent-moon so bright
Among the scattered stars.

Up goes my Boat among the stars
Through many a breathless field of light,
Through many a long blue field of ether,
Leaving ten thousand stars beneath her:
Up goes my little Boat so bright!

The Crab, the Scorpion, and the Bull —
We pry among them all; have shot
High o'er the red-haired race of Mars,
Covered from top to toe with scars;
Such company I like it not!

The towns in Saturn are decayed,
And melancholy Spectres throng them; —
The Pleiads, that appear to kiss
Each other in the vast abyss,
With joy I sail among them.

Swift Mercury resounds with mirth,
Great Jove is full of stately bowers;
But these, and all that they contain,
What are they to that tiny grain,
That little Earth of ours?

Then back to Earth, the dear green Earth: —
Whole ages if I here should roam,

The world for my remarks and me
Would not a whit the better be;
I 've left my heart at home.

See! there she is, the matchless Earth!
There spreads the famed Pacific Ocean!
Old Andes thrusts yon craggy spear
Through the gray clouds; the Alps are
    here,
Like waters in commotion!

Yon tawny slip is Libya's sands;
That silver thread the river Dnieper!
And look, where clothed in brightest
    green
Is a sweet Isle, of isles the Queen;
Ye fairies, from all evil keep her!

And see the town where I was born!
Around those happy fields we span
In boyish gambols; — I was lost
Where I have been, but on this coast
I feel I am a man.

Never did fifty things at once
Appear so lovely, never, never; —
How tunefully the forests ring!
To hear the earth's soft murmuring
Thus could I hang forever!

"Shame on you!" cried my little Boat,
"Was ever such a homesick Loon,
Within a living Boat to sit,
And make no better use of it;
A Boat twin-sister of the crescent-moon!

"Ne'er in the breast of full-grown Poet
Fluttered so faint a heart before; —
Was it the music of the spheres
That overpowered your mortal ears?
— Such din shall trouble them no more.

"These nether precincts do not lack
Charms of their own; — then come with
    me;
I want a comrade, and for you
There 's nothing that I would not do;
Nought is there that you shall not see.

"Haste! and above Siberian snows
We 'll sport amid the boreal morning;
Will mingle with her lustres gliding
Among the stars, the stars now hiding,
And now the stars adorning.

"I know the secrets of a land
Where human foot did never stray;
Fair is that land as evening skies,
And cool, though in the depth it lies
Of burning Africa.

"Or we 'll into the realm of Faery,
Among the lovely shades of things;
The shadowy forms of mountains bare,
And streams, and bowers, and ladies fair,
The shades of palaces and kings!

"Or, if you thirst with hardy zeal
Less quiet regions to explore,
Prompt voyage shall to you reveal
How earth and heaven are taught to feel
The might of magic lore!"

"My little vagrant Form of light,
My gay and beautiful Canoe,.
Well have you played your friendly part;
As kindly take what from my heart
Experience forces — then adieu!

"Temptation lurks among your words;
But, while these pleasures you 're pursu-
    ing
Without impediment or let,
No wonder if you quite forget
What on the earth is doing.

"There was a time when all mankind
Did listen with a faith sincere
To tuneful tongues in mystery versed;
Then Poets fearlessly rehearsed
The wonders of a wild career.

"Go — (but the world 's a sleepy world,
And 't is, I fear, an age too late)
Take with you some ambitious Youth!
For, restless Wanderer! I, in truth,
Am all unfit to be your mate.

" Long have I loved what I behold,
The night that calms, the day that cheers;
The common growth of mother-earth
Suffices me — her tears, her mirth,
Her humblest mirth and tears.

" The dragon's wing, the magic ring,
I shall not covet for my dower,
If I along that lowly way
With sympathetic heart may stray,
And with a soul of power.

" These given, what more need I desire
To stir, to soothe, or elevate?
What nobler marvels than the mind
May in life's daily prospect find,
May find or there create?

" A potent wand doth Sorrow wield;
What spell so strong as guilty Fear!
Repentance is a tender Sprite;
If aught on earth have heavenly might,
'T is lodged within her silent tear.

" But grant my wishes, — let us now
Descend from this ethereal height;
Then take thy way, adventurous Skiff,
More daring far than Hippogriff,
And be thy own delight!

" To the stone-table in my garden,
Loved haunt of many a summer hour,
The Squire is come: his daughter Bess
Beside him in the cool recess
Sits blooming like a flower.

" With these are many more convened;
They know not I have been so far; —
I see them there, in number nine,
Beneath the spreading Weymouth-pine!
I see them — there they are!

" There sits the Vicar and his Dame;
And there my good friend Stephen Otter;
And, ere the light of evening fail,
To them I must relate the Tale
Of Peter Bell the Potter."

Off flew the Boat — away she flees,
Spurning her freight with indignation!
And I, as well as I was able,
On two poor legs, toward my stone-table
Limped on with sore vexation.

" O, here he is! " cried little Bess —
She saw me at the garden-door;
" We 've waited anxiously and long,"
They cried, and all around me throng,
Full nine of them or more!

" Reproach me not — your fears be still —
Be thankful we again have met; —
Resume, my Friends! within the shade
Your seats, and quickly shall be paid
The well-remembered debt."

I spake with faltering voice, like one
Not wholly rescued from the pale
Of a wild dream, or worse illusion;
But, straight, to cover my confusion,
Began the promised Tale.

PART FIRST.

ALL by the moonlight riverside
Groaned the poor Beast — alas! in vain;
The staff was raised to loftier height,
And the blows fell with heavier weight
As Peter struck — and struck again.

" Hold!" cried the Squire, " against the
    rules
Of common sense you 're surely sinning;
This leap is for us all too bold;
Who Peter was, let that be told,
And start from the beginning."

— " A Potter,[1] Sir, he was by trade,"
Said I, becoming quite collected;
" And wheresoever he appeared,
Full twenty times was Peter feared
For once that Peter was respected.

" He, two and thirty years or more,
Had been a wild and woodland rover;
Had heard the Atlantic surges roar
On farthest Cornwall's rocky shore,
And trod the cliffs of Dover.

" And he had seen Caernarvon's towers,
And well he knew the spire of Sarum;
And he had been where Lincoln bell
Flings o'er the fen that ponderous knell —
A far-renowned alarum!

[1] In the dialect of the North, a hawker of
earthenware is thus designated.

" At Doncaster, at York, and Leeds,
And merry Carlisle had he been;
And all along the Lowlands fair,
All through the bonny shire of Ayr
And far as Aberdeen.

" And he had been at Inverness;
And Peter, by the mountain rills,
Had danced his round with Highland
　　　　lasses;
And he had lain beside his asses
On lofty Cheviot Hills:

" And he had trudged through Yorkshire
　　　　dales,
Among the rocks and winding *scars;*
Where deep and low the hamlets lie
Beneath their little patch of sky
And little lot of stars:

" And all along the indented coast,
Bespattered with the salt-sea foam;
Where'er a knot of houses lay
On headland, or in hollow bay; —
Sure never man like him did roam !

" As well might Peter, in the Fleet,
Have been fast bound, a begging debt-
　　　　or; —
He travelled here, he travelled there; —
But not the value of a hair
Was heart or head the better.

" He roved among the vales and streams,
In the green wood and hollow dell;
They were his dwellings night and day, —
But nature ne'er could find the way
Into the heart of Peter Bell.

" In vain, through every changeful year,
Did Nature lead him as before;
A primrose by a river's brim
A yellow primrose was to him,
And it was nothing more.

" Small change it made on Peter's heart
To see his gentle panniered train
With more than vernal pleasure feeding,
Where'er the tender grass was leading
Its earliest green along the lane.

" In vain, through water, earth, and air,
The soul of happy sound was spread,
When Peter on some April morn,
Beneath the broom or budding thorn,
Made the warm earth his lazy bed.

" At noon, when, by the forest's edge
He lay beneath the branches high,
The soft blue sky did never melt
Into his heart; he never felt
The witchery of the soft blue sky !

" On a fair prospect some have looked
And felt, as I have heard them say,
As if the moving time had been
A thing as steadfast as the scene
On which they gazed themselves away.

" Within the breast of Peter Bell
These silent raptures found no place;
He was a Carl as wild and rude
As ever hue-and-cry pursued,
As ever ran a felon's race.

" Of all that lead a lawless life,
Of all that love their lawless lives,
In city or in village small,
He was the wildest far of all; —
He had a dozen wedded wives.

" Nay, start not ! — wedded wives — and
　　　　twelve !
But how one wife could e'er come near
　　　　him,
In simple truth I cannot tell;
For, be it said of Peter Bell,
To see him was to fear him.

" Though Nature could not touch his
　　　　heart
By lovely forms, and silent weather,
And tender sounds, yet you might see
At once, that Peter Bell and she
Had often been together.

" A savage wildness round him hung
As of a dweller out of doors;
In his whole figure and his mien
A savage character was seen
Of mountains and of dreary moors.

"To all the unshaped half-human
        thoughts
Which solitary Nature feeds
'Mid summer storms or winter's ice,
Had Peter joined whatever vice
The cruel city breeds.

" His face was keen as is the wind
That cuts along the hawthorn-fence; —
Of courage you saw little there,
But, in its stead, a medley air
Of cunning and of impudence.

" He had a dark and sidelong walk,
And long and slouching was his gait;
Beneath his looks so bare and bold,
You might perceive, his spirit cold
Was playing with some inward bait.

" His forehead wrinkled was and furred;
A work, one half of which was done
By thinking of his ' *whens* ' and ' *hows* ; '
And half, by knitting of his brows
Beneath the glaring sun.

" There was a hardness in his cheek,
There was a hardness in his eye,
As if the man had fixed his face,
In many a solitary place,
Against the wind and open sky!"

ONE NIGHT, (and now my little Bess!
We 've reached at last the promised
        Tale:)
One beautiful November night,
When the full moon was shining bright
Upon the rapid river Swale,

Along the river's winding banks
Peter was travelling all alone; —
Whether to buy or sell, or led
By pleasure running in his head,
To me was never known.

He trudged along through copse and
        brake,
He trudged along o'er hill and dale;
Nor for the moon cared he a tittle,
And for the stars he cared as little,
And for the murmuring river Swale.

But, chancing to espy a path
That promised to cut short the way,
As many a wiser man hath done,
He left a trusty guide for one
That might his steps betray.

To a thick wood he soon is brought
Where cheerily his course he weaves,
And whistling loud may yet be heard,
Though often buried, like a bird
Darkling, among the boughs and leaves.

But quickly Peter's mood is changed,
And on he drives with cheeks that burn
In downright fury and in wrath; —
There 's little sign the treacherous path
Will to the road return!

The path grows dim, and dimmer still;
Now up, now down, the Rover wends,
With all the sail that he can carry,
Till brought to a deserted quarry —
And there the pathway ends.

He paused — for shadows of strange
        shape,
Massy and black, before him lay;
But through the dark, and through the
        cold,
And through the yawning fissures old,
Did Peter boldly press his way

Right through the quarry; — and behold
A scene of soft and lovely hue!
Where blue and gray, and tender green,
Together make as sweet a scene
As ever human eye did view.

Beneath the clear blue sky he saw
A little field of meadow ground;
But field or meadow name it not;
Call it of earth a small green plot,
With rocks encompassed round.

The Swale flowed under the gray rocks,
But he flowed quiet and unseen; —
You need a strong and stormy gale
To bring the noises of the Swale
To that green spot, so calm and green!

And is there no one dwelling here,
No hermit with his beads and glass?
And does no little cottage look
Upon this soft and fertile nook?
Does no one live near this green grass?

Across the deep and quiet spot
Is Peter driving through the grass —
And now has reached the skirting trees;
When, turning round his head, he sees
A solitary Ass.

"A Prize!" cries Peter — but he first
Must spy about him far and near:
There 's not a single house in sight,
No woodman's hut, no cottage light —
Peter, you need not fear!

There 's nothing to be seen but woods,
And rocks that spread a hoary gleam,
And this·one Beast, that from the bed
Of the green meadow hangs his head
Over the silent stream.

His head is with a halter bound;
The halter seizing, Peter leapt
Upon the Creature's back, and plied
With ready heels his shaggy side;
But still the Ass his station kept.

Then Peter gave a sudden jerk,
A jerk that from a dungeon-floor
Would have pulled up an iron ring;
But still the heavy-headed Thing
Stood just as he had stood before!

Quoth Peter, leaping from his seat,
"There is some plot against me laid;"
Once more the little meadow-ground
And all the hoary cliffs around
He cautiously surveyed.

All, all is silent — rocks and woods,
All still and silent — far and near!
Only the Ass, with motion dull,
Upon the pivot of his skull
Turns round his long left ear.

Thought Peter, What can mean all this?
Some ugly witchcraft must be here!
— Once more the Ass, with motion dull,
Upon the pivot of his skull
Turned round his long left ear.

Suspicion ripened into dread;
Yet with deliberate action slow,
His staff high-raising, in the pride
Of skill, upon the sounding hide,
He dealt a sturdy blow.

The poor Ass staggered with the shock;
And then, as if to take his ease,
In quiet uncomplaining mood,
Upon the spot where he had stood,
Dropped gently down upon his knees:

As gently on his side he fell;
And by the river's brink did lie;
And, while he lay like one that mourned,
The patient Beast on Peter turned
His shining hazel eye.

'T was but one mild, reproachful look,
A look more tender than severe;
And straight in sorrow, not in dread,
He turned the eyeball in his head
Towards the smooth river deep and clear.

Upon the Beast the sapling rings;
His lank sides heaved, his limbs they
        stirred;
He gave a groan, and then another,
Of that which went before the brother,
And then he gave a third.

All by the moonlight riverside
He gave three miserable groans;
And not till now hath Peter seen
How gaunt the Creature is, — how lean
And sharp his staring bones!

With legs stretched out and stiff he lay:—
No word of kind commiseration
Fell at the sight from Peter's tongue;
With hard contempt his heart was wrung,
With hatred and vexation.

The meagre beast lay still as death;
And Peter's lips with fury quiver;
Quoth he, "You little mulish dog,
I 'll fling your carcase like a log
Head-foremost down the river!"

An impious oath confirmed the threat —
Whereat from the earth on which he lay
To all the echoes, south and north,
And east and west, the Ass sent forth
A long and clamorous bray!

This outcry, on the heart of Peter,
Seems like a note of joy to strike, —
Joy at the heart of Peter knocks;
But in the echo of the rocks
Was something Peter did not like.

Whether to cheer his coward breast,
Or that he could not break the chain,
In this serene and solemn hour,
Twined round him by demoniac power,
To the blind work he turned again.

Among the rocks and winding crags;
Among the mountains far away;
Once more the ass will lengthen out
More ruefully a deep-drawn shout,
The hard dry see-saw of his horrible bray!

What is there now in Peter's heart!
Or whence the might of this strange sound?
The moon uneasy looked and dimmer,
The broad blue heavens appeared to glim-
    mer,
And the rocks staggered all around —

From Peter's hand the sapling dropped!
Threat has he none to execute;
" If any one should come and see
That I am here, they 'll think," quoth he,
" I 'm helping this poor dying brute."

He scans the ass from limb to limb,
And ventures now to uplift his eyes;
More steady looks the moon, and clear,
More like themselves the rocks appear
And touch more quiet skies.

His scorn returns — his hate revives;
He stoops the Ass's neck to seize
With malice — that again takes flight;
For in the pool a startling sight
Meets him, among the inverted trees.

Is it the moon's distorted face?
The ghost-like image of a cloud?
Is it a gallows there portrayed?
Is Peter of himself afraid?
Is it a coffin, — or a shroud?

A grisly idol hewn in stone?
Or imp from witch's lap let fall?
Perhaps a ring of shining fairies?
Such as pursue their fearèd vagaries
In sylvan bower, or haunted hall?

Is it a fiend that to a stake
Of fire his desperate self is tethering?
Or stubborn spirit doomed to yell
In solitary ward or cell,
Ten thousand miles from all his brethren?

Never did pulse so quickly throb,
And never heart so loudly panted;
He looks, he cannot choose but look;
Like some one reading in a book —
A book that is enchanted.

Ah, well-a-day for Peter Bell!
He will be turned to iron soon,
Meet Statue for the court of Fear!
His hat is up — and every hair
Bristles, and whitens in the moon!

He looks, he ponders, looks again;
He sees a motion — hears a groan;
His eyes will burst — his heart will
    break —
He gives a loud and frightful shriek,
And back he falls, as if his life were flown!

PART SECOND.

WE left our Hero in a trance,
Beneath the alders, near the river;
The Ass is by the riverside,
And, where the feeble breezes glide,
Upon the stream the moonbeams quiver.

A happy respite! but at length
He feels the glimmering of the moon;
Wakes with glazed eye, and feebly sigh-
    ing —
To sink, perhaps, where he is lying,
Into a second swoon!

He lifts his head, he sees his staff;
He touches — 't is to him a treasure!
Faint recollection seems to tell
That he is yet where mortals dwell —
A thought received with languid pleasure!

His head upon his elbow propped,
Becoming less and less perplexed,
Sky-ward he looks — to rock and wood —
And then — upon the glassy flood
His wandering eye is fixed.

Thought he, that is the face of one
In his last sleep securely bound!
So toward the stream his head he bent,
And downward thrust his staff, intent
The river's depth to sound.

Now — like a tempest-shattered bark,
That overwhelmed and prostrate lies,
And in a moment to the verge
Is lifted of a foaming surge —
Full suddenly the Ass doth rise!

His staring bones all shake with joy,
And close by Peter's side he stands:
While Peter o'er the river bends,
The little Ass his neck extends,
And fondly licks his hands.

Such life is in the Ass's eyes,
Such life is in his limbs and ears;
That Peter Bell, if he had been
The veriest coward ever seen,
Must now have thrown aside his fears.

The Ass looks on — and to his work
Is Peter quietly resigned;
He touches here — he touches there —
And now among the dead man's hair
His sapling Peter has intwined.

He pulls — and looks — and pulls again;
And he whom the poor Ass had lost,
The man who had been four days dead,
Head-foremost from the river's bed
Uprises like a ghost!

And Peter draws him to dry land;
And through the brain of Peter pass
Some poignant twitches, fast and faster;
" No doubt," quoth he, " he is the Master
Of this poor miserable Ass!"

The meagre Shadow that looks on —
What would he now? what is he doing?
His sudden fit of joy is flown, —
He on his knees hath laid him down,
As if he were his grief renewing;

But no — that Peter on his back
Must mount, he shows well as he can:
Thought Peter then, come weal or woe,
I 'll do what he would have me do,
In pity to this poor drowned man.

With that resolve he boldly mounts
Upon the pleased and thankful Ass;
And then, without a moment's stay,
That earnest Creature turned away
Leaving the body on the grass.

Intent upon his faithful watch,
The Beast four days and nights had past;
A sweeter meadow ne'er was seen,
And there the Ass four days had been,
Nor ever once did break his fast:

Yet firm his step, and stout his heart;
The mead is crossed — the quarry's mouth
Is reached; but there the trusty guide
Into a thicket turns aside,
And deftly ambles towards the south.

When hark a burst of doleful sound!
And Peter honestly might say,
The like came never to his ears,
Though he has been, full thirty years,
A rover — night and day!

'T is not a plover of the moors,
'T is not a bittern of the fen;
Nor can it be a barking fox,
Nor night-bird chambered in the rocks,
Nor wild-cat in a woody glen!

The Ass is startled — and stops short
Right in the middle of the thicket;
And Peter, wont to whistle loud
Whether alone or in a crowd,
Is silent as a silent cricket.

What ails you now, my little Bess?
Well may you tremble and look grave!
This cry — that rings along the wood,
This cry — that floats adown the flood,
Comes from the entrance of a cave:

I see a blooming Wood-boy there,
And if I had the power to say
How sorrowful the wanderer is,
Your heart would be as sad as his
Till you had kissed his tears away!

Grasping a hawthorn branch in hand,
All bright with berries ripe and red,
Into the cavern's mouth he peeps;
Thence back into the moonlight creeps;
Whom seeks he — whom? — the silent
    dead:

His father! — Him doth he require —
Him hath he sought with fruitless pains,
Among the rocks, behind the trees;
Now creeping on his hands and knees,
Now running o'er the open plains.

And hither is he come at last,
When he through such a day has gone,
By this dark cave to be distrest
Like a poor bird — her plundered nest
Hovering around with dolorous moan!

Of that intense and piercing cry
The listening Ass conjectures well;
Wild as it is, he there can read
Some intermingled notes that plead
With touches irresistible.

But Peter — when he saw the Ass
Not only stop but turn, and change
The cherished tenor of his pace
That lamentable cry to chase —
It wrought in him conviction strange;

A faith that, for the dead man's sake
And this poor slave who loved him well,
Vengeance upon his head will fall,
Some visitation worse than all
Which ever till this night befell.

Meanwhile the Ass to reach his home,
Is striving stoutly as he may;
But, while he climbs the woody hill,
The cry grows weak — and weaker still;
And now at last it dies away.

So with his freight the Creature turns
Into a gloomy grove of beech,
Along the shade with footsteps true
Descending slowly, till the two
The open moonlight reach.

And there, along the narrow dell,
A fair smooth pathway you discern,
A length of green and open road —

As if it from a fountain flowed —
Winding away between the fern.

The rocks that tower on either side
Build up a wild fantastic scene;
Temples like those among the Hindoos,
And mosques, and spires, and abbey
    windows,
And castles all with ivy green!

And, while the Ass pursues his way,
Along this solitary dell,
As pensively his steps advance,
The mosques and spires change counte-
    nance
And look at Peter Bell!

That unintelligible cry
Hath left him high in preparation, —
Convinced that he, or soon or late,
This very night will meet his fate —
And so he sits in expectation!

The strenuous Animal hath clomb
With the green path; and now he wends
Where, shining like the smoothest sea,
In undisturbed immensity
A level plain extends.

But whence this faintly rustling sound
By which the journeying pair are chased?
— A withered leaf is close behind,
Light plaything for the sportive wind
Upon that solitary waste.

When Peter spied the moving thing,
It only doubled his distress;
" Where there is not a bush or tree,
The very leaves they follow me —
So huge hath been my wickedness! "

To a close lane they now are come,
Where, as before, the enduring Ass
Moves on without a moment's stop,
Nor once turns round his head to crop
A bramble-leaf or blade of grass.

Between the hedges as they go,
The white dust sleeps upon the lane;
And Peter, ever and anon
Back-looking, sees, upon a stone,
Or in the dust, a crimson stain.

A stain — as of a drop of blood
By moonlight made more faint and wan;
Ha! why these sinkings of despair?
He knows not how the blood comes
    there —
And Peter is a wicked man.

At length he spies a bleeding wound,
Where he had struck the Ass's head;
He sees the blood, knows what it is, —
A glimpse of sudden joy was his,
But then it quickly fled;

Of him whom sudden death had seized
He thought, — of thee, O faithful Ass!
And once again those ghastly pains,
Shoot to and fro through heart and reins,
And through his brain like lightning pass.

PART THIRD.

I've heard of one, a gentle Soul,
Though given to sadness and to gloom,
And for the fact will vouch, — one night
It chanced that by a taper's light
This man was reading in his room;

Bending, as you or I might bend
At night o'er any pious book,
When sudden blackness overspread
The snow-white page on which he read,
And made the good man round him look.

The chamber walls were dark all round, —
And to his book he turned again;
— The light had left the lonely taper,
And formed itself upon the paper
Into large letters — bright and plain!

The godly book was in his hand —
And, on the page, more black than coal,
Appeared, set forth in strange array,
A *word* — which to his dying day
Perplexed the good man's gentle soul.

The ghostly word, thus plainly seen,
Did never from his lips depart;
But he hath said, poor gentle wight!
It brought full many a sin to light
Out of the bottom of his heart.

Dread Spirits! to confound the meek
Why wander from your course so far,

Disordering color, form, and stature!
— Let good men feel the soul of nature,
And see things as they are.

Yet, potent Spirits! well I know,
How ye, that play with soul and sense,
Are not unused to trouble friends
Of goodness, for most gracious ends —
And this I speak in reverence!

But might I give advice to you,
Whom in my fear I love so well;
From men of pensive virtue go,
Dread Beings! and your empire show
On hearts like that of Peter Bell.

Your presence often have I felt
In darkness and the stormy night;
And, with like force, if need there be,
Ye can put forth your agency
When earth is calm, and heaven is bright.

Then, coming from the wayward world,
That powerful world in which ye dwell,
Come, Spirits of the Mind! and try
To-night, beneath the moonlight sky,
What may be done with Peter Bell!

— O, would that some more skilful voice
My further labor might prevent!
Kind Listeners, that around me sit,
I feel that I am all unfit
For such high argument.

I've played, I've danced, with my narra-
    tion;
I loitered long ere I began:
Ye waited then on my good pleasure;
Pour out indulgence still, in measure
As liberal as ye can!

Our Travellers, ye remember well,
Are thridding a sequestered lane;
And Peter many tricks is trying,
And many anodynes applying,
To ease his conscience of its pain.

By this his heart is lighter far;
And, finding that he can account
So snugly for that crimson stain,
His evil spirit up again
Does like an empty bucket mount.

And Peter is a deep logician
Who hath no lack of wit mercurial;
"Blood drops — leaves rustle — yet,"
    quoth he,
"This poor man never, but for me,
Could have had Christian burial.

" And, say the best you can, 't is plain,
That here has been some wicked dealing;
No doubt the devil in me wrought;
I'm not the man who could have thought
An Ass like this was worth the stealing ! ' "

So from his pocket Peter takes
His shining horn tobacco-box;
And, in a light and careless way,
As men who with their purpose play,
Upon the lid he knocks.

Let them whose voice can stop the clouds,
Whose cunning eye can see the wind,
Tell to a curious world the cause
Why, making here a sudden pause,
The Ass turned round his head, and
    grinned.

Appalling process ! I have marked
The like on heath, in lonely wood;
And, verily, have seldom met
A spectacle more hideous — yct
It suited Peter's present mood.

And, grinning in his turn, his teeth
He in jocose defiance showed —
When, to upset his spiteful mirth,
A murmur, pent within the earth,
In the dead earth beneath the road

Rolled audibly ! it swept along,
A muffled noise — a rumbling sound ! —
'T was by a troop of miners made,
Plying with gunpowder their trade,
Some twenty fathoms under ground.

Small cause of dire effect ! for, surely,
If ever mortal, King or Cotter,
Believed that earth was charged to quake
And yawn for his unworthy sake,
'T was Peter Bell the Potter.

But, as an oak in breathless air
Will stand though to the centre hewn;
Or as the weakest things, if frost

Have stiffened them, maintain their post;
So he, beneath the gazing moon ! —

The Beast bestriding thus, he reached
A spot where, in a sheltering cove,
A little chapel stands alone,
With greenest ivy overgrown,
And tufted with an ivy grove;

Dying insensibly away
From human thoughts and purposes,
It seemed — wall, window, roof, and
    tower —
To bow to some transforming power,
And blend with the surrounding trees.

As ruinous a place it was,
Thought Peter, in the shire of Fife
That served my turn, when following still
From land to land a reckless will
I married my sixth wife !

The unheeding Ass moves slowly on,
And now is passing by an inn
Brim-full of a carousing crew,
That make, with curses not a few,
An uproar and a drunken din.

I cannot well express the thoughts
Which Peter in those noises found; —
A stifling power compressed his frame,
While-as a swimming darkness came
Over that dull and dreary sound.

For well did Peter know the sound;
The language of those drunken joys
To him, a jovial soul, I ween,
But a few hours ago, had been
A gladsome and a welcome noise.

Now, turned adrift into the past,
He finds no solace in his course;
Like planet-stricken men of yore,
He trembles, smitten to the core
By strong compunction and remorse.

But, more than all, his heart is stung
To think of one, almost a child;
A sweet and playful Highland girl,
As light and beauteous as a squirrel,
As beauteous and as wild !

Her dwelling was a lonely house,
A cottage in a heathy dell;
And she put on her gown of green,
And left her mother at sixteen,
And followed Peter Bell.

But many good and pious thoughts
Had she; and, in the kirk to pray,
Two long Scotch miles, through rain or
    snow
To kirk she had been used to go,
Twice every Sabbath-day.

And, when she followed Peter Bell,
It was to lead an honest life;
For he, with tongue not used to falter,
Had pledged his troth before the altar
To love her as his wedded wife.

A mother's hope is hers; — but soon
She drooped and pined like one forlorn;
From Scripture she a name did borrow;
Benoni, or the child of sorrow,
She called her babe unborn.

For she had learned how Peter lived,
And took it in most grievous part;
She to the very bone was worn,
And, ere that little child was born,
Died of a broken heart.

And now the Spirits of the Mind
Are busy with poor Peter Bell;
Upon the rights of visual sense
Usurping, with a prevalence
More terrible than magic spell.

Close by a brake of flowering furze
(Above it shivering aspens play)
He sees an unsubstantial creature,
His very self in form and feature,
Not four yards from the broad highway:

And stretched beneath the furze he sees
The Highland girl — it is no other;
And hears her crying as she cried,
The very moment that she died,
"My mother! oh my mother!"

The sweat pours down from Peter's face,
So grievous is his heart's contrition;
With agony his eye-balls ache
While he beholds by the furze-brake
This miserable vision!

Calm is the well-deserving brute,
His peace hath no offence betrayed;
But now, while down that slope he wends,
A voice to Peter's ear ascends,
Resounding from the woody glade:

The voice, though clamorous as a horn
Re-echoed by a naked rock,
Comes from that tabernacle — List!
Within, a fervent Methodist
Is preaching to no heedless flock!

" Repent! repent!" he cries aloud,
" While yet ye may find mercy; — strive
To love the Lord with all your might;
Turn to him, seek him day and night,
And save your souls alive!

" Repent! repent! though ye have gone,
Through paths of wickedness and woe,
After the Babylonian harlot;
And, though your sins be red as scarlet,
They shall be white as snow!"

Even as he passed the door, these words
Did plainly come to Peter's ears;
And they such joyful tidings were,
The joy was more than he could bear! —
He melted into tears.

Sweet tears of hope and tenderness!
And fast they fell, a plenteous shower!
His nerves, his sinews seemed to melt;
Through all his iron frame was felt
A gentle, a relaxing, power!

Each fibre of his frame was weak;
Weak all the animal\within;
But, in its helplessness, grew mild
And gentle as an infant child,
An infant that has known no sin.

'T is said, meek Beast! that, through
    Heaven's grace,
He not unmoved did notice now
The cross upon thy shoulder scored,
For lasting impress, by the Lord
To whom all human-kind shall bow;

Memorial of his touch — that day
When Jesus humbly deigned to ride,
Entering the proud Jerusalem.
By an immeasurable stream
Of shouting people deified!

Meanwhile the persevering Ass,
Turned towards a gate that hung in view
Across a shady lane; his chest
Against the yielding gate he pressed
And quietly passed through.

And up the stony lane he goes;
No ghost more softly ever trod;
Among the stones and pebbles, he
Sets down his hoofs inaudibly,
As if with felt his hoofs were shod.

Along the lane the trusty Ass
Went twice two hundred yards or more,
And no one could have guessed his aim, —
Till to a lonely house he came,
And stopped beside the door.

Thought Peter, 't is the poor man's home!
He listens — not a sound is heard
Save from the trickling household rill;
But, stepping o'er the cottage-sill,
Forthwith a little Girl appeared.

She to the Meeting-house was bound
In hopes some tidings there to gather:
No glimpse it is, no doubtful gleam;
She saw — and uttered with a scream,
"My father! here's my father!"

The very word was plainly heard,
Heard plainly by the wretched Mother —
Her joy was like a deep affright:
And forth she rushed into the light,
And saw it was another!

And, instantly, upon the earth,
Beneath the full moon shining bright,
Close to the Ass's feet she fell;
At the same moment Peter Bell
Dismounts in most unhappy plight.

As he beheld the Woman lie
Breathless and motionless, the mind
Of Peter sadly was confused;
But, though to such demands unused,
And helpless almost as the blind,

He raised her up; and, while he held
Her body propped against his knee,
The Woman waked — and when she spied
The poor Ass standing by her side,
She moaned most bitterly.

"Oh! God be praised — my heart's at
        ease —
For he is dead — I know it well!"
— At this she wept a bitter flood;
And, in the best way that he could,
His tale did Peter tell.

He trembles — he is pale as death;
His voice is weak with perturbation;
He turns aside his head, he pauses;
Poor Peter, from a thousand causes,
Is crippled sore in his narration.

At length she learned how he espied
The Ass in that small meadow-ground;
And that her Husband now lay dead,
Beside that luckless river's bed
In which he had been drowned.

A piercing look the Widow cast
Upon the Beast that near her stands;
She sees 't is he, that 't is the same;
She calls the poor Ass by his name,
And wrings, and wrings her hands.

"O wretched loss — untimely stroke!
If he had died upon his bed!
He knew not one forewarning pain;
He never will come home again —
Is dead, forever dead!"

Beside the woman Peter stands;
His heart is opening more and more;
A holy sense pervades his mind;
He feels what he for human kind
Had never felt before.

At length, by Peter's arm sustained,
The Woman rises from the ground —
"Oh, mercy! something must be done,
My little Rachel, you must run, —
Some willing neighbor must be found.

"Make haste — my little Rachel — do,
The first you meet with — bid him
        come,
Ask him to lend his horse to-night,
And this good Man, whom Heaven re-
        quite,
Will help to bring the body home."

Away goes Rachel weeping loud; —
An Infant, waked by her distress,
Makes in the house a piteous cry;
And Peter hears the Mother sigh,
"Seven are they, and all fatherless!"

And now is Peter taught to feel
That man's heart is a holy thing;
And Nature, through a world of death,
Breathes into him a second breath,
More searching than the breath of spring.

Upon a stone the Woman sits
In agony of silent grief —
From his own thoughts did Peter start;
He longs to press her to his heart,
From love that cannot find relief.

But roused, as if through every limb
Had passed a sudden shock of dread,
The Mother o'er the threshold flies,
And up the cottage stairs she hies,
And on the pillow lays her burning head.

And Peter turns his steps aside
Into a shade of darksome trees,
Where he sits down, he knows not how,
With his hands pressed against his brow,
His elbows on his tremulous knees.

There, self-involved, does Peter sit
Until no sign of life he makes,
As if his mind were sinking deep
Through years that have been long asleep
The trance is passed away — he wakes;

He lifts his head — and sees the Ass
Yet standing in the clear moonshine;
"When shall I be as good as thou?
Oh! would, poor beast, that I had now
A heart but half as good as thine!"

But *He* — who deviously hath sought
His Father through the lonesome woods,
Hath sought, proclaiming to the ear
Of night his grief and sorrowful fear —
He comes, escaped from fields and
    floods; —

With weary pace is drawing nigh;
He sees the Ass — and nothing living
Had ever such a fit of joy

As hath this little orphan Boy,
For he has no misgiving!

Forth to the gentle Ass he springs,
And up about his neck he climbs;
In loving words he talks to him,
He kisses, kisses face and limb, —
He kisses him a thousand times!

This Peter sees, while in the shade
He stood beside the cottage-door;
And Peter Bell, the ruffian wild,
Sobs loud, he sobs even like a child,
"O God! I can endure no more!"

— Here ends my Tale: for in a trice
Arrived a neighbor with his horse;
Peter went forth with him straightway;
And, with due care, ere break of day,
Together they brought back the Corse.

And many years did this poor Ass,
Whom once it was my luck to see
Cropping the shrubs of Leming-Lane,
Help by his labor to maintain
The Widow and her family.

And Peter Bell, who, till that night,
Had been the wildest of his clan,
Forsook his crimes, renounced his folly,
And, after ten months' melancholy,
Became a good and honest man.
1798.   1819.

THE SIMPLON PASS.[1]

                        — Brook and road
Were fellow-travellers in this gloomy
    Pass,
And with them did we journey several
    hours
At a slow step. The immeasurable
    height
Of woods decaying, never to be de-
    cayed,
The stationary blasts of waterfalls,
And in the narrow rent, at every turn,
Winds thwarting winds bewildered and
    forlorn,
The torrents shooting from the clear blue
    sky,

[1] See Prelude, book vi. p. 316.

The rocks that muttered close upon our
    ears,
Black drizzling crags that spake by the
    wayside
As if a voice were in them, the sick
    sight
And giddy prospect of the raving stream,
The unfettered clouds and region of the
    heavens,
Tumult and peace, the darkness and the
    light —
Were all like workings of one mind, the
    features
Of the same face, blossoms upon one
    tree,
Characters of the great Apocalypse,
The types and symbols of Eternity,
Of first, and last, and midst, and without
    end.
1799.   1845.

INFLUENCE OF NATURAL
OBJECTS

IN CALLING FORTH AND STRENGTHENING
THE IMAGINATION IN BOYHOOD AND
EARLY YOUTH.

WRITTEN IN GERMANY.[1]

This Extract is reprinted from "THE FRIEND."

WISDOM and Spirit of the universe!
Thou Soul, that art the Eternity of
    thought!
And giv'st to forms and images a breath
And everlasting motion! not in vain,
By day or star-light, thus from my first
    dawn
Of childhood didst thou intertwine for
    me
The passions that build up our human
    soul;
Not with the mean and vulgar works of
    Man;
But with high objects, with enduring
    things,
With life and nature; purifying thus
The elements of feeling and of thought,
And sanctifying by such discipline
Both pain and fear, — until we recog-
    nize
A grandeur in the beatings of the heart.

    [1] See Prelude, book i. p. 274.

Nor was this fellowship vouchsafed to
    me
With stinted kindness.   In November
    days,
When vapors rolling down the valleys
    made
A lonely scene more lonesome; among
    woods
At noon; and 'mid the calm of summer
    nights,
When, by the margin of the trembling
    lake,
Beneath the gloomy hills, homeward I
    went
In solitude, such intercourse was mine:
Mine was it in the fields both day and
    night,
And by the waters, all the summer long.
And in the frosty season, when the sun
Was set, and, visible for many a mile,
The cottage-windows through the twilight
    blazed,
I heeded not the summons: happy time
It was indeed for all of us; for me
It was a time of rapture!   Clear and loud
The village-clock tolled six — I wheeled
    about,
Proud and exulting like an untired horse
That cares not for his home. — All shod
    with steel
We hissed along the polished ice, in
    games
Confederate, imitative of the chase
And woodland pleasures, — the resound-
    ing horn,
The pack loud-chiming, and the hunted
    hare.
So through the darkness and the cold we
    flew,
And not a voice was idle: with the din
Smitten, the precipices rang aloud;
The leafless trees and every icy crag
Tinkled like iron; while far-distant hills
Into the tumult sent an alien sound
Of melancholy, not unnoticed while the
    stars,
Eastward, were sparkling clear, and in
    the west
The orange sky of evening died away.
    Not seldom from the uproar I retired
Into a silent bay, or sportively
Glanced sideway, leaving the tumultuous
    throng,

To cut across the reflex of a star;
Image, that, flying still before me,
    gleamed
Upon the glassy plain: and oftentimes,
When we had given our bodies to the
    wind,
And all the shadowy banks on either side
Came sweeping through the darkness,
    spinning still
The rapid line of motion, then at once
Have I, reclining back upon my heels,
Stopped short; yet still the solitary cliffs
Wheeled by me — even as if the earth
    had rolled
With visible motion her diurnal round!
Behind me did they stretch in solemn
    train,
Feebler and feebler, and I stood and
    watched
Till all was tranquil as a summer sea.

1799.   1809.

THERE WAS A BOY.

Written in Germany. This is an extract from
the poem on my own poetical education. This
practice of making an instrument of their own
fingers is known to most boys, though some are
more skilful at it than others. William Raincock
of Rayrigg, a fine spirited lad, took the lead of all
my schoolfellows in this art.

THERE was a Boy; ye knew him well,
    ye cliffs
And islands of Winander! — many a time,
At evening, when the earliest stars began
To move along the edges of the hills,
Rising or setting, would he stand alone,
Beneath the trees, or by the glimmering
    lake;
And there, with fingers interwoven, both
    hands
Pressed closely palm to palm and to his
    mouth
Uplifted, he, as through an instrument,
Blew mimic hootings to the silent owls,
That they might answer him. — And they
    would shout
Across the watery vale, and shout again,
Responsive to his call, — with quivering
    peals,
And loud halloos, and screams, and
    echoes loud

Redoubled and redoubled; concourse
    wild
Of jocund din! And, when there came a
    pause
Of silence such as baffled his best skill:
Then, sometimes, in that silence, while
    he hung
Listening, a gentle shock of mild surprise
Has carried far into his heart the voice
Of mountain-torrents; or the visible
    scene
Would enter unawares into his mind
With all its solemn imagery, its rocks,
Its woods, and that uncertain heaven
    received
Into the bosom of the steady lake.
    This boy was taken from his mates, and
    died
In childhood, ere he was full twelve years
    old.
Pre-eminent in beauty is the vale
Where he was born and bred: the church-
    yard hangs
Upon a slope above the village-school;
And, through that church-yard when my
    way has led
On summer-evenings, I believe, that there
A long half-hour together I have stood
Mute — looking at the grave in which he
    lies!

1799.   1800.

NUTTING.

Written in Germany; intended as part of a
poem on my own life, but struck out as not being
wanted there. Like most of my schoolfellows I
was an impassioned nutter. For this pleasure,
the vale of Esthwaite, abounding in coppice-wood,
furnished a very wide range. These verses arose
out of the remembrance of feelings I had often had
when a boy, and particularly in the extensive
woods that still stretch from the side of Esthwaite
Lake towards Graythwaite, the seat of the ancient
family of Sandys.

             IT seems a day
(I speak of one from many singled out)
One of those heavenly days that cannot
    die;
When, in the eagerness of boyish hope,
I left our cottage-threshold, sallying forth
With a huge wallet o'er my shoulders
    slung,

·A nutting-crook in hand; and turned my
 steps
Tow'rd some far-distant wood, a Figure
 quaint,
Tricked out in proud disguise of cast-off
 weeds
Which for that service had been hus-
 banded,
By exhortation of my frugal Dame —
Motley accoutrement, of power to smile
At thorns, and brakes, and brambles, —
 and, in truth,
More ragged than need was !   O'er path-
 less rocks,
Through beds of matted fern, and tangled
 thickets,
Forcing my way, I came to one dear nook
Unvisited, where not a broken bough
Drooped with its withered leaves, un-
 gracious sign
Of devastation; but the hazels rose
Tall and erect, with tempting clusters
 hung,
A virgin scene ! — A little while I stood,
Breathing with such suppression of the
 heart
As joy delights in; and, with wise re-
 straint
Voluptuous, fearless of a rival, eyed
The banquet; — or beneath the trees I
 sate
Among the flowers, and with the flowers
 I played;
A temper known to those, who, after long
And weary expectation, have been blest
With sudden happiness beyond all hope.
Perhaps it was a bower beneath whose
 leaves
The violets of five seasons re-appear
And fade, unseen by any human eye;
Where fairy water-breaks do murmur on
Forever; and I saw the sparkling foam,
And — with my cheek on one of those
 green stones
That, fleeced with moss, under the shady
 trees,
Lay round me, scattered like a flock of
 sheep —
I heard the murmur and the murmuring
 sound,
In that sweet mood when pleasure loves
 to pay
Tribute to ease; and, of its joy secure,

The heart luxuriates with indifferent
 things,
Wasting its kindliness on stocks and
 stones,
And on the vacant air.   Then up I rose,
And dragged to earth both branch and
 ·   bough, with crash
And merciless ravage : and the shady nook
Of hazels, and the green and mossy bower,
Deformed and sullied, patiently gave up
Their quiet being : and, unless I now
Confound my present feelings with the
 past;
Ere from the mutilated bower I turned
Exulting, rich beyond the wealth of kings,
I felt a sense of pain when I beheld
The silent trees, and saw the intruding
 sky —
Then, dearest Maiden, move along these
 shades
In gentleness of heart; with gentle hand
Touch — for there is a spirit in the woods.
1799.   1800.

The next three poems were written in
 Germany.

STRANGE fits of passion have I known:
And I will dare to tell,   .
But in the Lover's ear alone,
What once to me befell.

When she I loved looked every day
Fresh as a rose in June,
I to her cottage bent my way,
Beneath an evening-moon.

Upon the moon I fixed my eye,
All over the wide lea;
With quickening pace my horse drew nigh
Those paths so dear to me.

And now we reached the orchard-plot;
And, as we climbed the hill,
The sinking moon to Lucy's cot
Came near, and nearer still.

In one of those sweet dreams I slept,
Kind Nature's gentlest boon !
And all the while my eyes I kept
On the descending moon.

My horse moved on; hoof after hoof
He raised, and never stopped:
When down behind the cottage roof,
At once, the bright moon dropped.

What fond and wayward thoughts will
    slide
Into a Lover's head!
"O mercy!" to myself I cried,
"If Lucy should be dead!"
1799.   1800.

SHE dwelt among the untrodden ways
  Beside the springs of Dove,
A Maid whom there were none to praise
  And very few to love:

A violet by a mossy stone
  Half hidden from the eye!
— Fair as a star, when only one
  Is shining in the sky.

She lived unknown, and few could know
  When Lucy ceased to be;
But she is in her grave, and, oh,
  The difference to me!
1799.   1800.

I TRAVELLED among unknown men,
  In lands beyond the sea;
Nor, England! did I know till then
  What love I bore to thee.

'T is past, that melancholy dream!
  Nor will I quit thy shore
A second time; for still I seem
  To love thee more and more.

Among thy mountains did I feel
  The joy of my desire;
And she I cherished turned her wheel
  Beside an English fire.

Thy mornings showed, thy nights con-
    cealed
  The bowers where Lucy played;
And thine too is the last green field
  That Lucy's eyes surveyed.
1799.   1807.

Composed in the Hartz Forest.

THREE years she grew in sun and shower,
Then Nature said, "A lovelier flower
On earth was never sown;
This Child I to myself will take;
She shall be mine, and I will make
A Lady of my own.

"Myself will to my darling be
Both law and impulse: and with me
The Girl, in rock and plain,
In earth and heaven, in glade and bower,
Shall feel an overseeing power
To kindle or restrain.

"She shall be sportive as the fawn
That wild with glee across the lawn,
Or up the mountain springs;
And hers shall be the breathing balm,
And hers the silence and the calm
Of mute insensate things.

"The floating clouds their state shall lend
To her; for her the willow bend;
Nor shall she fail to see
Even in the motions of the Storm
Grace that shall mould the Maiden's form
By silent sympathy.

"The stars of midnight shall be dear
To her; and she shall lean her ear
In many a secret place
Where rivulets dance their wayward
    round,
And beauty born of murmuring sound
Shall pass into her face.

"And vital feelings of delight
Shall rear her form to stately height,
Her virgin bosom swell;
Such thoughts to Lucy I will give
While she and I together live
Here in this happy dell."

Thus Nature spake — The work was
    done —
How soon my Lucy's race was run!
She died, and left to me
This heath, this calm, and quiet scene;
The memory of what has been,
And nevermore will be.
1799.   1800.

Written in Germany.

A SLUMBER did my spirit seal;
  I had no human fears:
She seemed a thing that could not feel
  The touch of earthly years.

No motion has she now, no force;
  She neither hears nor sees;
Rolled round in earth's diurnal course,
  With rocks, and stones, and trees.
1799.   1800.

A POET'S EPITAPH

ART thou a Statist in the van
  Of public conflicts trained and bred?
— First learn to love one living man;
Then may'st thou think upon the dead.

A Lawyer art thou? — draw not nigh!
Go, carry to some fitter place
The keenness of that practised eye,
The hardness of that sallow face.

Art thou a Man of purple cheer?
A rosy Man, right plump to see?
Approach; yet, Doctor, not too near,
This grave no cushion is for thee.

Or art thou one of gallant pride,
A Soldier and no man of chaff?
Welcome! — but lay thy sword aside,
And lean upon a peasant's staff.

Physician art thou? one, all eyes,
Philosopher! a fingering slave,
One that would peep and botanize
Upon his mother's grave?

Wrapt closely in thy sensual fleece,
O turn aside, — and take, I pray,
That he below may rest in peace,
Thy ever-dwindling soul, away!

A Moralist perchance appears;
Led, Heaven knows how! to this poor
        sod:
And he has neither eyes nor ears;
Himself his world, and his own God;

One to whose smooth-rubbed soul can
        cling
Nor form, nor feeling, great or small;
A reasoning, self-sufficing thing,
An intellectual All-in-all!

Shut close the door; press down the
        latch;
Sleep in thy intellectual crust;
Nor lose ten tickings of thy watch
Near this unprofitable dust.

But who is He, with modest looks,
And clad in homely russet brown?
He murmurs near the running brooks
A music sweeter than their own.

He is retired as noontide dew,
Or fountain in a noon-day grove;
And you must love him, ere to you
He will seem worthy of your love.

The outward shows of sky and earth,
Of hill and valley, he has viewed;
And impulses of deeper birth
Have come to him in solitude.

In common things that round us lie
Some random truths he can impart, —
The harvest of a quiet eye
That broods and sleeps on his own heart.

But he is weak; both Man and Boy,
Hath been an idler in the land;
Contented if he might enjoy the things
The things which others understand.

— Come hither in thy hour of strength;
Come, weak as is a breaking wave!
Here stretch thy body at full length;
Or build thy house upon this grave.
1799.   1800.

ADDRESS TO THE SCHOLARS OF
THE VILLAGE SCHOOL OF ——

Composed at Goslar, in Germany.

I COME, ye little noisy Crew,
Not long your pastime to prevent;
I heard the blessing which to you
Our common Friend and Father sent.
I kissed his cheek before he died;

And when his breath was fled,
I raised, while kneeling by his side,
His hand: — it dropped like lead.
Your hands, dear Little-ones, do all
That can be done, will never fall
Like his till they are dead.
By night or day blow foul or fair,
Ne'er will the best of all your train
Play with the locks of his white hair,
Or stand between his knees again.

   Here did he sit confined for hours;
But he could see the woods and plains,
Could hear the wind and mark the showers
Come streaming down the streaming
    panes.
Now stretched beneath his grass-green
    mound
He rests a prisoner of the ground.
He loved the breathing air,
He loved the sun, but if it rise
Or set, to him where now he lies,
Brings not a moment's care.
Alas! what idle words; but take
The Dirge which for our Master's sake
And yours, love prompted me to make.
The rhymes so homely in attire
With learned ears may ill agree,
But chanted by your Orphan Choir
Will make a touching melody.

DIRGE.

Mourn, Shepherd, near thy old gray stone;
Thou Angler, by the silent flood;
And mourn when thou art all alone,
Thou Woodman, in the distant wood!

Thou one blind Sailor, rich in joy
Though blind, thy tunes in sadness hum;
And mourn, thou poor half-witted Boy!
Born deaf, and living deaf and dumb.

Thou drooping sick Man, bless the Guide
Who checked or turned thy headstrong
    youth,
As he before had sanctified
Thy infancy with heavenly truth.

Ye Striplings, light of heart and gay,
Bold settlers on some foreign shore,
Give, when your thoughts are turned this
    way,
A sigh to him whom we deplore.

For us who here in funeral strain
With one accord our voices raise,
Let sorrow overcharged with pain
Be lost in thankfulness and praise.

And when our hearts shall feel a sting
From ill we meet or good we miss,
May touches of his memory bring
Fond healing, like a mother's kiss.
   1799.   1845.

BY THE SIDE OF THE GRAVE SOME YEARS AFTER.

Long time his pulse hath ceased to beat
But benefits, his gift, we trace —
Expressed in every eye we meet
Round this dear Vale, his native place.

To stately Hall and Cottage rude
Flowed from his life what still they hold,
Light pleasures, every day, renewed;
And blessings half a century old.

Oh true of heart, of spirit gay,
Thy faults, where not already gone
From memory, prolong their stay
For charity's sweet sake alone.

Such solace find we for our loss;
And what beyond this thought we crave
Comes in the promise from the Cross,
Shining upon thy happy grave.

MATTHEW.

   In the School of —— is a tablet, on which are
inscribed, in gilt letters, the Names of the several
persons who have been Schoolmasters there since
the foundation of the School, with the time at
which they entered upon and quitted their office.
Opposite to one of those names the Author wrote
the following lines.

   Such a Tablet as is here spoken of continued to
be preserved in Hawkshead School, though the
inscriptions were not brought down to our time.
This and other poems connected with Matthew
would not gain by a literal detail of facts. Like
the Wanderer in "The Excursion," this School-
master was made up of several both of his class
and men of other occupations. I do not ask
pardon for what there is of untruth in such verses,
considered strictly as matters of fact. It is enough

if, being true and consistent in spirit, they move and teach in a manner not unworthy of a Poêt's calling.

IF Nature, for a favorite child,
In thee hath tempered so her clay,
That every hour thy heart runs wild,
Yet never once doth go astray,

Read o'er these lines; and then review
This tablet, that thus humbly rears
In such diversity of hue
Its history of two hundred years.

— When through this little wreck of fame,
Cipher and syllable! thine eye
Has travelled down to Matthew's name,
Pause with no common sympathy.

And, if a sleeping tear should wake,
Then be it neither checked nor stayed:
For Matthew a request I make
Which for himself he had not made.

Poor Matthew, all his frolics o'er,
Is silent as a standing pool;
Far from the chimney's merry roar,
And murmur of the village school.

The sighs which Matthew heaved were sighs
Of one tired out with fun and madness;
The tears which came to Matthew's eyes
Were tears of light, the dew of gladness.

Yet, sometimes, when the secret cup
Of still and serious thought went round,
It seemed as if he drank it up —
He felt with spirit so profound.

— Thou soul of God's best earthly mould!
Thou happy Soul! and can it be
That these two words of glittering gold
Are all that must remain of thee?
1799.   1800.

THE TWO APRIL MORNINGS.

WE walked along, while bright and red
Uprose the morning sun;
And Matthew stopped, he looked, and said,
"The will of God be done!"

A village schoolmaster was he,
With hair of glittering gray;
As blithe a man as you could see
On a spring holiday.

And on that morning, through the grass,
And by the steaming rills,
We travelled merrily, to pass
A day among the hills.

"Our work," said I, "was well begun;
Then, from thy breast what thought,
Beneath so beautiful a sun,
So sad a sigh has brought?"

A second time did Matthew stop;
And fixing still his eye
Upon the eastern mountain-top,
To me he made reply:

"Yon cloud with that long purple cleft
Brings fresh into my mind
A day like this which I have left
Full thirty years behind.

"And just above yon slope of corn
Such colors, and no other,
Were in the sky, that April morn,
Of this the very brother.

"With rod and line I sued the sport
Which that sweet season gave,
And, to the church-yard come, stopped short
Beside my daughter's grave.

"Nine summers had she scarcely seen,
The pride of all the vale;
And then she sang;— she would have been
A very nightingale.

"Six feet in earth my Emma lay;
And yet I loved her more,
For so it seemed, than till that day
I e'er had loved before.

"And, turning from her grave, I met,
Beside the church-yard yew,
A blooming Girl, whose hair was wet
With points of morning dew.

"A basket on her head she bare;
Her brow was smooth and white:
To see a child so very fair,
It was a pure delight!

"No fountain from its rocky cave
E'er tripped with foot so free;
She seemed as happy as a wave
That dances on the sea.

"There came from me a sigh of pain
Which I could ill confine;
I looked at her, and looked again:
And did not wish her mine!"

Matthew is in his grave, yet now,
Methinks, I see him stand,
As at that moment, with a bough
Of wilding in his hand.
1799.   1800.

THE FOUNTAIN.

A CONVERSATION.

WE talked with open heart, and tongue
Affectionate and true,
A pair of friends, though I was young,
And Matthew seventy-two.

We lay beneath a spreading oak,
Beside a mossy seat;
And from the turf a fountain broke,
And gurgled at our feet.

"Now, Matthew!" said I, "let us match
This water's pleasant tune
With some old border-song, or catch
That suits a summer's noon;

"Or of the church-clock and the chimes
Sing here beneath the shade,
That half-mad thing of witty rhymes
Which you last April made!"

In silence Matthew lay, and eyed
The spring beneath the tree;
And thus the dear old Man replied,
The gray-haired man of glee:

"No check, no stay, this Streamlet fears;
How merrily it goes!
'T will murmur on a thousand years,
And flow as now it flows.

"And here, on this delightful day,
I cannot choose but think
How oft, a vigorous man, I lay
Beside this fountain's brink.

"My eyes are dim with childish tears,
My heart is idly stirred,
For the same sound is in my ears
Which in those days I heard.

"Thus fares it still in our decay:
And yet the wiser mind
Mourns less for what age takes away
Than what it leaves behind.

"The blackbird amid leafy trees,
The lark above the hill,
Let loose their carols when they please,
Are quiet when they will.

"With Nature never do *they* wage
A foolish strife; they see
A happy youth, and their old age
Is beautiful and free:

"But we are pressed by heavy laws;
And often, glad no more,
We wear a face of joy, because
We have been glad of yore.

"If there be one who need bemoan
His kindred laid in earth,
The household hearts that were his own;
It is the man of mirth.

"My days, my Friend, are almost gone,
My life has been approved,
And many love me; but by none
Am I enough beloved."

"Now both himself and me he wrongs,
The man who thus complains;
I live and sing my idle songs
Upon these happy plains;

"And, Matthew, for thy children dead
I'll be a son to thee!"
At this he grasped my hand, and said,
"Alas! that cannot be."

We rose up from the fountain-side;
And down the smooth descent
Of the green sheep-track did we glide;
And through the wood we went;

And, ere we came to Leonard's rock,
He sang those witty rhymes
About the crazy old church-clock,
And the bewildered chimes.
1799. 1800.

TO A SEXTON.

Written in Germany.

LET thy wheel-barrow alone —
Wherefore, Sexton, piling still
In thy bone-house bone on bone?
'T is already like a hill
In a field of battle made,
Where three thousand skulls are laid;
These died in peace each with the other,—
Father, sister, friend, and brother.

Mark the spot to which I point!
From this platform, eight feet square,
Take not even a finger-joint:
Andrew's whole fire-side is there.
Here, alone, before thine eyes,
Simon's sickly daughter lies,
From weakness now, and pain defended,
Whom he twenty winters tended.

Look but at the gardener's pride —
How he glories, when he sees
Roses, lilies, side by side,
Violets in families!
By the heart of Man, his tears,
By his hopes and by his fears,
Thou, too heedless, art the Warden •
Of a far superior garden.

Thus then, each to other dear,
Let them all in quiet lie,
Andrew there, and Susan here,
Neighbors in mortality.
And, should I live through sun and rain
Seven widowed years without my Jane,
O Sexton, do not then remove her,
Let one grave hold the Loved and Lover!
1799. 1800.

THE DANISH BOY.

A FRAGMENT.

Written in Germany. It was entirely a fancy;
but intended as a prelude to a ballad-poem never
written.

I.

BETWEEN two sister moorland rills
There is a spot that seems to lie
Sacred to flowerets of the hills,
And sacred to the sky.
And in this smooth and open dell
There is a tempest-stricken tree;
A corner-stone by lightning cut,
The last stone of a lonely hut;
And in this dell you see
A thing no storm can e'er destroy,
The shadow of a Danish Boy.

II.

In clouds above, the lark is heard,
But drops not here to earth for rest;
Within this lonesome nook the bird
Did never build her nest.
No beast, no bird hath here his home;
Bees, wafted on the breezy air,
Pass high above those fragrant bells
To other flowers: — to other dells
Their burthens do they bear;
The Danish Boy walks here alone:
The lovely dell is all his own.

III.

A Spirit of noon-day is he;
Yet seems a form of flesh and blood;
Nor piping shepherd shall he be,
Nor herd-boy of the wood.
A regal vest of fur he wears,
In color like a raven's wing;
It fears not rain, nor wind, nor dew;
But in the storm 't is fresh and blue
As budding pines in spring;
His helmet has a vernal grace,
Fresh as the bloom upon his face.

IV.

A harp is from his shoulder slung;
Resting the harp upon his knee,
To words of a forgotten tongue
He suits its melody.
Of flocks upon the neighboring hill
He is the darling and the joy;
And often, when no cause appears,
The mountain-ponies prick their ears,
—They hear the Danish Boy,
While in the dell he sings alone
Beside the tree and corner-stone.

V.

There sits he; in his face you spy
No trace of a ferocious air,
Nor ever was a cloudless sky
So steady or so fair.
The lovely Danish Boy is blest

And happy in his flowery cove:
From bloody deeds his thoughts are far;
And yet he warbles songs of love,
That seem like songs of war,
For calm and gentle is his mien;
Like a dead Boy he is serene.

1799.   1800.

LUCY GRAY

OR, SOLITUDE.

Written at Goslar, in Germany. It was founded
on a circumstance told me by my Sister, of a little
girl who, not far from Halifax, in Yorkshire, was
bewildered in a snow-storm. Her footsteps were
traced by her parents to the middle of the lock of
a canal, and no other vestige of her, backward or
forward, could be traced. The body, however,
was found in the canal. The way in which the
incident was treated, and the spiritualizing of the
character might furnish hints for contrasting the
imaginative influences which I have endeavored
to throw over common life with Crabbe's matter-
of-fact style of treating subjects of the same kind.
This is not spoken to his disparagement, far from
it, but to direct the attention of thoughtful readers,
into whose hands these notes may fall, to a com-
parison that may both enlarge the circle of their
sensibilities, and tend to produce in them a catholic
judgment.

OFT I had heard of Lucy Gray:
And, when I crossed the wild,
I chanced to see at break of day
The solitary child.

No mate, no comrade Lucy knew;
She dwelt on a wide moor,
— The sweetest thing that ever grew
Beside a human door!

You yet may spy the fawn at play,
The hare upon the green;
But the sweet face of Lucy Gray
Will never more be seen.

" To-night will be a stormy night —
You to the town must go;
And take a lantern, Child, to light
Your mother through the snow."

" That, Father! will I gladly do:
'T is scarcely afternoon —
The minster-clock has just struck two,
And yonder is the moon!"

At this the Father raised his hook,
And snapped a fagot-band;
He plied his work; — and Lucy took
The lantern in her hand.

Not blither is the mountain roe:
With many a wanton stroke
Her feet disperse the powdery snow,
That rises up like smoke.

The storm came on before its time:
She wandered up and down;
And many a hill did Lucy climb:
But never reached the town.

The wretched parents all that night
Went shouting far and wide;
But there was neither sound nor sight
To serve them for a guide.

At day-break on a hill they stood
That overlooked the moor;
And thence they saw the bridge of wood,
A furlong from their door.

They wept — and, turning homeward,
          cried,
" In Heaven we all shall meet; "
— When in the snow the mother spied
The print of Lucy's feet.

Then downwards from the steep hill's
          edge
They tracked the footmarks small;
And through the broken hawthorn hedge,
And by the long stone-wall;

And then an open field they crossed:
The marks were still the same;
They tracked them on, nor ever lost;
And to the bridge they came.

They followed from the snowy bank
Those footmarks, one by one,
Into the middle of the plank;
And further there were none!

— Yet some maintain that to this day
She is a living child;
That you may see sweet Lucy Gray
Upon the lonesome wild.

O'er rough and smooth she trips along,
And never looks behind;
And sings a solitary song
That whistles in the wind.

   1799.   1800.

RUTH.

Written in Germany. Suggested by an account
    I had of a wanderer in Somersetshire.

WHEN Ruth was left half desolate,
Her Father took another Mate;
And Ruth, not seven years old,
A slighted child, at her own will
Went wandering over dale and hill,
In thoughtless freedom, bold.

And she had made a pipe of straw,
And music from that pipe could draw
Like sounds of winds and floods;
Had built a bower upon the green,
As if she from her birth had been
An infant of the woods.

Beneath her father's roof, alone
She seemed to live; her thoughts her own;
Herself her own delight;
Pleased with herself, nor sad, nor gay;
And, passing thus the live-long day,
She grew to woman's height.

There came a Youth from Georgia's
     shore —
A military casque he wore,
With splendid feathers drest;
He brought them from the Cherokees;
The feathers nodded in the breeze,
And made a gallant crest.

From Indian blood you deem him sprung:
But no! he spake the English tongue,
And bore a soldier's name;
And, when America was free
From battle and from jeopardy,
He 'cross the ocean came.

With hues of genius on his cheek
In finest tones the Youth could speak:
— While he was yet a boy,
The moon, the glory of the sun,
And streams that murmur as they run,
Had been his dearest joy.

He was a lovely Youth! I guess
The panther in the wilderness
Was not so fair as he;
And, when he chose to sport and play,
No dolphin ever was so gay
Upon the tropic sea.

Among the Indians he had fought,
And with him many tales he brought
Of pleasure and of fear;
Such tales as told to any maid
By such a Youth, in the green shade,
Were perilous to hear.

He told of girls — a happy rout!
Who quit their fold with dance and shout,
Their pleasant Indian town,
To gather strawberries all day long;
Returning with a choral song
When daylight is gone down.

He spake of plants that hourly change
Their blossoms, through a boundless range
Of intermingling hues;
With budding, fading, faded flowers
They stand the wonder of the bowers
From morn to evening dews.

He told of the magnolia, spread
High as a cloud, high over head!
The cypress and her spire;
— Of flowers that with one scarlet gleam
Cover a hundred leagues, and seem
To set the hills on fire.

The Youth of green savannahs spake,
And many an endless, endless lake,
With all its fairy crowds
Of islands, that together lie
As quietly as spots of sky
Among the evening clouds.

" How pleasant," then he said, " it were
A fisher or a hunter there,
In sunshine or in shade
To wander with an easy mind;
And build a household fire, and find
A home in every glade!

" What days and what bright years! Ah
     me!
Our life were life indeed, with thee
So passed in quiet bliss,

And all the while," said he, "to know
That we were in a world of woe,
On such an earth as this!"

And then he sometimes interwove
Fond thoughts about a father's love;
"For there," said he, "are spun
Around the heart such tender ties,
That our own children to our eyes
Are dearer than the sun.

"Sweet Ruth! and could you go with me
My helpmate in the woods to be,
Our shed at night to rear;
Or run, my own adopted bride,
A sylvan huntress at my side,
And drive the flying deer!

"Beloved Ruth!" — No more he said.
The wakeful Ruth at midnight shed
A solitary tear:
She thought again — and did agree
With him to sail across the sea,
And drive the flying deer.

"And now, as fitting is and right,
We in the church our faith will plight,
A husband and a wife."
Even so they did; and I may say
That to sweet Ruth that happy day
Was more than human life.

Through dream and vision did she sink,
Delighted all the while to think
That on those lonesome floods,
And green savannahs, she should share
His board with lawful joy, and bear
His name in the wild woods.

But, as you have before been told,
This Stripling, sportive, gay, and bold,
And, with his dancing crest,
So beautiful, through savage lands
Had roamed about, with vagrant bands
Of Indians in the West.

The wind, the tempest roaring high,
The tumult of a tropic sky,
Might well be dangerous food
For him, a Youth to whom was given
So much of earth — so much of heaven,
And such impetuous blood.

Whatever in those climes he found
Irregular in sight or sound
Did to his mind impart
A kindred impulse, seemed allied
To his own powers, and justified
The workings of his heart.

Nor less, to feed voluptuous thought,
The beauteous forms of nature wrought,
Fair trees and gorgeous flowers;
The breezes their own languor lent;
The stars had feelings, which they sent
Into those favored bowers.

Yet, in his worst pursuits, I ween
That sometimes there did intervene
Pure hopes of high intent:
For passions linked to forms so fair
And stately, needs must have their share
Of noble sentiment.

But ill he lived, much evil saw,
With men to whom no better law
Nor better life was known;
Deliberately, and undeceived,
Those wild men's vices he received,
And gave them back his own.

His genius and his moral frame
Were thus impaired, and he became
The slave of low desires:
A Man who without self-control
Would seek what the degraded soul
Unworthily admires.

And yet he with no feigned delight
Had wooed the Maiden, day and night
Had loved her, night and morn:
What could he less than love a Maid
Whose heart with so much nature played?
So kind and so forlorn!

Sometimes, most earnestly, he said,
"O Ruth! I have been worse than dead;
False thoughts, thoughts bold and vain,
Encompassed me on every side
When I, in confidence and pride,
Had crossed the Atlantic main.

"Before me shone a glorious world —
Fresh as a banner bright, unfurled
To music suddenly:
I looked upon those hills and plains,

And seemed as if let loose from chains,
To live at liberty.

"No more of this; for now, by thee,
Dear Ruth! more happily set free
With nobler zeal I burn;
My soul from darkness is released,
Like the whole sky when to the east
The morning doth return."

Full soon that better mind was gone;
No hope, no wish remained, not one, —
They stirred him now no more;
New objects did new pleasure give,
And once again he wished to live
As lawless as before.

Meanwhile, as thus with him it fared,
They for the voyage were prepared,
And went to the seashore;
But, when they thither came, the Youth
Deserted his poor Bride, and Ruth
Could never find him more.

God help thee, Ruth! — Such pains she
        had,
That she in half a year was mad,
And in a prison housed;
And there, with many a doleful song
Made of wild words, her cup of wrong
She fearfully caroused.

Yet sometimes milder hours she knew,
Nor wanted sun, nor rain, nor dew,
Nor pastimes of the May;
— They all were with her in her cell;
And a clear brook with cheerful knell
Did o'er the pebbles play.

When Ruth three seasons thus had lain,
There came a respite to her pain;
She from her prison fled;
But of the Vagrant none took thought;
And where it liked her best she sought
Her shelter and her bread.

Among the fields she breathed again:
The master-current of her brain
Ran permanent and free;
And, coming to the Banks of Tone,
There did she rest; and dwell alone
Under the greenwood tree.

The engines of her pain, the tools
That shaped her sorrow, rocks and pools,
And airs that gently stir
The vernal leaves — she loved them still;
Nor ever taxed them with the ill
Which had been done to her.

A Barn her *winter* bed supplies;
But, till the warmth of summer skies
And summer days is gone,
(And all do in this tale agree)
She sleeps beneath the greenwood tree,
And other home hath none.

An innocent life, yet far astray!
And Ruth will, long before her day,
Be broken down and old:
Sore aches she needs must have! but less
Of mind, than body's wretchedness,
From damp, and rain, and cold.

If she is prest by want of food,
She from her dwelling in the wood
Repairs to a roadside;
And there she begs at one steep place
Where up and down with easy pace
The horsemen-travellers ride.

That oaten pipe of hers is mute,
Or thrown away; but with a flute
Her loneliness she cheers:
This flute, made of a hemlock stalk,
At evening in his homeward walk
The Quantock woodman hears.

I, too, have passed her on the hills
Setting her little water-mills
By spouts and fountains wild —
Such small machinery as she turned
Ere she had wept, ere she had mourned,
A young and happy Child!

Farewell! and when thy days are told,
Ill-fated Ruth, in hallowed mould
Thy corpse shall buried be,
For thee a funeral bell shall ring,
And all the congregation sing
A Christian psalm for thee.

1799.   1800.

WRITTEN IN GERMANY

ON ONE OF THE COLDEST DAYS OF THE CENTURY.

A bitter winter it was when these verses were composed by the side of my Sister, in our lodgings at a draper's house in the romantic imperial town of Goslar, on the edge of the Hartz Forest. In this town the German emperors of the Franconian line were accustomed to keep their court, and it retains vestiges of ancient splendor. So severe was the cold of this winter, that when we passed out of the parlor warmed by the stove, our cheeks were struck by the air as by cold iron. I slept in a room over a passage which was not ceiled. The people of the house used to say, rather unfeelingly, that they expected I should be frozen to death some night; but, with the protection of a pelisse lined with fur, and a dog's-skin bonnet, such as was worn by the peasants, I walked daily on the ramparts, or in a sort of public ground or gardens in which was a pond. Here, I had no companion but a kingfisher, a beautiful creature, that used to glance by me. I consequently became much attached to it. During these walks I composed the poem that follows.

The Reader must be apprised, that the Stoves in North-Germany generally have the impression of a galloping horse upon them, this being part of the Brunswick Arms.

A PLAGUE on your languages, German
   and Norse!
Let me have the song of the kettle;
And the tongs and the poker, instead of
   that horse
That gallops away with such fury and force
On this dreary dull plate of black metal.

See that Fly, — a disconsolate creature!
   perhaps
A child of the field or the grove;
And, sorrow for him! the dull treacherous
   heat
Has seduced the poor fool from his winter
   retreat,
And he creeps to the edge of my stove.

Alas! how he fumbles about the domains
Which this comfortless oven environ!
He cannot find out in what track he must
   crawl,
Now back to the tiles, then in search of
   the wall,
And now on the brink of the iron.

Stock-still there he stands like a traveller
   bemazed:
The best of his skill he has tried;
His feelers, methinks, I can see him put
   forth
To the east and the west, to the south and
   the north;
But he finds neither guide-post nor guide.

His spindles sink under him, foot, leg,
   and thigh!
His eyesight and hearing are lost;
Between life and death his blood freezes
   and thaws;
And his two pretty pinions of blue dusky
   gauze
Are glued to his sides by the frost.

No brother, no mate has he near him —
   while I
Can draw warmth from the cheek of my
   Love;
As blest and as glad, in this desolate
   gloom,
As if green summer grass were the floor
   of my room,
And woodbines were hanging above.

Yet, God is my witness, thou small help-
   less Thing!
Thy life I would gladly sustain
Till summer come up from the south, and
   with crowds
Of thy brethren a march thou should'st
   sound through the clouds,
And back to the forests again!
1799.   1800.

THE BROTHERS.

This poem was composed in a grove at the north-eastern end of Grasmere lake, which grove was in a great measure destroyed by turning the high-road along the side of the water. The few trees that are left were spared at my intercession. The poem arose out of the fact, mentioned to me at Ennerdale, that a shepherd had fallen asleep upon the top of the rock called The Pillar, and perished as here described, his staff being left midway on the rock.

"THESE Tourists, heaven preserve us!
   needs must live
A profitable life: some glance along,

Rapid and gay, as if the earth were air,
And they were butterflies to wheel about
Long as the summer lasted: some, as
  wise,
Perched on the forehead of a jutting crag,
Pencil in hand and book upon the knee,
Will look and scribble, scribble on and
  look,
Until a man might travel twelve stout
  miles,
Or reap an acre of his neighbor's corn.
But, for that moping Son of Idleness,
Why can he tarry *yonder?* — In our
  churchyard
Is neither epitaph nor monument,
Tombstone nor name — only the turf we
  tread
And a few natural graves."
                          To Jane, his wife,
Thus spake the homely Priest of Enner-
  dale.
It was a July evening; and he sate
Upon the long stone-seat beneath the
  eaves
Of his old cottage, — as it chanced, that
  day,
Employed in winter's work.   Upon the
  stone
His wife sate near him, teasing matted
  wool,
While, from the twin cards toothed with
  glittering wire,
He fed the spindle of his youngest child,
Who, in the open air, with due accord
Of busy hands and back-and-forward
  steps,
Her large round wheel was turning.   To-
  wards the field
In which the Parish Chapel stood alone,
Girt round with a bare ring of mossy wall,
While half an hour went by, the Priest
  had sent
Many a long look of wonder: and at last,
Risen from his seat, beside the snow-
  white ridge
Of carded wool which the old man had
  piled
He laid his implements with gentle care,
Each in the other locked; and, down the
  path
That from his cottage to the churchyard
  led,
He took his way, impatient to accost

The Stranger, whom he saw still linger-
  ing there.
'T was one well known to him in for-
  mer days,
A Shepherd-lad; who ere his sixteenth
  year
Had left that calling, tempted to entrust
His expectations to the fickle winds
And perilous waters; with the mariners
A fellow-mariner; — and so had fared
Through twenty seasons; but he had been
  reared
Among the mountains, and he in his heart
Was half a shepherd on the stormy seas.
Oft in the piping shrouds had Leonard
  heard
The tones of waterfalls, and inland sounds
Of caves and trees: — and, when the
  regular wind
Between the tropics filled the steady sail,
And blew with the same breath through
  days and weeks,
Lengthening invisibly its weary line
Along the cloudless Main, he, in those
  hours
Of tiresome indolence, would often hang
Over the vessel's side, and gaze and gaze;
And, while the broad blue wave and
  sparkling foam
Flashed round him images and hues that
  wrought
In union with the employment of his heart,
He, thus by feverish passion overcome,
Even with the organs of his bodily eye,
Below him, in the bosom of the deep,
Saw mountains; saw the forms of sheep
  that grazed
On verdant hills — with dwellings among
  trees,
And shepherds clad in the same country
  gray
Which he himself had worn.[1]
                      And now, at last,
From perils manifold, with some small
  wealth
Acquired by traffic 'mid the Indian Isles,
To his paternal home he is returned,
With a determined purpose to resume

[1] This description of the Calenture is sketched
from an imperfect recollection of an admirable
one in prose, by Mr. Gilbert, author of the
Hurricane.

The life he had lived there; both for the
sake
Of many darling pleasures, and the love
Which to an only brother he has borne
In all his hardships, since that happy time
When, whether it blew foul or fair, they
two
Were brother-shepherds on their native
hills.
—They were the last of all their race:
and now,
When Leonard had approached his home,
his heart
Failed in him; and, not venturing to en-
quire
Tidings of one so long and dearly loved,
He to the solitary churchyard turned;
That, as he knew in what particular spot
His family were laid, he thence might learn
If still his Brother lived, or to the file
Another grave was added.—He had found
Another grave, — near which a full half-
hour
He had remained; but, as he gazed, there
grew
Such a confusion in his memory,
That he began to doubt; and even to hope
That he had seen this heap of turf be-
fore, —
That it was not another grave; but one
He had forgotten. He had lost his path,
As up the vale, that afternoon, he walked
Through fields which once had been well
known to him:
And oh what joy this recollection now
Sent to his heart! he lifted up his eyes,
And, looking round, imagined that he
saw
Strange alteration wrought on every side
Among the woods and fields, and that the
rocks,
And everlasting hills themselves were
changed.
   By this the Priest, who down the field
had come,
Unseen by Leonard, at the churchyard
gate
Stopped short, — and thence, at leisure,
limb by limb
Perused him with a gay complacency.
Ay, thought the Vicar, smiling to himself,
'T is one of those who needs must leave
the path

Of the world's business to go wild alone:
His arms have a perpetual holiday;
The happy man will creep about the fields,
Following his fancies by the hour, to
bring
Tears down his cheek, or solitary smiles
Into his face, until the setting sun
Write fool upon his forehead. — Planted
thus
Beneath a shed that over-arched the gate
Of this rude churchyard, till the stars
appeared
The good Man might have communed
with himself,
But that the Stranger, who had left the
grave,
Approached; he recognized the Priest at
once,
And, after greetings interchanged, and
given
By Leonard to the Vicar as to one
Unknown to him, this dialogue ensued.
   Leonard. You live, Sir, in these dales,
a quiet life:
Your years make up one peaceful family;
And who would grieve and fret, if, wel-
come come
And welcome gone, they are so like each
other,
They cannot be remembered? Scarce a
funeral
Comes to this churchyard once in eigh-
teen months;
And yet, some changes must take place
among you:
And you, who dwell here, even among
these rocks,
Can trace the finger of mortality,
And see, that with our threescore years
and ten
We are not all that perish. — I re-
member,
(For many years ago I passed this road)
There was a foot-way all along the fields
By the brook-side — 't is gone — and that
dark cleft!
To me it does not seem to wear the face
Which then it had!
   Priest. Nay, Sir, for aught I know,
That chasm is much the same —
   Leonard. But, surely, yonder —
   Priest. Ay, there, indeed, your mem-
ory is a friend

That does not play you false. — On that
    tall pike
(It is the loneliest place of all these hills)
There were two springs which bubbled
    side by side,
As if they had been made that they
    might be
Companions for each other: the huge
    crag
Was rent with lightning — one hath dis-
    appeared;
The other, left behind, is flowing still.
For accidents and changes such as these,
We want not store of them; — a water-
    spout
Will bring down half a mountain; what
    a feast
For folks that wander up and down like
    you,
To see an acre's breadth of that wide
    cliff
One roaring cataract! a sharp May-
    storm
Will come with loads of January snow,
And in one night send twenty score of
    sheep
To feed the ravens; or a shepherd dies
By some untoward death among the
    rocks:
The ice breaks up and sweeps away a
    bridge;
A wood is felled: — and then for our
    own homes!
A child is born or christened, a field
    ploughed,
A daughter sent to service, a web spun,
The old house-clock is decked with a
    new face;
And hence, so far from wanting facts or
    dates
To chronicle the time, we all have here
A pair of diaries, — one serving, Sir,
For the whole dale, and one for each
    fireside —
Yours was a stranger's judgment: for
    historians,
Commend me to these valleys!
    Leonard.   Yet your Churchyard
Seems, if such freedom may be used
    with you,
To say that you are heedless of the past:
An orphan could not find his mother's
    grave:

Here 's neither head nor foot stone,
    plate of brass,
Cross-bones nor skull, — type of our
    earthly state
Nor emblem of our hopes: the dead
    man's home
Is but a fellow to that pasture-field.
    Priest. Why, there, Sir, is a thought
    that 's new to me!
The stone-cutters, 't is true, might beg
    their bread
If every English churchyard were like
    ours;
Yet your conclusion wanders from the
    truth:
We have no need of names and epi-
    taphs;
We talk about the dead by our firesides.
And then, for our immortal part! *we*
    want
No symbols, Sir, to tell us that plain
    tale:
The thought of death sits easy on the
    man
Who has been born and dies among the
    mountains.
    Leonard. Your Dalesmen, then, do
    in each other's thoughts
Possess a kind of second life: no doubt
You, Sir, could help me to the history
Of half these graves?
    Priest.   For eightscore winters past,
With what I 've witnessed, and with what
    I 've heard,
Perhaps I might; and, on a winter-even-
    ing,
If you were seated at my chimney's
    nook,
By turning o'er these hillocks one by one,
We two could travel, Sir, through a
    strange round;
Yet all in the broad highway of the
    world.
Now there 's a grave — your foot is half
    upon it, —
It looks just like the rest; and yet that
    man
Died broken-hearted.
    Leonard.   'T is a common case.
We 'll take another: who is he that lies
Beneath yon ridge, the last of those three
    graves?
It touches on that piece of native rock

Left in the churchyard wall.

Priest.   That 's Walter Ewbank.
He had as white a head and fresh a
    cheek
As ever were produced by youth and age
Engendering in the blood of hale four-
    score.
Through five long generations had the
    heart
Of Walter's forefathers o'erflowed the
    bounds
Of their inheritance, that single cottage —
You see it yonder! and those few green
    fields.
They toiled and wrought, and still, from
    sire to son,
Each struggled, and each yielded as be-
    fore
A little — yet a little, — and old Walter,
They left to him the family heart, and
    land
With other burthens than the crop it
    bore.
Year after year the old man still kept up
A cheerful mind, — and buffeted with
    bond,
Interest, and mortgages; at last he sank,
And went into his grave before his time.
Poor Walter! whether it was care that
    spurred him
God only knows, but to the very last
He had the lightest foot in Ennerdale:
His pace was never that of an old man:
I almost see him tripping down the path
With his two grandsons after him: — but
    you,
Unless our Landlord be your host to-
    night,
Have far to travel, — and on these rough
    paths
Even in the longest day of midsummer —

Leonard. But those two Orphans!

Priest. Orphans! — Such they were —
Yet not while Walter lived: for, though
    their parents
Lay buried side by side as now they lie,
The old man was a father to the boys,
Two fathers in one father: and if tears,
Shed when he talked of them where they
    were not,
And hauntings from the infirmity of love,
Are aught of what makes up a mother's
    heart,

This old Man, in the day of his old age,
Was half a mother to them. — If you
    weep, Sir,
To hear a stranger talking about stran-
    gers,
Heaven bless you when you are among
    your kindred!
Ay — you may turn that way — it is a
    grave
Which will bear looking at.

Leonard.   These boys — I hope
They loved this good old Man? —

Priest.   They did — and truly:
But that was what we almost overlooked,
They were such darlings of each other.
    Yes,
Though from the cradle they had lived
    with Walter,
The only kinsman near them, and though
    he
Inclined to both by reason of his age,
With a more fond, familiar tenderness;
They, notwithstanding, had much love
    to spare,
And it all went into each other's hearts.
Leonard, the elder by just eighteen
    months,
Was two years taller: 't was a joy to
    see,
To hear, to meet them! — From their
    house to the school
Is distant three short miles, and in the
    time
Of storm and thaw, when every water-
    course
And unbridged stream, such as you may
    have noticed
Crossing our roads at every hundred
    steps,
Was swoln into a noisy rivulet,
Would Leonard then, when elder boys
    remained
At home, go staggering through the
    slippery fords,
Bearing his brother on his back. I have
    seen him,
On windy days, in one of those stray
    brooks,
Ay, more than once I have seen him,
    midleg deep,
Their two books lying both on a dry
    stone,
Upon the hither side: and once I said,

As I remember, looking round these
  rocks
And hills on which we all of us were
  born,
That God who made the great book of
  the world
Would bless such piety —
  Leonard.   It may be then —
  Priest. Never did worthier lads break
    English bread :
The very brightest Sunday Autumn saw
With all its mealy clusters of ripe nuts,
Could never keep those boys away from
  church,
Or tempt them to an hour of sabbath
  breach.
Leonard and James ! I warrant, every
  corner
Among these rocks, and every hollow
  place
That venturous foot could reach, to one or
  both
Was known as well as to the flowers that
  grow there.
Like roe-bucks they went bounding o'er
  the hills ;
They played like two young ravens on the
  crags :
Then they could write, ay and speak too,
  as well
As many of their betters — and for
  Leonard !
The very night before he went away,
In my own house I put into his hand
A Bible, and I 'd wager house and field
That, if he be alive, he has it yet.
    Leonard. It seems, these Brothers have
      not lived to be
A comfort to each other —
    Priest.   That they might
Live to such end is what both old and
  young
In this our valley all of us have wished,
And what, for my part, I have often
  prayed :
But Leonard —
    Leonard. Then James still is left among
      you !
    Priest. 'T is of the elder brother I am
      speaking :
They had an uncle ; — he was at that time
A thriving man, and trafficked on the seas :
And, but for that same uncle, to this hour

Leonard had never handled rope or
  shroud :
For the boy loved the life which we lead
  here ;
And though of unripe years, a stripling
  only,
His soul was knit to this his native soil.
But, as I said, old Walter was too weak
To strive with such a torrent ; when he
  died,
The estate and house were sold ; and all
  their sheep,
A pretty flock, and which, for aught I
  know,
Had clothed the Ewbanks for a thousand
  years : —
Well — all was gone, and they were des-
  titute,
And Leonard, chiefly for his Brother's
  sake,
Resolved to try his fortune on the seas.
Twelve years are past since we had tidings
  from him.
If there were one among us who had heard
That Leonard Ewbank was come home
  again,
From the Great Gavel,[1] down by Leeza's
  banks,
And down the Enna, far as Egremont,
The day would be a joyous festival ;
And those two bells of ours, which there
  you see —
Hanging in the open air — but, O good
  Sir !
This is sad talk — they 'll never sound for
  him —
Living or dead. — When last we heard of
  him,
He was in slavery among the Moors
Upon the Barbary coast. — 'T was not a
  little
That would bring down his spirit ; and no
  doubt,

[1] The Great Gavel, so called, I imagine, from
its resemblance to the gable end of a house, is one
of the highest of the Cumberland mountains. It
stands at the head of the several vales of Enner-
dale, Wastdale, and Borrowdale.
    The Leeza is a river which flows into the Lake
of Ennerdale : on issuing from the Lake, it
changes its name, and is called the End, Eyne,
or Enna. It falls into the sea a little below
Egremont.

Before it ended in his death, the Youth
Was sadly crossed. — Poor Leonard!
    when we parted,
He took me by the hand, and said to me,
If e'er he should grow rich, he would re-
    turn,
To live in peace upon his father's land,
And lay his bones among us.
    Leonard.   If that day
Should come, 't would needs be a glad
    day for him;
He would himself, no doubt, be happy
    then
As any that should meet him —
    Priest.   Happy! Sir —
    Leonard.   You said his kindred all were
    in their graves,
And that he had one Brother —
    Priest.   That is but
A fellow-tale of sorrow. From his youth
James, though not sickly, yet was delicate;
And Leonard being always by his side
Had done so many offices about him,
That, though he was not of a timid nature,
Yet still the spirit of a mountain-boy
In him was somewhat checked; and, when
    his Brother
Was gone to sea, and he was left alone,
The little color that he had was soon
Stolen from his cheek; he drooped, and
    pined, and pined —
    Leonard.   But these are all the graves
    of full-grown men!
    Priest.   Ay, Sir, that passed away: we
    took him to us;
He was the child of all the dale — he lived
Three months with one, and six months
    with another,
And wanted neither food, nor clothes, nor
    love:
And many, many happy days were his.
But, whether blithe or sad, 't is my belief
His absent Brother still was at his heart.
And, when he dwelt beneath our roof, we
    found
(A practice till this time unknown to him)
That often, rising from his bed at night,
He in his sleep would walk about, and
    sleeping
He sought his brother Leonard. — You
    are moved!
Forgive me, Sir: before I spoke to you,
I judged you most unkindly.

    Leonard.   But this Youth,
How did he die at last?
    Priest.   One sweet May-morning,
(It will be twelve years since when Spring
    returns)
He had gone forth among the new-
    dropped lambs,
With two or three companions, whom
    their course
Of occupation led from height to height
Under a cloudless sun — till he, at length,
Through weariness, or, haply, to indulge
The humor of the moment, lagged be-
    hind.
You see yon precipice; — it wears the
    shape
Of a vast building made of many crags;
And in the midst is one particular rock
That rises like a column from the vale,
Whence by our shepherds it is called, THE
    PILLAR.
Upon its summit crowned with heath,
The loiterer, not unnoticed by his com-
    rades,
Lay stretched at ease; but, passing by the
    place
On their return, they found that he was
    gone.
No ill was feared; till one of them by
    chance
Entering, when evening was far spent, the
    house
Which at that time was James's home,
    there learned
That nobody had seen him all that day:
The morning came, and still he was un-
    heard of:
The neighbors were alarmed, and to the
    brook
Some hastened; some ran to the lake: ere
    noon
They found him at the foot of that same
    rock
Dead, and with mangled limbs. The
    third day after
I buried him, poor Youth, and there he
    lies!
    Leonard. And that then *is* his grave! —
    Before his death
You say that he saw many happy years?
    Priest.   Ay, that he did —
    Leonard.   And all went well with
    him? —

Priest. If he had one, the Youth had
    twenty homes.
Leonard. And you believe, then, that
    his mind was easy? —
Priest. Yes, long before he died, he
    found that time
Is a true friend to sorrow; and unless
His thoughts were turned on Leonard's
    luckless fortune,
He talked about him with a cheerful love.
Leonard. He could not come to an
    unhallowed end!
Priest. Nay, God forbid! — You rec-
    ollect I mentioned
A habit which disquietude and grief
Had brought upon him; and we all con-
    jectured
That, as the day was warm, he had lain
    down
On the soft heath, — and, waiting for his
    comrades,
He there had fallen asleep; that in his
    sleep
He to the margin of the precipice
Had walked, and from the summit had
    fallen headlong:
And so no doubt he perished.   When the
    Youth
Fell, in his hand he must have grasped, we
    think,
His shepherd's staff; for on that Pillar of
    rock
It had been caught mid-way; and there
    for years
It hung; — and mouldered there.
                    The Priest here ended —
The Stranger would have thanked him,
    but he felt
A gushing from his heart, that took away
The power of speech.   Both left the spot
    in silence;
And Leonard, when they reached the
    churchyard gate,
As the Priest lifted up the latch, turned
    round, —
And, looking at the grave, he said, "My
    Brother!"
The Vicar did not hear the words: and
    now,
He pointed towards his dwelling-place,
    entreating
That Leonard would partake his homely
    fare:

The other thanked him with an earnest
    voice;
But added, that, the evening being calm,
He would pursue his journey.   So they
    parted.
    It was not long ere Leonard reached a
        grove
That overhung the road: he there stopped
    short,
And, sitting down beneath the trees, re-
    viewed
All that the Priest had said: his early years
Were with him: — his long absence, cher-
    ished hopes,
And thoughts which had been his an hour
    before,
All pressed on him with such a weight,
    that now,
This vale, where he had been so happy,
    seemed
A place in which he could not bear to live:
So he relinquished all his purposes.
He travelled back to Egremont: and
    thence,
That night, he wrote a letter to the Priest,
Reminding him of what had passed be-
    tween them;
And adding, with a hope to be forgiven,
That it was from the weakness of his heart
He had not dared to tell him who he was.
This done, he went on shipboard, and is
    now
A Seaman, a gray-headed Mariner.

1800.   1800.

MICHAEL.

A PASTORAL POEM.

Written at Town-end, Grasmere, about the
same time as "The Brothers." The Sheepfold,
on which so much of the poem turns, remains, or
rather the ruins of it.   The character and cir-
cumstances of Luke were taken from a family to
whom had belonged, many years before, the
house we lived in at Town-end, along with some
fields and woodlands on the eastern shore of
Grasmere.   The name of the Evening Star was
not in fact given to this house, but to another on
the same side of the valley, more to the north.

IF from the public way you turn your steps
Up the tumultuous brook of Greenhead
    Ghyll,

You will suppose that with an upright path
Your feet must struggle; in such bold
ascent
The pastoral mountains front you, face to
face.
But, courage! for around that boisterous
brook
The mountains have all opened out them-
selves,
And made a hidden valley of their own.
No habitation can be seen; but they
Who journey thither find themselves alone
With a few sheep, with rocks and stones,
and kites
That overhead are sailing in the sky.
It is in truth an utter solitude;
Nor should I have made mention of this
Dell
But for one object which you might pass
by,
Might see and notice not. Beside the
brook
Appears a straggling heap of unhewn
stones!
And to that simple object appertains
A story — unenriched with strange events,
Yet not unfit, I deem, for the fireside,
Or for the summer shade. It was the first
Of those domestic tales that spake to me
Of shepherds, dwellers in the valleys, men
Whom I already loved; not verily
For their own sakes, but for the fields and
hills
Where was their occupation and abode.
And hence this Tale, while I was yet a Boy
Careless of books, yet having felt the
power
Of Nature, by the gentle agency
Of natural objects, led me on to feel
For passions that were not my own, and
think
(At random and imperfectly indeed)
On man, the heart of man, and human
life.
Therefore, although it be a history
Homely and rude, I will relate the same
For the delight of a few natural hearts;
And, with yet fonder feeling, for the sake
Of youthful Poets, who among these hills
Will be my second self when I am gone.
UPON the forest-side in Grasmere Vale
There dwelt a Shepherd, Michael was his
name;

An old man, stout of heart, and strong of
limb.
His bodily frame had been from youth to
age
Of an unusual strength: his mind was keen,
Intense, and frugal, apt for all affairs,
And in his shepherd's calling he was
prompt
And watchful more than ordinary men.
Hence had he learned the meaning of all
winds,
Of blasts of every tone; and, oftentimes,
When others heeded not, he heard the
South
Make subterraneous music, like the noise
Of bagpipers on distant Highland hills.
The Shepherd, at such warning, of his
flock
Bethought him, and he to himself would
say,
"The winds are now devising work for
me!"
And, truly, at all times, the storm, that
drives
The traveller to a shelter, summoned him
Up to the mountains: he had been alone
Amid the heart of many thousand mists,
That came to him, and left him, on the
heights.
So lived he till his eightieth year was past.
And grossly that man errs, who should
suppose
That the green valleys, and the streams
and rocks,
Were things indifferent to the Shepherd's
thoughts.
Fields, where with cheerful spirits he had
breathed
The common air; hills, which with vigor-
ous step
He had so often climbed; which had
impressed
So many incidents upon his mind
Of hardship, skill or courage, joy or fear;
Which, like a book, preserved the memory
Of the dumb animals, whom he had saved,
Had fed or sheltered, linking to such acts
The certainty of honorable gain;
Those fields, those hills — what could they
less? had laid
Strong hold on his affections, were to him
A pleasurable feeling of blind love,
The pleasure which there is in life itself.

His days had not been passed in single-
  ness.
His Helpmate was a comely matron, old—
Though younger than himself full twenty
  years.
She was a woman of a stirring life,
Whose heart was in her house: two wheels
  she had
Of antique form; this large, for spinning
  wool;
That small, for flax; and if one wheel had
  rest
It was because the other was at work.
The Pair had but one inmate in their house,
An only Child, who had been born to them
When Michael, telling o'er his years, be-
  gan
To deem that he was old,—in shepherd's
  phrase,
With one foot in the grave. This only Son,
With two brave sheep-dogs tried in many
  a storm,
The one of an inestimable worth,
Made all their household. I may truly
  say,
That they were as a proverb in the vale
For endless industry. When day was
  gone,
And from their occupations out of doors
The Son and Father were come home,
  even then,
Their labor did not cease; unless when all
Turned to the cleanly supper-board, and
  there,
Each with a mess of pottage and skimmed
  milk,
Sat round the basket piled with oaten
  cakes,
And their plain home-made cheese. Yet
  when the meal
Was ended, Luke (for so the Son was
  named)
And his old Father both betook them-
  selves
To such convenient work as might employ
Their hands by the fireside; perhaps to
  card
Wool for the Housewife's spindle, or re-
  pair
Some injury done to sickle, flail, or scythe,
Or other implement of house or field.
  Down from the ceiling, by the chim-
    ney's edge,

That in our ancient uncouth country style
With huge and black projection over-
  browed
Large space beneath, as duly as the light
Of day grew dim the Housewife hung a
  lamp;
An aged utensil, which had performed
Service beyond all others of its kind.
Early at evening did it burn — and late,
Surviving comrade of uncounted hours,
Which, going by from year to year, had
  found,
And left, the couple neither gay perhaps
Nor cheerful, yet with objects and with
  hopes,
Living a life of eager industry.
And now, when Luke had reached his
  eighteenth year,
There by the light of this old lamp they
  sate,
Father and Son, while far into the night
The Housewife plied her own peculiar
  work,
Making the cottage through the silent
  hours
Murmur as with the sound of summer flies.
This light was famous in its neighbor-
  hood,
And was a public symbol of the life
That thrifty Pair had lived. For, as it
  chanced,
Their cottage on a plot of rising ground
Stood single, with large prospect, north
  and south,
High into Easedale, up to Dunmail-Raise,
And westward to the village near the lake;
And from this constant light, so regular
And so far seen, the House itself, by all
Who dwelt within the limits of the vale,
Both old and young, was named THE
  EVENING STAR.
  Thus living on through such a length of
    years,
The Shepherd, if he loved himself, must
  needs
Have loved his Helpmate; but to
  Michael's heart
This son of his old age was yet more
  dear —
Less from instinctive tenderness, the same
Fond spirit that blindly works in the blood
  of all —
Than that a child, more than all other gifts

That earth can offer to declining man,
Brings hope with it, and forward-looking
.thoughts,
And stirrings of inquietude, when they
By tendency of nature needs must fail.
Exceeding was the love he bare to him,
His heart and his heart's joy! For often-
times
Old Michael, while he was a babe in arms,
Had done him female service, not alone
For pastime and delight, as is the use
Of fathers, but with patient mind enforced
To acts of tenderness; and he had rocked
His cradle, as with a woman's gentle hand.

And, in a later time, ere yet the Boy
Had put on boy's attire, did Michael love,
Albeit of a stern unbending mind,
To have the Young-one in his sight, when
he
Wrought in the field, or on his shepherd's
stool
Sate with a fettered sheep before him
stretched
Under the large old oak, that near his door
Stood single, and, from matchless depth
of shade,
Chosen for the Shearer's covert from the
sun,
Thence in our rustic dialect was called
The CLIPPING TREE,[1] a name which yet
it bears.
There, while they two were sitting in the
shade,
With others round them, earnest all and
blithe,
Would Michael exercise his heart with
looks
Of fond correction and reproof bestowed
Upon the Child, if he disturbed the sheep
By catching at their legs, or with his shouts
Scared them, while they lay still beneath
the shears.

And when by Heaven's good grace the
boy grew up
A healthy Lad, and carried in his cheek
Two steady roses that were five years old;
Then Michael from a winter coppice cut
With his own hand a sapling, which he
hooped
With iron, making it throughout in all

[1] Clipping is the word used in the North of
England for shearing.

Due requisites a perfect shepherd's staff,
And gave it to the Boy; wherewith equipt
He as a watchman oftentimes was placed
At gate or gap, to stem or turn the flock;
And, to his office prematurely called,
There stood the urchin, as you will divine,
Something between a hindrance and a
help;
And for this cause not always, I believe,
Receiving from his Father hire of praise;
Though nought was left undone which
staff, or voice,
Or looks, or threatening gestures, could
perform.

But soon as Luke, full ten years old,
could stand
Against the mountain blasts; and to the
heights,
Not fearing toil, nor length of weary ways,
He with his Father daily went, and they
Were as companions, why should I relate
That objects which the Shepherd loved
before
Were dearer now? that from the Boy
there came
Feelings and emanations — things which
were
Light to the sun and music to the wind;
And that the old Man's heart seemed
born again?
Thus in his father's sight the Boy grew
up:
And now, when he had reached his eigh-
teenth year,
He was his comfort and his daily hope.

While in this sort the simple household
lived
From day to day, to Michael's ear there
came
Distressful tidings. Long before the time
Of which I speak, the Shepherd had been
bound
In surety for his brother's son, a man
Of an industrious life, and ample means;
But unforeseen misfortunes suddenly
Had prest upon him; and old Michael
now
Was summoned to discharge the for-
feiture,
A grievous penalty, but little less
Than half his substance. This unlooked-
for claim,
At the first hearing, for a moment took

More hope out of his life than he sup-
   posed
That any old man ever could have lost.
As soon as he had armed himself with
   strength
To look his troubles in the face, it seemed
The Shepherd's sole resource to sell at
   once
A portion of his patrimonial fields.
Such was his first resolve; he thought
   again,
And his heart failed him. "Isabel,"
   said he,
Two evenings after he had heard the
   news,
"I have been toiling more than seventy
   years,
And in the open sunshine of God's love
Have we all lived; yet if these fields of
   ours
Should pass into a stranger's hand, I think
That I could not lie quiet in my grave.
Our lot is a hard lot; the sun himself
Has scarcely been more diligent than I;
And I have lived to be a fool at last
To my own family. An evil man
That was, and made an evil choice, if he
Were false to us; and if he were not false,
There are ten thousand to whom loss like
   this
Had been no sorrow. I forgive him;—
   but
'T were better to be dumb than to talk
   thus.
   When I began, my purpose was to
   speak
Of remedies and of a cheerful hope.
Our Luke shall leave us, Isabel; the land
Shall not go from us, and it shall be free;
He shall possess it, free as is the wind
That passes over it. We have, thou
   know'st,
Another kinsman — he will be our friend
In this distress. He is a prosperous man,
Thriving in trade — and Luke to him
   shall go,
And with his kinsman's help and his own
   thrift
He quickly will repair this loss, and then
He may return to us. If here he stay,
What can be done? Where every one is
   poor,
What can be gained?"

      At this the old Man paused,
And Isabel sat silent, for her mind
Was busy, looking back into past times.
There's Richard Bateman, thought she
   to herself,
He was a parish-boy — at the church-door
They made a gathering for him, shillings,
   pence
And halfpennies, wherewith the neigh-
   bors bought
A basket, which they filled with pedlar's
   wares;
And, with this basket on his arm, the lad
Went up to London, found a master there,
Who, out of many, chose the trusty boy
To go and overlook his merchandise
Beyond the seas; where he grew won-
   drous rich,
And left estates and monies to the poor,
And, at his birthplace, built a chapel,
   floored
With marble which he sent from foreign
   lands.
These thoughts, and many others of like
   sort,
Passed quickly through the mind of
   Isabel,
And her face brightened. The old Man
   was glad,
And thus resumed:— "Well, Isabel!
   this scheme
These two days, has been meat and
   drink to me.
Far more than we have lost is left us yet.
— We have enough — I wish indeed
   that I
Were younger;— but this hope is a good
   hope.
— Make ready Luke's best garments, of
   the best
Buy for him more, and let us send him
   forth
To-morrow, or the next day, or to-night:
— If he *could* go, the Boy should go to-
   night."
   Here Michael ceased, and to the fields
   went forth
With a light heart. The Housewife for
   five days
Was restless morn and night, and all day
   long
Wrought on with her best fingers to pre-
   pare

Things needful for the journey of her son.
But Isabel was glad when Sunday came
To stop her in her work: for, when she
lay
By Michael's side, she through the last
two nights
Heard him, how he was troubled in his
sleep:
And when they rose at morning she
could see
That all his hopes were gone. That day
at noon
She said to Luke, while they two by
themselves
Were sitting at the door, "Thou must
not go:
We have no other Child but thee to lose,
None to remember — do not go away,
For if thou leave thy Father he will die."
The Youth made answer with a jocund
voice;
And Isabel, when she had told her fears,
Recovered heart. That evening her best
fare
Did she bring forth, and all together sat
Like happy people round a Christmas fire.
 With daylight Isabel resumed her
work;
And all the ensuing week the house ap-
peared
As cheerful as a grove in Spring: at
length
The expected letter from their kinsman
came,
With kind assurances that he would do
His utmost for the welfare of the Boy;
To which, requests were added, that
forthwith
He might be sent to him. Ten times or
more
The letter was read over; Isabel
Went forth to show it to the neighbors
round;
Nor was there at that time on English
land
A prouder heart than Luke's. When
Isabel
Had to her house returned, the old Man
said,
" He shall depart to-morrow." To this
word
The Housewife answered, talking much
of things

Which, if at such short notice he shoul(
go,
Would surely be forgotten. But at lengtl
She gave consent, and Michael was a
ease.
 Near the tumultuous brook of Green
head Ghyll,
In that deep valley, Michael had de
signed
To build a Sheepfold; and, before h(
heard
The tidings of his melancholy loss,
For this same purpose he had gatherec
up
A heap of stones, which by the stream
let's edge
Lay thrown together, ready for the work.
With Luke that evening thitherward he
walked:
And soon as they had reached the place
he stopped,
And thus the old Man spake to him:—
 " My Son,
To-morrow thou wilt leave me: with full
heart
I look upon thee, for thou art the same
That wert a promise to me ere thy birth,
And all thy life hast been my daily joy.
I will relate to thee some little part
Of our two histories; 't will do thee gooc
When thou art from me, even if I should
touch
On things thou canst not know of. —
After thou
First cam'st into the world — as oft be-
falls
To new-born infants — thou didst sleep
away
Two days, and blessings from thy
Father's tongue
Then fell upon thee. Day by day passed
on,
And still I loved thee with increasing
love.
Never to living ear came sweeter sounds
Than when I heard thee by our own fire-
side
First uttering, without words, a natural
tune;
While thou, a feeding babe, didst in thy
joy
Sing at thy Mother's breast. Month fol-
lowed month,

And in the open fields my life was passed
And on the mountains; else I think that
thou
Hadst been brought up upon thy Father's
knees.
But we were playmates, Luke: among
these hills,
As well thou knowest, in us the old and
young   .
Have played together, nor with me didst
thou
Lack any pleasure which a boy can know.''
Luke had a manly heart; but at these
words
He sobbed aloud.   The old Man grasped
his hand,
And said, '' Nay, do not take it so — I
see
That these are things of which I need
not speak.
— Even to the utmost I have been to
thee
A kind and a good Father: and herein
I but repay a gift which I myself
Received at others' hands; for, though
now old
Beyond the common life of man, I still
Remember them who loved me in my
youth.
Both of them sleep together: here they
lived,
As all their Forefathers had done; and
when
At length their time was come, they
were not loth
To give their bodies to the family mould.
I wished that thou should'st live the life
they lived:
But, 't is a long time to look back, my
Son,
And see so little gain from threescore
years.
These fields were burthened when they
came to me;
Till I was forty years of age, not more
Than half of my inheritance was mine.
I toiled and toiled; God blessed me in
my work,
And till these three weeks past the land
was free.
— It looks as if it never could endure
Another Master.   Heaven forgive me,
Luke,

If I judge ill for thee, but it seems good
That thou should'st go.''
                    At this the old Man paused;
Then, pointing to the stones near which
they stood,
Thus, after a short silence, he resumed:
'' This was a work for us; and now, my
Son,
It is a work for me.   But, lay one stone —
Here, lay it for me, Luke, with thine own
hands.
Nay, Boy, be of good hope; — we both
may live
To see a better day.   At eighty-four
I still am strong and hale; — do thou thy
part;
I will do mine. — I will begin again
With many tasks that were resigned to
thee:
Up to the heights, and in among the
storms,
Will I without thee go again, and do
All works which I was wont to do alone,
Before I knew thy face. — Heaven bless
thee, Boy !
Thy heart these two weeks has been
beating fast
With many hopes; it should be so —
yes — yes —
I knew that thou could'st never have a
wish
To leave me, Luke: thou hast been
bound to me
Only by links of love: when thou art
gone,
What will be left to us ! — But, I forget
My purposes.   Lay now the corner-stone,
As I requested; and hereafter, Luke,
When thou art gone away, should evil
men
Be thy companions, think of me, my
Son,
And of this moment; hither turn thy
thoughts,
And God will strengthen thee: amid all
fear
And all temptation, Luke, I pray that
thou
May'st bear in mind the life thy Fathers
lived,
Who, being innocent, did for that cause
Bestir them in good deeds.   Now, fare
thee well —   .

When thou return'st, thou in this place
wilt see
A work which is not here: a covenant
'T will be between us; but, whatever fate
Befall thee, I shall love thee to the last,
And bear thy memory with me to the
grave.''
The Shepherd ended here; and Luke
stooped down,
And, as his Father had requested, laid
The first stone of the Sheepfold. At the
sight
The old Man's grief broke from him; to
his heart
He pressed his Son, he kissèd him and
wept;
And to the house together they returned.
— Hushed was that House in peace, or
seeming peace,
Ere the night fell: — with morrow's dawn
the Boy
Began his journey, and when he had
reached
The public way, he put on a bold face;
And all the neighbors, as he passed their
doors,
Came forth with wishes and with farewell
prayers,
That followed him till he was out of sight.
A good report did from their Kinsman
come,
Of Luke and his well-doing: and the Boy
Wrote loving letters, full of wondrous
news,
Which, as the Housewife phrased it, were
throughout
"The prettiest letters that were ever
seen."
Both parents read them with rejoicing
hearts.
So, many months passed on: and once
again
The Shepherd went about his daily work
With confident and cheerful thoughts;
and now
Sometimes when he could find a leisure
hour
He to that valley took his way, and there
Wrought at the Sheepfold. Meantime
Luke began
To slacken in his duty; and, at length,
He in the dissolute city gave himself
To evil courses: ignominy and shame

Fell on him, so that he was driven at last
To seek a hiding-place beyond the seas.
There is a comfort in the strength of
love;
'T will make a thing endurable, which else
Would overset the brain, or break the
heart:
I have conversed with more than one who
well
Remember the old Man, and what he
was
Years after he had heard this heavy news.
His bodily frame had been from youth to
age
Of an unusual strength. Among the rocks
He went, and still looked up to sun and
cloud,
And listened to the wind; and, as before,
Performed all kinds of labor for his sheep,
And for the land, his small inheritance.
And to that hollow dell from time to time
Did he repair, to build the Fold of which
His flock had need. 'T is not forgotten
yet
The pity which was then in every heart
For the old Man — and 't is believed by
all
That many and many a day he thither
went,
And never lifted up a single stone.
There, by the Sheepfold, sometimes
was he seen
Sitting alone, or with his faithful Dog,
Then old, beside him, lying at his feet.
The length of full seven years, from time
to time,
He at the building of this Sheepfold
wrought,
And left the work unfinished when he
died.
Three years, or little more, did Isabel
Survive her Husband: at his death the
estate
Was sold, and went into a stranger's
hand.
The Cottage which was named the EVEN-
ING STAR
Is gone — the ploughshare has been
through the ground
On which it stood; great changes have
been wrought
In all the neighborhood: — yet the oak is
left

That grew beside their door; and the re-
     mains
Of the unfinished Sheepfold may be seen
Beside the boisterous brook of Greenhead
     Ghyll.

1800.   1800.

THE IDLE SHEPHERD–BOYS;

OR, DUNGEON-GHYLL FORCE.[1]

A PASTORAL.

Written at Town-end, Grasmere. I will only
add a little monitory anecdote concerning this sub-
ject. When Coleridge and Southey were walk-
ing together upon the Fells, Southey observed
that, if I wished to be considered a faithful painter
of rural manners, I ought not to have said that
my Shepherd-boys trimmed their rustic hats as
described in the poem. Just as the words had
passed his lips two boys appeared with the very
plant entwined round their hats. I have often
wondered that Southey, who rambled so much
about the mountains, should have fallen into this
mistake, and I record it as a warning for others
who, with far less opportunity than my dear
friend had of knowing what things are, and far
less sagacity, give way to presumptuous criticism,
from which he was free, though in this matter
mistaken. In describing a tarn under Helvellyn,
I say —

     "There sometimes doth a leaping fish
       Send through the tarn a lonely cheer."

This was branded by a critic of these days, in a
review ascribed to Mrs. Barbauld, as unnatural
and absurd. I admire the genius of Mrs. Bar-
bauld, and am certain that, had her education
been favorable to imaginative influences, no
female of her day would have been more likely to
sympathize with that image, and to acknowledge
the truth of the sentiment.

THE valley rings with mirth and joy;
Among the hills the echoes play
A never never ending song,
To welcome in the May.
The magpie chatters with delight;
The mountain raven's youngling brood

---

[1] *Ghyll*, in the dialect of Cumberland and
Westmoreland, is a short and, for the most part,
a steep narrow valley, with a stream running
through it. *Force* is the word universally em-
ployed in these dialects for waterfall.

Have left the mother and the nest;
And they go rambling east and west
In search of their own food;
Or through the glittering vapors dart
In very wantonness of heart.

Beneath a rock, upon the grass,
Two boys are sitting in the sun;
Their work, if any work they have,
Is out of mind — or done.
On pipes of sycamore they play
The fragments of a Christmas hymn;
Or with that plant which in our dale
We call stag-horn, or fox's tail,
Their rusty hats they trim:
And thus, as happy as the day,
Those Shepherds wear the time away.

Along the river's stony marge
The sand-lark chants a joyous song;
The thrush is busy in the wood,
And carols loud and strong.
A thousand lambs are on the rocks,
All newly born! both earth and sky
Keep jubilee, and more than all,
Those boys with their green coronal;
They never hear the cry,
That plaintive cry! which up the hill
Comes from the depth of Dungeon-Ghyll.

Said Walter, leaping from the ground,
"Down to the stump of yon old yew
We'll for our whistles run a race."
— Away the shepherds flew;
They leapt — they ran — and when they
     came
Right opposite to Dungeon-Ghyll,
Seeing that he should lose the prize,
"Stop!" to his comrade Walter cries —
James stopped with no good will:
Said Walter then, exulting; "Here
You'll find a task for half a year.

"Cross, if you dare, where I shall cross —
Come on, and tread where I shall tread."
The other took him at his word,
And followed as he led.
It was a spot which you may see
If ever you to Langdale go;
Into a chasm a mighty block
Hath fallen, and made a bridge of rock:
The gulf is deep below;

And, in a basin black and small,
Receives a lofty waterfall.

With staff in hand across the cleft
The challenger pursued his march;
And now, all eyes and feet, hath gained
The middle of the arch.
When list ! he hears a piteous moan —
Again ! — his heart within him dies —
His pulse is stopped, his breath is lost,
He totters, pallid as a ghost,
And, looking down, espies
A lamb, that in the pool is pent
Within that black and frightful rent.

The lamb had slipped into the stream,
And safe without a bruise or wound
The cataract had borne him down
Into the gulf profound.
His dam had seen him when he fell,
She saw him down the torrent borne;
And, while with all a mother's love
She from the lofty rocks above
Sent forth a cry forlorn,
The lamb, still swimming round and
    round,
Made answer to that plaintive sound.

When he had learnt what thing it was,
That sent this rueful cry; I ween
The Boy recovered heart, and told
The sight which he had seen.
Both gladly now deferred their task;
Nor was there wanting other aid —
A Poet, one who loves the brooks
Far better than the sages' books,
By chance had thither strayed;
And there the helpless lamb he found
By those huge rocks encompassed round.

He drew it from the troubled pool,
And brought it forth into the light:
The Shepherds met him with his charge,
An unexpected sight !
Into their arms the lamb they took,
Whose life and limbs the flood had spared;
Then up the steep ascent they hied,
And placed him at his mother's side;
And gently did the Bard
Those idle Shepherd-boys upbraid,
And bade them better mind their trade.

1800.

THE PET-LAMB.

A PASTORAL.

Written at Town-end, Grasmere. Barbara
Lewthwaite, now living at Ambleside (1843),
though much changed as to beauty, was one of
two most lovely sisters. Almost the first words
my poor brother John said, when he visited us for
the first time at Grasmere, were, "Were those
two Angels that I have just seen?" and from his
description I have no doubt they were those two
sisters. The mother died in childbed ; and one
of our neighbors at Grasmere told me that the
loveliest sight ,she had ever seen was that mother
as she lay in her coffin with her babe in her arm.
I mention this to notice what I cannot but think
a salutary custom once universal in these vales.
Every attendant on a funeral made it a duty to
look at the corpse in the coffin before the lid was
closed, which was never done (nor I believe is
now) till a minute or two before the corpse was
removed. Barbara Lewthwaite was not in fact
the child whom I had seen and overheard as
described in the poem. I chose the name for
reasons implied in the above ; and will here add
a caution against the use of names of living per-
sons. Within a few months after the publication
of this poem, I was much surprised, and more
hurt, to find it in a child's school-book which,
having been compiled by Lindley Murray, had
come into use at Grasmere School where Barbara
was a pupil; and, alas ! I had the mortification
of hearing that she was very vain of being thus
distinguished ; and, in after-life, she used to say
that she remembered the incident and what I said
to her upon the occasion.

THE dew was falling fast, the stars began
    to blink;
I heard a voice; it said, "Drink, pretty
    creature, drink ! "
And, looking o'er the hedge, before me
    I espied
A snow-white mountain-lamb with a
    Maiden at its side.

Nor sheep nor kine were near; the lamb
    was all alone,
And by a slender cord was tethered to a
    stone;
With one knee on the grass did the little
    Maiden kneel,
While to that mountain-lamb she gave its
    evening meal.

1800.

The lamb, while from her hand he thus his
    supper took,
Seemed to feast with head and ears; and
    his tail with pleasure shook.
"Drink, pretty creature, drink," she said
    in such a tone
That I almost received her heart into my
    own.

'T was little Barbara Lewthwaite, a child
    of beauty rare!
I watched them with delight, they were
    a lovely pair.
Now with her empty can the Maiden
    turned away:
But ere ten yards were gone her footsteps
    did she stay.

Right towards the lamb she looked; and
    from a shady place
I unobserved could see the workings of
    her face:
If Nature to her tongue could measured
    numbers bring,
Thus, thought I, to her lamb that little
    Maid might sing:

"What ails thee, young One? what?
    Why pull so at thy cord?
Is it not well with thee? well both for bed
    and board?
Thy plot of grass is soft, and green as
    grass can be;
Rest, little young One, rest; what is 't that
    aileth thee?

"What is it thou wouldst seek?   What is
    wanting to thy heart?
Thy limbs are they not strong?   And
    beautiful thou art:
This grass is tender grass; these flowers
    they have no peers;
And that green corn all day is rustling in
    thy ears!

"If the sun be shining hot, do but stretch
    thy woollen chain,
This beech is standing by, its covert thou
    canst gain;
For rain and mountain-storms! the like
    thou need'st not fear,
The rain and storm are things that scarce-
    ly can come here.

"Rest, little young One, rest; thou hast
    forgot the day
When my father found thee first in places
    far away;
Many flocks were on the hills, but thou
    wert owned by none,
And thy mother from thy side for ever-
    more was gone.

"He took thee in his arms, and in pity
    brought thee home:
A blessèd day for thee! then whither
    wouldst thou roam?
A faithful nurse thou hast; the dam that
    did thee yean
Upon the mountain-tops no kinder could
    have been.

"Thou know'st that twice a day I have
    brought thee in this can
Fresh water from the brook, as clear as
    ever ran;
And twice in the day, when the ground is
    wet with dew,
I bring thee draughts of milk, warm milk
    it is and new.

"Thy limbs will shortly be twice as stout
    as they are now,
Then I 'll yoke thee to my cart like a pony
    in the plough;
My playmate thou shalt be; and when the
    wind is cold
Our hearth shall be thy bed, our house
    shall be thy fold.

"It will not, will not rest! — Poor crea-
    ture, can it be
That 't is thy mother's heart which is
    working so in thee?
Things that I know not of belike to thee
    are dear,
And dreams of things which thou canst
    neither see nor hear.

"Alas, the mountain-tops that look so
    green and fair!
I 've heard of fearful winds and darkness
    that come there;
The little brooks that seem all pastime
    and all play,
When they are angry, roar like lions for
    their prey.

" Here thou need'st not dread the raven
    in the sky;
Night and day thou art safe, — our cot-
    tage is hard by.
Why bleat so after me? Why pull so at
    thy chain?
Sleep — and at break of day I will come
    to thee again ! "

As homeward through the lane I went
    with lazy feet,
This song to myself did I oftentimes re-
    peat;
And it seemed, as I retraced the ballad
    line by line,
That but half of it was hers, and one-half
    of it was *mine*.

Again, and once again, did I repeat the
    song;
" Nay," said I, " more than half to the
    damsel must belong,
For she looked with such a look and she
    spake with such a tone,
That I almost received her heart into my
    own."

1800.   1800.

POEMS ON THE NAMING OF PLACES.

ADVERTISEMENT.

By persons resident in the country and attached
to rural objects, many places will be found un-
named or of unknown names, where little Inci-
dents must have occurred, or feelings been expe-
rienced, which will have given to such places a
private and peculiar interest. From a wish to
give some sort of record to such Incidents, and
renew the gratification of such feelings, Names
have been given to Places by the Author and
some of his Friends, and the following Poems
written in consequence.

I.

Written at Grasmere. This poem was sug-
gested on the banks of the brook that runs through
Easedale, which is, in some parts of its course, as
wild and beautiful as brook can be. I have com-
posed thousands of verses by the side of it.

It was an April morning: fresh and clear
The Rivulet, delighting in its strength,
Ran with a young man's speed; and yet
    the voice
Of waters which the winter had supplied
Was softened down into a vernal tone.
The spirit of enjoyment and desire,
And hopes and wishes, from all living
    things
Went circling, like a multitude of sounds.
The budding groves seemed eager to
    urge on
The steps of June; as if their various hues
Were only hindrances that stood between
Them and their object: but, meanwhile,
    prevailed
Such an entire contentment in the air
That every naked ash, and tardy tree
Yet leafless, showed as if the countenance
With which it looked on this delightful
    day
Were native to the summer. — Up the
    brook
I roamed in the confusion of my heart,
Alive to all things and forgetting all.
At length I to a sudden turning came
In this continuous glen, where down a rock
The Stream, so ardent in its course before,
Sent forth such sallies of glad sound,
    that all
Which I till then had heard, appeared
    the voice
Of common pleasure: beast and bird, the
    lamb,
The shepherd's dog, the linnet and the
    thrush
Vied with this waterfall, and made a song,
Which, while I listened, seemed like the
    wild growth
Or like some natural produce of the air
That could not cease to be. Green leaves
    were here;
But 't was the foliage of the rocks — the
    birch,
The yew, the holly, and the bright green
    thorn,
With hanging islands of resplendent
    furze;
And, on a summit, distant a short space,
By any who should look beyond the dell,
A single mountain-cottage might be seen.
I gazed and gazed, and to myself I said,
" Our thoughts at least are ours; and
    this wild nook,
My Emma I will dedicate to thee."

—Soon did the spot become my other
        home,
My dwelling, and my out-of-doors abode.
And, of the Shepherds who have seen me
        there,
To whom I sometimes in our idle talk
Have told this fancy, two or three, per-
        haps,
Years after we are gone and in our graves,
When they have cause to speak of this
        wild place,
May call it by the name of EMMA'S DELL.

    1800.   1800.

II.

TO JOANNA.

Written at Grasmere. The effect of her laugh
is an extravagance; though the effect of the re-
verberation of voices in some parts of the moun-
tains is very striking. There is, in the "Excur-
sion," an allusion to the bleat of a lamb thus
re-echoed, and described without any exaggera-
tion, as I heard it, on the side of Stickle Tarn,
from the precipice that stretches on to Langdale
Pikes.

AMID the smoke of cities did you pass
The time of early youth; and there you
        learned,
From years of quiet industry, to love
The living Beings by your own fireside,
With such a strong devotion, that your
        heart
Is slow to meet the sympathies of them
Who look upon the hills with tenderness,
And make dear friendships with the
        streams and groves.
Yet we, who are transgressors in this
        kind,
Dwelling retired in our simplicity
Among the woods and fields, we love you
        well,
Joanna! and I guess, since you have been
So distant from us now for two long years,
That you will gladly listen to discourse,
However trivial, if you thence be taught
That they, with whom you once were
        happy, talk
Familiarly of you and of old times.
    While I was seated, now some ten days
        past,
Beneath those lofty firs, that overtop

Their ancient neighbor, the old steeple-
        tower,
The Vicar from his gloomy house hard by
Came forth to greet me; and when he
        had asked,
"How fares Joanna, that wild-hearted
        Maid!
And when will she return to us?" he
        paused;
And, after short exchanges of village
        news,
He with grave looks demanded, for what
        cause,
Reviving obsolete idolatry,
I, like a Runic Priest, in characters
Of formidable size had chiselled out
Some uncouth name upon the native rock,
Above the Rotha, by the forest-side.
— Now, by those dear immunities of heart
Engendered between malice and true
        love,
I was not loth to be so catechised,
And this was my reply:— "As it befell,
One summer morning we had walked
        abroad
At break of day, Joanna and myself.
— 'T was that delightful season when the
        broom,
Full-flowered, and visible on every steep,
Along the copses runs in veins of gold.
Our pathway led us on to Rotha's banks;
And when we came in front of that tall
        rock
That eastward looks, I there stopped short
        — and stood
Tracing the lofty barrier with my eye
From base to summit; such delight I
        found
To note in shrub and tree, in stone and
        flower
That intermixture of delicious hues,
Along so vast a surface, all at once,
In one impression, by connecting force
Of their own beauty, imaged in the heart.
—When I had gazed perhaps two minutes'
        space,
Joanna, looking in my eyes, beheld
That ravishment of mine, and laughed
        aloud.
The Rock, like something starting from
        a sleep,
Took up the Lady's voice, and laughed
        again;

That ancient Woman seated on Helm-
   crag
Was ready with her cavern; Hammar-
   scar,
And the tall Steep of Silver-how, sent
   forth
A noise of laughter; southern Loughrigg
   heard,
And Fairfield answered with a mountain
   tone;
Helvellyn far into the clear blue sky
Carried the Lady's voice, — old Skiddaw
   blew
His speaking-trumpet; — back out of the
   clouds
Of Glaramara southward came the voice;
And Kirkstone tossed it from his misty
   head.
— Now whether (said I to our cordial
   Friend,
Who, in the hey-day of astonishment
Smiled in my face) this were in simple
   truth
A work accomplished by the brotherhood
Of ancient mountains, or my ear was
   touched
With dreams and visionary impulses
To me alone imparted, sure I am
That there was a loud uproar in the hills.
And, while we both were listening, to my
   side
The fair Joanna drew, as if she wished
To shelter from some object of her fear.
— And hence, long afterwards, when
   eighteen moons
Were wasted, as I chanced to walk alone
Beneath this rock, at sunrise, on a calm
And silent morning, I sat down, and there,
In memory of affections old and true,
I chiselled out in those rude characters
Joanna's name deep in the living stone :—
And I, and all who dwell by my fireside,
Have called the lovely rock, JOANNA'S
   ROCK."
1800.   1800.

NOTE. — In Cumberland and Westmoreland
are several Inscriptions, upon the native rock,
which, from the wasting of time, and the rude-
ness of the workmanship, have been mistaken for
Runic. They are without doubt Roman.

The Rotha, mentioned in this poem, is the
River which, flowing through the lakes of Gras-
mere and Rydale, falls into Wynandermere. On
Helm-crag, that impressive single mountain at
the head of the Vale of Grasmere, is a rock
which from most points of view bears a striking
resemblance to an old Woman cowering. Close
by this rock is one of those fissures or caverns,
which in the language of the country are called
dungeons. Most of the mountains here men-
tioned immediately surround the Vale of Gras-
mere; of the others, some are at a considerable
distance, but they belong to the same cluster.

III.

It is not accurate that the Eminence here
alluded to could be seen from our orchard-seat.
It rises above the road by the side of Grasmere
lake, towards Keswick, and its name is Stone-
Arthur.

THERE is an Eminence, — of these our
   hills
The last that parleys with the setting sun;
We can behold it from our orchard-seat;
And, when at evening we pursue our
   walk
Along the public way, this Peak, so high
Above us, and so distant in its height,
Is visible; and often seems to send
Its own deep quiet to restore our hearts.
The meteors make of it a favorite haunt:
The star of Jove, so beautiful and large
In the mid heavens, is never half so fair
As when he shines above it.   'T is in
   truth
The loneliest place we have among the
   clouds.
And She who dwells with me, whom I
   have loved
With such communion, that no place on
   earth
Can ever be a solitude to me,
Hath to this lonely Summit given my
   Name.
1800.   1800.

IV.

The character of the eastern shore of Grasmere
lake is quite changed, since these verses were
written, by the public road being carried along
its side. The friends spoken of were Coleridge
and my Sister, and the facts occurred strictly as
recorded.

A NARROW girdle of rough stones and
   crags,
A rude and natural causeway, interposed
Between the water and a winding slope

Of copse and thicket, leaves the eastern
    shore
Of Grasmere safe in its own privacy:
And there myself and two belovèd
    Friends,
One calm September morning, ere the
    mist
Had altogether yielded to the sun,
Sauntered on this retired and difficult
    way.
— Ill suits the road with one in haste;
    but we
Played with our time; and, as we strolled
    along,
It was our occupation to observe
Such objects as the waves had tossed
    ashore —
Feather, or leaf, or weed, or withered
    bough,
Each on the other heaped, along the line
Of the dry wreck. And, in our vacant
    mood,   .
Not seldom did we stop to watch some
    tuft
Of dandelion seed or thistle's beard,
That skimmed the surface of the dead
    calm lake,
Suddenly halting now — a lifeless stand!
And starting off again with freak as sud-
    den;
In all its sportive wanderings, all the
    while,
Making report of an invisible breeze
That was its wings, its chariot, and its
    horse,
Its playmate, rather say, its moving soul.
— And often, trifling with a privilege
Alike indulged to all, we paused, one
    now,
And now the other, to point out, per-
    chance
To pluck, some flower or water-weed,
    too fair
Either to be divided from the place
On which it grew, or to be left alone
To its own beauty. Many such there
    are,   .
Fair ferns and flowers, and chiefly that
    tall fern,
So stately, of the queen Osmunda named;
Plant lovelier, in its own retired abode
On Grasmere's beach, than Naiad by the
    side

Of Grecian brook, or Lady of the Mere,
Sole-sitting by the shores of old ro-
    mance.
— So fared we that bright morning: from
    the fields
Meanwhile, a noise was heard, the busy
    mirth
Of reapers, men and women, boys and
    girls.
Delighted much to listen to those sounds,
And feeding thus our fancies, we ad-
    vanced
Along the indented shore; when sud-
    denly,
Through a thin veil of glittering haze was
    seen
Before us, on a point of jutting land,
The tall and upright figure of a Man
Attired in peasant's garb, who stood
    alone,
Angling beside the margin of the lake.
"Improvident and reckless," we ex-
    claimed,
"The Man must be, who thus can lose
    a day
Of the mid harvest, when the laborer's
    hire
Is ample, and some little might be stored
Wherewith to cheer him in the winter
    time."
Thus talking of that Peasant, we ap-
    proached
Close to the spot where with his rod and
    line
He stood alone; whereat he turned his
    head
To greet us — and we saw a Man worn
    down
By sickness, gaunt and lean, with sunken
    cheeks
And wasted limbs, his legs so long and
    lean
That for my single self I looked at them,
Forgetful of the body they sustained. —
Too weak to labor in the harvest field,
The Man was using his best skill to gain
A pittance from the dead unfeeling lake
That knew not of his wants. I will not
    say
What thoughts immediately were ours,
    nor how
The happy idleness of that sweet morn,
With all its lovely images, was changed

To serious musing and to self-reproach.
Nor did we fail to see within ourselves
What need there is to be reserved in
speech,
And temper all our thoughts with charity.
— Therefore, unwilling to forget that
day,
My Friend, Myself, and She who then
received
The same admonishment, have called the
place
By a memorial name, uncouth indeed
As e'er by mariner was given to bay
Or foreland, on a new-discovered coast;
And POINT RASH-JUDGMENT is the name
it bears.

1800.   1800.

V.

To M. H.

The pool alluded to is in Rydal Upper Park.

OUR walk was far among the ancient
trees:
There was no road, nor any woodman's
path;
But a thick umbrage — checking the
wild growth
Of weed and sapling, along soft green
turf
Beneath the branches — of itself had
made
A track, that brought us to a slip of lawn,
And a small bed of water in the woods.
All round this pool both flocks and herds
might drink
On its firm margin, even as from a well,
Or some stone-basin which the herds-
man's hand
Had shaped for their refreshment; nor
did sun,
Or wind from any quarter, ever come,
But as a blessing to this calm recess,
This glade of water and this one green
field.
The spot was made by Nature for herself;
The travellers know it not, and 't will
remain
Unknown to them; but it is beautiful;
And if a man should plant his cottage near,
Should sleep beneath the shelter of its
trees,
And blend its waters with his daily meal,

He would so love it, that in his death-
hour
Its image would survive among his
thoughts:
And therefore, my sweet MARY, this still
Nook,
With all its beeches, we have named
from You!

1800.   1800.

THE WATERFALL AND THE EGLANTINE.

Suggested nearer to Grasmere, on the same
mountain track as that referred to in the follow-
ing Note. The Eglantine remained many years
afterwards, but is now gone.

I.

" BEGONE, thou fond presumptuous Elf,"
Exclaimed an angry Voice,
" Nor dare to thrust thy foolish self
Between me and my choice ! "
A small Cascade fresh swoln with snows
Thus threatened a poor Briar-rose,
That, all bespattered with his foam,
And dancing high and dancing low,
Was living, as a child might know,
In an unhappy home.

II.

" Dost thou presume my course to block?
Off, off ! or, puny Thing !
I 'll hurl thee headlong with the rock
To which thy fibres cling."
The Flood was tyrannous and strong;
The patient Briar suffered long,
Nor did he utter groan or sigh,
Hoping the danger would be past;
But, seeing no relief, at last,
He ventured to reply.

III.

" Ah ! " said the Briar, " blame me not;
Why should we dwell in strife?
We who in this sequestered spot
Once lived a happy life !
You stirred me on my rocky bed —
What pleasure through my veins you
spread
The summer long, from day to day,
My leaves you freshened and bedewed;
Nor was it common gratitude
That did your cares repay.

IV.

" When spring came on with bud and bell,
Among these rocks did I
Before you hang my wreaths to tell
That gentle days were nigh!
And in the sultry summer hours,
I sheltered you with leaves and flowers;
And in my leaves — now shed and gone,
The linnet lodged, and for us two
Chanted his pretty songs, when you
Had little voice or none.

V.

" But now proud thoughts are in your
          breast —
What grief is mine you see,
Ah! would you think, even yet how blest
Together we might be!
Though of both leaf and flower bereft,
Some ornaments to me are left —
Rich store of scarlet hips is mine,
With which I, in my humble way,
Would deck you many a winter day,
A happy Eglantine! "

VI.

What more he said I cannot tell,
The Torrent down the rocky dell
Came thundering loud and fast;
I listened, nor aught else could hear;
The Briar quaked — and much I fear
Those accents were his last.
1800.   1800.

THE OAK AND THE BROOM.

A PASTORAL.

Suggested upon the mountain pathway that
leads from Upper Rydal to Grasmere. The pon-
derous block of stone which is mentioned in the
poem remains, I believe, to this day, a good way
up Nab-Scar. Broom grows under it, and in
many places on the side of the precipice.

I.

His simple truths did Andrew glean
Beside the babbling rills;
A careful student he had been
Among the woods and hills.
One winter's night, when through the
          trees
The wind was roaring, on his knees

His youngest born did Andrew hold:
And while the rest, a ruddy quire,
Were seated round their blazing fire,
This Tale the Shepherd told.

II.

" I saw a crag, a lofty stone
As ever tempest beat!
Out of its head an Oak had grown,
A Broom out of its feet.
The time was March, a cheerful noon —
The thaw-wind, with the breath of June,
Breathed gently from the warm south-
          west:
When, in a voice sedate with age,
This Oak, a giant and a sage,
His neighbor thus addressed: —

III.

" ' Eight weary weeks, through rock and
          clay,
Along this mountain's edge,
The Frost hath wrought both night and
          day,
Wedge driving after wedge.
Look up! and think, above your head
What trouble, surely, will be bred;
Last night I heard a crash — 't is true,
The splinters took another road —
I see them yonder — what a load
For such a Thing as you!

IV.

" ' You are preparing as before,
To deck your slender shape;
And yet, just three years back — no
          more —
You had a strange escape:
Down from yon cliff a fragment broke;
It thundered down, with fire and smoke,
And hitherward pursued its way;
This ponderous block was caught by me,
And o'er your head, as you may see,
'T is hanging to this day!

V.

" ' If breeze or bird to this rough steep
Your kind's first seed did bear;
The breeze had better been asleep,
The bird caught in a snare:
For you and your green twigs decoy
The little witless shepherd-boy

To come and slumber in your bower;
And, trust me, on some sultry noon,
Both you and he, Heaven knows how
    soon!
Will perish in one hour.

VI.

" ' From me this friendly warning take'—
The Broom began to doze,
And thus, to keep herself awake,
Did gently interpose:
' My thanks for your discourse are due;
That more than what you say is true,
I know, and I have known it long;
Frail is the bond by which we hold
Our being, whether young or old,
Wise, foolish, weak, or strong.

VII.

" ' Disasters, do the best we can,
Will reach both great and small;
And he is oft the wisest man,
Who is not wise at all.
For me, why should I wish to roam?
This spot is my paternal home,
It is my pleasant heritage;
My father many a happy year,
Spread here his careless blossoms, here
Attained a good old age.

VIII.

" ' Even such as his may be my lot.
What cause have I to haunt
My heart with terrors? Am I not
In truth a favored plant!
On me such bounty Summer pours,
That I am covered o'er with flowers;
And, when the Frost is in the sky,
My branches are so fresh and gay
That you might look at me and say,
This Plant can never die.

IX.

" ' The butterfly, all green and gold,
To me hath often flown,
Here in my blossoms to behold
Wings lovely as his own.
When grass is chill with rain or dew,
Beneath my shade, the mother-ewe
Lies with her infant lamb; I see
The love they to each other make,
And the sweet joy which they partake,
It is a joy to me.

X.

" Her voice was blithe, her heart was
    light;
The Broom might have pursued
Her speech, until the stars of night
Their journey had renewed;
But in the branches of the oak
Two ravens now began to croak
Their nuptial song, a gladsome air;
And to her own green bower the breeze
That instant brought two stripling bees
To rest, or murmur there.

XI.

" One night, my Children! from the north
There came a furious blast;
At break of day I ventured forth,
And near the cliff I passed.
The storm had fallen upon the Oak,
And struck him with a mighty stroke,
And whirled, and whirled him far away;
And, in one hospitable cleft,
The little careless Broom was left
To live for many a day."
    1800.   1800.

HART–LEAP WELL.

Written at Town-end, Grasmere. The first
eight stanzas were composed extempore one win-
ter evening in the cottage; when, after having
tired myself with laboring at an awkward passage
in " The Brothers," I started with a sudden im-
pulse to this to get rid of the other, and finished
it in a day or two. My Sister and I had passed the
place a few weeks before in our wild winter jour-
ney from Sockburn on the banks of the Tees to
Grasmere. A peasant whom we met near the
spot told us the story so far as concerned the
name of the Well, and the Hart, and pointed out
the Stones. Both the Stones and the Well are
objects that may easily be missed; the tradition
by this time may be extinct in the neighborhood:
the man who related it to us was very old.

Hart-Leap Well is a small spring of water,
about five miles from Richmond in Yorkshire, and
near the side of the road that leads from Rich-
mond to Askrigg. Its name is derived from a
remarkable Chase, the memory of which is pre-
served by the monuments spoken of in the second
Part of the following Poem, which monuments
do now exist as I have there described them.

THE Knight had ridden down from
       Wensley Moor
With the slow motion of a summer's cloud,

And now, as he approached a vassal's
door,
" Bring forth another horse ! " he cried
aloud.

" Another horse ! " — That shout the vas-
sal heard
And saddled his best Steed, a comely gray;
Sir Walter mounted him; he was the third
Which he had mounted on that glorious
day.

Joy sparkled in the prancing courser's
eyes;
The horse and horseman are a happy pair;
But, though Sir Walter like a falcon flies,
There is a doleful silence in the air.

A rout this morning left Sir Walter's Hall,
That as they galloped made the echoes
roar;
But horse and man are vanished, one and
all;
Such race, I think, was never seen before.

Sir Walter, restless as a veering wind,
Calls to the few tired dogs that yet remain:
Blanch, Swift, and Music, noblest of their
kind,
Follow, and up the weary mountain strain.

The Knight hallooed, he cheered and chid
them on
With suppliant gestures and upbraidings
stern;
But breath and eyesight fail; and, one by
one,
The dogs are stretched among the moun-
tain fern.

Where is the throng, the tumult of the
race?
The bugles that so joyfully were blown?
— This chase it looks not like an earthly
chase;
Sir Walter and the Hart are left alone.

The poor Hart toils along the mountain-
side;
I will not stop to tell how far he fled,
Nor will I mention by what death he died;
But now the Knight beholds him lying
dead.

Dismounting, then, he leaned against a
thorn;
He had no follower, dog, nor man, nor
boy:
He neither cracked his whip, nor blew
his horn,
But gazed upon the spoil with silent joy.

Close to the thorn on which Sir Walter
leaned,
Stood his dumb partner in this glorious
feat;
Weak as a lamb the hour that it is yeaned;
And white with foam as if with cleaving
sleet.

Upon his side the Hart was lying stretched:
His nostril touched a spring beneath a hill,
And with the last deep groan his breath
had fetched
The waters of the spring were trembling
still.

And now, too happy for repose or rest,
(Never had living man such joyful lot !)
Sir Walter walked all round, north, south,
and west,
And gazed and gazed upon that darling
spot.

And climbing up the hill —(it was at least
Four roods of sheer ascent) Sir Walter
found
Three several hoof-marks which the hunt-
ed Beast
Had left imprinted on the grassy ground.

Sir Walter wiped his face, and cried, " Till
now
Such sight was never seen by human eyes:
Three leaps have borne him from this lofty
brow,
Down to the very fountain where he lies.

" I 'll build a pleasure-house upon this
spot,
And a small arbor, made for rural joy;
'T will be the traveller's shed, the pil-
grim's cot,
A place of love for damsels that are coy.

" A cunning artist will I have to frame
A basin for that fountain in the dell !

And they who do make mention of the same,
From this day forth, shall call it HART-LEAP WELL.

" And, gallant Stag ! to make thy praises known,
Another monument shall here be raised;
Three several pillars, each a rough-hewn stone,
And planted where thy hoofs the turf have grazed.

" And, in the summer-time when days are long,
I will come hither with my Paramour;
And with the dancers and the minstrel's song
We will make merry in that pleasant bower.

" Till the foundations of the mountains fail
My mansion with its arbor shall endure; —
The joy of them who till the fields of Swale,
And them who dwell among the woods of Ure ! "

Then home he went, and left the Hart, stone-dead,
With breathless nostrils stretched above the spring.
— Soon did the Knight perform what he had said;
And far and wide the fame thereof did ring.

Ere thrice the Moon into her port had steered,
A cup of stone received the living well;
Three pillars of rude stone Sir Walter reared,
And built a house of pleasure in the dell.

And near the fountain, flowers of stature tall
With trailing plants and trees were inter-twined, —
Which soon composed a little sylvan hall,
A leafy shelter from the sun and wind.

And thither, when the summer days were long,
Sir Walter led his wondering Paramour;
And with the dancers and the minstrel's song
Made merriment within that pleasant bower.

The Knight, Sir Walter, died in course of time,
And his bones lie in his paternal vale. —
But there is matter for a second rhyme,
And I to this would add another tale.

PART SECOND.

THE moving accident is not my trade;
To freeze the blood I have no ready arts :
'T is my delight, alone in summer shade,
To pipe a simple song for thinking hearts.

As I from Hawes to Richmond did repair,
It chanced that I saw standing in a dell
Three aspens at three corners of a square;
And one, not four yards distant, near a well.

What this imported I could ill divine :
And, pulling now the rein my horse to stop,
I saw three pillars standing in a line, —
The last stone-pillar on a dark hill-top.

The trees were gray, with neither arms nor head;
Half wasted the square mound of tawny green;
So that you just might say, as then I said,
" Here in old time the hand of man hath been."

I looked upon the hill both far and near,
More doleful place did never eye survey;
It seemed as if the spring-time came not here,
And Nature here were willing to decay.

I stood in various thoughts and fancies lost,
When one, who was in shepherd's garb attired,
Came up the hollow : — him did I accost,
And what this place might be I then inquired.

The Shepherd stopped, and that same
   story told
Which in my former rhyme I have re-
   hearsed.
" A jolly place," said he, "in times of
   old !
But something ails it now: the spot is
   curst.

" You see these lifeless stumps of aspen
   wood —
Some say that they are beeches, others
   elms —
These were the bower; and here a man-
   sion stood,
The finest palace of a hundred realms !

" The arbor does its own condition tell;
You see the stones, the fountain, and the
   stream;
But as to the great Lodge ! you might as
   well
Hunt half a day for a forgotten dream.

" There 's neither dog nor heifer, horse
   nor sheep,
Will wet his lips within that cup of stone;
And oftentimes, when all are fast asleep,
This water doth send forth a dolorous
   groan.

" Some say that here a murder has been
   done,
And blood cries out for blood: but, for
   my part,
I 've guessed, when I 've been sitting in
   the sun,
That it was all for that unhappy Hart.

" What thoughts must through the crea-
   ture's brain have past !
Even from the topmost stone, upon the
   steep,
Are but three bounds — and look, Sir, at
   this last —
O Master ! it has been a cruel leap.

" For thirteen hours he ran a desperate
   race;
And in my simple mind we cannot tell
What cause the Hart might have to love
   this place,
And come and make his deathbed near
   the well.

" Here on the grass perhaps asleep he
   sank,
Lulled by the fountain in the summer-
   tide;
This water was perhaps the first he drank
When he had wandered from his mother's
   side.

" In April here beneath the flowering
   thorn
He heard the birds their morning carols
   sing;
And he, perhaps, for aught we know,
   was born
Not half a furlong from that self-same
   spring.

" Now, here is neither grass nor pleasant
   shade;
The sun on drearier hollow never shone;
So will it be, as I have often said,
Till trees, and stones, and fountain, all
   are gone."

" Gray-headed Shepherd, thou hast
   spoken well;
Small difference lies between thy creed
   and mine :
This Beast not unobserved by Nature fell;
His death was mourned by sympathy
   divine.

" The Being, that is in the clouds and air,
That is in the green leaves among the
   groves,
Maintains a deep and reverential care
For the unoffending creatures whom he
   loves.

" The pleasure-house is dust :— behind,
   before,
This is no common waste, no common
   gloom;
But Nature, in due course of time, once
   more
Shall here put on her beauty and her
   bloom.

" She leaves these objects to a slow decay,
That what we are, and have been, may
   be known;
But at the coming of the milder day,
These monuments shall all be overgrown.

"One lesson, Shepherd, let us two di-
        vide,
Taught both by what she shows, and
        what conceals;
Never to blend our pleasure or our pride
With sorrow of the meanest thing that
        feels."
1800.

"'T IS SAID, THAT SOME HAVE DIED FOR LOVE."

'T is said, that some have died for love:
And here and there a churchyard grave
        is found
In the cold north's unhallowed ground,
Because the wretched man himself had
        slain,
His love was such a grievous pain.
And there is one whom I five years have
        known;
He dwells alone
Upon Helvellyn's side:
He loved — the pretty Barbara died;
And thus he makes his moan:
Three years had Barbara in her grave
        been laid
When thus his moan he made:

"Oh, move, thou Cottage, from behind
        that oak!
Or let the aged tree uprooted lie.
That in some other way yon smoke
May mount into the sky!
The clouds pass on; they from the
        heavens depart.
I look — the sky is empty space;
I know not what I trace;
But when I cease to look, my hand is on
        my heart.

"Oh! what a weight is in these shades!
        Ye leaves,
That murmur once so dear, when will it
        cease?
Your sound my heart of rest bereaves,
It robs my heart of peace.
Thou Thrush, that singest loud — and
        loud and free,
Into yon row of willows flit,
Upon that alder sit;
Or sing another song, or choose another
        tree.

"Roll back, sweet Rill! back to thy
        mountain-bounds,
And there forever be thy waters chained!
For thou dost haunt the air with sounds
That cannot be sustained;
If still beneath that pine-tree's ragged
        bough
Headlong yon waterfall must come,
Oh let it then be dumb!
Be anything, sweet Rill, but that which
        thou art now.

"Thou Eglantine, so bright with sunny
        showers,
Proud as a rainbow spanning half the
        vale,
Thou one fair shrub, oh! shed thy
        flowers,
And stir not in the gale.
For thus to see thee nodding in the air,
To see thy arch thus stretch and bend,
Thus rise and thus descend, —
Disturbs me till the sight is more than I
        can bear."

The Man who makes this feverish com-
        plaint
Is one of giant stature, who could dance
Equipped from head to foot in iron mail.
Ah gentle Love! if ever thought was thine
To store up kindred hours for me, thy face
Turn from me, gentle Love! nor let me
        walk
Within the sound of Emma's voice, nor
        know
Such happiness as I have known to-day.
1800.

THE CHILDLESS FATHER.

Written at Town-end, Grasmere. When I was
a child at Cockermouth, no funeral took place
without a basin filled with sprigs of boxwood be-
ing placed upon a table covered with a white cloth
in front of the house. The huntings on foot, in
which the old man is supposed to join as here
described, were of common, almost habitual, oc-
currence in our vales when I was a boy; and the
people took much delight in them. They are
now less frequent.

"Up, Timothy, up with your staff and
        away!
Not a soul in the village this morning
        will stay;

The hare has just started from Hamilton's
    grounds,
And Skiddaw is glad with the cry of the
    hounds."
— Of coats and of jackets grey, scarlet,
    and green,
On the slopes of the pastures all colors
    were seen;
With their comely blue aprons, and caps
    white as snow,
The girls on the hills made a holiday show.

Fresh sprigs of green boxwood, not six
    months before,
Filled the funeral basin[1] at Timothy's
    door;
A coffin through Timothy's threshold had
    passed;
One Child did it bear, and that Child was
    his last.

Now fast up the dell came the noise and
    the fray,
The horse and the horn, and the hark!
    hark away!
Old Timothy took up his staff, and he
    shut
With a leisurely motion the door of his
    hut.

Perhaps to himself at that moment he
    said;
"The key I must take, for my Ellen is
    dead."
But of this in my ears not a word did he
    speak;
And he went to the chase with a tear on
    his cheek.
1800.   1800.

SONG

FOR THE WANDERING JEW.

THOUGH the torrents from their fountains
Roar down many a craggy steep,
Yet they find among the mountains
Resting-places calm and deep.

[1] In several parts of the North of England,
when a funeral takes place, a basin full of sprigs
of boxwood is placed at the door of the house
from which the coffin is taken up, and each person
who attends the funeral ordinarily takes a sprig
of this boxwood, and throws it into the grave of
the deceased.

Clouds that love through air to hasten,
Ere the storm its fury stills,
Helmet-like themselves will fasten
On the heads of towering hills.

What, if through the frozen center
Of the Alps the Chamois bound,
Yet he has a home to enter
In some nook of chosen ground:

And the Sea-horse, though the ocean
Yield him no domestic cave,
Slumbers without sense of motion,
Couched upon the rocking wave.

If on windy days the Raven
Gambol like a dancing skiff,
Not the less she loves her haven
In the bosom of the cliff.

The fleet Ostrich, till day closes,
Vagrant over desert sands,
Brooding on her eggs reposes
When chill night that care demands.

Day and night my toils redouble,
Never nearer to the goal;
Night and day, I feel the trouble
Of the Wanderer in my soul.
1800.   1800.

RURAL ARCHITECTURE.

Written at Town-end, Grasmere. These struc-
tures, as every one knows, are common amongst
our hills, being built by shepherds, as conspicuous
marks, and occasionally by boys in sport.

THERE'S George Fisher, Charles Flem-
    ing, and Reginald Shore,
Three rosy-cheeked school-boys, the high-
    est not more
Than the height of a counsellor's bag;
To the top of GREAT HOW[1] did it please
    them to climb:
And there they built up, without mortar
    or lime,
A Man on the peak of the crag.

[1] Great How is a single and conspicuous hill,
which rises towards the foot of Thirlmere, on the
western side of the beautiful dale of Legber-
thwaite, along the high road between Keswick
and Ambleside.

They built him of stones gathered up as
    they lay:
They built him and christened him all in
    one day,
An urchin both vigorous and hale;
And so without scruple they called him
    Ralph Jones.
Now Ralph is renowned for the length of
    his bones;
The Magog of Legberthwaite dale.

Just half a week after, the wind sallied
    forth,
And, in anger or merriment, out of the
    north,
Coming on with a terrible pother,
From the peak of the crag blew the giant
    away.
And what did these school-boys? — The
    very next day
They went and they built up another.

— Some little I 've seen of blind bois-
    terous works
By Christian disturbers more savage than
    Turks,
Spirits busy to do and undo:
At remembrance whereof my blood some-
    times will flag;
Then, light-hearted Boys, to the top of the
    crag!
And I 'll build up a giant with you.
    1800.   1800.

ELLEN IRWIN:

OR,

THE BRAES OF KIRTLE.[1]

It may be worth while to observe that as there
are Scotch Poems on this subject in simple ballad
strain, I thought it would be both presumptuous
and superfluous to attempt treating it in the same
way; and, accordingly, I chose a construction of
stanza quite new in our language; in fact, the
same as that of Bürger's *Leonora*, except that
the first and third lines do not, in my stanzas,
rhyme. At the outset I threw out a classical
image to prepare the reader for the style in which
I mean to treat the story, and so to preclude all
comparison.

[1] The Kirtle is a river in the southern part of
Scotland, on the banks of which the events here
related took place.

FAIR Ellen Irwin, when she sate
Upon the braes of Kirtle,
Was lovely as a Grecian maid
Adorned with wreaths of myrtle;
Young Adam Bruce beside her lay,
And there did they beguile the day
With love and gentle speeches,
Beneath the budding beeches.

From many knights and many squires
The Bruce had been selected;
And Gordon, fairest of them all,
By Ellen was rejected.
Sad tidings to that noble Youth!
For it may be proclaimed with truth,
If Bruce hath loved sincerely,
That Gordon loves as dearly.

But what are Gordon's form and face,
His shattered hopes and crosses,
To them, 'mid Kirtle's pleasant braes,
Reclined on flowers and mosses?
Alas that ever he was born!
The Gordon, couched behind a thorn,
Sees them and their caressing;
Beholds them blest and blessing.

Proud Gordon, maddened by the thoughts
That through his brain are travelling,
Rushed forth, and at the heart of Bruce
He launched a deadly javelin!
Fair Ellen saw it as it came,
And, starting up to meet the same,
Did with her body cover
The Youth, her chosen lover.

And, falling into Bruce's arms,
Thus died the beauteous Ellen,
Thus, from the heart of her True-love,
The mortal spear repelling.
And Bruce, as soon as he had slain
The Gordon, sailed away to Spain;
And fought with rage incessant,
Against the Moorish crescent.

But many days, and many months,
And many years ensuing,
This wretched Knight did vainly seek
The death that he was wooing.
So, coming his last help to crave,
Heart-broken, upon Ellen's grave
His body he extended,
And there his sorrow ended.

Now ye, who willingly have heard
The tale I have been telling,
May in Kirkconnel churchyard view
The grave of lovely Ellen:
By Ellen's side the Bruce is laid;
And, for the stone upon his head,
May no rude hand deface it,
And its forlorn 𝕳𝖎𝖈 𝖏𝖆𝖈𝖊𝖙!
1800.   1800.

ANDREW JONES.

I HATE that Andrew Jones; he 'll breed
His children up to waste and pillage.
I wish the press-gang or the drum
With its tantara sound would come,
And sweep him from the village!

I said not this, because he loves
Through the long day to swear and tipple;
But for the poor dear sake of one
To whom a foul deed he had done,
A friendless man, a travelling cripple!

For this poor crawling helpless wretch,
Some horseman who was passing by,
A penny on the ground had thrown;
But the poor cripple was alone
And could not stoop — no help was nigh.

Inch-thick the dust lay on the ground,
For it had long been droughty weather;
So with his staff the cripple wrought
Among the dust till he had brought
The half-pennies together.

It chanced that Andrew passed that way
Just at the time; and there he found
The cripple in the mid-day heat
Standing alone, and at his feet
He saw the penny on the ground.

He stopped and took the penny up:
And when the cripple nearer drew,
Quoth Andrew, "Under half-a-crown,
What a man finds is all his own,
And so, my Friend, good-day to you."

And *hence* I said, that Andrew's boys
Will all be trained to waste and pillage;
And wished the press-gang, or the drum
With its tantara sound, would come
And sweep him from the village.
1800.   1800.

THE TWO THIEVES;

OR, THE LAST STAGE OF AVARICE.

This is described from the life, as I was in the
habit of observing when a boy at Hawkshead
School. Daniel was more than eighty years
older than myself when he was daily, thus occu-
pied, under my notice. No book could have so
early taught me to think of the changes to which
human life is subject; and while looking at him
I could not but say to myself — we may, one of
us, I or the happiest of my playmates, live to
become still more the object of pity than this old
man, this half-doating pilferer!

O NOW that the genius of Bewick were
          mine,
And the skill which he learned on the
          banks of the Tyne.
Then the Muses might deal with me just
          as they chose,
For I 'd take my last leave both of verse
          and of prose.

What feats would I work with my magi-
          cal hand!
Book-learning and books should be ban-
          ished the land:
And, for hunger and thirst and such
          troublesome calls,
Every ale-house should then have a feast
          on its walls.

The traveller would hang his wet clothes
          on a chair;
Let them smoke, let them burn, not a
          straw would he care!
For the Prodigal Son, Joseph's Dream
          and his sheaves,
Oh, what would they be to my tale of
          two Thieves?

The One, yet unbreeched, is not three
          birthdays old,
His Grandsire that age more than thirty
          times told;
There are ninety good seasons of fair
          and foul weather
Between them, and both go a-pilfering
          together.

With chips is the carpenter strewing his
   floor?
Is a cart-load of turf at an old woman's
   door?
Old Daniel his hand to the treasure will
   slide!
And his Grandson's as busy at work by
   his side.

Old Daniel begins; he stops short — and
   his eye,
Through the lost look of dotage, is cun-
   ning and sly:
'T is a look which at this time is hardly
   his own,
But tells a plain tale of the days that
   are flown.

He once had a heart which was moved
   by the wires
Of manifold pleasures and many desires:
And what if he cherished his purse?
   'T was no more
Than treading a path trod by thousands
   before.

'T was a path trod by thousands; but
   Daniel is one
Who went something farther than others
   have gone,
And now with old Daniel you see how it
   fares;
You see to what end he has brought his
   gray hairs.

The pair sally forth hand in hand: ere
   the sun
Has peered o'er the beeches, their work
   is begun:
And yet, into whatever sin they may fall,
This child but half knows it, and that,
   not at all.

They hunt through the streets with delib-
   erate tread,
And each, in his turn, becomes leader or
   led;
And, wherever they carry their plots and
   their wiles,
Every face in the village is dimpled with
   smiles.

Neither checked by the rich nor the
   needy they roam;
For the gray-headed Sire has a daughter
   at home,
Who will gladly repair all the damage
   that 's done;
And three, were it asked, would be ren-
   dered for one.

Old Man! whom so oft I with pity have
   eyed,
I love thee, and love the sweet Boy at
   thy side:
Long yet may'st thou live! for a teacher
   we see
That lifts up the veil of our nature in thee.

1800.   1800.

A CHARACTER.

The principal features are taken from that of
my friend Robert Jones.

I MARVEL how Nature could ever find
   space
For so many strange contrasts in one
   human face:
There 's thought and no thought, and
   there 's paleness and bloom
And bustle and sluggishness, pleasure
   and gloom.

There 's weakness, and strength both re-
   dundant and vain;
Such strength as, if ever affliction and pain
Could pierce through a temper that 's soft
   to disease,
Would be rational peace — a philoso-
   pher's ease.

There 's indifference, alike when he fails
   or succeeds,
And attention full ten times as much as
   there needs;
Pride where there 's no envy, there 's so
   much of joy;
And mildness, and spirit both forward
   and coy.

There 's freedom, and sometimes a diffi-
   dent stare
Of shame scarcely seeming to know that
   she 's there,

There 's virtue, the title it surely may
  claim,
Yet wants heaven knows what to be
  worthy the name.

This picture from nature may seem to
  depart,
Yet the Man would at once run away
  with your heart;
And I for five centuries right gladly
  would be
Such an odd, such a kind happy creature
  as he.
            1800.   1800.

INSCRIPTIONS

FOR THE SPOT WHERE THE HERMITAGE
  STOOD ON ST. HERBERT'S ISLAND,
  DERWENTWATER.

IF thou in the dear love of some one
  Friend
Hast been so happy that thou know'st
  what thoughts
Will sometimes in the happiness of love
Make the heart sink, then wilt thou rever-
  ence
This quiet spot; and, Stranger! not un-
  moved
Wilt thou behold this shapeless heap of
  stones,
The desolate ruins of St. Herbert's Cell.
Here stood his threshold; here was
  spread the roof
That sheltered him, a self-secluded Man,
After long exercise in social cares
And offices humane, intent to adore
The Deity, with undistracted mind,
And meditate on everlasting things,
In utter solitude. — But he had left
A Fellow-laborer, whom the good Man
  loved
As his own soul. And, when with eye
  upraised
To heaven he knelt before the crucifix,
While o'er the lake the cataract of Lodore
Pealed to his orisons, and when he paced
Along the beach of this small isle and
  thought
Of his Companion, he would pray that
  both

(Now that their earthly duties were ful-
  filled)
Might die in the same moment. Nor in
  vain
So prayed he : — as our chronicles report,
Though here the Hermit numbered his
  last day
Far from St. Cuthbert his belovèd Friend,
Those holy Men both died in the same
  hour.
      1800.   1800.

WRITTEN WITH A PENCIL UPON A STONE
  IN THE WALL OF THE HOUSE (AN OUT-
  HOUSE), ON THE ISLAND AT GRASMERE.

RUDE is this Edifice, and Thou hast seen
Buildings, albeit rude, that have main-
  tained
Proportions more harmonious, and ap-
  proached
To closer fellowship with ideal grace.
But take it in good part : — alas ! the poor
Vitruvius of our village had no help
From the great City; never, upon leaves
Of red Morocco folio, saw displayed,
In long succession, pre-existing ghosts
Of Beauties yet unborn — the rustic Lodge
Antique, and Cottage with veranda
  graced,
Nor lacking, for fit company, alcove,
Green-house, shell-grot, and moss-lined
  hermitage.
Thou see'st a homely Pile, yet to these
  walls
The heifer comes in the snow-storm, and
  here
The new-dropped lamb finds shelter from
  the wind.
And hither does one Poet sometimes row
His pinnace, a small vagrant barge, up-
  piled
With plenteous store of heath and with-
  ered fern,
(A lading which he with his sickle cuts,
Among the mountains) and beneath this
  roof
He makes his summer couch, and here at
  noon
Spreads out his limbs, while, yet unshorn,
  the Sheep,
Panting beneath the burthen of their wool,
Lie round him, even as if they were a part

Of his own Household: nor, while from
    his bed
He looks, through the open door-place,
    toward the lake
And to the stirring breezes, does he want
Creations lovely as the work of sleep —
Fair sights, and visions of romantic joy!
1800.   1800.

WRITTEN WITH A SLATE PENCIL UPON A
    STONE, THE LARGEST OF A HEAP
    LYING NEAR A DESERTED QUARRY,
    UPON ONE OF THE ISLANDS AT RYDAL.

STRANGER! this hillock of mis-shapen
    stones
Is not a Ruin spared or made by time,
Nor, as perchance thou rashly deem'st,
    the Cairn
Of some old British Chief: 't is nothing
    more
Than the rude embryo of a little Dome
Or Pleasure-house, once destined to be
    built
Among the birch-trees of this rocky isle.
But, as it chanced, Sir William having
    learned
That from the shore a full-grown man
    might wade,
And make himself a freeman of this spot
At any hour he chose, the prudent Knight
Desisted, and the quarry and the mound
Are monuments of his unfinished task.
The block on which these lines are traced,
    perhaps,
Was once selected as the corner-stone
Of that intended Pile, which would have
    been
Some quaint odd plaything of elaborate
    skill,
So that, I guess, the linnet and the thrush,
And other little builders who dwell here,
Had wondered at the work. But blame
    him not,
For old Sir William was a gentle Knight,
Bred in this vale, to which he apper-
    tained
With all his ancestry. Then peace to
    him, ·
And for the outrage which he had devised
Entire forgiveness! — But if thou art
    one ·
On fire with thy impatience to become

An inmate of these mountains, — if, dis-
    turbed
By beautiful conceptions, thou hast hewn
Out of the quiet rock the elements
Of thy trim Mansion destined soon to
    blaze
In snow-white splendor, — think again;
    and, taught
By old Sir William and his quarry, leave
Thy fragments to the bramble and the
    rose;
There let the vernal slow-worm sun him-
    self,
And let the redbreast hop from stone to
    stone.
1800.   1800.

THE SPARROW'S NEST.

*Written in the Orchard, Town-end, Grasmere.
At the end of the garden of my father's house at
Cockermouth was a high terrace that commanded
a fine view of the river Derwent and Cockermouth
Castle. This was our favorite play-ground. The
terrace-wall, a low one, was covered with closely-
clipt privet and roses, which gave an almost
impervious shelter to birds that built their nests
there. The latter of these stanzas alludes to one
of those names.*

BEHOLD, within the leafy shade,
Those bright blue eggs together laid!
On me the chance-discovered sight
Gleamed like a vision of delight.
I started — seeming to espy
The home and sheltered bed,
The Sparrow's dwelling, which, hard by
My Father's house, in wet or dry
My sister Emmeline and I
    Together visited.

She looked at it and seemed to fear it;
Dreading, tho' wishing, to be near it:
Such heart was in her, being then
A little Prattler among men.
The Blessing of my later years
Was with me when a boy:
She gave me eyes, she gave me ears;
And humble cares, and delicate fears;
A heart, the fountain of sweet tears;
    And love, and thought, and joy.
1801.   1807.

"PELION AND OSSA FLOURISH SIDE BY SIDE."

PELION and Ossa flourish side by side,
Together in immortal books enrolled:
His ancient dower Olympus hath not sold;
And that inspiring Hill, which " did
    divide
Into two ample horns his forehead wide,"
Shines with poetic radiance as of old;
While not an English Mountain we behold
By the celestial Muses glorified.
Yet round our sea-girt shore they rise in
    crowds:
What was the great Parnassus' self to
    Thee,
Mount Skiddaw? In his natural sover-
    eignty
Our British Hill is nobler far; he shrouds
His double front among Atlantic clouds,
And pours forth streams more sweet than
    Castaly.
1801.   1815.

THE PRIORESS'S TALE.

FROM CHAUCER.

" Call up him who left half told
    The story of Cambuscan bold."

In the following Poem no further deviation
from the original has been made than was neces-
sary for the fluent reading and instant under-
standing of the Author: so much, however, is the
language altered since Chaucer's time, especially
in pronunciation, that much was to be removed,
and its place supplied with as little incongruity
as possible. The ancient accent has been retained
in a few conjunctions, as *alsò* and *alwày*, from a
conviction that such sprinklings of antiquity
would be admitted, by persons of taste, to have
a graceful accordance with the subject. The
fierce bigotry of the Prioress forms a fine back-
ground for her tender-hearted sympathies with
the Mother and Child; and the mode in which
the story is told amply atones for the extravagance
of the miracle.

I.

"O LORD, our Lord! how wondrously,"
    (quoth she)
" Thy name in this large world is spread
    abroad!
For not alone by men of dignity
Thy worship is performed and precious
    laud;

But by the mouths of children, gracious
    God!
Thy goodness is set forth; they when they
    lie
Upon the breast thy name do glorify.

II.

" Wherefore in praise, the worthiest that
    I may,
Jesu! of thee, and the white Lily-flower
Which did thee bear, and is a Maid for
    aye,
To tell a story I will use my power;
Not that I may increase her honor's
    dower,
For she herself is honor, and the root
Of goodness, next her Son, our soul's
    best boot.

III.

" O Mother Maid! O Maid and Mother
    free!
O bush unburnt! burning in Moses' sight!
That down didst ravish from the Deity,
Through humbleness, the spirit that did
    alight
Upon thy heart, whence, through that
    glory's might,
Conceivèd was the Father's sapience,
Help me to tell it in thy reverence!

IV.

" Lady! thy goodness, thy magnificence,
Thy virtue, and thy great humility,
Surpass all science and all utterance;
For sometimes, Lady! ere men pray to
    thee
Thou goest before in thy benignity,
The light to us vouchsafing of thy prayer,
To be our guide unto thy Son so dear.

V.

" My knowledge is so weak, O blissful
    Queen!
To tell abroad thy mighty worthiness,
That I the weight of it may not sustain;
But as a child of twelvemónths old or less,
That laboreth his language to express,
Even so fare I; and therefore, I thee pray,
Guide thou my song which I of thee shall
    say.

VI.

" There was in Asia, in a mighty town,
'Mong Christian folk, a street where Jews
    might be,
Assigned to them and given them for their
    own
By a great Lord, for gain and usury,
Hateful to Christ and to his company;
And through this street who list might
    ride and wend;
Free was it, and unbarred at either end.

VII.

" A little school of Christian people stood
Down at the farther end, in which there
    were
A nest of children come of Christian blood,
That learnèd in that school from year to
    year
Such sort of doctrine as men usèd there,
That is to say, to sing and read alsò,
As little children in their childhood do.

VIII.

" Among these children was a Widow's
    son,
A little scholar, scarcely seven years old,
Who day by day unto this school hath gone,
And eke, when he the image did behold
Of Jesu's Mother, as he had been told,
This Child was wont to kneel adown and
    say
Ave Maria, as he goeth by the way.

IX.

" This Widow thus her little Son hath
    taught
Our blissful Lady, Jesu's Mother dear,
To worship aye, and he forgat it not;
For simple infant hath a ready ear,
Sweet is the holiness of youth: and hence,
Calling to mind this matter when I may,
Saint Nicholas in my presence standeth
    aye,
For he so young to Christ did reverence.

X.

" This little Child, while in the school he
    sate
His Primer conning with an earnest cheer,
The whilst the rest their anthem-book
    repeat
The *Alma Redemptoris* did he hear;

And as he durst he drew him near and
    near,
And hearkened to the words and to the
    note,
Till the first verse he learned it all by rote.

XI.

" This Latin knew he nothing what it said,
For he too tender was of age to know;
But to his comrade he repaired, and prayed
That he the meaning of this song would
    show,
And unto him declare why men sing so;
This oftentimes, that he might be at ease,
This child did him beseech on his bare
    knees.

XII.

" His Schoolfellow, who elder was than
    he,
Answered him thus: — ' This song, I have
    heard say,
Was fashioned for our blissful Lady free;
Her to salute, and also her to pray
To be our help upon our dying day:
If there is more in this, I know it not;
Song do I learn, — small grammar I have
    got.'

XIII.

" ' And is this song fashioned in reverence
Of Jesu's Mother ? ' said this Innocent;
' Now, certès, I will use my diligence
To con it all ere Christmas-tide be spent;
Although I for my Primer shall be shent,
And shall be beaten three times in an hour,
Our Lady I will praise with all my power.'

XIV.

" His Schoolfellow, whom he had so
    besought,
As they went homeward taught him privily
And then he sang it well and fearlessly,
From word to word according to the note:
Twice in a day it passèd through his
    throat;
Homeward and schoolward whensoe'er
    he went,
On Jesu's Mother fixed was his intent.

XV.

" Through all the Jewry (this before said I
This little Child, as he came to and fro,

Full merrily then would he sing and cry,
O *Alma Redemptoris!* high and low:
The sweetness of Christ's Mother piercèd
    so
His heart, that her to praise, to her to
    pray,
He cannot stop his singing by the way.

XVI.

" The Serpent, Satan, our first foe, that
    hath
His wasp's nest in Jew's heart, upswelled
    — ' O woe,'
O Hebrew people ! ' said he in his wrath,
' Is it an honest thing ? Shall this be so ?
That such a Boy where'er he lists shall go
In your despite, and sing his hymns and
    saws,
Which is against the reverence of our
    laws ! '

XVII.

" From that day forward have the Jews
    conspired
Out of the world this Innocent to chase;
And to this end a Homicide they hired,
That in an alley had a privy place,
And, as the Child 'gan to the school to
    pace,
This cruel Jew him seized, and held him
    fast
And cut his throat, and in a pit him cast.

XVIII.

" I say that him into a pit they threw,
A loathsome pit, whence noisome scents
    exhale;
O cursèd folk ! away, ye Herods new !
What may your ill intentions you avail ?
Murder will out; certès it will not fail;
Know, that the honor of high God may
    spread,
The blood cries out on your accursèd deed.

XIX.

" O Martyr 'stablished in virginity !
Now may'st thou sing for aye before the
    throne,
Following the Lamb celestial," quoth she,
" Of which the great Evangelist, Saint
    John,
In Patmos wrote, who saith of them that
    go

Before the Lamb singing continually,
That never fleshly woman they did know.

XX.

" Now this poor widow waiteth all that
    night
After her little Child, and he came not;
For which, by earliest glimpse of morn-
    ing light,
With face all pale with dread and busy
    thought,
She at the School and elsewhere him hath
    sought
Until thus far she learned, that he had
    been
In the Jews' street, and there he last was
    seen.

XXI.

" With Mother's pity in her breast en-
    closed
She goeth, as she were half out of her
    mind,
To every place wherein she hath supposed
By likelihood her little Son to find;
And ever on Christ's Mother meek and
    kind
She cried, till to the Jewry she was
    brought,
And him among the accursèd Jews she
    sought.

XXII.

" She asketh, and she piteously doth pray
To every Jew that dwelleth in that place
To tell her if her child had passed that
    way;
They all said — Nay; but Jesu of his
    grace
Gave to her thought, that in a little space
She for her Son in that same spot did cry
Where he was cast into a pit hard by.

XXIII.

" O thou great God that dost perform thy
    laud
By mouths of Innocents, lo ! here thy
    might;
This gem of chastity, this emerald,
And eke of martyrdom this ruby bright,
There, where with mangled throat he lay
    upright,

The *Alma Redemptoris* 'gan to sing,
So loud, that with his voice the place did
    ring.

XXIV.

"The Christian folk that through the
    Jewry went
Come to the spot in wonder at the thing;
And hastily they for the Provost sent;
Immediately he came, not tarrying,
And praiseth Christ that is our heavenly
    King,
And eke his Mother, honor of Mankind:
Which done he bade that they the Jews
    should bind.

XXV.

"This Child with piteous lamentation
    then
Was taken up, singing his song alwày;
And with procession great and pomp of
    men
To the next Abbey him they bare away;
His Mother swooning by the body lay:
And scarcely could the people that were
    near
Remove this second Rachel from the bier.

XXVI.

"Torment and shameful death to every
    one
This Provost doth for those bad Jews
    prepare
That of this murder wist, and that anon:
Such wickedness his judgments cannot
    spare;
Who will do evil, evil shall he bear;
Them therefore with wild horses did he
    draw,
And after that he hung them by the law.

XXVII.

"Upon his bier this Innocent doth lie
Before the altar while the Mass doth last:
The Abbot with his convent's company
Then sped themselves to bury him full
    fast;
And, when they holy water on him cast,
Yet spake this Child when sprinkled was
    the water,
And sang, O *Alma Redemptoris Mater !*

XXVIII.

"This Abbot, for he was a holy man,
As all Monks are, or surely ought to be,
In supplication to the Child began
Thus saying, 'O dear Child!   I summon
    thee
In virtue of the holy Trinity
Tell me the cause why thou dost sing this
    hymn   .
Since that thy throat is cut, as it doth
    seem.'

XXIX.

"'My throat is cut unto the bone, I trow,'
Said this young Child, 'and by the law of
    kind
I should have died, yea many hours ago;
But Jesus Christ, as in the books ye find,
Will that his glory last, and be in mind;
And, for the worship of his Mother dear,
Yet may I sing O *Alma !* loud and clear.

XXX.

"'This well of mercy, Jesu's Mother
    sweet,
After my knowledge I have loved alwày;
And in the hour when I my death did meet
To me she came, and thus to me did say,
"Thou in thy dying sing this holy lay,"
As ye have heard; and soon as I had sung
Methought she laid a grain upon my
    tongue.

XXXI.

"'Wherefore I sing, nor can from song
    refrain,
In honor of that blissful Maiden free,
Till from my tongue off-taken is the grain;
And after that thus said she unto me;
'My little Child, then will I come for thee
Soon as the grain from off thy tongue
    they take:
Be not dismayed, I will not thee for-
    sake!'"'

XXXII.

"This holy Monk, this Abbot — him
    mean I,
Touched then his tongue, and took away
    the grain;
And he gave up the ghost full peacefully;
And, when the Abbot had this wonder
    seen,

His salt tears trickled down like showers
    of rain;
And on his face he dropped upon the
    ground,
And still he lay as if he had been bound.

XXXIII.

" Eke the whole Convent on the pave-
    . ment lay,
Weeping and praising Jesu's Mother dear;
And after that they rose, and took their
    way,
And lifted up this Martyr from the bier,
And in a tomb of precious marble clear
Enclosed his uncorrupted body sweet. —
Where'er he be, God grant us him to
    meet !

XXXIV.

" Young Hew of Lincoln ! in like sort
    laid low
By cursèd Jews — thing well and widely
    known,
For it was done a little while ago —
Pray also thou for us, while here we tarry
Weak sinful folk, that God, with pitying
    eye,
In mercy would his mercy multiply
On us, for reverence of his Mother Mary !''

DEC. 5, 1801.   1820.

THE CUCKOO AND THE NIGHTINGALE.

FROM CHAUCER.

I.

THE God of Love — *ah, benedicite!*
How mighty and how great a Lord is he !
For he of low hearts can make high, of
    high
He can make low, and unto death bring
    nigh;
And hard hearts he can make them kind
    and free.

II.

Within a little time, as hath been found,
He can make sick folk whole and fresh
    and sound:
Them who are whole in body and in mind,

He can make sick, — bind can he and un-
    bind
All that he will have bound, or have
    unbound.

III.

To tell his might my wit may not suffice;
Foolish men he can make them out of
    wise; —
For he may do all that he will devise;
Loose livers he can make abate their vice,
And proud hearts can make tremble in a
    trice.

IV.

In brief, the whole of what he will, he
    may;
Against him dare not any wight say nay;
To humble or afflict whome'er he will,
To gladden or to grieve, he hath like skill;
But most his might he sheds on the eve of
    May.

V.

For every true heart, gentle heart and
    free,
That with him is, or thinketh so to be,
Now against May shall have some stirring
    — whether
To joy, or be it to some mourning; never
At other time, methinks, in like degree.

VI.

For now when they may hear the small
    birds' song,
And see the budding leaves the branches
    throng,
This unto their remembrance doth bring
All kinds of pleasure mixed with sor-
    rowing;
And longing of sweet thoughts that ever
    long.

VII.

And of that longing heaviness doth come,
Whence oft great sickness grows of heart
    and home :
Sick are they all for lack of their desire;
And thus in May their hearts are set on
    fire,
So that they burn forth in great martyr-
    dom.

VIII.

In sooth, I speak from feeling, what
  though now
Old am I, and to genial pleasure slow;
Yet have I felt of sickness through the
  May,
Both hot and cold, and heart-aches every
  day, —
How hard, alas! to bear, I only know.

IX.

Such shaking doth the fever in me keep
Through all this May that I have little
  sleep;
And also 't is not likely unto me,
That any living heart should sleepy be
In which Love's dart its fiery point doth
  steep.

X.

But tossing lately on a sleepless bed,
I of a token thought which Lovers heed;
How among them it was a common tale,
That it was good to hear the Nightingale,
Ere the vile Cuckoo's note be utterèd.

XI.

And then I thought anon as it was day,
I gladly would go somewhere to essay
If I perchance a Nightingale might hear,
For yet had I heard none, of all that year,
And it was then the third night of the May.

XII.

And soon as I a glimpse of day espied,
No longer would I in my bed abide,
But straightway to a wood that was hard
  by,
Forth did I go, alone and fearlessly,
And held the pathway down by a brook-
  side;

XIII.

Till to a lawn I came all white and green,
I in so fair a one had never been.
The ground was green, with daisy pow-
  dered over;
Tall were the flowers, the grove a lofty
  cover,
All green and white; and nothing else
  was seen.

XIV.

There sate I down among the fair fresh
  flowers,
And saw the birds come tripping from
  their bowers,
Where they had rested them all night;
  and they,
Who were so joyful at the light of day,
Began to honor May with all their powers.

XV.

Well did they know that service all by
  rote,
And there was many and many a lovely
  note,
Some, singing loud, as if they had com-
  plained;
Some with their notes another manner
  feigned;
And some did sing all out with the full
  throat.

XVI.

They pruned themselves, and made them-
  selves right gay,
Dancing and leaping light upon the spray;
And ever two and two together were,
The same as they had chosen for the year,
Upon Saint Valentine's returning day.

XVII.

Meanwhile the stream, whose bank I sate
  upon,
Was making such a noise as it ran on
Accordant to the sweet Birds' harmony;
Methought that it was the best melody
Which ever to man's ear a passage won.

XVIII.

And for delight, but how I never wot,
I in a slumber and a swoon was caught,
Not all asleep and yet not waking wholly;
And as I lay, the Cuckoo, bird unholy,
Broke silence, or I heard him in my
  thought.

XIX.

And that was right upon a tree fast by,
And who was then ill satisfied but I?
Now, God, quoth I, that died upon the
  rood,
From thee and thy base throat, keep all
  that 's good,
Full little joy have I now of thy cry.

XX.

And, as I with the Cuckoo thus 'gan
    chide,
In the next bush that was me fast beside,
I heard the lusty Nightingale so sing,
That her clear voice made a loud rioting,
Echoing thorough all the green wood wide.

XXI.

Ah! good sweet Nightingale! for my
    heart's cheer,
Hence hast thou stayed a little while too
    long;
For we have had the sorry Cuckoo here,
And she hath been before thee with her
    song;
Evil light on her! she hath done me
    wrong.

XXII.

But hear you now a wondrous thing, I
    pray;
As long as in that swooning-fit I lay,
Methought I wist right well what these
    birds meant,
And had good knowing both of their in-
    tent,
And of their speech, and all that they
    would say.

XXIII.

The Nightingale thus in my hearing
    spake: —
Good Cuckoo, seek some other bush or
    brake,
And, prithee, let us that can sing dwell
    here;
For every wight eschews thy song to hear,
Such uncouth singing verily dost thou
    make.

XXIV.

What! quoth she then, what is 't that
    ails thee now?
It seems to me I sing as well as thou;
For mine 's a song that is both true and
    plain, —
Although I cannot quaver so in vain
As thou dost in thy throat, I wot not how.

XXV.

All men may understanding have of me,
But, Nightingale, so may they not of thee;
For thou hast many a foolish and quaint
    cry: —
Thou say'st OSEE, OSEE, then how may I
Have knowledge, I thee pray, what this
    may be?

XXVI.

Ah, fool! quoth she, wist thou not what
    it is?
Oft as I say OSEE, OSEE, I wis,
Then mean I, that I should be wondrous
    fain
That shamefully they one and all were
    slain,
Whoever against Love mean aught amiss.

XXVII.

And also would I that they all were dead,
Who do not think in love their life to
    lead;
For who is loth the God of Love to obey,
Is only fit to die, I dare well say,
And for that cause OSEE I cry; take heed!

XXVIII.

Ay, quoth the Cuckoo, that is a quaint law,
That all must love or die; but I withdraw,
And take my leave of all such company,
For mine intent it neither is to die,
Nor ever while I live Love's yoke to
    draw.

XXIX.

For lovers of all folk that be alive,
The most disquiet have and least do
    thrive;
Most feeling have of sorrow woe and care,
And the least welfare cometh to their
    share;
What need is there against the truth to
    strive?

XXX.

What! quoth she, thou art all out of thy
    mind,
That in thy churlishness a cause canst find
To speak of Love's true Servants in this
    mood;
For in this world no service is so good
To every wight that gentle is of kind.

XXXI.

For thereof comes all goodness and all
    worth;
All gentilesse and honor thence come
    forth;

Thence worship comes, content and true
heart's pleasure,
And full-assurèd trust, joy without
measure,
And jollity, fresh cheerfulness, and mirth;

XXXII.
And bounty, lowliness, and courtesy,
And seemliness, and faithful company,
And dread of shame that will not do amiss;
For he that faithfully Love's servant is,
Rather than be disgraced, would choose
to die.

XXXIII.
And that the very truth it is which I.
Now say — in such belief I 'll live and die;
And Cuckoo, do thou so, by my advice.
Then, quoth she, let me never hope for
bliss,
If with that counsel I do e'er comply.

XXXIV.
Good Nightingale ! thou speakest won-
. drous fair,
Yet for all that, the truth is found else-
where;
For Love in young folk is but rage, I wis:
And Love in old folk a great dotage is;
Who most it useth, him 't will most impair.

XXXV.
For thereof come all contraries to glad-
ness !
Thence sickness comes, and overwhelm-
ing sadness,
Mistrust and jealousy, despite, debate,
Dishonor, shame, envy importunate,
Pride, anger, mischief, poverty, and mad-
ness.

XXXVI.
Loving is aye an office of despair,
And one thing is therein which is not fair;
For whoso gets of love a little bliss,
Unless it alway stay with him, I wis
He may full soon go with an old man's
hair.

XXXVII.
And, therefore, Nightingale ! do thou
keep nigh,
For trust me well, in spite of thy quaint
cry,

If long time from thy mate thou be, or far,
Thou 'lt be as others that forsaken are;
Then shalt thou raise a clamor as do I.

XXXVIII.
Fie, quoth she, on thy name, Bird ill be-
seen !
The God of Love afflict thee with all teen,
For thou art worse than mad a thousand
fold;
For many a one hath virtues manifold,
Who had been nought, if Love had never
been.

XXXIX.
For evermore his servants Love amendeth,
And he from every blemish them de-
fendeth;
And maketh them to burn, as in a fire,
In loyalty, and worshipful desire,
And, when it likes him, joy enough them
sendeth.

XL.
Thou Nightingale ! the Cuckoo said, be
still,
For Love no reason hath but his own
will;
For to th' untrue he oft gives ease and joy;
True lovers doth so bitterly annoy,
He lets them perish through that grievous
ill.

XLI.
With such a master would I never be; [1]
For he, in sooth, is blind, and may not see,
And knows not when he hurts and when
he heals;
Within this court full seldom Truth avails,
So diverse in his wilfulness is he.

XLII.
Then of the Nightingale did I take note,
How from her inmost heart a sigh she
brought,
And said, Alas ! that ever I was born,
Not one word have I now, I am so for-
lorn, —
And with that word, she into tears burst
out.

[1] From a manuscript in the Bodleian, as are
also stanzas 44 and 45, which are necessary to
complete the sense.

XLIII.

Alas, alas ! my very heart will break, ·
Quoth she, to hear this churlish bird thus
    speak
Of Love, and of his holy services;
Now, God of Love; thou help me in some
    wise,
That vengeance on this Cuckoo I may
    wreak.

XLIV.

And so methought I started up anon,
And to the brook I ran and got a stone,
Which at the Cuckoo hardily I cast,
And he for dread did fly away full fast;
And glad, in sooth, was I when he was
    gone.

XLV.

And as he flew, the Cuckoo, ever and aye,
Kept crying " Farewell ! — farewell, Pop-
    injay ! "
As if in scornful mockery of me;
And on I hunted him from tree to tree,
Till he was far, all out of sight, away.

XLVI.

Then straightway came the Nightingale to
    me,
And said, Forsooth, my friend, do I thank
    thee,
That thou wert near to rescue me; and
    now,
Unto the God of Love I make a vow,
That all this May I will thy songstress be.

XLVII.

Well satisfied, I thanked her, and she said,
By this mishap no longer be dismayed,
Though thou the Cuckoo heard, ere thou
    heard'st me;
Yet if I live it shall amended be,
When next May comes, if I am not afraid.

XLVIII.

And one thing will I counsel thee alsò,
The Cuckoo trust not thou, nor his Love's
    saw;
All that she said is an outrageous lie.
Nay, nothing shall me bring thereto,
    quoth I,
For Love, and it hath done me mighty
    woe.

XLIX.

Yea, hath it ? use, quoth she, this medi·
    cine;
This May-time, every day before thou
    dine,
Go look on the fresh daisy; then say I,
Although for pain thou may'st be like to
    die,
Thou wilt be eased, and less wilt droop
    and pine.

L.

And mind always that thou be good and
    true,
And I will sing one song, of many new,
For love of thee, as loud as I may cry;
And then did she begin this song full high,
" Beshrew all them that are in love un-
    true."

LI.

And soon as she had sung it to the end,
Now farewell, quoth she, for I hence
    must wend;
And, God of Love, that can right well
    and may,
Send unto thee as mickle joy this day,
As ever he to Lover yet did send.

LII.

Thus takes the Nightingale her leave of
    · me;
I pray to God with her always to be,
And joy of love to send her evermore;
And shield us from the Cuckoo and her
    lore,
For there is not so false a bird as she.

LIII.

Forth then she flew, the gentle Nightin-
    gale,
To all the Birds that lodged within that
    dale,
And gathered each and all into one place;
And them besought to hear her doleful
    case,
And thus it was that she began her tale.

LIV.

The Cuckoo — 't is not well that I should
    hide
How she and I did each the other chide,

And without ceasing, since it was day-
light;
And now I pray you all to do me right
Of that false Bird whom Love cannot
abide.

LV.

Then spake one Bird, and full assent all
gave;
This matter asketh counsel good as grave,
For birds we are — all here together
brought;
And, in good sooth, the Cuckoo here is
not;
And therefore we a Parliament will have.

LVI.

And thereat shall the Eagle be our Lord,
And other Peers whose names are on
record;
A summons to the Cuckoo shall be sent,
And judgment there be given; or that
intent
Failing, we finally shall make accord.

LVII.

And all this shall be done, without a nay,
The morrow after Saint Valentine's day,
Under a maple that is well beseen,
Before the chamber-window of the Queen,
At Woodstock, on the meadow green and
gay.

LVIII.

She thankèd them; and then her leave
she took,
And flew into a hawthorn by that brook;
And there she sate and sung — upon that
tree —
" For term of life Love shall have hold
of me " —
So loudly, that I with that song awoke.

Unlearnèd Book and rude, as well I know,
For beauty thou hast none, nor eloquence,
Who did on thee the hardiness bestow
To appear before my Lady? but a sense
Thou surely hast of her benevolence,
Whereof her hourly bearing proof doth
give;
For of all good she is the best alive.

Alas, poor Book! for thy unworthiness,
To show to her some pleasant meanings
writ
In winning words, since through her gen-
tiles,
Thee she accepts as for her service fit!
Oh! it repents me I have neither wit
Nor leisure unto thee more worth to give;
For of all good she is the best alive.

Beseech her meekly with all lowliness,
Though I be far from her I reverence,
To think upon my truth and steadfastness,
And to abridge my sorrow's violence,
Caused by the wish, as knows your sa-
pience,
She of her liking proof to me would give;
For of all good she is the best alive.

L'ENVOY.

Pleasure's Aurora, Day of gladsomeness!
Luna by night, with heavenly influence
Illumined! root of beauty and goodnesse,
Write, and allay, by your beneficence,
My sighs breathed forth in silence, —
comfort give!
Since of all good, you are the best alive.

EXPLICIT.
Dec. 8, 1801. 1842.

TROILUS AND CRESIDA.

FROM CHAUCER.

Next morning Troilus began to clear
His eyes from sleep, at the first break of
day,
And unto Pandarus, his own Brother dear,
For love of God, full piteously did say,
We must the Palace see of Cresida;
For since we yet may have no other feast,
Let us behold her Palace at the least!

And therewithal to cover his intent
A cause he found into the Town to go,
And they right forth to Cresid's Palace
went;
But, Lord, this simple Troilus was woe,
Him thought his sorrowful heart would
break in two;
For when he saw her doors fast bolted all,
Well nigh for sorrow down he 'gan to fall.

Therewith when this true Lover 'gan be-
　　hold,
How shut was every window of the place,
Like frost he thought his heart was icy
　　cold;
For which, with changèd, pale, and
　　deadly face,
Without word uttered, forth he 'gan to
　　pace;
And on his purpose bent so fast to ride,
That no wight his continuance espied.

Then said he thus, — O Palace desolate!
O house of houses, once so richly dight!
O Palace empty and disconsolate!
Thou lamp of which extinguished is the
　　light;
O Palace whilom day that now art night,
Thou ought'st to fall and I to die; since
　　she
Is gone who held us both in sovereignty.

O, of all houses once the crownèd boast!
Palace illumined with the sun of bliss;
O ring of which the ruby now is lost,
O cause of woe, that cause has been of
　　bliss:
Yet, since I may no better, would I kiss
Thy cold doors; but I dare not for this
　　rout;
Farewell, thou shrine of which the Saint
　　is out.

Therewith he cast on Pandarus an eye,
With changèd face, and piteous to be-
　　hold;
And when he might his time aright espy,
Aye as he rode, to Pandarus he told
Both his new sorrow and his joys of old,
So piteously, and with so dead a hue,
That every wight might on his sorrow rue.

Forth from the spot he rideth up and
　　down,
And everything to his rememberànce
Came as he rode by places of the town
Where he had felt such perfect pleasure
　　once.
Lo, yonder saw I mine own Lady dance,
And in that Temple she with her bright
　　eyes,
My Lady dear, first bound me captive-
　　wise.

And yonder with joy-smitten heart have I
Heard my own Cresid's laugh; and once
　　at play
I yonder saw her eke full blissfully;
And yonder once she unto me 'gan say —
Now, my sweet Troilus, love me well, I
　　pray!
And there so graciously did me behold,
That hers unto the death my heart I hold.

And at the corner of that self-same house
Heard I my most belovèd Lady dear,
So womanly, with voice melodious
Singing so well, so goodly, and so clear,
That in my soul methinks I yet do hear
The blissful sound; and in that very place
My Lady first me took unto her grace.

O blissful God of Love! then thus he
　　cried,
When I the process have in memory,
How thou hast wearied me on every side,
Men thence a book might make, a his-
　　tory;
What need to seek a conquest over me,
Since I am wholly at thy will? what joy
Hast thou thy own liege subjects to
　　destroy?

Dread Lord! so fearful when provoked,
　　thine ire
Well hast thou wreaked on me by pain
　　and grief.
Now mercy, Lord! thou know'st well I
　　desire
Thy grace above all pleasures first and
　　chief;
And live and die I will in thy belief;
For which I ask for guerdon but one boon,
That Cresida again thou send me soon.

Constrain her heart as quickly to return,
As thou dost mine with longing her to see,
Then know I well that she would not so-
　　journ.
Now, blissful Lord, so cruel do not be
Unto the blood of Troy, I pray of thee,
As Juno was unto the Theban blood,
From whence to Thebes came griefs in
　　multitude.

And after this he to the gate did go,
Whence Cresid rode, as if in haste she
was;
And up and down there went, and to and
fro,
And to himself full oft he said, alas!
From hence my hope, and solace forth
did pass.
O would the blissful God now for his joy,
I might her see again coming to Troy!

And up to yonder hill was I her guide;
Alas, and there I took of her my leave;
Yonder I saw her to her Father ride,
For very grief of which my heart shall
cleave; —
And hither home I came when it was eve;
And here I dwell an outcast from all joy,
And shall, unless I see her soon in Troy.

And of himself did he imagine oft,
That he was blighted, pale, and waxen
less
Than he was wont; and that in whispers
soft
Men said, what may it be, can no one
guess
Why Troilus hath all this heaviness?
All which he of himself conceited wholly
Out of his weakness and his melancholy.

Another time he took into his head,
That every wight, who in the way passed
by,
Had of him ruth, and fancied that they
said,
I am right sorry Troilus will die:
And thus a day or two drove wearily;
As ye have heard; such life 'gan he to
lead
As one that standeth betwixt hope and
dread.

For which it pleased him in his songs to
show
The occasion of his woe, as best he might;
And made a fitting song, of words but few,
Somewhat his woeful heart to make more
light;
And when he was removed from all men's
sight,

With a soft night voice, he of his Lady
dear,
That absent was, 'gan sing as ye may hear.

O star, of which I lost have all the light,
With a sore heart well ought I to be-
wail,
That ever dark in torment, night by night,
Toward my death with wind I steer and
sail;
For which upon the tenth night if thou
fail
With thy bright beams to guide me but
one hour,
My ship and me Charybdis will devour.

As soon as he this song had thus sung
through,
He fell again into his sorrows old;
And every night, as was his wont to do,
Troilus stood the bright moon to be-
hold;
And all his trouble to the moon he told,
And said; I wis, when thou art horn'd
anew,
I shall be glad if all the world be true.

Thy horns were old as now upon that
morrow,
When hence did journey my bright Lady
dear,
That cause is of my torment and my
sorrow;
For which, oh, gentle Luna, bright and
clear;
For love of God, run fast above thy
sphere;
For when thy horns begin once more to
spring,
Then shall she come, that with her bliss
may bring.

The day is more, and longer every night
Than they were wont to be — for he
thought so;
And that the sun did take his course not
right,
By longer way than he was wont to go;
And said, I am in constant dread I trow,
That Phaëton his son is yet alive,
His too fond father's car amiss to drive.

Upon the walls fast also would he walk,
To the end that he the Grecian host might
    see;
And ever thus he to himself would talk :—
Lo! yonder is my own bright Lady free;
Or yonder is it that the tents must be;
And thence does come this air which is so
    sweet,
That in my soul I feel the joy of it.

And certainly this wind, that more and
    more
By moments thus increaseth in my face,
Is of my Lady's sighs heavy and sore;
I prove it thus; for in no other space
Of all this town, save only in this place,
Feel I a wind, that soundeth so like pain;
It saith, Alas, why severed are we twain?

A weary while in pain he tosseth thus,
Till fully past and gone was the ninth
    night;
And ever at his side stood Pandarus,
Who busily made use of all his might
To comfort him, and make his heart more
    light;
Giving him always hope, that she the
    morrow
Of the tenth day will come, and end his
    sorrow.

1801.   1842.

THE SAILOR'S MOTHER.

Written at Town-end, Grasmere. I met this
woman near the Wishing-gate, on the high-road
that then led from Grasmere to Ambleside. Her
appearance was exactly as here described, and
such was her account, nearly to the letter.

ONE morning (raw it was and wet —
A foggy day in winter time)
A Woman on the road I met,
Not old, though something past her
    prime :
Majestic in her person, tall and straight;
And like a Roman matron's was her mien
    and gait.

The ancient spirit is not dead;
Old times, thought I, are breathing
    there;
Proud was I that my country bred

Such strength, a dignity so fair :
She begged an alms, like one in poor
    estate;
I looked at her again, nor did my pride
    abate.

When from these lofty thoughts I woke,
"What is it," said I, "that you bear,
Beneath the covert of your Cloak,
Protected from this cold damp air?"
She answered, soon as she the question
    heard,
"A simple burthen, Sir, a little Singing-
    bird."

And, thus continuing, she said,
"I had a Son, who many a day
Sailed on the seas, but he is dead;
In Denmark he was cast away :
And I have travelled weary miles to see
If aught which he had owned might still
    remain for me.

"The bird and cage they both were his :
'T was my Son's bird; and neat and trim
He kept it : many voyages
The singing-bird had gone with him;
When last he sailed, he left the bird
    behind;
From bodings, as might be, that hung
    upon his mind.

"He to a fellow-lodger's care
Had left it, to be watched and fed,
And pipe its song in safety; — there
I found it when my Son was dead;
And now, God help me for my little wit!
I bear it with me, Sir; — he took so much
    delight in it."

MARCH, 1802.   1807.

ALICE FELL;

OR, POVERTY.

Written to gratify Mr. Graham of Glasgow,
brother of the Author of "The Sabbath." He
was a zealous coadjutor of Mr. Clarkson, and a
man of ardent humanity. The incident had hap-
pened to himself, and he urged me to put it into
verse, for humanity's sake. The humbleness,
meanness if you like, of the subject, together
with the homely mode of treating it, brought

upon me a world of ridicule by the small critics, so that in policy I excluded it from many editions of my Poems, till it was restored at the request of some of my friends, in particular my son-in-law, Edward Quillinan.

THE post-boy drove with fierce career,
For threatening clouds the moon had
    drowned;
When, as we hurried on, my ear
Was smitten with a startling sound.

As if the wind blew many ways,
I heard the sound, — and more and more,
It seemed to follow with the chaise,
And still I heard it as before.

At length I to the boy called out;
He stopped his horses at the word,
But neither cry, nor voice, nor shout,
Nor aught else like it, could be heard.

The boy then smacked his whip, and fast
The horses scampered through the rain;
But, hearing soon upon the blast
The cry, I bade him halt again.

Forthwith alighting on the ground,
" Whence comes," said I, " this piteous
    moan ? "
And there a little Girl I found,
Sitting behind the chaise, alone.

" My cloak ! " no other word she spake,
But loud and bitterly she wept,
As if her innocent heart would break;
And down from off her seat she leapt.

" What ails you, child ? " — she sobbed
    " Look here ! "
I saw it in the wheel entangled,
A weather-beaten rag as e'er
From any garden scare-crow dangled.

There, twisted between nave and spoke,
It hung, nor could at once be freed;
But our joint pains unloosed the cloak,
A miserable rag indeed !

" And whither are you going, child,
To-night along these lonesome ways ? "
" To Durham," answered she, half wild—
" Then come with me into the chaise."

Insensible to all relief
Sat the poor girl, and forth did send
Sob after sob, as if her grief
Could never, never have an end.

" My child, in Durham do you dwell ? "
She checked herself in her distress,
And said, " My name is Alice Fell;
I 'm fatherless and motherless.

" And I to Durham, Sir, belong."
Again, as if the thought would choke
Her very heart, her grief grew strong;
And all was for her tattered cloak !

The chaise drove on; our journey's end
Was nigh; and, sitting by my side,
As if she had lost her only friend
She wept, nor would be pacified.

Up to the tavern-door we post;
Of Alice and her grief I told;
And I gave money to the host,
To buy a new cloak for the old.

" And let it be of duffil gray,
As warm a cloak as man can sell ! "
Proud creature was she the next day,
The little orphan, Alice Fell !
   MARCH, 1802.   1807.

BEGGARS.

Written at Town-end, Grasmere. Met, and described to me by my Sister, near the quarry at the head of Rydal lake, a place still a chosen resort of vagrants travelling with their families.

SHE had a tall man's height or more;
Her face from summer's noontide heat
No bonnet shaded, but she wore
A mantle, to her very feet
Descending with a graceful flow,
And on her head a cap as white as new-
    fallen snow.

Her skin was of Egyptian brown:
Haughty, as if her eye had seen
Its own light to a distance thrown,
She towered, fit person for a Queen
To lead those ancient Amazonian files;
Or ruling Bandit's wife among the Gre-
    cian isles.

Advancing, forth she stretched her hand
And begged an alms with doleful plea
That ceased not; on our English land
Such woes, I knew, could never be;
And yet a boon I gave her, for the crea-
    ture
Was beautiful to see — a weed of glorious
    feature.

I left her, and pursued my way;
And soon before me did espy
A pair of little Boys at play,
Chasing a crimson butterfly;
The taller followed with his hat in hand,
Wreathed round with yellow flowers the
    gayest of the land.

The other wore a rimless crown
With leaves of laurel stuck about;
And, while both followed up and down,
Each whooping with a merry shout,
In their fraternal features I could trace
Unquestionable lines of that wild Sup-
    pliant's face.

Yet *they*, so blithe of heart, seemed fit
For finest tasks of earth or air:
Wings let them have, and they might flit
Precursors to Aurora's car,
Scattering fresh flowers; though happier
    far, I ween,
To hunt their fluttering game o'er rock
    and level green.

They dart across my path — but lo,
Each ready with a plaintive whine!
Said I, "not half an hour ago
Your Mother has had alms of mine."
"That cannot be," one answered —
    "she is dead:" —
I looked reproof — they saw — but neither
    hung his head.

" She has been dead, Sir, many a day." —
" Hush, boys! you 're telling me a lie;
It was your Mother, as I say!"
And, in the twinkling of an eye,
" Come! Come!" cried one, and with-
    out more ado,
Off to some other play the joyous Va-
    grants flew!

MARCH, 1802.   1807.

TO A BUTTERFLY.

Written in the orchard, Town-end, Grasmere.
My sister and I were parted immediately after
the death of our mother, who died in 1778, both
being very young.

STAY near me — do not take thy flight!
A little longer stay in sight!
Much converse do I find in thee,
Historian of my infancy!
Float near me; do not yet depart!
Dead times revive in thee:
Thou bring'st, gay creature as thou art!
A solemn image to my heart,
My father's family!

Oh! pleasant, pleasant were the days,
The time, when, in our childish plays,
My sister Emmeline and I
Together chased the butterfly!
A very hunter did I rush
Upon the prey: — with leaps and springs
I followed on from brake to bush;
But she, God love her, feared to brush
The dust from off its wings.

MARCH, 1802.   1807.

THE EMIGRANT MOTHER.

Suggested by what I have noticed in more than
one French fugitive during the time of the French
Revolution. If I am not mistaken, the lines
were composed at Sockburn, when I was on a
visit to Mrs. Wordsworth and her brother.

ONCE in a lonely hamlet I sojourned
In which a Lady driven from France did
    dwell;
The big and lesser griefs with which she
    mourned,
In friendship she to me would often tell.
This Lady, dwelling upon British ground,
Where she was childless, daily would re-
    pair

To a poor neighboring cottage; as I
    found,
For sake of a young Child whose home
    was there.
Once having seen her clasp with fond
    embrace
This Child, I chanted to myself a lay,

Endeavoring, in our English tongue, to
    trace
Such things as she unto the Babe might
    say:
And thus, from what I heard and knew,
    or guessed,
My song the workings of her heart ex-
    pressed.

I.

" Dear Babe, thou daughter of another,
One moment let me be thy mother!
An infant's face and looks are thine,
And sure a mother's heart is mine:
Thy own dear mother's far away,
At labor in the harvest field:
Thy little sister is at play; —
What warmth, what comfort would it
    yield
To my poor heart, if thou wouldst be
One little hour a child to me!

II.

" Across the waters I am come,
And I have left a babe at home:
A long, long way of land and sea!
Come to me — I 'm no enemy:
I am the same who at thy side
Sate yesterday, and made a nest
For thee, sweet Baby! — thou hast tried,
Thou know'st the pillow of my breast;
Good, good art thou: — alas! to me .
Far more than I can be to thee.

III.

" Here, little Darling, dost thou lie;
An infant thou, a mother I!
Mine wilt thou be, thou hast no fears;
Mine art thou — spite of these my tears.
Alas! before I left the spot,
My baby and its dwelling-place;
The nurse said to me, ' Tears should not
Be shed upon an infant's face,
It was unlucky ' — no, no, no;
No truth is in them who say so!

IV.

" My own dear Little-one will sigh,
Sweet Babe! and they will let him die.
' He pines,' they 'll say, ' it is his doom,
And you may see his hour is come.'
Oh! had he but thy cheerful smiles,
Limbs stout as thine, and lips as gay,
Thy looks, thy cunning, and thy wiles,
And countenance like a summer's day,
They would have hopes of him; — and
    then
I should behold his face again!

V.

" ' T is gone — like dreams that we forget;
There was a smile or two — yet — yet
I can remember them, I see
The smiles, worth all the world to me.
Dear Baby! I must lay thee down;
Thou troublest me with strange alarms;
Smiles hast thou, bright ones of thy own;
I cannot keep thee in my arms;
For they confound me; — where — where
    is
That last, that sweetest smile of his?

VI.

" Oh! how I love thee! — we will stay
Together here this one half day.
My sister's child, who bears my name,
From France to sheltering England came;
She with her mother crossed the sea;
The babe and mother near me dwell:
Yet does my yearning heart to thee
Turn rather, though I love her well:
Rest, little Stranger, rest thee here!
Never was any child more dear!

VII.

" — I cannot help it; ill intent
I 've none, my pretty Innocent!
I weep — I know they do thee wrong,
These tears — and my poor idle tongue.
Oh, what a kiss was that! my cheek
How cold it is! but thou art good;
Thine eyes are on me — they would speak,
I think, to help me if they could.
Blessings upon that soft, warm face,
My heart again is in its place!

VIII.

" While thou art mine, my little Love,
This cannot be a sorrowful grove;
Contentment, hope, and mother's glee,
I seem to find them all in thee:
Here's grass to play with, here are flowers;
I 'll call thee by my darling's name;
Thou hast, I think, a look of ours,

Thy features seem to me the same;
His little sister thou shalt be;
And, when once more my home I see,
I 'll tell him many tales of Thee."
MARCH, 1802.   1807.

"MY HEART LEAPS UP WHEN I BEHOLD."

Written at Town-end, Grasmere.

My heart leaps up when I behold
    A rainbow in the sky:
So was it when my life began;
So is it now I am a man;
So be it when I shall grow old,
    Or let me die!
The Child is father of the Man;
And I could wish my days to be
Bound each to each by natural piety.
MARCH 26, 1802.   1807.

"AMONG ALL LOVELY THINGS MY LOVE HAD BEEN."

AMONG all lovely things my Love had
    been;
Had noted well the stars, all flowers that
    grew
About her home; but she had never seen
A glow-worm, never one, and this I knew.

While riding near her home one stormy
    night
A single glow-worm did I chance to espy;
I gave a fervent welcome to the sight,
And from my horse I leapt; great joy
    had I.

Upon a leaf the glow-worm did I lay,
To bear it with me through the stormy
    night:
And, as before, it shone without dismay;
Albeit putting forth a fainter light.
When to the dwelling of my Love I came,
I went into the orchard quietly;
And left the glow-worm, blessing it by
    name,
Laid safely by itself, beneath a tree.

The whole next day, I hoped, and hoped
    with fear;
At night the glow-worm shone beneath
    the tree;
I led my Lucy to the spot, "Look here,"
Oh! joy it was for her, and joy for me!
APRIL 12, 1802.   1807.

WRITTEN IN MARCH,

WHILE RESTING ON THE BRIDGE AT THE FOOT OF BROTHER'S WATER.

Extempore. This little poem was a favorite with Joanna Baillie.

THE Cock is crowing,
The stream is flowing,
The small birds twitter,
The lake doth glitter,
The green field sleeps in the sun;
    The oldest and youngest
    Are at work with the strongest;
The cattle are grazing,
Their heads never raising;
There are forty feeding like one!

Like an army defeated
The snow hath retreated,
And now doth fare ill
On the top of the bare hill;
The ploughboy is whooping — anon —
    anon:
There 's joy in the mountains;
There 's life in the fountains;
Small clouds are sailing,
Blue sky prevailing;
The rain is over and gone!
1802.   1807.

THE REDBREAST CHASING THE BUTTERFLY.

Observed, as described, in the then beautiful orchard, Town-end, Grasmere.

ART thou the bird whom Man loves best,
The pious bird with the scarlet breast,
    Our little English robin;
The bird that comes about our doors
When Autumn winds are sobbing?
Art thou the Peter of Norway Boors?
    Their Thomas in Finland,
    And Russia far inland?

The bird, that by some name or other
All men who know thee call their brother,
The darling of children and men?
Could Father Adam [1] open his eyes
And see this sight beneath the skies,
He 'd wish to close them again.
—If the Butterfly knew but his friend,
Hither his flight he would bend;
And find his way to me,
Under the branches of the tree:
In and out, he darts about;
· Can this be the bird, to man so good,
That, after their bewildering,
Covered with leaves the little children,
    So painfully in the wood?
What ailed thee, Robin, thàt thou could'st
        pursue
    A beautiful creature,
That is gentle by nature?
Beneath the summer sky
From flower to flower let him fly;
'T is all that he wishes to do.
The cheerer Thou of our in-door sadness,
He is the friend of our summer gladness:
What hinders, then, that ye should be
Playmates in the sunny weather,
And fly about in the air together!
His beautiful wings in crimson are drest,
A crimson as bright as thine own:
Would'st thou be happy in thy nest,
O pious Bird! whom man loves best,
Love him, or leave him alone!
    APRIL 18, 1802.   1807.

TO A BUTTERFLY.

Written in the orchard, Town-end, Grasmere.

I 'VE watched you now a full half-hour,
Self-poised upon that yellow flower;
And, little Butterfly! indeed
I know not if you sleep or feed.
How motionless! — not frozen seas
More motionless! and then
What joy awaits you, when the breeze
Hath found you out among the trees,
And calls you forth again!

[1] See *Paradise Lost*, Book XI., where Adam
points out to Eve the ominous sign of the Eagle
chasing "two birds of gayest plume," and the
gentle Hart and Hind pursued by their enemy.

This plot of orchard-ground is ours;
My trees they are, my Sister's flowers;
Here rest your wings when they are
        weary;
Here lodge as in a sanctuary!
Come often to us, fear no wrong;
Sit near us on the bough!
We 'll talk of sunshine and of song,
And summer days, when we were young;
Sweet childish days, that were as long
As twenty days are now.
    APRIL 20, 1802.   1807.

FORESIGHT.

Also composed in the orchard, Town-end,
Grasmere.

THAT is work of waste and ruin —
Do as Charles and I are doing!
Strawberry-blossoms, one and all,
We must spare them — here are many:
Look at it — the flower is small,
Small and low, though fair as any:
Do not touch it! summers two
I am older, Anne, than you.

Pull the primrose, sister Anne!
Pull as many as you can.
— Here are daisies, take your fill;
Pansies, and the cuckoo-flower:
Of the lofty daffodil
Make your bed, or make your bower;
Fill your lap, and fill your bosom;
Only spare the strawberry-blossom!

Primroses, the Spring may love them —
Summer knows but little of them:
Violets, a barren kind,
Withered on the ground must lie;
Daisies leave no fruit behind
When the pretty flowerets die;
Pluck them, and another year
As many will be blowing here.

God has given a kindlier power
To the favored strawberry-flower.
Hither soon as spring is fled
You and Charles and I will walk;
Lurking berries, ripe and red,
Then will hang on every stalk,
Each within its leafy bower;
And for that promise spare the flower!
    APRIL 28, 1802.   1807.

TO THE SMALL CELANDINE.[1]

Written at Town-end, Grasmere. It is remarkable that this flower, coming out so early in the spring as it does, and so bright and beautiful, and in such profusion, should not have been noticed earlier in English verse. What adds much to the interest that attends it is its habit of shutting itself up and opening out according to the degree of light and temperature of the air.

PANSIES, lilies, kingcups, daisies,
Let them live upon their praises;
Long as there 's a sun that sets,
Primroses will have their glory;
Long as there are violets,
They will have a place in story:
There 's a flower that shall be mine,
'T is the little Celandine.

Eyes of some men travel far
For the finding of a star;
Up and down the heavens they go,
Men that keep a mighty rout!
I 'm as great as they, I trow,
Since the day I found thee out,
Little Flower! — I 'll make a stir,
Like a sage astronomer.

Modest, yet withal an Elf
Bold, and lavish of thyself;
Since we needs must first have met
I have seen thee, high and low,
Thirty years or more, and yet
'T was a face I did not know;
Thou hast now, go where I may,
Fifty greetings in a day.

Ere a leaf is on a bush,
In the time before the thrush
Has a thought about her nest,
Thou wilt come with half a call,
Spreading out thy glossy breast
Like a careless Prodigal;
Telling tales about the sun,
When we 've little warmth, or none.

Poets, vain men in their mood!
Travel with the multitude:
Never heed them; I aver
That they all are wanton wooers;

[1] Common Pilewort.

But the thrifty cottager,
Who stirs little out of doors,
Joys to spy thee near her home;
Spring is coming, Thou art come!

Comfort have thou of thy merit,
Kindly, unassuming Spirit!
Careless of thy neighborhood,
Thou dost show thy pleasant face
On the moor, and in the wood,
In the lane; — there 's not a place,
Howsoever mean it be,
But 't is good enough for thee.

Ill befall the yellow flowers,
Children of the flaring hours!
Buttercups, that will be seen,
Whether we will see or no;
Others, too, of lofty mien;
They have done as worldings do,
Taken praise that should be thine,
Little, humble Celandine!

Prophet of delight and mirth,
Ill-requited upon earth;
Herald of a mighty band,
Of a joyous train ensuing,
Serving at my heart's command,
Tasks that are no tasks renewing,
I will sing, as doth behove,
Hymns in praise of what I love!
APRIL 30, 1802.   1807

TO THE SAME FLOWER.

PLEASURES newly found are sweet
When they lie about our feet:
February last, my heart
First at sight of thee was glad;
All unheard of as thou art,
Thou must needs, I think, have had,
Celandine! and long ago,
Praise of which I nothing know.

I have not a doubt but he,
Whosoe'er the man might be,
Who the first with pointed rays
(Workman worthy to be sainted)
Set the sign-board in a blaze,
When the rising sun he painted,
Took the fancy from a glance
At thy glittering countenance.

Soon as gentle breezes bring
News of winter's vanishing,
And the children build their bowers,
Sticking 'kerchief-plots of mould
All about with full-blown flowers,
Thick as sheep in shepherd's fold!
With the proudest thou art there,
Mantling in the tiny square.

Often have I sighed to measure
By myself a lonely pleasure,
Sighed to think, I read a book
Only read, perhaps, by me;
Yet I long could overlook
Thy bright coronet and Thee,
And thy arch and wily ways,
And thy store of other praise.

Blithe of heart, from week to week
Thou dost play at hide-and-seek;
While the patient primrose sits
Like a beggar in the cold,
Thou, a flower of wiser wits,
Slipp'st into thy sheltering hold;
Liveliest of the vernal train
When ye all are out again.

Drawn by what peculiar spell,
By what charm of sight or smell,
Does the dim-eyed curious Bee,
Laboring for her waxen cells,
Fondly settle upon Thee
Prized above all buds and bells
Opening daily at thy side,
By the season multiplied?

Thou art not beyond the moon,
But a thing " beneath our shoon: "
Let the bold Discoverer thrid
In his bark the polar sea;
Rear who will a pyramid;
Praise it is enough for me,
If there be but three or four
Who will love my little Flower.

MAY 1, 1802.   1807.

RESOLUTION AND INDE-
PENDENCE.

Written at Town-end Grasmere. This old
man I met a few hundred yards from my cottage;
and the account of him is taken from his own
mouth. I was in the state of feeling described in
the beginning of the poem, while crossing over
Barton Fell from Mr. Clarkson's, at the foot of
Ullswater, towards Askham. The image of the
hare I then observed on the ridge of the Fell.

I.

THERE was a roaring in the wind all night;
The rain came heavily and fell in floods;
But now the sun is rising calm and bright;
The birds are singing in the distant woods;
Over his own sweet voice the Stock-dove
        broods;
The Jay makes answer as the Magpie
        chatters;
And all the air is filled with pleasant
        noise of waters.

II.

All things that love the sun are out of
        doors;
The sky rejoices in the morning's birth;
The grass is bright with rain-drops; — on
        the moors
The hare is running races in her mirth;
And with her feet she from the plashy
        earth
Raises a mist, that, glittering in the sun,
Runs with her all the way, wherever she
        doth run.

III.

I was a Traveller then upon the moor,
I saw the hare that raced about with joy;
I heard the woods and distant waters
        roar;
Or heard them not, as happy as a boy:
The pleasant season did my heart employ:
My old remembrances went from me
        wholly;
And all the ways of men, so vain and
        melancholy.

IV.

But, as it sometimes chanceth, from the
        might
Of joy in minds that can no further go,
As high as we have mounted in delight
In our dejection do we sink as low;
To me that morning did it happen so;
And fears and fancies thick upon me
        came;
Dim sadness — and blind thoughts, I
        knew not, nor could name.

V.

I heard the sky-lark warbling in the sky;
And I bethought me of the playful hare:
Even such a happy Child of earth am I;
Even as these blissful creatures do I fare;
Far from the world I walk, and from all
    care;
But there may come another day to me —
Solitude, pain of heart, distress, and
    poverty.

VI.

My whole life I have lived in pleasant
    thought,
As if life's business were a summer mood;
As if all needful things would come un-
    sought
To genial faith, still rich in genial good;
But how can He expect that others should
Build for him, sow for him, and at his call
Love him, who for himself will take no
    heed at all?

VII.

I thought of Chatterton, the marvellous
    Boy,
The sleepless Soul that perished in his
    pride;
Of Him who walked in glory and in joy
Following his plough, along the mountain-
    side:
By our own spirits are we deified:
We Poets in our youth begin in gladness;
But thereof come in the end despondency
    and madness.

VIII.

Now, whether it were by peculiar grace,
A leading from above, a something given,
Yet it befell, that, in this lonely place,
When I with these untoward thoughts
    had striven,
Beside a pool bare to the eye of heaven
I saw a Man before me unawares:
The oldest man he seemed that ever wore
    gray hairs.

IX.

As a huge stone is sometimes seen to lie
Couched on the bald top of an eminence;
Wonder to all who do the same espy,
By what means it could thither come, and
    whence;

So that it seems a thing endued with
    sense:
Like a sea-beast crawled forth, that on a
    shelf
Of rock or sand reposeth, there to sun
    itself;

X.

Such seemed this Man, not all alive nor
    dead,
Nor all asleep — in his extreme old age:
His body was bent double, feet and head
Coming together in life's pilgrimage;
As if some dire constraint of pain, or rage
Of sickness felt by him in times long past,
A more than human weight upon his frame
    had cast.

XI.

Himself he propped, limbs, body, and
    pale face,
Upon a long gray staff of shaven wood:
And, still as I drew near with gentle
    pace,
Upon the margin of that moorish flood
Motionless as a cloud the old Man stood,
That heareth not the loud winds when
    they call
And moveth all together, if it move at all.

XII.

At length, himself unsettling, he the pond
Stirred with his staff, and fixedly did look
Upon the muddy water, which he conned,
As if he had been reading in a book:
And now a stranger's privilege I took;
And, drawing to his side, to him did say,
"This morning gives us promise of a
    glorious day."

XIII.

A gentle answer did the old Man make,
In courteous speech which forth he slowly
    drew:
And him with further words I thus be-
    spake,
"What occupation do you there pursue?
This is a lonesome place for one like you."
Ere he replied, a flash of mild surprise
Broke from the sable orbs of his yet-vivid
    eyes.

XIV.

His words came feebly, from a feeble
    chest,
But each in solemn order followed each,
With something of a lofty utterance
    drest —
Choice word and measured phrase, above
    the reach
Of ordinary men; a stately speech;
Such as grave Livers do in Scotland use,
Religious men, who give to God and man
    their dues.

XV.

He told, that to these waters he had come
To gather leeches, being old and poor:
Employment hazardous and wearisome!
And he had many hardships to endure:
From pond to pond he roamed, from
    moor to moor;
Housing, with God's good help, by
    choice or chance,
And in this way he gained an honest
    maintenance.

XVI.

The old Man still stood talking by my
    side;
But now his voice to me was like a stream
Scarce heard; nor word from word could
    I divide;
And the whole body of the Man did seem
Like one whom I had met with in a
    dream;
Or like a man from some far region sent,
To give me human strength, by apt ad-
    monishment.

XVII.

My former thoughts returned: the fear
    that kills;
And hope that is unwilling to be fed;
Cold, pain, and labor, and all fleshly ills;
And mighty Poets in their misery dead.
— Perplexed, and longing to be com-
    forted,
My question eagerly did I renew,
"How is it that you live, and what is it
    you do?"

XVIII.

He with a smile did then his words re-
    peat;
And said, that, gathering leeches, far and
    wide

He travelled; stirring thus about his feet
The waters of the pools where they abide.
"Once I could meet with them on every
    side;
But they have dwindled long by slow
    decay;
Yet still I persevere, and find them where
    I may."

XIX.

While he was talking thus, the lonely
    place,
The old Man's shape, and speech — all
    troubled me:
In my mind's eye I seemed to see him pace
About the weary moors continually,
Wandering about alone and silently,
While I these thoughts within myself
    pursued,
He, having made a pause, the same dis-
    course renewed.

XX.

And soon with this he other matter
    blended,
Cheerfully uttered, with demeanor kind,
But stately in the main; and when he
    ended,
I could have laughed myself to scorn to
    find
In that decrepit Man so firm a mind.
"God," said I, "be my help and stay
    secure;
I 'll think of the Leech-gatherer on the
    lonely moor!"

MAY 7, 1802.   1807.

"I GRIEVED FOR BUONAPARTÉ."

I GRIEVED for Buonaparté, with a vain
And an unthinking grief! The tenderest
    mood
Of that Man's mind — what can it be?
    what food
Fed his first hopes? what knowledge could
    he gain?
'T is not in battles that from youth we
    train
The Governor who must be wise and good,
And temper with the sternness of the brain
Thoughts motherly, and meek as woman-
    hood.

Wisdom doth live with children round her
    knees:
Books, leisure, perfect freedom, and the
    talk
Man holds with week-day man in the
    hourly walk
Of the mind's business: these are the
    degrees
By which true Sway doth mount; this is
    the stalk
True Power doth grow on; and her rights
    are these.

    MAY 21, 1802.　　　　　　　　1807.

A FAREWELL.

Composed just before my sister and I went to
fetch Mrs. Wordsworth from Gallow-hill, near
Scarborough.

FAREWELL, thou little Nook of mountain-
    ground,
Thou rocky corner in the lowest stair
Of that magnificent temple which doth
    bound
One side of our whole vale with grandeur
    rare;
Sweet garden-orchard, eminently fair,
The loveliest spot that man hath ever
    found,
Farewell! — we leave thee to Heaven's
    peaceful care,
Thee, and the Cottage which thou dost
    surround.

Our boat is safely anchored by the shore,
And there will safely ride when we are
    gone;
The flowering shrubs that deck our hum-
    ble door
Will prosper, though untended and alone:
Fields, goods, and far-off chattels we have
    none:
These narrow bounds contain our private
    store
Of things earth makes, and sun doth shine
    upon;
Here are they in our sight — we have no
    more.

Sunshine and shower be with you, bud
    and bell!
For two months now in vain we shall be
    sought:

We leave you here in solitude to dwell
With these our latest gifts of tender
    thought;
Thou, like the morning, in thy saffron
    coat,
Bright gowan, and marsh-marigold, fare-
    well!
Whom from the borders of the Lake we
    brought,
And placed together near our rocky Well.

We go for One to whom ye will be dear;
And she will prize this Bower, this Indian
    shed,
Our own contrivance, Building without
    peer!
— A gentle Maid, whose heart is lowly
    bred,
Whose pleasures are in wild fields gath-
    erèd,
With joyousness, and with a thoughtful
    cheer,
Will come to you; to you herself will wed;
And love the blessed life that we lead
    here.

Dear Spot! which we have watched with
    tender heed,
Bringing thee chosen plants and blossoms
    blown
Among the distant mountains, flower and
    weed,
Which thou hast taken to thee as thy
    own,
Making all kindness registered and
    known;
Thou for our sakes, though Nature's child
    indeed,
Fair in thyself and beautiful alone,
Hast taken gifts which thou dost little
    need.

And O most constant, yet most fickle
    Place,
Thou hast thy wayward moods, as thou
    dost show
To them who look not daily on thy face;
Who, being loved, in love no bounds dost
    know,
And say'st, when we forsake thee, "Let
    them go!"

Thou easy-hearted Thing, with thy wild
    race
Of weeds and flowers, till we return be
    slow,
And travel with the year at a soft pace.

Help us to tell Her tales of years gone by,
And this sweet spring, the best beloved
    and best;
Joy will be flown in its mortality;
Something must stay to tell us of the rest.
Here, thronged with primroses, the steep
    rock's breast
Glittered at evening like a starry sky;
And in this bush our sparrow built her
    nest,
Of which I sang one song that will not die.

O happy Garden! whose seclusion deep
Hath been so friendly to industrious
    hours;
And to soft slumbers, that did gently steep
Our spirits, carrying with them dreams of
    flowers,
And wild notes warbled among leafy
    bowers;
Two burning months let summer overleap,
And, coming back with Her who will be
    ours,
Into thy bosom we again shall creep.
    MAY 29, 1802.   1815.

"THE SUN HAS LONG BEEN SET."

Reprinted at the request of my Sister, in whose
presence the lines were thrown off.
This *Impromptu* appeared, many years ago,
among the Author's poems, from which, in sub-
sequent editions, it was excluded.

THE sun has long been set,
  The stars are out by twos and threes,
The little birds are piping yet
  Among the bushes and trees;
There's a cuckoo, and one or two thrushes,
And a far-off wind that rushes,
And a sound of water that gushes,
And the cuckoo's sovereign cry
Fills all the hollow of the sky.
  Who would "go parading"
In London, "and masquerading,"

On such a night of June
With that beautiful soft half-moon,
And all these innocent blisses?
On such a night as this is!
    JUNE 8, 1802.   1807.

COMPOSED UPON WESTMINSTER BRIDGE, SEPT. 3, 1802.

Written on the roof of a coach, on my way to
France.

EARTH has not anything to show more
    fair:
Dull would he be of soul who could pass by
A sight so touching in its majesty:
This City now doth, like a garment, wear
The beauty of the morning; silent, bare,
Ships, towers, domes, theatres, and tem-
    ples lie
Open unto the fields, and to the sky;
All bright and glittering in the smokeless
    air.
Never did sun more beautifully steep
In his first splendor, valley, rock, or hill;
Ne'er saw I, never felt, a calm so deep!
The river glideth at his own sweet will:
Dear God! the very houses seem asleep;
And all that mighty heart is lying still!
    1802.   1807.

COMPOSED BY THE SEA-SIDE, NEAR CALAIS, AUGUST, 1802.

FAIR Star of evening, Splendor of the
    west,
Star of my Country! — on the horizon's
    brink
Thou hangest, stooping, as might seem,
    to sink
On England's bosom; yet well pleased to
    rest,
Meanwhile, and be to her a glorious crest
Conspicuous to the Nations. Thou, I
    think,
Should'st be my Country's emblem; and
    should'st wink,
Bright Star! with laughter on her ban-
    ners, drest
In thy fresh beauty. There! that dusky
    spot

Beneath thee, that is England; there she
  lies.
Blessings be on you both! one hope, one
  lot,
One life, one glory!—I, with many a
  fear
For my dear Country, many heartfelt
  sighs,
Among men who do not love her, linger
  here.
1802.   1807.

CALAIS, AUGUST, 1802.

Is it a reed that 's shaken by the wind,
Or what is it that ye go forth to see?
Lords, lawyers, statesmen, squires of low
  degree,
Men known, and men unknown, sick,
  lame, and blind,
Post forward all, like creatures of one
  kind,
With first-fruit offerings crowd to bend
  the knee
In France, before the new-born Majesty.
'T is ever thus. Ye men of prostrate
  mind,
A seemly reverence may be paid to power;
But that 's a loyal virtue, never sown
In haste, nor springing with a transient
  shower:
When truth, when sense, when liberty
  were flown,
What hardship had it been to wait an
  hour?
Shame on you, feeble Heads, to slavery
  prone!
1802.   1807.

COMPOSED NEAR CALAIS, ON THE ROAD LEADING TO ARDRES, AUGUST 7, 1802.

JONES! as from Calais southward you
  and I
Went pacing side by side, this public Way
Streamed with the pomp of a too-credu-
  lous day,[1]
When faith was pledged to new-born
  Liberty:
A homeless sound of joy was in the sky:

[1] 14th July, 1790.

From hour to hour the antiquated Earth
Beat like the heart of Man: songs, gar-
  lands, mirth,
Banners, and happy faces, far and nigh!
And now, sole register that these things
  were,
Two solitary greetings have I heard,
" Good-morrow, Citizen!" a hollow
  word,
As if a dead man spake it! Yet despair
Touches me not, though pensive as a bird
Whose vernal coverts winter hath laid
  bare.[2]
1802.   1807.

CALAIS, AUGUST 15, 1802.

FESTIVALS have I seen that were not
  names:
This is young Buonaparté's natal day,
And his is henceforth an established
  sway—
Consul for life. With worship France
  proclaims
Her approbation, and with pomps and
  games.
Heaven grant that other Cities may be
  gay!
Calais is not: and I have bent my way
To the sea-coast, noting that each man
  frames
His business as he likes. Far other show
My youth here witnessed, in a prouder
  time;
The senselessness of joy was then sublime!
Happy is he, who, caring not for Pope,
Consul, or King, can sound himself to
  know
The destiny of Man, and live in hope.
1802.   1807.

"IT IS A BEAUTEOUS EVENING, CALM AND FREE."

This was composed on the beach near Calais,
in the autumn of 1802.

IT is a beauteous evening, calm and free,
The holy time is quiet as a Nun
Breathless with adoration; the broad sun
Is sinking down in its tranquillity;
The gentleness of heaven broods o'er the
  Sea:

[2] See Note.

Listen! the mighty Being is awake,
And doth with his eternal motion make
A sound like thunder — everlastingly.
Dear Child! dear Girl! that walkest with
    me here,
If thou appear untouched by solemn
    thought,
Thy nature is not therefore less divine:
Thou liest in Abraham's bosom all the
    year;
And worship'st at the Temple's inner
    shrine,
God being with thee when we know it
    not.

AUGUST, 1802.   1807.

ON THE EXTINCTION OF THE VENETIAN REPUBLIC.

ONCE did She hold the gorgeous east in
    fee;
And was the safeguard of the west: the
    worth
Of Venice did not fall below her birth,
Venice, the eldest Child of Liberty.
She was a maiden City, bright and free;
No guile seduced, no force could violate;
And, when she took unto herself a Mate,
She must espouse the everlasting Sea.
And what if she had seen those glories
    fade,
Those titles vanish, and that strength
    decay;
Yet shall some tribute of regret be paid
When her long life hath reached its final
    day:
Men are we, and must grieve when even
    the Shade
Of that which once was great, is passed
    away.

AUGUST, 1802.   1807.

THE KING OF SWEDEN.

THE Voice of song from distant lands
    shall call
To that great King; shall hail the crownèd
    Youth
Who, taking counsel of unbending Truth,
By one example hath set forth to all
How they with dignity may stand; or fall,

If fall they must.   Now, whither doth it
    tend?
And what to him and his shall be the end?
That thought is one which neither can
    appal
Nor cheer him; for the illustrious Swede
    hath done
The thing which ought to be; is raised
    above
All consequences: work he hath begun
Of fortitude, and piety, and love,
Which all his glorious ancestors approve:
The heroes bless him, him their rightful
    son.[1]

AUGUST, 1802.   1807.

TO TOUSSAINT L'OUVERTURE.

TOUSSAINT, the most unhappy man of
    men!
Whether the whistling Rustic tend his
    plough
Within thy hearing, or thy head be now
Pillowed in some deep dungeon's earless
    den; —
O miserable Chieftain! where and when
Wilt thou find patience?   Yet die not;
    do thou
Wear rather in thy bonds a cheerful brow:
Though fallen thyself, never to rise again,
Live, and take comfort.   Thou hast left
    behind
Powers that will work for thee; air, earth,
    and skies;
There's not a breathing of the common
    wind
That will forget thee; thou hast great
    allies;
Thy friends are exultations, agonies,
And love, and man's unconquerable mind.

AUGUST, 1802.   1807.

COMPOSED IN THE VALLEY NEAR DOVER, ON THE DAY OF LAND-ING.

HERE, on our native soil, we breathe
    once more.
The cock that crows, the smoke that curls,
    that sound
Of bells; those boys who in yon meadow-
    ground

[1] See Note.

In white-sleeved shirts are playing; and
　　the roar
Of the waves breaking on the chalky
　　shore; —
All, all are English. Oft have I looked
　　round
With joy in Kent's green vales; but never
　　found
Myself so satisfied in heart before.
Europe is yet in bonds; but let that pass,
Thought for another moment. Thou art
　　free,
My Country! and 't is joy enough and
　　pride
For one hour's perfect bliss, to tread the
　　grass
Of England once again, and hear and see,
With such a dear Companion at my side.

　　AUGUST 29, 1802.　　　　　　　1807.

SEPTEMBER 1, 1802.

Among the capricious acts of tyranny that dis-
graced those times, was the chasing of all Negroes
from France by decree of the government: we
had a Fellow-passenger who was one of the
expelled.

WE had a female Passenger who came
From Calais with us, spotless in array, —
A white-robed Negro, like a lady gay,
Yet downcast as a woman fearing blame;
Meek, destitute, as ..med, of hope or
　　aim
She sate, from notice turning not away,
But on all proffered intercourse did lay
A weight of languid speech, or to the same
No sign of answer made by word or face:
Yet still her eyes retained their tropic fire,
That, burning independent of the mind,
Joined with the lustre of her rich attire
To mock the Outcast. — O ye Heavens, be
　　kind!
And feel, thou Earth, for this afflicted
　　Race!

　　1802.　　　　　　　　　　　1807.

NEAR DOVER, SEPTEMBER, 1802.

INLAND, within a hollow vale, I stood;
And saw, while sea was calm and air was
　　clear,
The　coast　of　France — the　coast　of
　　France how near!

Drawn almost into frightful neighborhood.
I shrunk; for verily the barrier flood
Was like a lake, or river bright and fair,
A span of waters; yet what power is
　　there!
What mightiness for evil and for good!
Even so doth God protect us if we be
Virtuous and wise. Winds blow, and
　　waters roll,
Strength to the brave, and Power, and
　　Deity;
Yet in themselves are nothing! One de-
　　cree
Spake laws to *them*, and said that by the
　　soul
Only, the Nations shall be great and free.

　　1802.　　　　　　　　　　　1807.

WRITTEN IN LONDON, SEPTEMBER, 1802.

This was written immediately after my return
from France to London, when I could not but
be struck, as here described, with the vanity and
parade of our own country, especially in great
towns and cities, as contrasted with the quiet, and
I may say the desolation, that the revolution had
produced in France. This must be borne in
mind, or else the reader may think that in this
and the succeeding Sonnets I have exaggerated
the mischief engendered and fostered among us
by undisturbed wealth. It would not be easy to
conceive with what a depth of feeling I entered
into the struggle carried on by the Spaniards for
their deliverance from the usurped power of the
French. Many times have I gone from Allan
Bank in Grasmere vale, where we were then re-
siding, to the top of the Raise-gap as it is called,
so late as two o'clock in the morning, to meet the
carrier bringing the newspaper from Keswick.
Imperfect traces of the state of mind in which I
then was may be found in my Tract on the Con-
vention of Cintra, as well as in these Sonnets.

O FRIEND! I know not which way I
　　must look
For comfort, being, as I am, opprest,
To think that now our life is only drest
For show; mean handy-work of crafts-
　　man, cook,
Or groom! — We must run glittering like
　　a brook
In the open sunshine, or we are unblest:
The wealthiest man among us is the best:
No grandeur now in nature or in book

Delights us.   Rapine, avarice, expense,
This is idolatry; and these we adore:
Plain living and high thinking are no more:
The homely beauty of the good old cause
Is gone; our peace, our fearful innocence,
And pure religion breathing household
    laws.

1802.   1807.

LONDON, 1802.

MILTON! thou should'st be living at this
    hour:
England hath need of thee: she is a fen
Of stagnant waters! altar, sword, and
    pen,
Fireside, the heroic wealth of hall and
    bower,
Have forfeited their ancient English dower
Of inward happiness.   We are selfish men;
Oh! raise us up, return to us again;
And give us manners, virtue, freedom,
    power.
Thy soul was like a Star, and dwelt apart:
Thou hadst a voice whose sound was like
    the sea:
Pure as the naked heavens, majestic, free,
So didst thou travel on life's common way,
In cheerful godliness; and yet thy heart
The lowliest duties on herself did lay.

SEPTEMBER, 1802.   1807.

"GREAT MEN HAVE BEEN AMONG US."

GREAT men have been among us; hands
    that penned
And tongues that uttered wisdom — better
    none:
The later Sidney, Marvel, Harrington,
Young Vane, and others who called Mil-
    ton friend.
These moralists could act and compre-
    hend:
They knew how genuine glory was put on;
Taught us how rightfully a nation shone
In splendor: what strength was, that
    would not bend
But in magnanimous meekness.   France,
    't is strange,
Hath brought forth no such souls as we
    had then.

Perpetual emptiness! unceasing change!
No single volume paramount, no code,
No master spirit, no determined road;
But equally a want of books and men!

SEPTEMBER, 1802.   1807.

" IT IS NOT TO BE THOUGHT OF."

IT is not to be thought of that the Flood
Of British freedom, which, to the open
    sea
Of the world's praise, from dark antiquity
Hath flowed, "with pomp of waters, un-
    withstood,"
Roused though it be full often to a mood
Which spurns the check of salutary bands,
That this most famous Stream in bogs and
    sands
Should perish; and to evil and to good
Be lost forever.   In our halls is hung
Armory of the invincible Knights of old:
We must be free or die, who speak the
    tongue
That Shakspeare spake; the faith and
    morals hold
Which Milton held. — In everything we
    are sprung
Of Earth's first blood, have titles mani-
    fold.

SEPTEMBER, 1802.   1807.

"WHEN I HAVE BORNE IN MEMORY."

WHEN I have borne in memory what has
    tamed
Great Nations, how ennobling thoughts
    depart
When men change swords for ledgers,
    and desert
The student's bower for gold, some fears
    unnamed
I had, my Country! — am I to be blamed?
Now, when I think of thee, and what
    thou art,
Verily, in the bottom of my heart,
Of those unfilial fears I am ashamed.
For dearly must we prize thee; we who
    find
In thee a bulwark for the cause of men:

And I by my affection was beguiled:
What wonder if a Poet now and then,
Among the many movements of his mind,
Felt for thee as a lover or a child!

SEPTEMBER, 1802.   1807.

COMPOSED   AFTER   A   JOURNEY
    ACROSS   THE   HAMBLETON
HILLS, YORKSHIRE.

Composed October 4th, 1802, after a journey
over the Hambleton Hills, on a day memorable
to me — the day of my marriage. The horizon
commanded by those hills is most magnificent. —
The next day, while we were travelling in a post-
chaise up Wensleydale, we were stopt by one of
the horses proving restive, and were obliged to
wait two hours in a severe storm before the post-
boy could fetch from the inn another to supply
its place. The spot was in front of Bolton Hall,
where Mary Queen of Scots was kept prisoner
soon after her unfortunate landing at Working-
ton. The place then belonged to the Scroopes,
and memorials of her are yet preserved there.
To beguile the time I composed a Sonnet. The
subject was our own confinement contrasted with
hers; but it was not thought worthy of being
preserved.

DARK and more dark the shades of even-
        ing fell;
The wished-for point was reached — but
        at an hour
When little could be gained from that
        rich dower
Of prospect, whereof many thousands
        tell.
Yet did the glowing west with marvellous
        power
Salute us; there stood Indian citadel,
Temple of Greece, and minster with its
        tower
Substantially expressed — a place for bell
Or clock to toll from! Many a tempting
        isle,
With groves that never were imagined, lay
'Mid seas how steadfast! objects all for
        the eye
Of silent rapture; but we felt the while
We should forget them; they are of the
        sky,
And from our earthly memory fade away.

OCT. 4, 1802.   1807.

STANZAS.

WRITTEN IN MY POCKET-COPY OF THOM-
SON'S " CASTLE OF INDOLENCE."

Composed in the orchard, Town-end, Gras-
mere, Coleridge living with us much at the time :
his son Hartley has said, that his father's char-
acter and habits are here preserved in a livelier
way than in anything that has been written about
him.

WITHIN our happy Castle there dwelt One
Whom without blame I may not overlook;
For never sun on living creature shone
Who more devout enjoyment with us took:
Here on his hours he hung as on a book,
On his own time here would he float away,
As doth a fly upon a summer brook;   .
But go to-morrow, or belike to-day,
Seek for him, — he is fled; and whither
        none can say.

Thus often would he leave our peaceful
        home,
And find elsewhere his business or delight;
Out of our Valley's limits did he roam:
Full many a time, upon a stormy night,
His voice came to us from the neighbor-
        ing height:
Oft could we see him driving full in view
At mid-day when the sun was shining
  .   bright;
What ill was on him, what he had to do,
A mighty wonder bred among our quiet
        crew.

Ah! piteous sight it was to see this Man
When he came back to us, a withered
        flower, —
Or like a sinful creature, pale and wan.
Down would he sit; and without strength
        or power
Look at the common grass from hour to
        hour:
And oftentimes, how long I fear to say,
Where apple-trees in blossom made a
        bower,
Retired in that sunshiny shade he lay;
And, like a naked Indian, slept himself
        away.

Great wonder to our gentle tribe it was
Whenever from our Valley he withdrew;

For happier soul no living creature has
Than he had, being here the long day
    through.
Some thought he was a lover, and did woo:
Some thought far worse of him, and
    judged him wrong;
But verse was what he had been wedded
    to;
And his own mind did like a tempest
    strong
Come to him thus, and drove the weary
    Wight along.

With him there often walked in friendly
    guise,
Or lay upon the moss by brook or tree,
A noticeable Man with large gray eyes,
And a pale face that seemed undoubtedly
As if a blooming face it ought to be;
Heavy his low-hung lip did oft appear,
Deprest by weight of musing Phantasy;
Profound his forehead was, though not
    severe;
Yet some did think that he had little busi-
    ness here:

Sweet heaven forfend! his was a lawful
    right;
Noisy he was, and gamesome as a boy;
His limbs would toss about him with de-
    light
Like branches when strong winds the trees
    annoy.
Nor lacked his calmer hours device or toy
To banish listlessness and irksome care;
He would have taught you how you might
    employ
Yourself; and many did to him repair, —
And certes not in vain; he had inventions
    rare.

Expedients, too, of simplest sort he tried:
Long blades of grass, plucked round him
    as he lay,
Made, to his ear attentively applied,
A pipe on which the wind would deftly
    play;
Glasses he had, that little things display,
The beetle panoplied in gems and gold,
A mailèd angel on a battle-day;
The mysteries that cups of flowers enfold,
And all the gorgeous sights which fairies
    do behold.

He would entice that other Man to hear
His music, and to view his imagery:
And, sooth, these two were each to the
    other dear:
No livelier love in such a place could be:
There did they dwell — from earthly labor
    free,
As happy spirits as were ever seen;
If but a bird, to keep them company,
Or butterfly sate down, they were, I ween,
As pleased as if the same had been a
    Maiden-queen.
1802.   1815

TO H. C.

SIX YEARS OLD.

O THOU! whose fancies from afar are
    brought;
Who of thy words dost make a mock ap-
    parel,
And fittest to unutterable thought
The breeze-like motion and the self-born
    carol;
Thou faery voyager! that dost float
In such clear water, that thy boat
May rather seem
To brood on air than on an earthly stream;
Suspended in a stream as clear as sky,
Where earth and heaven do make one
    imagery;
O blessed vision! happy child!
Thou art so exquisitely wild,
I think of thee with many fears
For what may be thy lot in future years.
    I thought of times when Pain might be
        thy guest,
Lord of thy house and hospitality;
And Grief, uneasy lover! never rest
But when she sate within the touch of thee.
O too industrious folly!
O vain and causeless melancholy!
Nature will either end thee quite;
Or, lengthening out thy season of delight,
Preserve for thee, by individual right,
A young lamb's heart among the full-
    grown flocks.
What hast thou to do with sorrow,
Or the injuries of to-morrow?
Thou art a dew-drop, which the morn
    brings forth,
Ill fitted to sustain unkindly shocks,

Or to be trailed along the soiling earth;
A gem that glitters while it lives,
And no forewarning gives;
But, at the touch of wrong, without a strife
Slips in a moment out of life.

1802.   1807.

TO THE DAISY.[1]

This and the two following were composed in
the orchard, Town-end, Grasmere, where the bird
was often seen as here described.

> " Her [2] divine skill taught me this,
>   That from everything I saw
>   I could some instruction draw,
>   And raise pleasure to the height
>   Through the meanest object's sight.
>   By the murmur of a spring,
>   Or the least bough's rustelling;
>   By a Daisy whose leaves spread
>   Shut when Titan goes to bed;
>   Or a shady bush or tree;
>   She could more infuse in me
>   Than all Nature's beauties can
>   In some other wiser man."
>   G. WITHER.

IN youth from rock to rock I went,
From hill to hill in discontent
Of pleasure high and turbulent,
    Most pleased when most uneasy;
But now my own delights I make, —
My thirst at every rill can slake,
And gladly Nature's love partake,
    Of Thee, sweet Daisy!

Thee Winter in the garland wears
That thinly decks his few gray hairs;
Spring parts the clouds with softest airs,
    That she may sun thee;
Whole Summer-fields are thine by right;
And Autumn, melancholy Wight!
Doth in thy crimson head delight
    When rains are on thee.

In shoals and bands, a morrice train,
Thou greet'st the traveller in the lane;
Pleased at his greeting thee again;
    Yet nothing daunted,
Nor grieved if thou be set at nought:
And oft alone in nooks remote
We meet thee, like a pleasant thought,
    When such are wanted.

[1] See Note.   [2] His muse.

Be violets in their secret mews
The flowers the wanton Zephyrs choose;
Proud be the rose, with rains and dews
    Her head impearling,
Thou liv'st with less ambitious aim,
Yet hast not gone without thy fame;
Thou art indeed by many a claim
    The Poet's darling.

If to a rock from rains he fly,
Or, some bright day of April sky,
Imprisoned by hot sunshine lie
    Near the green holly,
And wearily at length should fare;
He needs but look about, and there
Thou art ! — a friend at hand, to scare
    His melancholy.

A hundred times, by rock or bower,
Ere thus I have lain couched an hour,
Have I derived from thy sweet power
    Some apprehension;
Some steady love; some brief delight;
Some memory that had taken flight;
Some chime of fancy wrong or right;
    Or stray invention.

If stately passions in me burn,
And one chance look to Thee should turn,
I drink out of an humbler urn
    A lowlier pleasure;
The homely sympathy that heeds
The common life, our nature breeds;
A wisdom fitted to the needs
    Of hearts at leisure.

Fresh-smitten by the morning ray,
When thou art up, alert and gay,
Then, cheerful Flower ! my spirits play
    With kindred gladness:
And when, at dusk, by dews opprest
Thou sink'st, the image of thy rest
Hath often eased my pensive breast
    Of careful sadness.

And all day long I number yet,
All seasons through, another debt,
Which I, wherever thou art met,
    To thee am owing;
An instinct call it, a blind sense;
A happy, genial influence,
Coming one knows not how, nor whence,
    Nor whither going.

Child of the Year! that round dost run
Thy pleasant course,— when day 's begun
As ready to salute the sun
    As lark or leveret,
Thy long-lost praise thou shalt regain;
Nor be less dear to future men
Than in old time;— thou not in vain
    Art Nature's favorite.[1]
1802.   1807.

TO THE SAME FLOWER.

WITH little here to do or see
Of things that in the great world be,
Daisy! again I talk to thee,
    For thou art worthy,
Thou unassuming Common-place
Of Nature, with that homely face,
And yet with something of a grace,
    Which Love makes for thee!

Oft on the dappled turf at ease
I sit, and play with similes,
Loose types of things through all degrees,
    Thoughts of thy raising:
And many a fond and idle name
I give to thee, for praise or blame,
As is the humor of the game,
    While I am gazing.

A nun demure of lowly port;
Or sprightly maiden, of Love's court,
In thy simplicity the sport
    Of all temptations;
A queen in crown of rubies drest;
A starveling in a scanty vest;
Are all, as seems to suit thee best,
    Thy appellations.

A little cyclops, with one eye
Staring to threaten and defy,
That thought comes next — and instantly
    The freak is over,
The shape will vanish — and behold
A silver shield with boss of gold,
That spreads itself, some faery bold
    In fight to cover!

I see thee glittering from afar —
And then thou art a pretty star;

[1] See, in Chaucer and the elder Poets, the honors formerly paid to this flower.

Not quite so fair as many are
    In heaven above thee!
Yet like a star, with glittering crest,
Self-poised in air thou seem'st to rest; —
May peace come never to his nest,
    Who shall reprove thee!

Bright *Flower!* for by that name at last,
When all my reveries are past,
I call thee, and to that cleave fast,
    Sweet silent creature!
That breath'st with me in sun and air,
Do thou, as thou art wont, repair
My heart with gladness, and a share
    Of thy meek nature!
1802.   1807.

TO THE DAISY.

This and the other Poems addressed to the same flower were composed at Town-end, Grasmere, during the earlier part of my residence there. I have been censured for the last line but one — "thy function apostolical" — as being little less than profane. How could it be thought so? The word is adopted with reference to its derivation, implying something sent on a mission; and assuredly this little flower, especially when the subject of verse, may be regarded, in its humble degree, as administering both to moral and to spiritual purposes.

BRIGHT Flower! whose home is every-
    where,
Bold in maternal Nature's care,
And all the long year through the heir
    Of joy or sorrow;
Methinks that there abides in thee
Some concord with humanity,
Given to no other flower I see
    The forest thorough!

Is it that Man is soon deprest?
A thoughtless Thing! who, once unblest,
Does little on his memory rest,
    Or on his reason,
And Thou would'st teach him how to find
A shelter under every wind,
A hope for times that are unkind
    And every season?

Thou wander'st the wide world about,
Unchecked by pride or scrupulous doubt,

With friends to greet thee, or without,
  Yet pleased and willing;
Meek, yielding to the occasion's call,
And all things suffering from all
Thy function apostolical
  In peace fulfilling.
1802.   1807.

THE GREEN LINNET.

BENEATH these fruit-tree boughs that
    shed
Their snow-white blossoms on my head,
With brightest sunshine round me spread
    Of spring's unclouded weather,
In this sequestered nook how sweet
To sit upon my orchard-seat!
And birds and flowers once more to greet,
    My last year's friends together.

One have I marked, the happiest guest
In all this covert of the blest:
Hail to Thee, far above the rest
    In joy of voice and pinion!
Thou, Linnet! in thy green array,
Presiding Spirit here to-day,
Dost lead the revels of the May;
    And this is thy dominion.

While birds, and butterflies, and flowers,
Make all one band of paramours,
Thou, ranging up and down the bowers,
    Art sole in thy employment:
A Life, a Presence like the Air,
Scattering thy gladness without care,
Too blest with any one to pair;
    Thyself thy own enjoyment.

Amid yon tuft of hazel trees,
That twinkle to the gusty breeze,
Behold him perched in ecstasies,
    Yet seeming still to hover;
There! where the flutter of his wings
Upon his back and body flings
Shadows and sunny glimmerings,
    That cover him all over.

My dazzled sight he oft deceives,
A Brother of the dancing leaves;
Then flits, and from the cottage-eaves
    Pours forth his song in gushes;

As if by that exulting strain
He mocked and treated with disdain
The voiceless Form he chose to feign,
    While fluttering in the bushes.
1803.   1807.

YEW-TREES.

Written at Grasmere. These yew-trees are still standing, but the spread of that at Lorton is much diminished by mutilation. I will here mention that a little way up the hill, on the road leading from Rosthwaite to Stonethwaite (in Borrowdale), lay the trunk of a yew-tree, which appeared as you approached, so vast was its diameter, like the entrance of a cave, and not a small one. Calculating upon what I have observed of the slow growth of this tree in rocky situations, and of its durability, I have often thought that the one I am describing must have been as old as the Christian era. The tree lay in the line of a fence. Great masses of its ruins were strewn about, and some had been rolled down the hillside and lay near the road at the bottom. As you approached the tree, you were struck with the number of shrubs and young plants, ashes, etc., which had found a bed upon the decayed trunk and grew to no inconsiderable height, forming, as it were, a part of the hedge-row. In no part of England, or of Europe, have I ever seen a yew-tree at all approaching this in magnitude, as it must have stood. By the bye, Hutton, the old Guide, of Keswick, had been so impressed with the remains of this tree, that he used gravely to tell strangers that there could be no doubt of its having been in existence before the flood.

THERE is a Yew-tree, pride of Lorton
    Vale,
Which to this day stands single, in the
    midst
Of its own darkness, as it stood of yore;
Not loth to furnish weapons for the bands
Of Umfraville or Percy ere they marched
To Scotland's heaths; or those that
    crossed the sea
And drew their sounding bows at Azin-
    cour,
Perhaps at earlier Crecy, or Poictiers.
Of vast circumference and gloom profound
This solitary Tree! a living thing
Produced too slowly ever to decay;
Of form and aspect too magnificent
To be destroyed. But worthier still of
    note

Are those fraternal Four of Borrowdale,
Joined in one solemn and capacious grove;
Huge trunks! and each particular trunk a
    growth
Of intertwisted fibres serpentine
Up-coiling, and inveterately convolved;
Nor uniformed with Phantasy, and looks
That threaten the profane; — a pillared
    shade,
Upon whose grassless floor of red-brown
    hue,
By sheddings from the pining umbrage
    tinged
Perennially — beneath whose sable roof
Of boughs, as if for festal purpose, decked
With unrejoicing berries — ghostly Shapes
May meet at noontide; Fear and trem-
    bling Hope,
Silence and Foresight; Death the Skele-
    ton
And Time the Shadow; — there to cele-
    brate,
As in a natural temple scattered o'er
With altars undisturbed of mossy stone,
United worship; or in mute repose
To lie, and listen to the mountain flood
Murmuring from Glaramara's inmost
    caves.

1803.   1815.

"WHO FANCIED WHAT A PRETTY SIGHT."

WHO fancied what a pretty sight
This Rock would be if edged around
With living snow-drops? circlet bright!
How glorious to this orchard-ground!
Who loved the little Rock, and set
Upon its head this coronet?

Was it the humor of a child?
Or rather of some gentle maid,
Whose brows, the day that she was styled
The shepherd-queen, were thus arrayed?
Of man mature, or matron sage?
Or old man toying with his age!

I asked — 't was whispered; The device
To each and all might well belong:
It is the Spirit of Paradise
That prompts such work, a Spirit strong,
That gives to all the self-same bent
Where life is wise and innocent.

1803.   1807.

"IT IS NO SPIRIT WHO FROM HEAVEN HATH FLOWN."

Written at Town-end, Grasmere. I remember the instant my sister, S. H., called me to the window of our Cottage, saying, "Look how beautiful is yon star! It has the sky all to itself." I composed the verses immediately.

IT is no Spirit who from heaven hath
    flown,
And is descending on his embassy;
Nor Traveller gone from earth the heavens
    to espy!
'T is Hesperus — there he stands with
    glittering crown,
First admonition that the sun is down!
For yet it is broad daylight: clouds pass
    by;
A few are near him still — and now the
    sky,
He hath it to himself — 't is all his own.
O most ambitious Star! an inquest
    wrought
Within me when I recognized thy light;
A moment I was startled at the sight:
And, while I gazed, there came to me a
    thought
That I might step beyond my natural race
As thou seem'st now to do; might one day
    trace
Some ground not mine; and, strong her
    strength above,
My Soul, an Apparition in the place,
Tread there with steps that no one shall
    reprove!

1803.   1807.

MEMORIALS OF A TOUR IN SCOTLAND.

1803.

Mr. Coleridge, my Sister, and myself started together from Town-end to make a tour in Scotland. Poor Coleridge was at that time in bad spirits, and somewhat too much in love with his own dejection; and he departed from us, as is recorded in my Sister's Journal, soon after we left Loch Lomond. The verses that stand foremost among these Memorials were not actually written for the occasion, but transplanted from my "Epistle to Sir George Beaumont,"

I.

DEPARTURE FROM THE VALE OF GRASMERE.

AUGUST, 1803.

THE gentlest Shade that walked Elysian
        plains
Might sometimes covet dissoluble chains;
Even for the tenants of the zone that lies
Beyond the stars, celestial Paradise,
Methinks 't would heighten joy, to over-
        leap
At will the crystal battlements, and peep
Into some other region, though less fair,
To see how things are made and managed
        there.
Change for the worse might please, incur-
        sion bold
Into the tracts of darkness and of cold;
O'er Limbo lake with aëry flight to steer,
And on the verge of Chaos hang in fear.
Such animation often do I find,
Power in my breast, wings growing in my
        mind,
Then, when some rock or hill is overpast,
Perchance without one look behind me
        cast.
Some barrier with which Nature, from the
        birth
Of things, has fenced this fairest spot on
        earth.
O pleasant transit, Grasmere! to resign
Such happy fields, abodes so calm as thine;
Not like an outcast with himself at strife;
The slave of business, time, or care for life,
But moved by choice; or, if constrained
        in part,
Yet still with Nature's freedom at the
        heart; —
To cull contentment upon wildest shores,
And luxuries extract from bleakest moors;
With prompt embrace all beauty to en-
        fold.
And having rights in all that we behold.
— Then why these lingering steps? — A
        bright adieu,
For a brief absence, proves that love is
        true;
Ne'er can the way be irksome or forlorn
That winds into itself for sweet return.

1803.   1827.

II.

AT THE GRAVE OF BURNS,
1803,

SEVEN YEARS AFTER HIS DEATH.

For illustration, see my Sister's Journal. It
may be proper to add that the second of these
pieces, though *felt* at the time, was not composed
till many years after.

I SHIVER, Spirit fierce and bold,
At thought of what I now behold:
As vapors breathed from dungeons cold,
        Strike pleasure dead,
So sadness comes from out the mould
        Where Burns is laid.

And have I then thy bones so near,
And thou forbidden to appear?
As if it were thyself that 's here
        I shrink with pain;
And both my wishes and my fear
        Alike are vain.

Off weight — nor press on weight! —
        away
Dark thoughts! — they came, but not to
        stay;
With chastened feelings would I pay
        The tribute due
To him, and aught that hides his clay
        From mortal view.

Fresh as the flower, whose modest worth
He sang, his genius " glinted " forth,
Rose like a star that touching earth,
        For so it seems,
Doth glorify its humble birth
        With matchless beams.

The piercing eye, the thoughtful brow,
The struggling heart, where be they
        now? —
Full soon the Aspirant of the plough,
        The prompt, the brave,
Slept, with the obscurest, in the low
        And silent grave.

I mourned with thousands, but as one
More deeply grieved, for He was gone
Whose light I hailed when first it shone,
        And showed my youth

How Verse may build a princely throne
    On humble truth.

Alas! where'er the current tends,
Regret pursues and with it blends, —
Huge Criffel's hoary top ascends
    By Skiddaw seen, —
Neighbors we were, and loving friends
    We might have been;

True friends though diversely inclined;
But heart with heart and mind with mind,
Where the main fibres are entwined,
    Through Nature's skill,
May even by contraries be joined
    More closely still.

The tear will start, and let it flow;
Thou " poor Inhabitant below,"
At this dread moment — even so —
    Might we together
Have sate and talked where gowans blow,
    Or on wild heather.

What treasures would have then been
    placed
Within my reach; of knowledge graced
By fancy what a rich repast!
    But why go on? —
Oh! spare to sweep, thou mournful blast,
    His grave grass-grown.

There, too, a Son, his joy and pride,
(Not three weeks past the Stripling died,)
Lies gathered to his Father's side,
    Soul-moving sight!
Yet one to which is not denied
    Some sad delight:

For *he* is safe, a quiet bed
Hath early found among the dead,
Harbored where none can be misled,
    Wronged, or distrest;
And surely here it may be said
    That such are blest.

And oh for Thee, by pitying grace
Checked oft-times in a devious race,
May He who halloweth the place
    Where Man is laid
Receive thy Spirit in the embrace
    For which it prayed!

Sighing I turned away; but ere
Night fell I heard, or seemed to hear,
Music that sorrow comes not near,
    A ritual hymn,
Chanted in love that casts out fear
    By Seraphim.

1803.   1845.

III.

THOUGHTS.

SUGGESTED THE DAY FOLLOWING, ON
THE BANKS OF NITH, NEAR THE
POET'S RESIDENCE.

Too frail to keep the lofty vow
That must have followed when his brow
Was wreathed — "The Vision" tells us
    how —
    With holly spray,
He faltered, drifted to and fro,
    And passed away.

Well might such thoughts, dear Sister,
    throng
Our minds when, lingering all too long,
Over the grave of Burns we hung
    In social grief —
Indulged as if it were a wrong
    To seek relief.

But, leaving each unquiet theme
Where gentlest judgments may misdeem,
And prompt to welcome every gleam
    Of good and fair,
Let us beside this limpid Stream
    Breathe hopeful air.

Enough of sorrow, wreck, and blight;
Think rather of those moments bright
When to the consciousness of right
    His course was true,
When Wisdom prospered in his sight
    And virtue grew.

Yes, freely let our hearts expand,
Freely as in youth's season bland,
When side by side, his Book in hand,
    We wont to stray,
Our pleasure varying at command
    Of each sweet Lay.

How oft inspired must he have trod
These pathways, yon far-stretching road!
There lurks his home; in that Abode,
        With mirth elate,
Or in his nobly-pensive mood,
        The Rustic sate.

Proud thoughts that Image overawes,
Before it humbly let us pause,
And ask of Nature, from what cause
        And by what rules
She trained her Burns to win applause
        That shames the Schools.

Through busiest street and loneliest glen
Are felt the flashes of his pen;
He rules 'mid winter snows, and when
        Bees fill their hives;
Deep in the general heart of men
        His power survives.

What need of fields in some far clime
Where Heroes, Sages, Bards sublime,
And all that fetched the flowing rhyme
        From genuine springs,
Shall dwell together till old Time
        Folds up his wings?

Sweet Mercy! to the gates of Heaven
This Minstrel lead, his sins forgiven;
The rueful conflict, the heart riven
        With vain endeavor,
And memory of Earth's bitter leaven,
        Effaced forever.

But why to Him confine the prayer,
When kindred thoughts and yearnings
        bear
On the frail heart the purest share
        With all that live? —
The best of what we do and are,
        Just God, forgive![1]

1803.   1845.

IV.

TO THE SONS OF BURNS

AFTER VISITING THE GRAVE OF THEIR
FATHER.

The Poet's grave is in a corner of the church-
yard. We looked at it with melancholy and

[1] See Note.

painful reflections, repeating to each other his
own verses —

"'Is there a man whose judgment clear,' etc."
        Extract from the Journal of my
        Fellow-Traveller.

'MID crowded obelisks and urns
I sought the untimely grave of Burns;
Sons of the Bard, my heart still mourns
        With sorrow true;
And more would grieve, but that it turns
        Trembling to you!

Through twilight shades of good and ill
Ye now are panting up life's hill,
And more than common strength and
        skill
        Must ye display;
If ye would give the better will
        Its lawful sway.

Hath Nature strung your nerves to bear
Intemperance with less harm, beware!
But if the Poet's wit ye share,
        Like him can speed
The social hour — of tenfold care
        There will be need;

For honest men delight will take
To spare your failings for his sake,
Will flatter you, — and fool and rake
        Your steps pursue;
And of your Mother's name will make
        A snare for you.

Far from their noisy haunts retire,
And add your voices to the quire
That sanctify the cottage fire
        With service meet;
There seek the genius of your Sire,
        His spirit greet;

Or where, 'mid "lonely heights and
        hows,"
He paid to Nature tuneful vows;
Or wiped his honorable brows
        Bedewed with toil,
While reapers strove, or busy ploughs
        Upturned the soil;

His judgment with benignant ray
Shall guide, his fancy cheer, your way;

But ne'er to a seductive lay
    Let faith be given;
Nor deem that " light which leads astray,
    Is light from Heaven.''

Let no mean hope your souls enslave;
Be independent, generous, brave;
Your Father such example gave,
    And such revere;
But be admonished by his grave,
    And think, and fear!
1803.   1807.

V.

TO A HIGHLAND GIRL

AT INVERSNEYDE, UPON LOCH LOMOND.

This delightful creature and her demeanor are particularly described in my Sister's Journal. The sort of prophecy with which the verses conclude has, through God's goodness, been realized; and now, approaching the close of my 73d year, I have a most vivid remembrance of her and the beautiful objects with which she was surrounded. She is alluded to in the Poem of "The Three Cottage Girls" among my Continental Memorials. In illustration of this class of Poems I have scarcely anything to say beyond what is anticipated in my Sister's faithful and admirable Journal.

SWEET Highland Girl, a very shower
Of beauty is thy earthly dower!
Twice seven consenting years have shed
Their utmost bounty on thy head:
And these gray rocks; that household
    lawn;
Those trees, a veil just half withdrawn;
This fall of water that doth make
A murmur near the silent lake;
This little bay; a quiet road
That holds in shelter Thy abode —
In truth together do ye seem
Like something fashioned in a dream;
Such Forms as from their covert peep
When earthly cares are laid asleep!
But, O fair Creature! in the light
Of common day, so heavenly bright,
I bless Thee, Vision as thou art,
I bless thee with a human heart;
God shield thee to thy latest years!
Thee, neither know I, nor thy peers;

And yet my eyes are filled with tears.
  With earnest feeling I shall pray
For thee when I am far away:
For never saw I mien, or face,
In which more plainly I could trace
Benignity and home-bred sense
Ripening in perfect innocence.
Here scattered, like a random seed,
Remote from men, Thou dost not need
The embarrassed look of shy distress,
And maidenly shamefacedness:
Thou wear'st upon thy forehead clear
The freedom of a Mountaineer:
A face with gladness overspread!
Soft smiles, by human kindness bred!
And seemliness complete, that sways
Thy courtesies, about thee plays;
With no restraint, but such as springs
From quick and eager visitings
Of thoughts that lie beyond the reach
Of thy few words of English speech:
A bondage sweetly brooked, a strife
That gives thy gestures grace and life!
So have I, not unmoved in mind,
Seen birds of tempest-loving-kind —
Thus beating up against the wind.
  What hand but would a garland cull
For thee who art so beautiful?
O happy pleasure! here to dwell
Beside thee in some heathy dell;
Adopt your homely ways, and dress,
A Shepherd, thou a Shepherdess!
But I could frame a wish for thee
More like a grave reality:
Thou art to me but as a wave
Of the wild sea; and I would have
Some claim upon thee, if I could,
Though but of common neighborhood.
What joy to hear thee, and to see!
Thy elder Brother I would be,
Thy Father — anything to thee!
  Now thanks to Heaven! that of its grace
Hath led me to this lonely place.
Joy have I had; and going hence
I bear away my recompense.
In spots like these it is we prize
Our Memory, feel that she hath eyes:
Then, why should I be loth to stir?
I feel this place was made for her;
To give new pleasure like the past,
Continued long as life shall last.
Nor am I loth, though pleased at heart,
Sweet Highland Girl! from thee to part:

For I, methinks, till I grow old,
As fair before me shall behold,
As I do now, the cabin small,
The lake, the bay, the waterfall;
And Thee, the Spirit of them all!

1803.   1807.

VI.

GLEN-ALMAIN;

OR, THE NARROW GLEN.

IN this still place, remote from men,
Sleeps Ossian, in the NARROW GLEN;
In this still place, where murmurs on
But one meek streamlet, only one:
He sang of battles, and the breath
Of stormy war, and violent death;
And should, methinks, when all was past,
Have rightfully been laid at last
Where rocks were rudely heaped, and rent
As by a spirit turbulent;
Where sights were rough, and sounds were
        wild,
And everything unreconciled;
In some complaining, dim retreat,
For fear and melancholy meet;
But this is calm; there cannot be
A more entire tranquillity.
Does then the Bard sleep here indeed?
Or is it but a groundless creed?
What matters it? — I blame them not
Whose Fancy in this lonely Spot
Was moved; and in such way expressed
Their notion of its perfect rest.
A convent, even a hermit's cell,
Would break the silence of this Dell:
It is not quiet, is not ease;
But something deeper far than these:
The separation that is here
Is of the grave; and of austere
Yet happy feelings of the dead:
And, therefore, was it rightly said
That Ossian, last of all his race!
Lies buried in this lonely place.

1803.   1807.

VII.

STEPPING WESTWARD.

While my Fellow-traveller and I were walking
by the side of Loch Ketterine, one fine evening
after sunset, in our road to a Hut where, in the
course of our Tour, we had been hospitably en-
tertained some weeks before, we met, in one of
the loneliest parts of that solitary region, two
well-dressed Women, one of whom said to us, by
way of greeting, " What, are you stepping west-
ward ? "

" *What, you are stepping westward ?* " —
        " *Yea.*"
— 'T would be a *wildish* destiny,
If we, who thus together roam
In a strange Land, and far from home,
Were in this place the guests of Chance:
Yet who would stop, or fear to advance,
Though home or shelter he had none,
With such a sky to lead him on?

The dewy ground was dark and cold;
Behind, all gloomy to behold;
And stepping westward seemed to be
A kind of *heavenly* destiny:
I liked the greeting; 't was a sound
Of something without place or bound;
And seemed to give me spiritual right
To travel through that region bright.

The voice was soft, and she who spake
Was walking by her native lake:
The salutation had to me
The very sound of courtesy:
Its power was felt; and while my eye
Was fixed upon the glowing Sky,
The echo of the voice enwrought
A human sweetness with the thought
Of travelling through the world that lay
Before me in my endless way.

1803.   1807.

VIII.

THE SOLITARY REAPER.

BEHOLD her, single in the field,
Yon solitary Highland Lass!
Reaping and singing by herself;
Stop here, or gently pass!
Alone she cuts and binds the grain,
And sings a melancholy strain;
O listen! for the Vale profound
Is overflowing with the sound.

No Nightingale did ever chaunt
More welcome notes to weary bands

Of travellers in some shady haunt,
Among Arabian sands:
A voice so thrilling ne'er was heard,
In spring-time from the Cuckoo-bird,
Breaking the silence of the seas
Among the farthest Hebrides.

Will no one tell me what she sings? —
Perhaps the plaintive numbers flow
For old, unhappy, far-off things,
And battles long ago:
Or is it some more humble lay,
Familiar matter of to-day?
Some natural sorrow, loss, or pain,
That has been, and may be again?

Whate'er the theme, the Maiden sang
As if her song could have no ending;
I saw her singing at her work,
And o'er the sickle bending; —
I listened, motionless and still;
And, as I mounted up the hill,
The music in my heart I bore,
Long after it was heard no more.

1803.   1807.

IX.

ADDRESS TO KILCHURN CASTLE, UPON LOCH AWE.

The first three lines were thrown off at the moment I first caught sight of the Ruin from a small eminence by the wayside; the rest was added many years after.

"From the top of the hill a most impressive scene opened upon our view, — a ruined Castle on an Island (for an Island the flood had made it) at some distance from the shore, backed by a Cove of the Mountain Cruachan, down which came a foaming stream. The Castle occupied every foot of the Island that was visible to us, appearing to rise out of the water, — mists rested upon the mountain side, with spots of sunshine; there was a mild desolation in the low grounds, a solemn grandeur in the mountains, and the Castle was wild, yet stately — not dismantled of turrets — nor the walls broken down, though obviously a ruin." — *Extract from the Journal of my Companion.*

CHILD of loud-throated War! the mountain Stream
Roars in thy hearing; but thy hour of rest
Is come, and thou art silent in thy age;

Save when the wind sweeps by and sounds are caught
Ambiguous, neither wholly thine nor theirs.
Oh! there is life that breathes not; Powers there are
That touch each other to the quick in modes
Which the gross world no sense hath to perceive,
No soul to dream of. What art Thou, from care
Cast off — abandoned by thy rugged Sire,
Nor by soft Peace adopted; though, in place
And in dimension, such that thou might'st seem
But a mere footstool to yon sovereign Lord,
Huge Cruachan, (a thing that meaner hills
Might crush, nor know that it had suffered harm;)
Yet he, not loth, in favor of thy claims
To reverence, suspends his own; submitting
All that the God of Nature hath conferred,
All that he holds in common with the stars,
To the memorial majesty of Time
Impersonated in thy calm decay!
Take, then, thy seat, Vicegerent unreproved!
Now, while a farewell gleam of evening light
Is fondly lingering on thy shattered front,
Do thou, in turn, be paramount; and rule
Over the pomp and beauty of a scene
Whose mountains, torrents, lake, and woods, unite
To pay thee homage; and with these are joined
In willing admiration and respect,
Two Hearts, which in thy presence might be called
Youthful as Spring. — Shade of departed Power,
Skeleton of unfleshed humanity,
The chronicle were welcome that should call
Into the compass of distinct regard

The toils and struggles of thy infant
    years!
Yon foaming flood seems motionless as
    ice;
Its dizzy turbulence eludes the eye,
Frozen by distance; so, majestic Pile,
To the perception of this Age, appear
Thy fierce beginnings, softened and sub-
    dued
And quieted in character — the strife,
The pride, the fury uncontrollable,
Lost on the aërial heights of the Cru-
    sades! [1]

  1803.   1827.

X.

ROB ROY'S GRAVE.

I have since been told that I was misinformed
as to the burial-place of Rob Roy. If so, I may
plead in excuse that I wrote on apparently good
authority, namely, that of a well-educated Lady
who lived at the head of the Lake, within a mile
or less of the point indicated as containing the
remains of One so famous in the neighborhood.

The history of Rob Roy is sufficiently known;
his grave is near the head of Loch Ketterine, in
one of those small pinfold-like Burial-grounds, of
neglected and desolate appearance, which the
traveller meets with in the Highlands of Scotland.

A FAMOUS man is Robin Hood,
  The English ballad-singer's joy!
And Scotland has a thief as good,
An outlaw of as daring mood;
    She has her brave ROB ROY!

Then clear the weeds from off his Grave,
And let us chant a passing stave,
  In honor of that Hero brave!

Heaven gave Rob Roy a dauntless heart
And wondrous length and strength of arm:
Nor craved he more to quell his foes,
  Or keep his friends from harm.

Yet was Rob Roy as *wise* as brave;
Forgive me if the phrase be strong; —
A Poet worthy of Rob Roy
    Must scorn a timid song.

[1] The tradition is, that the Castle was built
by a Lady during the absence of her Lord in
Palestine.

Say, then, that he was wise as brave;
As wise in thought as bold in deed:
For in the principles of things
    He sought his moral creed.

Said generous Rob, "What need of
    books?
Burn all the statutes and their shelves:
They stir us up against our kind;
    And worse, against ourselves.

"We have a passion — make a law,
Too false to guide us or control!
And for the law itself we fight
    In bitterness of soul.

"And, puzzled, blinded thus, we lose
Distinctions that are plain and few:
These find I graven on my heart:
    That tells me what to do.

"The creatures see of flood and field,
And those that travel on the wind!
With them no strife can last; they live
    In peace, and peace of mind.

"For why? — because the good old rule
Sufficeth them, the simple plan,
That they should take, who have the
    power,
    And they should keep who can.

"A lesson that is quickly learned,
A signal this which all can see!
Thus nothing here provokes the strong
    To wanton cruelty.

"All freakishness of mind is checked;
He tamed, who foolishly aspires;
While to the measure of his might
    Each fashions his desires.

"All kinds, and creatures, stand and fall
By strength of prowess or of wit:
'T is God's appointment who must sway,
    And who is to submit.

"Since, then, the rule of right is plain,
And longest life is but a day;
To have my ends, maintain my rights,
    I 'll take the shortest way."

And thus among these rocks he lived,
Through summer heat and winter snow:
The Eagle, he was lord above,
    And Rob was lord below.

So was it — *would*, at least, have been
But through untowardness of fate;
For Polity was then too strong —
    He came an age too late;

Or shall we say an age too soon?
For, were the bold Man living *now*,
How might he flourish in his pride,
    With buds on every bough!

Then rents and factors, rights of chase,
Sheriffs, and lairds and their domains,
Would all have seemed but paltry things,
    Not worth a moment's pains.

Rob Roy had never lingered here,
To these few meagre Vales confined;
But thought how wide the world, the times
    How fairly to his mind!

And to his Sword he would have said,
" Do Thou my sovereign will enact
From land to land through half the earth!
    Judge thou of law and fact!

" 'T is fit that we should do our part,
Becoming, that mankind should learn
That we are not to be surpassed
    In fatherly concern.

" Of old things all are over old,
Of good things none are good enough: —
We 'll show that we can help to frame
    A world of other stuff.

" I, too, will have my kings that take
From me the sign of life and death:
Kingdoms shall shift about, like clouds,
    Obedient to my breath."

And, if the word had been fulfilled,
As *might* have been, then, thought of joy!
France would have had her present Boast,
    And we our own Rob Roy!

Oh! say not so; compare them not;
I would not wrong thee, Champion brave!
Would wrong thee nowhere; least of all
    Here standing by thy grave.

For Thou, although with some wild thoughts,
Wild Chieftain of a savage Clan!
Hadst this to boast of; thou didst love
    The *liberty* of man.

And, had it been thy lot to live
With us who now behold the light,
Thou would'st have nobly stirred thyself,
    And battled for the Right.

For thou wert still the poor man's stay,
The poor man's heart, the poor man's hand;
And all the oppressed, who wanted strength,
    Had thine at their command.

Bear witness many a pensive sigh
Of thoughtful Herdsman when he strays
Alone upon Loch Veol's heights,
    And by Loch Lomond's braes!

And, far and near, through vale and hill,
Are faces that attest the same;
The proud heart flashing through the eyes,
    At sound of ROB ROY's name.
1803.   1807.

XI.

SONNET.

COMPOSED AT ——— CASTLE.

The Castle here mentioned was Nidpath near Peebles. The person alluded to was the then Duke of Queensbury. The fact was told me by Walter Scott.

DEGENERATE Douglas! oh, the unworthy Lord!
Whom mere despite of heart could so far please,
And love of havoc, (for with such disease
Fame taxes him,) that he could send forth word
To level with the dust a noble horde,
A brotherhood of venerable Trees,

Leaving an ancient dome, and towers like
    these,
Beggared and outraged! — Many hearts
    deplored
The fate of those old Trees; and oft with
    pain
The traveller, at this day, will stop and
    gaze
On wrongs, which Nature scarcely seems
    to heed:
For sheltered places, bosoms, nooks, and
    bays,
And the pure mountains, and the gentle
    Tweed,
And the green silent pastures, yet remain.

    SEPT. 18, 1803.   1807.

XII.

YARROW UNVISITED.

    See the various Poems the scene of which is
laid upon the banks of the Yarrow; in particular,
the exquisite ballad of Hamilton beginning
" Busk ye, busk ye, my bonny, bonny Bride,
  Busk ye, busk ye, my winsome Marrow! — "

FROM Stirling castle we had seen
The mazy Forth unravelled;
Had trod the banks of Clyde, and Tay,
And with the Tweed had travelled;
And when we came to Clovenford,
Then said my " *winsome Marrow*,"
" Whate'er betide, we 'll turn aside,
And see the Braes of Yarrow."

" Let Yarrow folk, *frae* Selkirk town,
Who have been buying, selling,
Go back to Yarrow, 't is their own;
Each maiden to her dwelling!
On Yarrow's banks let herons feed,
Hares couch, and rabbits burrow!
But we will downward with the Tweed,
Nor turn aside to Yarrow.

" There 's Galla Water, Leader Haughs,
Both lying right before us;
And Dryborough, where with chiming
    Tweed
The lintwhites sing in chorus;
There 's pleasant Tiviot-dale, a land
Made blithe with plough and harrow:

Why throw away a needful day
To go in search of Yarrow?

" What 's Yarrow but a river bare,
That glides the dark hills under?
There are a thousand such elsewhere
As worthy of your wonder."
— Strange words they seemed of slight
    and scorn
My True-love sighed for sorrow;
And looked me in the face, to think
I thus could speak of Yarrow!

" Oh! green," said I, "are Yarrow's
    holms,
And sweet is Yarrow flowing!
Fair hangs the apple frae the rock,[1]
But we will leave it growing.
O'er hilly path, and open Strath,
We 'll wander Scotland thorough;
But, though so near, we will not turn
Into the dale of Yarrow.

" Let beeves and home-bred kine partake
The sweets of Burn-mill meadow;
The swan on still St. Mary's Lake
Float double, swan and shadow!
We will not see them; will not go,
To-day, nor yet to-morrow,
Enough if in our hearts we know
There 's such a place as Yarrow.

" Be Yarrow stream unseen, unknown!
It must, or we shall rue it:
We have a vision of our own;
Ah! why should we undo it?
The treasured dreams of times long past,
We 'll keep them, winsome Marrow!
For when we 're there, although 't is fair,
'T will be another Yarrow!

" If Care with freezing years should come,
And wandering seem but folly, —
Should we be loth to stir from home,
And yet be melancholy;
Should life be dull, and spirits low,
'T will soothe us in our sorrow,
That earth has something yet to show,
The bonny holms of Yarrow! "

    1803.   1807.

    [1] See Hamilton's Ballad as above.

XIII.

THE MATRON OF JEDBOROUGH AND HER HUSBAND.

At Jedborough, my companion and I went into private lodgings for a few days: and the following Verses were called forth by the character and domestic situation of our Hostess.

AGE! twine thy brows with fresh spring
    flowers,
And call a train of laughing Hours;
And bid them dance, and bid them sing;
And thou, too, mingle in the ring!
Take to thy heart a new delight;
If not, make merry in despite
That there is One who scorns thy
    power: —
But dance! for under Jedborough Tower,
A Matron dwells who, though she bears
The weight of more than seventy years,
Lives in the light of youthful glee,
And she will dance and sing with thee.

    Nay! start not at that Figure — there!
Him who is rooted to his chair!
Look at him — look again! for he
Hath long been of thy family.
With legs that move not, if they can,
And useless arms, a trunk of man,
He sits, and with a vacant eye;
A sight to make a stranger sigh!
Deaf, drooping, that is now his doom:
His world is in this single room:
Is this a place for mirthful cheer?
Can merry-making enter here?

    The joyous Woman is the Mate
Of him in that forlorn estate!
He breathes a subterranean damp;
But bright as Vesper shines her lamp;
He is as mute as Jedborough Tower:
She jocund as it was of yore,
With all its bravery on; in times
When all alive with merry chimes,
Upon a sun-bright morn of May,
It roused the Vale to holiday.

    I praise thee, Matron! and thy due
Is praise, heroic praise, and true!
With admiration I behold
Thy gladness unsubdued and bold:
Thy looks, thy gestures, all present
The picture of a life well spent:
This do I see; and something more;
A strength unthought of heretofore!

Delighted am I for thy sake;
And yet a higher joy partake:
Our Human-nature throws away
Its second twilight, and looks gay;
A land of promise and of pride
Unfolding, wide as life is wide.

    Ah! see her helpless Charge! enclosed
Within himself it seems, composed;
To fear of loss, and hope of gain,
The strife of happiness and pain,
Utterly dead! yet in the guise
Of little infants, when their eyes
Begin to follow to and fro
The persons that before them go,
He tracks her motions, quick or slow,
Her buoyant spirit can prevail
Where common cheerfulness would fail;
She strikes upon him with the heat
Of July suns; he feels it sweet;
An animal delight though dim!
'T is all that now remains for him!

    The more I looked, I wondered more —
And, while I scanned them o'er and o'er,
Some inward trouble suddenly
Broke from the Matron's strong black
    eye —
A remnant of uneasy light,
A flash of something over-bright!
Nor long this mystery did detain
My thoughts; — she told in pensive strain
That she had borne a heavy yoke,
Been stricken by a twofold stroke;
Ill health of body; and had pined
Beneath worse ailments of the mind.

    So be it! — but let praise ascend
To Him who is our lord and friend!
Who from disease and suffering
Hath called for thee a second spring;
Repaid thee for that sore distress
By no untimely joyousness;
Which makes of thine a blissful state;
And cheers thy melancholy Mate!
   1803.   1807.

XIV.

"FLY, SOME KIND HARBINGER, TO GRASMERE-DALE!"

This was actually composed the last day of our tour between Dalston and Grasmere.

FLY, some kind Harbinger, to Grasmere-
    dale!
Say that we come, and come by this day's
    light;

Fly upon swiftest wing round field and
    height,
But chiefly let one Cottage hear the tale;
There let a mystery of joy prevail,
The kitten frolic, like a gamesome sprite,
And Rover whine, as at a second sight
Of near-approaching good that shall not
    fail:
And from that Infant's face let joy appear;
Yea, let our Mary's one companion
    child —
That hath her six weeks' solitude beguiled
With intimations manifold and dear,
While we have wandered over wood and
    wild —
Smile on his Mother now with bolder
    cheer.
1803.   1815.

XV.

THE BLIND HIGHLAND BOY.

A TALE TOLD BY THE FIRESIDE, AFTER
RETURNING TO THE VALE OF GRASMERE.

The story was told me by George Mackereth,
for many years parish-clerk of Grasmere. He
had been an eye-witness of the occurrence. The
vessel in reality was a washing-tub, which the
little fellow had met with on the shore of the
Loch.

Now we are tired of boisterous joy,
Have romped enough, my little Boy!
Jane hangs her head upon my breast,
And you shall bring your stool and rest;
    This corner is your own.

There! take your seat, and let me see
That you can listen quietly:
And, as I promised, I will tell
That strange adventure which befell
    A poor blind Highland Boy.

A *Highland* Boy! — why call him so?
Because, my Darlings, ye must know
That, under hills which rise like towers,
Far higher hills than these of ours!
    He from his birth had lived.

He ne'er had seen one earthly sight
The sun, the day; the stars, the night;
Or tree, or butterfly, or flower,
Or fish in stream, or bird in bower,
    Or woman, man, or child.

And yet he neither drooped nor pined,
Nor had a melancholy mind;
For God took pity on the Boy,
And was his friend; and gave him joy
    Of which we nothing know.

His Mother, too, no doubt, above
Her other children him did love:
For, was she here, or was she there,
She thought of him with constant care,
    And more than mother's love.

And proud she was of heart, when, clad
In crimson stockings, tartan plaid,
And bonnet with a feather gay,
To Kirk he on the Sabbath day
    Went hand in hand with her.

A dog too, had he; not for need,
But one to play with and to feed;
Which would have led him, if bereft
Of company or friends, and left
    Without a better guide.

And then the bagpipes he could blow —
And thus from house to house would go;
And all were pleased to hear and see,
For none made sweeter melody
    Than did the poor blind Boy.

Yet he had many a restless dream;
Both when he heard the eagles scream,
And when he heard the torrents roar,
And heard the water beat the shore
    Near which their cottage stood.

Beside a lake their cottage stood,
Not small like ours, a peaceful flood;
But one of mighty size, and strange;
That, rough or smooth, is full of change,
    And stirring in its bed.

For to this lake, by night and day,
The great Sea-water finds its way
Through long, long windings of the hills
And drinks up all the pretty rills
    And rivers large and strong:

Then hurries back the road it came —
Returns, on errand still the same;
This did it when the earth was new;
And this for evermore will do
    As long as earth shall last.

And, with the coming of the tide,
Come boats and ships that safely ride
Between the woods and lofty rocks;
And to the shepherds with their flocks
    Bring tales of distant lands.

And of those tales, whate'er they were,
The blind Boy always had his share;
Whether of mighty towns, or vales
With warmer suns and softer gales,
    Or wonders of the Deep.

Yet more it pleased him, more it stirred,
When, from the water-side he heard
The shouting, and the jolly cheers;
The bustle of the mariners
    In stillness or in storm.

But what do his desires avail?
For He must never handle sail;
Nor mount the mast, nor row, nor float,
In sailor's ship, or fisher's boat,
    Upon the rocking waves.

His Mother often thought, and said,
What sin would be upon her head
If she should suffer this: "My Son,
Whate'er you do, leave this undone;
    The danger is so great.

Thus lived he by Loch Leven's side,
Still sounding with the sounding tide,
And heard the billows leap and dance,
Without a shadow of mischance,
    Till he was ten years old.

When one day (and now mark me well,
Ye soon shall know how this befell)
He in a vessel of his own,
On the swift flood is hurrying down,
    Down to the mighty Sea.

In such a vessel never more
May human creature leave the shore!
If this or that way he should stir,
Woe to the poor blind Mariner!
    For death will be his doom.

But say what bears him? — Ye have seen
The Indian's bow, his arrows keen,
Rare beasts, and birds with plumage
    bright;

Gifts which, for wonder or delight,
    Are brought in ships from far.

Such gifts had those seafaring men
Spread round that haven in the glen;
Each hut, perchance, might have its own;
And to the Boy they all were known —
    He knew and prized them all.

The rarest was a Turtle-shell
Which he, poor Child, had studied well;
A shell of ample size, and light
As the pearly car of Amphitrite,
    That sportive dolphins drew.

And, as a Coracle that braves
On Vaga's breast the fretful waves,
This shell upon the deep would swim,
And gayly lift its fearless brim
    Above the tossing surge.

And this the little blind Boy knew:
And he a story strange yet true
Had heard, how in a shell like this
An English Boy, O thought of bliss!
    Had stoutly launched from shore;

Launched from the margin of a bay
Among the Indian isles, where lay
His father's ship, and had sailed far —
To join that gallant ship of war,
    In his delightful shell.

Our Highland Boy oft visited
The house that held this prize; and, led
By choice or chance, did thither come
One day when no one was at home,
    And found the door unbarred.

While there he sate, alone and blind,
That story flashed upon his mind; —
A bold thought roused him, and he took
The shell from out its secret nook,
    And bore it on his head.

He launched his vessel, — and in pride
Of spirit, from Loch Leven's side,
Stepped into it — his thoughts all free
As the light breezes that with glee
    Sang through the adventurer's hair.

A while he stood upon his feet;
He felt the motion — took his seat;

Still better pleased as more and more
The tide retreated from the shore,
   And sucked, and sucked him in.

And there he is in face of Heaven.
How rapidly the Child is driven!
The fourth part of a mile, I ween,
He thus had gone, ere he was seen
   By any human eye.

But when he was first seen, oh me
What shrieking and what misery!
For many saw; among the rest
His Mother, she who loved him best,
   She saw her poor blind Boy.

But for the child, the sightless Boy,
It is the triumph of his joy!
The bravest traveller in balloon,
Mounting as if to reach the moon,
   Was never half so blessed.

And let him, let him go his way,
Alone, and innocent, and gay!
For, if good Angels love to wait
On the forlorn unfortunate,
   This Child will take no harm.

But now the passionate lament,
Which from the crowd on shore was sent,
The cries which broke from old and young
In Gaelic, or the English tongue,
   Are stifled — all is still.

And quickly with a silent crew
A boat is ready to pursue;
And from the shore their course they take,
And swiftly down the running lake
   They follow the blind Boy.

But soon they move with softer pace;
So have ye seen the fowler chase
On Grasmere's clear unruffled breast
A youngling of the wild-duck's nest
   With deftly-lifted oar;

Or as the wily sailors crept
To seize (while on the Deep it slept)
The hapless creature which did dwell
Erewhile within the dancing shell,
   They steal upon their prey.

With sound the least that can be made,
They follow, more and more afraid,
More cautious as they draw more near;
But in his darkness he can hear,
   And guesses their intent.

"*Lei-gha — Lei-gha*" — he then cried out,
"*Lei-gha — Lei-gha*" — with eager shout;
Thus did he cry, and thus did pray,
And what he meant was, "Keep away,
   And leave me to myself!"

Alas! and when he felt their hands —
You 've often heard of magic wands,
That with a motion overthrow
A palace of the proudest show,
   Or melt it into air:

So all his dreams — that inward light
With which his soul had shone so bright —
All vanished; — 't was a heartfelt cross
To him, a heavy, bitter loss,
   As he had ever known.

But hark! a gratulating voice,
With which the very hills rejoice:
'T is from the crowd, who tremblingly
Have watched the event, and now can
   see
   That he is safe at last.

And then, when he was brought to land,
Full sure they were a happy band,
Which, gathering round, did on the banks
Of that great Water give God thanks,
   And welcomed the poor Child.

And in the general joy of heart
The blind Boy's little dog took part;
He leapt about, and oft did kiss
His master's hands in sign of bliss,
   With sound like lamentation.

But most of all, his Mother dear,
She who had fainted with her fear,
Rejoiced when waking she espies
The Child; when she can trust her eyes,
   And touches the blind Boy.

She led him home, and wept amain,
When he was in the house again:

Tears flowed in torrents from her eyes;
She kissed him — how could she chastise?
    She was too happy far.

Thus, after he had fondly braved
The perilous Deep, the Boy was saved;
And, though his fancies had been wild,
Yet he was pleased and reconciled
    To live in peace on shore.

And in the lonely Highland dell
Still do they keep the Turtle-shell
And long the story will repeat
Of the blind Boy's adventurous feat,
    And how he was preserved.
1803.   1807.

NOTE. — It is recorded in Dampier's *Voyages*,
that a boy, son of the captain of a Man-of-War,
seated himself in a Turtle-shell, and floated in it
from the shore to his father's ship, which lay at
anchor at the distance of half a mile. In defer-
ence to the opinion of a Friend, I have substituted
such a shell for the less elegant vessel in which
my blind Voyager did actually entrust himself to
the dangerous current of Loch Leven, as was
related to me by an eye-witness.

OCTOBER, 1803.

ONE might believe that natural miseries
Had blasted France, and made of it a land
Unfit for men; and that in one great band
Her sons were bursting forth, to dwell at
    ease.
But 't is a chosen soil, where sun and
    breeze
Shed gentle favors: rural works are there,
And ordinary business without care;
Spot rich in all things that can soothe and
    please!
How piteous then that there should be
    such dearth
Of knowledge; that whole myriads should
    unite
To work against themselves such fell
    despite:
Should come in phrensy and in drunken
    mirth,
Impatient to put out the only light
Of Liberty that yet remains on earth!
1803.   1807.

"THERE IS A BONDAGE WORSE, FAR WORSE, TO BEAR."

THERE is a bondage worse, far worse, to
    bear
Than his who breathes, by roof, and floor,
    and wall,
Pent in, a Tyrant's solitary Thrall:
'T is his who walks about in the open air,
One of a Nation who, henceforth, must
    wear
Their fetters in their souls. For who
    could be,
Who, even the best, in such condition, free
From self-reproach, reproach that he must
    share
With Human-nature? Never be it ours
To see the sun how brightly it will shine,
And know that noble feelings, manly
    powers,
Instead of gathering strength, must droop
    and pine;
And earth with all her pleasant fruits and
    flowers
Fade, and participate in man's decline.
OCTOBER, 1803.   1807.

OCTOBER, 1803.

THESE times strike monied worldlings
    with dismay:
Even rich men, brave by nature, taint the
    air
With words of apprehension and despair:
While tens of thousands, thinking on the
    affray,
Men unto whom sufficient for the day
And minds not stinted or untilled are
    given,
Sound, healthy, children of the God of
    heaven,
Are cheerful as the rising sun in May.
What do we gather hence but firmer faith
That every gift of noble origin
Is breathed upon by Hope's perpetual
    breath;
That virtue and the faculties within
Are vital, — and that riches are akin
To fear, to change, to cowardice, and
    death?
1803.   1807.

"ENGLAND! THE TIME IS COME WHEN THOU SHOULD'ST WEAN."

ENGLAND! the time is come when thou
          should'st wean
Thy heart from its emasculating food;
The truth should now be better under-
          stood;
Old things have been unsettled; we have
          seen
Fair seed-time, better harvest might have
          been
But for thy trespasses; and, at this day,
If for Greece, Egypt, India, Africa,
Aught good were destined, thou would'st
          step between.
England! all nations in this charge agree:
But worse, more ignorant in love and
          hate,
Far — far more abject, is thine Enemy:
Therefore the wise pray for thee, though
          the freight
Of thy offences be a heavy weight:
Oh grief that Earth's best hopes rest all
          with Thee!

OCTOBER, 1803.   1807.

OCTOBER, 1803.

WHEN, looking on the present face of
          things,
I see one Man, of men the meanest too!
Raised up to sway the world, to do, undo,
With mighty Nations for his underlings,
The great events with which old story rings
Seem vain and hollow; I find nothing
          great:
Nothing is left which I can venerate;
So that a doubt almost within me springs
Of Providence, such emptiness at length
Seems at the heart of all things. But,
          great God!
I measure back the steps which I have
          trod:
And tremble, seeing whence proceeds the
          strength
Of such poor Instruments, with thoughts
          sublime
I tremble at the sorrow of the time.

  1803.   1807.

TO THE MEN OF KENT.

OCTOBER, 1803.

VANGUARD of Liberty, ye men of Kent,
Ye children of a Soil that doth advance
Her haughty brow against the coast of
          France,
Now is the time to prove your hardiment!
To France be words of invitation sent!
They from their fields can see the coun-
          tenance
Of your fierce war, may ken the glittering
          lance
And hear you shouting forth your brave
          intent.
Left single, in bold parley, ye, of yore,
Did from the Norman win a gallant
          wreath;
Confirmed the charters that were yours
          before; —
No parleying now!   In Britain is one
          breath;
We all are with you now from shore to
          shore: —
Ye men of Kent, 't is victory or death!
  1803.   1807.

IN THE PASS OF KILLICRANKY.

An invasion being expected, October, 1803.

SIX thousand veterans practised in war's
          game,
Tried men, at Killicranky were arrayed
Against an equal host that wore the plaid,
Shepherds and herdsmen. — Like a whirl-
          wind came
The Highlanders, the slaughter spread like
          flame;
And Garry, thundering down his moun-
          tain-road,
Was stopped, and could not breathe be-
          neath the load
Of the dead bodies. — 'T was a day of
          shame
For them whom precept and the pedantry
Of cold mechanic battle do enslave.
O for a single hour of that Dundee,
Who on that day the word of onset gave!
Like conquest would the Men of England
          see;
And her Foes find a like inglorious grave.
  1803.   1807.

ANTICIPATION, October, 1803.

SHOUT, for a mighty Victory is won!
On British ground the Invaders are laid
    low;
The breath of Heaven has drifted them
    like snow,
And left them lying in the silent sun,
Never to rise again! — the work is done.
Come forth, ye old men, now in peaceful
    show
And greet your sons! drums beat and
    trumpets blow!
Make merry, wives! ye little children, stun
Your grandame's ears with pleasure of
    your noise!
Clap, infants, clap your hands! Divine
    must be
That triumph, when the very worst, the
    pain,
And even the prospect of our brethren
    slain,
Hath something in it which the heart
    enjoys: —
In glory will they sleep and endless sanc-
    tity.
1803.   1807.

LINES ON THE EXPECTED INVASION, 1803.

COME ye — who, if (which Heaven
    avert!) the Land
Were with herself at strife, would take
    your stand,
Like gallant Falkland, by the Monarch's
    side,
And, like Montrose, make Loyalty your
    pride —
Come ye — who, not less zealous, might
    display
Banners at enmity with regal sway,
And, like the Pyms and Miltons of that
    day,
Think that a State would live in sounder
    health
If Kingship bowed its head to Common-
    wealth —
Ye too — whom no discreditable fear
Would keep, perhaps with many a fruitless
    tear,

Uncertain what to choose and how to
    steer —
And ye — who might mistake for sober
    sense
And wise reserve the plea of indolence —
Come ye — whate'er your creed — O
    waken all,
Whate'er your temper, at your Country's
    call;
Resolving (this a free-born Nation can)
To have one Soul, and perish to a man,
Or save this honored Land from every
    Lord
But British reason and the British sword.
1803.   1845.

THE FARMER OF TILSBURY VALE.[1]

The character of this man was described to
me, and the incident upon which the verses turn
was told me, by Mr. Pool of Nether Stowey, with
whom I became acquainted through our common
friend, S. T. Coleridge. During my residence at
Alfoxden I used to see much of him and had fre-
quent occasions to admire the course of his daily
life, especially his conduct to his laborers and
poor neighbors: their virtues he carefully encour-
aged, and weighed their faults in the scales of
charity. If I seem in these verses to have treated
the weaknesses of the farmer, and his transgres-
sion, too tenderly, it may in part be ascribed to
my having received the story from one so averse
to all harsh judgment. After his death, was
found in his escritoir a lock of gray hair carefully
preserved, with a notice that it had been cut from
the head of his faithful shepherd, who had served
him for a length of years. I need scarcely add
that he felt for all men as his brothers. He was
much beloved by distinguished persons — Mr.
Coleridge, Mr. Southey, Sir H. Davy, and many
others; and in his own neighborhood was highly
valued as a magistrate, a man of business, and in
every other social relation. The latter part of the
poem, perhaps, requires some apology as being
too much of an echo to the "Reverie of Poor
Susan."

'T IS not for the unfeeling, the falsely re-
    fined,
The squeamish in taste, and the narrow of
    mind,
And the small critic wielding his delicate
    pen,
That I sing of old Adam, the pride of old
    men.

[1] See Note.

He dwells in the centre of London's wide
Town;
His staff is a sceptre — his gray hairs a
crown;
And his bright eyes look brighter, set off
by the streak
Of the unfaded rose that still blooms on
his cheek.

'Mid the dews, in the sunshine of morn, —
'mid the joy
Of the fields, he collected that bloom,
when a boy,
That countenance there fashioned, which,
spite of a stain
That his life hath received, to the last will
remain.

A Farmer he was; and his house far and
near
Was the boast of the country for excellent
cheer:
How oft have I heard in sweet Tilsbury
Vale
Of the silver-rimmed horn whence he
dealt his mild ale!

Yet Adam was far as the farthest from ruin,
His fields seemed to know what their
Master was doing:
And turnips, and corn-land, and meadow,
and lea,
All caught the infection — as generous
as he.

Yet Adam prized little the feast and the
bowl, —
The fields better suited the ease of his
soul:
He strayed through the fields like an in-
dolent wight,
The quiet of nature was Adam's delight.

For Adam was simple in thought; and
the poor,
Familiar with him, made an inn of his
door:
He gave them the best that he had; or,
to say
What less may mislead you, they took it
away.

Thus thirty smooth years did he thrive on
his farm:
The Genius of plenty preserved him from
harm:
At length, what to most is a season of
sorrow,
His means are run out, — he must beg, or
must borrow.

To the neighbors he went, — all were free
with their money;
For his hive had so long been replenished
with honey,
That they dreamt not of dearth; — He
continued his rounds,
Knocked here — and knocked there,
pounds still adding to pounds.

He paid what he could with his ill-gotten
pelf,
And something, it might be, reserved for
himself:
Then (what is too true) without hinting
a word,
Turned his back on the country — and off
like a bird.

You lift up your eyes! — but I guess that
you frame
A judgment too harsh of the sin and the
shame;
In him it was scarcely a business of art,
For this he did all in the *ease* of his heart.

To London — a sad emigration I ween —
With his gray hairs he went from the
brook and the green;
And there, with small wealth but his legs
and his hands,
As lonely he stood as a crow on the sands.

All trades, as need was, did old Adam
assume, —
Served as stable-boy, errand-boy, porter,
and groom;
But nature is gracious, necessity kind,
And, in spite of the shame that may lurk
in his mind,

He seems ten birthdays younger, is green
and is stout;
Twice as fast as before does his blood run
about;

You would say that each hair of his beard
    was alive,
And his fingers are busy as bees in a hive.

For he 's not like an Old Man that leisurely
    goes
About work that he knows, in a track that
    he knows;
But often his mind is compelled to demur,
And you guess that the more then his body
    must stir.

In the throng of the town like a stranger
    is he,
Like one whose own country's far over
    the sea;
And Nature, while through the great city
    he hies,
Full ten times a day takes his heart by
    surprise.

This gives him the fancy of one that is
    young,
More of soul in his face than of words on
    his tongue;
Like a maiden of twenty he trembles and
    sighs,
And tears of fifteen will come into his
    eyes.

What 's a tempest to him, or the dry
    parching heats?
Yet he watches the clouds that pass over
    the streets;
With a look of such earnestness often will
    stand,
You might think he 'd twelve reapers at
    work in the Strand.

Where proud Covent-garden, in desolate
    hours
Of snow and hoar-frost, spreads her fruits
    and her flowers,
Old Adam will smile at the pains that have
    made
Poor winter look fine in such strange
    masquerade.

'Mid coaches and chariots, a wagon of
    straw,
Like a magnet, the heart of old Adam can
    draw;

With a thousand soft pictures his memory
    will teem,
And his hearing is touched with the
    sounds of a dream.

Up the Haymarket hill he oft whistles his
    way,
Thrusts his hands in a wagon, and smells
    at the hay;
He thinks of the fields he so often hath
    mown,
And is happy as if the rich freight were
    his own.

But chiefly to Smithfield he loves to re-
    pair, —
If you pass by at morning, you 'll meet
    with him there.
The breath of the cows you may see him
    inhale,
And his heart all the while is in Tilsbury
    Vale.

Now farewell, old Adam! when low thou
    art laid,
May one blade of grass spring up over thy
    head;
And I hope that thy grave, wheresoever
    it be,
Will hear the wind sigh through the leaves
    of a tree.
    1803.   1815.

TO THE CUCKOO.

Composed in the Orchard, Town-end, Grasmere.

O BLITHE New-comer! I have heard,
I hear thee and rejoice.
O Cuckoo! shall I call thee Bird,
Or but a wandering Voice?

While I am lying on the grass
Thy twofold shout I hear,
From hill to hill it seems to pass,
At once far off, and near.

Though babbling only to the Vale,
Of sunshine and of flowers,
Thou bringest unto me a tale
Of visionary hours.

Thrice welcome, darling of the Spring!
Even yet thou art to me

No bird, but an invisible thing,
A voice, a mystery;

The same whom in my school-boy days
I listened to; that Cry
Which made me look a thousand ways
In bush, and tree, and sky.

To seek thee did I often rove
Through woods and on the green;
And thou wert still a hope, a love;
Still longed for, never seen.

And I can listen to thee yet;
Can lie upon the plain
And listen, till I do beget
That golden time again.

O blessèd Bird! the earth we pace
Again appears to be
An unsubstantial, faery place;
That is fit home for Thee!
1804.   1807.

"SHE WAS A PHANTOM OF DELIGHT."

Written at Town-end, Grasmere. The germ of this poem was four lines composed as a part of the verses on the Highland Girl. Though beginning in this way, it was written from my heart, as is sufficiently obvious.

SHE was a Phantom of delight
When first she gleamed upon my sight;
A lovely Apparition, sent
To be a moment's ornament;
Her eyes as stars of Twilight fair;
Like Twilight's, too, her dusky hair;
But all things else about her drawn
From May-time and the cheerful Dawn;
A dancing Shape, an Image gay,
To haunt, to startle, and waylay.

I saw her upon nearer view,
A Spirit, yet a Woman too!
Her household motions light and free,
And steps of virgin-liberty;
A countenance in which did meet
Sweet records, promises as sweet;
A Creature not too bright or good
For human nature's daily food;

For transient sorrows, simple wiles,
Praise, blame, love, kisses, tears, and
  smiles.

And now I see with eye serene
The very pulse of the machine;
A Being breathing thoughtful breath,
A Traveller between life and death;
The reason firm, the temperate will,
Endurance, foresight, strength, and skill;
A perfect Woman, nobly planned,
To warn, to comfort, and command;
And yet a Spirit still, and bright
With something of angelic light.
1804.   1807.

"I WANDERED LONELY AS A CLOUD."

Written at Town-end, Grasmere. The Daffodils grew and still grow on the margin of Ullswater, and probably may be seen to this day as beautiful in the month of March, nodding their golden heads beside the dancing and foaming waves.

I WANDERED lonely as a cloud
That floats on high o'er vales and hills,
When all at once I saw a crowd,
A host, of golden daffodils;
Beside the lake, beneath the trees,
Fluttering and dancing in the breeze.

Continuous as the stars that shine
And twinkle on the milky way,
They stretched in never-ending line
Along the margin of a bay:
Ten thousand saw I at a glance,
Tossing their heads in sprightly dance.

The waves beside them danced; but they
Out-did the sparkling waves in glee:
A poet could not but be gay,
In such a jocund company:
I gazed — and gazed — but little thought
What wealth the show to me had brought:

For oft, when on my couch I lie
In vacant or in pensive mood,
They flash upon that inward eye
Which is the bliss of solitude;
And then my heart with pleasure fills,
And dances with the daffodils.
1804.   1807.

THE AFFLICTION OF MARGARET ——

Written at Town-end, Grasmere. This was taken from the case of a poor widow who lived in the town of Penrith. Her sorrow was well known to Mrs. Wordsworth, to my Sister, and, I believe, to the whole town. She kept a shop, and when she saw a stranger passing by, she was in the habit of going out into the street to inquire of him after her son.

I.

WHERE art thou, my belovèd Son,
Where art thou, worse to me than dead?
Oh find me, prosperous or undone!
Or, if the grave be now thy bed,
Why am I ignorant of the same,
That I may rest; and neither blame
Nor sorrow may attend thy name?

II.

Seven years, alas! to have received
No tidings of an only child;
To have despaired, have hoped, believed,
And been for evermore beguiled,
Sometimes with thoughts of very bliss!
I catch at them, and then I miss;
Was ever darkness like to this?

III.

He was among the prime in worth,
An object beauteous to behold;
Well born, well bred; I sent him forth
Ingenuous, innocent, and bold:
If things ensued that wanted grace,
As hath been said, they were not base;
And never blush was on my face.

IV.

Ah! little doth the young one dream,
When full of play and childish cares,
What power is in his wildest scream,
Heard by his mother unawares!
He knows it not, he cannot guess:
Years to a mother bring distress;
But do not make her love the less.

V.

Neglect me! no, I suffered long
From that ill thought; and, being blind,
Said, "Pride shall help me in my wrong;
Kind mother have I been, as kind

As ever breathed:" and that is true;
I 've wet my path with tears like dew,
Weeping for him when no one knew.

VI.

My Son, if thou be humbled, poor,
Hopeless of honor and of gain,
Oh! do not dread thy mother's door;
Think not of me with grief and pain:
I now can see with better eyes;
And worldly grandeur I despise,
And fortune with her gifts and lies.

VII.

Alas! the fowls of heaven have wings,
And blasts of heaven will aid their flight;
They mount — how short a voyage brings
The wanderers back to their delight!
Chains tie us down by land and sea;
And wishes, vain as mine, may be
All that is left to comfort thee.

VIII.

Perhaps some dungeon hears thee groan,
Maimed, mangled by inhuman men;
Or thou upon a desert thrown
Inheritest the lion's den;
Or hast been summoned to the deep,
Thou, thou and all thy mates, to keep
An incommunicable sleep.

IX.

I look for ghosts; but none will force
Their way to me: 't is falsely said
That there was ever intercourse
Between the living and the dead;
For, surely, then I should have sight
Of him I wait for day and night,
With love and longings infinite.

X.

My apprehensions come in crowds;
I dread the rustling of the grass;
The very shadows of the clouds
Have power to shake me as they pass:
I question things and do not find
One that will answer to my mind;
And all the world appears unkind.

XI.

Beyond participation lie
My troubles, and beyond relief:

If any chance to heave a sigh,
They pity me, and not my grief.
Then come to me, my Son, or send
Some tidings that my woes may end;
I have no other earthly friend!
1804.   1807.

THE FORSAKEN.

This was an overflow from the "Affliction of Margaret ——," and was excluded as superfluous there, but preserved in the faint hope that it may turn to account by restoring a shy lover to some forsaken damsel. My poetry has been complained of as deficient in interests of this sort, — a charge which the piece beginning, "Lyre! though such power do in thy magic live," will scarcely tend to obviate. The natural imagery of these verses was supplied by frequent, I might say intense, observation of the Rydal torrent. What an animating contrast is the ever-changing aspect of that, and indeed of every one of our mountain brooks, to the monotonous tone and unmitigated fury of such streams among the Alps as are fed all the summer long by glaciers and melting snows. A traveller observing the exquisite purity of the great rivers, such as the Rhine at Geneva, and the Reuss at Lucerne, when they issue out of their respective lakes, might fancy for a moment that some power in nature produced this beautiful change, with a view to make amends for those Alpine sullyings which the waters exhibit near their fountain heads; but, alas! how soon does that purity depart before the influx of tributary waters that have flowed through cultivated plains and the crowded abodes of men.

THE peace which others seek they find;
The heaviest storms not longest last;
Heaven grants even to the guiltiest mind
An amnesty for what is past;
When will my sentence be reversed?
I only pray to know the worst;
And wish as if my heart would burst.

O weary struggle! silent years
Tell seemingly no doubtful tale;
And yet they leave it short, and fears
And hopes are strong and will prevail.
My calmest faith escapes not pain;
And, feeling that the hope is vain,
I think that he will come again.
1804.   1845.

REPENTANCE.

A PASTORAL BALLAD.

Written at Town-end, Grasmere. Suggested by the conversation of our next neighbor, Margaret Ashburner.

THE fields which with covetous spirit we
    sold,
Those beautiful fields, the delight of the
    day,
Would have brought us more good than
    a burthen of gold,
Could we but have been as contented as
    they.

When the troublesome Tempter beset us,
    said I,
"Let him come, with his purse proudly
    grasped in his hand;
But, Allan, be true to me, Allan, — we'll
    die
Before he shall go with an inch of the
    land!"

There dwelt we, as happy as birds in their
    bowers;
Unfettered as bees that in gardens abide;
We could do what we liked with the land,
    it was ours;
And for us the brook murmured that ran
    by its side.

But now we are strangers; go early or late;
And often, like one overburthened with
    sin,
With my hand on the latch of the half-
    opened gate,
I look at the fields, but I cannot go in!

When I walk by the hedge on a bright
    summer's day,
Or sit in the shade of my grandfather's
    tree,
A stern face it puts on, as if ready to say,
"What ails you, that you must come
    creeping to me!"

With our pastures about us, we could not
    be sad;
Our comfort was near if we ever were
    crost;

But the comfort, the blessings, and wealth
   that we had,
We slighted them all, — and our birth-
   right was lost.

Oh, ill-judging sire of an innocent son
Who must now be a wanderer! but peace
   to that strain!
Think of evening's repose when our labor
   was done,
The sabbath's return; and its leisure's soft
   chain!

And in sickness, if night had been spar-
   ing of sleep,
How cheerful, at sunrise, the hill where
   I stood,
Looking down on the kine, and our treas-
   ure of sheep
That besprinkled the field; 't was like
   youth in my blood!

Now I cleave to the house, and am dull
   as a snail;
And, oftentimes, hear the church-bell
   with a sigh,
That follows the thought — We 've no land
   in the vale,
Save six feet of earth where our forefathers
   lie!

1804.   1820.

THE SEVEN SISTERS;[1]

OR, THE SOLITUDE OF BINNORIE.

I.

SEVEN Daughters had Lord Archibald,
All children of one mother:
You could not say in one short day
What love they bore each other.
A garland, of seven lilies, wrought!
Seven Sisters that together dwell;
But he, bold Knight as ever fought,
Their Father, took of them no thought,
He loved the wars so well.
Sing, mournfully, oh! mournfully,
The solitude of Binnorie!

II.

Fresh blows the wind, a western wind,
And from the shores of Erin,

[1] See Note.

Across the wave, a Rover brave
To Binnorie is steering:
Right onward to the Scottish strand
The gallant ship is borne;
The warriors leap upon the land,
And hark! the Leader of the band
Hath blown his bugle horn.
Sing, mournfully, oh! mournfully,
The solitude of Binnorie.

III.

Beside a grotto of their own,
With boughs above them closing,
The Seven are laid, and in the shade
They lie like fawns reposing.
But now, upstarting with affright
At noise of man and steed,
Away they fly to left, to right —
Of your fair household, Father-knight,
Methinks you take small heed!
Sing, mournfully, oh! mournfully,
The solitude of Binnorie.

IV.

Away the seven fair Campbells fly,
And, over hill and hollow,
With menace proud, and insult loud,
The youthful Rovers follow.
Cried they, " Your Father loves to roam:
Enough for him to find
The empty house when he comes home;
For us your yellow ringlets comb,
For us be fair and kind! "
Sing, mournfully, oh! mournfully,
The solitude of Binnorie.

V.

Some close behind, some side to side,
Like clouds in stormy weather;
They run, and cry, " Nay, let us die,
And let us die together."
A lake was near; the shore was steep;
There never foot had been;
They ran, and with a desperate leap
Together plunged into the deep,
Nor ever more were seen.
Sing, mournfully, oh! mournfully,
The solitude of Binnorie.

VI.

The stream that flows out of the lake,
As through the glen it rambles,

Repeats a moan o'er moss and stone,
For those seven lovely Campbells.
Seven little Islands, green and bare,
Have risen from out the deep:
The fishers say, those sisters fair,
By faeries all are buried there,
And there together sleep.
Sing, mournfully, oh! mournfully,
The solitude of Binnorie.

1804.   •   1807.

ADDRESS TO MY INFANT DAUGHTER, DORA,

ON BEING REMINDED THAT SHE WAS A MONTH OLD THAT DAY, SEPTEMBER 16.

— HAST thou then survived —
Mild Offspring of infirm humanity,
Meek Infant! among all forlornest things
The most forlorn — one life of that bright
    star,
The second glory of the Heavens? —
    Thou hast,
Already hast survived that great decay,
That transformation through the wide
    earth felt,
And by all nations.   In that Being's sight
From whom the Race of human kind pro-
    ceed,
A thousand years are but as yesterday;
And one day's narrow circuit is to Him
Not less capacious than a thousand years.
But what is time?   What outward glory?
    neither
A measure is of Thee, whose claims extend
Through " heaven s eternal year." — Yet
    hail to Thee,
Frail, feeble Monthling! — by that name,
    methinks,
Thy scanty breathing-time is portioned out
Not idly. — Hadst thou been of Indian
    birth,
Couched on a casual bed of moss and
    leaves,
And rudely canopied by leafy boughs,
Or to the churlish elements exposed
On the blank plains, — the coldness of the
    night,
Or the night's darkness, or its cheerful
    face
Of beauty, by the changing moon adorned,
Would, with imperious admonition, then

Have scored thine age, and punctually
    timed
Thine infant history, on the minds of those
Who might have wandered with thee. —
    Mother's love,
Nor less than mother's love in other
    breasts,
Will, among us warm-clad and warmly
    housed,
Do for thee what the finger of the heavens
Doth all too often harshly execute
For thy unblest coevals, amid wilds
Where fancy hath small liberty to grace
The affections, to exalt them or refine;
And the maternal sympathy itself,
Though strong, is, in the main, a joyless
    tie
Of naked instinct, wound about the heart.
Happier, far happier is thy lot and ours!
Even now — to solemnize thy helpless
    state,
And to enliven in the mind's regard
Thy passive beauty — parallels have risen,
Resemblances, or contrasts, that con-
    nect,
Within the region of a father's thoughts,
Thee and thy mate and sister of the sky.
And first; — thy sinless progress, through
    a world
By sorrow darkened and by care disturbed,
Apt likeness bears to hers, through gath-
    ered clouds,
Moving untouched in silver purity,
And cheering oft-times their reluctant
    gloom.
Fair are ye both, and both are free from
    stain:
But thou, how leisurely thou fill'st thy
    horn
With brightness! leaving her to post
    along,
And range about, disquieted in change,
And still impatient of the shape she wears.
Once up, once down the hill, one journey,
    Babe,
That will suffice thee; and it seems that
    now
Thou hast fore-knowledge that such task
    is thine;
Thou travellest so contentedly, and
    sleep'st
In such a heedless peace.   Alas! full soon
Hath this conception, grateful to behold,

Changed countenance, like an object
   sullied o'er
By breathing mist; and thine appears to be
A mournful labor, while to her is given
Hope, and a renovation without end.
— That smile forbids the thought; for on
   thy face
Smiles are beginning, like the beams of
   dawn,
To shoot and circulate; smiles have there
   been seen
Tranquil assurances that Heaven supports
The feeble motions of thy life, and cheers
Thy loneliness: or shall those smiles be
   called
Feelers of love, put forth as if to explore
This untried world, and to prepare thy
   way
Through a strait passage intricate and dim?
Such are they; and the same are tokens,
   signs,
Which, when the appointed season hath
   arrived,
Joy, as her holiest language, shall adopt;
And Reason's godlike Power be proud to
   own.
  1804.   1815.

THE KITTEN AND FALLING LEAVES.

Seen at Town-end, Grasmere. The elder-bush
has long since disappeared: it hung over the wall
near the Cottage; and the Kitten continued to
leap up, catching the leaves as here described.
The infant was Dora.

THAT way look, my Infant, lo!
What a pretty baby-show!
See the Kitten on the wall,
Sporting with the leaves that fall,
Withered leaves — one — two — and
   three —
From the lofty elder-tree!
Through the calm and frosty air
Of this morning bright and fair,
Eddying round and round they sink
Softly, slowly: one might think,
From the motions that are made,
Every little leaf conveyed
Sylph or Faery hither tending, —
To this lower world descending,
Each invisible and mute,

In his wavering parachute.
— But the Kitten, how she starts,
Crouches, stretches, paws, and darts!
First at one, and then its fellow
Just as light and just as yellow;
There are many now — now one —
Now they stop and there are none.
What intenseness of desire
In her upward eye of fire!
With a tiger-leap half-way
Now she meets the coming prey,
Lets it go as fast, and then
Has it in her power again:
Now she works with three or four,
Like an Indian conjurer;
Quick as he in feats of art,
Far beyond in joy of heart.
Were her antics played in the eye
Of a thousand standers-by,
Clapping hands with shout and stare,
What would little Tabby care
For the plaudits of the crowd?
Over happy to be proud,
Over wealthy in the treasure
Of her own exceeding pleasure!
'T is a pretty baby-treat;
Nor, I deem, for me unmeet;
Here, for neither Babe nor me,
Other playmate can I see.
Of the countless living things,
That with stir of feet and wings
(In the sun or under shade,
Upon bough or grassy blade)
And with busy revellings,
Chirp and song, and murmurings,
Made this orchard's narrow space,
And this vale so blithe a place;
Multitudes are swept away
Never more to breathe the day:
Some are sleeping; some in bands
Travelled into distant lands;
Others slunk to moor and wood,
Far from human neighborhood;
And, among the Kinds that keep
With us closer fellowship,
With us openly abide,
All have laid their mirth aside.
  Where is he that giddy Sprite,
Blue-cap, with his colors bright,
Who was blest as bird could be,
Feeding in the apple-tree;
Made such wanton spoil and rout,
Turning blossoms inside out;

Hung — head pointing towards the
    ground —
Fluttered, perched, into a round
Bound himself, and then unbound;
Lithest, gaudiest Harlequin!
Prettiest Tumbler ever seen!
Light of heart and light of limb;
What is now become of Him?
Lambs, that through the mountains went
Frisking, bleating merriment,
When the year was in its prime,
They are sobered by this time.
If you look to vale or hill,
If you listen, all is still,
Save a little neighboring rill,
That from out the rocky ground
Strikes a solitary sound.
Vainly glitter hill and plain,
And the air is calm in vain;
Vainly Morning spreads the lure
Of a sky serene and pure;
Creature none can she decoy
Into open sign of joy:
Is it that they have a fear
Of the dreary season near?
Or that other pleasures be
Sweeter even than gayety?
    Yet, whate'er enjoyments dwell
In the impenetrable cell
Of the silent heart which Nature
Furnishes to every creature;
Whatsoe'er we feel and know
Too sedate for outward show,
Such a light of gladness breaks,
Pretty Kitten! from thy freaks, —
Spreads with such a living grace
O'er my little Dora's face;
Yes, the sight so stirs and charms
Thee, Baby, laughing in my arms,
That almost I could repine
That your transports are not mine,
That I do not wholly fare
Even as ye do, thoughtless pair!
And I will have my careless season
Spite of melancholy reason,
Will walk through life in such a way
That, when time brings on decay,
Now and then I may possess
Hours of perfect gladsomeness.
— Pleased by any random toy;
By a kitten's busy joy,
Or an infant's laughing eye
Sharing in the ecstasy;

I would fare like that or this,
Find my wisdom in my bliss;
Keep the sprightly soul awake,
And have faculties to take,
Even from things by sorrow wrought,
Matter for a jocund thought,
Spite of care, and spite of grief,
To gambol with Life's falling Leaf.
    1804.   1807.

TO THE SPADE OF A FRIEND
(AN AGRICULTURIST).

COMPOSED WHILE WE WERE LABORING
TOGETHER IN HIS PLEASURE-GROUND.

    This person was Thomas Wilkinson, a Quaker
by religious profession; by natural constitution
of mind, or shall I venture to say, by God's grace,
he was something better. He had inherited a
small estate, and built a house upon it near
Yanwath, upon the banks of the Emont. I have
heard him say that his heart used to beat, in his
boyhood, when he heard the sound of a drum and
fife. Nevertheless, the spirit of enterprise in him
confined itself to tilling his ground, and conquer-
ing such obstacles as stood in the way of its
fertility. Persons of his religious persuasion do
now, in a far greater degree than formerly, attach
themselves to trade and commerce. He kept the
old track. As represented in this poem, he
employed his leisure hours in shaping pleasant
walks by the side of his beloved river, where he
also built something between a hermitage and a
summer-house, attaching to it inscriptions after
the manner of Shenstone at his Leasowes. He
used to travel from time to time, partly from love
of nature, and partly with religious friends in the
service of humanity. His admiration of genius
in every department did him much honor.
Through his connection with the family in which
Edmund Burke was educated, he became ac-
quainted with that great man, who used to receive
him with great kindness and consideration; and
many times have I heard Wilkinson speak of
those interesting interviews. He was honored
also by the friendship of Elizabeth Smith, and of
Thomas Clarkson and his excellent wife, and was
much esteemed by Lord and Lady Lonsdale, and
every member of that family. Among his verses
(he wrote many) are some worthy of preservation
— one little poem in particular upon disturbing,
by prying curiosity, a bird while hatching her
young in his garden. The latter part of this
innocent and good man's life was melancholy.
He became blind, and also poor by becoming

surety for some of his relations. He was a bachelor. He bore, as I have often witnessed, his calamities with unfailing resignation. I will only add that, while working in one of his fields, he unearthed a stone of considerable size, then another, then two more, and, observing that they had been placed in order as if forming the segment of a circle, he proceeded carefully to uncover the soil, and brought into view a beautiful Druid's temple of perfect though small dimensions. In order to make his farm more compact, he exchanged this field for another; and, I am sorry to add, the new proprietor destroyed this interesting relic of remote ages for some vulgar purpose.

SPADE! with which Wilkinson hath tilled
    his lands,
And shaped these pleasant walks by
    Emont's side,
Thou art a tool of honor in my hands;
I press thee, through the yielding soil,
    with pride.

Rare master has it been thy lot to know;
Long hast Thou served a man to reason
    true;
Whose life combines the best of high and
    low,
The laboring many and the resting few;

Health, meekness, ardor, quietness secure,
And industry of body and of mind;
And elegant enjoyments, that are pure
As nature is; too pure to be refined.

Here often hast Thou heard the Poet sing
In concord with his river murmuring by;
Or in some silent field, while timid spring
Is yet uncheered by other minstrelsy.

Who shall inherit Thee when death has
    laid
Low in the darksome cell thine own dear
    lord?
That man will have a trophy, humble
    Spade!
A trophy nobler than a conqueror's sword.

If he be one that feels, with skill to part
False praise from true, or, greater from
    the less,
Thee will he welcome to his hand and
    heart,
Thou monument of peaceful happiness!

He will not dread with Thee a toilsome
    day —
Thee his loved servant, his inspiring mate!
And, when thou art past service, worn
    away,
No dull oblivious nook shall hide thy fate.

His thrift thy uselessness will never scorn;
An *heir-loom* in his cottage wilt thou
    be: —
High will he hang thee up, well pleased
    to adorn
His rustic chimney with the last of Thee!
1804.   1807.

THE SMALL CELANDINE.

THERE is a Flower, the lesser Celandine,
That shrinks, like many more, from cold
    and rain;
And, the first moment that the sun may
    shine,
Bright as the sun himself, 't is out again!

When hailstones have been falling, swarm
    on swarm,
Or blasts the green field and the trees
    distrest,
Oft have I seen it muffled up from harm,
In close self-shelter like a Thing at rest.

But lately, one rough day, this Flower I
    passed
And recognized it, though an altered form,
Now standing forth an offering to the
    blast,
And buffeted at will by rain and storm.

I stopped, and said with inly-muttered
    voice,
"It doth not love the shower, nor seek
    the cold:
This neither is its courage nor its choice,
But its necessity in being old.

"The sunshine may not cheer it, nor the
    dew;
It cannot help itself in its decay;
Stiff in its members, withered, changed
    of hue."
And, in my spleen, I smiled that it was
    gray.

To be a Prodigal's Favorite — then, worse
truth,
A Miser's Pensioner — behold our lot!
O Man, that from thy fair and shining
youth
Age might but take the things Youth
needed not!

1804.   ·   1807.

AT APPLETHWAITE, NEAR KES-
WICK.

This place was presented to me by Sir George
Beaumont with a view to the erection of a house
upon it, for the sake of being near to Coleridge,
then living, and likely to remain, at Greta Hall
near Keswick. The *severe* necessities that pre-
vented this arose from his domestic situation.
This little property, with a considerable addition
that still leaves it very small, lies beautifully upon
the banks of a rill that gurgles down the side of
Skiddaw, and the orchard and other parts of the
grounds command a magnificent prospect of Der-
went Water, and of the mountains of Borrowdale
and Newlands. Many years ago I gave the place
to my daughter.

BEAUMONT! it was thy wish that I should
rear
A seemly Cottage in this sunny Dell,
On favored ground, thy gift, where I
might dwell
In neighborhood with One to me most
dear,
That undivided we from year to year
Might work in our high Calling — a bright
hope
To which our fancies, mingling, gave free
scope
Till checked by some necessities severe.
And should these slacken, honored BEAU-
MONT! still
Even then we may perhaps in vain im-
plore
Leave of our fate thy wishes to fulfil.
Whether this boon be granted us or
not,
Old Skiddaw will look down upon the
Spot
With pride, the Muses love it evermore.

1804.   1845.

TO THE SUPREME BEING.

FROM THE ITALIAN OF MICHAEL ANGELO.

THE prayers I make will then be sweet
indeed
If Thou the spirit give by which I pray:
My unassisted heart is barren clay,
That of its native self can nothing feed:
Of good and pious works thou art the
seed,
That quickens only where thou say'st it
may:
Unless Thou show to us thine own true
way
No man can find it: Father! Thou must
lead.
Do Thou, then, breathe those thoughts
into my mind
By which such virtue may in me be bred
That in thy holy footsteps I may tread;
The fetters of my tongue do Thou unbind,
That I may have the power to sing of thee,
And sound thy praises everlastingly.

1804.   1807.

ODE TO DUTY.

This ode is on the model of Gray's Ode to
Adversity, which is copied from Horace's Ode
to Fortune. Many and many a time have I been
twitted by my wife and sister for having forgotten
this dedication of myself to the stern lawgiver.
Transgressor indeed I have been, from hour to
hour, from day to day: I would fain hope, how-
ever, not more flagrantly or in a worse way than
most of my tuneful brethren. But these last
words are in a wrong strain. We should be
rigorous to ourselves and forbearing, if not in-
dulgent, to others, and, if we make comparisons
at all, it ought to be with those who have morally
excelled us.
"Jam non consilio bonus, sed more eò perduc-
tus, ut non tantum rectè facere possim, sed nisi
rectè facere non possim."

STERN Daughter of the Voice of God!
O Duty! if that name thou love
Who art a light to guide, a rod
To check the erring, and reprove;
Thou, who art victory and law
When empty terrors overawe;

From vain temptations dost set free;
And calm'st the weary strife of frail
   humanity!

There are who ask not if thine eye
Be on them; who, in love and truth,
Where no misgiving is, rely
Upon the genial sense of youth:
Glad Hearts! without reproach or blot
Who do thy work, and know it not:
Oh! if through confidence misplaced
They fail, thy saving arms, dread Power!
   around them cast.

Serene will be our days and bright,
And happy will our nature be,
When love is an unerring light,
And joy its own security.
And they a blissful course may hold
Even now, who, not unwisely bold,
Live in the spirit of this creed;
Yet seek thy firm support, according to
   their need.

I, loving freedom, and untried;
No sport of every random gust,
Yet being to myself a guide,
Too blindly have reposed my trust:
And oft, when in my heart was heard
Thy timely mandate, I deferred
The task, in smoother walks to stray;
But thee I now would serve more strictly,
   if I may.

Through no disturbance of my soul,
Or strong compunction in me wrought,
I supplicate for thy control;
But in the quietness of thought:
Me this unchartered freedom tires;
I feel the weight of chance-desires:
My hopes no more must change their
   name,
I long for a repose that ever is the same.

Stern Lawgiver! yet thou dost wear
The Godhead's most benignant grace;
Nor know we anything so fair
As is the smile upon thy face:
Flowers laugh before thee on their beds
And fragrance in thy footing treads;
Thou dost preserve the stars from wrong;
And the most ancient heavens, through
   Thee, are fresh and strong.

To humbler functions, awful Power!
I call thee: I myself commend
Unto thy guidance from this hour;
Oh, let my weakness have an end!
Give unto me, made lowly wise,
The spirit of self-sacrifice;
The confidence of reason give;
And in the light of truth thy Bondman
   let me live!
   1805.   1807.

TO A SKY-LARK.

Up with me! up with me into the clouds!
   For thy song, Lark, is strong;
Up with me, up with me into the clouds!
   Singing, singing,
With clouds and sky about thee ringing,
   Lift me, guide me till I find
That spot which seems so to thy mind!

I have walked through wildernesses dreary
And to-day my heart is weary;
Had I now the wings of a Faery,
Up to thee would I fly.
There is madness about thee, and joy
   divine
In that song of thine;
Lift me, guide me high and high
To thy banqueting-place in the sky.

      Joyous as morning
Thou art laughing and scorning;
Thou hast a nest for thy love and thy rest,
And, though little troubled with sloth,
Drunken Lark! thou would'st be loth
To be such a traveller as I.
Happy, happy Liver,
With a soul as strong as a mountain river
Pouring out praise to the Almighty Giver,
   Joy and jollity be with us both!

Alas! my journey, rugged and uneven,
Through prickly moors or dusty ways
   must wind;
But hearing thee, or others of thy kind,
As full of gladness and as free of heaven,
I, with my fate contented, will plod on,
And hope for higher raptures, when life's
   day is done.
   1805.   1807.

FIDELITY.

The young man whose death gave occasion to this poem was named Charles Gough, and had come early in the spring to Paterdale for the sake of angling. While attempting to cross over Helvellyn to Grasmere he slipped from a steep part of the rock where the ice was not thawed, and perished. His body was discovered as is told in this poem. Walter Scott heard of the accident, and both he and I, without either of us knowing that the other had taken up the subject, each wrote a poem in admiration of the dog's fidelity. His contains a most beautiful stanza :—

" How long didst thou think that his silence was
        slumber,
When the wind waved his garment how oft didst
        thou start."

I will add that the sentiment in the last four lines of the last stanza in my verses was uttered by a shepherd with such exactness, that a traveller, who afterwards reported his account in print, was induced to question the man whether he had read them, which he had not.

A BARKING sound the Shepherd hears,
A cry as of a dog or fox;
He halts — and searches with his eyes
Among the scattered rocks:
And now at distance can discern
A stirring in a brake of fern;
And instantly a dog is seen,
Glancing through that covert green.

The Dog is not of mountain breed;
Its motions, too, are wild and shy;
With something, as the Shepherd thinks,
Unusual in its cry:
Nor is there any one in sight
All round, in hollow or on height;
Nor shout, nor whistle strikes his ear;
What is the creature doing here?

It was a cove, a huge recess,
That keeps, till June, December's snow;
A lofty precipice in front,
A silent tarn [1] below!
Far in the bosom of Helvellyn,
Remote from public road or dwelling,

[1] Tarn is a *small* Mere or Lake, mostly high up in the mountains.

Pathway, or cultivated land;
From trace of human foot or hand.

There sometimes doth a leaping fish
Send through the tarn a lonely cheer;
The crags repeat the raven's croak,
In symphony austere;
Thither the rainbow comes — the cloud —
And mists that spread the flying shroud;
And sunbeams; and the sounding blast,
That, if it could, would hurry past;
But that enormous barrier holds it fast.

Not free from boding thoughts, a while
The Shepherd stood; then makes his way
O'er rocks and stones, following the Dog
As quickly as he may;
Nor far had gone before he found
A human skeleton on the ground;
The appalled Discoverer with a sigh
Looks round, to learn the history.

From those abrupt and perilous rocks
The Man had fallen, that place of fear!
At length upon the Shepherd's mind
It breaks, and all is clear:
He instantly recalled the name,
And who he was, and whence he came;
Remembered, too, the very day
On which the Traveller passed this way.

But hear a wonder, for whose sake
This lamentable tale I tell!
A lasting monument of words
This wonder merits well.
The Dog, which still was hovering nigh,
Repeating the same timid cry,
This Dog, had been through three months'
        space
A dweller in that savage place.

Yes, proof was plain that, since the day
When this ill-fated Traveller died,
The Dog had watched about the spot,
Or by his master's side:
How nourished here through such long
        time
He knows, who gave that love sublime;
And gave that strength of feeling, great
Above all human estimate!

1805.   1807.

INCIDENT

CHARACTERISTIC OF A FAVORITE DOG.

This Dog I knew well. It belonged to Mrs.
Wordsworth's brother, Mr. Thomas Hutchinson,
who then lived at Sockburn on the Tees, a
beautiful retired situation where I used to visit
him and his sisters before my marriage. My
sister and I spent many months there after our
return from Germany in 1799.

On his morning rounds the Master
Goes to learn how all things fare;
Searches pasture after pasture,
Sheep and cattle eyes with care;
And, for silence or for talk,
He hath comrades in his walk;
Four dogs, each pair of different breed,
Distinguished two for scent, and two for
    speed.

See a hare before him started!
— Off they fly in earnest chase;
Every dog is eager-hearted,
All the four are in the race:
And the hare whom they pursue,
Knows from instinct what to do;
Her hope is near: no turn she makes;
But, like an arrow, to the river takes.

Deep the river was, and crusted
Thinly by a one night's frost;
But the nimble Hare hath trusted
To the ice, and safely crost;
She hath crost, and without heed
All are following at full speed,
When, lo! the ice, so thinly spread,
Breaks — and the greyhound, Dart, is
    overhead!

Better fate have Prince and Swallow —
See them cleaving to the sport!
Music has no heart to follow,
Little Music, she stops short.
She hath neither wish nor heart,
Hers is now another part:
A loving creature she, and brave!
And fondly strives her struggling friend to
    save.

From the brink her paws she stretches,
Very hands as you would say!
And afflicting moans she fetches,
As he breaks the ice away.
For herself she hath no fears, —
Him alone she sees and hears, —
Makes efforts with complainings; nor
    gives o'er
Until her fellow sinks to re-appear no
    more.
1805.   1807.

TRIBUTE.

TO THE MEMORY OF THE SAME DOG.

Lie here, without a record of thy worth,
Beneath a covering of the common earth!
It is not from unwillingness to praise,
Or want of love, that here no Stone we
    raise;
More thou deserv'st; but *this* man gives
    to man,
Brother to brother, *this* is all we can.
Yet they to whom thy virtues made thee
    dear
Shall find thee through all changes of the
    year:
This Oak points out thy grave; the silent
    tree
Will gladly stand a monument of thee.
  We grieved for thee, and wished thy
    end were past;
And willingly have laid thee here at last:
For thou hadst lived till everything that
    cheers
In thee had yielded to the weight of years;
Extreme old-age had wasted thee away,
And left thee but a glimmering of the day;
Thy ears were deaf, and feeble were thy
    knees, —
I saw thee stagger in the summer breeze,
Too weak to stand against its sportive
    breath,
And ready for the gentlest stroke of death.
It came, and we were glad; yet tears were
    shed;
Both man and woman wept when thou
    wert dead;
Not only for a thousand thoughts that
    were,
Old household thoughts, in which thou
    hadst thy share;
But for some precious boons vouchsafed
    to thee,

Found scarcely anywhere in like degree!
For love, that comes wherever life and
    sense
Are given by God, in thee was most in-
    tense;
A chain of heart, a feeling of the mind,
A tender sympathy, which did thee bind
Not only to us Men, but to thy Kind:
Yea, for thy fellow-brutes in thee we saw
A soul of love, love's intellectual law: —
Hence, if we wept, it was not done in
    shame;
Our tears from passion and from reason
    came,
And, therefore, shalt thou be an honored
    name!

  1805.   1807.

TO THE DAISY.

Sweet Flower! belike one day to have
A place upon thy Poet's grave,
I welcome thee once more:
But He, who was on land, at sea,
My Brother, too, in loving thee,
Although he loved more silently,
Sleeps by his native shore.

Ah! hopeful, hopeful was the day
When to that Ship he bent his way,
To govern and to guide:
His wish was gained: a little time
Would bring him back in manhood's
    prime
And free for life, these hills to climb;
With all his wants supplied.

And full of hope day followed day
While that stout Ship at anchor lay
Beside the shores of Wight;
The May had then made all things green;
And, floating there, in pomp serene,
That Ship was goodly to be seen,
His pride and his delight!

Yet then, when called ashore, he sought
The tender peace of rural thought:
In more than happy mood
To your abodes, bright daisy Flowers!
He then would steal at leisure hours,
And loved you glittering in your bowers
A starry multitude.

But hark the word! — the ship is gone; —
Returns from her long course: — anon
Sets sail: — in season due,
Once more on English earth they stand:
But, when a third time from the land
They parted, sorrow was at hand
For Him and for his crew.

Ill-fated Vessel! — ghastly shock!
— At length delivered from the rock,
The deep she hath regained;
And through the stormy night they steer;
Laboring for life, in hope and fear,
To reach a safer shore — how near,
Yet not to be attained!

" Silence! " the brave Commander cried:
To that calm word a shriek replied,
It was the last death-shriek.
— A few (my soul oft sees that sight)
Survive upon the tall mast's height;
But one dear remnant of the night —
For Him in vain I seek.

Six weeks beneath the moving sea
He lay in slumber quietly;
Unforced by wind or wave
To quit the Ship for which he died,
(All claims of duty satisfied;)
And there they found him at her side;
And bore him to the grave.

Vain service! yet not vainly done
For this, if other end were none,
That He, who had been cast
Upon a way of life unmeet
For such a gentle Soul and sweet,
Should find an undisturbed retreat
Near what he loved, at last —

That neighborhood of grove and field
To Him a resting-place should yield,
A meek man and a brave!
The birds shall sing and ocean make
A mournful murmur for *his* sake;
And Thou, sweet Flower, shalt sleep and
    wake
Upon his senseless grave.

  1805.   1815.

ELEGIAC STANZAS.

SUGGESTED BY A PICTURE OF PEELE
CASTLE, IN A STORM, PAINTED BY SIR
GEORGE BEAUMONT.

Sir George Beaumont painted two pictures of
this subject, one of which he gave to Mrs.
Wordsworth, saying she ought to have it; but
Lady Beaumont interfered, and after Sir George's
death she gave it to Sir Uvedale Price, in whose
house at Foxley I have seen it.

I WAS thy neighbor once, thou rugged
    Pile!
Four summer weeks I dwelt in sight of
    thee:
I saw thee every day; and all the while
Thy Form was sleeping on a glassy sea.

So pure the sky, so quiet was the air!
So like, so very like, was day to day!
Whene'er I looked, thy Image still was
    there;
It trembled, but it never passed away.

How perfect was the calm! it seemed no
    sleep;
No mood, which season takes away, or
    brings:
I could have fancied that the mighty Deep
Was even the gentlest of all gentle Things.

Ah! THEN, if mine had been the Painter's
    hand,
To express what then I saw; and add the
    gleam,
The light that never was, on sea or land,
The consecration, and the Poet's dream;

I would have planted thee, thou hoary
    Pile
Amid a world how different from this!
Beside a sea that could not cease to smile;
On tranquil land, beneath a sky of bliss.

Thou shouldst have seemed a treasure-
    house divine
Of peaceful years; a chronicle of
    heaven;—
Of all the sunbeams that did ever shine
The very sweetest had to thee been given.

A Picture had it been of lasting ease,
Elysian quiet, without toil or strife;
No motion but the moving tide, a breeze,
Or merely silent Nature's breathing life.

Such, in the fond illusion of my heart,
Such Picture would I at that time have
    made:
And seen the soul of truth in every part,
A steadfast peace that might not be be-
    trayed.

So once it would have been,—'t is so no
    more;
I have submitted to a new control:
A power is gone, which nothing can re-
    store;
A deep distress hath humanized my Soul.

Not for a moment could I now behold
A smiling sea, and be what I have been:
The feeling of my loss will ne'er be old;
This, which I know, I speak with mind
    serene.

Then, Beaumont, Friend! who would
    have been the Friend,
If he had lived, of Him whom I deplore,
This work of thine I blame not, but
    commend;
This sea in anger, and that dismal shore.

O 't is a passionate Work!—yet wise
    and well,
Well chosen is the spirit that is here;
That Hulk which labors in the deadly
    swell,
This rueful sky, this pageantry of fear!

And this huge Castle, standing here sub-
    lime,
I love to see the look with which it
    braves,
Cased in the unfeeling armor of old time,
The lightning, the fierce wind, and tramp-
    ling waves.

Farewell, farewell the heart that lives
    alone,
Housed in a dream, at distance from the
    Kind!
Such happiness, wherever it be known,
Is to be pitied; for 't is surely blind.

But welcome fortitude, and patient cheer,
And frequent sights of what is to be
    borne!
Such sights, or worse, as are before me
    here. —
Not without hope we suffer and we mourn.
    1805.   1807.

"WHEN TO THE ATTRACTIONS OF THE BUSY WORLD."

The grove still exists, but the plantation has
been walled in. and is not so accessible as when
my brother John wore the path in the manner
here described. The grove was a favorite haunt
with us all while we lived at Town-end.

WHEN, to the attractions of the busy
    world,
Preferring studious leisure, I had chosen
A habitation in this peaceful Vale,
Sharp season followed of continual storm
In deepest winter; and, from week to
    week,
Pathway, and lane, and public road, were
    clogged
With frequent showers of snow. Upon a
    hill
At a short distance from my cottage,
    stands
A stately Fir-grove, whither I was wont
To hasten, for I found, beneath the roof
Of that perennial shade, a cloistral place
Of refuge, with an unincumbered floor.
Here, in safe covert, on the shallow snow,
And, sometimes, on a speck of visible
    earth,
The redbreast near me hopped; nor was
    I loth
To sympathize with vulgar coppice birds
That, for protection from the nipping
    blast,
Hither repaired. — A single beech-tree
    grew
Within this grove of firs! and, on the fork
Of that one beech, appeared a thrush's
    nest;
A last year's nest, conspicuously built
At such small elevation from the ground
As gave sure sign that they, who in that
    house
Of nature and of love had made their home
Amid the fir-trees, all the summer long

Dwelt in a tranquil spot. And oftentimes,
A few sheep, stragglers from some moun-
    tain-flock,
Would watch my motions with suspicious
    stare,
From the remotest outskirts of the
    grove, —
Some nook where they had made their
    final stand,
Huddling together from two fears — the
    fear
Of me and of the storm. Full many an
    hour
Here did I lose. But in this grove the
    trees
Had been so thickly planted, and had
    thriven
In such perplexed and intricate array;
That vainly did I seek, beneath their stems
A length of open space, where to and fro
My feet might move without concern or
    care;
And, baffled thus, though earth from day
    to day
Was fettered, and the air by storm dis-
    turbed,
I ceased the shelter to frequent, — and
    prized,
Less than I wished to prize, that calm
    recess.
    The snows dissolved, and genial Spring
    returned
To clothe the fields with verdure. Other
    haunts
Meanwhile were mine; till, one bright
    April day,
By chance retiring from the glare of noon
To this forsaken covert, there I found
A hoary pathway traced between the trees,
And winding on with such an easy line
Along a natural opening, that I stood
Much wondering how I could have sought
    in vain
For what was now so obvious. To abide,
For an allotted interval of ease,
Under my cottage-roof, had gladly come
From the wild sea a cherished Visitant;
And with the sight of this same path —
    begun,
Begun and ended, in the shady grove,
Pleasant conviction flashed upon my mind
That, to this opportune recess allured,
He had surveyed it with a finer eye,

A heart more wakeful; and had worn the track
By pacing here, unwearied and alone,
In that habitual restlessness of foot
That haunts the Sailor measuring o'er and o'er
His short domain upon the vessel's deck,
While she pursues her course through the dreary sea.
When thou hadst quitted Esthwaite's pleasant shore,
And taken thy first leave of those green hills
And rocks that were the play-ground of thy youth,
Year followed year, my Brother! and we two,
Conversing not, knew little in what mould
Each other's mind was fashioned; and at length,
When once again we met in Grasmere Vale,
Between us there was little other bond
Than common feelings of fraternal love.
But thou, a Schoolboy, to the sea hadst carried
Undying recollections! Nature there
Was with thee; she, who loved us both, she still
Was with thee; and even so didst thou become
A *silent* Poet; from the solitude
Of the vast sea didst bring a watchful heart
Still couchant, an inevitable ear,
And an eye practised like a blind man's touch.
— Back to the joyless Ocean thou art gone;
Nor from this vestige of thy musing hours
Could I withhold thy honored name, — and now
I love the fir-grove with a perfect love.
Thither do I withdraw when cloudless suns
Shine hot, or wind blows troublesome and strong;
And there I sit at evening, when the steep
Of Silver-how, and Grasmere's peaceful lake,
And one green island, gleam between the stems
Of the dark firs, a visionary scene!

And, while I gaze upon the spectacle
Of clouded splendor, on this dream-like sight
Of solemn loveliness, I think on thee,
My Brother, and on all which thou hast lost.
Nor seldom, if I rightly guess, while Thou,
Muttering the verses which I muttered first
Among the mountains, through the midnight watch
Art pacing thoughtfully the vessel's deck
In some far region, here, while o'er my head,
At every impulse of the moving breeze,
The fir-grove murmurs with a sea-like sound,
Alone I tread this path; — for aught I know,
Timing my steps to thine; and, with a store
Of undistinguishable sympathies,
Mingling most earnest wishes for the day
When we, and others whom we love, shall meet
A second time, in Grasmere's happy Vale.

1805.   1815.

NOTE. — This wish was not granted; the lamented Person not long after perished by shipwreck, in discharge of his duty as commander of the Honorable East India Company's Vessel, the Earl of Abergavenny.

ELEGIAC VERSES.

IN MEMORY OF MY BROTHER, JOHN WORDSWORTH.

COMMANDER OF THE E.I. COMPANY'S SHIP THE EARL OF ABERGAVENNY, IN WHICH HE PERISHED BY CALAMITOUS SHIPWRECK, FEB. 6, 1805.

Composed near the Mountain track that leads from Grasmere through Grisdale Hawes, where it descends towards Paterdale.

" Here did we stop; and here looked round,
While each into himself descends."

The point is two or three yards below the outlet of Grisdale tarn, on a foot-road by which a horse may pass to Paterdale — a ridge of Helvellyn on the left, and the summit of Fairfield on the right.

I.

THE Sheep-boy whistled loud, and lo!
That instant, startled by the shock,

The Buzzard mounted from the rock
Deliberate and slow:
Lord of the air, he took his flight;
Oh! could he on that woful night
Have lent his wing, my Brother dear,
For one poor moment's space to Thee,
And all who struggled with the Sea,
When safety was so near.

II.

Thus in the weakness of my heart
I spoke (but let that pang be still)
When rising from the rock at will,
I saw the Bird depart.
And let me calmly bless the Power
That meets me in this unknown Flower.
Affecting type of him I mourn!
With calmness suffer and believe,
And grieve, and know that I must grieve,
Not cheerless, though forlorn.

III.

Here did we stop; and here looked round
While each into himself descends,
For that last thought of parting Friends
That is not to be found.
Hidden was Grasmere Vale from sight,
Our home and his, his heart's delight,
His quiet heart's selected home.
But time before him melts away,
And he hath feeling of a day
Of blessedness to come.

IV.

Full soon in sorrow did I weep,
Taught that the mutual hope was dust,
In sorrow, but for higher trust,
How miserably deep!
All vanished in a single word,
A breath, a sound, and scarcely heard:
Sea — Ship — drowned — Shipwreck —
  so it came,
The meek, the brave, the good, was gone;
He who had been our living John
Was nothing but a name.

V.

That was indeed a parting! oh,
Glad am I, glad that it is past;
For there were some on whom it cast
Unutterable woe.
But they as well as I have gains; —
From many a humble source, to pains

Like these, there comes a mild release;
Even here I feel it, even this Plant
Is in its beauty ministrant
To comfort and to peace.

VI.

He would have loved thy modest grace,
Meek Flower! To Him I would have
  said,
" It grows upon its native bed
Beside our Parting-place;
There, cleaving to the ground, it lies
With multitude of purple eyes,
Spangling a cushion green like moss;
But we will see it, joyful tide!
Some day, to see it in its pride,
The mountain will we cross."

VII.

— Brother and Friend, if verse of mine
Have power to make thy virtues known,
Here let a monumental Stone
Stand — sacred as a Shrine;
And to the few who pass this way,
Traveller or Shepherd, let it say,
Long as these mighty rocks endure, —
Oh do not Thou too fondly brood,
Although deserving of all good,
On any earthly hope, however pure! [1]
1805.   1845.

LOUISA.

AFTER ACCOMPANYING HER ON A
MOUNTAIN EXCURSION.

Written at Town-end, Grasmere.

I MET Louisa in the shade,
And, having seen that lovely Maid,
Why should I fear to say
That, nymph-like, she is fleet and strong,
And down the rocks can leap along
Like rivulets in May?

She loves her fire, her cottage-home;
Yet o'er the moorland will she roam
In weather rough and bleak;
And, when against the wind she strains,
Oh! might I kiss the mountain rains
That sparkle on her cheek.

[1] The plant alluded to is the Moss Campion
(*Silene acaulis* of Linnæus). See Note.

Take all that's mine " beneath the moon,"
If I with her but half a noon
May sit beneath the walls
Of some old cave, or mossy nook,
When up she winds along the brook
To hunt the waterfalls.

1805.   1807.

TO A YOUNG LADY

WHO HAD BEEN REPROACHED FOR TAK-
ING LONG WALKS IN THE COUNTRY.

Composed at the same time and on the same
view as " I met Louisa in the shade : " indeed,
they were designed to make one piece.

DEAR Child of Nature, let them rail !
— There is a nest in a green dale,
A harbor and a hold;
Where thou, a Wife and Friend, shalt see
Thy own heart-stirring days, and be
A light to young and old.

There, healthy as a shepherd boy,
And treading among flowers of joy
Which at no season fade,
Thou, while thy babes around thee cling,
Shalt show us how divine a thing
A Woman may be made.

Thy thoughts and feelings shall not die,
Nor leave thee, when gray hairs are nigh,
A melancholy slave;
But an old age serene and bright,
And lovely as a Lapland night,
Shall lead thee to thy grave.

1805.   1807.

VAUDRACOUR AND JULIA.[1]

Written at Town-end, Grasmere. Faithfully
narrated, though with the omission of many
pathetic circumstances, from the mouth of a
French lady, who had been an eye-and-ear-witness
of all that was done and said. Many long years
after, I was told that Dupligne was then a monk
in the Convent of La Trappe.

The following tale was written as an Episode,
in a work from which its length may perhaps ex-
clude it. The facts are true ; no invention as to
these has been exercised, as none was needed.

[1] The first four lines occur in The Prelude,
book ix. p. 346.

O HAPPY time of youthful lovers (thus
My story may begin) O balmy time,
In which a love-knot on a lady's brow
Is fairer than the fairest star in heaven !
To such inheritance of blessed fancy
(Fancy that sports more desperately with
        minds
Than ever fortune hath been known to do)
The high-born Vaudracour was brought,
        by years
Whose progress had a little overstepped
His stripling prime. A town of small
        repute,
Among the vine-clad mountains of Au-
        vergne,
Was the Youth's birth-place. There he
        wooed a Maid
Who heard the heart-felt music of his suit
With answering vows. Plebeian was the
        stock,
Plebeian, though ingenuous, the stock,
From which her graces and her honors
        sprung :
And hence the father of the enamored
        Youth,
With haughty indignation, spurned the
        thought
Of such alliance. — From their cradles up,
With but a step between their several
        homes,
Twins had they been in pleasure; after
        strife
And petty quarrels, had grown fond again;
Each other's advocate, each other's stay;
And, in their happiest moments, not con-
        tent,
If more divided than a sportive pair
Of sea-fowl, conscious both that they are
        hovering
Within the eddy of a common blast,
Or hidden only by the concave depth
Of neighboring billows from each other's
        sight.
    Thus, not without concurrence of an age
Unknown to memory, was an earnest given
By ready nature for a life of love,
For endless constancy, and placid truth;
But whatsoe'er of such rare treasure lay
Reserved, had fate permitted, for support
Of their maturer years, his present mind
Was under fascination; — he beheld
A vision, and adored the thing he saw.
Arabian fiction never filled the world

With half the wonders that were wrought
    for him.
Earth breathed in one great presence of
    the spring;
Life turned the meanest of her imple-
    ments,
Before his eyes, to price above all gold;
The house she dwelt in was a sainted
    shrine;
Her chamber-window did surpass in glory
The portals of the dawn; all paradise
Could, by the simple opening of a door,
Let itself in upon him: — pathways,
    walks,
Swarmed with enchantment, till his spirit
    sank,
Surcharged, within him, overblest to move
Beneath a sun that wakes a weary world
To its dull round of ordinary cares;
A man too happy for mortality!
    So passed the time, till whether through
    effect
Of some unguarded moment that dissolved
Virtuous restraint — ah, speak it, think
    it, not!
Deem rather that the fervent Youth, who
    saw
So many bars between his present state
And the dear haven where he wished to be
In honorable wedlock with his Love,
Was in his judgment tempted to decline
To perilous weakness, and entrust his
    cause
To nature for a happy end of all;
Deem that by such fond hope the Youth
    was swayed,
And bear with their transgression, when I
    add
That Julia, wanting yet the name of wife,
Carried about her for a secret grief
The promise of a mother.
               To conceal
The threatened shame, the parents of the
    Maid
Found means to hurry her away by night,
And unforewarned, that in some distant
    spot
She might remain shrouded in privacy,
Until the babe was born. When morning
    came
The Lover, thus bereft, stung with his
    loss,
And all uncertain whither he should turn,

Chafed like a wild beast in the toils; but
    soon
Discovering traces of the fugitives,
Their steps he followed to the Maid's re-
    treat.
Easily may the sequel be divined —
Walks to and fro — watchings at every
    hour;
And the fair Captive, who, whene'er she
    may,
Is busy at her casement as the swallow
Fluttering its pinions, almost within reach,
About the pendent nest, did thus espy
Her Lover! — thence a stolen interview,
Accomplished under friendly shade of
    night.
    I pass the raptures of the pair; — such
    theme
Is, by innumerable poets, touched
In more delightful verse than skill of mine
Could fashion; chiefly by that darling
    bard
Who told of Juliet and her Romeo,
And of the lark's note heard before its
    time,
And of the streaks that laced the severing
    clouds
In the unrelenting east. — Through all her
    courts
The vacant city slept; the busy winds,
That keep no certain intervals of rest,
Moved not; meanwhile the galaxy dis-
    played
Her fires, that like mysterious pulses beat
Aloft; — momentous but uneasy bliss!
To their full hearts the universe seemed
    hung
On that brief meeting's slender filament!
    They parted; and the generous Vau-
    dracour
Reached speedily the native threshold,
    bent
On making (so the Lovers had agreed)
A sacrifice of birthright to attain
A final portion from his father's hand;
Which granted, Bride and Bridegroom
    then would flee
To some remote and solitary place,
Shady as night, and beautiful as heaven,
Where they may live, with no one to be-
    hold
Their happiness, or to disturb their love.
But *now* of this no whisper; not the less,

If ever an obtrusive word were dropped
Touching the matter of his passion, still,
In his stern father's hearing, Vaudracour
Persisted openly that death alone
Should abrogate his human privilege
Divine, of swearing everlasting truth,
Upon the altar, to the Maid he loved.
    " You shall be baffled in your mad in-
        tent
If there be justice in the court of France,"
Muttered the Father.— From these words
        the Youth
Conceived a terror; and, by night or day,
Stirred nowhere without weapons, that
        full soon
Found dreadful provocation: for at night
When to his chamber he retired, attempt
Was made to seize him by three armèd
        men,
Acting, in furtherance of the father's will,
Under a private signet of the State.
One the rash Youth's ungovernable hand
Slew, and as quickly to a second gave
A perilous wound— he shuddered to be-
        hold
The breathless corse; then peacefully re-
        signed
His person to the law, was lodged in
        prison,
And wore the fetters of a criminal.
    Have you observed a tuft of wingèd
        seed
That, from the dandelion's naked stalk,
Mounted aloft, is suffered not to use
Its natural gifts for purposes of rest,
Driven by the autumnal whirlwind to and
        fro
Through the wide element? or have you
        marked
The heavier substance of a leaf-clad bough,
Within the vortex of a foaming flood,
Tormented? by such aid you may conceive
The perturbation that ensued; — ah, no !
Desperate the Maid— the Youth is
        stained with blood;
Unmatchable on earth is their disquiet !
Yet as the troubled seed and tortured
        bough
Is Man, subjected to despotic sway.
    For him, by private influence with the
        Court,
Was pardon gained, and liberty procured;
But not without exaction of a pledge,

Which liberty and love dispersed in air.
He flew to her from whom they would
        divide him —
He clove to her who could not give him
        peace —
Yea, his first word of greeting was, —
        " All right
Is gone from me; my lately-towering
        hopes,
To the least fibre of their lowest root,
Are withered; thou no longer canst be
        mine,
I thine— the conscience-stricken must
        not woo
The unruffled Innocent, — I see thy face,
Behold thee, and my misery is complete !''
    " One, are we not? '' exclaimed the
        Maiden— " One,
For innocence and youth, for weal and
        woe? ''
Then with the father's name she coupled
        words
Of vehement indignation; but the Youth
Checked her with filial meekness; for no
        thought
Uncharitable crossed his mind, no sense
Of hasty anger rising in the eclipse
Of true domestic loyalty, did e'er
Find place within his bosom. — Once
        again
The persevering wedge of tyranny
Achieved their separation: and once more
Were they united, — to be yet again
Disparted, pitiable lot ! But here
A portion of the tale may well be left
In silence, though my memory could
        add
Much how the Youth, in scanty space of
        time,
Was traversed from without; much, too,
        of thoughts
That occupied his days in solitude
Under privation and restraint; and what,
Through dark and shapeless fear of things
        to come,
And what, through strong compunction
        for the past,
He suffered— breaking down in heart
        and mind !
    Doomed to a third and last captivity,
His freedom he recovered on the eve
Of Julia's travail. When the babe was
        born,

Its presence tempted him to cherish
  schemes
Of future happiness. "You shall return,
Julia," said he, "and to your father's
  house
Go with the child. — You have been
  wretched; yet
The silver shower, whose reckless burthen
  weighs
Too heavily upon the lily's head,
Oft leaves a saving moisture at its root.
Malice, beholding you, will melt away.
Go! — 't is a town where both of us were
  born;
None will reproach you, for our truth is
  known;
And if, amid those once-bright bowers,
  our fate
Remain unpitied, pity is not in man.
With ornaments — the prettiest, nature
  yields
Or art can fashion, shall you deck our boy,
And feed his countenance with your own
  sweet looks
Till no one can resist him. — Now, even
  now,
I see him sporting on the sunny lawn;
My father from the window sees him too;
Startled, as if some new-created thing
Enriched the earth, or Faery of the woods
Bounded before him; — but the unweet-
  ing Child
Shall by his beauty win his grandsire's
  heart
So that it shall be softened, and our loves
End happily, as they began!"
                    These gleams
Appeared but seldom; oftener was he seen
Propping a pale and melancholy face
Upon the Mother's bosom; resting thus
His head upon one breast, while from the
  other
The Babe was drawing in its quiet food.
— That pillow is no longer to be thine,
Fond Youth! that mournful solace now
  must pass
Into the list of things that cannot be!
Unwedded Julia, terror-smitten, hears
The sentence, by her mother's lip pro-
  nounced,
That dooms her to a convent. — Who
  shall tell,
Who dares report, the tidings to the lord

Of her affections? so they blindly asked
Who knew not to what quiet depths a
  weight
Of agony had pressed the Sufferer down:
The word, by others dreaded, he can hear
Composed and silent, without visible sign
Of even the least emotion. Noting this,
When the impatient object of his love
Upbraided him with slackness, he returned
No answer, only took the mother's hand
And kissed it; seemingly devoid of pain,
Or care, that what so tenderly he pressed,
Was a dependant on the obdurate heart
Of one who came to disunite their lives
Forever — sad alternative! preferred,
By the unbending Parents of the Maid,
To secret 'spousals meanly disavowed.
— So be it!
                    In the city he remained
A season after Julia had withdrawn
To those religious walls. He, too, de-
  parts —
Who with him? — even the senseless
  Little-one.
With that sole charge he passed the city-
  gates,
For the last time, attendant by the side
Of a close chair, a litter, or sedan,
In which the Babe was carried. To a hill,
That rose a brief league distant from the
  town,
The dwellers in that house where he had
  lodged
Accompanied his steps, by anxious love
Impelled; — they parted from him there,
  and stood
Watching below till he had disappeared
On the hill top. His eyes he scarcely
  took,
Throughout that journey, from the vehicle
(Slow-moving ark of all his hopes!) that
  veiled
The tender infant: and, at every inn,
And under every hospitable tree
At which the bearers halted or reposed,
Laid him with timid care upon his knees,
And looked, as mothers ne'er were known
  to look,
Upon the nursling which his arms em-
  braced.
    This was the manner in which Vau-
  dracour
Departed with his infant; and thus reached

His father's house, where to the innocent child
Admittance was denied.   The young man spake
No word of indignation or reproof,
But of his father begged, a last request,
That a retreat might be assigned to him
Where in forgotten quiet he might dwell,
With such allowance as his wants required;
For wishes he had none.   To a lodge that stood
Deep in a forest, with leave given, at the age
Of four-and-twenty summers he withdrew;
And thither took with him his motherless Babe,
And one domestic for their common needs,
An aged woman.   It consoled him here
To attend upon the orphan, and perform
Obsequious service to the precious child,
Which, after a short time, by some mistake
Or indiscretion of the Father, died. —
The Tale I follow to its last recess
Of suffering or of peace, I know not which:
Theirs be the blame who caused the woe, not mine!
  From this time forth he never shared a smile
With mortal creature.   An Inhabitant
Of that same town, in which the pair had left
So lively a remembrance of their griefs,
By chance of business, coming within reach
Of his retirement, to the forest lodge
Repaired, but only found the matron there,
Who told him that his pains were thrown away,
For that her Master never uttered word
To living thing — not even to her. — Behold!
While they were speaking, Vaudracour approached;
But, seeing some one near, as on the latch
Of the garden-gate his hand was laid, he shrunk —
And, like a shadow, glided out of view.
Shocked at his savage aspect, from the place

The visitor retired.
                          Thus lived the Youth
Cut off from all intelligence with man,
And shunning even the light of common day;
Nor could the voice of Freedom, which through France
Full speedily resounded, public hope,
Or personal memory of his own deep wrongs,
Rouse him: but in those solitary shades
His days he wasted, an imbecile mind!
1805.   1820.

THE COTTAGER TO HER INFANT.

BY MY SISTER.

Suggested to her while beside my sleeping children.

THE days are cold, the nights are long,
The north-wind sings a doleful song;
Then hush again upon my breast;
All merry things are now at rest,
        Save thee, my pretty Love!

The kitten sleeps upon the hearth,
The crickets long have ceased their mirth;
There's nothing stirring in the house
Save one *wee*, hungry, nibbling mouse,
        Then why so busy thou?

Nay! start not at that sparkling light;
'T is but the moon that shines so bright
On the window pane bedropped with rain:
Then, little Darling! sleep again,
        And wake when it is day.
1805.   1815.

THE WAGGONER.[1]

Written at Town-end, Grasmere.   The characters and story from fact.

            In Cairo's crowded streets
The impatient Merchant, wondering, waits in vain,
And Mecca saddens at the long delay.
                              THOMSON.
                  TO
        CHARLES LAMB, ESQ.

MY DEAR FRIEND,
            When I sent you, a few weeks ago,
the tale of Peter Bell, you asked "why THE

            [1] See Note.

WAGGONER was not added?"—To say the truth
—from the higher tone of imagination, and the
deeper touches of passion aimed at in the former,
I apprehended this little Piece could not accom-
pany it without disadvantage. In the year 1806,
if I am not mistaken, THE WAGGONER was read
to you in manuscript, and, as you have remem-
bered it for so long a time, I am the more en-
couraged to' hope, that, since the localities on
which the Poem partly depends did not prevent
its being interesting to you, it may prove accept-
able to others. Being therefore in some measure
the cause of its present appearance, you must
allow me the gratification of inscribing it to you;
in acknowledgment of the pleasure I have derived
from your Writings, and of the high esteem with
which

I am very truly yours,
WILLIAM WORDSWORTH.

Rydal Mount, May 20, 1819.

CANTO FIRST.

'T IS spent — this burning day of June!
Soft darkness o'er its latest gleams is
    stealing;
The buzzing dor-hawk, round and round,
    is wheeling,[1] —
That solitary bird
Is all that can be heard
In silence deeper far than that of deepest
    noon!
   Confiding Glow-worms, 't is a night
Propitious to your earth-born light!
But, where the scattered stars are seen
In hazy straits the clouds between,
Each, in his station twinkling not,
Seems changed into a pallid spot.
The mountains against heaven's grave
    weight
Rise up, and grow to wondrous height.
The air, as in a lion's den,
Is close and hot; — and now and then
Comes a tired and sultry breeze
With a haunting and a panting,
Like the stifling of disease;
But the dews allay the heat,
And the silence makes it sweet.
Hush, there is some one on the stir!
'T is Benjamin the Waggoner;
Who long hath trod this toilsome way,
Companion of the night and day.
That far-off tinkling's drowsy cheer,
Mixed with a faint yet grating sound

[1] See Note.

In a moment lost and found,
The Wain announces — by whose side
Along the banks of Rydal Mere
He paces on, a trusty Guide, —
Listen! you can scarcely hear!
Hither he his course is bending; —
Now he leaves the lower ground,
And up the craggy hill ascending
Many a stop and stay he makes,
Many a breathing-fit he takes; —
Steep the way and wearisome,
Yet all the while his whip is dumb!
   The Horses have worked with right
    good-will,
And so have gained the top of the hill;
He was patient, they were strong,
And now they smoothly glide along,
Recovering breath, and pleased to win
The praises of mild Benjamin.
Heaven shield him from mishap and
    snare!
But why so early with this prayer? —
Is it for threatenings in the sky?
Or for some other danger nigh?
No; none is near him yet, though he
Be one of much infirmity;
For at the bottom of the brow,
Where once the DOVE and OLIVE-BOUGH
Offered a greeting of good ale
To all who entered Grasmere Vale;
And called on him who must depart
To leave it with a jovial heart;
There, where the DOVE and OLIVE-BOUGH
Once hung, a Poet harbors now,
A simple water-drinking Bard;
Why need our Hero then (though frail
His best resolves) be on his guard?
He marches by, secure and bold;
Yet while he thinks on times of old,
It seems that all looks wondrous cold;
He shrugs his shoulders, shakes his head,
And, for the honest folk within,
It is a doubt with Benjamin
Whether they be alive or dead!
   Here is no danger, — none at all!
Beyond his wish he walks secure;
But pass a mile — and *then* for trial, —
Then for the pride of self-denial;
If he resist that tempting door,
Which with such friendly voice will call;
If he resist those casement panes,
And that bright gleam which thence will
    fall

Upon his Leaders' bells and manes,
Inviting him with cheerful lure:
For still, though all be dark elsewhere,
Some shining notice will be *there*,
Of open house and ready fare.
  The place to Benjamin right well
Is known, and by as strong a spell
As used to be that sign of love
And hope — the OLIVE - BOUGH and
    DOVE;
He knows it to his cost, good Man!
Who does not know the famous SWAN?
Object uncouth! and yet our boast,
For it was painted by the Host;
His own conceit the figure planned,
'T was colored all by his own hand;
And that frail Child of thirsty clay,
Of whom I sing this rustic lay,
Could tell with self-dissatisfaction
Quaint stories of the bird's attraction![1]
  Well! that is past — and in despite
Of open door and shining light.
And now the conqueror essays
The long ascent of Dunmail-raise;
And with his team is gentle here
As when he clomb from Rydal Mere;
His whip they do not dread — his voice
They only hear it to rejoice.
To stand or go is at *their* pleasure;
Their efforts and their time they measure
By generous pride within the breast;
And, while they strain, and while they
    rest,
He thus pursues his thoughts at leisure.
  Now am I fairly safe to-night —
And with proud cause my heart is light:
I trespassed lately worse than ever —
But Heaven has blest a good endeavor;
And, to my soul's content, I find
The evil One is left behind.
Yes, let my master fume and fret,
Here am I — with my horses yet!
My jolly team, he finds that ye
Will work for nobody but me!
Full proof of this the Country gained;
It knows how ye were vexed and strained,
And forced unworthy stripes to bear,
When trusted to another's care.
Here was it — on this rugged slope,

Which now ye climb with heart and hope,
I saw you, between rage and fear,
Plunge, and fling back a spiteful ear,
And ever more and more confused,
As ye were more and more abused:
As chance would have it, passing by
I saw you in that jeopardy:
A word from me was like a charm;
Ye pulled together with one mind;
And your huge burthen, safe from harm,
Moved like a vessel in the wind!
— Yes, without me, up hills so high
'T is vain to strive for mastery.
Then grieve not, jolly team! though tough
The road we travel, steep, and rough;
Though Rydal-heights and Dunmail-raise,
And all their fellow banks and braes,
Full often make you stretch and strain,
And halt for breath and halt again,
Yet to their sturdiness 't is owing
That side by side we still are going!
  While Benjamin in earnest mood
His meditations thus pursued,
A storm, which had been smothered long,
Was growing inwardly more strong;
And, in its struggles to get free,
Was busily employed as he.
The thunder had begun to growl —
He heard not, too intent of soul;
The air was now without a breath —
He marked not that 't was still as death,
But soon large rain-drops on his head
Fell with the weight of drops of lead; —
He starts — and takes, at the admonition,
A sage survey of his condition.
The road is black before his eyes,
Glimmering faintly where it lies;
Black is the sky — and every hill,
Up to the sky, is blacker still —
Sky, hill, and dale, one dismal room,
Hung round and overhung with gloom;
Save that above a single height
Is to be seen a lurid light,
Above Helm-crag[1] — a streak half dead,
A burning of portentous red;
And near that lurid light, full well
The ASTROLOGER, sage Sidrophel,
Where at his desk and book he sits,

---

[1] This rude piece of self-taught art (such is the progress of refinement) has been supplanted by a professional production.

[1] A mountain of Grasmere, the broken summit of which presents two figures, full as distinctly shaped as that of the famous Cobbler near Arroquhar in Scotland.

Puzzling aloft his curious wits;
He whose domain is held in common
With no one but the ANCIENT WOMAN,
Cowering beside her rifted cell,
As if intent on magic spell;—
Dread pair, that, spite of wind and
   weather,
Still sit upon Helm-crag together!
  The ASTROLOGER was not unseen
By solitary Benjamin;
But total darkness came anon,
And he and everything was gone:
And suddenly a ruffling breeze,
(That would have rocked the sounding
   trees
Had aught of sylvan growth been there)
Swept through the Hollow long and
   bare:
The rain rushed down—the road was
   battered,
As with the force of billows shattered;
The horses are dismayed, nor know
Whether they should stand or go;
And Benjamin is groping near them
Sees nothing, and can scarcely hear
   them.
He is astounded, — wonder not, —
With such a charge in such a spot;
Astounded in the mountain gap
With thunder-peals, clap after clap,
Close-treading on the silent flashes—
And somewhere, as he thinks, by crashes
Among the rocks; with weight of rain,
And sullen motions long and slow,
That to a dreary distance go—
Till, breaking in upon the dying strain,
A rending o'er his head begins the fray
   again.
  Meanwhile, uncertain what to do,
And oftentimes compelled to halt,
The horses cautiously pursue
Their way, without mishap or fault;
And now have reached that pile of stones,
Heaped over brave King Dunmail's
   bones;
His who had once supreme command,
Last king of rocky Cumberland;
His bones, and those of all his Power,
Slain here in a disastrous hour!
  When, passing through this narrow
   strait,
Stony, and dark, and desolate,
Benjamin can faintly hear

A voice that comes from some one near,
A female voice: — "Who e'er you be,
Stop," it exclaimed, " and pity me!"
And, less in pity than in wonder,
Amid the darkness and the thunder,
The Waggoner, with prompt command,
Summons his horses to a stand.
  While, with increasing agitation,
The Woman urged her supplication,
In rueful words, with sobs between —
The voice of tears that fell unseen;
There came a flash — a startling glare,
And all Seat-Sandal was laid bare!
'T is not a time for nice suggestion,
And Benjamin, without a question,
Taking her for some way-worn rover,
Said, "Mount, and get you under
   cover!"
  Another voice, in tone as hoarse
As a swoln brook with rugged course,
Cried out, "Good brother, why so fast?
I've had a glimpse of you — avast!
Or, since it suits you to be civil,
Take her at once — for good and evil!"
  "It is my Husband," softly said
The Woman, as if half afraid:
By this time she was snug within,
Through help of honest Benjamin;
She and her Babe, which to her breast
With thankfulness the Mother pressed;
And now the same strong voice more
   near
Said cordially, " My Friend, what cheer?
Rough doings these! as God's my judge,
The sky owes somebody a grudge!
We've had in half an hour or less
A twelvemonth's terror and distress!"
  Then Benjamin entreats the Man
Would mount, too, quickly as he can:
The Sailor — Sailor now no more,
But such he had been heretofore —
To courteous Benjamin replied,
" Go you your way, and mind not me;
For I must have, whate'er betide,
My Ass and fifty things beside, —
Go, and I'll follow speedily!"
  The Wagon moves — and with its load
Descends along the sloping road;
And the rough Sailor instantly
Turns to a little tent hard by:
For when, at closing-in of day,
The family had come that way,
Green pasture and the soft warm air

Tempted them to settle there. —
Green is the grass for beast to graze,
Around the stones of Dunmail-raise!
 The Sailor gathers up his bed,
Takes down the canvas overhead;
And, after farewell to the place,
A parting word — though not of grace,
Pursues, with Ass and all his store,
The way the Wagon went before.

CANTO SECOND.

IF Wytheburn's modest House of prayer,
As lowly as the lowliest dwelling,
Had, with its belfry's humble stock,
A little pair that hang in air,
Been mistress also of a clock,
(And one, too, not in crazy plight)
Twelve strokes that clock would have
    been telling
Under the brow of old Helvellyn —
Its bead-roll of midnight,
Then, when the Hero of my tale
Was passing by, and, down the vale
(The vale now silent, hushed I ween
As if a storm had never been)
Proceeding with a mind at ease;
While the old Familiar of the seas,
Intent to use his utmost haste,
Gained ground upon the Wagon fast,
And gives another lusty cheer;
For spite of rumbling of the wheels,
A welcome greeting he can hear; —
It is a fiddle in its glee
Dinning from the CHERRY TREE!
 Thence the sound — the light is there —
As Benjamin is now aware,
Who, to his inward thoughts confined,
Had almost reached the festive door,
When, startled by the Sailor's roar,
He hears a sound and sees a light,
And in a moment calls to mind
That 't is the village MERRY-NIGHT! [1]
 Although before in no dejection,
At this insidious recollection
His heart with sudden joy is filled, —
His ears are by the music thrilled,
His eyes take pleasure in the road

[1] A term well known in the North of England,
and applied to rural Festivals where young per-
sons meet in the evening for the purpose of dan-
cing.

Glittering before him bright and broad;
And Benjamin is wet and cold,
And there are reasons manifold
That make the good, tow'rds which he's
    yearning,
Look fairly like a lawful earning.
 Nor has thought time to come and go,
To vibrate between yes and no;
For, cries the Sailor, " Glorious chance
That blew us hither ! — let him dance,
Who can or will ! — my honest soul,
Our treat shall be a friendly bowl ! "
He draws him to the door — " Come in,
Come, come," cries he to Benjamin !
And Benjamin — ah, woe is me !
Gave the word — the horses heard
And halted, though reluctantly.
 " Blithe souls and lightsome hearts
    have we,
Feasting at the CHERRY TREE ! "
This was the outside proclamation,
This was the inside salutation;
What bustling — jostling — high and low !
A universal overflow !
What tankards foaming from the tap !
What store of cakes in every lap !
What thumping — stumping — overhead !
The thunder had not been more busy:
With such a stir you would have said,
This little place may well be dizzy !
'T is who can dance with greatest vigor —
'T is what can be most prompt and eager;
As if it heard the fiddle's call,
The pewter clatters on the wall;
The very bacon shows its feeling,
Swinging from the smoky ceiling !
 A steaming bowl, a blazing fire,
What greater good can heart desire?
'T were worth a wise man's while to try
The utmost anger of the sky:
To *seek* for thoughts of a gloomy cast,
If such the bright amends at last.
Now should you say I judge amiss,
The CHERRY TREE shows proof of this;
For soon of all the happy there,
Our Travellers are the happiest pair;
All care with Benjamin is gone —
A Cæsar past the Rubicon !
He thinks not of his long, long strife; —
The Sailor, Man by nature gay,
Hath no resolves to throw away;
And he hath now forgot his Wife,
Hath quite forgotten her — or may be

Thinks her the luckiest soul on earth,
Within that warm and peaceful berth,
Under cover,
Terror over,
Sleeping by her sleeping Baby.
With bowl that sped from hand to hand,
The gladdest of the gladsome band,
Amid their own delight and fun,
They hear — when every dance is done,
When every whirling bout is o'er —
The fiddle's *squeak* [1] — that call to bliss,
Ever followed by a kiss;
They envy not the happy lot,
But enjoy their own the more!
While thus our jocund Travellers fare,
Up springs the Sailor from his chair —
Limps (for I might have told before
That he was lame) across the floor —
Is gone — returns — and with a prize;
With what? — a Ship of lusty size;
A gallant stately Man-of-war,
Fixed on a smoothly-sliding car.
Surprise to all, but most surprise
To Benjamin, who rubs his eyes,
Not knowing that he had befriended
A Man so gloriously attended!
"This," cries the Sailor, "a Third-
rate is —
Stand back, and you shall see her gratis!
This was the Flag-ship at the Nile,
The Vanguard — you may smirk and
smile,
But, pretty Maid, if you look near,
You'll find you've much in little here!
A nobler ship did never swim,
And you shall see her in full trim:
I'll set, my friends, to do you honor,
Set every inch of sail upon her."
So said, so done; and masts, sails, yards,
He names them all; and interlards
His speech with uncouth terms of art,
Accomplished in the showman's part;
And then, as from a sudden check,
Cries out — "'Tis there, the quarter-
deck
On which brave Admiral Nelson stood —
A sight that would have roused your
blood!
One eye he had, which, bright as ten,
Burned like a fire among his men;

[1] At the close of each strathspey, or jig, a par-
ticular note from the fiddle summons the Rustic
to the agreeable duty of saluting his partner.

Let this be land, and that be sea,
Here lay the French — and *thus* came
we!"
Hushed was by this the fiddle's sound,
The dancers all were gathered round,
And, such the stillness of the house,
You might have heard a nibbling mouse;
While, borrowing helps where'er he may,
The Sailor through the story runs
Of ships to ships and guns to guns;
And does his utmost to display
The dismal conflict, and the might
And terror of that marvellous night!
"A bowl, a bowl of double measure,"
Cries Benjamin, "a draught of length,
To Nelson, England's pride and treasure,
Her bulwark and her tower of strength!"
When Benjamin had seized the bowl,
The mastiff, from beneath the wagon,
Where he lay, watchful as a dragon,
Rattled his chain; — 't was all in vain,
For Benjamin, triumphant soul!
He heard the monitory growl;
Heard — and in opposition quaffed
A deep, determined, desperate draught!
Nor did the battered Tar forget,
Or flinch from what he deemed his debt:
Then, like a hero crowned with laurel,
Back to her place the ship he led;
Wheeled her back in full apparel;
And so, flag flying at mast head,
Re-yoked her to the Ass: — anon,
Cries Benjamin, "We must be gone."
Thus, after two hours' hearty stay,
Again behold them on their way!

CANTO THIRD.

RIGHT gladly had the horses stirred,
When they the wished-for greeting heard,
The whip's loud notice from the door,
That they were free to move once more.
You think, those doings must have bred
In them disheartening doubts and dread;
No, not a horse of all the eight,
Although it be a moonless night,
Fears either for himself or freight;
For this they know (and let it hide,
In part, the offences of their guide)
That Benjamin, with clouded brains,
Is worth the best with all their pains;
And, if they had a prayer to make,
The prayer would be that they may take

With him whatever comes in course,
The better fortune or the worse;
That no one else may have business near
    them,
And, drunk or sober, he may steer them.
  So, forth in dauntless mood they fare,
And with them goes the guardian pair.
  Now, heroes, for the true commotion,
The triumph of your late devotion
Can aught on earth impede delight,
Still mounting to a higher height;
And higher still — a greedy flight!
Can any low-born care pursue her.
Can any mortal clog come to her? [1]
No notion have they — not a thought,
That is from joyless regions brought!
And, while they coast the silent lake,
Their inspiration I partake;
Share their empyreal spirits — yea,
With their enraptured vision, see —
O fancy — what a jubilee!
What shifting pictures — clad in gleams
Of color bright as feverish dreams!
Earth, spangled sky, and lake serene,
Involved and restless all — a scene
Pregnant with mutual exaltation,
Rich change, and multiplied creation!
This sight to me the Muse imparts; —
And then, what kindness in their hearts!
What tears of rapture, what vow-making,
Profound entreaties, and hand-shaking!
What solemn, vacant, interlacing,
As if they 'd fall asleep embracing!
Then, in the turbulence of glee,
And in the excess of amity,
Says Benjamin, "That Ass of thine,
He spoils thy sport, and hinders mine:
If he were tethered to the wagon,
He 'd drag as well what he is dragging,
And we, as brother should with brother,
Might trudge it alongside each other!"
  Forthwith, obedient to command,
The horses made a quiet stand;
And to the wagon's skirts was tied
The Creature, by the Mastiff's side,
The Mastiff wondering, and perplex
With dread of what will happen next;
And thinking it but sorry cheer,
To have such company so near!
  This new arrangement made, the Wain
Through the still night proceeds again;
No Moon hath risen her light to lend;

[1] See Note.

But indistinctly may be kenned
The VANGUARD, following close behind,
Sails spread, as if to catch the wind!
  "Thy wife and child are snug and warm,
Thy ship will travel without harm; .
I like," said Benjamin, "her shape and
    stature:
And this of mine — this bulky creature
Of which I have the steering — this,
Seen fairly, is not much amiss!
We want your streamers, friend, you
    know;
But, altogether as we go,
We make a kind of handsome show!
Among these hills, from first to last,
We 've weathered many a furious blast;
Hard passage forcing on, with head
Against the storm, and canvas spread.
I hate a boaster; but to thee
Will say 't, who know'st both land and
    sea,
The unluckiest hulk that stems the brine
Is hardly worse beset than mine,
When cross-winds on her quarter beat;
And, fairly lifted from my feet,
I stagger onward — heaven knows how;
But not so pleasantly as now:
Poor pilot I, by snows confounded,
And many a foundrous pit surrounded!
Yet here we are, by night and day
Grinding through rough and smooth our
    way;
Through foul and fair our task fulfilling:
And long shall be so yet — God willing!"
  "Ay," said the Tar, "through fair and
    foul —
But save us from yon screeching owl!"
That instant was begun a fray
Which called their thoughts another way:
The mastiff, ill-conditioned carl!
What must he do but growl and snarl,
Still more and more dissatisfied
With the meek comrade at his side!
Till, not incensed though put to proof,
The Ass, uplifting a hind hoof,
Salutes the Mastiff on the head;
And so were better manners bred,
And all was calmed and quieted.
  "Yon screech-owl," says the Sailor,
    turning
Back to his former cause of mourning,
"Yon owl! — pray God that all be well!
'T is worse than any funeral bell;

As sure as I 've the gift of sight,
We shall be meeting ghosts to-night ! ''
— Said Benjamin, " This whip shall lay
A thousand, if they cross our way.
I know that Wanton's noisy station,
I know him and his occupation;
The jolly bird hath learned his cheer
Upon the banks of Windermere;
Where a tribe of them make merry,
Mocking the Man that keeps the ferry;
Hallooing from an open throat,
Like travellers shouting for a boat.
— The tricks he learned at Windermere
This vagrant owl is playing here —
That is the worst of his employment:
He 's at the top of his enjoyment ! ''
This explanation stilled the alarm,
Cured the foreboder like a charm;
This, and the manner, and the voice,
Summoned the Sailor to rejoice;
His heart is up — he fears no evil
From life or death, from man or devil;
He wheels — and, making many stops,
Brandished his crutch against the moun-
tain tops;
And, while he talked of blows and scars,
Benjamin, among the stars,
Beheld a dancing — and a glancing;
Such retreating and advancing
As, I ween, was never seen
In bloodiest battle since the days of Mars !

CANTO FOURTH.

THUS they, with freaks of proud delight,
Beguile the remnant of the night;
And many a snatch of jovial song
Regales them as they wind along;
While to the music, from on high,
The echoes make a glad reply. —
But the sage Muse the revel heeds
No farther than her story needs;
Nor will she servilely attend
The loitering journey to its end.
— Blithe spirits of her own impel
The Muse, who scents the morning air,
To take of this transported pair
A brief and unreproved farewell;
To quit the slow-paced wagon's side,
And wander down yon hawthorn dell,
With murmuring Greta for her guide.
— There doth she ken the awful form
Of Raven-crag — black as a storm —

Glimmering through the twilight pale;
And Ghimmer-crag,[1] his tall twin brother,
Each peering forth to meet the other: —
And, while she roves through St. John's
        Vale,
Along the smooth unpathwayed plain,
By sheep-track or through cottage lane,
Where no disturbance comes to intrude
Upon the pensive solitude,
Her unsuspecting eye, perchance,
With the rude shepherd's favored glance,
Beholds the faeries in array,
Whose party-colored garments gay
The silent company betray:
Red, green, and blue; a moment's sight !
For Skiddaw-top with rosy light
Is touched — and all the band take flight.
— Fly also, Muse ! and from the dell
Mount to the ridge of Nathdale Fell;
Thence, look thou forth o'er wood and
        lawn
Hoar with the frost-like dews of dawn;
Across yon meadowy bottom look,
Where close fogs hide their parent brook;
And see, beyond that hamlet small,
The ruined towers of Threlkeld-hall,
Lurking in a double shade,
By trees and lingering twilight made !
There, at Blencathara's rugged feet,
Sir Lancelot gave a safe retreat
To noble Clifford; from annoy
Concealed the persecuted boy,
Well pleased in rustic garb to feed
His flock, and pipe on shepherd's reed
Among this multitude of hills,
Crags, woodlands, waterfalls, and rills;
Which soon the morning shall enfold,
From east to west, in ample vest
Of massy gloom and radiance bold.
    The mists, that o'er the streamlet's bed
Hung low, begin to rise and spread;
Even while I speak, their skirts of gray
Are smitten by a silver ray;
And lo ! — up Castrigg's naked steep
(Where, smoothly urged, the vapors
        sweep
Along — and scatter and divide,
Like fleecy clouds self-multiplied)
The stately wagon is ascending,
With faithful Benjamin attending,
Apparent now beside his team —
Now lost amid a glittering steam:

[1] The crag of the ewe lamb.

And with him goes his Sailor-friend,
By this time near their journey's end;
And, after their high-minded riot,
Sickening into thoughtful quiet;
As if the morning's pleasant hour
Had for their joys a killing power.
And, sooth, for Benjamin a vein
Is opened of still deeper pain
As if his heart by notes were stung
From out the lowly hedge-rows flung;
As if the Warbler lost in light
Reproved his soarings of the night,
In strains of rapture pure and holy
Upbraided his distempered folly.

  Drooping is he, his step is dull;
But the horses stretch and pull;
With increasing vigor climb,
Eager to repair lost time;
Whether, by their own desert,
Knowing what cause there is for shame,
They are laboring to avert
As much as may be of the blame,
Which, they foresee, must soon alight
Upon *his* head, whom, in despite
Of all his failings, they love best;
Whether for him they are distrest,
Or, by length of fasting roused,
Are impatient to be housed:
Up against the hill they strain
Tugging at the iron chain,
Tugging all with might and main,
Last and foremost, every horse
To the utmost of his force!
And the smoke and respiration,
Rising like an exhalation,
Blend with the mist — a moving shroud
To form, an undissolving cloud;
Which, with slant ray, the merry sun
Takes delight to play upon.
Never golden-haired Apollo,
Pleased some favorite chief to follow
Through accidents of peace or war,
In a perilous moment threw
Around the object of his care
Veil of such celestial hue;
Interposed so bright a screen —
Him and his enemies between!

  Alas! what boots it? — who can hide,
When the malicious Fates are bent
On working out an ill intent?
Can destiny be turned aside?
No — sad progress of my story!
Benjamin, this outward glory

Cannot shield thee from thy Master,
Who from Keswick has pricked forth,
Sour and surly as the north;
And, in fear of some disaster,
Comes to give what help he may,
And to hear what thou canst say;
If, as needs he must forbode,
Thou hast been loitering on the road!
His fears, his doubts, may now take
    flight —
The wished-for object is in sight;
Yet, trust the Muse, it rather hath
Stirred him up to livelier wrath;
Which he stifles, moody man!
With all the patience that he can;
To the end that, at your meeting,
He may give thee decent greeting.

  There he is — resolved to stop,
Till the wagon gains the top;
But stop he cannot — must advance:
Him Benjamin, with lucky glance,
Espies — and instantly is ready,
Self-collected, poised, and steady:
And, to be the better seen,
Issues from his radiant shroud,
From his close-attending cloud,
With careless air and open mien.
Erect his port, and firm his going;
So struts yon cock that now is crowing;
And the morning light in grace
Strikes upon his lifted face,
Hurrying the pallid hue away
That might his trespasses betray.
But what can all avail to clear him,
Or what need of explanation,
Parley or interrogation?
For the Master sees, alas!
That unhappy Figure near him,
Limping o'er the dewy grass,
Where the road it fringes, sweet,
Soft and cool to way-worn feet;
And, O indignity! an Ass,
By his noble Mastiff's side,
Tethered to the wagon's tail:
And the ship, in all her pride,
Following after in full sail!
Not to speak of babe and mother;
Who, contented with each other,
And snug as birds in leafy arbor,
Find, within, a blessed harbor!

  With eager eyes the Master pries;
Looks in and out, and through and
    through;

Says nothing — till at last he spies
A wound upon the Mastiff's head,
A wound, where plainly might be read
What feats an Ass's hoof can do!
But drop the rest: — this aggravation,
This complicated provocation,
A hoard of grievances unsealed;
All past forgiveness it repealed;
And thus, and through distempered blood
On both sides, Benjamin the good,
The patient, and the tender-hearted,
Was from his team and wagon parted;
When duty of that day was o'er,
Laid down his whip — and served no
        more. —
Nor could the wagon long survive,
Which Benjamin had ceased to drive:
It lingered on; — guide after guide
Ambitiously the office tried;
But each unmanageable hill
Called for *his* patience and *his* skill; —
And sure it is, that through this night,
And what the morning brought to light,
Two losses had we to sustain,
We lost both WAGGONER and WAIN!

———

Accept, O Friend, for praise or blame,
The gift of this adventurous song;
A record which I dared to frame,
Though timid scruples checked me long;
They checked me — and I left the theme
Untouched — in spite of many a gleam
Of fancy which thereon was shed,
Like pleasant sunbeams shifting still
Upon the side of a distant hill:
But Nature might not be gainsaid;
For what I have and what I miss
I sing of these; — it makes my bliss!
Nor is it I who play the part,
But a shy spirit in my heart,
That comes and goes — will sometimes
        leap
From hiding-places ten years deep;
Or haunts me with familiar face,
Returning, like a ghost unlaid,
Until the debt I owe be paid.
Forgive me, then; for I had been
On friendly terms with this Machine:
In him, while he was wont to trace
Our roads, through many a long year's
        space,

A living almanac had we;
We had a speaking diary,
That in this uneventful place
Gave to the days a mark and name
By which we knew them when they came.
— Yes, I, and all about me here,
Through all the changes of the year,
Had seen him through the mountains
        go,
In pomp of mist or pomp of snow,
Majestically huge and slow:
Or, with a milder grace adorning
The landscape of a summer's morning;
While Grasmere smoothed her liquid plain
The moving image to detain;
And mighty Fairfield, with a chime
Of echoes, to his march kept time;
When little other business stirred,
And little other sound was heard;
In that delicious hour of balm,
Stillness, solitude, and calm,
While yet the valley is arrayed,
On this side with a sober shade;
On that is prodigally bright —
Crag, lawn, and wood — with rosy light.
— But most of all, thou Lordly Wain!
I wish to have thee here again,
When windows flap and chimney roars,
And all is dismal out of doors;
And, sitting by my fire, I see
Eight sorry carts, no less a train;
Unworthy successors of thee,
Come straggling through the wind and
        rain!
And oft, as they pass slowly on,
Beneath my windows, one by one,
See, perched upon the naked height
The summit of a cumbrous freight,
A single traveller — and there
Another; then perhaps a pair —
The lame, the sickly, and the old;
Men, women, heartless with the cold;
And babes in wet and starveling plight:
Which once, be weather as it might,
Had still a nest within a nest,
Thy shelter — and their mother's breast:
Then most of all, then far the most,
Do I regret what we have lost;
Am grieved for that unhappy sin
Which robbed us of good Benjamin;
And of his stately Charge, which none
Could keep alive when He was gone!

1805.   1819.

FRENCH REVOLUTION

AS IT APPEARED TO ENTHUSIASTS AT ITS COMMENCEMENT.[1] REPRINTED FROM "THE FRIEND." [2]

An extract from the long poem on my own poetical education. It was first published by Coleridge in his "Friend," which is the reason of its having had a place in every edition of my poems since.

OH! pleasant exercise of hope and joy!
For mighty were the auxiliars which then
    stood
Upon our side, we who were strong in
    love!
Bliss was it in that dawn to be alive,
But to be young was very heaven! — Oh!
    times,
In which the meagre, stale, forbidding
    ways
Of custom, law, and statute, took at once
The attraction of a country in romance!
When Reason seemed the most to assert
    her rights,
When most intent on making of herself
A prime Enchantress — to assist the work,
Which then was going forward in her
    name!
Not favored spots alone, but the whole
    earth,
The beauty wore of promise, that which
    sets
(As at some moment might not be unfelt
Among the bowers of paradise itself)
The budding rose above the rose full
    blown.
What temper at the prospect did not wake
To happiness unthought of? The inert
Were roused, and lively natures rapt
    away!
They who had fed their childhood upon
    dreams,
The playfellows of fancy, who had made
All powers of swiftness, subtilty, and
    strength
Their ministers, — who in lordly wise had
    stirred

[1] This and the Extract, p. 136, and the first Piece of this Class, are from the [then] unpublished Poem of which some account is given in the Preface to the EXCURSION.

[2] Prelude, book xi. p. 357.

Among the grandest objects of the sense,
And dealt with whatsoever they found
    there
As if they had within some lurking right
To wield it; — they, too, who, of gentle
    mood,
Had watched all gentle motions, and to
    these
Had fitted their own thoughts, schemers
    more mild,
And in the region of their peaceful
    selves; —
Now was it that both found, the meek
    and lofty
Did both find, helpers to their heart's
    desire,
And stuff at hand, plastic as they could
    wish;
Were called upon to exercise their skill,
Not in Utopia, subterranean fields,
Or some secreted island, Heaven knows
    where!
But in the very world, which is the world
Of all of us, — the place where in the end
We find our happiness, or not at all!
1805.   1810.

THE PRELUDE

OR, GROWTH OF A POET'S MIND;

AN AUTOBIOGRAPHICAL POEM.

ADVERTISEMENT.

The following Poem was commenced in the beginning of the year 1799, and completed in the summer of 1805.

The design and occasion of the work are described by the Author in his Preface to the EXCURSION, first published in 1814, where he thus speaks: —

"Several years ago, when the Author retired to his native mountains with the hope of being enabled to construct a literary work that might live, it was a reasonable thing that he should take a review of his own mind, and examine how far Nature and Education had qualified him for such an employment.

"As subsidiary to this preparation, he undertook to record, in verse, the origin and progress of his own powers, as far as he was acquainted with them.

"That work, addressed to a dear friend, most distinguished for his knowledge and genius, and to whom the Author's intellect is deeply indebted, has been long finished; and the result of the investigation which gave rise to it, was a determination to compose a philosophical Poem, containing views of Man, Nature, and Society, and to be entitled the ' Recluse '.; as having for its principal subject the sensations and opinions of a poet living in retirement.

"The preparatory poem is biographical, and conducts the history of the Author's mind to the point when he was emboldened to hope that his faculties were sufficiently matured for entering upon the arduous labor which he had proposed to himself; and the two works have the same kind of relation to each other, if he may so express himself, as the Ante-chapel has to the body of a Gothic church. Continuing this allusion, he may be permitted to add, that his minor pieces, which have been long before the public, when they shall be properly arranged, will be found by the attentive reader to have such connection with the main work as may give them claim to be likened to the little cells, oratories, and sepulchral recesses, ordinarily included in those edifices."

Such was the Author's language in the year 1814.

It will thence be seen, that the present Poem was intended to be introductory to the RECLUSE, and that the RECLUSE, if completed, would have consisted of Three Parts. Of these, the Second Part alone, viz. the EXCURSION, was finished, and given to the world by the Author.

The First Book of the First Part of the RECLUSE still remains in manuscript;[1] but the Third Part was only planned. The materials of which it would have been formed have, however, been incorporated, for the most part, in the Author's other Publications, written subsequently to the EXCURSION.

The Friend, to whom the present Poem is addressed, was the late SAMUEL TAYLOR COLERIDGE, who was resident in Malta, for the restoration of his health, when the greater part of it was composed.

Mr. Coleridge read a considerable portion of the Poem while he was abroad; and his feelings, on hearing it recited by the Author (after his return to his own country), are recorded in his Verses, addressed to Mr. Wordsworth, which will be found in the *Sibylline Leaves*, p. 197, ed. 1817, or *Poetical Works by S. T. Coleridge*, vol. i. p. 206.

RYDAL MOUNT,
July 13th, 1850.

[1] Now printed, see p. 378.

BOOK FIRST.

INTRODUCTION — CHILDHOOD AND SCHOOL–TIME.

OH there is a blessing in this gentle breeze,
A visitant that while it fans my cheek
Doth seem half-conscious of the joy it
    brings
From the green fields, and from yon azure
    sky.
Whate'er its mission, the soft breeze can
    come
To none more grateful than to me; es-
    caped
From the vast city, where I long had pined
A discontented sojourner: now free,
Free as a bird to settle where I will.
What dwelling shall receive me? in what
    vale
Shall be my harbor? underneath what
    grove
Shall I take up my home? and what clear
    stream
Shall with its murmur lull me into rest?
The earth is all before me. With a heart
Joyous, nor scared at its own liberty,
I look about; and should the chosen guide
Be nothing better than a wandering cloud,
I cannot miss my way. I breathe again!
Trances of thought and mountings of the
    mind
Come fast upon me: it is shaken off,
That burthen of my own unnatural self,
The heavy weight of many a weary day
Not mine, and such as were not made for
    me.
Long months of peace (if such bold word
    accord
With any promises of human life),
Long months of ease and undisturbed
    delight
Are mine in prospect; whither shall I turn,
By road or pathway, or through trackless
    field,
Up hill or down, or shall some floating
    thing
Upon the river point me out my course?

Dear Liberty! Yet what would it avail
But for a gift that consecrates the joy?
For I, methought, while the sweet breath
    of heaven

Was blowing on my body, felt within
A correspondent breeze, that gently
     moved
With quickening virtue, but is now be-
     come
A tempest, a redundant energy,
Vexing its own creation. Thanks to both,
And their congenial powers, that, while
     they join
In breaking up a long-continued frost,
Bring with then vernal promises, the hope
Of active days urged on by flying hours,—
Days of sweet leisure, taxed with patient
     thought
Abstruse, nor wanting punctual service
     high,
Matins and vespers of harmonious verse!

     Thus far, O Friend! did I, not used to
     make
A present joy the matter of a song,
Pour forth that day my soul in measured
     strains
That would not be forgotten, and are here
Recorded: to the open fields I told
A prophecy: poetic numbers came
Spontaneously to clothe in priestly robe
A renovated spirit singled out,
Such hope was mine, for holy services.
My own voice cheered me, and, far more,
     the mind's
Internal echo of the imperfect sound;
To both I listened, drawing from them
     both
A cheerful confidence in things to come.

     Content and not unwilling now to give
A respite to this passion, I paced on
With brisk and eager steps; and came,
     at length,
To a green shady place, where down I sate
Beneath a tree, slackening my thoughts
     by choice
And settling into gentler happiness.
'T was autumn, and a clear and placid day,
With warmth, as much as needed, from a
     sun
Two hours declined towards the west; a
     day
With silver clouds, and sunshine on the
     grass,
And in the sheltered and the sheltering
     grove

A perfect stillness. Many were the
     thoughts
Encouraged and dismissed, till choice was
     made
Of a known Vale, whither my feet should
     turn,
Nor rest till they had reached the very door
Of the one cottage which methought I
     saw.
No picture of mere memory ever looked
So fair; and while upon the fancied scene
I gazed with growing love, a higher power
Than Fancy gave assurance of some work
Of glory there forthwith to be begun,
Perhaps too there performed. Thus long
     I mused,
Nor e'er lost sight of what I mused upon,
Save when, amid the stately grove of oaks,
Now here, now there, an acorn, from its
     cup
Dislodged, through sere leaves rustled, or
     at once
To the bare earth dropped with a startling
     sound.
From that soft couch I rose not, till the
     sun
Had almost touched the horizon; casting
     then
A backward glance upon the curling cloud
Of city smoke, by distance ruralized;
Keen as a Truant or a Fugitive,
But as a Pilgrim resolute, I took,
Even with the chance equipment of that
     hour,
The road that pointed toward the chosen
     Vale.
It was a splendid evening, and my soul
Once more made trial of her strength, nor
     lacked
Æolian visitations; but the harp
Was soon defrauded, and the banded host
Of harmony dispersed in straggling
     sounds,
And lastly utter silence! " Be it so;
Why think of anything but present
     good?"
So, like a home-bound laborer, I pursued
My way beneath the mellowing sun, that
     shed
Mild influence; nor left in me one wish
Again to bend the Sabbath of that time
To a servile yoke. What need of many
     words?

A pleasant loitering journey, through three
   days
Continued, brought me to my hermitage.
I spare to tell of what ensued, the life
In common things — the endless store of
   things,
Rare, or at least so seeming, every day
Found all about me in one neighbor-
   hood —
The self-congratulation, and, from morn
To night, unbroken cheerfulness serene.
But speedily an earnest longing rose
To brace myself to some determined aim,
Reading or thinking; either to lay up
New stores, or rescue from decay the old
By timely interference: and therewith
Came hopes still higher, that with out-
   ward life
I might endue some airy phantasies
That had been floating loose about for
   years,
And to such beings temperately deal forth
The many feelings that oppressed my
   heart.
That hope hath been discouraged; wel-
   come light
Dawns from the east, but dawns to dis-
   appear
And mock me with a sky that ripens not
Into a steady morning: if my mind,
Remembering the bold promise of the
   past,
Would gladly grapple with some noble
   theme,
Vain is her wish; where'er she turns she
   finds
Impediments from day to day renewed.

   And now it would content me to yield
      up
Those lofty hopes awhile, for present gifts
Of humbler industry.   But, oh, dear
   Friend!
The Poet, gentle creature as he is,
Hath, like the Lover, his unruly times;
His fits when he is neither sick nor well,
Though no distress be near him but his
   own
Unmanageable thoughts: his mind, best
   pleased
While she as duteous as the mother dove
Sits brooding, lives not always to that
   end,

But like the innocent bird, hath goadings
   on
That drive her as in trouble through the
   groves;
With me is now such passion, to be blamed
No otherwise than as it lasts too long.

   When, as becomes a man who would
      prepare
For such an arduous work, I through my-
   self
Make rigorous inquisition, the report
Is often cheering; for I neither seem
To lack that first great gift, the vital soul,
Nor general Truths, which are themselves
   a sort
Of Elements and Agents, Under-powers,
Subordinate helpers of the living mind:
Nor am I naked of external things,
Forms, images, nor numerous other aids
Of less regard, though won perhaps with
   toil
And needful to build up a Poet's praise.
Time, place, and manners do I seek, and
   these
Are found in plenteous store, but nowhere
   such
As may be singled out with steady choice;
No little band of yet remembered names
Whom I, in perfect confidence, might
   hope
To summon back from lonesome banish-
   ment,
And make them dwellers in the hearts of
   men
Now living, or to live in future years.
Sometimes the ambitious Power of choice,
   mistaking
Proud spring-tide swellings for a regular
   sea,
Will settle on some British theme, some
   old
Romantic tale by Milton left unsung;
More often turning to some gentle place
Within the groves of Chivalry, I pipe
To shepherd swains, or seated harp in
   hand,
Amid reposing knights by a river side
Or fountain, listen to the grave reports
Of dire enchantments faced and over-
   come
By the strong mind, and tales of warlike
   feats,

Where spear encountered spear, and
    sword with sword
Fought, as if conscious of the blazonry
That the shield bore, so glorious was the
    strife;
Whence inspiration for a song that winds
Through ever-changing scenes of votive
    quest
Wrongs to redress, harmonious tribute
    paid
To patient courage and unblemished
    truth,
To firm devotion, zeal unquenchable,
And Christian meekness hallowing faith-
    ful loves.
Sometimes, more sternly moved, I would
    relate
How vanquished Mithridates northward
    passed,
And, hidden in the cloud of years, became
Odin, the Father of a race by whom
Perished the Roman Empire: how the
    friends
And followers of Sertorius, out of Spain
Flying, found shelter in the Fortunate
    Isles,
And left their usages, their arts and laws,
To disappear by a slow gradual death,
To dwindle and to perish one by one,
Starved in those narrow bounds: but not
    the soul
Of Liberty, which fifteen hundred years
Survived, and, when the European came
With skill and power that might not be
    withstood,
Did, like a pestilence, maintain its hold
And wasted down by glorious death that
    race
Of natural heroes: or I would record
How, in tyrannic times, some high-souled
    man,
Unnamed among the chronicles of kings,
Suffered in silence for Truth's sake: or
    tell,
How that one Frenchman,[1] through con-
    tinued force
Of meditation on the inhuman deeds
Of those who conquered first the Indian
    Isles,

[1] Dominique de Gourgues, a French gentleman
who went in 1568 to Florida to avenge the mas-
sacre of the French by the Spaniards there.

Went single in his ministry across
The Ocean; not to comfort the oppressed,
But, like a thirsty wind, to roam about
Withering the Oppressor: how Gustavus
    sought
Help at his need in Dalecarlia's mines:
How Wallace fought for Scotland; left
    the name
Of Wallace to be found, like a wild flower,
All over his dear Country; left the deeds
Of Wallace, like a family of Ghosts,
To people the steep rocks and river banks,
Her natural sanctuaries, with a local soul
Of independence and stern liberty.
Sometimes it suits me better to invent
A tale from my own heart, more near akin
To my own passions and habitual
    thoughts;
Some variegated story, in the main
Lofty, but the unsubstantial structure
    melts
Before the very sun that brightens it,
Mist into air dissolving! Then a wish,
My last and favorite aspiration, mounts
With yearning toward some philosophic
    song
Of Truth that cherishes our daily life;
With meditations passionate from deep
Recesses in man's heart, immortal verse
Thoughtfully fitted to the Orphean lyre;
But from this awful burthen I full soon
Take refuge and beguile myself with trust
That mellower years will bring a riper
    mind
And clearer insight. Thus my days are
    past
In contradiction; with no skill to part
Vague longing, haply bred by want of
    power,
From paramount impulse not to be with-
    stood,
A timorous capacity, from prudence,
From circumspection, infinite delay.
Humility and modest awe, themselves
Betray me, serving often for a cloak
To a more subtle selfishness; that now
Locks every function up in blank reserve,
Now dupes me, trusting to an anxious eye
That with intrusive restlessness beats off
Simplicity and self-presented truth.
Ah! better far than this, to stray about
Voluptuously through fields and rural
    walks,

And ask no record of the hours, resigned
To vacant musing, unreproved neglect
Of all things, and deliberate holiday.
Far better never to have heard the name
Of zeal and just ambition, than to live
Baffled and plagued by a mind that every
  hour
Turns recreant to her task; takes heart
  again,
Then feels immediately some hollow
  thought
Hang like an interdict upon her hopes.
This is my lot; for either still I find
Some imperfection in the chosen theme,
Or see of absolute accomplishment
Much wanting, so much wanting, in my-
  self,
That I recoil and droop, and seek repose
In listlessness from vain perplexity,
Unprofitably travelling toward the grave,
Like a false steward who hath much re-
  ceived
And renders nothing back.
                        Was it for this
That one, the fairest of all rivers, loved
To blend his murmurs with my nurse's
  song,
And, from his alder shades and rocky falls,
And from his fords and shallows, sent a
  voice
That flowed along my dreams? For this,
  didst thou,
O Derwent! winding among grassy holms
Where I was looking on, a babe in arms,
Make ceaseless music that composed my
  thoughts
To more than infant softness, giving me
Amid the fretful dwellings of mankind
A foretaste, a dim earnest, of the calm
That Nature breathes among the hills and
  groves.

When he had left the mountains and
  received
On his smooth breast the shadow of those
  towers
That yet survive, a shattered monument
Of feudal sway, the bright blue river
  passed
Along the margin of our terrace walk;
A tempting playmate whom we dearly
  loved.

Oh, many a time have I, a five years'
  child,
In a small mill-race severed from his
  stream,
Made one long bathing of a summer's day;
Basked in the sun, and plunged and
  basked again
Alternate, all a summer's day, or scoured
The sandy fields, leaping through flowery
  groves
Of yellow ragwort; or, when rock and hill,
The woods, and distant Skiddaw's lofty
  height,
Were bronzed with deepest radiance,
  stood alone
Beneath the sky, as if I had been born
On Indian plains, and from my mother's
  hut
Had run abroad in wantonness, to sport
A naked savage, in the thunder shower.

Fair seed-time had my soul, and I grew
  up
Fostered alike by beauty and by fear:
Much favored in my birth-place, and no
  less
In that belovèd Vale to which erelong
We were transplanted; — there were we
  let loose
For sports of wider range. Ere I had told
Ten birth-days, when among the moun-
  tain slópes
Frost, and the breath of frosty wind, had
  snapped
The last autumnal crocus, 't was my joy
With store of springes o'er my shoulder
  hung
To range the open heights where wood-
  cocks run
Along the smooth green turf. Through
  half the night,
Scudding away from snare to snare, I plied
That anxious visitation; — moon and stars
Were shining o'er my head. I was alone,
And seemed to be a trouble to the peace
That dwelt among them. Sometimes it
  befell
In these night wanderings, that a strong
  desire
O'erpowered my better reason, and the
  bird
Which was the captive of another's toil

Became my prey; and when the deed was
    done
I heard among the solitary hills
Low breathings coming after me, and
    sounds
Of undistinguishable motion, steps
Almost as silent as the turf they trod.

    Nor less, when spring had warmed the
        cultured Vale,
Moved we as plunderers where the moth-
    er-bird
Had in high places built her lodge; though
    mean
Our object and inglorious, yet the end
Was not ignoble. Oh! when I have hung
Above the raven's nest, by knots of grass
And half-inch fissures in the slippery rock
But ill sustained, and almost (so it seemed)
Suspended by the blast that blew amain,
Shouldering the naked crag, oh, at that
    time
While on the perilous ridge I hung alone,
With what strange utterance did the loud
    dry wind
Blow through my ear! the sky seemed not
    a sky
Of earth — and with what motion moved
    the clouds!

    Dust as we are, the immortal spirit
        grows
Like harmony in music; there is a dark
Inscrutable workmanship that reconciles
Discordant elements, makes them cling
    together
In one society. How strange, that all
The terrors, pains, and early miseries,
Regrets, vexations, lassitudes interfused
Within my mind, should e'er have borne
    a part,
And that a needful part, in making up
The calm existence that is mine when I
Am worthy of myself! Praise to the end!
Thanks to the means which Nature deigned
    to employ;
Whether her fearless visitings, or those
That came with soft alarm, like hurtless
    light
Opening the peaceful clouds; or she
    would use
Severer interventions, ministry
More palpable, as best might suit her aim.

    One summer evening (led by her) I
        found
A little boat tied to a willow tree
Within a rocky cave, its usual home.
Straight I unloosed her chain, and step-
    ping in
Pushed from the shore. It was an act of
    stealth
And troubled pleasure, nor without the
    voice
Of mountain-echoes did my boat move on;
Leaving behind her still, on either side,
Small circles glittering idly in the moon,
Until they melted all into one track
Of sparkling light. But now, like one
    who rows,
Proud of his skill, to reach a chosen point
With an unswerving line, I fixed my view
Upon the summit of a craggy ridge,
The horizon's utmost boundary; far above
Was nothing but the stars and the gray
    sky.
She was an elfin pinnace; lustily
I dipped my oars into the silent lake,
And, as I rose upon the stroke, my boat
Went heaving through the water like a
    swan;
When, from behind that craggy steep till
    then
The horizon's bound, a huge peak, black
    and huge,
As if with voluntary power instinct,
Upreared its head. I struck and struck
    again,
And growing still in stature the grim shape
Towered up between me and the stars,
    and still,
For so it seemed, with purpose of its own
And measured motion like a living thing
Strode after me. With trembling oars I
    turned,
And through the silent water stole my way
Back to the covert of the willow tree;
There in her mooring-place I left my
    bark, —
And through the meadows homeward
    went, in grave
And serious mood; but after I had seen
That spectacle, for many days, my brain
Worked with a dim and undetermined
    sense
Of unknown modes of being; o'er my
    thoughts

There hung a darkness, call it solitude
Or blank desertion. No familiar shapes
Remained, no pleasant images of trees,
Of sea or sky, no colors of green fields;
But huge and mighty forms, that do not
    live
Like living men, moved slowly through
    the mind
By day, and were a trouble to my dreams.

   [1] Wisdom and Spirit of the universe!
Thou Soul that art the eternity of thought
That givest to forms and images a breath
And everlasting motion, not in vain
By day or star-light thus from my first
    dawn
Of childhood didst thou intertwine for me
The passions that build up our human
    soul;
Not with the mean and vulgar works of
    man,
But with high objects, with enduring
    things —
With life and nature — purifying thus
The elements of feeling and of thought,
And sanctifying, by such discipline,
Both pain and fear, until we recognize
A grandeur in the beatings of the heart.
Nor was this fellowship vouchsafed to me
With stinted kindness. In November
    days,
When vapors rolling down the valley
    made
A lonely scene more lonesome, among
    woods,
At noon and 'mid the calm of summer
    nights,
When, by the margin of the trembling
    lake,
Beneath the gloomy hills homeward I
    went
In solitude, such intercourse was mine;
Mine was it in the fields both day and
    night,
And by the waters, all the summer long.

   And in the frosty season, when the sun
Was set, and visible for many a mile
The cottage windows blazed through twi-
    light gloom,

[1] These lines have been printed before. See
p. 136.

I heeded not their summons: happy time
It was indeed for all of us — for me
It was a time of rapture! Clear and loud
The village clock tolled six, — I wheeled
    about,
Proud and exulting like an untired horse
That cares not for his home. All shod
    with steel,
We hissed along the polished ice in games
Confederate, imitative of the chase
And woodland pleasures, — the resound-
    ing horn,
The pack loud chiming, and the hunted
    hare.
So through the darkness and the cold we
    flew,
And not a voice was idle; with the din
Smitten, the precipices rang aloud;
The leafless trees and every icy crag
Tinkled like iron; while far distant hills
Into the tumult sent an alien sound
Of melancholy not unnoticed, while the
    stars
Eastward were sparkling clear, and in
    the west
The orange sky of evening died away.
Not seldom from the uproar I retired
Into a silent bay, or sportively
Glanced sideway, leaving the tumultuous
    throng,
To cut across the reflex of a star
That fled, and, flying still before me,
    gleamed
Upon the glassy plain; and oftentimes,
When we had given our bodies to the
    wind,
And all the shadowy banks on either side
Came sweeping through the darkness,
    spinning still
The rapid line of motion, then at once
Have I, reclining back upon my heels,
Stopped short; yet still the solitary cliffs
Wheeled by me — even as if the earth had
    rolled
With visible motion her diurnal round!
Behind me did they stretch in solemn train,
Feebler and feebler, and I stood and
    watched
Till all was tranquil as a dreamless sleep.

   Ye Presences of Nature in the sky
And on the earth! Ye Visions of the hills!
And Souls of lonely places! can I think

A vulgar hope was yours when ye em-
    ployed
Such ministry, when ye, through many a
    year
Haunting me thus among my boyish
    sports,
On caves and trees, upon the woods and
    hills,
Impressed, upon all forms, the characters
Of danger or desire; and thus did make
The surface of the universal earth,
With triumph and delight, with hope and
    fear,
Work like a sea?
            Not uselessly employed,
Might I pursue this theme through every
    change
Of exercise and play, to which the year
Did summon us in his delightful round.

    We were a noisy crew; the sun in heaven
Beheld not vales more beautiful than ours;
Nor saw a band in happiness and joy
Richer, or worthier of the ground they
    trod.
I could record with no reluctant voice
The woods of autumn, and their hazel
    bowers
With milk-white clusters hung; the rod
    and line,
True symbol of hope's foolishness, whose
    strong
And unreproved enchantment led us on
By rocks and pools shut out from every
    star,
All the green summer, to forlorn cascades
Among the windings hid of mountain
    brooks.
— Unfading recollections! at this hour
The heart is almost mine with which I felt,
From some hill-top on sunny afternoons,
The paper kite high among fleecy clouds
Pull at her rein like an impetuous courser;
Or, from the meadows sent on gusty days,
Beheld her breast the wind, then suddenly
Dashed headlong, and rejected by the
    storm.

Ye lowly cottages wherein we dwelt,
A ministration of your own was yours;
Can I forget you, being as you were
So beautiful among the pleasant fields

In which ye stood? or can I here forget
The plain and seemly countenance with
    which
Ye dealt out your plain comforts? Yet
    had ye
Delights and exultations of your own.
Eager and never weary we pursued
Our home-amusements by the warm peat-
    fire
At evening, when with pencil, and smooth
    slate
In square divisions parcelled out and all
With crosses and with ciphers scribbled
    o'er,
We schemed and puzzled, head opposed
    to head
In strife too humble to be named in verse:
Or round the naked table, snow-white
    deal,
Cherry or maple, sate in close array,
And to the combat, Loo or Whist, led on
A thick-ribbed army; not, as in the world,
Neglected and ungratefully thrown by
Even for the very service they had
    wrought,
But husbanded through many a long cam-
    paign.
Uncouth assemblage was it, where no few
Had changed their functions: some, ple-
    beian cards
Which Fate, beyond the promise of their
    birth,
Had dignified, and called to represent
The persons of departed potentates.
Oh, with what echoes on the board they
    fell!
Ironic diamonds, — clubs, hearts, dia-
    monds, spades,
A congregation piteously akin!
Cheap matter offered they to boyish wit,
Those sooty knaves, precipitated down
With scoffs and taunts, like Vulcan out of
    heaven:
The paramount ace, a moon in her
    eclipse,
Queens gleaming through their splendor's
    last decay,
And monarchs surly at the wrongs sus-
    tained
By royal visages. Meanwhile abroad
Incessant rain was falling, or the frost
Raged bitterly, with keen and silent tooth;
And, interrupting oft that eager game,

From under Esthwaite's splitting fields of
    ice
The pent-up air, struggling to free itself,
Gave out to meadow grounds and hills a
    loud
Protracted yelling, like the noise of wolves
Howling in troops along the Bothnic
    Main.

Nor, sedulous as I have been to trace
How Nature by extrinsic passion first
Peopled the mind with forms sublime or
    fair,
And made me love them, may I here
    omit
How other pleasures have been mine, and
    joys
Of subtler origin; how I have felt,
Not seldom even in that tempestuous time,
Those hallowed and pure motions of the
    sense
Which seem, in their simplicity, to own
An intellectual charm; that calm delight
Which, if I err not, surely must belong
To those first-born affinities that fit
Our new existence to existing things,
And, in our dawn of being, constitute
The bond of union between life and joy.

Yes, I remember when the changeful
    earth,
And twice five summers on my mind had
    stamped
The faces of the moving year, even then
I held unconscious intercourse with beauty
Old as creation, drinking in a pure
Organic pleasure from the silver wreaths
Of curling mist, or from the level plain
Of waters colored by impending clouds.

The sands of Westmoreland, the creeks
    and bays
Of Cumbria's rocky limits, they can tell
How, when the Sea threw off his evening
    shade,
And to the shepherd's hut on distant hills
Sent welcome notice of the rising moon,
How I have stood, to fancies such as these
A stranger, linking with the spectacle
No conscious memory of a kindred sight,
And bringing with me no peculiar sense
Of quietness or peace; yet have I stood,

Even while mine eye hath moved o'er
    many a league
Of shining water, gathering as it seemed,
Through every hair-breadth in that field
    of light,
New pleasure like a bee among the flowers.

Thus oft amid those fits of vulgar joy
Which, through all seasons, on a child's
    pursuits
Are prompt attendants, 'mid that giddy
    bliss
Which, like a tempest, works along the
    blood
And is forgotten; even then I felt
Gleams like the flashing of a shield; —
    the earth
And common face of Nature spake to me
Rememberable things; sometimes, 't is
    true,
By chance collisions and quaint accidents
(Like those ill-sorted unions, work sup-
    posed
Of evil-minded fairies), yet not vain
Nor profitless, if haply they impressed
Collateral objects and appearances,
Albeit lifeless then, and doomed to sleep
Until maturer seasons call them forth
To impregnate and to elevate the mind.
— And if the vulgar joy by its own weight
Wearied itself out of the memory,
The scenes which were a witness of that
    joy
Remained in their substantial lineaments
Depicted on the brain, and to the eye
Were visible, a daily sight; and thus
By the impressive discipline of fear,
By pleasure and repeated happiness,
So frequently repeated, and by force
Of obscure feelings representative
Of things forgotten, these same scenes
    so bright,
So beautiful, so majestic in themselves,
Though yet the day was distant, did be-
    come
Habitually dear, and all their forms
And changeful colors by invisible links
Were fastened to the affections.
                            I began
My story early — not misled, I trust,
By an infirmity of love for days
Disowned by memory — ere the breath
    of spring

Planting my snowdrops among winter
   snows:
Nor will it seem to thee, O Friend! so
   prompt
In sympathy, that I have lengthened out
With fond and feeble tongue a tedious tale.
Meanwhile, my hope has been, that I
   might fetch
Invigorating thoughts from former years;
Might fix the wavering balance of my
   mind,
And haply meet reproaches too, whose
   power
May spur me on, in manhood now mature
To honorable toil. Yet should these
   hopes
Prove vain, and thus should neither I be
   taught
To understand myself, nor thou to know
With better knowledge how the heart
   was framed
Of him thou lovest; need I dread from
   thee
Harsh judgments, if the song be loth to
   quit
Those recollected hours that have the
   charm
Of visionary things, those lovely forms
And sweet sensations that throw back
   our life,
And almost make remotest infancy
A visible scene, on which the sun is shin-
   ing?

One end at least hath been attained;
   my mind
Hath been revived, and if this genial
   mood
Desert me not, forthwith shall be brought
   down
Through later years the story of my life.
The road lies plain before me;—'t is a
   theme
Single and of determined bounds; and
   hence
I choose it rather at this time, than work
Of ampler or more varied argument,
Where I might be discomfited and lost:
And certain hopes are with me, that to
   thee
This labor will be welcome, honored
   Friend!

BOOK SECOND.

SCHOOL-TIME (*continued*).

THUS far, O Friend! have we, though
   leaving much
Unvisited, endeavored to retrace
The simple ways in which my childhood
   walked;
Those chiefly that first led me to the love
Of rivers, woods, and fields. The pas-
   sion yet
Was in its birth, sustained as might befall
By nourishment that came unsought; for
   still
From week to week, from month to
   month, we lived
A round of tumult. Duly were our games
Prolonged in summer till the daylight
   failed:
No chair remained before the doors; the
   bench
And threshold steps were empty; fast
   asleep
The laborer, and the old man who had
   sate
A later lingerer; yet the revelry
Continued and the loud uproar: at last,
When all the ground was dark, and
   twinkling stars
Edged the black clouds, home and to bed
   we went,
Feverish with weary joints and beating
   minds.
Ah! is there one who ever has been
   young,
Nor needs a warning voice to tame the
   pride
Of intellect and virtue's self-esteem?
One is there, though the wisest and the
   best
Of all mankind, who covets not at times
Union that cannot be;—who would not
   give
If so he might, to duty and to truth
The eagerness of infantine desire?
A tranquillizing spirit presses now
On my corporeal frame, so wide appears
The vacancy between me and those days
Which yet have such self-presence in my
   mind,
That, musing on them, often do I seem
Two consciousnesses, conscious of myself
And of some other Being. A rude mass

Of native rock, left midway in the square
Of our small market village, was the goal
Or centre of these sports; and when, re-
turned
After long absence, thither I repaired,
Gone was the old gray stone, and in its
place
A smart Assembly-room usurped the
ground
That had been ours.   There let the fid-
dle scream,
And be ye happy! Yet, my Friends! I
know
That more than one of you will think
with me
Of those soft starry nights, and that old
Dame
From whom the stone was named, who
there had sate,
And watched her table with its huckster's
wares
Assiduous, through the length of sixty
years.

We ran a boisterous course; the year
span round
With giddy motion. But the time ap-
proached
That brought with it a regular desire
For calmer pleasures, when the winning
forms
Of Nature were collaterally attached
To every scheme of holiday delight
And every boyish sport, less grateful else
And languidly pursued.
                    When summer came,
Our pastime was, on bright half-holidays,
To sweep along the plain of Windermere
With rival oars; and the selected bourne
Was now an Island musical with birds
That sang and ceased not; now a Sister
Isle
Beneath the oaks' umbrageous covert,
sown
With lilies of the valley like a field;
And now a third small Island, where sur-
vived
In solitude the ruins of a shrine
Once to Our Lady dedicate, and served
Daily with chaunted rites.   In such a
race
So ended, disappointment could be none,
Uneasiness, or pain, or jealousy:

We rested in the shade, all pleased alike,
Conquered and conqueror.   Thus the
pride of strength,
And the vain-glory of superior skill,
Were tempered; thus was gradually pro-
duced
A quiet independence of the heart;
And to my Friend who knows me I may
add,
Fearless of blame, that hence for future
days
Ensued a diffidence and modesty,
And I was taught to feel, perhaps too
much,
The self-sufficing power of Solitude.

Our daily meals were frugal, Sabine
fare!
More than we wished we knew the bless-
ing then
Of vigorous hunger — hence corporeal
strength
Unsapped by delicate viands; for, exclude
A little weekly stipend, and we lived
Through three divisions of the quartered
year
In penniless poverty.   But now to school
From the half-yearly holidays returned,
We came with weightier purses, that suf-
ficed
To furnish treats more costly than the
Dame
Of the old gray stone, from her scant
board, supplied.
Hence rustic dinners on the cool green
ground,
Or in the woods, or by a river side
Or shady fountains, while among the
leaves
Soft airs were stirring, and the mid-day
sun
Unfelt shone brightly round us in our joy.
Nor is my aim neglected if I tell
How sometimes, in the length of those
half-years,
We from our funds drew largely; — proud
to curb,
And eager to spur on, the galloping steed;
And with the courteous inn-keeper, whose
stud
Supplied our want, we haply might em-
ploy
Sly subterfuge, if the adventure's bound

Were distant: some famed temple where
    of yore
The Druids worshipped, or the antique
    walls
Of that large abbey, where within the
    Vale
Of Nightshade, to St. Mary's honor built,
Stands yet a mouldering pile with frac-
    tured arch,
Belfry, and images, and living trees;
A holy scene! — Along the smooth green
    turf
Our horses grazed. To more than in-
    land peace,
Left by the west wind sweeping overhead
From a tumultuous ocean, trees and
    towers
In that sequestered valley may be seen,
Both silent and both motionless alike;
Such the deep shelter that is there, and
    such
The safeguard for repose and quietness.

    Our steeds remounted and the sum-
      mons given,
With whip and spur. we through the
    chauntry flew
In uncouth race, and left the cross-legged
    knight,
And the stone-abbot, and that single
    wren
Which one day sang so sweetly in the
    nave
Of the old church, that — though from
    recent showers
The earth was comfortless, and, touched
    by faint
Internal breezes, sobbings of the place
And respirations, from the roofless walls
The shuddering ivy dripped large drops
    — yet still
So sweetly 'mid the gloom the invisible
    bird
Sang to herself, that there I could have
    made
My dwelling-place, and lived for ever
    there
To hear such music. Through the walls
    we flew
And down the valley, and, a circuit made
In wantonness of heart, through rough
    and smooth

We scampered homewards. Oh, ye
    rocks and streams,
And that still spirit shed from evening air!
Even in this joyous time I sometimes felt
Your presence, when with slackened step
    we breathed
Along the sides of the steep hills, or when
Lighted by gleams of moonlight from the
    sea
We beat with thundering hoofs the level
    sand.

    Midway on long Winander's eastern
    shore,
Within the crescent of a pleasant bay,
A tavern stood; no homely-featured
    house,
Primeval like its neighboring cottages,
But 't was a splendid place, the door
    beset
With chaises, grooms, and liveries, and
    within
Decanters, glasses, and the blood-red
    wine.
In ancient times, and ere the Hall was
    built
On the large island, had this dwelling
    been
More worthy of a poet's love, a hut,
Proud of its own bright fire and syca-
    more shade.
But — though the rhymes were gone that
    once inscribed
The threshold, and large golden charac-
    ters,
Spread o'er the spangled sign-board, had
    dislodged
The old Lion and usurped his place, in
    slight
And mockery of the rustic painter's
    hand —
Yet, to this hour, the spot to me is dear
With all its foolish pomp. The garden
    lay
Upon a slope surmounted by a plain
Of a small bowling-green; beneath us
    stood
A grove, with gleams of water through
    the trees
And over the tree-tops; nor did we want
Refreshment, strawberries and mellow
    cream.

There, while through half an afternoon
  we played
On the smooth platform, whether skill
  prevailed
Or happy blunder triumphed, bursts of
  glee
Made all the mountains ring. But, ere
  night-fall,
When in our pinnace we returned at
  leisure
Over the shadowy lake, and to the beach
Of some small island steered our course
  with one,
The Minstrel of the troop, and left him
  there,
And rowed off gently, while he blew his
  flute
Alone upon the rock — oh, then, the
  calm
And dead still water lay upon my mind
Even with a weight of pleasure, and the
  sky,
Never before so beautiful, sank down
Into my heart, and held me like a dream !
Thus were my sympathies enlarged, and
  thus
Daily the common range of visible things
Grew dear to me: already I began
To love the sun; a boy I loved the sun,
Not as I since have loved him, as a pledge
And surety of our earthly life, a light
Which we behold and feel we are alive;
Nor for his bounty to so many worlds —
But for this cause, that I had seen him lay
His beauty on the morning hills, had seen
The western mountain touch his setting
  orb,
In many a thoughtless hour, when, from
  excess
Of happiness, my blood appeared to flow
For its own pleasure, and I breathed
  with joy.
And, from like feelings, humble though
  intense,
To patriotic and domestic love
Analogous, the moon to me was dear;
For I could dream away my purposes,
Standing to gaze upon her while she hung
Midway between the hills, as if she knew
No other region, but belonged to thee,
Yea, appertained by a peculiar right
To thee and thy gray huts, thou one dear
  Vale !

Those incidental charms which first
  attached
My heart to rural objects, day by day
Grew weaker, and I hasten on to tell
How Nature, intervenient till this time
And secondary, now at length was sought
For her own sake. But who shall par-
  cel out
His intellect by geometric rules,
Split like a province into round and
  square?
Who knows the individual hour in which
His habits were first sown, even as a seed?
Who that shall point as with a wand and
  say
" This portion of the river of my mind
Came from yon fountain?" Thou, my
  Friend ! art one
More deeply read in thy own thoughts;
  to thee
Science appears but what in truth she
  is,
Not as our glory and our absolute boast,
But as a succedaneum, and a prop
To our infirmity. No officious slave
Art thou of that false secondary power
By which we multiply distinctions, then
Deem that our puny boundaries are things
That we perceive, and not that we have
  made.
To thee, unblinded by these formal arts,
The unity of all hath been revealed,
And thou wilt doubt, with me less aptly
  skilled
Than many are to range the faculties
In scale and order, class the cabinet
Of their sensations, and in voluble phrase
Run through the history and birth of each
As of a single independent thing.
Hard task, vain hope, to analyze the mind,
If each most obvious and particular
  thought,
Not in a mystical and idle sense,
But in the words of Reason deeply
  weighed,
Hath no beginning.
                    Blest the infant Babe,
(For with my best conjecture I would
  trace
Our Being's earthly progress,) blest the
  Babe,
Nursed in his Mother's arms, who sinks
  to sleep

Rocked on his Mother's breast; who with
    his soul
Drinks in the feelings of his Mother's
    eye!
For him, in one dear Presence, there
    exists
A virtue which irradiates and exalts
Objects through widest intercourse of
    sense.
No outcast he, bewildered and depressed:
Along his infant veins are interfused
The gravitation and the filial bond
Of nature that connect him with the
    world.
Is there a flower, to which he points with
    hand
Too weak to gather it, already love
Drawn from love's purest earthly fount
    for him
Hath beautified that flower; already
    shades
Of pity cast from inward tenderness
Do fall around him upon aught that bears
Unsightly marks of violence or harm.
Emphatically such a Being lives,
Frail creature as he is, helpless as frail,
An inmate of this active universe:
For, feeling has to him imparted power
That through the growing faculties of
    sense
Doth like an agent of the one great Mind
Create, creator and receiver both,
Working but in alliance with the works
Which it beholds. — Such, verily, is the
    first
Poetic spirit of our human life,
By uniform control of after years,
In most, abated or suppressed; in some,
Through every change of growth and of
    decay,
Pre-eminent till death.

               From early days,
Beginning not long after that first time
In which, a Babe, by intercourse of touch
I held mute dialogues with my Mother's
    heart,
I have endeavored to display the means
Whereby this infant sensibility,
Great birthright of our being, was in me
Augmented and sustained. Yet is a path
More difficult before me; and I fear
That in its broken windings we shall
    need

The chamois' sinews, and the eagle's
    wing:
For now a trouble came into my mind
From unknown causes. I was left alone
Seeking the visible world, nor knowing
    why.
The props of my affections were removed,
And yet the building stood, as if sustained
By its own spirit! All that I beheld
Was dear, and hence to finer influxes
The mind lay open to a more exact
And close communion. Many are our
    joys
In youth, but oh! what happiness to live
When every hour brings palpable access
Of knowledge, when all knowledge is
    delight,
And sorrow is not there! the seasons
    came,
And every season wheresoe'er I moved
Unfolded transitory qualities,
Which, but for this most watchful power
    of love,
Had been neglected; left a register
Of permanent relations, else unknown.
Hence life, and change, and beauty, soli-
    tude
More active ever than " best society " —
Society made sweet as solitude
By silent inobtrusive sympathies,
And gentle agitations of the mind
From manifold distinctions, difference
Perceived in things, where, to the un-
    watchful eye,
No difference is, and hence, from the
    same source,
Sublimer joy; for I would walk alone,
Under the quiet stars, and at that time
Have felt what e'er there is of power in
    sound
To breathe an elevated mood, by form
Or image unprofaned; and I would stand,
If the night blackened with a coming
    storm,
Beneath some rock, listening to notes that
    are
The ghostly language of the ancient earth,
Or make their dim abode in distant winds.
Thence did I drink the visionary power;
And deem not profitless those fleeting
    moods
Of shadowy exultation: not for this,
That they are kindred to our purer mind

And intellectual life; but that the soul,
Remembering how she felt, but what she
felt
Remembering not, retains an obscure
sense
Of possible sublimity, whereto
With growing faculties she doth aspire,
With faculties still growing, feeling still
That whatsoever point they gain, they yet
Have something to pursue.
                          And not alone,
'Mid gloom and tumult, but no less 'mid
fair
And tranquil scenes, that universal power
And fitness in the latent qualities
And essences of things, by which the mind
Is moved with feelings of delight, to me
Came strengthened with a superadded
soul,
A virtue not its own. My morning walks
Were early; — oft before the hours of
school
I travelled round our little lake, five miles
Of pleasant wandering. Happy time!
more dear
For this, that one was by my side, a
Friend,[1]
Then passionately loved; with heart how
full
Would he puruse these lines ! For many
years
Have since flowed in between us, and,
our minds
Both silent to each other, at this time
We live as if those hours had never been.
Nor seldom did I lift our cottage latch
Far earlier, ere one smoke-wreath had
risen
From human dwelling, or the vernal
thrush
Was audible; and sate among the woods
Alone upon some jutting eminence,
At the first gleam of dawn-light, when
the Vale,
Yet slumbering, lay in utter solitude.
How shall I seek the origin? where
find
Faith in the marvellous things which then
I felt?
Oft in these moments such a holy calm

[1] The late Rev. John Fleming, of Rayrigg,
Windermere.

Would overspread my soul, that bodily
eyes
Were utterly forgotten, and what I saw
Appeared like something in myself, a
dream,
A prospect in the mind.
                          'T were long to tell
What spring and autumn, what the winter
snows,
And what the summer shade, what day
and night,
Evening and morning, sleep and waking,
thought
From sources inexhaustible, poured forth
To feed the spirit of religious love.
In which I walked with Nature. But let
this
Be not forgotten, that I still retained
My first creative sensibility;
That by the regular action of the world
My soul was unsubdued. A plastic power
Abode with me; a forming hand, at times
Rebellious, acting in a devious mood;
A local spirit of his own, at war
With general tendency, but, for the most,
Subservient strictly to external things
With which it communed. An auxiliar
light
Came from my mind, which on the setting
sun
Bestowed new splendor; the melodious
birds,
The fluttering breezes, fountains that run
on
Murmuring so sweetly in themselves,
obeyed
A like dominion, and the midnight storm
Grew darker in the presence of my eye:
Hence my obeisance, my devotion hence,
And hence my transport.
                          Nor should this, perchance,
Pass unrecorded, that I still had loved
The exercise and produce of a toil,
Than analytic industry to me
More pleasing, and whose character I
deem
Is more poetic as resembling more
Creative agency. The song would speak
Of that interminable building reared
By observation of affinities
In objects where no brotherhood exists
To passive minds. My seventeenth year
was come

And, whether from this habit rooted now
So deeply in my mind, or from excess
In the great social principle of life
Coercing all things into sympathy,
To unorganic natures were transferred
My own enjoyments; or the power of
    truth
Coming in revelation, did converse
With things that really are; I, at this
    time,
Saw blessings spread around me like a sea.
Thus while the days flew by, and years
    passed on,
From Nature and her overflowing soul,
I had received so much, that all my
    thoughts
Were steeped in feeling; I was only then
Contented, when with bliss ineffable
I felt the sentiment of Being spread
O'er all that moves and all that seemeth
    still;
O'er all that, lost beyond the reach of
    thought
And human knowledge, to the human eye
Invisible, yet liveth to the heart;
O'er all that leaps and runs, and shouts
    and sings,
Or beats the gladsome air; o'er all that
    glides
Beneath the wave, yea, in the wave itself,
And mighty depth of waters. Wonder
    not
If high the transport, great the joy I felt,
Communing in this sort through earth and
    heaven
With every form of creature, as it looked
Towards the Uncreated with a counte-
    nance
Of adoration, with an eye of love.
One song they sang, and it was audible,
Most audible, then, when the fleshly ear,
O'ercome by humblest prelude of that
    strain,
Forgot her functions, and slept undis-
    turbed.

If this be error, and another faith
Find easier access to the pious mind,
Yet were I grossly destitute of all
Those human sentiments that make this
    earth
So dear, if I should fail with grateful voice

To speak of you, ye mountains, and ye
    lakes
And sounding cataracts, ye mists and
    winds
That dwell among the hills where I was
    born.
If in my youth I have been pure in heart,
If, mingling with the world, I am content
With my own modest pleasures, and have
    lived
With God and Nature communing, re-
    moved
From little enmities and low desires —
The gift is yours; if in these times of
    fear,
This melancholy waste of hopes o'er-
    thrown,
If, 'mid indifference and apathy,
And wicked exultation when good men
On every side fall off, we know not how,
To selfishness, disguised in gentle names
Of peace and quiet and domestic love
Yet mingled not unwillingly with sneers
On visionary minds; if, in this time
Of dereliction and dismay, I yet
Despair not of our nature, but retain
A more than Roman confidence, a faith
That fails not, in all sorrow my support,
The blessing of my life — the gift is yours,
Ye winds and sounding cataracts! 't is
    yours,
Ye mountains! thine, O Nature! Thou
    hast fed
My lofty speculations; and in thee,
For this uneasy heart of ours, I find
A never-failing principle of joy
And purest passion.
            Thou, my Friend! wert reared
In the great city, 'mid far other scenes;
But we, by different roads, at length have
    gained
The selfsame bourne. And for this cause
    to thee
I speak, unapprehensive of contempt,
The insinuated scoff of coward tongues,
And all that silent language which so oft
In conversation between man and man
Blots from the human countenance all
    trace
Of beauty and of love. For thou hast
    sought
The truth in solitude, and, since the days
That gave thee liberty, full long desired,

To serve in Nature's temple, thou hast
    been
The most assiduous of her ministers;
In many things my brother, chiefly here
In this our deep devotion.
                Fare thee well!
Health and the quiet of a healthful mind
Attend thee! seeking oft the haunts of
    men,
And yet more often living with thyself,
And for thyself, so haply shall thy days
Be many, and a blessing to mankind.

BOOK THIRD.

RESIDENCE AT CAMBRIDGE.

IT was a dreary morning when the wheels
Rolled over a wide plain o'erhung with
    clouds,
And nothing cheered our way till first we
    saw
The long-roofed chapel of King's College
    lift
Turrets and pinnacles in answering files,
Extended high above a dusky grove.

Advancing, we espied upon the road
A student clothed in gown and tasselled
    cap,
Striding along as if o'ertasked by Time,
Or covetous of exercise and air;
He passed — nor was I master of my eyes
Till he was left an arrow's flight behind.
As near and nearer to the spot we drew,
It seemed to suck us in with an eddy's
    force.
Onward we drove beneath the Castle;
    caught,
While crossing Magdalene Bridge, a
    glimpse of Cam;
And at the *Hoop* alighted, famous Inn.

My spirit was up, my thoughts were
    full of hope;
Some friends I had, acquaintances who
    there
Seemed friends, poor simple schoolboys,
    now hung round
With honor and importance: in a world
Of welcome faces up and down I roved;
Questions, directions, warnings and ad-
    vice,

Flowed in upon me, from all sides; fresh
    day
Of pride and pleasure! to myself I seemed
A man of business and expense, and went
From shop to shop about my own affairs,
To Tutor or to Tailor, as befell,
From street to street with loose and care-
    less mind.

I was the Dreamer, they the Dream; I
    roamed
Delighted through the motley spectacle;
Gowns grave, or gaudy, doctors, students,
    streets,
Courts, cloisters, flocks of churches, gate-
    ways, towers:
Migration strange for a stripling of the
    hills,
A northern villager.
                As if the change
Had waited on some Fairy's wand, at
    once
Behold me rich in monies, and attired
In splendid garb, with hose of silk, and
    hair
Powdered like rimy trees, when frost is
    keen.
My lordly dressing-gown, I pass it by,
With other signs of manhood that supplied
The lack of beard. — The weeks went
    roundly on,
With invitations, suppers, wine and fruit,
Smooth housekeeping within, and all
    without
Liberal, and suiting gentleman's array.

The Evangelist St. John my patron was:
Three Gothic courts are his, and in the
    first
Was my abiding-place, a nook obscure;
Right underneath, the College kitchens
    made
A humming sound, less tuneable than
    bees,
But hardly less industrious; with shrill
    notes
Of sharp command and scolding inter-
    mixed.
Near me hung Trinity's loquacious clock,
Who never let the quarters, night or day,
Slip by him unproclaimed, and told the
    hours
Twice over with a male and female voice

Her pealing organ was my neighbor too;
And from my pillow, looking forth by
    light
Of moon or favoring stars, I could behold
The antechapel where the statue stood
Of Newton with his prism and silent face,
The marble index of a mind forever
Voyaging through strange seas of
    Thought, alone.

Of College labors, of the Lecturer's
    room
All studded round, as thick as chairs
    could stand,
With loyal students, faithful to their
    books,
Half-and-half idlers, hardy recusants,
And honest dunces — of important days,
Examinations, when the man was weighed
As in a balance! of excessive hopes,
Tremblings withal and commendable
    fears,
Small jealousies, and triumphs good or
    bad —
Let others that know more speak as they
    know.
Such glory was but little sought by me,
And little won. Yet from the first crude
    days
Of settling time in this untried abode,
I was disturbed at times by prudent
    thoughts,
Wishing to hope without a hope, some
    fears
About my future worldly maintenance,
And, more than all, a strangeness in the
    mind,
A feeling that I was not for that hour,
Nor for that place. But wherefore be
    cast down?
For (not to speak of Reason and her pure
Reflective acts to fix the moral law
Deep in the conscience, nor of Christian
    Hope,
Bowing her head before her sister Faith
As one far mightier), hither I had come,
Bear witness Truth, endowed with holy
    powers
And faculties, whether to work or feel.
Oft when the dazzling show no longer
    new
Had ceased to dazzle, oft-times did I quit

My comrades, leave the crowd, buildings
    and groves,
And as I paced alone the level fields
Far from those lovely sights and sounds
    sublime
With which I had been conversant, the
    mind
Drooped not; but there into herself re-
    turning,
With prompt rebound seemed fresh as
    heretofore.
At least I more distinctly recognized
Her native instincts: let me dare to speak
A higher language, say that now I felt
What independent solaces were mine,
To mitigate the injurious sway of place
Or circumstance, how far soever changed
In youth, or to be changed in after years.
As if awakened, summoned, roused, con-
    strained,
I looked for universal things; perused
The common countenance of earth and
    sky:
Earth, nowhere unembellished by some
    trace
Of that first Paradise whence man was
    driven;
And sky, whose beauty and bounty are
    expressed
By the proud name she bears — the name
    of Heaven.
I called on both to teach me what they
    might;
Or, turning the mind in upon herself,
Pored, watched, expected, listened,
    spread my thoughts
And spread them with a wider creeping;
    felt
Incumbencies more awful, visitings
Of the Upholder of the tranquil soul,
That tolerates the indignities of Time,
And, from the centre of Eternity
All finite motions overruling, lives
In glory immutable. But peace! enough
Here to record that I was mounting now
To such community with highest truth —
A track pursuing, not untrod before,
From strict analogies by thought supplied
Or consciousnesses not to be subdued.
To every natural form, rock, fruits, or
    flower,
Even the loose stones that cover the high-
    way,

I gave a moral life: I saw them feel,
Or linked them to some feeling: the great
    mass
Lay bedded in a quickening soul, and all
That I beheld respired with inward mean-
    ing.
Add that whate'er of Terror or of Love
Or Beauty, Nature's daily face put on
From transitory passion, unto this
I was as sensitive as waters are
To the sky's influence in a kindred mood
Of passion; was obedient as a lute
That waits upon the touches of the wind.
Unknown, unthought of, yet I was most
    rich —
I had a world about me — 'twas my own;
I made it, for it only lived to me,
And to the God who sees into the heart.
Such sympathies, though rarely, were be-
    trayed
By outward gestures and by visible looks:
Some called it madness — so indeed it
    was,
If child-like fruitfulness in passing joy,
If steady moods of thoughtfulness matured
To inspiration, sort with such a name;
If prophecy be madness; if things viewed
By poets in old time, and higher up
By the first men, earth's first inhabitants,
May in these tutored days no more be seen
With undisordered sight. But leaving
    this,
It was no madness, for the bodily eye
Amid my strongest workings evermore
Was searching out the lines of difference
As they lie hid in all external forms,
Near or remote, minute or vast; an eye
Which, from a tree, a stone, a withered
    leaf,
To the broad ocean and the azure heavens
Spangled with kindred multitudes of stars,
Could find no surface where its power
    might sleep;
Which spake perpetual logic to my soul,
And by an unrelenting agency
Did bind my feelings even as in a chain.

And here, O Friend! have I retraced
    my life
Up to an eminence, and told a tale
Of matters which not falsely may be
    called

The glory of my youth. Of genius, power,
Creation and divinity itself
I have been speaking, for my theme has
    been
What passed within me. Not of outward
    things
Done visibly for other minds, words, signs,
Symbols or actions, but of my own heart
Have I been speaking, and my youthful
    mind.
O Heavens! how awful is the might of
    souls,
And what they do within themselves while
    yet
The yoke of earth is new to them, the
    world
Nothing but a wild field where they were
    sown.
This is, in truth, heroic argument,
This genuine prowess, which I wished to
    touch
With hand however weak, but in the main
It lies far hidden from the reach of words.
Points have we all of us within our souls
Where all stand single; this I feel, and
    make .
Breathings for incommunicable powers;
But is not each a memory to himself,
And, therefore, now that we must quit
    this theme,
I am not heartless, for there's not a man
That lives who hath not known his god-
    like hours,
And feels not what an empire we inherit
As natural beings in the strength of
    Nature.

No more: for now into a populous plain
We must descend. A Traveller I am,
Whose tale is only of himself; even so,
So be it, if the pure of heart be prompt
To follow, and if thou, my honored
    Friend!
Who in these thoughts art ever at my side,
Support, as heretofore, my fainting steps.

It hath been told, that when the first
    delight
That flashed upon me from this novel show
Had failed, the mind returned into her-
    self;
Yet true it is, that I had made a change
In climate, and my nature's outward coat

Changed also slowly and insensibly.
Full oft the quiet and exalted thoughts
Of loneliness gave way to empty noise
And superficial pastimes; now and then
Forced labor, and more frequently forced
    hopes;
And, worst of all, a treasonable growth
Of indecisive judgments, that impaired
And shook the mind's simplicity. — And
    yet
This was a gladsome time. Could I be-
    hold —
Who, less insensible than sodden clay
In a sea-river's bed at ebb of tide,
Could have beheld, — with undelighted
    heart,
So many happy youths, so wide and fair
A congregation in its budding-time
Of health, and hope, and beauty, all at
    once
So many divers samples from the growth
Of life's sweet season — could have seen
    unmoved
That miscellaneous garland of wild flow-
    ers
Decking the matron temples of a place
So famous through the world? To me,
    at least,
It was a goodly prospect: for, in sooth,
Though I had learnt betimes to stand un-
    propped,
And independent musings pleased me so
That spells seemed on me when I was
    alone,
Yet could I only cleave to solitude
In lonely places; if a throng was near
That way I leaned by nature; for my
    heart
Was social, and loved idleness and joy.

Not seeking those who might participate
My deeper pleasures (nay, I had not once,
Though not unused to mutter lonesome
    songs,
Even with myself divided such delight,
Or looked that way for aught that might
    be clothed
In human language), easily I passed
From the remembrances of better things,
And slipped into the ordinary works
Of careless youth, unburthened, un-
    alarmed.

Caverns there were within my mind which
    sun
Could never penetrate, yet did there not
Want store of leafy *arbors* where the light
Might enter in at will. Companionships,
Friendships, acquaintances, were wel-
    come all.
We sauntered, played, or rioted; we
    talked
Unprofitable talk at morning hours;
Drifted about along the streets and walks,
Read lazily in trivial books, went forth
To gallop through the country in blind
    zeal
Of senseless horsemanship, or on the
    breast
Of Cam sailed boisterously, and let the
    stars
Come forth, perhaps without one quiet
    thought.

Such was the tenor of the second act
In this new life. Imagination slept,
And yet not utterly. I could not print
Ground where the grass had yielded to
    the steps
Of generations of illustrious men,
Unmoved. I could not always lightly pass
Through the same gateways, sleep where
    they had slept,
Wake where they waked, range that in-
    closure old,
That garden of great intellects, undis-
    turbed.
Place also by the side of this dark sense
Of noble feeling, that those spiritual men,
Even the great Newton's own ethereal
    self,
Seemed humbled in these precincts thence
    to be
The more endeared. Their several memo-
    ries here
(Even like their persons in their portraits
    clothed
With the accustomed garb of daily life)
Put on a lowly and a touching grace
Of more distinct humanity, that left
All genuine admiration unimpaired.

Beside the pleasant Mill of Tromp-
    ington
I laughed with Chaucer in the hawthorn
    shade;

Heard him, while birds were warbling,
     tell his tales
Of amorous passion. And that gentle
     Bard,
Chosen by the Muses for their Page of
     State —
Sweet Spenser, moving through his
     clouded heaven
With the moon's beauty and the moon's
     soft pace,
I called him Brother, Englishman, and
     Friend!
Yea, our blind Poet, who in his later day,
Stood almost single ; uttering odious
     truth —
Darkness before, and danger's voice
     behind,
Soul awful — if the earth has ever lodged
An awful soul — I seemed to see him here
Familiarly, and in his scholar's dress
Bounding before me, yet a stripling
     youth —
A boy, no better, with his rosy cheeks
Angelical, keen eye, courageous look,
And conscious step of purity and pride.
Among the band of my compeers was one
Whom chance had stationed in the very
     room
Honored by Milton's name. O temper-
     ate Bard!
Be it confest that, for the first time, seated
Within thy innocent lodge and oratory,
One of a festive circle, I poured out
Libations, to thy memory drank, till pride
And gratitude grew dizzy in a brain
Never excited by the fumes of wine
Before that hour, or since. Then, forth
     I ran
From the assembly; through a length of
     streets,
Ran, ostrich-like, to reach our chapel
     door
In not a desperate or opprobrious time,
Albeit long after the importunate bell
Had stopped, with wearisome Cassandra
     voice
No longer haunting the dark winter night.
Call back, O Friend! a moment to thy
     mind,
The place itself and fashion of the rites.
With careless ostentation shouldering up
My surplice, through the inferior throng
     I clove

Of the plain Burghers, who in audience
     stood
On the last skirts of their permitted
     ground,
Under the pealing organ. Empty
     thoughts!
I am ashamed of them: and that great
     Bard,
And thou, O Friend! who in thy ample
     mind
Hast placed me high above my best
     deserts,
Ye will forgive the weakness of that hour,
In some of its unworthy vanities,
Brother to many more.
                    In this mixed sort
The months passed on, remissly, not
     given up
To wilful alienation from the right,
Or walks of open scandal, but in vague
And loose indifference, easy likings, aims
Of a low pitch — duty and zeal dismissed,
Yet Nature, or a happy course of things
Not doing in their stead the needful work.
The memory languidly revolved, the heart
Reposed in noontide rest, the inner pulse
Of contemplation almost failed to beat.
Such life might not inaptly be compared
To a floating island, an amphibious spot
Unsound, of spongy texture, yet withal
Not wanting a fair face of water weeds
And pleasant flowers. The thirst of
     living praise,
Fit reverence for the glorious Dead, the
     sight
Of those long vistas, sacred catacombs,
Where mighty *minds* lie visibly en-
     tombed,
Have often stirred the heart of youth,
     and bred
A fervent love of rigorous discipline. —
Alas! such high emotion touched me not.
Look was there none within these walls
     to shame
My easy spirits, and discountenance
Their light composure, far less to instil
A calm resolve of mind, firmly addressed
To puissant efforts. Nor was this the
     blame
Of others but my own; I should, in truth,
As far as doth concern my single self,
Misdeem most widely, lodging it else-
     where:

For I, bred up 'mid Nature's luxuries,
Was a spoiled child, and, rambling like
the wind,
As I had done in daily intercourse
With those crystalline rivers, solemn
heights,
And mountains, ranging like a fowl of
the air,
I was ill-tutored for captivity;
To quit my pleasure, and, from month
to month,
Take up a station calmly on the perch
Of sedentary peace. Those lovely forms
Had also left less space within my mind,
Which, wrought upon instinctively, had
found
A freshness in those objects of her love,
A winning power, beyond all other power.
Not that I slighted books, — that were
to lack
All sense, — but other passions in me
ruled,
Passions more fervent, making me less
prompt
To in-door study than was wise or well,
Or suited to those years. Yet I, though
used
In magisterial liberty to rove,
Culling such flowers of learning as might
tempt
A random choice, could shadow forth a
place
(If now I yield not to a flattering dream)
Whose studious aspect should have bent
me down
To instantaneous service; should at once
Have made me pay to science and to arts
And written lore, acknowledged my liege
lord,
A homage frankly offered up, like that
Which I had paid to Nature. Toil and
pains
In this recess, by thoughtful Fancy built,
Should spread from heart to heart; and
stately groves,
Majestic edifices, should not want
A corresponding dignity within.
The congregating temper that pervades
Our unripe years, not wasted, should be
taught
To minister to works of high attempt —
Works which the enthusiast would per-
form with love.

Youth should be awed, religiously pos-
sessed
With a conviction of the power that waits
On knowledge, when sincerely sought
and prized
For its own sake, on glory and on praise
If but by labor won, and fit to endure
The passing day; should learn to put aside
Her trappings here, should strip them off
abashed
Before antiquity and steadfast truth
And strong book-mindedness; and over
all
A healthy sound simplicity should reign,
A seemly plainness, name it what you will,
Republican or pious.
If these thoughts
Are a gratuitous emblazonry
That mocks the recreant age *we* live in,
then
Be Folly and False-seeming free to affect
Whatever formal gait of discipline
Shall raise them highest in their own
esteem —
Let them parade among the Schools at
will,
But spare the House of God. Was ever
known
The witless shepherd who persists to drive
A flock that thirsts not to a pool disliked?
A weight must surely hang on days begun
And ended with such mockery. Be wise,
Ye Presidents and Deans, and, till the
spirit
Of ancient times revive, and youth be
trained
At home in pious service, to your bells
Give seasonable rest, for 't is a sound
Hollow as ever vexed the tranquil air;
And your officious doings bring disgrace
On the plain steeples of our English
Church,
Whose worship, 'mid remotest village
trees,
Suffers for this. Even Science, too, at
hand
In daily sight of this irreverence,
Is smitten thence with an unnatural taint,
Loses her just authority, falls beneath
Collateral suspicion, else unknown.
This truth escaped me not, and I confess,
That having 'mid my native hills given
loose

To a schoolboy's vision, I had raised a
  pile
Upon the basis of the coming time,
That fell in ruins round me. Oh, what
  joy
To see a sanctuary for our country's
  youth
Informed with such a spirit as might be
Its own protection; a primeval grove,
Where, though the shades with cheer-
  fulness were filled,
Nor indigent of songs warbled from
  crowds
In under-coverts, yet the countenance
Of the whole place should bear a stamp
  of awe;
A habitation sober and demure
For ruminating creatures; a domain
For quiet things to wander in; a haunt
In which the heron should delight to feed
By the shy rivers, and the pelican
Upon the cypress spire in lonely thought
Might sit and sun himself. — Alas! Alas!
In vain for such solemnity I looked;
Mine eyes were crossed by butterflies, ears
  vexed
By chattering popinjays; the inner heart
Seemed trivial, and the impresses with-
  out
Of a too gaudy region.
                      Different sight
Those venerable Doctors saw of old,
When all who dwelt within these famous
  walls
Led in abstemiousness a studious life;
When, in forlorn and naked chambers
  cooped
And crowded, o'er the ponderous books
  they hung
Like caterpillars eating out their way
In silence, or with keen devouring noise
Not to be tracked or fathered. Princes
  then
At matins froze, and couched at curfew-
  time,
Trained up through piety and zeal to prize
Spare diet, patient labor, and plain weeds.
O seat of Arts! renowned throughout the
  world!
Far different service in those homely days
The Muses' modest nurslings underwent
From their first childhood: in that glorious
  time

When Learning, like a stranger come from
  far,
Sounding through Christian lands her
  trumpet, roused
Peasant and king; when boys and youths,
  the growth
Of ragged villages and crazy huts,
Forsook their homes, and, errant in the
  quest
Of Patron, famous school or friendly nook,
Where, pensioned, they in shelter might
  sit down,
From town to town and through wide
  scattered realms
Journeyed with ponderous folios in their
  hands;
And often, starting from some covert
  place,
Saluted the chance comer on the road,
Crying, "An obolus, a penny give
To a poor scholar!" — when illustrious
  men,
Lovers of truth, by penury constrained,
Bucer, Erasmus, or Melanchthon, read
Before the doors or windows of their cells
By moonshine through mere lack of taper
  light.

But peace to vain regrets! We see but
  darkly
Even when we look behind us, and best
  things
Are not so pure by nature that they needs
Must keep to all, as fondly all believe,
Their highest promise. If the mariner,
When at reluctant distance he hath passed
Some tempting island, could but know the
  ills
That must have fallen upon him had he
  brought
His bark to land upon the wished-for
  shore,
Good cause would oft be his to thank the
  surf
Whose white belt scared him thence, or
  wind that blew
Inexorably adverse: for myself
I grieve not; happy is the gownèd youth,
Who only misses what I missed, who falls
No lower than I fell.
                      I did not love,
Judging not ill perhaps, the timid course

Of our scholastic studies; could have
    wished
To see the river flow with ampler range
And freer pace; but more, far more, I
    grieved
To see displayed among an eager few,
Who in the field of contest persevered,
Passions unworthy of youth's generous
    heart
And mounting spirit, pitiably repaid,
When so disturbed, whatever palms are
    won.
From these I turned to travel with the
    shoal
Of more unthinking natures, easy minds
And pillowy; yet not wanting love that
    makes
The day pass lightly on, when foresight
    sleeps,
And wisdom and the pledges interchanged
With our own inner being are forgot.

Yet was this deep vacation not given up
To utter waste.   Hitherto I had stood
In my own mind remote from social life
(At least from what we commonly so
    name),
Like a lone shepherd on a promontory
Who lacking occupation looks far forth
Into the boundless sea, and rather makes
Than finds what he beholds. And sure it is,
That this first transit from the smooth de-
    lights
And wild outlandish walks of simple youth
To something that resembles an approach
Towards human business, to a privileged
    world
Within a world, a midway residence
With all its intervenient imagery,
Did better suit my visionary mind,
Far better, than to have been bolted forth,
Thrust out abruptly into Fortune's way
Among the conflicts of substantial life;
By a more just gradation did lead on
To higher things; more naturally matured,
For permanent possession, better fruits,
Whether of truth or virtue, to ensue.
In serious mood, but oftener, I confess,
With playful zest of fancy, did we note
(How could we less?) the manners and
    the ways
Of those who lived distinguished by the
    badge

Of good or ill report; or those with whom
By frame of Academic discipline
We were perforce connected, men whose
    sway
And known authority of office served
To set our minds on edge, and did no
    more.
Nor wanted we rich pastime of this kind,
Found everywhere, but chiefly in the ring
Of the grave Elders, men unscoured, gro-
    tesque
In character, tricked out like aged trees
Which through the lapse of their infirmity
Give ready place to any random seed
That chooses to be reared upon their
    trunks.

Here on my view, confronting vividly
Those shepherd swains whom I had lately .
    left
Appeared a different aspect of old age;
How different! yet both distinctly marked,
Objects embossed to catch the general eye,
Or portraitures for special use designed,
As some might seem, so aptly do they
    serve
To illustrate Nature's book of rudiments—
That book upheld as with maternal care
When she would enter on her tender
    scheme
Of teaching comprehension with delight,
And mingling playful with pathetic
    thoughts.

The surfaces of artificial life
And manners finely wrought, the delicate
    race
Of colors, lurking, gleaming up and down
Through that state arras woven with silk
    and gold;
This wily interchange of snaky hues,
Willingly or unwillingly revealed,
I neither knew nor cared for; and as such
Were wanting here, I took what might be
    found
Of less elaborate fabric.   At this day
I smile, in many a mountain solitude
Conjuring up scenes as obsolete in freaks
Of character, in points of wit as broad,
As aught by wooden images performed
For entertainment of the gaping crowd
At wake or fair.   And oftentimes do flit
Remembrances before me of old men —

Old humorists, who have been long in
    their graves,
And having almost in my mind put off
Their human names, have into phantoms
    passed
Of texture midway between life and books.

I play the loiterer: 't is enough to note
That here in dwarf proportions were ex-
    pressed
The limbs of the great world; its eager
    strifes
Collaterally portrayed, as in mock fight,
A tournament of blows, some hardly dealt
Though short of mortal combat; and what-
    e'er
Might in this pageant be supposed to hit
An artless rustic's notice, this way less,
More that way, was not wasted upon me —
And yet the spectacle may well demand
A more substantial name, no mimic show,
Itself a living part of a live whole,
A creek in the vast sea; for, all degrees
And shapes of spurious fame and short-
    lived praise
Here sate in state, and fed with daily
    alms
Retainers won away from solid good;
And here was Labor, his own bond-slave;
    Hope,
That never set the pains against the prize;
Idleness halting with his weary clog,
And poor misguided Shame, and witless
    Fear,
And simple Pleasure foraging for Death;
Honor misplaced, and Dignity astray;
Feuds, factions, flatteries, enmity, and
    guile,
Murmuring submission, and bald govern-
    ment
(The idol weak as the idolater),
And Decency and Custom starving Truth,
And blind Authority beating with his staff
The child that might have led him;
    Emptiness
Followed as of good omen, and meek
    Worth
Left to herself unheard of and unknown.

Of these and other kindred notices
I cannot say what portion is in truth
The naked recollection of that time,

And what may rather have been called to
    life
By after-meditation.   But delight
That, in an easy temper lulled asleep,
Is still with Innocence its own reward,
This was not wanting.   Carelessly I
    roamed
As through a wide museum from whose
    stores
A casual rarity is singled out
And has its brief perusal, then gives way
To others, all supplanted in their turn;
Till 'mid this crowded neighborhood of
    things
That are by nature most unneighborly,
The head turns round and cannot right
    itself;
And though an aching and a barren sense
Of gay confusion still be uppermost,
With few wise longings and but little love,
Yet to the memory something cleaves at
    last,
Whence profit may be drawn in times to
    come.

Thus in submissive idleness, my Friend!
The laboring time of autumn, winter,
    spring,
Eight months! rolled pleasingly away;
    the ninth
Came and returned me to my native hills.

BOOK FOURTH.

SUMMER VACATION.

BRIGHT was the summer's noon when
    quickening steps
Followed each other till a dreary moor
Was crossed, a bare ridge clomb, upon
    whose top
Standing alone, as from a rampart's edge,
I overlooked the bed of Windermere,
Like a vast river, stretching in the sun.
With exultation, at my feet I saw
Lake, islands, promontories, gleaming
    bays,
A universe of Nature's fairest forms
Proudly revealed with instantaneous
    burst,
Magnificent, and beautiful, and gay.
I bounded down the hill shouting amain

For the old Ferryman; to the shout the rocks
Replied, and when the Charon of the flood
Had stayed his oars, and touched the jutting pier,
I did not step into the well-known boat
Without a cordial greeting.   Thence with speed
Up the familiar hill I took my way
Towards that sweet Valley[1] where I had been reared;
'T was but a short hour's walk, ere veering round
I saw the snow-white church upon her hill
Sit like a thronèd Lady, sending out
A gracious look all over her domain.
Yon azure smoke betrays the lurking town;   •
With eager footsteps I advance and reach
The cottage threshold where my journey closed.
Glad welcome had I, with some tears, perhaps,
From my old Dame, so kind and motherly,
While she perused me with a parent's pride.
The thoughts of gratitude shall fall like dew
Upon thy grave, good creature!   While my heart
Can beat never will I forget thy name.
Heaven's blessing be upon thee where thou liest
After thy innocent and busy stir
In narrow cares, thy little daily growth
Of calm enjoyments, after eighty years,
And more than eighty, of untroubled life;
Childless, yet by the strangers to thy blood
Honored with little less than filial love.
What joy was mine to see thee once again,
Thee and thy dwelling, and a crowd of things
About its narrow precincts all beloved,
And many of them seeming yet my own!
Why should I speak of what a thousand hearts
Have felt, and every man alive can guess?
The rooms, the court, the garden were not left

[1] Hawkshead.

Long unsaluted, nor the sunny seat
Round the stone table under the dark pine,
Friendly to studious or to festive hours;
Nor that unruly child of mountain birth,
The famous brook, who, soon as he was boxed
Within our garden, found himself at once,
As if by trick insidious and unkind,
Stripped of his voice and left to dimple down
(Without an effort and without a will)
A channel paved by man's officious care.
I looked at him and smiled, and smiled again,
And in the press of twenty thousand thoughts,
"Ha," quoth I, "pretty prisoner, are you there!"
Well might sarcastic Fancy then have whispered,
"An emblem here behold of thy own life;
In its late course of even days with all
Their smooth enthralment;" but the heart was full,
Too full for that reproach.   My aged Dame
Walked proudly at my side: she guided me;
I willing, nay — nay, wishing to be led.
— The face of every neighbor whom I met
Was like a volume to me; some were hailed
Upon the road, some busy at their work,
Unceremonious greetings interchanged
With half the length of a long field between.
Among my schoolfellows I scattered round
Like recognitions, but with some constraint
Attended, doubtless, with a little pride,
But with more shame, for my habiliments,
The transformation wrought by gay attire.
Not less delighted did I take my place
At our domestic table: and, dear Friend!
In this endeavor simply to relate
A Poet's history, may I leave untold
The thankfulness with which I laid me down
In my accustomed bed, more welcome now
Perhaps than if it had been more desired

Or been more often thought of with re-
gret;
That lowly bed whence I had heard the
wind
Roar, and the rain beat hard; where I so
oft
Had lain awake on summer nights to
watch
The moon in splendor couched among the
leaves
Of a tall ash, that near our cottage stood;
Had watched her with fixed eyes while to
and fro
In the dark summit of the waving tree
She rocked with every impulse of the
breeze.

Among the favorites whom it pleased
me well
To see again, was one by ancient right
Our inmate, a rough terrier of the hills;
By birth and call of nature pre-ordained
To hunt the badger and unearth the fox
Among the impervious crags, but having
been
From youth our own adopted, he had
passed
Into a gentler service.   And when first
The boyish spirit flagged, and day by day
Along my veins I kindled with the stir,
The fermentation, and the vernal heat
Of poesy, affecting private shades
Like a sick Lover, then this dog was used
To watch me, an attendant and a friend,
Obsequious to my steps early and late,
Though often of such dilatory walk
Tired, and uneasy at the halts I made.
A hundred times when, roving high and
low,
I have been harassed with the toil of verse,
Much pains and little progress, and at
once
Some lovely Image in the song rose up
Full-formed, like Venus rising from the
sea;
Then have I darted forwards to let loose
My hand upon his back with stormy joy,
Caressing him again and yet again.
And when at evening on the public way
I sauntered, like a river murmuring
And talking to itself when all things else
Are still, the creature trotted on before;

Such was his custom; but whene'er he
met
A passenger approaching, he would turn
To give me timely notice, and straight-
way,
Grateful for that admonishment, I hushed
My voice, composed my gait, and, with
the air
And mien of one whose thoughts are free,
advanced
To give and take a greeting that might
save
My name from piteous rumors, such as
wait
On men suspected to be crazed in brain.

Those walks well worthy to be prized
and loved —
Regretted! — that word, too, was on my
tongue,
But they were richly laden with all good,
And cannot be remembered but with
thanks
And gratitude, and perfect joy of heart —
Those walks in all their freshness now
came back
Like a returning Spring.   When first I
made
Once more the circuit of our little lake,
If ever happiness hath lodged with man,
That day consummate happiness was mine,
Wide-spreading, steady, calm, contem-
plative.
The sun was set, or setting, when I left
Our cottage door, and evening soon
brought on
A sober hour, not winning or serene,
For cold and raw the air was, and untuned:
But as a face we love is sweetest then
When sorrow damps it, or, whatever look
It chance to wear, is sweetest if the heart
Have fulness in herself; even so with me
It fared that evening.   Gently did my soul
Put off her veil, and, self-transmuted,
stood
Naked, as in the presence of her God.
While on I walked, a comfort seemed to
touch
A heart that had not been disconsolate:
Strength came where weakness was not
known to be,
At least not felt; and restoration came
Like an intruder knocking at the door

Of unacknowledged weariness. I took
The balance, and with firm hand weighed
   myself.
— Of that external scene which round me
   lay,
Little, in this abstraction, did I see;
Remembered less; but I had inward hopes
And swellings of the spirit, was rapt and
   soothed,
Conversed with promises, had glimmering
   views
How life pervades the undecaying mind;
How the immortal soul with God-like
   power
Informs, creates, and thaws the deepest
   sleep
That time can lay upon her; how on earth,
Man, if he do but live within the light
Of high endeavors, daily spreads abroad
His being armed with strength that cannot
   fail.
Nor was there want of milder thoughts, of
   love,
Of innocence, and holiday repose;
And more than pastoral quiet,' mid the stir
Of boldest projects, and a peaceful end
At last, or glorious, by endurance won.
Thus musing, in a wood I sate me down
Alone, continuing there to muse: the
   slopes
And heights meanwhile were slowly over-
   spread
With darkness, and before a rippling
   breeze
The long lake lengthened out its hoary
   line,
And in the sheltered coppice where I sate,
Around me from among the hazel leaves,
Now here, now there, moved by the strag-
   gling wind,
Came ever and anon a breath-like sound,
Quick as the pantings of the faithful dog,
The off and on companion of my walk;
And such, at times, believing them to be,
I turned my head to look if he were there;
Then into solemn thought I passed once
   more.

A freshness also found I at this time
In human Life, the daily life of those
Whose occupations really I loved;
The peaceful scene oft filled me with sur-
   prise

Changed like a garden in the heat of spring
After an eight-days' absence. For (to
   omit
The things which were the same and yet
   appeared
Far otherwise) amid this rural solitude,
A narrow Vale where each was known to
   all,
'T was not indifferent to a youthful mind
To mark some sheltering bower or sunny
   nook
Where an old man had used to sit alone,
Now vacant; pale-faced babes whom I had
   left
In arms, now rosy prattlers at the feet
Of a pleased grandame tottering up and
   down;
And growing girls whose beauty, filched
   away
With all its pleasant promises, was gone
To deck some slighted playmate's homely
   cheek.

Yes, I had something of a subtler sense,
And often looking round was moved to
   smiles
Such as a delicate work of humor breeds;
I read, without design, the opinions,
   thoughts,
Of those plain-living people now observed
With clearer knowledge; with another eye
I saw the quiet woodman in the woods,
The shepherd roam the hills. With new
   delight,
This chiefly, did I note my gray-haired
   Dame;
Saw her go forth to church or other work
Of state equipped in monumental trim;
Short velvet cloak, (her bonnet of the like),
A mantle such as Spanish Cavaliers
Wore in old times. Her smooth domestic
   life,
Affectionate without disquietude,
Her talk, her business, pleased me; and no
   less
Her clear though shallow stream of piety
That ran on Sabbath days a fresher course;
With thoughts unfelt till now I saw her
   read
Her Bible on hot Sunday afternoons,
And loved the book, when she had
   dropped asleep
And made of it a pillow for her head.

Nor less do I remember to have felt,
Distinctly manifested at this time,
A human-heartedness about my love
For objects hitherto the absolute wealth
Of my own private being and no more;
Which I had loved, even as a blessed spirit
Or Angel, if he were to dwell on earth,
Might love in individual happiness.
But now there opened on me other
          thoughts
Of change, congratulation or regret,
A pensive feeling ! It spread far and wide;
The trees, the mountains shared it, and
          the brooks,
The stars of Heaven, now seen in their old
          haunts —
White Sirius glittering o'er the southern
          crags,
Orion with his belt, and those fair Seven,
Acquaintances of every little child,
And Jupiter, my own belovèd star !
Whatever shadings of mortality,
Whatever imports from the world of death
Had come among these objects heretofore,
Were, in the main, of mood less tender:
          strong,
Deep, gloomy were they, and severe; the
          scatterings
Of awe or tremulous dread, that had given
          way
In later youth to yearnings of a love
Enthusiastic, to delight and hope.

    As one who hangs down-bending from
          the side
Of a slow-moving boat, upon the breast
Of a still water, solacing himself
With such discoveries as his eye can make
Beneath him in the bottom of the deep,
Sees many beauteous sights — weeds,
          fishes, flowers,
Grots, pebbles, roots of trees, and fancies
          more,
Yet often is perplexed, and cannot part
The shadow from the substance, rocks and
          sky,
Mountains and clouds, reflected in the
          depth
Of the clear flood, from things which there
          abide
In their true dwelling; now is crossed by
          gleam
Of his own image, by a sunbeam now,

And wavering motions sent he knows not
          whence,
Impediments that make his task more
          sweet;
Such pleasant office have we long pursued
Incumbent o'er the surface of past time
With like success, nor often have appeared
Shapes fairer or less doubtfully discerned
Than these to which the Tale, indulgent
          Friend !
Would now direct thy notice. Yet in spite
Of pleasure won, and knowledge not with-
          held,
There was an inner falling off — I loved,
Loved deeply all that had been loved
          before,
More deeply even than ever : but a swarm
Of heady schemes jostling each other,
          gawds,
And feast and dance, and public revelry,
And sports and games (too grateful in
          themselves,
Yet in themselves less grateful, I believe,
Than as they were a badge glossy and fresh
Of manliness and freedom) all conspired
To lure my mind from firm habitual quest
Of feeding pleasures, to depress the zeal
And damp those yearnings which had once
          been mine —
A wild, unworldly-minded youth, given
          up
To his own eager thoughts. It would
          demand
Some skill, and longer time than may be
          spared
To paint these vanities, and how they
          wrought
In haunts where they, till now, had been
          unknown.
It seemed the very garments that I wore
Preyed on my strength, and stopped the
          quiet stream
Of self-forgetfulness.
                    Yes, that heartless chase
Of trivial pleasures was a poor exchange
For books and nature at that early age.
'T is true, some casual knowledge might
          be gained
Of character or life; but at that time,
Of manners put to school I took small
          note,
And all my deeper passions lay elsewhere.
Far better had it been to exalt the mind

By solitary study, to uphold
Intense desire through meditative peace;
And yet, for chastisement of these regrets,
The memory of one particular hour
Doth here rise up against me. 'Mid a
    throng
Of maids and youths, old men, and
    matrons staid,
A medley of all tempers, I had passed
The night in dancing, gayety, and mirth,
With din of instruments and shuffling feet,
And glancing forms, and tapers glitter-
    ing,
And unaimed prattle flying up and down;
Spirits upon the stretch, and here and
    there
Slight shocks of young love-liking inter-
    spersed,
Whose transient pleasure mounted to the
    head,
And tingled through the veins. Ere we
    retired,
The cock had crowed, and now the east-
    ern sky
Was kindling, not unseen, from humble
    copse
And open field, through which the path-
    way wound,
And homeward led my steps. Magnificent
The morning rose, in memorable pomp,
Glorious as e'er I had beheld — in front,
The sea lay laughing at a distance; near,
The solid mountains shone, bright as the
    clouds,
Grain-tinctured, drenched in empyrean
    light;
And in the meadows and the lower
    grounds
Was all the sweetness of a common
    dawn —
Dews, vapors, and the melody of birds,
And laborers going forth to till the fields.
Ah! need I say, dear Friend! that to
    the brim
My heart was full; I made no vows, but
    vows
Were then made for me; bond unknown
    to me
Was given, that I should be, else sinning
    greatly,
A dedicated Spirit. On I walked
In thankful blessedness, which yet sur-
    vives.

Strange rendezvous! My mind was at
    that time
A parti-colored show of grave and gay,
Solid and light, short-sighted and pro-
    found;
Of inconsiderate habits and sedate,
Consorting in one mansion unreproved.
The worth I knew of powers that I pos-
    sessed,
Though slighted and too oft misused.
    Besides,
That summer, swarming as it did with
    thoughts
Transient and idle, lacked not intervals
When Folly from the frown of fleeting
    Time
Shrunk, and the mind experienced in
    herself
Conformity as just as that of old
To the end and written spirit of God's
    works,
Whether held forth in Nature or in Man,
Through pregnant vision, separate or
    conjoined.

When from our better selves we have
    too long
Been parted by the hurrying world, and
    droop,
Sick of its business, of its pleasures tired,
How gracious, how benign, is Solitude;
How potent a mere image of her sway;
Most potent when impressed upon the
    mind
With an appropriate human centre —
    hermit,
Deep in the bosom of the wilderness;
Votary (in vast cathedral, where no foot
Is treading, where no other face is seen)
Kneeling at prayers; or watchman on
    the top
Of lighthouse, beaten by Atlantic waves;
Or as the soul of that great Power is met
Sometimes embodied on a public road,
When, for the night deserted, it assumes
A character of quiet more profound
Than pathless wastes.

Once, when those summer months
Were flown, and autumn brought its an-
    nual show
Of oars with oars contending, sails with
    sails,

Upon Winander's spacious breast, it chanced
That — after I had left a flower-decked room
(Whose in-door pastime, lighted up, survived
To a late hour), and spirits overwrought
Were making night do penance for a day
Spent in a round of strenuous idleness —
My homeward course led up a long ascent,
Where the road's watery surface, to the top
Of that sharp rising, glittered to the moon
And bore the semblance of another stream
Stealing with silent lapse to join the brook
That murmured in the vale. All else was still;
No living thing appeared in earth or air,
And, save the flowing water's peaceful voice,
Sound there was none — but, lo! an uncouth shape,
Shown by a sudden turning of the road,
So near that, slipping back into the shade
Of a thick hawthorn, I could mark him well,
Myself unseen. He was of stature tall,
A span above man's common measure, tall,
Stiff, lank, and upright; a more meagre man
Was never seen before by night or day.
Long were his arms, pallid his hands; his mouth
Looked ghastly in the moonlight: from behind,
A mile-stone propped him; I could also ken
That he was clothed in military garb,
Though faded, yet entire. Companionless,
No dog attending, by no staff sustained,
He stood, and in his very dress appeared
A desolation, a simplicity,
To which the trappings of a gaudy world
Make a strange background. From his lips, ere long,
Issued low muttered sounds, as if of pain
Or some uneasy thought; yet still his form
Kept the same awful steadiness — at his feet
His shadow lay, and moved not. From self-blame
Not wholly free, I watched him thus; at length
Subduing my heart's specious cowardice,
I left the shady nook where I had stood
And hailed him. Slowly from his resting-place
He rose, and with a lean and wasted arm
In measured gesture lifted to his head
Returned my salutation; then resumed
His station as before; and when I asked
His history, the veteran, in reply,
Was neither slow nor eager; but, unmoved,
And with a quiet uncomplaining voice,
A stately air of mild indifference,
He told in few plain words a soldier's tale —
That in the Tropic Islands he had served,
Whence he had landed scarcely three weeks past;
That on his landing he had been dismissed,
And now was travelling towards his native home.
This heard, I said, in pity, " Come with me."
He stooped, and straightway from the ground took up
An oaken staff by me yet unobserved —
A staff which must have dropped from his slack hand
And lay till now neglected in the grass.
Though weak his step and cautious, he appeared
To travel without pain, and I beheld,
With an astonishment but ill suppressed,
His ghostly figure moving at my side;
Nor could I, while we journeyed thus, forbear
To turn from present hardships to the past,
And speak of war, battle, and pestilence,
Sprinkling this talk with questions, better spared,
On what he might himself have seen or felt.
He all the while was in demeanor calm,
Concise in answer; solemn and sublime
He might have seemed, but that in all he said
There was a strange half-absence, as of one

Knowing too well the importance of his
    theme,
But feeling it no longer. Our discourse
Soon ended, and together on we passed
In silence through a wood gloomy and
    still.
Up-turning, then, along an open field,
We reached a cottage. At the door I
    knocked,
And earnestly to charitable care
Commended him as a poor friendless man,
Belated and by sickness overcome.
Assured that now the traveller would
    repose
In comfort, I entreated that henceforth
He would not linger in the public ways,
But ask for timely furtherance and help
Such as his state required. At this reproof,
With the same ghastly mildness in his look,
He said, " My trust is in the God of
    Heaven,
And in the eye of him who passes me ! "

The cottage door was speedily unbarred,
And now the soldier touched his hat once
    more
With his lean hand, and in a faltering
    voice,
Whose tone bespake reviving interests
Till then unfelt, he thanked me; I returned
The farewell blessing of the patient man,
And so we parted. Back I cast a look,
And lingered near the door a little space,
Then sought with quiet heart my distant
    home.

BOOK FIFTH.

BOOKS.

WHEN Contemplation, like the night-calm
    felt
Through earth and sky, spreads widely,
    and sends deep
Into the soul its tranquillizing power,
Even then I sometimes grieve for thee, O
    Man,
Earth's paramount Creature ! not so much
    for woes
That thou endurest; heavy though that
    weight be,
Cloud-like it mounts, or touched with light
    divine

Doth melt away; but for those palms
    achieved
Through length of time, by patient exercise
Of study and hard thought; there, there,
    it is
That sadness finds its fuel. Hitherto,
In progress through this Verse, my mind
    hath looked
Upon the speaking face of earth and
    heaven
As her prime teacher, intercourse with man
Established by the sovereign Intellect,
Who through that bodily image hath dif-
    fused,
As might appear to the eye of fleeting time,
A deathless spirit. Thou also, man ! hast
    wrought,
For commerce of thy nature with herself,
Things that aspire to unconquerable life;
And yet we feel — we cannot choose but
    feel —
That they must perish. Tremblings of the
    heart
It gives, to think that our immortal being
No more shall need such garments; and
    yet man,
As long as he shall be the child of earth,
Might almost " weep to have " what he
    may lose,
Nor be himself extinguished, but survive,
Abject, depressed, forlorn, disconsolate.
A thought is with me sometimes, and I
    say, —
Should the whole frame of earth by inward
    throes
Be wrenched, or fire come down from far
    to scorch
Her pleasant habitations, and dry up
Old ocean, in his bed left singed and bare,
Yet would the living Presence still subsist
Victorious, and composure would ensue,
And kindlings like the morning — presage
    sure
Of day returning and of life revived.
But all the meditations of mankind,
Yea, all the adamantine holds of truth
By reason built, or passion, which itself
Is highest reason in a soul sublime;
The consecrated works of Bard and Sage,
Sensuous or intellectual, wrought by men,
Twin laborers and heirs of the same hopes;
Where would they be ? Oh ! why hath not
    the Mind

Some element to stamp her image on
In nature somewhat nearer to her own?
Why, gifted with such powers to send
      abroad
Her spirit, must it lodge in shrines so frail?

   One day, when from my lips a like
      complaint
Had fallen in presence of a studious friend,
He with a smile made answer, that in truth
'T was going far to seek disquietude;
But on the front of his reproof confessed
That he himself had oftentimes given way
To kindred hauntings. Whereupon I told,
That once in the stillness of a summer's
      noon,
While I was seated in a rocky cave
By the seaside, perusing, so it chanced,
The famous history of the errant knight
Recorded by Cervantes, these same
      thoughts
Beset me, and to height unusual rose,
While listlessly I sate, and, having closed
The book, had turned my eyes toward the
      wide sea.
On poetry and geometric truth,
And their high privilege of lasting life,
From all internal injury exempt,
I mused; upon these chiefly: and at length,
My senses yielding to the sultry air,
Sleep seized me, and I passed into a dream.
I saw before me stretched a boundless
      plain
Of sandy wilderness, all black and void,
And as I looked around, distress and fear
Came creeping over me, when at my side,
Close at my side, an uncouth shape ap-
      peared
Upon a dromedary, mounted high.
He seemed an Arab of the Bedouin tribes:
A lance he bore, and underneath one arm
A stone, and in the opposite hand a shell
Of a surpassing brightness. At the sight
Much I rejoiced, not doubting but a guide
Was present, one who with unerring skill
Would through the desert lead me; and
      while yet
I looked and looked, self-questioned what
      this freight
Which the new-comer carried through the
      waste
Could mean, the Arab told me that the
      stone

(To give it in the language of the dream)
Was "Euclid's Elements," and "This,"
      said he,
"Is something of more worth;" and at
      the word
Stretched forth the shell, so beautiful in
      shape,
In color so resplendent, with command
That I should hold it to my ear. I did so,
And heard that instant in an unknown
      tongue,
Which yet I understood, articulate sounds,
A loud prophetic blast of harmony;
An Ode, in passion uttered, which foretold
Destruction to the children of the earth
By deluge, now at hand. No sooner ceased
The song, than the Arab with calm look
      declared
That all would come to pass of which the
      voice
Had given forewarning, and that he him-
      self
Was going then to bury those two books:
The one that held acquaintance with the
      stars,
And wedded soul to soul in purest bond
Of reason, undisturbed by space or time;
The other that was a god, yea many gods,
Had voices more than all the winds, with
      power
To exhilarate the spirit, and to soothe,
Through every clime, the heart of human
      kind.
While this was uttering, strange as it may
      seem,
I wondered not, although I plainly saw
The one to be a stone, the other a shell;
Nor doubted once but that they both were
      books,
Having a perfect faith in all that passed.
Far stronger, now, grew the desire I felt
To cleave unto this man; but when I prayed
To share his enterprise, he hurried on
Reckless of me: I followed, not unseen,
For oftentimes he cast a backward look,
Grasping his twofold treasure.— Lance in
      rest,
He rode, I keeping pace with him; and
      now
He, to my fancy, had become the knight
Whose tale Cervantes tells; yet not the
      knight,
But was an Arab of the desert too;

Of these was neither, and was both at once.
His countenance, meanwhile, grew more
    disturbed;
And, looking backwards when he looked,
    mine eyes
Saw, over half the wilderness diffused,
A bed of glittering light: I asked the cause:
" It is," said he, " the waters of the deep
Gathering upon us;" quickening then the
    pace
Of the unwieldy creature he bestrode,
He left me: I called after him aloud;
He heeded not; but, with his twofold
    charge
Still in his grasp, before me, full in view,
Went hurrying o'er the illimitable waste,
With the fleet waters of a drowning world
In chase of him; whereat I waked in terror,
And saw the sea before me, and the book,
In which I had been reading, at my side.

Full often, taking from the world of
    sleep
This Arab phantom, which I thus beheld,
This semi-Quixote, I to him have given
A substance, fancied him a living man,
A gentle dweller in the desert, crazed
By love and feeling, and internal thought
Protracted among endless solitudes;
Have shaped him wandering upon this
    quest!
Nor have I pitied him; but rather felt
Reverence was due to a being thus em-
    ployed;
And thought that, in the blind and awful
    lair
Of such a madness, reason did lie couched.
Enow there are on earth to take in charge
Their wives, their children, and their vir-
    gin loves,
Or whatsoever else the heart holds dear;
Enow to stir for these; yea, will I say,
Contemplating in soberness the approach
Of an event so dire, by signs in earth
Or heaven made manifest, that I could
    share
That maniac's fond anxiety, and go
Upon like errand. Oftentimes at least
Me hath such strong entrancement over-
    come,
When I have held a volume in my hand,
Poor earthly casket of immortal verse,
Shakespeare, or Milton, laborers divine!

Great and benign, indeed, must be the
    power
Of living nature, which could thus so long
Detain me from the best of other guides
And dearest helpers, left unthanked, un-
    praised,
Even in the time of lisping infancy;
And later down, in prattling childhood
    even,
While I was travelling back among those
    days,
How could I ever play an ingrate's part?
Once more should I have made those
    bowers resound,
By intermingling strains of thankfulness
With their own thoughtless melodies; at
    least
It might have well beseemed me to repeat
Some simply fashioned tale, to tell again,
In slender accents of sweet verse, some tale
That did bewitch me then, and soothes me
    now.
O Friend! O Poet! brother of my soul,
Think not that I could pass along un-
    touched
By these remembrances. Yet wherefore
    speak?
Why call upon a few weak words to say
What is already written in the hearts
Of all that breathe?—what in the path of
    all
Drops daily from the tongue of every child,
Wherever man is found? The trickling
    tear
Upon the cheek of listening Infancy
Proclaims it, and the insuperable look
That drinks as if it never could be full.

That portion of my story I shall leave
There registered: whatever else of power
Or pleasure sown, or fostered thus, may be
Peculiar to myself, let that remain
Where still it works, though hidden from
    all search
Among the depths of time. Yet is it just
That here, in memory of all books which
    lay
Their sure foundations in the heart of man,
Whether by native prose, or numerous
    verse,
That in the name of all inspirèd souls—
From Homer the great Thunderer, from
    the voice

That roars along the bed of Jewish song,
And that more varied and elaborate,
Those trumpet-tones of harmony that shake
Our shores in England, — from those lofti-
est notes
Down to the low and wren-like warblings,
made
For cottagers and spinners at the wheel,
And sun-burnt travellers resting their tired
limbs,
Stretched under wayside hedge-rows, bal-
lad tunes,
Food for the hungry ears of little ones,
And of old men who have survived their
joys —
'T is just that in behalf of these, the works,
And of the men that framed them, whether
known
Or sleeping nameless in their scattered
graves,
That I should here assert their rights, attest
Their honors, and should, once for all,
pronounce
Their benediction; speak of them as
Powers
Forever to be hallowed; only less,
For what we are and what we may become,
Than Nature's self, which is the breath of
God,
Or His pure Word by miracle revealed.

Rarely and with reluctance would I
stoop
To transitory themes; yet I rejoice,
And, by these thoughts admonished, will
pour out
Thanks with uplifted heart, that I was
reared
Safe from an evil which these days have
laid
Upon the children of the land, a pest
That might have dried me up, body and
soul.
This verse is dedicate to Nature's self,
And things that teach as Nature teaches:
then,
Oh! where had been the Man, the Poet
where,
Where had we been, we two, belovèd
Friend!
If in the season of unperilous choice,

In lieu of wandering, as we did, through
vales
Rich with indigenous produce, open
ground
Of Fancy, happy pastures ranged at will,
We had been followed, hourly watched,
and noosed,
Each in his several melancholy walk
Stringed like a poor man's heifer at its feed,
Led through the lanes in forlorn servitude;
Or rather like a stallèd ox debarred
From touch of growing grass, that may
not taste
A flower till it have yielded up its sweets
A prelibation to the mower's scythe.

Behold the parent hen amid her brood,
Though fledged and feathered, and well
pleased to part
And straggle from her presence, still a
brood,
And she herself from the maternal bond
Still undischarged; yet doth she little more
Than move with them in tenderness and
love,
A centre to the circle which they make;
And now and then, alike from need of
theirs
And call of her own natural appetites,
She scratches, ransacks up the earth for
food,
Which they partake at pleasure. Early
died
My honored Mother, she who was the
heart
And hinge of all our learnings and our
loves:
She left us destitute, and, as we might,
Trooping together. Little suits it me
To break upon the sabbath of her rest
With any thought that looks at others'
blame;
Nor would I praise her but in perfect love.
Hence am I checked: but let me boldly
say,
In gratitude, and for the sake of truth,
Unheard by her, that she, not falsely
taught,
Fetching her goodness rather from times
past,
Than shaping novelties for times to come,
Had no presumption, no such jealousy,
Nor did by habit of her thoughts mistrust

Our nature, but had virtual faith that He
Who fills the mother's breast with inno-
cent milk,
Doth also for our nobler part provide,
Under His great correction and control,
As innocent instincts, and as innocent
food;
Or draws, for minds that are left free to
trust
In the simplicities of opening life,
Sweet honey out of spurned or dreaded
weeds.
This was her creed, and therefore she was
pure
From anxious fear of error or mishap,
And evil, overweeningly so called;
Was not puffed up by false unnatural
hopes,
Nor selfish with unnecessary cares,
Nor with impatience from the season asked
More than its timely produce; rather loved
The hours for what they are, than from
regard
Glanced on their promises in restless
pride.
Such was she — not from faculties more
strong
Than others have, but from the times,
perhaps,
And spot in which she lived, and through
a grace
Of modest meekness, simple-mindedness,
A heart that found benignity and hope,
Being itself benign.
                    My drift I fear
Is scarcely obvious; but, that common
sense
May try this modern system by its fruits,
Leave let me take to place before her sight
A specimen portrayed with faithful hand.
Full early trained to worship seemliness,
This model of a child is never known
To mix in quarrels; that were far beneath
Its dignity; with gifts he bubbles o'er
As generous as a fountain; selfishness
May not come near him, nor the little
throng
Of flitting pleasures tempt him from his
path;
The wandering beggars propagate his
name,
Dumb creatures find him tender as a nun,
And natural or supernatural fear,

Unless it leap upon him in a dream,
Touches him not.   To enhance the
wonder, see
How arch his notices, how nice his sense
Of the ridiculous; not blind is he
To the broad follies of the licensed world,
Yet innocent himself withal, though
shrewd,
And can read lectures upon innocence;
A miracle of scientific lore,
Ships he can guide across the pathless sea,
And tell you all their cunning; he can read
The inside of the earth, and spell the stars;
He knows the policies of foreign lands;
Can string you names of districts, cities,
towns,
The whole world over, tight as beads of
dew
Upon a gossamer thread; he sifts, he
weighs;
All things are put to question; he must
live
Knowing that he grows wiser every day
Or else not live at all, and seeing too
Each little drop of wisdom as it falls
Into the dimpling cistern of his heart:
For this unnatural growth the trainer
blame,
Pity the tree. — Poor human vanity,
Wert thou extinguished, little would be
left
Which he could truly love; but how
escape?
For, ever as a thought of purer birth
Rises to lead him toward a better clime,
Some intermeddler still is on the watch
To drive him back, and pound him, like
a stray,
Within the pinfold of his own conceit.
Meanwhile old grandame earth is grieved
to find
The playthings, which her love designed
for him,
Unthought of: in their woodland beds
the flowers
Weep, and the river sides are all forlorn.
Oh! give us once again the wishing-cap
Of Fortunatus, and the invisible coat
Of Jack the Giant-killer, Robin Hood,
And Sabra in the forest with St. George!
The child, whose love is here, at least,
doth reap
One precious gain, that he forgets himself.

These mighty workmen of our later age,
Who, with a broad highway, have over-
bridged
The froward chaos of futurity,
Tamed to their bidding; they who have
the skill
To manage books, and things, and make
them act
On infant minds as surely as the sun
Deals with a flower; the keepers of our
time,
The guides and wardens of our faculties,
Sages who in their prescience would
control
All accidents, and to the very road
Which they have fashioned would confine
us down,
Like engines; when will their presump-
tion learn,
That in the unreasoning progress of the
world
A wiser spirit is at work for us,
A better eye than theirs, most prodigal
Of blessings, and most studious of our
good,
Even in what seem our most unfruitful
hours ?

[1] There was a Boy: ye knew him well,
ye cliffs
And islands of Winander ! — many a time
At evening, when the earliest stars began
To move along the edges of the hills,
Rising or setting, would he stand alone
Beneath the trees or by the glimmering
lake,
And there, with fingers interwoven, both
hands
Pressed closely palm to palm, and to his
mouth
Uplifted, he, as through an instrument,
Blew mimic hootings to the silent owls,
That they might answer him; and they
would shout
Across the watery vale, and shout again,
Responsive to his call, with quivering
peals,
And long halloos and screams, and echoes
loud,
Redoubled and redoubled, concourse wild
Of jocund din; and, when a lengthened
pause

[1] See p. 137.

Of silence came and baffled his best skill,
Then sometimes, in that silence while he
hung
Listening, a gentle shock of mild surprise
Has carried far into his heart the voice
Of mountain torrents; or the visible scene
Would enter unawares into his mind,
With all its solemn imagery, its rocks,
Its woods, and that uncertain heaven,
received
Into the bosom of the steady lake.

This Boy was taken from his mates,
and died
In childhood, ere he was full twelve years
old.
Fair is the spot, most beautiful the vale
Where he was born; the grassy church-
yard hangs
Upon a slope above the village school,
And through that churchyard when my
way has led
On summer evenings, I believe that there
A long half hour together I have stood
Mute, looking at the grave in which he
lies !
Even now appears before the mind's
clear eye
That self-same village church; I see her
sit
(The thronèd Lady whom erewhile we
hailed)
On her green hill, forgetful of this Boy
Who slumbers at her feet, — forgetful,
too,
Of all her silent neighborhood of graves,
And listening only to the gladsome sounds
That, from the rural school ascending,
play
Beneath her and about her. May she long
Behold a race of young ones like to those
With whom I herded ! — (easily, indeed,
We might have fed upon a fatter soil
Of arts and letters — but be that for-
given) —
A race of real children; not too wise,
Too learned, or too good; but wanton,
fresh,
And bandied up and down by love and
hate;
Not unresentful where self-justified;
Fierce, moody, patient, venturous,
modest, shy;

Mad at their sports like withered leaves
    in winds;
Though doing wrong and suffering, and
    full oft
Bending beneath our life's mysterious
    weight
Of pain, and doubt, and fear, yet yielding
    not
In happiness to the happiest upon earth.
Simplicity in habit, truth in speech,
Be these the daily strengtheners of their
    minds;
May books and Nature be their early joy!
And knowledge, rightly honored with
    that name —
Knowledge not purchased by the loss of
    power!

Well do I call to mind the very week
When I was first intrusted to the care
Of that sweet Valley; when its paths,
    its shores,
And brooks were like a dream of novelty
To my half-infant thoughts; that very
    week,
While I was roving up and down alone,
Seeking I knew not what, I chanced to
    cross
One of those open fields, which, shaped
    like ears,
Make green peninsulas on Esthwaite's
    Lake:
Twilight was coming on, yet through the
    gloom
Appeared distinctly on the opposite shore
A heap of garments, as if left by one
Who might have there been bathing.
    Long I watched,
But no one owned them; meanwhile the
    calm lake
Grew dark with all the shadows on its
    breast,
And, now and then, a fish up-leaping
    snapped
The breathless stillness. The succeed-
    ing day,
Those unclaimed garments telling a plain
    tale
Drew to the spot an anxious crowd;
    some looked
In passive expectation from the shore,
While from a boat others hung o'er the
    deep,

Sounding with grappling irons and long
    poles.
At last, the dead man, 'mid that beaute-
    ous scene
Of trees and hills and water, bolt upright
Rose, with his ghastly face, a spectre
    shape
Of terror; yet no soul-debasing fear,
Young as I was, a child not nine years
    old,
Possessed me, for my inner eye had seen
Such sights before, among the shining
    streams
Of faëry land, the forest of romance.
Their spirit hallowed the sad spectacle
With decoration of ideal grace;
A dignity, a smoothness, like the works
Of Grecian art, and purest poesy.

A precious treasure had I long pos-
    sessed,
A little yellow, canvas-covered book,
A slender abstract of the Arabian tales;
And, from companions in a new abode,
When first I learnt that this dear prize
    of mine
Was but a block hewn from a mighty
    quarry —
That there were four large volumes,
    laden all
With kindred matter, 't was to me, in
    truth,
A promise scarcely earthly. Instantly,
With one not richer than myself, I made
A covenant that each should lay aside
The moneys he possessed, and hoard up
    more,
Till our joint savings had amassed enough
To make this book our own. Through
    several months,
In spite of all temptation, we preserved
Religiously that vow; but firmness failed,
Nor were we ever masters of our wish.

And when thereafter to my father's
    house
The holidays returned me, there to find
That golden store of books which I had
    left,
What joy was mine! How often in the
    course
Of those glad respites, though a soft
    west wind

Ruffled the waters to the angler's wish,
For a whole day together, have I lain
Down by thy side, O Derwent! murmur-
    ing stream,
On the hot stones, and in the glaring sun,
And there have read, devouring as I read,
Defrauding the day's glory, desperate!
Till with a sudden bound of smart re-
    proach,
Such as an idler deals with in his shame,
I to the sport betook myself again.

A gracious spirit o'er this earth pre-
    sides,
And o'er the heart of man; invisibly
It comes, to works of unreproved delight,
And tendency benign, directing those
Who care not, know not, think not,
    what they do.
The tales that charm away the wakeful
    night
In Araby, romances; legends penned
For solace by dim light of monkish lamps;
Fictions, for ladies of their love, devised
By youthful squires; adventures endless,
    spun
By the dismantled warrior in old age,
Out of the bowels of those very schemes
In which his youth did first extravagate;
These spread like day, and something in
    the shape .
Of these will live till man shall be no
    more.
Dumb yearnings, hidden appetites, are
    ours,
And *they must* have their food. Our
    childhood sits,
Our simple childhood, sits upon a throne
That hath more power than all the
    elements.
I guess not what this tells of Being past,
Nor what it augurs of the life to come;
But so it is; and, in that dubious hour —
That twilight — when we first begin to
    see
This dawning earth, to recognize, expect,
And, in the long probation that ensues,
The time of trial, ere we learn to live
In reconcilement with our stinted powers;
To endure this state of meagre vassalage,
Unwilling to forego, confess, submit,
Uneasy and unsettled, yoke-fellows

To custom, mettlesome, and not yet
    tamed
And humbled down — oh! then we feel,
    we feel,
We know where we have friends. Ye
    dreamers, then,
Forgers of daring tales! we bless you
    then,
Impostors, drivellers, dotards, as the ape
Philosophy will call you: *then* we feel
With what and how great might ye are
    in league,
Who make our wish, our power, our
    thought a deed,
An empire, a possession, — ye whom
    time
And seasons serve; all Faculties to whom
Earth crouches, the elements are potter's
    clay,
Space like a heaven filled up with north-
    ern lights,
Here, nowhere, there, and everywhere
    at once.

Relinquishing this lofty eminence
For ground, though humbler, not the
    less a tract
Of the same isthmus, which our spirits
    cross
In progress from their native continent
To earth and human life, the Song
    might dwell
On that delightful time of growing youth,
When craving for the marvellous gives
    way
To strengthening love for things that we
    have seen;
When sober truth and steady sympathies,
Offered to notice by less daring pens,
Take firmer hold of us, and words them-
    selves
Move us with conscious pleasure.
                                I am sad
At thought of rapture now forever flown;
Almost to tears I sometimes could be sad
To think of, to read over, many a page,
Poems withal of name, which at that time
Did never fail to entrance me, and are
    now
Dead in my eyes, dead as a theatre
Fresh emptied of spectators. Twice five
    years

Or less I might have seen, when first my
mind
With conscious pleasure opened to the
charm
Of words in tuneful order, found them
sweet
For their own *sakes*, a passion, and a
power;
And phrases pleased me chosen for
delight,
For pomp, or love. Oft, in the public
roads
Yet unfrequented, while the morning
light
Was yellowing the hill tops, I went
abroad
With a dear friend, and for the better part
Of two delightful hours we strolled along
By the still borders of the misty lake,
Repeating favorite verses with one voice,
Or conning more, as happy as the birds
That round us chanted. Well might we
be glad,
Lifted above the ground by airy fancies,
More bright than madness or the dreams
of wine;
And, though full oft the objects of our
love
Were false, and in their splendor over-
wrought,
Yet was there surely then no ·vulgar
power
Working within us, — nothing less, in
truth,
Than that most noble attribute of man,
Though yet untutored and inordinate,
That wish for something loftier, more
adorned,
Than is the common aspect, daily garb,
Of human life. What wonder, then, if
sounds
Of exultation echoed through the groves!
For, images, and sentiments, and words,
And everything encountered or pursued
In that delicious world of poesy,
Kept holiday, a never-ending show,
With music, incense, festival, and flowers!

Here must we pause: this only let me
add,
From heart-experience, and in humblest
sense
Of modesty, that he, who in his youth

A daily wanderer among woods and fields
With living Nature hath been intimate,
Not only in that raw unpractised time
Is stirred to ecstasy, as others are,
By glittering verse; but further, doth
receive,
In measure only dealt out to himself,
Knowledge and increase of enduring joy
From the great Nature that exists in works
Of mighty Poets. Visionary power
Attends the motions of the viewless
winds,
Embodied in the mystery of words:
There, darkness makes abode, and all
the host
Of shadowy things work endless changes,
— there,
As in a mansion like their proper home,
Even forms and substances are circum-
fused
By that transparent veil with light divine,
And, through the turnings intricate of
verse,
Present themselves as objects recognized,
In flashes, and with glory not their own.

BOOK SIXTH.

CAMBRIDGE AND THE ALPS.

THE leaves were fading when to Esth-
waite's banks
And the simplicities of cottage life
I bade farewell; and, one among the
youth
Who, summoned by that season, reunite
As scattered birds troop to the fowler's
lure,
Went back to Granta's cloisters, not so
prompt
Or eager, though as gay and undepressed
In mind, as when I thence had taken flight
A few short months before. I turnéd my
face
Without repining from the coves and
heights
Clothed in the sunshine of the withering
fern;
Quitted, not loth, the mild magnificence
Of calmer lakes and louder streams; and
you,
Frank-hearted maids of rocky Cumber-
land,

You and your not unwelcome days of
  mirth,
Relinquished, and your nights of revelry,
And in my own unlovely cell sate down
In lightsome mood — such privilege has
  youth
That cannot take long leave of pleasant
  thoughts.

  The bonds of indolent society
Relaxing in their hold, henceforth I lived
More to myself. Two winters may be
  passed
Without a separate notice: many books
Were skimmed, devoured, or studiously ·
  perused,
But with no settled plan. I was detached
Internally from academic cares;
Yet independent study seemed a course
Of hardy disobedience toward friends
And kindred, proud rebellion and unkind.
This spurious virtue, rather let it bear
A name it now deserves, this cowardice,
Gave treacherous sanction to that over-
  love
Of freedom which encouraged me to turn
From regulations even of my own
As from restraints and bonds. Yet who
  can tell —
Who knows what thus may have been
  gained, both then
And at a later season, or preserved;
What love of nature, what original
  strength
Of contemplation, what intuitive truths
The deepest and the best, what keen re-
  search,
Unbiassed, unbewildered, and unawed?

  The Poet's soul was with me at that
  time;
Sweet meditations, the still overflow
Of present happiness, while future years
Lacked not anticipations, tender dreams,
No few of which have since been realized;
And some remain, hopes for my future
  life.
Four years and thirty, told this very week,
Have I been now a sojourner on earth,
By sorrow not unsmitten; yet for me
Life's morning radiance hath not left the
  hills,

Her dew is on the flowers. Those were
  the days
Which also first emboldened me to trust
With firmness, hitherto but slightly
  touched
By such a daring thought, that I might
  leave
Some monument behind me which pure
  hearts
Should reverence. The instinctive hum-
  bleness,
Maintained even by the very name and
  thought
Of printed books and authorship, began
To melt away; and further, the dread awe
Of mighty names was softened down and
  seemed
Approachable, admitting fellowship
Of modest sympathy. Such aspect now,
Though not familiarly, my mind put on,
Content to observe, to achieve, and to
  enjoy.

  All winter long, whenever free to
  choose,
Did I by night frequent the College grove
And tributary walks; the last, and oft
The only one, who had been lingering
  there
Through hours of silence, till the porter's
  bell,
A punctual follower on the stroke of nine,
Rang with its blunt unceremonious voice;
Inexorable summons! Lofty elms,
Inviting shades of opportune recess,
Bestowed composure on a neighborhood
Unpeaceful in itself. A single tree
With sinuous trunk, boughs exquisitely
  wreathed,
Grew there; an ash which Winter for him-
  self
Decked out with pride, and with outland-
  ish grace:
Up from the ground, and almost to the
  top,
The trunk and every master branch were
  green
With clustering ivy, and the lightsome
  twigs
And outer spray profusely tipped with
  seeds
That hung in yellow tassels, while the air

Stirred them, not voiceless. Often have
    I stood
Foot-bound uplooking at this lovely tree
Beneath a frosty moon. The hemisphere
Of magic fiction, verse of mine perchance
May never tread; but scarcely Spenser's
    self
Could have more tranquil visions in his
    youth,
Or could more bright appearances create
Of human forms with superhuman pow-
    ers,
Than I beheld, loitering on calm clear
    nights
Alone, beneath this fairy work of earth.

    On the vague reading of a truant youth
'T were idle to descant. My inner judg-
    ment
Not seldom differed from my taste in
    books,
As if it appertained to another mind,
And yet the books which then I valued
    most
Are dearest to me *now;* for, having
    scanned,
Not heedlessly, the laws, and watched
    the forms
Of Nature, in that knowledge I possessed
A standard, often usefully applied,
Even when unconsciously, to things re-
    moved
From a familiar sympathy. — In fine,
I was a better judge of thoughts than
    words,
Misled in estimating words, not only
By common inexperience of youth,
But by the trade in classic niceties,
The dangerous craft, of culling term and
    phrase
From languages that want the living voice
To carry meaning to the natural heart;
To tell us what is passion, what is truth,
What reason, what simplicity and sense.

    Yet may we not entirely overlook
The pleasure gathered from the rudiments
Of geometric science. Though advanced
In these inquiries, with regret I speak,
No farther than the threshold, there I
    found
Both elevation and composed delight:

With Indian awe and wonder, ignorance
    pleased
With its own struggles, did I meditate
On the relation those abstractions bear
To Nature's laws, and by what process
    led,
Those immaterial agents bowed their
    heads
Duly to serve the mind of earth-born man;
From star to star, from kindred sphere to
    sphere,
From system on to system without end.

    More frequently from the same source I
    drew
A pleasure quiet and profound, a sense
Of permanent and universal sway,
And paramount belief; there, recognized
A type, for finite natures, of the one
Supreme Existence, the surpassing life
Which — to the boundaries of space and
    time,
Of melancholy space and doleful time,
Superior and incapable of change,
Nor touched by welterings of passion — is,
And hath the name, of, God. Transcen-
    dent peace
And silence did await upon these thoughts
That were a frequent comfort to my youth.

    'T is told by one whom stormy waters
    threw,
With fellow-sufferers by the shipwreck
    spared,
Upon a desert coast, that having brought
To land a single volume, saved by chance,
A treatise of Geometry, he wont,
Although of food and clothing destitute,
And beyond common wretchedness de-
    pressed,
To part from company and take this book
(Then first a self-taught pupil in its truths)
To spots remote, and draw his diagrams
With a long staff upon the sand, and thus
Did oft beguile his sorrow, and almost
Forget his feeling: so (if like effect
From the same cause produced, 'mid out-
    ward things
So different, may rightly be compared),
So was it then with me, and so will be
With Poets ever. Mighty is the charm
Of those abstractions to a mind beset
With images and haunted by herself,

And specially delightful unto me
Was that clear synthesis built up aloft
So gracefully; even then when it appeared
Not more than a mere plaything, or a toy
To sense embodied: not the thing it is
In verity, an independent world,
Created out of pure intelligence.

Such dispositions then were mine un-
    earned
By aught, I fear, of genuine desert —
Mine, through heaven's grace and inborn
    aptitudes.
And not to leave the story of that time
Imperfect, with these habits must be
    joined,
Moods melancholy, fits of spleen, that
    loved
A pensive sky, sad days, and piping winds,
The twilight more than dawn, autumn than
    spring;
A treasured and luxurious gloom of choice
And inclination mainly, and the mere
Redundancy of youth's contentedness.
— To time thus spent, add multitudes of
    hours
Pilfered away, by what the Bard who sang
Of the Enchanter Indolence hath called
"Good-natured lounging," and behold a
    map
Of my collegiate life — far less intense
Than duty called for, or, without regard
To duty, *might* have sprung up of itself
By change of accidents, or even, to speak
Without unkindness, in another place.
Yet why take refuge in that plea? — the
    fault,
This I repeat, was mine; mine be the
    blame.

In summer, making quest for works of
    art,
Or scenes renowned for beauty, I explored
That streamlet whose blue current works
    its way
Between romantic Dovedale's spiry rocks;
Pried into Yorkshire dales, or hidden
    tracts
Of my own native region, and was blest
Between these sundry wanderings with a
    joy
Above all joys, that seemed another morn

Risen on mid noon; blest with the pres-
    ence, Friend!
Of that sole Sister, her who hath been
    long
Dear to thee also, thy true friend and
    mine,
Now, after separation desolate,
Restored to me — such absence that she
    seemed
A gift then first bestowed.   The varied
    banks
Of Emont, hitherto unnamed in song,
And that monastic castle, 'mid tall trees,
Low standing by the margin of the stream,
A mansion visited (as fame reports)
By Sidney, where, in sight of our Hel-
    vellyn,
Or stormy Cross-fell, snatches he might
    pen
Of his Arcadia, by fraternal love
Inspired; — that river and those moulder-
    ing towers
Have seen us side by side, when, having
    clomb
The darksome windings of a broken stair,
And crept along a ridge of fractured wall,
Not without trembling, we in safety looked
Forth, through some Gothic window's
    open space,
And gathered with one mind a rich reward
From the far-stretching landscape, by the
    light
Of morning beautified, or purple eve;
Or, not less pleased, lay on some turret's
    head,
Catching from tufts of grass and hare-bell
    flowers
Their faintest whisper to the passing
    breeze,
Given out while mid-day heat oppressed
    the plains.

Another maid there was, who also shed
A gladness o'er that season, then to me,
By her exulting outside look of youth
And placid under-countenance, first en-
    deared;
That other spirit, Coleridge! who is now
So near to us, that meek confiding heart,
So reverenced by us both.   O'er paths
    and fields
In all that neighborhood, through narrow
    lanes

Of eglantine, and through the shady
    woods,
And o'er the Border Beacon, and the
    waste
Of naked pools, and common crags that
    lay
Exposed on the bare fell, were scattered
    love,
The spirit of pleasure, and youth's golden
    gleam.
O Friend! we had not seen thee at that
    time,
And yet a power is on me, and a strong
Confusion, and I seem to plant thee there.
Far art thou wandered now in search of
    health
And milder breezes, — melancholy lot!
But thou art with us, with us in the past,
The present, with us in the times to come.
There is no grief, no sorrow, no despair,
No languor, no dejection, no dismay,
No absence scarcely can there be, for
    those
Who love as we do. Speed thee well!
    divide
With us thy pleasure; thy returning
    strength,
Receive it daily as a joy of ours;
Share with us thy fresh spirits, whether
    gift
Of gales Etesian or of tender thoughts.

I, too, have been a wanderer; but, alas!
How different the fate of different men.
Though mutually unknown, yea nursed
    and reared
As if in several elements, we were framed
To bend at last to the same discipline,
Predestined, if two beings ever were,
To seek the same delights, and have one
    health,
One happiness. Throughout this narra-
    'ive,
Else sooner ended, I have borne in mind
For whom it registers the birth, and
    marks the growth,
Of gentleness, simplicity, and truth,
And joyous loves, that hallow innocent
    days
Of peace and self-command. Of rivers,
    fields,
And groves I speak to thee, my Friend! to
    thee,

Who, yet a liveried schoolboy, in the
    depths
Of the huge city, on the leaded roof
Of that wide edifice, thy school and home,
Wert used to lie and gaze upon the clouds
Moving in heaven; or, of that pleasure
    tired,
To shut thine eyes, and by internal light
See trees, and meadows, and thy native
    stream,
Far distant, thus beheld from year to year
Of a long exile. Nor could I forget,
In this late portion of my argument,
That scarcely, as my term of pupilage
Ceased, had I left those academic bowers
When thou wert thither guided. From the
    heart
Of London, and from cloisters there, thou
    camest,
And didst sit down in temperance and
    peace,
A rigorous student. What a stormy course
Then followed. Oh! it is a pang that calls
For utterance, to think what easy change
Of circumstances might to thee have
    spared
A world of pain, ripened a thousand hopes,
Forever withered. Through this ret-
    rospect
Of my collegiate life I still have had
Thy after-sojourn in the self-same place
Present before my eyes, have played with
    times
And accidents as children do with cards,
Or as a man, who, when his house is built,
A frame locked up in wood and stone, doth
    still,
As impotent fancy prompts, by his fireside,
Rebuild it to his liking. I have thought
Of thee, thy learning, gorgeous eloquence,
And all the strength and plumage of thy
    youth,
Thy subtle speculations, toils abstruse
Among the schoolmen, and Platonic forms
Of wild ideal pageantry, shaped out
From things well-matched or ill, and
    words for things,
The self-created sustenance of a mind
Debarred from Nature's living images,
Compelled to be a life unto herself,
And unrelentingly possessed by thirst
Of greatness, love, and beauty. Not
    alone,

Ah! surely not in singleness of heart
Should I have seen the light of evening
        fade
From smooth Cam's silent waters: had we
        met,
Even at that early time, needs must I trust
In the belief, that my maturer age,
My calmer habits, and more steady voice,
Would with an influence benign have
        soothed,
Or chased away, the airy wretchedness
That battened on thy youth.   But thou
        hast trod
A march of glory, which doth put to
        shame
These vain regrets; health suffers in thee,
        else
Such grief for thee would be the weakest
        thought
That ever harbored in the breast of man.

        A passing word erewhile did lightly
        touch
On wanderings of my own, that now
        embraced
With livelier hope a region wider far.

        When the third summer freed us from
        restraint,
A youthful friend, he too a mountaineer,
Not slow to share my wishes, took his
        staff,
And sallying forth, we journeyed side by
        side,
Bound to the distant Alps. A hardy slight,
Did this unprecedented course imply,
Of college studies and their set rewards;
Nor had, in truth, the scheme been
        formed by me
Without uneasy forethought of the pain,
The censures, and ill-omening, of those
To whom my worldly interests were dear.
But Nature then was sovereign in my
        mind,
And mighty forms, seizing a youthful
        fancy,
Had given a charter to irregular hopes.
In any age of uneventful calm
Among the nations, surely would my heart
Have been possessed by similar desire;
But Europe at that time was thrilled
        with joy,

France standing on the top of golden
        hours,
And human nature seeming born again.

        Lightly equipped, and but a few brief
        looks
Cast on the white cliffs of our native shore
From the receding vessel's deck, we
        chanced
To land at Calais on the very eve
Of that great federal day; and there we
        saw,
In a mean city, and among a few,
How bright a face is worn when joy of one
Is joy for tens of millions.   Southward
        thence
We held our way, direct through hamlets,
        towns,
Gaudy with reliques of that festival,
Flowers left to wither on triumphal arcs,
And window-garlands.   On the public
        roads,
And, once, three days successively,
        through paths
By which our toilsome journey was
        abridged,
Among sequestered villages we walked
And found benevolence and blessedness
Spread like a fragrance everywhere, when
        spring
Hath left no corner of the land untouched;
Where elms for many and many a league
        in files
With their thin umbrage, on the stately
        roads
Of that great kingdom, rustled o'er our
        heads,
Forever near us as we paced along:
How sweet at such a time, with such de-
        light
On every side, in prime of youthful
        strength,
To feed a Poet's tender melancholy
And fond conceit of sadness, with the
        sound
Of undulations varying as might please
The wind that swayed them; once, and
        more than once,
Unhoused beneath the evening star we
        saw
Dances of liberty, and, in late hours
Of darkness, dances in the open air

Deftly prolonged, though gray-haired
    lookers on
Might waste their breath in chiding.
               Under hills —
The vine-clad hills and slopes of Burgundy,
Upon the bosom of the gentle Saône
We glided forward with the flowing
    stream.
Swift Rhone! thou wert the *wings* on
    which we cut
A winding passage with majestic ease
Between thy lofty rocks. Enchanting
    show
Those woods and farms and orchards did
    present,
And single cottages and lurking towns,
Reach after reach, succession without end
Of deep and stately vales! A lonely pair
Of strangers, till day closed, we sailed
    along
Clustered together with a merry crowd
Of those emancipated, a blithe host
Of travellers, chiefly delegates, returning
From the great spousals newly solemnized
At their chief city, in the sight of Heaven.
Like bees they swarmed, gaudy and gay
    as bees;
Some vapored in the unruliness of joy,
And with their swords flourished as if to
    fight
The saucy air. In this proud company
We landed — took with them our evening
    meal,
Guests welcome almost as the angels were
To Abraham of old. The supper done,
With flowing cups elate and happy
    thoughts
We rose at signal given, and formed a
    ring
And, hand in hand, danced round and
    round the board;
All hearts were open, every tongue was
    loud
With amity and glee; we bore a name
Honored in France, the name of English-
    men,
And hospitably did they give us hail,
As their forerunners in a glorious course;
And round and round the board we danced
    again.
With these blithe friends our voyage we
    renewed
At early dawn. The monastery bells

Made a sweet jingling in our youthful ears;
The rapid river flowing without noise,
And each uprising or receding spire
Spake with a sense of peace, at intervals
Touching the heart amid the boisterous
    crew
By whom we were encompassed. Taking
    leave
Of this glad throng, foot-travellers side
    by side,
Measuring our steps in quiet, we pursued
Our journey, and ere twice the sun had set
Beheld the Convent of Chartreuse, and
    there
Rested within an awful *solitude :*
Yes; for even then no other than a place
Of soul-affecting *solitude* appeared
That far-famed region, though our eyes
    had seen,
As toward the sacred mansion we ad-
    vanced,
Arms flashing, and a military glare
Of riotous men commissioned to expel
The blameless inmates, and belike subvert
That frame of social being, which so long
Had bodied forth the ghostliness of things
In silence visible and perpetual calm.
— "Stay, stay your sacrilegious hands!"
    — The voice
Was Nature's, uttered from her Alpine
    throne;
I heard it then and seem to hear it now —
"Your impious work forbear, perish what
    may,
Let this one temple last, be this one spot
Of earth devoted to eternity!"
She ceased to speak, but while St. Bruno's
    pines
Waved their dark tops, not silent as they
    waved,
And while below, along their several beds,
Murmured the sister streams of Life and
    Death,
Thus by conflicting passions pressed, my
    heart
Responded; "Honor to the patriot's zeal!
Glory and hope to new-born Liberty!
Hail to the mighty projects of the time!
Discerning sword that Justice wields, do
    thou
Go forth and prosper; and, ye purging
    fires,
Up to the loftiest towers of Pride ascend,

Fanned by the breath of angry Providence.
But oh! if Past and Future be the wings
On whose support harmoniously conjoined
Moves the great spirit of human knowl-
edge, spare
These courts of mystery, where a step
advanced
Between the portals of the shadowy rocks
Leaves far behind life's treacherous
vanities,
For penitential tears and trembling hopes
Exchanged — to equalize in God's pure
sight
Monarch and peasant: be the house re-
deemed
With its unworldly votaries, for the sake
Of conquest over sense, hourly achieved
Through faith and meditative reason,
resting
Upon the word of heaven-imparted truth,
Calmly triumphant; and for humbler claim
Of that imaginative impulse sent
From these majestic floods, yon shining
cliffs,
The untransmuted shapes of many worlds,
Cerulean ether's pure inhabitants,
These forests unapproachable by death,
That shall endure as long as man endures,
To think, to hope, to worship, and to feel,
To struggle, to be lost within himself
In trepidation, from the blank abyss
To look with bodily eyes, and be con-
soled."
Not seldom since that moment have I
wished
That thou, O Friend! the trouble or the
calm
Hadst shared, when, from profane regards
apart,
In sympathetic reverence we trod
The floors of those dim cloisters, till that
hour,
From their foundation, strangers to the
presence
Of unrestricted and unthinking man.
Abroad, how cheeringly the sunshine lay
Upon the open lawns! Vallombre's
groves
Entering, we fed the soul with darkness;
thence
Issued, and with uplifted eyes beheld,
In different quarters of the bending sky,
The cross of Jesus stand erect, as if

Hands of angelic powers had fixed it there,
Memorial reverenced by a thousand
storms;
Yet then, from the undiscriminating sweep
And rage of one State-whirlwind, in-
secure.

'T is not my present purpose to retrace
That variegated journey step by step.
A march it was of military speed,
And Earth did change her images and
forms
Before us, fast as clouds are changed in
heaven.
Day after day, up early and down late,
From hill to vale we dropped, from vale
to hill
Mounted — from province on to province
swept,
Keen hunters in a chase of fourteen weeks,
Eager as birds of prey, or as a ship
Upon the stretch, when winds are blow-
ing fair:
Sweet coverts did we cross of pastoral life,
Enticing valleys, greeted them and left
Too soon, while yet the very flash and
gleam
Of salutation were not passed away.
Oh! sorrow for the youth who could
have seen,
Unchastened, unsubdued, unawed, un-
raised
To patriarchal dignity of mind,
And pure simplicity of wish and will,
Those sanctified abodes of peaceful man,
Pleased (though to hardship born, and
compassed round
With danger, varying as the seasons
change),
Pleased with his daily task, or, if not
pleased,
Contented, from the moment that the
dawn
(Ah! surely not without attendant gleams
Of soul-illumination) calls him forth
To industry, by glistenings flung on rocks,
Whose evening shadows lead him to
repose.

Well might a stranger look with
bounding heart
Down on a green recess, the first I saw
Of those deep haunts, an aboriginal vale,

Quiet and lorded over and possessed
By naked huts, wood-built, and sown like
    tents
Or Indian cabins over the fresh lawns
And by the river side.
                        That very day,
From a bare ridge we also first beheld
Unveiled the summit of Mont Blanc, and
    grieved
To have a soulless image on the eye
That had usurped upon a living thought
That never more could be. The won-
    drous Vale
Of Chamouny stretched far below, and
    soon
With its dumb cataracts and streams of ice,
A motionless array of mighty waves,
Five rivers broad and vast, made rich
    amends,
And reconciled us to realities;
There small birds warble from the leafy
    trees,
The eagle soars high in the element,
There doth the reaper bind the yellow
    sheaf,
The maiden spread the haycock in the sun,
While Winter like a well-tamed lion
    walks,
Descending from the mountain to make
    sport
Among the cottagers by beds of flowers.

Whate'er in this wide circuit we beheld,
Or heard, was fitted to our unripe state
Of intellect and heart. With such a book
Before our eyes, we could not choose but
    read
Lessons of genuine brotherhood, the plain
And universal reason of mankind,
The truths of young and old. Nor, side
    by side
Pacing, two social pilgrims, or alone
Each with his humor, could we fail to
    abound
In. dreams and fictions, pensively com-
    posed:
Dejection taken up for pleasure's sake,
And gilded sympathies, the willow wreath,
And sober posies of funereal flowers,
Gathered among those solitudes sublime
From formal gardens of the lady Sorrow,
Did sweeten many a meditative hour.

Yet still in me with those soft luxuries
Mixed something of stern mood, an
    underthirst
Of vigor seldom utterly allayed:
And from that source how different a
    sadness
Would issue, let one incident make
    known.
When from the Vallais we had turned,
    and clomb
Along the Simplon's steep and rugged
    road,
Following a band of muleteers, we reached
A halting-place, where all together took
Their noon-tide meal. Hastily rose our
    guide,
Leaving us at the board; awhile we
    lingered,
Then paced the beaten downward way
    that led
Right to a rough stream's edge, and
    there broke off;
The only track now visible was one
That from the torrent's further brink
    held forth
Conspicuous invitation to ascend
A lofty mountain. After brief delay
Crossing the unbridged stream, that road
    we took,
And clomb with eagerness, till anxious
    fears
Intruded, for we failed to overtake
Our comrades gone before. By fortunate
    chance,
While every moment added doubt to
    doubt,
A peasant met us, from whose mouth we
    learned
That to the spot which had perplexed us
    first
We must descend, and there should find
    the road,
Which in the stony channel of the stream
Lay a few steps, and then along its banks;
And, that our future course, all plain to
    sight,
Was downwards, with the current of that
    stream.
Loth to believe what we so grieved to
    hear,
For still we had hopes that pointed to
    the clouds,
We questioned him again, and yet again;

But every word that from the peasant's lips
Came in reply, translated by our feelings,
Ended in this, — *that we had crossed the Alps.*

Imagination — here the Power so called
Through sad incompetence of human speech,
That awful Power rose from the mind's abyss
Like an unfathered vapor that enwraps,
At once, some lonely traveller. I was lost;
Halted without an effort to break through;
But to my conscious soul I now can say —
" I recognize thy glory : " in such strength
Of usurpation, when the light of sense
Goes out, but with a flash that has revealed
The invisible world, doth greatness make abode,
There harbors; whether we be young or old,
Our destiny, our being's heart and home,
Is with infinitude, and only there;
With hope it is, hope that can never die,
Effort, and expectation, and desire,
And something evermore about to be.
Under such banners militant, the soul
Seeks for no trophies, struggles for no spoils
That may attest her prowess, blest in thoughts
That are their own perfection and reward,
Strong in herself and in beatitude
That hides her, like the mighty flood of Nile
Poured from his fount of Abyssinian clouds
To fertilize the whole Egyptian plain.

The melancholy slackening that ensued
Upon those tidings by the peasant given
Was soon dislodged. Downwards we hurried fast,
And, with the half-shaped road which we 'had missed,
Entered a narrow chasm. [1] The brook and road
Were fellow-travellers in this gloomy strait,
And with them did we journey several hours
At a slow pace. The immeasurable height

[1] See p. 135.

Of woods decaying, never to be decayed,
The stationary blasts of waterfalls,
And in the narrow rent at every turn
Winds thwarting winds, bewildered and forlorn,
The torrents shooting from the clear blue sky,
The rocks that muttered close upon our ears,
Black drizzling crags that spake by the wayside
As if a voice were in them, the sick sight
And giddy prospect of the raving stream,
The unfettered clouds and region of the Heavens,
Tumult and peace, the darkness and the light —
Were all like workings of one mind, the features
Of the same face, blossoms upon one tree;
Characters of the great Apocalypse,
The types and symbols of Eternity,
Of first, and last, and midst, and without end.

That night our lodging was a house that stood
Alone within the valley, at a point
Where, tumbling from aloft, a torrent swelled
The rapid stream whose margin we had trod;
A dreary mansion, large beyond all need,
With high and spacious 'rooms, deafened and stunned
By noise of waters, making innocent sleep
Lie melancholy among weary bones.

Uprisen betimes, our journey we renewed,
Led by the stream, ere noon-day magnified
Into a lordly river, broad and deep,
Dimpling along in silent majesty,
With mountains for its neighbors, and in view
Of distant mountains and their snowy tops,
And thus proceeding to Locarno's Lake,
Fit resting-place for such a visitant.
Locarno! spreading out in width like Heaven,
How dost thou cleave to the poetic heart,
Bask in the sunshine of the memory;

And Como! thou, a treasure whom the earth
Keeps to herself, confined as in a depth
Of Abyssinian privacy. I spake
Of thee, thy chestnut woods, and garden plots
Of Indian corn tended by dark-eyed maids;
Thy lofty steeps, and pathways roofed with vines,
Winding from house to house, from town to town,
Sole link that binds them to each other; walks,
League after league, and cloistral avenues,
Where silence dwells if music be not there:
While yet a youth undisciplined in verse,
Through fond ambition of that hour I strove
To chant your praise; nor can approach you now
Ungreeted by a more melodious Song,
Where tones of Nature smoothed by learnèd Art
May flow in lasting current. Like a breeze
Or sunbeam over your domain I passed
In motion without pause; but ye have left
Your beauty with me, a serene accord
Of forms and colors, passive, yet endowed
In their submissiveness with power as sweet
And gracious, almost, might I dare to say,
As virtue is, or goodness; sweet as love,
Or the remembrance of a generous deed,
Or mildest visitations of pure thought,
When God, the giver of all joy, is thanked
Religiously, in silent blessedness;
Sweet as this last herself, for such it is.

With those delightful pathways we advanced,
For two days' space, in presence of the Lake,
That, stretching far among the Alps, assumed
A character more stern. The second night,
From sleep awakened, and misled by sound
Of the church clock telling the hours with strokes
Whose import then we had not learned, we rose
By moonlight, doubting not that day was nigh,

And that meanwhile, by no uncertain path,
Along the winding margin of the lake,
Led, as before, we should behold the scene
Hushed in profound repose. We left the town
Of Gravedona with this hope; but soon
Were lost, bewildered among woods immense,
And on a rock sate down, to wait for day.
An open place it was, and overlooked,
From high, the sullen water far beneath,
On which a dull red image of the moon
Lay bedded, changing oftentimes its form.
Like an uneasy snake. From hour to hour
We sate and sate, wondering, as if the night
Had been ensnared by witchcraft. On the rock
At last we stretched our weary limbs for sleep,
But *could not* sleep, tormented by the stings
Of insects, which, with noise like that of noon,
Filled all the woods: the cry of unknown birds;
The mountains more by blackness visible
And their own size, than any outward light;
The breathless wilderness of clouds; the clock
That told, with unintelligible voice,
The widely parted hours; the noise of streams,
And sometimes rustling motions nigh at hand,
That did not leave us free from personal fear;
And, lastly, the withdrawing moon, that set
Before us, while she still was high in heaven;—
These were our food; and such a summer's night
Followed that pair of golden days that shed
On Como's Lake, and all that round it lay,
Their fairest, softest, happiest influence.

But here I must break off, and bid farewell
To days, each offering some new sight, or fraught

With some untried adventure, in a course
Prolonged till sprinklings of autumnal
    snow
Checked our unwearied steps.   Let this
    alone
Be mentioned as a parting word, that not
In hollow exultation, dealing out
Hyperboles of praise comparative,
Not rich one moment to be poor forever;
Not prostrate, overborne, as if the mind
Herself were nothing, a mere pensioner
On outward forms — did we in presence
    stand
Of that magnificent region.   On the front
Of this whole Song is written that my heart
Must, in such Temple, needs have offered
    up
A different worship.   Finally, whate'er
I saw, or heard, or felt, was but a stream
That flowed into a kindred stream; a gale,
Confederate with the current of the soul,
To speed my voyage; every sound or sight,
In its degree of power, administered
To grandeur or to tenderness, — to the one
Directly, but to tender thoughts by means
Less often instantaneous in effect;
Led me to these by paths that, in the main,
Were more circuitous, but not less sure
Duly to reach the point marked out by
    Heaven.

Oh, most belovèd Friend! a glorious
    time,
A happy time that was; triumphant looks
Were then the common language of all
    eyes;
As if awaked from sleep, the Nations hailed
Their great expectancy; the fife of war
Was then a spirit-stirring sound indeed,
A blackbird's whistle in a budding grove.
We left the Swiss exulting in the fate
Of their near neighbors; and, when short-
    ening fast
Our pilgrimage, nor distant far from home,
We crossed the Brabant armies on the fret
For battle in the cause of Liberty.
A stripling, scarcely of the household then
Of social life, I looked upon these things
As from a distance; heard, and saw, and
    felt,
Was touched, but with no intimate con-
    cern;
I seemed to move along them, as a bird

Moves through the air, or as a fish pursues
Its sport, or feeds in its proper element;
I wanted not that joy, I did not need
Such help; the ever-living universe,
Turn where I might, was opening out its
    glories,
And the independent spirit of pure youth
Called forth, at every season, new delights,
Spread round my steps like sunshine o'er
    green fields.

BOOK SEVENTH.

RESIDENCE IN LONDON.

Six changeful years have vanished since I
    first
Poured out (saluted by that quickening
    breeze
Which met me issuing from the City's [1]
    walls)
A glad preamble to this Verse: I sang
Aloud, with fervor irresistible
Of short-lived transport, like a torrent
    bursting,
From a black thunder-cloud, down Sca-
    fell's side
To rush and disappear.   But soon broke
    forth
(So willed the Muse) a less impetuous
    stream,
That flowed awhile with unabating
    strength,
Then stopped for years; not audible
    again
Before last primrose-time.   Belovèd
    Friend!
The assurance which then cheered some
    heavy thoughts
On thy departure to a foreign land
Has failed; too slowly moves the prom-
    ised work.
Through the whole summer have I been
    at rest,
Partly from voluntary holiday,
And part through outward hindrance.
    But I heard,
After the hour of sunset yester-even,
Sitting within doors between light and
    dark,
A choir of redbreasts gathered some-
    where near

[1] The City of Goslar, in Lower Saxony.

My threshold, — minstrels from the dis-
tant woods
Sent in on Winter's service, to announce,
With preparation artful and benign,
That the rough lord had left the surly
North
On his accustomed journey. The delight,
Due to this timely notice, unawares
Smote me, and, listening, I in whispers
said,
" Ye heartsome Choristers, ye and I
will be
Associates, and, unscared by blustering
winds,
Will chant together." Thereafter, as
the shades
Of twilight deepened, going forth, I spied
A glow-worm underneath a dusky plume
Or canopy of yet unwithered fern,
Clear-shining, like a hermit's taper seen
Through a thick forest. Silence touched
me here
No less than sound had done before; the child
Of Summer, lingering, shining, by her-
self,
The voiceless worm on the unfrequented
hills,
Seemed sent on the same errand with
the choir
Of Winter that had warbled at my door,
And the whole year breathed tenderness
and love.

The last night's genial feeling over-
flowed
Upon this morning, and my favorite
grove,
Tossing in sunshine its dark boughs aloft,
As if to make the strong wind visible,
Wakes in me agitations like its own,
A spirit friendly to the Poet's task,
Which we will now resume with lively
hope,
Nor checked by aught of tamer argument
That lies before us, needful to be told.

Returned from that excursion,[1] soon I
bade
Farewell forever to the sheltered seats
Of gownèd students, quitted hall and
bower,

[1] See p. 312.

And every comfort of that privileged
ground,
Well pleased to pitch a vagrant tent
among
The unfenced regions of society.

Yet, undetermined to what course of
life
I should adhere, and seeming to possess
A little space of intermediate time
At full command, to London first I
turned,
In no disturbance of excessive hope,
By personal ambition unenslaved,
Frugal as there was need, and, though
self-willed,
From dangerous passions free. Three
years had flown
Since I had felt in heart and soul the
shock
Of the huge town's first presence, and
had paced
Her endless streets, a transient visitant:
Now, fixed amid that concourse of man-
kind
Where Pleasure whirls about incessantly,
And life and labor seem but one, I filled
An idler's place; an idler well content
To have a house (what matter for a
home?)
That owned him; living cheerfully abroad
With unchecked fancy ever on the stir,
And all my young affections out of doors.

There was a time when whatsoe'er is
feigned
Of airy palaces, and gardens built
By Genii of romance; or hath in grave
Authentic history been set forth of Rome,
Alcairo, Babylon, or Persepolis;
Or given upon report by pilgrim friars,
Of golden cities ten months' journey deep
Among Tartarian wilds — fell short, far
short,
Of what my fond simplicity believed
And thought of London — held me by a
chain
Less strong of wonder and obscure
delight.
Whether the bolt of childhood's Fancy
shot
For me beyond its ordinary mark,

'T were vain to ask; but in our flock of
    boys
Was One, a cripple from his birth, whom
    chance
Summoned from school to London; for-
    tunate
And envied traveller! When the Boy
    returned,
After short absence, curiously I scanned
His mien and person, nor was free, in
    sooth,
From disappointment, not to find some
    change
In look and air, from that new region
    brought,
As if from Fairy-land. Much I ques-
    tioned him;
And every word he uttered, on my ears
Fell flatter than a cagèd parrot's note,
That answers unexpectedly awry,
And mocks the prompter's listening.
    Marvellous things
Had vanity (quick Spirit that appears
Almost as deeply seated and as strong
In a Child's heart as fear itself) con-
    ceived
For my enjoyment. Would that I could
    now
Recall what then I pictured to myself,
Of mitred Prelates, Lords in ermine clad,
The King, and the King's Palace, and,
    not last,
Nor least, Heaven bless him! the re-
    nowned Lord Mayor.
Dreams not unlike to those which once
    begat
A change of purpose in young Whit-
    tington,
When he, a friendless and a drooping boy,
Sate on a stone, and heard the bells
    speak out
Articulate music. Above all, one thought
Baffled my understanding: how men lived
Even next-door neighbors, as we say,
    yet still
Strangers, not knowing each the other's
    name.

Oh, wondrous power of words, by
    simple faith
Licensed to take the meaning that we
    love!

Vauxhall and Ranelagh! I then had
    heard
Of your green groves, and wilderness of
    lamps
Dimming the stars, and fireworks magi-
    cal,
And gorgeous ladies, under splendid
    domes,
Floating in dance, or warbling high in air
The songs of spirits! Nor had Fancy fed
With less delight upon that other class
Of marvels, broad-day wonders perma-
    nent:
The River proudly bridged; the dizzy top
And Whispering Gallery of St. Paul's;
    the tombs
Of Westminster; the Giants of Guildhall;
Bedlam, and those carved maniacs at the
    gates,
Perpetually recumbent; Statues — man,
And the horse under him — in gilded
    pomp
Adorning flowery gardens, 'mid vast
    squares;
The Monument, and that Chamber of
    the Tower
Where England's sovereigns sit in long
    array,
Their steeds bestriding, — every mimic
    shape
Cased in the gleaming mail the monarch
    wore,
Whether for gorgeous tournament ad-
    dressed,
Or life or death upon the battle-field.
Those bold imaginations in due time
Had vanished, leaving others in their
    stead:
And now I looked upon the living scene;
Familiarly perused it; oftentimes,
In spite of strongest disappointment,
    pleased
Through courteous self-submission, as a
    tax
Paid to the object by prescriptive right.

Rise up, thou monstrous ant-hill on
    the plain
Of a too busy world! Before me flow,
Thou endless stream of men and moving
    things!
Thy every-day appearance, as it strikes —

With wonder heightened, or sublimed by
    awe —
On strangers, of all ages; the quick
    dance
Of colors, lights, and forms; the deafen-
    ing din;
The comers and the goers face to face,
Face after face; the string of dazzling
    wares,
Shop after shop, with symbols, blazoned
    names,
And all the tradesman's honors over-
    head:
Here, fronts of houses, like a title-page,
With letters huge inscribed from top to
    toe,
Stationed above the door, like guardian
    saints;
There, allegoric shapes, female or male,
Or physiognomies of real men,
Land-warriors, kings, or admirals of the
    sea,
Boyle, Shakspeare, Newton, or the
    attractive head
Of some quack-doctor, famous in his day.

Meanwhile the roar continues, till at
    length,
Escaped as from an enemy, we turn
Abruptly into some sequestered nook,
Still as a sheltered place when winds blow
    loud!
At leisure, thence, through tracts of thin
    resort,
And sights and sounds that come at inter-
    vals,
We take our way. A raree-show is here,
With children gathered round; another
    street
Presents a company of dancing dogs,
Or dromedary, with an antic pair
Of monkeys on his back; a minstrel band
Of Savoyards; or, single and alone,
An English ballad-singer. Private courts,
Gloomy as coffins, and unsightly lanes
Thrilled by some female vendor's scream,
    belike
The very shrillest of all London cries,
May then entangle our impatient steps;
Conducted through those labyrinths, un-
    awares,
To privileged regions and inviolate,

Where from their airy lodges studious
    lawyers
Look out on waters, walks, and gardens
    green.

Thence back into the throng, until we
    reach,
Following the tide that slackens by de-
    grees,
Some half-frequented scene, where wider
    streets
Bring straggling breezes of suburban air.
Here files of ballads dangle from dead
    walls;
Advertisements, of giant-size, from high
Press forward, in all colors, on the sight;
These, bold in conscious merit, lower
    down;
That, fronted with a most imposing word,
Is, peradventure, one in masquerade.
As on the broadening causeway we ad-
    vance,
Behold, turned upwards, a face hard and
    strong
In lineaments, and red with over-toil.
'T is one encountered here and every-
    where;
A travelling cripple, by the trunk cut
    short,
And stumping on his arms. In sailor's
    garb
Another lies at length, beside a range
Of well-formed characters, with chalk in-
    scribed
Upon the smooth flat stones: the Nurse
    is here,
The Bachelor, that loves to sun himself,
The military Idler, and the Dame,
That field-ward takes her walk with
    decent steps.

Now homeward through the thickening
    hubbub, where
See, among less distinguishable shapes,
The begging scavenger, with hat in hand;
The Italian, as he thrids his way with care,
Steadying, far-seen, a frame of images
Upon his head; with basket at his breast
The Jew; the stately and slow-moving
    Turk,
With freight of slippers piled beneath his
    arm!

Enough; — the mighty concourse I sur-
    veyed
With no unthinking mind, well pleased
    to note
Among the crowd all specimens of man,
Through all the colors which the sun
    bestows,
And every character of form and face:
The Swede, the Russian; from the genial
    south,
The Frenchman and the Spaniard; from
    remote
America, the Hunter-Indian; Moors,
Malays, Lascars, the Tartar, the Chinese,
And Negro Ladies in white muslin gowns.

At leisure, then, I viewed, from day to
    day,
The spectacles within doors, — birds and
    beasts
Of every nature, and strange plants con-
    vened
From every clime; and, next, those sights
    that ape
The absolute presence of reality,
Expressing, as in mirror, sea and land,
And what earth is, and what she has to
    show.
I do not here allude to subtlest craft,
By means refined attaining purest ends,
But imitations, fondly made in plain
Confession of man's weakness and his
    loves.
Whether the Painter, whose ambitious
    .   skill
Submits to nothing less than taking in
A whole horizon's circuit, do with power,
Like that of angels or commissioned
    spirits,
Fix us upon some lofty pinnacle,
Or in a ship on waters, with a world
Of life, and life-like mockery beneath,
Above, behind, far stretching and before;
Or more mechanic artist represent
By scale exact, in model, wood or clay,
From blended colors also borrowing help,
Some miniature of famous spots or
    things, —
St. Peter's Church; or, more aspiring aim,
In microscopic vision, Rome herself;
Or, haply, some choice rural haunt, —
    the Falls
Of Tivoli; and, high upon that steep,

The Sibyl's mouldering Temple! every
    tree,
Villa, or cottage, lurking among rocks
Throughout the landscape; tuft, stone
    scratch minute —
All that the traveller sees when he is there.

Add to these exhibitions, mute and still,
Others of wider scope, where living men,
Music, and shifting pantomimic scenes,
Diversified the allurement.   Need I fear
To mention by its name, as in degree,
Lowest of these and humblest in attempt,
Yet richly graced with honors of her own,
Half-rural Sadler's Wells?   Though at
    that time
Intolerant, as is the way of youth
Unless itself be pleased, here more than
    once
Taking my seat, I saw (nor blush to add,
With ample recompense) giants and
    dwarfs,
Clowns, conjurers, posture-masters, har-
    lequins,
Amid the uproar of the rabblement,
Perform their feats.   Nor was it mean
    delight
To watch crude Nature work in untaught
    minds;
To note the laws and progress of belief;
Though obstinate on this way, yet on that
How willingly we travel, and how far!
To have, for instance, brought upon the
    scene
The champion, Jack the Giant-killer:
    Lo!
He dons his coat of darkness; on the
    stage
Walks and achieves his wonders, from the
    eye
Of living Mortal covert, " as the moon
Hid in her vacant interlunar cave."
Delusion bold! and how can it be
    wrought?
The garb he wears is black as death, the
    word
" Invisible " flames forth upon his chest.

Here, too, were " forms and pressures
    of the time,"
Rough, bold, as Grecian comedy dis-
    played

When Art was young; dramas of living
  men,
And recent things yet warm with life; a
  sea-fight,
Shipwreck, or some domestic incident
Divulged by Truth and magnified by
  Fame;
Such as the daring brotherhood of late
Set forth, too serious theme for that light
  place —
I mean, O distant Friend! a story drawn
From our own ground, — the Maid of
  Buttermere, —
And how, unfaithful to a virtuous wife
Deserted and deceived, the Spoiler came
And wooed the artless daughter of the
  hills,
And wedded her, in cruel mockery
Of love and marriage bonds. These
  words to thee
Must needs bring back the moment when
  we first,
Ere the broad world rang with the
  maiden's name,
Beheld her serving at the cottage inn;
Both stricken, as she entered or withdrew,
With admiration of her modest mien
And carriage, marked by unexampled
  grace.
We since that time not unfamiliarly
Have seen her, — her discretion have ob-
  served,
Her just opinions, delicate reserve,
Her patience, and humility of mind
Unspoiled by commendation and the
  excess
Of public notice — an offensive light
To a meek spirit suffering inwardly.

From this memorial tribute to my theme
I was returning, when, with sundry forms
Commingled — shapes which met me in
  the way
That we must tread — thy image rose
  again,
Maiden of Buttermere! She lives in
  peace
Upon the spot where she was born and
  reared;
Without contamination doth she live
In quietness, without anxiety:
Beside the mountain chapel, sleeps in
  earth

Her new-born infant, fearless as a lamb
That, thither driven from some un-
  sheltered place,
Rests underneath the little rock-like pile
When storms are raging. Happy are they
  both —
Mother and child! — These feelings, in
  themselves
Trite, do yet scarcely seem so when I
  think
On those ingenuous moments of our youth
Ere we have learnt by use to slight the
  crimes
And sorrows of the world. Those simple
  days
Are now my theme; and, foremost of the
  scenes,
Which yet survive in memory, appears
One, at whose centre sate a lovely Boy,
A sportive infant, who, for six months'
  space,
Not more, had been of age to deal about
Articulate prattle — Child as beautiful
As ever clung around a mother's neck,
Or father fondly gazed upon with pride.
There, too, conspicuous for stature tall
And large dark eyes, beside her infant
  stood
The mother; but, upon her cheeks dif-
  fused,
False tints too well accorded with the glare
From playhouse lustres thrown without
  reserve
On every object near. The Boy had been
The pride and pleasure of all lookers-on
In whatsoever place, but seemed in this
A sort of alien scattered from the clouds.
Of lusty vigor, more than infantine
He was in limb, in cheek a summer rose
Just three parts blown — a cottage-child
  — if e'er,
By cottage-door on breezy mountain-side,
Or in some sheltering vale, was seen a
  babe
By Nature's gifts so favored. Upon a
  board
Decked with refreshments had this child
  been placed
His little stage in the vast theatre,
And there he sate, surrounded with a
  throng
Of chance spectators, chiefly dissolute
  men

And shameless women, treated and
  caressed;
Ate, drank, and with the fruit and glasses
  played,
While oaths and laughter and indecent
  speech.
Were rife about him as the songs of birds
Contending after showers. The mother
  now
Is fading out of memory, but I see
The lovely Boy as I beheld him then
Among the wretched and the falsely gay,
Like one of those who walked with hair
  unsinged
Amid the fiery furnace. Charms and
  spells
Muttered on black and spiteful instigation
Have stopped, as some believe, the kind-
  liest growths.
Ah, with how different spirit might a
  prayer
Have been preferred, that this fair crea-
  ture, checked
By special privilege of Nature's love,
Should in his childhood be detained for-
  ever!
But with its universal freight the tide
Hath rolled along, and this bright inno-
  cent,
Mary! may now have lived till he could
  look
With envy on thy nameless babe that
  sleeps,
Beside the mountain chapel, undisturbed.

  Four rapid years had scarcely then been
    told
Since, travelling southward from our
  pastoral hills,
I heard, and for the first time in my life,
The voice of woman utter blasphemy —
Saw woman as she is, to open shame
Abandoned, and the pride of public vice;
I shuddered, for a barrier seemed at once
Thrown in that from humanity divorced
Humanity, splitting the race of man
In twain, yet leaving the same outward
  form.
Distress of mind ensued upon the sight,
And ardent meditation. Later years
Brought to such spectacle a milder sad-
  ness,
Feelings of pure commiseration, grief

For the individual and the overthrow
Of her soul's beauty; farther I was then
But seldom led, or wished to go; in truth
The sorrow of the passion stopped me
  there.

  But let me now, less moved, in order
    take
Our argument. Enough is said to show
How casual incidents of real life,
Observed where pastime only had been
  sought,
Outweighed, or put to flight, the set
  events
And measured passions of the stage,
  albeit
By Siddons trod in the fulness of her
  power.
Yet was the theatre my dear delight;
The very gilding, lamps and painted
  scrolls,
And all the mean upholstery of the place,
Wanted not animation, when the tide
Of pleasure ebbed but to return as fast
With the ever-shifting figures of the scene,
Solemn or gay: whether some beauteous
  dame
Advanced in radiance through a deep
  recess
Of thick entangled forest, like the moon
Opening the clouds; or sovereign king,
  announced
With flourishing trumpet, came in full-
  blown state
Of the world's greatness, winding round
  with train
Of courtiers, banners, and a length of
  guards;
Or captive led in abject weeds, and jin-
  gling
His slender manacles; or romping girl
Bounced, leapt, and pawed the air; or
  mumbling sire,
A scare-crow pattern of old age dressed up
In all the tatters of infirmity
All loosely put together, hobbled in,
Stumping upon a cane with which he
  smites,
From time to time, the solid boards, and
  makes them
Prate somewhat loudly of the whereabout
Of one so overloaded with his years.

But what of this! the laugh, the grin,
grimace,
The antics striving to outstrip each other,
Were all received, the least of them not
lost,
With an unmeasured welcome. Through
the night,
Between the show, and many-headed
mass
Of the spectators, and each several nook
Filled with its fray or brawl, how eagerly
And with what flashes, as it were, the
mind
Turned this way — that way! sportive and
alert
And watchful, as a kitten when at play,
While winds are eddying round her,
among straws
And rustling leaves. Enchanting age and
sweet!
Romantic almost, looked at through a
space,
How small, of intervening years! For
then,
Though surely no mean progress had been
made
In meditations holy and sublime,
Yet something of a girlish child-like gloss
Of novelty survived for scenes like these;
Enjoyment haply handed down from times
When at a country-playhouse, some rude
barn
Tricked out for that proud use, if I per-
chance
Caught, on a summer evening through a
chink
In the old wall, an unexpected glimpse
Of daylight, the bare thought of where I
was
Gladdened me more than if I had been led
Into a dazzling cavern of romance,
Crowded with Genii busy among works
Not to be looked at by the common sun.

The matter that detains us now may
seem,
To many, neither dignified enough
Nor arduous, yet will not be scorned by
them,
Who, looking inward, have observed the
ties
That bind the perishable hours of life
Each to the other, and the curious props

By which the world of memory and
thought
Exists and is sustained. More lofty
themes,
Such as at least do wear a prouder face,
Solicit our regard; but when I think
Of these, I feel the imaginative power
Languish within me; even then it slept,
When, pressed by tragic sufferings, the
heart
Was more than full; amid my sobs and
tears
It slept, even in the pregnant season of
youth.
For though I was most passionately moved
And yielded to all changes of the scene
With an obsequious promptness, yet the
storm
Passed not beyond the suburbs of the
mind;
Save when realities of act and mien,
The incarnation of the spirits that move
In harmony amid the Poet's world,
Rose to ideal grandeur, or, called forth
By power of contrast, made me recognize,
As at a glance, the things which I had
shaped,
And yet not shaped, had seen and scarcely
seen,
When, having closed the mighty Shak-
speare's page,
I mused, and thought, and felt, in solitude.

Pass we from entertainments, that are
such
Professedly, to others titled higher,
Yet, in the estimate of youth at least,
More near akin to those than names im-
ply, —
I mean the brawls of lawyers in their
courts
Before the ermined judge, or that great
stage
Where senators, tongue-favored men, per-
form,
Admired and envied. Oh! the beating
heart,
When one among the prime of these rose
up, —
One, of whose name from childhood we
had heard
Familiarly, a household term, like those,
The Bedfords, Glosters, Salisburys, of old,

Whom the fifth Harry talks of. Silence!
   hush!
This is no trifler, no short-flighted wit,
No stammerer of a minute, painfully
Delivered. No! the Orator hath yoked
The Hours, like young Aurora, to his car:
Thrice welcome Presence! how can pa-
   tience e'er
Grow weary of attending on a track
That kindles with such glory! All are
   charmed,
Astonished; like a hero in romance,
He winds away his never-ending horn;
Words follow words, sense seems to follow
   sense:
What memory and what logic! till the
   strain
Transcendent, superhuman as it seemed,
Grows tedious even in a young man's ear.

   Genius of Burke! forgive the pen
   seduced
By specious wonders, and too slow to tell
Of what the ingenuous, what bewildered
   men,
Beginning to mistrust their boastful guides,
And wise men, willing to grow wiser,
   caught,
Rapt auditors! from thy most eloquent
   tongue —
Now mute, forever mute in the cold
   grave.
I see him, — old, but vigorous in age, —
Stand like an oak whose stag - horn
   branches start
Out of its leafy brow, the more to awe
The younger brethren of the grove. But
   some —
While he forewarns, denounces, launches
   forth,
Against all systems built on abstract
   rights,
Keen ridicule; the majesty proclaims
Of Institutes and Laws, hallowed by time;
Declares the vital power of social ties
Endeared by Custom; and with high dis-
   dain,
Exploding upstart Theory, insists
Upon the allegiance to which men are
   born —
Some — say at once a froward multitude —
Murmur (for truth is hated, where not
   loved)

As the winds fret within the Æolian cave,
Galled by their monarch's chain. The
   times were big
With ominous change, which, night by
   night, provoked
Keen struggles, and black clouds of pas-
   sion raised;
But memorable moments intervened,
When Wisdom, like the Goddess from
   Jove's brain,
Broke forth in armor of resplendent
   words,
Startling the Synod. Could a youth, and
   one
In ancient story versed, whose breast had
   heaved
Under the weight of classic eloquence,
Sit, see, and hear, unthankful, unin-
   spired?

   Nor did the Pulpit's oratory fail
To achieve its higher triumph. Not unfelt
Were its admonishments, nor lightly
   heard
The awful truths delivered thence by
   tongues
Endowed with various power to search the
   soul;
Yet ostentation, domineering, oft
Poured forth harangues, how sadly out of
   place! —
There have I seen a comely bachelor,
Fresh from a toilette of two hours, ascend
His rostrum, with seraphic glance look up,
And, in a tone elaborately low
Beginning, lead his voice through many a
   maze
A minuet course; and, winding up his
   mouth,
From time to time, into an orifice
Most delicate, a lurking eyelet, small,
And only not invisible, again
Open it out, diffusing thence a smile
Of rapt irradiation, exquisite.
Meanwhile the Evangelists, Isaiah, Job,
Moses, and he who penned, the other day,
The Death of Abel, Shakspeare, and the
   Bard
Whose genius spangled o'er a gloomy
   theme
With fancies thick as his inspiring stars,
And Ossian (doubt not — 't is the naked
   truth)

Summoned from streamy Morven — each
   and all
Would, in their turns, lend ornaments and
   flowers
To entwine the crook of eloquence that
   helped
This pretty Shepherd, pride of all the
   plains,
To rule and guide his captivated flock.

   I glance but at a few conspicuous
      marks,
Leaving a thousand others, that, in hall,
Court, theatre, conventicle, or shop,
In public room or private, park or street,
Each fondly reared on his own pedestal,
Looked out for admiration. Folly, vice,
Extravagance in gesture, mien, and dress,
And all the strife of singularity,
Lies to the ear, and lies to every sense —
Of these, and of the living shapes they
   wear,
There is no end. Such candidates for re-
   gard,
Although well pleased to be where they
   were found,
I did not hunt after, nor greatly prize,
Nor made unto myself a secret boast
Of reading them with quick and curious
   eye;
But, as a common produce, things that are
To-day, to-morrow will be, took of them
Such willing note, as, on some errand
   bound
That asks not speed, a traveller might be-
   stow
On sea-shells that bestrew the sandy
   beach,
Or daisies swarming through the fields of
   June.

   But foolishness and madness in parade,
Though most at home in this their dear
   domain,
Are scattered everywhere, no rarities,
Even to the rudest novice of the Schools.
Me, rather, it employed, to note, and
   keep
In memory, those individual sights
Of courage, or integrity, or truth,
Or tenderness, which there, set off by
   foil,

Appeared more touching. One will I
   select —
A Father — for he bore that sacred
   name; —
Him saw I, sitting in an open square,
Upon a corner-stone of that low wall,
Wherein were fixed the iron pales that
   fenced
A spacious grass-plot; there, in silence,
   sate
This One Man, with a sickly babe out-
   stretched
Upon his knee, whom he had thither
   brought
For sunshine, and to breathe the fresher
   air.
Of those who passed, and me who looked
   at him,
He took no heed; but in his brawny arms
(The Artificer was to the elbow bare,
And from his work this moment had been
   stolen)
He held the child, and, bending over it,
As if he were afraid both of the sun
And of the air, which he had come to
   seek,
Eyed the poor babe with love unutterable.

   As the black storm upon the mountain
      top
Sets off the sunbeam in the valley, so
That huge fermenting mass of human-
   kind
Serves as a solemn background or relief,
To single forms and objects, whence they
   draw,
For feeling and contemplative regard,
More than inherent liveliness and power.
How oft, amid those overflowing streets,
Have I gone forward with the crowd, and
   said
Unto myself, "The face of every one
That passes by me is a mystery!"
Thus have I looked, nor ceased to look,
   oppressed
By thoughts of what and whither, when
   and how,
Until the shapes before my eyes became
A second-sight procession, such as glides
Over still mountains, or appears in
   dreams;
And once, far-travelled in such mood,
   beyond

The reach of common indication, lost
Amid the moving pageant, I was smitten
Abruptly, with the view (a sight not rare)
Of a blind Beggar, who, with upright face,
Stood, propped against a wall, upon his chest
Wearing a written paper, to explain
His story, whence he came, and who he was.
Caught by the spectacle my mind turned round
As with the might of waters; and apt type
This label seemed of the utmost we can know,
Both of ourselves and of the universe;
And, on the shape of that unmoving man,
His steadfast face and sightless eyes, I gazed,
As if admonished from another world.

Though reared upon the base of outward things,
Structures like these the excited spirit mainly
Builds for herself; scenes different there are,
Full-formed, that take, with small internal help,
Possession of the faculties, — the peace
That comes with night; the deep solemnity
Of nature's intermediate hours of rest,
When the great tide of human life stands still:
The business of the day to come, unborn,
Of that gone by, locked up, as in the grave;
The blended calmness of the heavens and earth,
Moonlight and stars, and empty streets, and sounds
Unfrequent as in deserts; at late hours
Of winter evenings, when unwholesome rains
Are falling hard, with people yet astir,
The feeble salutation from the voice
Of some unhappy woman, now and then
Heard as we pass, when no one looks about,
Nothing is listened to. But these, I fear,
Are falsely catalogued; things that are,
are not, .
As the mind answers to them, or the heart
Is prompt, or slow, to feel. What say you, then,

To times, when half the city shall break out
Full of one passion, vengeance, rage, or fear?
To executions, to a street on fire,
Mobs, riots, or rejoicings? From these sights
Take one, — that ancient festival, the Fair,
Holden where martyrs suffered in past time,
And named of St. Bartholomew; there, see
A work completed to our hands, that lays,
If any spectacle on earth can do,
The whole creative powers of man asleep! —
For once, the Muse's help will we implore,
And she shall lodge us, wafted on her wings,
Above the press and danger of the crowd,
Upon some showman's platform. What a shock
For eyes and ears! what anarchy and din,
Barbarian and infernal, — a phantasma,
Monstrous in color, motion, shape, sight, sound!
Below, the open space, through every nook
Of the wide area, twinkles, is alive
With heads; the midway region, and above,
Is thronged with staring pictures and huge scrolls,
Dumb proclamations of the Prodigies;
With chattering monkeys dangling from their poles,
And children whirling in their roundabouts;
With those that stretch the neck and strain the eyes,
And crack the voice in rivalship, the crowd
Inviting; with buffoons against buffoons
Grimacing, writhing, screaming, — him who grinds
The hurdy-gurdy, at the fiddle weaves,
Rattles the salt-box, thumps the kettledrum,
And him who at the trumpet puffs his cheeks,
The silver-collared Negro with his timbrel,
Equestrians, tumblers, women, girls, and boys,

Blue-breeched, pink-vested, with high-
    towering plumes. —
All movables of wonder, from all parts,
Are here — Albinos, painted Indians,
    Dwarfs,
The Horse of knowledge, and the learned
    Pig,
The Stone-eater, the man that swallows
    fire,
Giants, Ventriloquists, the Invisible Girl,
The Bust that speaks and moves its gog-
    gling eyes,
The Wax-work, Clock-work, all the mar-
    vellous craft
Of modern Merlins, Wild Beasts, Puppet-
    shows,
All out-o'-the-way, far-fetched, perverted
    things,
All freaks of nature, all Promethean
    thoughts
Of man, his dulness, madness, and their
    feats
All jumbled up together, to compose
A Parliament of Monsters. Tents and
    Booths
Meanwhile, as if the whole were one vast
    mill,
Are vomiting, receiving on all sides,
Men, Women, three-years' Children,
    Babes in arms.

Oh, blank confusion! true epitome
Of what the mighty City is herself,
To thousands upon thousands of her sons,
Living amid the same perpetual whirl
Of trivial objects, melted and reduced
To one identity, by differences
That have no law, no meaning, and no
    end —
Oppression, under which even highest
    minds
Must labor, whence the strongest are not
    free.
But though the picture weary out the eye,
By nature an unmanageable sight,
It is not wholly so to him who looks
In steadiness, who hath among least things
An under-sense of greatest; sees the parts
As parts, but with a feeling of the whole.
This, of all acquisitions, first awaits
On sundry and most widely different
    modes
Of education, nor with least delight

On that through which I passed. Atten-
    tion springs,
And comprehensiveness and memory
    flow,
From early converse with the works of
    God
Among all regions; chiefly where appear
Most obviously simplicity and power.
Think, how the everlasting streams and
    woods,
Stretched and still stretching far and
    wide, exalt
The roving Indian, on his desert sands:
What grandeur not unfelt, what pregnant
    show
Of beauty, meets the sun-burnt Arab's
    eye:
And, as the sea propels, from zone to zone,
Its currents; magnifies its shoals of life
Beyond all compass; spreads, and sends
    aloft
Armies of clouds, — even so, its powers
    and aspects
Shape for mankind, by principles as fixed,
The views and aspirations of the soul
To majesty. Like virtue have the forms
Perennial of the ancient hills; nor less
The changeful language of their counte-
    nances
Quickens the slumbering mind, and aids
    the thoughts,
However multitudinous, to move
With order and relation. This, if still,
As hitherto, in freedom I may speak,
Not violating any just restraint,
As may be hoped, of real modesty, —
This did I feel, in London's vast domain.
The Spirit of Nature was upon me there;
The soul of Beauty and enduring Life
Vouchsafed her inspiration, and diffused,
Through meagre lines and colors, and
    the press
Of self-destroying, transitory things,
Composure, and ennobling Harmony.

BOOK EIGHTH.

RETROSPECT. — LOVE OF NATURE LEAD-
    ING TO LOVE OF MAN.

WHAT sounds are those, Helvellyn, that
    are heard
Up to thy summit, through the depth of
    air

Ascending, as if distance had the power
To make the sounds more audible?
     What crowd
Covers, or sprinkles o'er, yon village
     green?
Crowd seems it, solitary hill! to thee,
Though but a little family of men,
Shepherds and tillers of the ground —
     betimes
Assembled with their children and their
     wives,
And here and there a stranger inter-
     spersed.
They hold a rustic fair — a festival,
Such as, on this side now, and now on
     that,
Repeated through his tributary vales,
Helvellyn, in the silence of his rest,
Sees annually, if clouds towards either
     ocean
Blown from their favorite resting-place,
     or mists
Dissolved, have left him an unshrouded
     head.
Delightful day it is for all who dwell
In this secluded glen, and eagerly
They give it welcome.   Long ere heat of
     noon,
From byre or field the kine were brought;
     the sheep
Are penned in cotes;   the chaffering is
     begun.
The heifer lows, uneasy at the voice
Of a new master; bleat the flocks aloud.
Booths are there none; a stall or two is
     here;
A lame man or a blind, the one to beg,
The other to make music; hither, too,
From far, with basket, slung upon her
     arm,
Of hawker's wares — books, pictures,
     combs, and pins —
Some aged woman finds her way again,
Year after year, a punctual visitant!
There also stands a speech-maker by rote,
Pulling the strings of his boxed raree-
     show;
And in the lapse of many years may come
Prouder itinerant, mountebank, or he
Whose wonders in a covered wain lie hid.
But one there is, the loveliest of them
     all,
Some sweet lass of the valley, looking out

For gains, and who that sees her would
     not buy?
Fruits of her father's orchard are her
     wares,
And with the ruddy produce she walks
     round
Among the crowd, half pleased with,
     half ashamed
Of, her new office, blushing restlessly.
The children now are rich, for the old
     to-day
Are generous as the young; and, if
     content
With looking on, some ancient wedded
     pair
Sit in the shade together; while they gaze,
" A cheerful smile unbends the wrinkled
     brow,
The days departed start again to life,
And all the scenes of childhood reappear,
Faint, but more tranquil, like the chan-
     ging sun
To him who slept at noon, and wakes at
     eve." [1]
Thus gayety and cheerfulness prevail,
Spreading from young to old, from old
     to young,
And no one seems to want his share. —
     Immense
Is the recess, the circumambient world
Magnificent, by which they are embraced:
They move about upon the soft green turf:
How little they, they and their doings,
     seem,
And all that they can further or obstruct!
Through utter weakness pitiably dear,
As tender infants are: and yet how great!
For all things serve them: them the
     morning light
Loves, as it glistens on the silent rocks;
And them the silent rocks, which now
     from high
Look down upon them; the reposing
     clouds;
The wild brooks prattling from invisible
     haunts;
And old Helvellyn, conscious of the stir
Which animates this day their calm abode.

     With deep devotion, Nature, did I feel,
In that enormous City's turbulent world

---

[1] These lines are from a descriptive Poem —
" Malvern Hills " — by one of Mr. Wordsworth's
oldest friends, Mr. Joseph Cottle.

Of men and things, what benefit I owed
To thee, and those domains of rural peace,
Where to the sense of beauty first my
    heart
Was opened; tract more exquisitely fair
Than that famed paradise of ten thousand
    trees,
Or Gehol's matchless gardens, for delight
Of the Tartarian dynasty composed
(Beyond that mighty wall, not fabulous,
China's stupendous mound) by patient toil
Of myriads and boon nature's lavish help;
There, in a clime from widest empire
    chosen,
Fulfilling (could enchantment have done
    more?)
A sumptuous dream of flowery lawns,
    with domes
Of pleasure sprinkled over, shady dells
For eastern monasteries, sunny mounts
With temples crested, bridges, gondolas,
Rocks, dens, and groves of foliage taught
    to melt
Into each other their obsequious hues,
Vanished and vanishing in subtle chase,
Too fine to be pursued; or standing forth
In no discordant opposition, strong
And gorgeous as the colors side by side
Bedded among rich plumes of tropic birds;
And mountains over all, embracing all;
And all the landscape, endlessly enriched
With waters running, falling, or asleep.

But lovelier far than this, the paradise
Where I was reared; in Nature's primi-
    tive gifts
Favored no less, and more to every sense
Delicious, seeing that the sun and sky,
The elements, and seasons as they change,
Do find a worthy fellow-laborer there —
Man free, man working for himself, with
    choice
Of time, and place, and object; by his
    wants,
His comforts, native occupations, cares,
Cheerfully led to individual ends
Or social, and still followed by a train
Unwooed, unthought - of even — sim-
    plicity,
And beauty, and inevitable grace.

Yea, when a glimpse of those imperial
    bowers

Would to a child be transport over-great,
When but a half-hour's roam through
    such a place
Would leave behind a dance of images,
That shall break in upon his sleep for
    weeks;
Even then the common haunts of the
    green earth,
And ordinary interests of man,
Which they embosom, all without regard
As both may seem, are fastening on the
    heart
Insensibly, each with the other's help.
For me, when my affections first were
    led
From kindred, friends, and playmates,
    to partake
Love for the human creature's absolute
    self,
That noticeable kindliness of heart
Sprang out of fountains, there abounding
    most,
Where sovereign Nature dictated the
    tasks
And occupations which her beauty
    adorned,
And Shepherds were the men that pleased
    me first;
Not such as Saturn ruled 'mid Latian
    wilds,
With arts and laws so tempered, that
    their lives
Left, even to us toiling in this late day,
A bright tradition of the golden age;
Not such as, 'mid Arcadian fastnesses
Sequestered, handed down among them-
    selves
Felicity, in Grecian song renowned;
Nor such as — when an adverse fate had
    driven,
From house and home, the courtly band
    whose fortunes
Entered, with Shakspeare's genius, the
    wild woods
Of Arden — amid sunshine or in shade
Culled the best fruits of Time's uncounted
    hours,
Ere Phœbe sighed for the false Gany-
    mede;
Or there where Perdita and Florizel
Together danced, Queen of the feast,
    and King;
Nor such as Spenser fabled. True it is,

That I had heard (what he perhaps had
    seen)
Of maids at sunrise bringing in from far
Their May-bush, and along the streets
    in flocks
Parading with a song of taunting rhymes,
Aimed at the laggards slumbering within
    doors;
Had also heard, from those who yet re-
    membered,
Tales of the May-pole dance, and wreaths
    that decked
Porch, door-way, or kirk-pillar; and of
    youths,
Each with his maid, before the sun was up,
By annual custom, issuing forth in troops,
To drink the waters of some sainted well,
And hang it round with garlands. Love
    survives;
But, for such purpose, flowers no longer
    grow:
The times, too sage, perhaps too proud,
    have dropped
These lighter graces; and the rural ways
And manners which my childhood looked
    upon
Were the unluxuriant produce of a life
Intent on little but substantial needs,
Yet rich in beauty, beauty that was felt.
But images of danger and distress,
Man suffering among awful Powers and
    Forms;
Of this I heard, and saw enough to make
Imagination restless; nor was I free
Myself from frequent perils; nor were tales
Wanting,— the tragedies of former times,
Hazards and strange escapes, of which the
    rocks
Immutable, and everflowing streams,
Where'er I roamed, were speaking monu-
    ments.

Smooth life had flock and shepherd in
    old time,
Long springs and tepid winters, on the
    banks
Of delicate Galesus; and no less
Those scattered along Adria's myrtle
    shores:
Smooth life had herdsman, and his snow-
    white herd
To triumphs and to sacrificial rites
Devoted, on the inviolable stream

Of rich Clitumnus; and the goat-herd lived
As calmly, underneath the pleasant brows
Of cool Lucretilis, where the pipe was
    heard
Of Pan, Invisible God, thrilling the rocks
With tutelary music, from all harm
The fold protecting. I myself, mature
In manhood then, have seen a pastoral
    tract
Like one of these, where Fancy might run
    wild,
Though under skies less generous, less
    serene:
There, for her own delight had Nature
    framed
A pleasure-ground, diffused a fair expanse
Of level pasture, islanded with groves
And banked with woody risings; but the
    Plain
Endless, here opening widely out, and
    there
Shut up in lesser lakes or beds of lawn
And intricate recesses, creek or bay
Sheltered within a shelter, where at large
The shepherd strays, a rolling hut his home.
Thither he comes with spring-time, there
    abides
All summer, and at sunrise ye may hear
His flageolet to liquid notes of love
Attuned, or sprightly fife resounding far.
Nook is there none, nor tract of that vast
    space
Where passage opens, but the same shall
    have
In turn its visitant, telling there his hours
In unlaborious pleasure, with no task
More toilsome than to carve a beechen
    bowl
For spring or fountain, which the traveller
    finds,
When through the region he pursues at will
His devious course. A glimpse of such
    sweet life
I saw when, from the melancholy walls
Of Goslar, once imperial, I renewed
My daily walk along that wide champaign,
That, reaching to her gates, spreads east
    and west,
And northwards, from beneath the moun-
    tainous verge
Of the Hercynian forest. Yet, hail to you
Moors, mountains, headlands, and ye
    hollow vales,

Ye long deep channels for the Atlantic's
 voice,
Powers of my native region ! Ye that seize
The heart with firmer grasp ! Your snows
 and streams
Ungovernable, and your terrifying winds,
That howl so dismally for him who treads
Companionless your awful solitudes !
There, 't is the shepherd's task the winter
 long
To wait upon the storms : of their approach
Sagacious, into sheltering coves he drives
His flock, and thither from the homestead
 bears
A toilsome burden up the craggy ways,
And deals it out, their regular nourishment
Strewn on the frozen snow. And when the
 spring
Looks out, and all the pastures dance with
 lambs,
And when the flock, with warmer weather,
 climbs
Higher and higher, him his office leads
To watch their goings, whatsoever track
The wanderers choose. For this he quits
 his home
At day-spring, and no sooner doth the sun
Begin to strike him with a fire-like heat,
Than he lies down upon some shining rock,
And breakfasts with his dog. When they
 have stolen,
As is their wont, a pittance from strict time,
For rest not needed or exchange of love,
Then from his couch he starts; and now
 his feet
Crush out a livelier fragrance from the
 flowers
Of lowly thyme, by Nature's skill en-
 wrought
In the wild turf : the lingering dews of morn
Smoke round him, as from hill to hill he
 hies,
His staff protending like a hunter's spear,
Or by its aid leaping from crag to crag,
And o'er the brawling beds of unbridged
 streams.
Philosophy, methinks, at Fancy's call,
Might deign to follow him through what
 he does
Or sees in his day's march; himself he feels,
In those vast regions where his service lies,
A freeman, wedded to his life of hope
And hazard, and hard labor interchanged

With that majestic indolence so dear
To native man. A rambling schoolboy,
 thus,
I felt his presence in his own domain,
As of a lord and master, or a power,
Or genius, under Nature, under God,
Presiding; and severest solitude
Had more commanding looks when he
 was there.
When up the lonely brooks on rainy days
Angling I went, or trod the trackless hills
By mists bewildered, suddenly mine eyes
Have glanced upon him distant a few steps,
In size a giant, stalking through thick fog,
His sheep like Greenland bears; or, as he
 stepped
Beyond the boundary line of some hill-
 shadow,
His form hath flashed upon me, glorified
By the deep radiance of the setting sun :
Or him have I descried in distant sky,
A solitary object and sublime,
Above all height ! like an aerial cross
Stationed alone upon a spiry rock
Of the Chartreuse, for worship. Thus
 was man
Ennobled outwardly before my sight,
And thus my heart was early introduced
To an unconscious love and reverence
Of human nature; hence the human form
To me became an index of delight,
Of grace and honor, power and worthiness.
Meanwhile this creature—spiritual almost
As those of books, but more exalted far;
Far more of an imaginative form
Than the gay Corin of the groves, who lives
For his own fancies, or to dance by the
 hour,
In coronal, with Phyllis in the midst —
Was, for the purposes of kind, a man
With the most common; husband, father;
 learned,
Could teach, admonish; suffered with the
 rest
From vice and folly, wretchedness and
 fear;
Of this I little saw, cared less for it,
But something must have felt.
                    Call ye these appearances —
Which I beheld of shepherds in my youth,
This sanctity of Nature given to man —
A shadow, a delusion, ye who pore
On the dead letter, miss the spirit of things;

Whose truth is not a motion or a shape
Instinct with vital functions, but a block
Or waxen image which yourselves have
     made,
And ye adore! But blessèd be the God
Of Nature and of Man that this was so;
That men before my inexperienced eyes
Did first present themselves thus purified,
Removed, and to a distance that was fit:
And so we all of us in some degree
Are led to knowledge, wheresoever led,
And howsoever; were it otherwise,
And we found evil fast as we find good
In our first years, or think that it is found,
How could the innocent heart bear up and
     live!
But doubly fortunate my lot; not here
Alone, that something of a better life
Perhaps was round me than it is the privi-
     lege
Of most to move in, but that first I looked
At Man through objects that were great or
     fair;
First communed with him by their help.
     And thus
Was founded a sure safeguard and defence
Against the weight of meanness, selfish
     cares,
Coarse manners, vulgar passions, that
     beat in
On all sides from the ordinary world
In which we traffic. Starting from this
     point
I had my face turned toward the truth,
     began
With an advantage furnished by that kind
Of prepossession, without which the soul
Receives no knowledge that can bring
     forth good,
No genuine insight ever comes to her.
From the restraint of over-watchful eyes
Preserved, I moved about, year after year,
Happy, and now most thankful that my
     walk
Was guarded from too early intercourse
With the deformities of crowded life,
And those ensuing laughters and con-
     tempts,
Self-pleasing, which, if we would wish
     to think
With a due reverence on earth's rightful
     lord,
Here placed to be the inheritor of heaven,

Will not permit us; but pursue the mind,
That to devotion willingly would rise,
Into the temple and the temple's heart.

Yet deem not, Friend! that human
     kind with me
Thus early took a place pre-eminent;
Nature herself was, at this unripe time,
But secondary to my own pursuits
And animal activities, and all
Their trivial pleasures; and when these
     had drooped
And gradually expired, and Nature,
     prized
For her own sake, became my joy, even
     then —
And upwards through late youth, until
     not less
Than two and twenty summers had been
     told —
Was Man in my affections and regards
Subordinate to her, her visible forms
And viewless agencies: a passion, she,
A rapture often, and immediate love
Ever at hand; he, only a delight
Occasional, an accidental grace,
His hour being not yet come. Far less
     had then
The inferior creatures, beast or bird,
     attuned
My spirit to that gentleness of love
(Though they had long been carefully
     observed),
Won from me those minute obeisances
Of tenderness, which I may number now
With my first blessings. Nevertheless,
     on these
The light of beauty did not fall in vain,
Or grandeur circumfuse them to no end.

But when that first poetic faculty
Of plain Imagination and severe,
No longer a mute influence of the soul,
Ventured, at some rash Muse's earnest
     call,
To try her strength among harmonious
     words;
And to book-notions and the rules of art
Did knowingly conform itself; there came
Among the simple shapes of human life
A wilfulness of fancy and conceit;
And Nature and her objects beautified

These fictions, as in some sort, in their
    turn,
They burnished her.   From touch of
    this new power
Nothing was safe: the elder-tree that grew
Beside the well-known charnel-house had
    then
A dismal look: the yew-tree had its ghost,
That took his station there for ornament:
The dignities of plain occurrence then
Were tasteless, and truth's golden mean,
    a point
Where no sufficient pleasure could be
    found.
Then, if a widow, staggering with the
    blow   .
Of her distress, was known to have
    turned her steps
To the cold grave in which her husband
    slept,
One night, or haply more than one,
    through pain
Or half-insensate impotence of mind,
The fact was caught at greedily, and there
She must be visitant the whole year
    . through,
Wetting the turf with never-ending tears.

    Through quaint obliquities I might
        pursue
These cravings; when the foxglove, one
    by one,
Upwards through every stage of the tall
    stem,
Had shed beside the public way its bells,
And stood of all dismantled, save the last
Left at the tapering ladder's top, that
    seemed
To bend as doth a slender blade of grass
Tipped with a rain-drop, Fancy loved to
    seat,
Beneath the plant despoiled, but crested
    still
With this last relic, soon itself to fall,
Some vagrant mother, whose arch little
    ones,
All unconcerned by her dejected plight,
Laughed as with rival eagerness their
    hands
Gathered the purple cups that round
    them lay,
Strewing the turf's green slope.

                         A diamond light
(Whene'er the summer sun, declining,
    smote
A smooth rock wet with constant springs)
    was seen
Sparkling from out a copse-clad bank
    that rose
Fronting our cottage.   Oft beside the
    hearth
Seated, with open door, often and long
Upon this restless lustre have I gazed,
That made my fancy restless as itself.
'T was now for me a burnished silver
    shield
Suspended over a knight's tomb, who lay
Inglorious, buried in the dusky wood:
An entrance now into some magic cave
Or palace built by fairies of the rock;
Nor could I have been bribed to disen-
    chant
The spectacle, by visiting the spot.
Thus wilful Fancy, in no hurtful mood,
Engrafted far-fetched shapes on feelings
    bred
By pure Imagination: busy Power
She was, and with her ready pupil turned
Instinctively to human passions, then
Least understood.   Yet, 'mid the fer-
    vent swarm
Of these vagaries, with an eye so rich
As mine was through the bounty of a
    grand
And lovely region, I had forms distinct
To steady me: each airy thought revolved
Round a substantial centre, which at once
Incited it to motion, and controlled.
I did not pine like one in cities bred,
As was thy melancholy lot, dear Friend!
Great Spirit as thou art, in endless dreams
Of sickliness, disjoining, joining, things
Without the light of knowledge.   Where
    the harm,
If, when the woodman languished with
    disease
Induced by sleeping nightly on the
    ground
Within his sod-built cabin, Indian-wise,
I called the pangs of disappointed love,
And all the sad etcetera of the wrong,
To help him to his grave?   Meanwhile
    the man,
If not already from the woods retired
To die at home, was haply, as I knew,

Withering by slow degrees, 'mid gentle
    airs,
Birds, running streams, and hills so beau-
    tiful
On golden evenings, while the charcoal
    pile
Breathed up its smoke, an image of his
    ghost
Or spirit that full soon must take her
    flight.
Nor shall we not be tending towards
    that point
Of sound humanity to which our Tale
Leads, though by sinuous ways, if here
    I show
How Fancy, in a season when she wove
Those slender cords, to guide the un-
    conscious Boy
For the Man's sake, could feed at Na-
    ture's call
Some pensive musings which might well
    beseem
Maturer years.
         A grove there is whose boughs
Stretch from the western marge of
    Thurstonmere,
With length of shade so thick, that
    whoso glides
Along the line of low-roofed water, moves
As in a cloister. Once — while, in that
    shade
Loitering, I watched the golden beams
    of light
Flung from the setting sun, as they re-
    posed
In silent beauty on the naked ridge
Of a high eastern hill — thus flowed my
    thoughts
In a pure stream of words fresh from
    the heart:
[1] Dear native Regions, wheresoe'er shall
    close
My mortal course, there will I think on
    you;
Dying, will cast on you a backward look;
Even as this setting sun (albeit the Vale
Is nowhere touched by one memorial
    gleam)
Doth with the fond remains of his last
    power
Still linger, and a farewell lustre sheds,

[1] See page 19.

On the dear mountain-tops where first
    he rose.

    Enough of humble arguments; recall,
My Song ! those high emotions which thy
    voice
Has heretofore made known; that burst-
    ing forth
Of sympathy, inspiring and inspired,
When everywhere a vital pulse was felt,
And all the several frames of things, like
    stars,
Through every magnitude distinguishable,
Shone mutually indebted, or half lost
Each in the other's blaze, a galaxy
Of life and glory. In the midst stood
    Man,
Outwardly, inwardly contemplated,
As, of all visible natures, crown, though
    born
Of dust, and kindred to the worm; a
    Being,
Both in perception and discernment, first
In every capability of rapture,
Through the divine effect of power and
    love;
As, more than anything we know, instinct
With godhead, and, by reason and by will,
Acknowledging dependency sublime.

    Ere long, the lonely mountains left, I
    moved,
Begirt, from day to day, with temporal
    shapes
Of vice and folly thrust upon my view,
Objects of sport, and ridicule, and scorn,
Manners and characters discriminate,
And little bustling passions that eclipse,
As well they might, the impersonated
    thought,
The idea, or abstraction of the kind.

    An idler among academic bowers,
Such was my new condition, as at large
Has been set forth; yet here the vulgar
    light
Of present, actual, superficial life,
Gleaming through coloring of other times,
Old usages and local privilege,
Was welcomed, softened, if not solem-
    nized.
This notwithstanding, being brought more
    near

To vice and guilt, forerunning wretched-
ness,
I trembled, — thought, at times, of human
life
With an indefinite terror and dismay,
Such as the storms and angry elements
Had bred in me; but gloomier far, a dim
Analogy to uproar and misrule,
Disquiet, danger, and obscurity.

It might be told (but wherefore speak
of things
Common to all?) that, seeing, I was led
Gravely to ponder — judging between
good
And evil, not as for the mind's delight
But for her guidance — one who was to
act,
As sometimes to the best of feeble means
I did, by human sympathy impelled:
And, through dislike and most offensive
pain,
Was to the truth conducted; of this faith
Never forsaken, that, by acting well,
And understanding, I should learn to love
The end of life, and everything we know.

Grave Teacher, stern Preceptress! for
at times
Thou canst put on an aspect most severe;
London, to thee I willingly return.
Erewhile my verse played idly with the
flowers
Enwrought upon thy mantle; satisfied
With that amusement, and a simple look
Of child-like inquisition now and then
Cast upwards on thy countenance, to de-
tect
Some inner meanings which might harbor
there.
But how could I in mood so light indulge,
Keeping such fresh remembrance of the
day,
When, having thridded the long labyrinth
Of the suburban villages, I first
Entered thy vast dominion? On the roof
Of an itinerant vehicle I sate,
With vulgar men about me, trivial forms
Of houses, pavement, streets, of men
and things, —
Mean shapes on every side: but, at the
instant,
When to myself it fairly might be said,

The threshold now is overpast (how
strange
That aught external to the living mind
Should have such mighty sway! yet so
it was),
A weight of ages did at once descend
Upon my heart; no thought embodied, no
Distinct remembrances, but weight and
power, —
Power growing under weight: alas! I
feel
That I am trifling: 't was a moment's
pause, —
All that took place within me came and
went
As in a moment; yet with Time it dwells,
And grateful memory, as a thing divine.

The curious traveller, who, from open
day,
Hath passed with torches into some huge
cave,
The Grotto of Antiparos, or the Den
In old time haunted by that Danish Witch,
Yordas; he looks around and sees the
vault
Widening on all sides; sees, or thinks he
sees,
Erelong, the massy roof above his head,
That instantly unsettles and recedes, —
Substance and shadow, light and dark-
ness, all
Commingled, making up a canopy
Of shapes and forms and tendencies to
shape
That shift and vanish, change and inter-
change
Like spectres, — ferment silent and sub-
lime!
That after a short space works less and
less,
Till, every effort, every motion gone,
The scene before him stands in perfect
view
Exposed, and lifeless as a written book! —
But let him pause awhile, and look again,
And a new quickening shall succeed, at
first
Beginning timidly, then creeping fast,
Till the whole cave, so late a senseless
mass,
Busies the eye with images and forms

Boldly assembled, — here is shadowed
    forth
From the projections, wrinkles, cavities,
A variegated landscape, — there the shape
Of some gigantic warrior clad in mail,
The ghostly semblance of a hooded monk,
Veiled nun, or pilgrim resting on his staff:
Strange congregation! yet not slow to
    meet
Eyes that perceive through minds that can
    inspire.

    Even in such sort had I at first been
        moved,
Nor otherwise continued to be moved,
As I explored the vast metropolis,
Fount of my country's destiny and the
    world's;
That great emporium, chronicle at once
And burial-place of passions, and their
    home
Imperial, their chief living residence.

    With strong sensations teeming as it
        did
Of past and present, such a place must
    needs
Have pleased me, seeking knowledge at
    that time
Far less than craving power; yet knowl-
    edge came,
Sought or unsought, and influxes of power
Came, of themselves, or at her call de-
    rived
In fits of kindliest apprehensiveness,
From all sides, when whate'er was in it-
    self
Capacious found, or seemed to find, in me
A correspondent amplitude of mind;
Such is the strength and glory of our
    youth!
The human nature unto which I felt
That I belonged, and reverenced with
    love,
Was not a punctual presence, but a spirit
Diffused through time and space, with aid
    derived
Of evidence from monuments, erect,
Prostrate, or leaning towards their com-
    mon rest
In earth, the widely scattered wreck sub-
    lime

Of vanished nations, or more clearly
    drawn
From books and what they picture and
    record.

    'T is true, the history of our native
        land —
With those of Greece compared and pop-
    ular Rome,
And in our high-wrought modern narra-
    tives
Stript of their harmonizing soul, the life
Of manners and familiar incidents —
Had never much delighted me.   And less
Than other intellects had mine been used
To lean upon extrinsic circumstance
Of record or tradition; but a sense
Of what in the Great City had been done
And suffered, and was doing, suffering,
    still,
Weighed with me, could support the test
    of thought;
And, in despite of all that had gone by,
Or was departing never to return,
There I conversed with majesty and power
Like independent natures.   Hence the
    place
Was thronged with impregnations like the
    Wilds
In which my early feelings had been
    nursed —
Bare hills and valleys, full of caverns,
    rocks,
And audible seclusions, dashing lakes,
Echoes and waterfalls, and pointed crags
That into music touch the passing wind.
Here then my young imagination found
No uncongenial element; could here
Among new objects serve or give com-
    mand,
Even as the heart's occasions might re-
    quire,
To forward reason's else too-scrupulous
    march.
The effect was, still more elevated views
Of human nature.   Neither vice nor
    guilt, ·
Debasement undergone by body or mind,
Nor all the misery forced upon my sight,
Misery not lightly passed, but sometimes
    scanned
Most feelingly, could overthrow my trust
In what we *may* become; induce belief

That I was ignorant, had been falsely
taught,
A solitary, who with vain conceits
Had been inspired, and walked about in
dreams.
From those sad scenes when meditation
turned,
Lo! everything that was indeed divine
Retained its purity inviolate,
Nay brighter shone, by this portentous
gloom
Set off; such opposition as aroused
The mind of Adam, yet in Paradise
Though fallen from bliss, when in the East
he saw
[1] Darkness ere day's mid-course, and
morning light
More orient in the western cloud, that
drew
O'er the blue firmament a radiant white,
Descending slow with something heavenly
fraught.

Add also, that among the multitudes
Of that huge city, oftentimes was seen
Affectingly set forth, more than elsewhere
Is possible, the unity of man,
One spirit over ignorance and vice
Predominant, in good and evil hearts;
One sense for moral judgments, as one eye
For the sun's light. The soul when smit-
ten thus
By a sublime *idea*, whencesoe'er
Vouchsafed for union or communion,
feeds
On the pure bliss, and takes her rest with
God.

Thus from a very early age, O Friend!
My thoughts by slow gradations had been
drawn
To human-kind, and to the good and ill
Of human life: Nature had led me on;
And oft amid the "busy hum" I seemed
To travel independent of her help,
As if I had forgotten her; but no,
The world of human-kind outweighed not
hers
In my habitual thoughts; the scale of love,
Though filling daily, still was light, com-
pared
With that in which *her* mighty objects lay.

[1] From Milton, *Par. Lost*, xi. 204.

Book Ninth.

RESIDENCE IN FRANCE.

EVEN as a river, — partly (it might seem)
Yielding to old remembrances, and swayed
In part by fear to shape a way direct,
That would engulph him soon in the raven-
ous sea —
Turns, and will measure back his course,
far back,
Seeking the very regions which he crossed
In his first outset; so have we, my Friend!
Turned and returned with intricate delay.
Or as a traveller, who has gained the brow
Of some aerial Down, while there he halts
For breathing-time, is tempted to review
The region left behind him; and, if aught
Deserving notice have escaped regard,
Or been regarded with too careless eye,
Strives, from that height, with one and
yet one more
Last look, to make the best amends he
may:
So have we lingered. Now we start afresh
With courage, and new hope risen on our
toil.
Fair greetings to this shapeless eagerness,
Whene'er it comes! needful in work so
long,
Thrice needful to the argument which now
Awaits us! Oh, how much unlike the
past!

Free as a colt at pasture on the hill,
I ranged at large, through London's wide
domain,
Month after month. Obscurely did I live,
Not seeking frequent intercourse with men,
By literature, or elegance, or rank,
Distinguished. Scarcely was a year thus
spent
Ere I forsook the crowded solitude,
With less regret for its luxurious pomp,
And all the nicely-guarded shows of art,
Than for the humble book-stalls in the
streets,
Exposed to eye and hand where'er I
turned.

France lured me forth; the realm that
I had crossed
So lately, journeying toward the snow-
clad Alps.

But now, relinquishing the scrip and staff,
And all enjoyment which the summer sun
Sheds round the steps of those who meet
    the day
With motion constant as his own, I went
Prepared to sojourn in a pleasant town,
Washed by the current of the stately Loire.

    Through Paris lay my readiest course,
    and there
Sojourning a few days, I visited
In haste, each spot of old or recent fame,
The latter chiefly; from the field of Mars
Down to the suburbs of St. Antony,
And from Mont Martre southward to the
    Dome
Of Geneviève.   In both her clamorous
    Halls,
The National Synod and the Jacobins,
I saw the Revolutionary Power
Toss like a ship at anchor, rocked by
    storms;
The Arcades I traversed, in the Palace
    huge
Of Orleans; coasted round and round the
    line
Of Tavern, Brothel, Gaming-house, and
    Shop,
Great rendezvous of worst and best, the
    walk
Of all who had a purpose, or had not;
I stared and listened, with a stranger's
    ears,
To Hawkers and Haranguers, hubbub
    wild!
And hissing Factionists with ardent eyes,
In knots, or pairs, or single.   Not a look
Hope takes, or Doubt or Fear is forced to
    wear,
But seemed there present; and I scanned
    them all,
Watched every gesture uncontrollable,
Of anger, and vexation, and despite,
All side by side, and struggling face to
    face,
With gayety and dissolute idleness.

    Where silent zephyrs sported with the
    dust
Of the Bastille, I sate in the open sun,
And from the rubbish gathered up a stone,
And pocketed the relic, in the guise
Of an enthusiast; yet, in honest truth,

I looked for something that I could not
    find,
Affecting more emotion than I felt;
For 't is most certain, that these various
    sights,
However potent their first shock, with me
Appeared to recompense the traveller's
    pains
Less than the painted Magdalene of Le
    Brun,
A beauty exquisitely wrought, with hair
Dishevelled, gleaming eyes, and rueful
    cheek
Pale and bedropped with overflowing
    tears.

    But hence to my more permanent abode
I hasten; there, by novelties in speech,
Domestic manners, customs, gestures,
    looks,
And all the attire of ordinary life,
Attention was engrossed; and, thus
    amused,
I stood 'mid those concussions, uncon-
    cerned,
Tranquil almost, and careless as a flower
Glassed in a green-house, or a parlor
    shrub
That spreads its leaves in unmolested
    peace,
While every bush and tree, the country
    through,
Is shaking to the roots: indifference this
Which may seem strange: but I was un-
    prepared
With needful knowledge, had abruptly
    passed
Into a theatre, whose stage was filled
And busy with an action far advanced.
Like others, I had skimmed, and some-
    times read
With care, the master pamphlets of the
    day;
Nor wanted such half-insight as grew wild
Upon that meagre soil, helped out by talk
And public news; but having never seen
A chronicle that might suffice to show
Whence the main organs of the public
    power
Had sprung, their transmigrations, when
    and how
Accomplished, giving thus unto events
A form and body; all things were to me

Loose and disjointed, and the affections
  left
Without a vital interest. At that time,
Moreover, the first storm was overblown,
And the strong hand of outward violence
Locked up in quiet. For myself, I fear
Now, in connection with so great a theme,
To speak (as I must be compelled to do)
Of one so unimportant; night by night
Did I frequent the formal haunts of men,
Whom, in the city, privilege of birth
Sequestered from the rest, societies
Polished in arts, and in punctilio versed;
Whence, and from deeper causes, all dis-
  course
Of good and evil of the time was shunned
With scrupulous care; but these restric-
  tions soon
Proved tedious, and I gradually withdrew
Into a noisier world, and thus ere long
Became a patriot; and my heart was all
Given to the people, and my love was
  theirs.

  A band of military Officers,
Then stationed in the city, were the chief
Of my associates: some of these wore
  swords
That had been seasoned in the wars, and
  all
Were men well-born; the chivalry of
  France.
In age and temper differing, they had yet
One spirit ruling in each heart; alike
(Save only one, hereafter to be named)
Were bent upon undoing what was done:
This was their rest and only hope; there-
  with
No fear had they of bad becoming worse,
For worst to them was come; nor would
  have stirred,
Or deemed it worth a moment's thought
  to stir,
In anything, save only as the act
Looked thitherward. One, reckoning by
  years,
Was in the prime of manhood, and ere-
  while
He had sate lord in many tender hearts;
Though heedless of such honors now, and
  changed:
His temper was quite mastered by the
  times,

And they had blighted him, had eaten
  away
The beauty of his person, doing wrong
Alike to body and to mind: his port,
Which once had been erect and open, now
Was stooping and contracted, and a face,
Endowed by Nature with her fairest gifts
Of symmetry and light and bloom, ex-
  pressed,
As much as any that was ever seen,
A ravage out of season, made by thoughts
Unhealthy and vexatious. With the hour,
That from the press of Paris duly brought
Its freight of public news, the fever came,
A punctual visitant, to shake this man,
Disarmed his voice and fanned his yellow
  cheek
Into a thousand colors; while he read,
Or mused, his sword was haunted by his
  touch
Continually, like an uneasy place
In his own body. 'T was in truth an hour
Of universal ferment; mildest men
Were agitated; and commotions, strife
Of passion and opinion, filled the walls
Of peaceful houses with unquiet sounds.
The soil of common life was, at that time,
Too hot to tread upon. Oft said I then,
And not then only, "What a mockery this
Of history, the past and that to come!
Now do I feel how all men are deceived,
Reading of nations and their works, in
  faith,
Faith given to vanity and emptiness;
Oh! laughter for the page that would
  reflect
To future times the face of what now is!"
The land all swarmed with passion, like a
  plain
Devoured by locusts, — Carra, Gorsas, —
  add
A hundred other names, forgotten now,
Nor to be heard of more; yet, they were
  powers,
Like earthquakes, shocks repeated day by
  day,
And felt through every nook of town and
  field.

  Such was the state of things. Mean-
  while the chief
Of my associates stood prepared for flight
To augment the band of emigrants in arms

Upon the borders of the Rhine, and
  leagued
With foreign foes mustered for instant war.
This was their undisguised intent, and
  they
Were waiting with the whole of their
  desires
The moment to depart.
                    An Englishman,
Born in a land whose very name appeared
To license some unruliness of mind;
A stranger, with youth's further privilege,
And the indulgence that a half-learnt
  speech
Wins from the courteous; I, who had
  been else
Shunned and not tolerated, freely lived
With these defenders of the Crown, and
  talked,   .
And heard their notions; nor did they dis-
  dain
The wish to bring me over to their cause.

  But though untaught by thinking or by
    books
To reason well of polity or law,
And nice distinctions, then on every
  tongue,
Of natural rights and civil; and to acts
Of nations and their passing interests
(If with unworldly ends and aims com-
  pared),
Almost indifferent, even the historian's
  tale
Prizing but little otherwise than I prized
Tales of the poets, as it made the heart
Beat high, and filled the fancy with fair
  forms,
Old heroes and their sufferings and their
  deeds;
Yet in the regal sceptre, and the pomp
Of orders and degrees, I nothing found
Then, or had ever, even in crudest youth,
That dazzled me, but rather what I
  mourned
And ill could brook, beholding that the
  best   .
Ruled not, and feeling that they ought to
  rule.

  For, born in a poor district, and which
    yet
Retaineth more of ancient homeliness,

Than any other nook of English ground,
It was my fortune scarcely to have seen,
Through the whole tenor of my school-
  day time,
The face of one, who, whether boy or
  man,
Was vested with attention or respect
Through claims of wealth or blood; nor
  was it least
Of many benefits, in later years
Derived from academic institutes
And rules, that they held something up to
  view
Of a Republic, where all stood thus far
Upon equal ground; that we were broth-
  ers all
In honor, as in one community,
Scholars and gentlemen; where, further-
  more,
Distinction open lay to all that came,
And wealth and titles were in less esteem
Than talents, worth, and prosperous in-
  dustry.
Add unto this, subservience from the first
To presences of God's mysterious power
Made manifest in Nature's sovereignty,
And fellowship with venerable books,·
To sanction the proud workings of the
  soul,
And mountain liberty. It could not be
But that one tutored thus should look with
  awe
Upon the faculties of man, receive
Gladly the highest promises, and hail,
As best, the government of equal rights
And individual worth. And hence, O
  Friend !
If at the first great outbreak I rejoiced
Less than might well befit my youth, the
  cause
In part lay here, that unto me the events
Seemed nothing out of nature's certain
  course,
A gift that was come rather late than soon.
No wonder, then, if advocates like these,
Inflamed by passion, blind with prejudice,
And stung with injury, at this riper day,
Were impotent to make my hopes put on
The shape of theirs, my understanding
  bend
In honor to their honor: zeal, which yet
Had slumbered, now in opposition burst
Forth like a Polar summer: every word

They uttered was a dart, by counter-winds
Blown back upon themselves; their rea-
son seemed
Confusion-stricken by a higher power
Than human understanding, their dis-
course
Maimed, spiritless; and, in their weak-
ness strong,
I triumphed.
　　　　Meantime, day by day, the roads
Were crowded with the bravest youth of
France,
And all the promptest of her spirits, linked
In gallant soldiership, and posting on
To meet the war upon her frontier bounds.
Yet at this very moment do tears start
Into mine eyes: I do not say I weep —
I wept not then, — but tears have dimmed
my sight,
In memory of the farewells of that time,
Domestic severings, female fortitude
At dearest separation, patriot love
And self-devotion, and terrestrial hope,
Encouraged with a martyr's confidence;
Even files of strangers merely seen but
once,
And for a moment, men from far with
sound
Of music, martial tunes, and banners
spread,
Entering the city, here and there a face,
Or person, singled out among the rest,
Yet still a stranger and beloved as such;
Even by these passing spectacles my heart
Was oftentimes uplifted, and they seemed
Arguments sent from Heaven to prove
the cause
Good, pure, which no one could stand
up against,
Who was not lost, abandoned, selfish,
proud,
Mean, miserable, wilfully depraved,
Hater perverse of equity and truth.

Among that band of Officers was one,
Already hinted at, of other mould —
A patriot, thence rejected by the rest,
And with an oriental loathing spurned,
As of a different caste. A meeker man
Than this lived never, nor a more benign,
Meek though enthusiastic. Injuries
Made *him* more gracious, and his nature
then

Did breathe its sweetness out most sen-
sibly,
As aromatic flowers on Alpine turf,
When foot hath crushed them. He
through the events
Of that great change wandered in per-
fect faith,
As through a book, an old romance, or
tale
Of Fairy, or some dream of actions
wrought
Behind the summer clouds. By birth he
ranked
With the most noble, but unto the poor
Among mankind he was in service bound,
As by some tie invisible, oaths professed
To a religious order. Man he loved
As man; and, to the mean and the obscure,
And all the homely in their homely works,
Transferred a courtesy which had no air
Of condescension; but did rather seem
A passion and a gallantry, like that
Which he, a soldier, in his idler day
Had paid to woman: somewhat vain he
was,
Or seemed so, yet it was not vanity,
But fondness, and a kind of radiant joy
Diffused around him, while he was intent
On works of love or freedom, or revolved
Complacently the progress of a cause,
Whereof he was a part: yet this was meek
And placid, and took nothing from the
man
That was delightful. Oft in solitude
With him did I discourse about the end
Of civil government, and its wisest forms;
Of ancient loyalty, and chartered rights,
Custom and habit, novelty and change;
Of self-respect, and virtue in the few
For patrimonial honor set apart,
And ignorance in the laboring multitude.
For he, to all intolerance indisposed,
Balanced these contemplations in his
mind;
And I, who at that time was scarcely
dipped
Into the turmoil, bore a sounder judgment
Than later days allowed; carried about me,
With less alloy to its integrity,
The experience of past ages, as, through
help
Of books and common life, it makes sure
way

To youthful minds, by objects over near
Not pressed upon, nor dazzled or misled
By struggling with the crowd for present
ends.

But though not deaf, nor obstinate to
find
Error without excuse upon the side
Of them who strove against us, more
delight
We took, and let this freely be confessed,
In painting to ourselves the miseries
Of royal courts, and that voluptuous life
Unfeeling, where the man who is of soul
The meanest thrives the most; where
dignity,
True personal dignity, abideth not;
A light, a cruel, and vain world cut off
From the natural inlets of just sentiment,
From lowly sympathy and chastening
truth;
Where good and evil interchange their
names,
And thirst for bloody spoils abroad is
paired
With vice at home. We added dearest
themes —
Man and his noble nature, as it is
The gift which God has placed within
his power,
His blind desires and steady faculties
Capable of clear truth, the one to break
Bondage, the other to build liberty
On firm foundations, making social life,
Through knowledge spreading and im-
perishable,
As just in regulation, and as pure
As individual in the wise and good.

We summoned up the honorable deeds
Of ancient Story, thought of each bright
spot,
That would be found in all recorded time,
Of truth preserved and error passed away;
Of single spirits that catch the flame
from Heaven,
And how the multitudes of men will feed
And fan each other; thought of sects,
how keen
They are to put the appropriate nature on,
Triumphant over every obstacle
Of custom, language, country, love, or
hate.

And what they do and suffer for their
creed;
How far they travel, and how long
endure;
How quickly mighty Nations have been
formed,
From least beginnings; how, together
locked
By new opinions, scattered tribes have
made
One body, spreading wide as clouds in
heaven.
To aspirations then of our own minds
Did we appeal; and, finally, beheld
A living confirmation of the whole
Before us, in a people from the depth
Of shameful imbecility uprisen,
Fresh as the morning star. Elate we
looked
Upon their virtues; saw, in rudest men,
Self-sacrifice the firmest; generous love,
And continence of mind, and sense of
right,
Uppermost in the midst of fiercest strife.

Oh, sweet it is, in academic groves,
Or such retirement, Friend! as we have
known
In the green dales beside our Rotha's
stream,
Greta, or Derwent, or some nameless rill,
To ruminate, with interchange of talk,
On rational liberty, and hope in man,
Justice and peace. But far more sweet
such toil —
Toil, say I, for it leads to thoughts
abstruse —
If nature then be standing on the brink
Of some great trial, and we hear the voice
Of one devoted,—one whom circumstance
Hath called upon to embody his deep sense
In action, give it outwardly a shape,
And that of benediction, to the world.
Then doubt is not, and truth is more than
truth, —
A hope it is, and a desire; a creed
Of zeal, by an authority Divine
Sanctioned, of danger, difficulty, or death.
Such conversation, under Attic shades,
Did Dion hold with Plato; ripened thus
For a Deliverer's glorious task, — and
such
He, on that ministry already bound,

Held with Eudemus and Timonides,
Surrounded by adventurers in arms,
When those two vessels with their daring
    freight,
For the Sicilian Tyrant's overthrow,
Sailed from Zacynthus, — philosophic
    war,
Led by Philosophers. With harder fate,
Though like ambition, such was he, O
    Friend!
Of whom I speak. So Beaupuis (let the
    name
Stand near the worthiest of Antiquity)
Fashioned his life; and many a long dis-
    course,
With like persuasion honored, we main-
    tained:
He, on his part, accoutred for the worst,
He perished fighting, in supreme com-
    mand,
Upon the borders of the unhappy Loire,
For liberty, against deluded men,
His fellow-countrymen; and yet most
    blessed
In this, that he the fate of later times
Lived not to see, nor what we now
    behold,
Who have as ardent hearts as he had then.

Along that very Loire, with festal mirth
Resounding at all hours, and innocent yet
Of civil slaughter, was our frequent walk;
Or in wide forests of continuous shade,
Lofty and over-arched, with open space
Beneath the trees, clear footing many a
    mile —
A solemn region. Oft amid those haunts,
From earnest dialogues I slipped in
    thought,
And let remembrance steal to other times,
When, o'er those interwoven roots, moss-
    clad,
And smooth as marble or a waveless sea,
Some Hermit, from his cell forth-strayed,
    might pace
In sylvan meditation undisturbed;
As on the pavement of a Gothic church
Walks a lone Monk, when service hath
    expired,
In peace and silence. But if e'er was
    heard, —
Heard, though unseen, — a devious trav-
    eller,

Retiring or approaching from afar
With speed and echoes loud of trampling
    hoofs
From the hard floor reverberated, then
It was Angelica thundering through the
    woods
Upon her palfrey, or that gentle maid
Erminia, fugitive as fair as she.
Sometimes methought I saw a pair of
    knights
Joust underneath the trees, that as in storm
Rocked high above their heads; anon, the
    din
Of boisterous merriment, and music's roar,
In sudden proclamation, burst from haunt
Of Satyrs in some viewless glade, with
    dance
Rejoicing o'er a female in the midst,
A mortal beauty, their unhappy thrall.
The width of those huge forests, unto me
A novel scene, did often in this way
Master my fancy while I wandered on
With that revered companion. And some-
    times —
When to a convent in a meadow green,
By a brook-side, we came, a roofless pile,
And not by reverential touch of Time
Dismantled, but by violence abrupt —
In spite of those heart-bracing colloquies,
In spite of real fervor, and of that
Less genuine and wrought up within
    myself —
I could not but bewail a wrong so harsh,
And for the Matin-bell to sound no more
Grieved, and the twilight taper, and the
    cross
High on the topmost pinnacle, a sign
(How welcome to the weary traveller's
    eyes!)
Of hospitality and peaceful rest.
And when the partner of those varied
    walks
Pointed upon occasion to the site
Of Romorentin, home of ancient kings,
To the imperial edifice of Blois,
Or to that rural castle, name now slipped
From my remembrance, where a lady
    lodged,
By the first Francis wooed, and bound to
    him
In chains of mutual passion, from the
    tower,
As a tradition of the country tells,

Practised to commune with her royal
    knight
By cressets and love-beacons, intercourse
'Twixt her high-seated residence and his
Far off at Chambord on the plain beneath;
Even here, though less than with the
    peaceful house
Religious,'mid these frequent monuments
Of Kings,their vices and their better deeds,
Imagination, potent to inflame
At times with virtuous wrath and noble
    scorn,
Did also often mitigate the force
Of civic prejudice, the bigotry,
So call it, of a youthful patriot's mind;
And on these spots with many gleams I
    looked
Of chivalrous delight.   Yet not the less,
Hatred of absolute rule, where will of one
Is law for all, and of that barren pride
In them who, by immunities unjust,
Between the sovereign and the people
    stand,
His helper and not theirs, laid stronger
    hold
Daily upon me, mixed with pity too
And love; for where hope is, there love
    will be
For the abject multitude.   And when we
    chanced
One day to meet a hunger-bitten girl,
Who crept along fitting her languid gait
Unto a heifer's motion, by a cord
Tied to her arm, and picking thus from
    the lane
Its sustenance, while the girl with pallid
    hands
Was busy knitting in a heartless mood
Of solitude, and at the sight my friend
In agitation said, " 'T is against *that*
That we are fighting," I with him believed
That a benignant spirit was abroad
Which might not be withstood, that
    poverty
Abject as this would in a little time
Be found no more, that we should see the
    earth
Unthwarted in her wish to recompense
The meek, the lowly, patient child of toil,
All institutes forever blotted out
That legalized exclusion, empty pomp
Abolished, sensual state and cruel power
Whether by edict of the one or few;

And finally, as sum and crown of all,
Should see the people having a strong
    hand
In framing their own laws; whence better
    days
To all mankind.   But, these things set
    apart,
Was not this single confidence enough
To animate the mind that ever turned
A thought to human welfare?   That hence-
    forth
Captivity by mandate without law
Should cease; and open accusation lead
To sentence in the hearing of the world,
And open punishment, if not the air
Be free to breathe in, and the heart of man
Dread nothing.   From this height I shall
    not stoop
To humbler matter that detained us oft
In thought or conversation, public acts,
And public persons,and emotions wrought
Within the breast, as ever-varying winds
Of record or report swept over us;
But I might here, instead, repeat a tale,[1]
Told by my Patriot friend, of sad events,
That prove to what low depth had struck
    the roots,
How widely spread the boughs, of that
    old tree
Which, as a deadly mischief, and a foul
And black dishonor, France was weary of.

Oh,happy time of youthful lovers (thus
The story might begin), oh, balmy time,
In which a love-knot, on a lady's brow,
Is fairer than the fairest star in Heaven!
So might—and with that prelude *did* begin
The record; and, in faithful verse, was
    given
The doleful sequel.
                    But our little bark
On a strong river boldly hath been
    launched;
And from the driving current should we
    turn
To loiter wilfully within a creek,
Howe'er attractive, Fellow voyager!
Would'st thou not chide?   Yet deem not
    my pains lost:
For Vaudracour and Julia (so were named
The ill-fated pair) in that plain tale will
    draw

[1] See " Vaudracour and Julia," p. 253.

Tears from the hearts of others, when
    their own
Shall beat no more. Thou, also, there
    may'st read,
At leisure, how the enamoured youth was
    driven,
By public power abased, to fatal crime,
Nature's rebellion against monstrous law;
How, between heart and heart, oppression
    thrust
Her mandates, severing whom true love
    had joined,
Harassing both; until he sank and pressed
The couch his fate had made for him;
    supine,
Save when the stings of viperous remorse,
Trying their strength, enforced him to
    start up,
Aghast and prayerless. Into a deep wood
He fled, to shun the haunts of human kind;
There dwelt, weakened in spirit more and
    more;
Nor could the voice of Freedom, which
    through France
Full speedily resounded, public hope,
Or personal memory of his own worst
    wrongs,
Rouse him; but, hidden in those gloomy
    shades,
His days he wasted, — an imbecile mind.

BOOK TENTH.

RESIDENCE IN FRANCE (*continued*).

IT was a beautiful and silent day
That overspread the countenance of earth,
Then fading with unusual quietness. —
A day as beautiful as e'er was given
To soothe regret, though deepening what
    it soothed,
When by the gliding Loire I paused, and
    cast
Upon his rich domains, vineyard and tilth,
Green meadow-ground, and many-colored
    woods,
Again, and yet again, a farewell look;
Then from the quiet of that scene passed
    on,
Bound to the fierce Metropolis. From his
    throne

The King had fallen, and that invading
    host —
Presumptuous cloud, on whose black front
    was written
The tender mercies of the dismal wind
That bore it — on the plains of Liberty
Had burst innocuous. Say in bolder
    words,
They — who had come elate as eastern
    hunters
Banded beneath the Great Mogul, when he
Erewhile went forth from Agra or Lahore,
Rajahs and Omrahs in his train, intent
To drive their prey enclosed within a ring
Wide as a province, but, the signal given,
Before the point of the life-threatening
    spear
Narrowing itself by moments — they, rash
    men,
Had seen the anticipated quarry turned
Into avengers, from whose wrath they fled
In terror. Disappointment and dismay
Remained for all whose fancies had run
    wild
With evil expectations; confidence
And perfect triumph for the better cause.

    The State — as if to stamp the final
        seal
On her security, and to the world
Show what she was, a high and fearless
    soul,
Exulting in defiance, or heart-stung
By sharp resentment, or belike to taunt
With spiteful gratitude the baffled League,
That had stirred up her slackening facul-
    ties
To a new transition — when the King was
    crushed,
Spared not the empty throne, and in
    proud haste
Assumed the body and venerable name
Of a Republic. Lamentable crimes,
'T is true, had gone before this hour, dire
    work
Of massacre, in which the senseless sword
Was prayed to as a judge; but these were
    past,
Earth free from them forever, as was
    thought, —
Ephemeral monsters, to be seen but once!
Things that could only show themselves
    and die.

Cheered with this hope, to Paris I re-
    turned,
And ranged, with ardor heretofore unfelt,
The spacious city, and in progress passed
The prison where the unhappy Monarch
    lay,
Associate with his children and his wife
In bondage; and the palace, lately stormed
With roar of cannon by a furious host.
I crossed the square (an empty area
    then!)
Of the Carrousel, where so late had lain
The dead, upon the dying heaped, and
    gazed
On this and other spots, as doth a man
Upon a volume whose contents he knows
Are memorable, but from him locked up,
Being written in a tongue he cannot read,
So that he questions the mute leaves with
    pain,
And half upbraids their silence.   But that
    night
I felt most deeply in what world I was,
What ground I trod on, and what air I
    breathed.
High was my room and lonely, near the
    roof
Of a large mansion or hôtel, a lodge
That would have pleased me in more quiet
    times;
Nor was it wholly without pleasure then.
With unextinguished taper I kept watch,
Reading at intervals; the fear gone by
Pressed on me almost like a fear to come.
I thought of those September massacres,
Divided from me by one little month,
Saw them and touched: the rest was con-
    jured up
From tragic fictions or true history,
Remembrances and dim admonishments.
The horse is taught his manage, and no star
Of wildest course but treads back his own
    steps;
For the spent hurricane the air provides
As fierce a successor; the tide retreats
But to return out of its hiding-place
In the great deep; all things have second
    birth;
The earthquake is not satisfied at once;
And in this way I wrought upon myself,
Until I seemed to hear a voice that cried,
To the whole city, " Sleep no more."
    The trance

Fled with the voice to which it had given
    birth;
But vainly comments of a calmer mind
Promised soft peace and sweet forgetful-
    ness.
The place, all hushed and silent as it was,
Appeared unfit for the repose of night,
Defenceless as a wood where tigers roam.

With early morning towards the Palace-
    walk
Of Orleans eagerly I turned: as yet
The streets were still; not so those long
    Arcades;
There, ' mid a peal of ill-matched sounds
    and cries,
That greeted me on entering, I could hear
Shrill voices from the hawkers in the
    throng,
Bawling, " Denunciation of the Crimes
Of Maximilian Robespierre; " the hand,
Prompt as the voice, held forth a printed
    speech,
The same that had been recently pro-
    nounced,
When Robespierre, not ignorant for what
    mark
Some words of indirect reproof had been
Intended, rose in hardihood, and dared
The man who had an ill surmise of him
To bring his charge in openness; whereat,
When a dead pause ensued, and no one
    stirred,
In silence of all present, from his seat
Louvet walked single through the avenue,
And took his station in the Tribune, say-
    ing,
" I, Robespierre, accuse thee! " Well is
    known
The inglorious issue of that charge, and
    how
He, who had launched the startling
    thunderbolt,
The one bold man, whose voice the attack
    had sounded,
Was left without a follower to discharge
His perilous duty, and retire lamenting
That Heaven's best aid is wasted upon
    men
Who to themselves are false.
                    But these are things
Of which I speak, only as they were storm
Or sunshine to my individual mind,

No further. Let me then relate that
    now —
In some sórt seeing with my proper eyes
That Liberty, and Life, and Death, would
    soon
To the remotest corners of the land
Lie in the arbitrement of those who ruled
The capital City; what was struggled for,
And by what combatants victory must be
    won;
The indecision on their part whose aim
Seemed best, and the straightforward path
    of those
Who in attack or in defence were strong
Through their impiety — my inmost soul
Was agitated; yea, I could almost
Have prayed that throughout earth upon
    all men,
By patient exercise of reason made
Worthy of liberty, all spirits filled
With zeal expanding in Truth's holy light,
The gift of tongues might fall, and power
    arrive
From the four quarters of the winds to do
For France, what without help she could
    not do,
A work of honor; think not that to this
I added, work of safety: from all doubt
Or trepidation for the end of things
Far was I, far as angels are from guilt.

Yet did I grieve, nor only grieved, but
    thought
Of opposition and of remedies:
An insignificant stranger and obscure,
And one, moreover, little graced with
    power
Of eloquence even in my native speech,
And all unfit for tumult or intrigue,
Yet would I at this time with willing heart
Have undertaken for a cause so great
Service however dangerous. I revolved,
How much the destiny of Man had still
Hung upon single persons; that there was,
Transcendent to all local patrimony,
One nature, as there is one sun in heaven;
That objects, even as they are great, there-
    by
Do come within the reach of humblest
    eyes;
That Man is only weak through his mis-
    trust
And want of hope where evidence divine

Proclaims to him that hope should be most
    sure;
Nor did the inexperience of my youth
Preclude conviction, that a spirit strong
In hope, and trained to noble aspirations,
A spirit thoroughly faithful to itself,
Is for Society's unreasoning herd
A domineering instinct, serves at once
For way and guide, a fluent receptacle
That gathers up each petty straggling rill
And vein of water, glad to be rolled on
In safe obedience; that a mind, whose rest
Is where it ought to be, in self-restraint,
In circumspection and simplicity,
Falls rarely in entire discomfiture
Below its aim, or meets with, from with-
    out,
A treachery that foils it or defeats;
And, lastly, if the means on human will,
Frail human will, dependent should betray
Him who too boldly trusted them, I felt
That 'mid the loud distractions of the
    world
A sovereign voice subsists within the soul,
Arbiter undisturbed of right and wrong,
Of life and death, in majesty severe
Enjoining, as may best promote the aims
Of truth and justice, either sacrifice,
From whatsoever region of our cares
Or our infirm affections Nature pleads,
Earnest and blind, against the stern
    decree.

On the other side, I called to mind
    those truths
That are the commonplaces of the
    schools —
(A theme for boys, too hackneyed for
    their sires,)
Yet, with a revelation's liveliness,
In all their comprehensive bearings known
And visible to philosophers of old,
Men who, to business of the world un-
    trained,
Lived in the shade; and to Harmodius
    known
And his compeer Aristogiton, known
To Brutus — that tyrannic power is weak,
Hath neither gratitude, nor faith, nor love,
Nor the support of good or evil men
To trust in; that the godhead which is ours
Can never utterly be charmed or stilled;
That nothing hath a natural right to last

But equity and reason; that all else
Meets foes irreconcilable, and at best
Lives only by variety of disease.

Well might my wishes be intense, my
    thoughts
Strong and perturbed, not doubting at
    that time
But that the virtue of one paramount mind
Would have abashed those impious crests
    — have quelled
Outrage and bloody power, and — in
    despite
Of what the People long had been and
    were
Through ignorance and false teaching,
    sadder proof
Of immaturity, and — in the teeth
Of desperate opposition from without —
Have cleared a passage for just govern-
    ment,
And left a solid birthright to the State,
Redeemed, according to example given
By ancient lawgivers.
                    In this frame of mind,
Dragged by a chain of harsh necessity,
So seemed it, — now I thankfully
    acknowledge,
Forced by the gracious providence of
    Heaven, —
To England I returned, else (though
    assured
That I, both was and must be of small
    weight,
No better than a landsman on the deck
Of a ship struggling with a hideous storm)
Doubtless, I should have then made
    common cause
With some who perished; haply perished
    too,
A poor mistaken and bewildered offer-
    ing, —
Should to the breast of Nature have
    gone back,
With all my resolutions, all my hopes,
A Poet only to myself, to men
Useless, and even, beloved Friend ! a soul
To thee unknown !
                    Twice had the trees let fall
Their leaves, as often Winter had put on
His hoary crown, since I had seen the
    surge

Beat against Albion's shore, since ear of
    mine
Had caught the accents of my native
    speech
Upon our native country's sacred ground.
A patriot of the world, how could I glide
Into communion with her sylvan shades,
Erewhile my tuneful haunt ? It pleased
    me more
To abide in the great City, where I found
The general air still busy with the stir
Of that first memorable onset made
By a strong levy of humanity
Upon the traffickers in Negro blood;
Effort which, though defeated, had re-
    called
To notice old forgotten principles,
And through the nation spread a novel
    heat
Of virtuous feeling.   For myself, I own
That this particular strife had wanted
    power
To rivet my affections; nor did now
Its unsuccessful issue much excite
My sorrow; for I brought with me the
    faith
That, if France prospered, good men
    would not long
Pay fruitless worship to humanity,
And this most rotten branch of human
    shame,
Object, so seemed it, of superfluous pains
Would fall together with its parent tree.
What, then, were my emotions, when in
    arms
Britain put forth her free-born strength
    in league,
Oh, pity and shame ! with those confed-
    erate Powers !
Not in my single self alone I found,
But in the minds of all ingenuous youth,
Change and subversion from that hour.
    No shock
Given to my moral nature had I known
Down to that very moment; neither lapse
Nor turn of sentiment that might be named
A revolution, save at this one time;
All else was progress on the self-same path
On which, with a diversity of pace,
I had been travelling : this a stride at once
Into another region.   As a light
And pliant harebell, swinging in the
    breeze

On some gray rock — its birthplace —
so had I
Wantoned, fast rooted on the ancient
tower
Of my beloved country, wishing not
A happier fortune than to wither there:
Now was I from that pleasant station torn
And tossed about in whirlwind. I re-
joiced,
Yea, afterwards — truth most painful to
record! —
Exulted, in the triumph of my soul,
When Englishmen by thousands were
o'erthrown,
Left without glory on the field, or driven,
Brave hearts! to shameful flight. It was
a grief, —
Grief call it not, 'twas anything but
that, —
A conflict of sensations without name,
Of which *he* only, who may love the
sight
Of a village steeple, as I do, can judge,
When, in the congregation bending all
To their great Father, prayers were
offered up,
Or praises for our country's victories;
And, 'mid the simple worshippers, per-
chance
I only, like an uninvited guest
Whom no one owned, sate silent, shall
I add,
Fed on the day of vengeance yet to come.

Oh! much have they to account for,
who could tear,
By violence, at one decisive rent,
From the best youth in England their
dear pride,
Their joy, in England; this, too, at a time
In which worst losses easily might wean
The best of names, when patriotic love
Did of itself in modesty give way,
Like the Precursor when the Deity
Is come Whose harbinger he was; a time
In which apostasy from ancient faith
Seemed but conversion to a higher creed;
Withal a season dangerous and wild,
A time when sage Experience would have
snatched
Flowers out of any hedge-row to compose
A chaplet in contempt of his gray locks.

When the proud fleet that bears the
red-cross flag
In that unworthy service was prepared
To mingle, I beheld the vessels lie,
A brood of gallant creatures, on the deep;
I saw them in their rest, a sojourner
Through a whole month of calm and
glassy days
In that delightful island which protects
Their place of convocation — there I
heard,
Each evening, pacing by the still sea-
shore,
A monitory sound that never failed, —
The sunset cannon. While the orb went
down
In the tranquillity of nature, came
That voice, ill requiem! seldom heard by
me
Without a spirit overcast by dark
Imaginations, sense of woes to come,
Sorrow for human kind, and pain of
heart.

In France, the men, who, for their
desperate ends,
Had plucked up mercy by the roots, were
glad
Of this new enemy. Tyrants, strong be-
fore
In wicked pleas, were strong as demons
now;
And thus, on every side beset with foes,
The goaded land waxed mad; the crimes
of few
Spread into madness of the many; blasts
From hell came sanctified like airs from
heaven.
The sternness of the just, the faith of those
Who doubted not that Providence had
times
Of vengeful retribution, theirs who
throned
The human Understanding paramount
And made of that their God, the hopes
of men
Who were content to barter short-lived
pangs
For a paradise of ages, the blind rage
Of insolent tempers, the light vanity
Of intermeddlers, steady purposes
Of the suspicious, slips of the indiscreet,

And all the accidents of life — were
    pressed
Into one service, busy with one work.
The Senate stood aghast, her prudence
    quenched,
Her wisdom stifled, and her justice scared,
Her frenzy only active to extol
Past outrages, and shape the way for new,
Which no one dared to oppose or mitigate.

    Domestic carnage now filled the whole
      year
With feast-days; old men from the chim-
    ney-nook,
The maiden from the bosom of her love,
The mother from the cradle of her babe,
The warrior from the field — all perished,
    all —
Friends, enemies, of all parties, ages,
    ranks,
Head after head, and never heads enough
For those that bade them fall. They
    found their joy,
They made it proudly, eager as a child,
(If like desires of innocent little ones
May with such heinous appetites be com-
    pared),
Pleased in some open field to exercise
A toy that mimics with revolving wings
The motion of a wind-mill; though the air
Do of itself blow fresh, and make the vanes
Spin in his eyesight, *that* contents him not,
But with the plaything at arm's length,
    he sets
His front against the blast, and runs
    amain,
That it may whirl the faster.
                Amid the depth
Of those enormities, even thinking minds
Forgot, at seasons, whence they had their
    being
Forgot that such a sound was ever heard
As Liberty upon earth: yet all beneath
Her innocent authority was wrought,
Nor could have been, without her blessed
    name.
The illustrious wife of Roland, in the hour
Of her composure, felt that agony,
And gave it vent in her last words. O
    Friend!
It was a lamentable time for man,
Whether a hope had e'er been his or not:

A woful time for them whose hopes sur-
    vived
The shock; most woful for those few
    who still
Were flattered, and had trust in human
    kind:
They had the deepest feeling of the grief.
Meanwhile the Invaders fared as they
    deserved:
The Herculean Commonwealth had put
    forth her arms,
And throttled with an infant godhead's
    might
The snakes about her cradle; that was
    well,
And as it should be; yet no cure for them
Whose souls were sick with pain of what
    would be
Hereafter brought in charge against man-
    kind.
Most melancholy at that time, O Friend!
Were my day-thoughts, — my nights were
    miserable;
Through months, through years, long
    after the last beat
Of those atrocities, the hour of sleep
To me came rarely charged with natural
    gifts,
Such ghastly visions had I of despair
And tyranny, and implements of death;
And innocent victims sinking under fear,
And momentary hope, and worn-out
    prayer,
Each in his separate cell, or penned in
    crowds
For sacrifice, and struggling with fond
    mirth
And levity in dungeons, where the dust
Was laid with tears. Then suddenly the
    scene
Changed, and the unbroken dream en-
    tangled me
In long orations, which I strove to plead
Before unjust tribunals, — with a voice
Laboring, a brain confounded, and a
    sense,
Death-like, of treacherous desertion, felt
In the last place of refuge — my own soul.

    When I began in youth's delightful
      prime
To yield myself to Nature, when that
    strong

And holy passion overcame me first,
Nor day nor night, evening or morn, was
    free
From its oppression. But, O Power
    Supreme!
Without Whose call this world would
    cease to breathe
Who from the fountain of Thy grace dost
    fill
The veins that branch through every
    frame of life,
Making man what he is, creature divine,
In single or in social eminence,
Above the rest raised infinite ascents
When reason that enables him to be
Is not sequestered — what a change is
    here!
How different ritual for this after-worship,
What countenance to promote this second
    love!
The first was service paid to things which
    lie
Guarded within the bosom of Thy will.
Therefore to serve was high beatitude;
Tumult was therefore gladness, and the
    fear
Ennobling, venerable; sleep secure,
And waking thoughts more rich than
    happiest dreams.

But as the ancient Prophets, borne
    aloft
In vision, yet constrained by natural laws
With them to take a troubled human heart,
Wanted not consolations, nor a creed
Of reconcilement, then when they de-
    nounced,
On towns and cities, wallowing in the
    abyss
Of their offences, punishment to come;
Or saw, like other men, with bodily eyes,
Before them, in some desolated place,
The wrath consummate and the threat
    fulfilled ;
So, with devout humility be it said,
So, did a portion of that spirit fall
On me uplifted from the vantage-ground
Of pity and sorrow to a state of being
That through the time's exceeding fierce-
    ness saw
Glimpses of retribution, terrible,
And in the order of sublime behests:
But, even if that were not, amid the awe

Of unintelligible chastisement,
Not only acquiescences of faith
Survived, but daring sympathies with
    power,
Motions not treacherous or profane, else
    why
Within the folds of no ungentle breast
Their dread vibration to this hour pro-
    longed?
Wild blasts of music thus could find their
    way
Into the midst of turbulent events;
So that worst tempests might be listened
    to.
Then was the truth received into my heart,
That, under heaviest sorrow earth can
    bring,
If from the affliction somewhere do not
    grow
Honor which could not else have been, a
    faith,
An elevation, and a sanctity,
If new strength be not given nor old
    restored,
The blame is ours, not Nature's. When
    a taunt
Was taken up by scoffers in their pride,
Saying, " Behold the harvest that we reap
From popular government and equality,"
I clearly saw that neither these nor aught
Of wild belief engrafted on their names
By false philosophy had caused the woe,
But a terrific reservoir of guilt
And ignorance filled up from age to age,
That could no longer hold its loathsome
    charge,
But burst and spread in deluge through
    the land.

And as the desert hath green spots, the
    sea
Small islands scattered amid stormy
    waves,
So that disastrous period did not want
Bright sprinklings of all human excel-
    lence,
To which the silver wands of saints in
    Heaven
Might point with rapturous joy. Yet not
    the less,
For those examples, in no age surpassed,
Of fortitude and energy and love,
And human nature faithful to herself

Under worst trials, was I driven to think
Of the glad times when first I traversed
    France
A youthful pilgrim; above all reviewed
That eventide, when under windows
    bright
With happy faces and with garlands
    hung,
And through a rainbow-arch that spanned
    the street,
Triumphal pomp for liberty confirmed,
I paced, a dear companion at my side,
The town of Arras, whence with promise
    high
Issued, on delegation to sustain
Humanity and right, *that* Robéspierre,
He who thereafter, and in how short time !
Wielded the sceptre of the Atheist crew.
When the calamity spread far and wide —
And this same city, that did then appear
To outrun the rest in exultation, groaned
Under the vengeance of her cruel son,
As Lear reproached the winds — I could
    almost
Have quarrelled with that blameless spec-
    tacle
For lingering yet an image in my mind
To mock me under such a strange reverse.

O Friend ! few happier moments have
    been mine
Than that which told the downfall of this
    Tribe
So dreaded, so abhorred.   The day
    deserves
A separate record.   Over the smooth sands
Of Leven's ample estuary lay
My journey, and beneath a genial sun,
With distant prospect among gleams of sky
And clouds and intermingling mountain
    tops,
In one inseparable glory clad,
Creatures of one ethereal substance met
In consistory, like a diadem
Or crown of burning seraphs as they sit
In the empyrean.   Underneath that pomp
Celestial, lay unseen the pastoral vales
Among whose happy fields I had grown up
From childhood.   On the fulgent spec-
    tacle,
That neither passed away nor changed, I
    gazed

Enrapt; but brightest things are wont to
    draw
Sad opposites out of the inner heart,
As even their pensive influence drew from
    mine.
How could it otherwise? for not in vain
That very morning had I turned aside
To seek the ground where, 'mid a throng
    of graves,
An honored teacher of my youth was laid,
And on the stone were graven by his de-
    sire
Lines from the churchyard elegy of Gray.
This faithful guide, speaking from his
    death-bed,
Added no farewell to his parting counsel,
But said to me, " My head will soon lie
    low;"
And when I saw the turf that covered him,
After the lapse of full eight years, those
    words,
With sound of voice and countenance of
    the Man,
Came back upon me, so that some few tears
Fell from me in my own despite.   But
    now
I thought, still traversing that widespread
    plain,
With tender pleasure of the verses graven
Upon his tombstone, whispering to my-
    self:
He loved the Poets, and, if now alive,
Would have loved me, as one not destitute
Of promise, nor belying the kind hope
That he had formed, when I, at his com-
    mand,
Began to spin, with toil, my earliest songs.

   As I advanced, all that I saw or felt
Was gentleness and peace.   Upon a small
And rocky island near, a fragment stood,
(Itself like a sea rock) the low remains
(With shells encrusted, dark with briny
    weeds)
Of a dilapidated structure, once
A Romish chapel, where the vested priest
Said matins at the hour that suited those
Who crossed the sands with ebb of morn-
    ing tide.
Not far from that still ruin all the plain
Lay spotted with a variegated crowd
Of vehicles and travellers, horse and foot,
Wading beneath the conduct of their guide

In loose procession through the shallow
   stream
Of inland waters; the great sea meanwhile
Heaved at safe distance, far retired. I
   paused,
Longing for skill to paint a scene so bright
And cheerful, but the foremost of the band
As he approached, no salutation given
In the familiar language of the day,
·Cried, "Robespierre is dead!" nor was
   a doubt,
After strict question, left within my mind
That he and his supporters all were fallen.

   Great was my transport, deep my grati-
     tude
To everlasting Justice, by this fiat
Made manifest. "Come now, ye golden
   times,"
Said I forth-pouring on those open sands
A hymn of triumph: "as the morning
   comes
From out the bosom of the night, come ye:
Thus far our trust is verified; behold!
They who with clumsy desperation
   brought
A river of Blood, and preached that noth-
   ing else
Could cleanse the Augean stable, by the
   might
Of their own helper have been swept
   away;
Their madness stands declared and visible;
Elsewhere will safety now be sought, and
   earth
March firmly towards righteousness and
   peace." —
Then schemes I framed more calmly,
   when and how
The madding factions might be tranquil-
   lized,
And how through hardships manifold and
   long
The glorious renovation would proceed.
Thus interrupted by uneasy bursts
Of exultation, I pursued my way
Along that very shore which I had
   skimmed
In former days, when — spurring from
   the Vale
Of Nightshade, and St. Mary's moulder-
   ing fane,
And the stone abbot, after circuit made

In wantonness of heart, a joyous band
Of schoolboys hastening to their distant
   home
Along the margin of the moonlight sea —
We beat with thundering hoofs the level
   sand.

BOOK ELEVENTH.

FRANCE *(concluded)*.

FROM that time forth, Authority in France
Put on a milder face; Terror had ceased,
Yet everything was wanting that might give
Courage to them who looked for good by
   light
Of rational Experience, for the shoots
And hopeful blossoms of a second spring:
Yet, in me, confidence was unimpaired;
The Senate's language, and the public acts
And measures of the Government, though
   both
Weak, and of heartless omen, had not
   power
To daunt me; in the People was my trust:
And, in the virtues which mine eyes had
   seen,
I knew that wound external could not take
Life from the young Republic; that new
   foes
Would only follow, in the path of shame,
Their brethren, and her triumphs be in
  · the end
Great, universal, irresistible.
This intuition led me to confound
One victory with another, higher far, —
Triumphs of unambitious peace at home,
And noiseless fortitude. Beholding still
Resistance strong as heretofore, I thought
That what was in degree the same was
   likewise
The same in quality, — that, as the worse
Of the two spirits then at strife remained
Untired, the better, surely, would preserve
The heart that first had roused him.
     Youth maintains,
In all conditions of society,
Communion more direct and intimate
With Nature, — hence, oft-times, ' with
   reason too —
Than age or manhood, even. To Nature,
   then,

Power had reverted: habit, custom, law,
Had left an interregnum's open space
For *her* to move about in, uncontrolled.
Hence could I see how Babel-like their
    task,
Who, by the recent deluge stupefied,
With their whole souls went culling from
    the day
Its petty promises, to build a tower
For their own safety; laughed with my
    compeers
At gravest heads, by enmity to France
Distempered, till they found, in every blast
Forced from the street-disturbing news-
    man's horn,
For her great cause record or prophecy
Of utter ruin. How might we believe
That wisdom could, in any shape, come
    near
Men clinging to delusions so insane?
And thus, experience proving that no few
Of our opinions had been just, we took
Like credit to ourselves where less was due,
And thought that other notions were as
    sound
Yea, could not but be right, because we
    saw
That foolish men opposed them.
                            To a strain
More animated I might here give way,
And tell, since juvenile errors are my
    theme,
What in those days, through Britain, was
    performed
To turn *all* judgments out of their right
    course;
But this is passion over-near ourselves,
Reality too close and too intense,
And intermixed with something, in my
    mind,
Of scorn and condemnation personal,
That would profane the sanctity of verse.
Our Shepherds, this say merely, at that
    time
Acted, or seemed at least to act, like men
Thirsting to make the guardian crook of
    law
A tool of murder; they who ruled the
    State —
Though with such awful proof before their
    eyes
That he, who would sow death, reaps
    death, or worse,

And can reap nothing better — child-like
    longed
To imitate, not wise enough to avoid;
Or left (by mere timidity betrayed)
The plain straight road, for one no better
    chosen
Than if their wish had been to undermine
Justice, and make an end of Liberty.

  . But from these bitter truths I must re-
    turn
To my own history. It hath been told
That I was led to take an eager part
In arguments of civil polity,
Abruptly, and indeed before my time:
I had approached, like other youths, the
    shield
Of human nature from the golden side,
And would have fought, even to the death,
    to attest
The quality of the metal which I saw.
What there is best in individual man,
Of wise in passion, and sublime in power,
Benevolent in small societies,
And great in large ones, I had oft re-
    volved,
Felt deeply, but not thoroughly under-
    stood
By reason: nay, far from it; they were
    yet,
As cause was given me afterwards to
    learn,
Not proof against the injuries of the day;
Lodged only at the sanctuary's door,
Not safe within its bosom. Thus pre-
    pared,
And with such general insight into evil,
And of the bounds which sever it from
    good,
As books and common intercourse with
    life
Must needs have given — to the inexpe-
    rienced mind,
When the world travels in a beaten road,
Guide faithful as is needed — I began
To meditate with ardor on the rule
And management of nations; what it is
And ought to be; and strove to learn how
    far
Their power or weakness, wealth or
    poverty,
Their happiness or misery, depends
Upon their laws, and fashion of the State.

[1] O pleasant exercise of hope and joy!
For mighty were the auxiliars which then
    stood
Upon our side, us who were strong in
    love!
Bliss was it in that dawn to be alive,
But to be young was very Heaven! O
    times,
In which the meagre, stale, forbidding
    ways
Of custom, law, and statute, took at once
The attraction of a country in romance!
When Reason seemed the most to assert
    her rights
When most intent on making of herself
A prime enchantress — to assist the work,
Which then was going forward in her
    name!
Not favored spots alone, but the whole
    Earth,
The beauty wore of promise — that which
    sets
(As at some moments might not be unfelt
Among the bowers of Paradise itself)
The budding rose above the rose full
    blown.
What temper at the prospect did not wake
To happiness unthought of? The inert
Were roused, and lively natures rapt
    away!
They who had fed their childhood upon
    dreams,
The play-fellows of fancy, who had made
All powers of swiftness, subtilty, and
    strength
Their ministers, — who in lordly wise had
    stirred
Among the grandest objects of the sense,
And dealt with whatsoever they found
    there
As if they had within some lurking right
To wield it; — they, too, who of gentle
    mood
Had watched all gentle motions, and to
    these
Had fitted their own thoughts, schemers
    more mild,
And in the region of their peaceful
    selves; —
Now was it that *both* found, the meek and
    lofty

[1] See p. 267.

Did both find, helpers to their hearts' de-
    sire,
And stuff at hand, plastic as they could
    wish, —
Were called upon to exercise their skill,
Not in Utopia, — subterranean fields, —
Or some secreted island, Heaven knows
    where!
But in the very world, which is the world
Of all of us, — the place where, in the
    end,
We find our happiness, or not at all!

Why should I not confess that Earth
    was then
To me, what an inheritance, new-fallen,
Seems, when the first time visited, to one
Who thither comes to find in it his home?
He walks about and looks upon the spot
With cordial transport, moulds it and
    remoulds,
And is half-pleased with things that are
    amiss,
'T will be such joy to see them disappear.

An active partisan, I thus convoked
From every object pleasant circumstance
To suit my ends; I moved among man-
    kind
With genial feelings still predominant;
When erring, erring on the better part,
And in the kinder spirit; placable,
Indulgent, as not uninformed that men
See as they have been taught — Antiquity
Gives rights to error; and aware, no less,
That throwing off oppression must be
    work
As well of License as of Liberty;
And above all — for this was more than
    all —
Not caring if the wind did now and then
Blow keen upon an eminence that gave
Prospects so large into futurity;
In brief, a child of Nature, as at first,
Diffusing only those affections wider
That from the cradle had grown up with
    me,
And losing, in no other way than light
Is lost in light, the weak in the more
    strong.

In the main outline, such it might be
    said
Was my condition, till with open war

Britain opposed the liberties of France.
This threw me first out of the pale of love;
Soured and corrupted, upwards to the
　　source,
My sentiments; was not, as hitherto,
A swallowing up of lesser things in great,
But change of them into their contraries;
And thus a way was opened for mistakes
And false conclusions, in degree as gross,
In kind more dangerous.　What had been
　　a pride,
Was now a shame; my likings and my
　　loves
Ran in new channels, leaving old ones
　　dry;
And hence a blow that, in maturer age,
Would but have touched the judgment,
　　struck more deep
Into sensations near the heart: meantime,
As from the first, wild theories were afloat,
To whose pretensions, sedulously urged,
I had but lent a careless ear, assured
That time was ready to set all things right,
And that the multitude, so long oppressed,
Would be oppressed no more.
　　　　　　　　But when events
Brought less encouragement, and unto
　　these
The immediate proof of principles no
　　more
Could be entrusted, while the events
　　themselves,
Worn out in greatness, stripped of
　　novelty,
Less occupied the mind, and sentiments
Could through my understanding's natural
　　growth
No longer keep their ground, by faith
　　maintained
Of inward consciousness, and hope that
　　laid
Her hand upon her object — evidence
Safer, of universal application, such
As could not be impeached, was sought
　　elsewhere.

　　But now, become oppressors in their
　　　　turn,
Frenchmen had changed a war of self-
　　defence
For one of conquest, losing sight of all
Which they had struggled for: up
　　mounted now,

Openly in the eye of earth and heaven,
The scale of liberty.　I read her doom,
With anger vexed, with disappointment
　　sore,
But not dismayed, nor taking to the shame
Of a false prophet.　While resentment rose
Striving to hide, what nought could heal,-
　　the wounds
Of mortified presumption, I adhered
More firmly to old tenets, and, to prove
Their temper, strained them more; and
　　thus, in heat
Of contest, did opinions every day
Grow into consequence, till round my
　　mind
They clung, as if they were its life, nay
　　more,
The very being of the immortal soul.

　　This was the time, when, all things
　　　　tending fast
To depravation, speculative schemes —
That promised to abstract the hopes of
　　Man
Out of his feelings, to be fixed thence-
　　forth
Forever in a purer element —
Found ready welcome.　Tempting region
　　　　that
For Zeal to enter and refresh herself,
Where passions had the privilege to work,
And never hear the sound of their own
　　names.
But, speaking more in charity, the dream
Flattered the young, pleased with ex-
　　tremes, nor least
With that which makes our Reason's
　　naked self
The object of its fervor.　What delight!
How glorious! in self-knowledge and
　　self-rule,
To look through all the frailties of the
　　world,
And, with a resolute mastery shaking off
Infirmities of nature, time, and place,
Build social upon personal Liberty,
Which, to the blind restraints of general
　　laws
Superior, magisterially adopts
One guide, the light of circumstances,
　　flashed
Upon an independent intellect.
Thus expectation rose again; thus hope,

From her first ground expelled, grew
    proud once more.
Oft, as my thoughts were turned to human
    kind,
I scorned indifference; but, inflamed with
    thirst
Of a secure intelligence, and sick
Of other longing, I pursued what seemed
A more exalted nature; wished that Man
Should start out of his earthy, worm-like
    state,
And spread abroad the wings of Liberty,
Lord of himself, in undisturbed delight —
A noble aspiration ! *yet* I feel
(Sustained by worthier as by wiser
    thoughts)
The aspiration, nor shall ever cease
To feel it; — but return we to our course.

    Enough, 't is true — could such a plea
      excuse
Those aberrations — had the clamorous
    friends
Of ancient Institutions said and done
To bring disgrace upon their very names;
Disgrace, of which, custom and written
    law,
And sundry moral sentiments as props
Or emanations of those institutes,
Too justly bore a part. A veil had been
Uplifted; why deceive ourselves? in sooth,
'T was even so; and sorrow for the man
Who either had not eyes wherewith to see,
Or, seeing, had forgotten ! A strong
    shock
Was given to old opinions; all men's
    minds
Had felt its power, and mine was both let
    loose,
Let loose and goaded. After what hath
    been
Already said of patriotic love,
Suffice it here to add, that, somewhat stern
In temperament, withal a happy man,
And therefore bold to look on painful
    things,
Free likewise of the world, and thence
    more bold,
I summoned my best skill, and toiled,
    intent
To anatomize the frame of social life;
Yea, the whole body of society

Searched to its heart. Share with me,
    Friend ! the wish
That some dramatic tale, endued with
    shapes
Livelier, and flinging out less guarded
    words
Than suit the work we fashion, might set
    forth ·
What then I learned, or think I learned,
    of truth,
And the errors into which I fell, betrayed
By present objects, and by reasonings false
From their beginnings, inasmuch as drawn
Out of a heart that had been turned aside
From Nature's way by outward accidents,
And which was thus confounded, more
    and more
Misguided, and misguiding. So I fared,
Dragging all precepts, judgments,
    maxims, creeds,
Like culprits to the bar; calling the mind,
Suspiciously, to establish in plain day
Her titles and her honors; now believing,
Now disbelieving; endlessly perplexed
With impulse, motive, right and wrong,
    the ground
Of obligation, what the rule and whence
The sanction; till, demanding formal
    proof,
And seeking it in everything, I lost
All feeling of conviction, and, in fine,
Sick, wearied out with contrarieties,
Yielded up moral questions in despair.

    This was the crisis of that strong disease,
This the soul's last and lowest ebb; I
    drooped,
Deeming our blessèd reason of least use
Where wanted most: " The lordly attri-
    butes
Of will and choice," I bitterly exclaimed,
" What are they but a mockery of a Being
Who hath in no concerns of his a test
Of good and evil; knows not what to fear
Or hope for, what to covet or to shun;
And who, if those could be discerned,
    would yet
Be little profited, would see, and ask
Where is the obligation to enforce?
And, to acknowledged law rebellious,
    still,
As selfish passion urged, would act amiss;
The dupe of folly, or the slave of crime."

Depressed, bewildered thus, I did not
    walk
With scoffers, seeking light and gay re-
    venge
From indiscriminate laughter, nor sate
    down
In reconcilement with an utter waste
Of intellect; such sloth I could not brook
(Too well I loved, in that my spring of
    life,
Pains-taking thoughts, and truth, their
    dear reward),
But turned to abstract science, and there
    sought
Work for the reasoning faculty enthroned
Where the disturbances of space and
    time —
Whether in matters various, properties
Inherent, or from human will and power
Derived — find no admission.   Then it
    was —
Thanks to the bounteous Giver of all
    good ! —
That the belovèd Sister in whose sight
Those days were passed, now speaking in
    a voice
Of sudden admonition — like a brook
That did but *cross* a lonely road, and now
Is seen, heard, felt, and caught at every
    turn,
Companion never lost through many a
    league —
Maintained for me a saving intercourse
With my true self; for, though bedimmed
    and changed
Much, as it seemed, I was no further
    changed
Than as a clouded and a waning moon:
She whispered still that brightness would
    return;
She, in the midst of all, preserved me still
A Poet, made me seek beneath that name,
And that alone, my office upon earth;
And, lastly, as hereafter will be shown,
If willing audience fail not, Nature's self,
By all varieties of human love
Assisted, led me back through opening day
To those sweet counsels between head and
    heart
Whence grew that genuine knowledge,
    fraught with peace,
Which, through the later sinkings of this
    cause,

Hath still upheld me, and upholds me now
In the catastrophe (for so they dream,
And nothing less), when, finally to close
And seal up all the gains of France, a
    Pope
Is summoned in, to crown an Emperor —
This last opprobrium, when we see a
    people,
That once looked up in faith, as if to
    Heaven
For manna, to take a lesson from the dog
Returning to his vomit; when the sun
That rose in splendor, was alive, and
    moved
In exultation with a living pomp
Of clouds — his glory's natural retinue —
Hath dropped all functions by the gods
    bestowed,
And, turned into a gewgaw, a machine,
Sets like an Opera phantom.
                    Thus, O Friend !
Through times of honor and through
    times of shame
Descending, have I faithfully retraced
The perturbations of a youthful mind
Under a long-lived storm of great events —
A story destined for thy ear, who now,
Among the fallen of nations, dost abide
Where Etna, over hill and valley, casts
His shadow stretching towards Syracuse,
The city of Timoleon ! Righteous Heaven!
How are the mighty prostrated !   They
    first,
They first of all that breathe should have
    awaked
When the great voice was heard from
    out the tombs
Of ancient heroes.   If I suffered grief
For ill-requited France, by many deemed
A trifler only in her proudest day;
Have been distressed to think of what
    she once
Promised, now is; a far more sober cause
Thine eyes must see of sorrow in a land,
To the reanimating influence lost
Of memory, to virtue lost and hope,
Though with the wreck of loftier years
    bestrewn.

    But indignation works where hope is
        not,
And thou, O Friend ! wilt be refreshed.
    There is

One great society alone on earth:
The noble Living and the noble Dead.

Thine be such converse strong and
sanative,
A ladder for thy spirit to reascend
To health and joy and pure contented-
ness;
To me the grief confined, that thou art
gone
From this last spot of earth, where Free-
dom now
Stands single in her only sanctuary;
A lonely wanderer, art gone, by pain
Compelled and sickness, at this latter day,
This sorrowful reverse for all mankind.
I feel for thee, must utter what I feel:
The sympathies erewhile in part dis-
charged,
Gather afresh, and will have vent again:
My own delights do scarcely seem to me
My own delights; the lordly Alps them-
selves,
Those rosy peaks, from which the Morn-
ing looks
Abroad on many nations, are no more
For me that image of pure gladsomeness
Which they were wont to be. Through
kindred scenes,
For purpose, at a time, how different!
Thou tak'st thy way, carrying the heart
and soul
That Nature gives to Poets, now by
thought
Matured, and in the summer of their
strength.
Oh! wrap him in your shades, ye giant
woods,
On Etna's side; and thou, O flowery field
Of Enna! is there not some nook of thine,
From the first play-time of the infant
world
Kept sacred to restorative delight,
When from afar invoked by anxious love?

Child of the mountains, among shep-
herds reared,
Ere yet familiar with the classic page,
I learnt to dream of Sicily; and lo,
The gloom, that, but a moment past, was
deepened
At thy command, at her command gives
way;

A pleasant promise, wafted from her
shores,
Comes o'er my heart: in fancy I behold
Her seas yet smiling, her once happy
vales;
Nor can my tongue give utterance to a
name
Of note belonging to that honored isle,
Philosopher or Bard, Empedocles,
Or Archimedes, pure abstracted soul!
That doth not yield a solace to my grief:
And, O Theocritus,[1] so far have some
Prevailed among the powers of heaven
and earth,
By their endowments, good or great, that
they
Have had, as thou reportest, miracles
Wrought for them in old time: yea,
not unmoved,
When thinking on my own beloved friend,
I hear thee tell how bees with honey fed
Divine Comates, by his impious lord
Within a chest imprisoned; how they came
Laden from blooming grove or flowery
field,
And fed him there, alive, month after
month,
Because the goatherd, blessèd man! had
lips
Wet with the Muses' nectar.
　　　　　　　Thus I soothe
The pensive moments by this calm fire-
side,
And find a thousand bounteous images
To cheer the thoughts of those I love,
and mine.
Our prayers have been accepted; thou
wilt stand
On Etna's summit, above earth and sea,
Triumphant, winning from the invaded
heavens
Thoughts without bound, magnificent
designs,
Worthy of poets who attuned their harps
In wood or echoing cave, for discipline
Of heroes; or, in reverence to the gods,
'Mid temples, served by sapient priests,
and choirs
Of virgins crowned with roses. Not in
vain
Those temples, where they in their ruins
yet

[1] *Theocrit. Idyll.* vii. 78.

Survive for inspiration, shall attract
Thy solitary steps: and on the brink
Thou wilt recline of pastoral Arethuse;
Or, if that fountain be in truth no more,
Then, near some other spring — which,
    by the name
Thou gratulatest, willingly deceived —
I see thee linger a glad votary,
And not a captive pining for his home.

Book Twelfth.

IMAGINATION AND TASTE, HOW IM-
PAIRED AND RESTORED.

Long time have human ignorance and
    guilt
Detained us, on what spectacles of woe
Compelled to look, and inwardly op-
    pressed
With sorrow, disappointment, vexing
    thoughts,
Confusion of the judgment, zeal decayed,
And, lastly, utter loss of hope itself
And things to hope for! Not with these
    began
Our song, and not with these our song
    must end. —
Ye motions of delight, that haunt the sides
Of the green hills; ye breezes and soft airs,
Whose subtle intercourse with breathing
    flowers,
Feelingly watched, might teach Man's
    haughty race
How without injury to take, to give
Without offence; ye who, as if to show
The wondrous influence of power gently
    used,
Bend the complying heads of lordly pines,
And, with a touch, shift the stupendous
    clouds
Through the whole compass of the sky;
    ye brooks,
Muttering along the stones, a busy noise
By day, a quiet sound in silent night;
Ye waves, that out of the great deep steal
    forth
In a calm hour to kiss the pebbly shore,
Not mute, and then retire, fearing no
    storm;
And you, ye groves, whose ministry it is
To interpose the covert of your shades,

Even as a sleep, between the heart of man
And outward troubles, between man him-
    self,
Not seldom, and his own uneasy heart:
Oh! that I had a music and a voice
Harmonious as your own, that I might tell
What ye have done for me. The morn-
    ing shines,
Nor heedeth Man's perverseness; Spring
    returns, —
I saw the Spring return, and could rejoice,
In common with the children of her love,
Piping on boughs, or sporting on fresh
    fields,
Or boldly|seeking pleasure nearer heaven
On wings that navigate cerulean skies.
So neither were complacency, nor peace,
Nor tender yearnings, wanting for my
    good
Through these distracted times; in Nature
    still   ·
Glorying, I found a counterpoise in her,
Which, when the spirit of evil reached
    its height,
Maintained for me a secret happiness.

   This narrative, my Friend! hath chiefly
    told
Of intellectual power, fostering love,
Dispensing truth, and, over men and
    things,
Where reason yet might hesitate, diffusing
Prophetic sympathies of genial faith:
So was I favored — such my happy lot —
Until that natural graciousness of mind
Gave way to overpressure from the times
And their disastrous issues. What availed,
When spells forbade the voyager to land,
That fragrant notice of a pleasant shore
Wafted, at intervals, from many a bower
Of blissful gratitude and fearless love?
Dare I avow that wish was mine to see,
And hope that future times *would* surely
    see,
The man to come, parted, as by a gulph,
From him who had been; that I could
    no more
Trust the elevation which had made me
    one
With the great family that still survives
To illuminate the abyss of ages past,
Sage, warrior, patriot, hero; for it seemed

That their best virtues were not free
    from taint
Of something false and weak, that could
    not stand
The open eye of Reason.   Then I said,
"Go to the Poets, they will speak to thee
More perfectly of purer creatures; — yet
If reason be nobility in man,
Can aught be more ignoble than the man
Whom they delight in, blinded as he is
By prejudice, the miserable slave
Of low ambition or distempered love?"

  In such strange passion, if I may once
    more
Review the past, I warred against my-
    self —
A bigot to a new idolatry —
Like a cowled monk who hath forsworn
    the world,
Zealously labored to cut off my heart
From all the sources of her former
    strength;
And as, by simple waving of a wand,
The wizard instantaneously dissolves
Palace or grove, even so could I unsoul
As readily by syllogistic words
Those mysteries of being which have
    made,
And shall continue evermore to make,
Of the whole human race one brother-
    hood.

  What wonder, then, if, to a mind so far
Perverted, even the visible Universe
Fell under the dominion of a taste
Less spiritual, with microscopic view
Was scanned, as I had scanned the
    moral world?

  O Soul of Nature! excellent and fair!
That didst rejoice with me, with whom
    I, too,
Rejoiced through early youth, before the
    winds
And roaring waters, and in lights and
    shades
That marched and countermarched about
    the hills
In glorious apparition, Powers on whom
I daily waited, now all eye and now
All ear; but never long without the heart
Employed, and man's unfolding intellect:

O Soul of Nature! that, by laws divine
Sustained and governed, still dost over-
    flow
With an impassioned life, what feeble
    ones
Walk on this earth! how feeble have I
    been
When thou wert in thy strength!   Nor
    this through stroke
Of human suffering, such as justifies
Remissness and inaptitude of mind,
But through presumption; even in pleas-
    ure pleased
Unworthily, disliking here, and there
Liking; by rules of mimic art transferred.
To things above all art; but more, — for
    this,
Although a strong infection of the age,
Was never much my habit — giving way
To a comparison of scene with scene,
Bent overmuch on superficial things,
Pampering myself with meagre novelties
Of color and proportion; to the moods
Of time and season, to the moral power,
The affections and the spirit of the place,
Insensible.   Nor only did the love
Of sitting thus in judgment interrupt
My deeper feelings, but another cause,
More subtle and less easily explained,
That almost seems inherent in the crea-
    ture,
A twofold frame of body and of mind.
I speak in recollection of a time
When the bodily eye, in every stage of life
The most despotic of our senses, gained
Such strength in *me* as often held my mind
In absolute dominion.   Gladly here,
Entering upon abstruser argument,
Could I endeavor to unfold the means
Which Nature studiously employs to
    thwart
This tyranny, summons all the senses each
To counteract the other, and themselves,
And makes them all, and the objects
    with which all
Are conversant, subservient in their turn
To the great ends of Liberty and Power.
But leave we this: enough that my
    delights
(Such as they were) were sought in-
    satiably.
Vivid the transport, vivid though not
    profound;

I roamed from hill to hill, from rock to
　　rock,
Still craving combinations of new forms,
New pleasure, wider empire for the sight,
Proud of her own endowments, and re-
　　joiced
To lay the inner faculties asleep.
Amid the turns and counterturns, the
　　strife
And various trials of our complex being,
As we grow up, such thraldom of that
　　sense
Seems hard to shun.　And yet I knew a
　　maid,
A young enthusiast, who escaped these
　　bonds;
Her eye was not the mistress of her heart;
Far less did rules prescribed by passive
　　taste,
Or barren intermeddling subtleties,
Perplex her mind; but, wise as women are
When genial circumstance hath favored
　　them,
She welcomed what was given, and
　　craved no more;
Whate'er the scene presented to her view
That was the best, to that she was attuned
By her benign simplicity of life,
And through a perfect happiness of soul,
Whose variegated feelings were in this
Sisters, that they were each some new
　　delight.
Birds in the bower, and lambs in the
　　green field,
Could they have known her, would have
　　loved; methought
Her very presence such a sweetness
　　breathed,
That flowers, and trees, and even the
　　silent hills,
And everything she looked on, should
　　have had
An intimation how she bore herself
Towards them and to all creatures.　God
　　delights
In such a being; for, her common thoughts
Are piety, her life is gratitude.

　　Even like this maid, before I was
　　　　called forth
From the retirement of my native hills,
I loved whate'er I saw: nor lightly loved,
But most intensely; never dreamt of aught

More grand, more fair, more exquisitely
　　framed
Than those few nooks to which my
　　happy feet
Were limited.　I had not at that time
Lived long enough, nor in the least sur-
　　vived
The first diviner influence of this world,
As it appears to unaccustomed eyes.
Worshipping them among the depth of
　　things,
As piety ordained, could I submit
To measured admiration, or to aught
That should preclude humility and love?
I felt, observed, and pondered; did not
　　judge,
Yea, never thought of judging; with the
　　gift
Of all this glory filled and satisfied.
And afterwards, when through the gor-
　　geous Alps
Roaming, I carried with me the same
　　heart:
In truth, the degradation — howsoe'er
Induced, effect, in whatsoe'er degree,
Of custom that prepares a partial scale
In which the little oft outweighs the great;
Or any other cause that hath been named;
Or lastly, aggravated by the times
And their impassioned sounds, which
　　well might make
The milder minstrelsies of rural scenes
Inaudible — was transient; I had known
Too forcibly, too early in my life,
Visitings of imaginative power
For this to last: I shook the habit off
Entirely and forever, and again
In Nature's presence stood, as now I
　　stand,
A sensitive being, a *creative* soul.

　　There are in our existence spots of time,
That with distinct pre-eminence retain
A renovating virtue, whence — depressed
By false opinion and contentious thought,
Or aught of heavier or more deadly weight,
In trivial occupations, and the round
Of ordinary intercourse — our minds
Are nourished and invisibly repaired;
A virtue, by which pleasure is enhanced,
That penetrates, enables us to mount,
When high, more high, and lifts us up
　　when fallen.

This efficacious spirit chiefly lurks
Among those passages of life that give
Profoundest knowledge to what point,
    and how,
The mind is lord and master — outward
    sense
The obedient servant of her will.   Such
    moments
Are scattered everywhere, taking their date
From our first childhood. I remember
    well,
That once, while yet my inexperienced
    hand
Could scarcely hold a bridle, with proud
    hopes
I mounted, and we journeyed towards the
    hills:
An ancient servant of my father's house
Was with me, my encourager and guide:
We had not travelled long, ere some mis-
    chance
Disjoined me from my comrade; and,
    through fear
Dismounting, down the rough and stony
    moor
I led my horse, and, stumbling on, at
    length
Came to a bottom, where in former times
A murderer had been hung in iron chains.
The gibbet-mast had mouldered down, the
    bones
And iron case were gone; but on the turf,
Hard by, soon after that fell deed was
    wrought,
Some unknown hand had carved the
    murderer's name.
The monumental letters were inscribed
In times long past; but still, from year to
    year
By superstition of the neighborhood,
The grass is cleared away, and to this hour
The characters are fresh and visible:
A casual glance had shown them, and I
    fled,
Faltering and faint, and ignorant of the
    road:
Then, reascending the bare common, saw
A naked pool that lay beneath the hills,
The beacon on the summit, and, more
    near,
A girl, who bore a pitcher on her head,
And seemed with difficult steps to force
    her way

Against the blowing wind.   It was, in
    truth,
An ordinary sight; but I should need
Colors and words that are unknown to
    man,
To paint the visionary dreariness
Which, while I looked all round for my
    lost guide,
Invested moorland waste and naked pool,
The beacon crowning the lone eminence,
The female and her garments vexed and
    tossed
By the strong wind. When, in the blessèd
    hours
Of early love, the loved one at my side,
I roamed, in daily presence of this scene,
Upon the naked pool and dreary crags,
And on the melancholy beacon, fell
A spirit of pleasure and youth's golden
    gleam;
And think ye not with radiance more sub-
    lime
For these remembrances, and for the power
They had left behind?   So feeling comes
    in aid
Of feeling, and diversity of strength
Attends us, if but once we have been
    strong.
Oh! mystery of man, from what a depth
Proceed thy honors.   I am lost, but see
In simple childhood something of the base
On which thy greatness stands; but this I
    feel,
That from thyself it comes, that thou must
    give,
Else never canst receive. The days gone by
Return upon me almost from the dawn
Of life: the hiding-places of man's power
Open; I would approach them, but they
    close.
I see by glimpses now; when age comes on,
May scarcely see at all; and I would give,
While yet we may, as far as words can
    give,
Substance and life to what I feel, en-
    shrining,
Such is my hope, the spirit of the Past
For future restoration. — Yet another
Of these memorials: —
                    One Christmas-time,
On the glad eve of its dear holidays,
Feverish, and tired, and restless, I went
    forth

Into the fields, impatient for the sight
Of those led palfreys that should bear us
    home;
My brothers and myself. There rose a
    crag,
That, from the meeting-point of two high-
    ways
Ascending, overlooked them both, far
    stretched;
Thither, uncertain on which road to fix
My expectation, thither I repaired,
Scout-like, and gained the summit; 't was
    a day
Tempestuous, dark, and wild, and on the
    grass
I sate half-sheltered by a naked wall;
Upon my right hand couched a single
    sheep,
Upon my left a blasted hawthorn stood;
With those companions at my side, I
    watched,
Straining my eyes intensely, as the mist
Gave intermitting prospect of the copse
And plain beneath. Ere we to school
    returned, —
That dreary time, — ere we had been ten
    days
Sojourners in my father's house, he died;
And I and my three brothers, orphans then,
Followed his body to the grave. The
    event,
With all the sorrow that it brought,
    appeared
A chastisement; and when I called to
    mind
That day so lately past, when from the crag
I looked in such anxiety of hope;
With trite reflections of morality,
Yet in the deepest passion, I bowed low
To God, Who thus corrected my desires;
And, afterwards, the wind and sleety rain,
And all the business of the elements,
The single sheep, and the one blasted tree,
And the bleak music from that old stone
    wall,
The noise of wood and water, and the mist
That on the line of each of those two roads
Advanced in such indisputable shapes;
All these were kindred spectacles and
    sounds
To which I oft repaired, and thence would
    drink,
As at a fountain; and on winter nights,

Down to this very time, when storm and
    rain
Beat on my roof, or, haply, at noon-day,
While in a grove I walk, whose lofty trees,
Laden with summer's thickest foliage, rock
In a strong wind, some working of the
    spirit,
Some inward agitations thence are
    brought,
Whate'er their office, whether to beguile
Thoughts over busy in the course they
    took,
Or animate an hour of vacant ease.

BOOK THIRTEENTH.

IMAGINATION AND TASTE, HOW IMPAIRED AND RESTORED (*concluded*).

FROM Nature doth emotion come, and
    moods
Of calmness equally are Nature's gift:
This is her glory; these two attributes
Are sister horns that constitute her
    strength.
Hence Genius, born to thrive by inter-
    change
Of peace and excitation, finds in her
His best and purest friend; from her
    receives
That energy by which he seeks the truth,
From her that happy stillness of the mind
Which fits him to receive it when unsought.

Such benefit the humblest intellects
Partake of, each in their degree; 't is mine
To speak, what I myself have known and
    felt;
Smooth task! for words find easy way,
    inspired
By gratitude, and confidence in truth.
Long time in seach of knowledge did I
    range
The field of human life, in heart and mind
Benighted; but, the dawn beginning now
To re-appear, 't was proved that not in vain
I had been taught to reverence a Power
That is the visible quality and shape
And image of right reason; that matures
Her processes by steadfast laws; gives birth
To no impatient or fallacious hopes,
No heat of passion or excessive zeal.

No vain conceits; provokes to no quick
    turns
Of self-applauding intellect; but trains
To meekness, and exalts by humble faith;
Holds up before the mind intoxicate
With present objects, and the busy dance
Of things that pass away, a temperate
    show
Of objects that endure; and by this course
Disposes her, when over-fondly set
On throwing off incumbrances, to seek
In man, and in the frame of social life,
Whate'er there is desirable and good
Of kindred permanence, unchanged in
    form
And function, or, through strict vicissitude
Of life and death, revolving. Above all
Were re-established now those watchful
    thoughts
Which, seeing little worthy or sublime
In what the Historian's pen so much
    delights
To blazon — power and energy detached
From moral purpose — early tutored me
To look with feelings of fraternal love
Upon the unassuming things that hold
A silent station in this beauteous world.

    Thus moderated, thus composed, I
    found
Once more in Man an object of delight,
Of pure imagination, and of love;
And, as the horizon of my mind enlarged,
Again I took the intellectual eye
For my instructor, studious more to see
Great truths, than touch and handle little
    ones.
Knowledge was given accordingly; my
    trust
Became more firm in feelings that had
    stood
The test of such a trial: clearer far
My sense of excellence — of right and
    wrong:
The promise of the present time retired
Into its true proportion; sanguine
    schemes,
Ambitious projects, pleased me less; I
    sought
For present good in life's familiar face,
And built thereon my hopes of good to
    come.

With settling judgments now of what
    would last
And what would disappear; prepared to
    find
Presumption, folly, madness, in the men
Who thrust themselves upon the passive
    world
As Rulers of the world; to see in these,
Even when the public welfare is their aim,
Plans without thought, or built on theories
Vague and unsound; and having brought
    the books
Of modern statists to their proper test,
Life, human life, with all its sacred claims
Of sex and age, and heaven-descended
    rights,
Mortal, or those beyond the reach of
    death;
And having thus discerned how dire a
    thing
Is worshipped in that idol proudly named
"The Wealth of Nations," *where* alone
    that wealth
Is lodged, and how increased; and having
    gained
A more judicious knowledge of the worth
And dignity of individual man,
No composition of the brain, but man
Of whom we read, the man whom we
    behold
With our own eyes — I could not but in-
    quire —
Not with less interest than heretofore,
But greater, though in spirit more sub-
    dued —
Why is this glorious creature to be found
One only in ten thousand? What one is,
Why may not millions be? What bars
    are thrown
By Nature in the way of such a hope?
Our animal appetites and daily wants,
Are these obstructions insurmountable?
If not, then others vanish into air.
"Inspect the basis of the social pile:
Inquire," said I, "how much of mental
    power
And genuine virtue they possess who live
By bodily toil, labor exceeding far
Their due proportion, under all the weight
Of that injustice which upon ourselves
Ourselves entail." Such estimate to frame
I chiefly looked (what need to look be-
    yond?)

Among the natural abodes of men,
Fields with their rural works; recalled to
mind
My earliest notices; with these compared
The observations made in later youth,
And to that day continued. — For, the
time
Had never been when throes of mighty
Nations
And the world's tumult unto me could
yield,
How far soe'er transported and possessed,
Full measure of content; but still I craved
An intermingling of distinct regards
And truths of individual sympathy
Nearer ourselves. Such often might be
gleaned
From the great City, else it must have
proved
To me a heart-depressing wilderness;
But much was wanting: therefore did I
turn
To you, ye pathways, and ye lonely roads;
Sought you enriched with everything I
prized,
With human kindnesses and simple joys.

Oh! next to one dear state of bliss,
vouchsafed,
Alas! to few in this untoward world,
The bliss of walking daily in life's prime
Through field or forest with the maid we
love,
While yet our hearts are young, while yet
we breathe
Nothing but happiness, in some lone nook,
Deep vale, or anywhere, the home of both,
From which it would be misery to stir:
Oh! next to such enjoyment of our youth,
In my esteem, next to such dear delight,
Was that of wandering on from day to day
Where I could meditate in peace, and cull
Knowledge that step by step might lead
me on
To wisdom; or, as lightsome as a bird
Wafted upon the wind from distant lands,
Sing notes of greeting to strange fields or
groves,
Which lacked not voice to welcome me in
turn:
And, when that pleasant toil had ceased
to please,

Converse with men, where if we meet a
face
We almost meet a friend, on naked heaths
With long long ways before, by cottage
bench,
Or well-spring where the weary traveller
rests.

Who doth not love to follow with his
eye
The windings of a public way? the sight,
Familiar object as it is, hath wrought
On my imagination since the morn
Of childhood, when a disappearing line,
One daily present to my eyes, that crossed
The naked summit of a far-off hill
Beyond the limits that my feet had trod,
Was like an invitation into space
Boundless, or guide into eternity.
Yes, something of the grandeur which
invests
The mariner, who sails the roaring sea
Through storm and darkness, early in
my mind
Surrounded, too, the wanderers of the
earth;
Grandeur as much, and loveliness far
more.
Awed have I been by strolling Bedlamites;
From many other uncouth vagrants
(passed
In fear) have walked with quicker step;
but why
Take note of this? When I began to
enquire,
To watch and question those I met, and
speak
Without reserve to them, the lonely roads
Were open schools in which I daily read
With most delight the passions of man-
kind,
Whether by words, looks, sighs, or tears,
revealed;
There saw into the depth of human souls,
Souls that appear to have no depth at all
To careless eyes. And — now convinced
at heart
How little those formalities, to which
With overweening trust alone we give
The name of Education, have to do
With real feeling and just sense; how vain
A correspondence with the talking world

Proves to the most; and called to make
    good search
If man's estate, by doom of Nature yoked
With toil, be therefore yoked with igno-
    rance;
If virtue be indeed so hard to rear,
And intellectual strength so rare a boon —
I prized such walks still more, for there I
    found
Hope to my hope, and to my pleasure
    peace
And steadiness, and healing and repose
To every angry passion. There I heard,
From mouths of men obscure and lowly,
    truths
Replete with honor; sounds in unison
With loftiest promises of good and fair.

There are who think that strong affec-
    tion, love
Known by whatever name, is falsely
    deemed
A gift, to use a term which they would use,
Of vulgar nature; that its growth requires
Retirement, leisure, language purified
By manners studied and elaborate;
That whoso feels such passion in its
    strength
Must live within the very light and air
Of courteous usages refined by art.
True is it, where oppression worse than
    death
Salutes the being at his birth, where grace
Of culture hath been utterly unknown,
And poverty and labor in excess
From day to day pre-occupy the ground
Of the affections, and to Nature's self
Oppose a deeper nature; there, indeed,
Love cannot be; nor does it thrive with
    ease
Among the close and overcrowded haunts
Of cities, where the human heart is sick,
And the eye feeds it not, and cannot feed.
— Yes, in those wanderings deeply did I
    feel
How we mislead each other; above all,
How books mislead us, seeking their re-
    ward
From judgments of the wealthy Few, who
    see
By artificial lights; how they debase
The Many for the pleasure of those Few;
Effeminately level down the truth

To certain general notions, for the sake
Of being understood at once, or else
Through want of better knowledge in the
    heads
That framed them; flattering self-conceit
    with words,
That, while they most ambitiously set forth
Extrinsic differences, the outward marks
Whereby society has parted man
From man, neglect the universal heart.

Here, calling up to mind what then I
    saw,
A youthful traveller, and see daily now
In the familiar circuit of my home,
Here might I pause, and bend in reverence
To Nature, and the power of human minds,
To men as they are men within themselves.
How oft high service is performed within,
When all the external man is rude in
    show, —
Not like a temple rich with pomp and gold,
But a mere mountain chapel, that protects
Its simple worshippers from sun and
    shower.
Of these, said I, shall be my song; of these,
If future years mature me for the task,
Will I record the praises, making verse
Deal boldly with substantial things; in
    truth
And sanctity of passion, speak of these,
That justice may be done, obeisance paid
Where it is due: thus haply shall I teach,
Inspire; through unadulterated ears
Pour rapture, tenderness, and hope, —
    my theme
No other than the very heart of man,
As found among the best of those who
    live —
Not unexalted by religious faith,
Nor uninformed by books, good books,
    though few —
In Nature's presence: thence may I select
Sorrow, that is not sorrow, but delight;
And miserable love, that is not pain
To hear of, for the glory that redounds
Therefrom to human kind, and what we
    are.
Be mine to follow with no timid step
Where knowledge leads me: it shall be
    my pride
That I have dared to tread this holy ground,
Speaking no dream, but things oracular;

Matter not lightly to be heard by those
Who to the letter of the outward promise
Do read the invisible soul; by men adroit
In speech, and for communion with the world
Accomplished; minds whose faculties are then
Most active when they are most eloquent,
And elevated most when most admired.
Men may be found of other mould than these,
Who are their own upholders, to themselves
Encouragement, and energy, and will,
Expressing liveliest thoughts in lively words
As native passion dictates. Others, too,
There are among the walks of homely life
Still higher, men for contemplation framed,
Shy, and unpractised in the strife of phrase;
Meek men, whose very souls perhaps would sink
Beneath them, summoned to such intercourse :
Theirs is the language of the heavens, the power,
The thought, the image, and the silent joy :
Words are but under-agents in their souls;
When they are grasping with their greatest strength,
They do not breathe among them : this I speak
In gratitude to God, Who feeds our hearts
For His own service; knoweth, loveth us,
When we are unregarded by the world.

Also, about this time did I receive
Convictions still more strong than heretofore,
Not only that the inner frame is good,
And graciously composed, but that, no less,
Nature for all conditions wants not power
To consecrate, if we have eyes to see,
The outside of her creatures, and to breathe
Grandeur upon the very humblest face
Of human life. I felt that the array
Of act and circumstance, and visible form,
Is mainly to the pleasure of the mind

What passion makes them; that meanwhile the forms
Of Nature have a passion in themselves,
That intermingles with those works of man
To which she summons him; although the works
Be mean, have nothing lofty of their own;
And that the Genius of the Poet hence
May boldly take his way among mankind
Wherever Nature leads; that he hath stood
By Nature's side among the men of old,
And so shall stand forever.   Dearest Friend !
If thou partake the animating faith
That Poets, even as Prophets, each with each
Connected in a mighty scheme of truth,
Have each his own peculiar faculty,
Heaven's gift, a sense that fits him to perceive
Objects unseen before, thou wilt not blame
The humblest of this band who dares to hope
That unto him hath also been vouchsafed
An insight that in some sort he possesses,
A privilege whereby a work of his,
Proceeding from a source of untaught things,
Creative and enduring, may become
A power like one of Nature's.   To a hope
Not less ambitious once among the wilds
Of Sarum's Plain, my youthful spirit was raised;
There, as I ranged at will the pastoral downs
Trackless and smooth, or paced the bare white roads
Lengthening in solitude their dreary line,
Time with his retinue of ages fled
Backwards, nor checked his flight until I saw
Our dim ancestral Past in vision clear;
Saw multitudes of men, and, here and there,
A single Briton clothed in wolf-skin vest,
With shield and stone-axe, stride across the wold;
The voice of spears was heard, the rattling spear.
Shaken by arms of mighty bone, in strength,
Long mouldered, of barbaric majesty.

I ealled on Darkness—but before the word
Was uttered, midnight darkness seemed
   to take
All objects from my sight; and lo! again
The Desert visible by dismal flames;
It is the sacrificial altar, fed
With living men — how deep the groans!
   the voice
Of those that crowd the giant wicker thrills
The monumental hillocks, and the pomp
Is for both worlds, the living and the dead.
At other moments — (for through that
   wide waste
Three summer days I roamed) where'er
   the Plain
Was figured o'er with circles, lines, or
   mounds,
That yet survive, a work, as some divine,
Shaped by the Druids, so to represent
Their knowledge of the heavens, and im-
   age forth
The constellations—gently was I charmed
Into a waking dream, a reverie
That, with believing eyes, where'er I
   turned,
Beheld long-bearded teachers, with white
   wands
Uplifted, pointing to the starry sky,
Alternately, and plain below, while breath
Of music swayed their motions, and the
   waste
Rejoiced with them and me in those sweet
   sounds.

   This for the past, and things that may
     be viewed
Or fancied in the obscurity of years
From monumental hints: and thou, O
   Friend!
Pleased with some unpremeditated strains
That served those wanderings to beguile,
   hast said
That then and there my mind had exercised
Upon the vulgar forms of present things,
The actual world of our familiar days,
Yet higher power; had caught from them
   a tone,
An image, and a character, by books
Not hitherto reflected. Call we this
A partial judgment — and yet why? for
   then
We were as strangers; and I may not
   speak

Thus wrongfully of verse, however rude,
Which on thy young imagination, trained
In the great City, broke like light from far.
Moreover, each man's Mind is to herself
Witness and judge; and I remember well
That in life's every-day appearances
I seemed about this time to gain clear
   sight
Of a new world — a world, too, that was
   fit
To be transmitted, and to other eyes
Made visible; as ruled by those fixed laws
Whence spiritual dignity originates,
Which do both give it being and maintain
A balance, an ennobling interchange
Of action from without and from within;
The excellence, pure function, and best
   power
Both of the objects seen, and eye that sees.

BOOK FOURTEENTH.

CONCLUSION.

IN one of those excursions (may they ne'er
Fade from remembrance!) through the
   Northern tracts
Of Cambria ranging with a youthful
   friend,
I left Bethgelert's huts at couching-time,
And westward took my way, to see the
   sun
Rise, from the top of Snowdon. To the
   door
Of a rude cottage at the mountain's base
.We came, and roused the shepherd who
   attends
The adventurous stranger's steps, a trusty
   guide;
Then, cheered by short refreshment, sal-
   lied forth.

   It was a close, warm, breezeless sum-
     mer night,
Wan, dull, and glaring, with a dripping
   fog
Low-hung and thick that covered all the
   sky;
But, undiscouraged, we began to climb
The mountain-side. The mist soon girt
   us round,
And, after ordinary travellers' talk

With our conductor, pensively we sank
Each into commerce with his private
    thoughts:
Thus did we breast the ascent, and by my-
    self
Was nothing either seen or heard that
    checked
Those musings or diverted, save that once
The shepherd's lurcher, who, among the
    crags,
Had to his joy unearthed a hedgehog,
    teased
His coiled-up prey with barkings turbu-
    lent.
This small adventure, for even such it
    seemed
In that wild place and at the dead of night,
Being over and forgotten, on we wound
In silence as before.   With forehead bent
Earthward, as if in opposition set
Against an enemy, I panted up
With eager pace, and no less eager
    thoughts.
Thus might we wear a midnight hour
    away,
Ascending at loose distance each from
    each,
And I, as chanced, the foremost of the
    band;
When at my feet the ground appeared to
    brighten,
And with a step or two seemed brighter
    still;
Nor was time given to ask or learn the
    cause,
For instantly a light upon the turf
Fell like a flash, and lo! as I looked up,
The Moon hung naked in a firmament
Of azure without cloud, and at my feet
Rested a silent sea of hoary mist.
A hundred hills their dusky backs up-
    heaved
All over this still ocean; and beyond,
Far, far beyond, the solid vapors stretched,
In headlands, tongues, and promontory
    shapes,
Into the main Atlantic, that appeared
To dwindle, and give up his majesty,
Usurped upon far as the sight could reach.
Not so the ethereal vault; encroachment
    none
Was there, nor loss; only the inferior stars
Had disappeared, or shed a fainter light

In the clear presence of the full-orbed
    Moon,
Who, from her sovereign elevation, gazed
Upon the billowy ocean, as it lay
All meek and silent, save that through a
    · rift —
Not distant from the shore whereon we
    stood,
·A fixed, abysmal, gloomy, breathing-
    place —
Mounted the roar of waters, torrents,
    streams
Innumerable, roaring with one voice!
Heard over earth and sea, and, in that
    hour,
For so it seemed, felt by the starry heavens.

When into air had partially dissolved
That vision, given to spirits of the night
And three chance human wanderers, in
    calm thought
Reflected, it appeared to me the type
Of a majestic intellect, its acts
And its possessions, what it has and
    craves,
What in itself it is, and would become.
There I beheld the emblem of a mind
That feeds upon infinity, that broods
Over the dark abyss, intent to hear
Its voices issuing forth to silent light
In one continuous stream; a mind sus-
    tained
By recognitions of transcendent power,
In sense conducting to ideal form,
In soul of more than mortal privilege.
One function, above all, of such a mind
Had Nature shadowed there, by putting
    forth,
'Mid circumstances awful and sublime,
That mutual domination which she loves
To exert upon the face of outward things,
So moulded, joined, abstracted, so en-
    dowed
With interchangeable supremacy,
That men, least sensitive, see, hear, per-
    ceive,
And cannot choose but feel.   The power,
    which all
Acknowledge when thus moved, which
    Nature thus
To bodily sense exhibits, is the express
Resemblance of that glorious faculty

That higher minds bear with them as their
    own.
This is the very spirit in which they deal
With the whole compass of the universe:
They from their native selves can send
    abroad
Kindred mutations; for themselves create
A like existence; and, whene'er it dawns
Created for them, catch it, or are caught
By its inevitable mastery,
Like angels stopped upon the wing by
    sound
Of harmony from Heaven's remotest
    spheres.
Them the enduring and the transient both
Serve to exalt; they build up greatest
    things
From least suggestions; ever on the
    watch,
Willing to work and to be wrought upon,
They need not extraordinary calls
To rouse them; in a world of life they live,
By sensible impressions not enthralled,
But by their quickening impulse made
    more prompt
To hold fit converse with the spiritual
    world,
And with the generations of mankind
Spread over time, past, present, and to
    come,
Age after age, till Time shall be no more.
Such minds are truly from the Deity,
For they are Powers; and hence the high-
    est bliss
That flesh can know is theirs — the con-
    sciousness
Of Whom they are, habitually infused
Through every image and through every
    thought,
And all affections by communion raised
From earth to heaven, from human to
    divine;
Hence endless occupation for the Soul,
Whether discursive or intuitive;
Hence cheerfulness for acts of daily life,
Emotions which best foresight need not
    fear,
Most worthy then of trust when most in-
    tense.
Hence, amid ills that vex and wrongs that
    crush
Our hearts — if here the words of Holy
    Writ

May with fit reverence be applied — that
    peace
Which passeth understanding, that repose
In moral judgments which from this pure
    source
Must come, or will by man be sought in
    vain.

Oh! who is he that hath his whole life
    long
Preserved, enlarged, this freedom in him-
    self?
For this alone is genuine liberty:
Where is the favored being who hath held
That course unchecked, unerring, and un-
    tired,
In one perpetual progress smooth and
    bright? —
A humbler destiny have we retraced,
And told of lapse and hesitating choice,
And backward wanderings along thorny
    ways:
Yet — compassed round by mountain soli-
    tudes,
Within whose solemn temple I received
My earliest visitations, careless then
Of what was given me; and which now I
    range,
A meditative, oft a suffering, man —
Do I declare — in accents which, from
    truth
Deriving cheerful confidence, shall blend
Their modulation with these vocal
    streams —
That, whatsoever falls my better mind,
Revolving with the accidents of life,
May have sustained, that, howso'er mis-
    led,
Never did I, in quest of right and wrong,
Tamper with conscience from a private
    aim;
Nor was in any public hope the dupe
Of selfish passions; nor did ever yield
Wilfully to mean cares or low pursuits,
But shrunk with apprehensive jealousy
From every combination which might aid
The tendency, too potent in itself,
Of use and custom to bow down the soul
Under a growing weight of vulgar sense,
And substitute a universe of death
For that which moves with light and life
    informed,

Actual, divine, and true. To fear and
love,
To love as prime and chief, for there fear
ends,
Be this ascribed; to early intercourse,
In presence of sublime or beautiful forms,
With the adverse principles of pain and
joy —
Evil as one is rashly named by men
Who know not what they speak. By love
subsists
All lasting grandeur, by pervading love;
That gone, we are as dust. — Behold the
fields
In balmy springtime full of rising flowers
And joyous creatures; see that pair, the
lamb
And the lamb's mother, and their tender
ways
Shall touch thee to the heart; thou callest
this love,
And not inaptly so, for love it is,
Far as it carries thee. In some green
bower
Rest, and be not alone, but have thou
there
The One who is thy choice of all the
world:
There linger, listening, gazing, with de-
light
Impassioned, but delight how pitiable!
Unless this love by a still higher love
Be hallowed, love that breathes not with-
out awe;
Love that adores, but on the knees of
prayer,
By heaven inspired; that frees from chains
the soul,
Lifted, in union with the purest, best,
Of earth-born passions, on the wings of
praise
Bearing a tribute to the Almighty's
Throne.

This spiritual Love acts not nor can
exist
Without Imagination, which, in truth,
Is but another name for absolute power
And clearest insight, amplitude of mind,
And Reason in her most exalted mood.
This faculty hath been the feeding source
Of our long labor: we have traced the
stream

From the blind cavern whence is faintly
heard
Its natal murmur; followed it to light
And open day; accompanied its course
Among the ways of Nature, for a time
Lost sight of it bewildered and engulphed;
Then given it greeting as it rose once more
In strength, reflecting from its placid
breast
The works of man and face of human life;
And lastly, from its progress have we
drawn
Faith in life endless, the sustaining
thought
Of human Being, Eternity, and God.

Imagination having been our theme,
So also hath that intellectual Love,
For they are each in each, and cannot
stand
Dividually. — Here must thou be, O Man!
Power to thyself; no Helper hast thou
here;
Here keepest thou in singleness thy state:
No other can divide with thee this work:
No secondary hand can intervene
To fashion this ability; 't is thine,
The prime and vital principle is thine
In the recesses of thy nature, far
From any reach of outward fellowship,
Else is not thine at all. But joy to him,
Oh, joy to him who here hath sown, hath
laid
Here, the foundation of his future years!
For all that friendship, all that love can
do,
All that a darling countenance can look
Or dear voice utter, to complete the man,
Perfect him, made imperfect in himself,
All shall be his: and he whose soul hath
risen
Up to the height of feeling intellect
Shall want no humbler tenderness; his
heart
Be tender as a nursing mother's heart;
Of female softness shall his life be full,
Of humble cares and delicate desires,
Mild interests and gentlest sympathies.

Child of my parents! Sister of my soul!
Thanks in sincerest verse have been else-
where
Poured out for all the early tenderness

Which I from thee imbibed: and 't is most
true
That later seasons owed to thee no less;
For, spite of thy sweet influence and the
touch
Of kindred hands that opened out the
springs
Of genial thought in childhood, and in
spite
Of all that unassisted I had marked
In life or nature of those charms minute
That win their way into the heart by
stealth
(Still to the very going-out of youth)
I too exclusively esteemed *that* love,
And sought *that* beauty, which, as Milton
sings,
Hath terror in it. Thou didst soften down
This over-sternness; but for thee, dear
Friend!
My soul, too reckless of mild grace, had
stood
In her original self too confident,
Retained too long a countenance severe;
A rock with torrents roaring, with the
clouds
Familiar, and a favorite of the stars:
But thou didst plant its crevices with
flowers,
Hang it with shrubs that twinkle in the
breeze,
And teach the little birds to build their
nests
And warble in its chambers. At a time
When Nature, destined to remain so long
Foremost in my affections, had fallen back
Into a second place, pleased to become
A handmaid to a nobler than herself,
When every day brought with it some new
sense
Of exquisite regard for common things,
And all the earth was budding with these
gifts
Of more refined humanity, thy breath,
Dear Sister! was a kind of gentler spring
That went before my steps. Thereafter
came
One whom with thee friendship had early
paired;
She came, no more a phantom to adorn
A moment, but an inmate of the heart,
And yet a spirit, there for me enshrined
To penetrate the lofty and the low;

Even as one essence of pervading light
Shines, in the brightest of ten thousand
stars
And the meek worm that feeds her lonely
lamp
Couched in the dewy grass.
                          With such a theme,
Coleridge! with this my argument, of thee
Shall I be silent? O capacious Soul!
Placed on this earth to love and under-
stand,
And from thy presence shed the light of
love,
Shall I be mute, ere thou be spoken of?
Thy kindred influence to my heart of
hearts
Did also find its way. Thus fear relaxed
Her overweening grasp; thus thoughts
and things
In the self-haunting spirit learned to take
More rational proportions; mystery,
The incumbent mystery of sense and soul,
Of life and death, time and eternity,
Admitted more habitually a mild
Interposition — a serene delight
In closelier gathering cares, such as
become
A human creature, howso'er endowed,
Poet, or destined for a humbler name;
And so the deep enthusiastic joy,
The rapture of the hallelujah sent
From all that breathes and is, was
chastened, stemmed
And balanced by pathetic truth, by trust
In hopeful reason, leaning on the stay
Of Providence; and in reverence for duty,
Here, if need be, struggling with storms,
and there
Strewing in peace life's humblest ground
with herbs,
At every season green, sweet at all hours.

And now, O Friend! this history is
brought
To its appointed close: the discipline
And consummation of a Poet's mind,
In everything that stood most prominent,
Have faithfully been pictured; we have
reached
The time (our guiding object from the
first)
When we may, not presumptuously, I
hope,

Suppose my powers so far confirmed,
and such
My knowledge, as to make me capable
Of building up a Work that shall endure.
Yet much hath been omitted, as need
was;
Of books how much! and even of the
other wealth
That is collected among woods and fields,
Far more: for Nature's secondary grace
Hath hitherto been barely touched upon,
The charm more superficial that attends
Her works, as they present to Fancy's
choice
Apt illustrations of the moral world,
Caught at a glance, or traced with curi-
ous pains.

Finally, and above all, O Friend!
(I speak
With due regret) how much is overlooked
In human nature and her subtle ways,
As studied first in our own hearts, and
then
In life among the passions of mankind,
Varying their composition and their hue,
Where'er we move, under the diverse
shapes
That individual character presents
To an attentive eye. For progress meet,
Along this intricate and difficult path,
Whate'er was wanting, something had I
gained,
As one of many schoolfellows compelled,
In hardy independence, to stand up
Amid conflicting interests, and the shock
Of various tempers; to endure and note
What was not understood, though known
to be;
Among the mysteries of love and hate,
Honor and shame, looking to right and
left,
Unchecked by innocence too delicate,
And moral notions too intolerant,
Sympathies too contracted. Hence,
when called
To take a station among men, the step
Was easier, the transition more secure,
More profitable also; for, the mind
Learns from such timely exercise to keep
In wholesome separation the two natures,
The one that feels, the other that ob-
serves.

Yet one word more of personal con-
cern; —
Since I withdrew unwillingly from
France,
I led an undomestic wanderer's life,
In London chiefly harbored, whence I
roamed,
Tarrying at will in many a pleasant spot
Of rural England's cultivated vales
Or Cambrian solitudes. A youth — (he
bore
The name of Calvert — it shall live, if
words
Of mine can give it life,) in firm belief
That by endowments not from me with-
held
Good might be furthered — in his last
decay
By a bequest sufficient for my needs
Enabled me to pause for choice, and walk
At large and unrestrained, nor damped
too soon
By mortal cares. Himself no Poet, yet
Far less a common follower of the world,
He deemed that my pursuits and labors
lay
Apart from all that leads to wealth, or
even
A necessary maintenance insures,
Without some hazard to the finer sense;
He cleared a passage for me, and the
stream
Flowed in the bent of Nature.
                                  Having now
Told what best merits mention, further
pains
Our present purpose seems not to re-
quire,
And I have other tasks. Recall to mind
The mood in which this labor was begun,
O Friend! The termination of my course
Is nearer now, much nearer; yet even
then,
In that distraction and intense desire,
I said unto the life which I had lived,
Where art thou? Hear I not a voice
from thee
Which 't is reproach to hear? Anon I
rose
As if on wings, and saw beneath me
stretched
Vast prospect of the world which I had
been

And was; and hence this Song, which, like a lark,
I have protracted, in the unwearied heavens
Singing, and often with more plaintive voice
To earth attempered and her deep-drawn sighs,
Yet centring all in love, and in the end
All gratulant, if rightly understood.

Whether to me shall be allotted life,
And, with life, power to accomplish aught of worth,
That will be deemed no insufficient plea
For having given the story of myself,
Is all uncertain: but, belovèd Friend!
When, looking back, thou seest, in clearer view
Than any liveliest sight of yesterday,
That summer, under whose indulgent skies,
Upon smooth Quantock's airy ridge we roved
Unchecked, or loitered 'mid her sylvan combs,
Thou in bewitching words, with happy heart,
Didst chant the vision of that Ancient Man,
The bright-eyed Mariner, and rueful woes
Didst utter of the Lady Christabel;
And I, associate with such labor, steeped
In soft forgetfulness the livelong hours,
Murmuring of him who, joyous hap, was found,
After the perils of his moonlight ride,
Near the loud waterfall; or her who sate
In misery near the miserable Thorn —
When thou dost to that summer turn thy thoughts,
And hast before thee all which then we were,
To thee, in memory of that happiness,
It will be known, by thee at least, my Friend!
Felt, that the history of a Poet's mind
Is labor not unworthy of regard;
To thee the work shall justify itself.

The last and later portions of this gift
Have been prepared, not with the buoyant spirits
That were our daily portion when we first
Together wantoned in wild Poesy,
But, under pressure of a private grief,
Keen and enduring, which the mind and heart,
That in this meditative history
Have been laid open, needs must make me feel
More deeply, yet enable me to bear
More firmly; and a comfort now hath risen
From hope that thou art near, and wilt be soon
Restored to us in renovated health;
When, after the first mingling of our tears,
'Mong other consolations, we may draw
Some pleasure from this offering of my love.

Oh! yet a few short years of useful life,
And all will be complete, thy race be run,
Thy monument of glory will be raised;
Then, though (too weak to tread the ways of truth)
This age fall back to old idolatry,
Though men return to servitude as fast
As the tide ebbs, to ignominy and shame,
By nations, sink together, we shall still
Find solace — knowing what we have learnt to know,
Rich in true happiness if allowed to be
Faithful alike in forwarding a day
Of firmer trust, joint laborers in the work
(Should Providence such grace to us vouchsafe)
Of their deliverance, surely yet to come.
Prophets of Nature, we to them will speak
A lasting inspiration, sanctified
By reason, blest by faith: what we have loved,
Others will love, and we will teach them how;
Instruct them how the mind of man becomes
A thousand times more beautiful than the earth
On which he dwells, above this frame of things
(Which, 'mid all revolution in the hopes
And fears of men, doth still remain unchanged)
In beauty exalted, as it is itself
Of quality and fabric more divine.

1799–1805.   1850.

THE RECLUSE.

PART FIRST.

BOOK FIRST — HOME AT GRASMERE.

ONCE to the verge of yon steep barrier
  came
A roving school-boy; what the adven-
  turer's age
Hath now escaped his memory — but
  the hour,
One of a golden summer holiday,
He well remembers, though the year be
  gone —
Alone and devious from afar he came;
And, with a sudden influx overpowered
At sight of this seclusion, he forgot
His haste, for hasty had his footsteps been
As boyish his pursuits; and sighing said,
" What happy fortune were it here to live !
And, if a thought of dying, if a thought
Of mortal separation, could intrude
With paradise before him, here to die ! "
No Prophet was he, had not even a hope,
Scarcely a wish, but one bright pleasing
  thought,
A fancy in the heart of what might be
The lot of others, never could be his.
 The station whence he looked was soft
  and green,
Not giddy yet aërial, with a depth
Of vale below, a height of hills above.
For rest of body perfect was the spot,
All that luxurious nature could desire;
But stirring to the spirit; who could gaze
And not feel motions there? He thought
  of clouds
That sail on winds: of breezes that delight
To play on water, or in endless chase
Pursue each other through the yielding
  plain
Of grass or corn, over and through and
  through,
In billow after billow, evermore
Disporting — nor unmindful was the boy-
Of sunbeams, shadows, butterflies and
  birds;
Of fluttering sylphs and softly-gliding
  Fays,
Genii, and wingèd angels that are Lords
Without restraint of all which they behold.

The illusion strengthening as he gazed,
  he felt
That such unfettered liberty was his,
Such power and joy; but only for this end,
To flit from field to rock, from rock to
  field,
From shore to island, and from isle to
  shore,
From open ground to covert, from a bed
Of meadow-flowers into a tuft of wood;
From high to low, from low to high, yet
  still
Within the bound of this huge concave;
  here
Must be his home, this valley be his
  world.
 Since that day forth the Place to him
  — to me
(For I who live to register the truth
Was that same young and happy Being)
  became
As beautiful to thought, as it had been
When present, to the bodily sense; a
  haunt
Of pure affections, shedding upon joy
A brighter joy; and through such damp
  and gloom
Of the gay mind, as oft-times splenetic
  youth
Mistakes for sorrow, darting beams of
  light
That no self-cherished sadness could
  withstand;
And now 't is mine, perchance for life,
  dear Vale,
Beloved Grasmere (let the wandering
  streams
Take up, the cloud-capt hills repeat, the
  Name)
One of thy lowly Dwellings is my Home.
 And was the cost so great? and could
  it seem
An act of courage, and the thing itself
A conquest? who must bear the blame?
  Sage man
Thy prudence, thy experience, thy desires,
Thy apprehensions — blush thou for
  them all.
 Yes the realities of life so cold,
So cowardly, so ready to betray,
So stinted in the measure of their grace
As we pronounce them, doing them much
  wrong,

Have been to me more bountiful than
    hope,
Less timid than desire — but that is past.
On Nature's invitation do I come,
By Reason sanctioned. Can the choice
    mislead,
That made the calmest fairest spot of
    earth
With all its unappropriated good
My own; and not mine only, for with me
Entrenched, say rather peacefully em-
    bowered,
Under yon orchard, in yon humble cot,
A younger Orphan of a home extinct,
The only Daughter of my Parents dwells.
    Ay, think on that, my heart, and cease
    to stir,
Pause upon that and let the breathing
    frame
No longer breathe, but all be satisfied.
— Oh, if such silence be not thanks to
    God
For what hath been bestowed, then
    where, where then
Shall gratitude find rest? Mine eyes did
    ne'er
Fix on a lovely object, nor my mind
Take pleasure in the midst of happy
    thoughts,
But either She whom now I have, who now
Divides with me this loved abode, was
    there,
Or not far off. Where'er my footsteps
    turned,
Her voice was like a hidden Bird that sang.
The thought of her was like a flash of light,
Or an unseen companionship, a breath
Of fragrance independent of the Wind.
In all my goings, in the new and old
Of all my meditations, and in this
Favorite of all, in this the most of all.
— What being, therefore, since the birth
    of Man
Had ever more abundant cause to speak
Thanks, and if favors of the Heavenly
    Muse
Make him more thankful, then to call on
    Verse
To aid him and in song resound his joy?
The boon is absolute; surpassing grace
To me hath been vouchsafed; among the
    bowers
Of blissful Eden this was neither given

Nor could be given, possession of the good
Which had been sighed for, ancient
    thought fulfilled,
And dear Imaginations realized,
Up to their highest measure, yea and
    more.
    Embrace me then, ye Hills, and close
    me in;
Now in the clear and open day I feel
Your guardianship; I take it to my heart;
'T is like the solemn shelter of the night.
But I would call thee beautiful, for mild,
And soft, and gay, and beautiful thou
    art
Dear Valley, having in thy face a smile
Though peaceful, full of gladness. Thou
    art pleased,
Pleased with thy crags and woody steeps,
    thy Lake,
Its one green island and its winding
    shores;
The multitude of little rocky hills,
Thy Church and cottages of mountain
    stone
Clustered like stars some few, but single
    most,
And lurking dimly in their shy retreats,
Or glancing at each other cheerful looks
Like separated stars with clouds between.
What want we? have we not perpetual
    streams,
Warm woods, and sunny hills, and fresh
    green fields,
And mountains not less green, and flocks
    and herds,
And thickets full of songsters, and the
    voice
Of lordly birds, an unexpected sound
Heard now and then from morn to latest
    eve,
Admonishing the man who walks below
Of solitude and silence in the sky?
These have we, and a thousand nooks of
    earth
Have also these, but nowhere else is
    found,
Nowhere (or is it fancy?) can be found
The one sensation that is here; 't is here,
Here as it found its way into my heart
In childhood, here as it abides by day,
By night, here only; or in chosen minds
That take it with them hence, where'er
    they go.

—'T is, but I cannot name it, 't is the
　　sense
Of majesty, and beauty, and repose,
A blended holiness of earth and sky,
Something that makes this individual spot,
This small abiding-place of many men,
A termination, and a last retreat,
A centre, come from whereso'er you will,
A whole without dependence or defect,
Made for itself, and happy in itself,
Perfect contentment, Unity entire.

　　Bleak season was it, turbulent and
　　　bleak,
When hitherward we journeyed side by
　　side
Through burst of sunshine and through
　　flying showers;
Paced the long vales — how long they
　　were — and yet
How fast that length of way was left
　　behind,
Wensley's rich Vale, and Sedbergh's
　　naked heights.
The frosty wind, as if to make amends
For its keen breath, was aiding to our
　　steps,
And drove us onward like two ships at sea,
Or like two birds, companions in mid-air,
Parted and reunited by the blast.
Stern was the face of nature; we rejoiced
In that stern countenance, for our souls
　　thence drew
A feeling of their strength. The naked
　　trees,
The icy brooks, as on we passed, appeared
To question us. "Whence come ye, to
　　what end?"
They seemed to say, "What would ye,"
　　said the shower,
"Wild Wanderers, whither through my
　　dark domain?"
The sunbeam said, "Be happy." When
　　this vale
We entered, bright and solemn was the sky
That faced us with a passionate welcom-
　　ing,
And led us to our threshold. Daylight
　　failed
Insensibly, and round us gently fell
Composing darkness, with a quiet load
Of full contentment, in a little shed
Disturbed, uneasy in itself as seemed,
And wondering at its new inhabitants.

It loves us now, this Vale so beautiful
Begins to love us! by a sullen storm,
Two months unwearied of severest storm,
It put the temper of our minds to proof,
And found us faithful through the gloom,
　　and heard
The poet mutter his prelusive songs
With cheerful heart, an unknown voice of
　　joy
Among the silence of the woods and hills;
Silent to any gladsomeness of sound
With all their shepherds.
　　　　　　　But the gates of Spring
Are opened; churlish winter hath given
　　leave
That she should entertain for this one day,
Perhaps for many genial days to come,
His guests, and make them jocund.—They
　　are pleased,
But most of all the birds that haunt the
　　flood
With the mild summons; inmates though
　　they be
Of Winter's household, they keep festival
This day, who drooped, or seemed to
　　droop, so long;
They show their pleasure, and shall I do
　　less?
Happier of happy though I be, like them
I cannot take possession of the sky,
Mount with a thoughtless impulse, and
　　wheel there
One of a mighty multitude, whose way
Is a perpetual harmony and dance
Magnificent. Behold how with a grace
Of ceaseless motion, that might scarcely
　　seem
Inferior to angelical, they prolong
Their curious pastime, shaping in mid-air,
And sometimes with ambitious wing that
　　soars
High as the level of the mountain tops,
A circuit ampler than the lake beneath,
Their own domain;—but ever, while intent
On tracing and retracing that large round,
Their jubilant activity evolves
Hundreds of curves and circlets, to and fro,
Upwards and downwards; progress intri-
　　cate
Yet unperplexed, as if one spirit swayed
Their indefatigable flight. 'T is done,
Ten times and more I fancied it had ceased.
But lo! the vanished company again

Ascending, they approach. I hear their
 wings
Faint, faint at first; and then an eager
 sound
Passed in a moment — and as faint again!
They tempt the sun to sport among their
 plumes;
Tempt the smooth water, or the gleaming
 ice,
To show them a fair image, — 't is them-
 selves,
Their own fair forms upon the glimmering
 plain
Painted more soft and fair as they descend,
Almost to touch, — then up again aloft,
Up with a sally and a flash of speed,
As if they scorned both resting-place and
 rest!
— This day is a thanksgiving, 't is a day
Of glad emotion and deep quietness;
Not upon me alone hath been bestowed,
Me rich in many onward-looking thoughts,
The penetrating bliss; oh surely these
Have felt it, not the happy choirs of spring,
Her own peculiar family of love
That sport among green leaves, a blither
 train!
 But two are missing, two, a lonely pair
Of milk-white Swans; wherefore are they
 not seen
Partaking this day's pleasure? From afar
They came, to sojourn here in solitude,
Choosing this Valley, they who had the
 choice
Of the whole world. We saw them day
 by day,
Through those two months of unrelenting
 storm,
Conspicuous at the centre of the Lake
Their safe retreat, we knew them well, I
 guess
That the whole valley knew them; but
 to us
They were more dear than may be well
 believed,
Not only for their beauty, and their still
And placid way of life, and constant love
Inseparable, not for these alone,
But that *their* state so much resembled
 ours,
They having also chosen this abode;
They strangers, and we strangers, they a
 pair,

And we a solitary pair like them.
They should not have departed; many days
Did I look forth in vain, nor on the
 wing
Could see them, nor in that small open
 space
Of blue unfrozen water, where they lodged
And lived so long and quiet, side by side.
Shall we behold them consecrated friends,
Faithful companions, yet another year
Surviving, they for us, and we for them,
And neither pair be broken? nay perchance
It is too late already for such hope;
The Dalesmen may have aimed the deadly
 tube,
And parted them; or haply both are gone
One death, and that were mercy given to
 both.
Recall, my song, the ungenerous thought;
 forgive,
Thrice favored Region, the conjecture
 harsh
Of such inhospitable penalty
Inflicted upon confidence so pure.
Ah! if I wished to follow where the sight
Of all that is before my eyes, the voice
Which speaks from a presiding spirit here,
Would lead me, I should whisper to my-
 self:
They who are dwellers in this holy place
Must needs themselves be hallowed, they
 require
No benediction from the stranger's lips,
For they are blessed already; none would
 give
The greeting " peace be with you " unto
 them,
For peace they have; it cannot but be
 theirs,
And mercy, and forbearance — nay — not
 these —
Their healing offices a pure good-will
Precludes, and charity beyond the bounds
Of charity — an overflowing love;
Not for the creature only, but for all
That is around them; love for everything
Which in their happy Region they behold!
 Thus do we soothe ourselves, and when
 the thought
Is passed, we blame it not for having
 come.
— What if I floated down a pleasant
 stream,

And now am landed, and the motion gone,
Shall I reprove myself? Ah no, the stream
Is flowing, and will never cease to flow,
And I shall float upon that stream again.
By such forgetfulness the soul becomes,
Words cannot say how beautiful: then
    hail,
Hail to the visible Presence, hail to thee,
Delightful Valley, habitation fair!
And to whatever else of outward form
Can give an inward help, can purify,
And elevate, and harmonize, and soothe,
And steal away, and for a while deceive
And lap in pleasing rest, and bear us on
Without desire in full complacency,
Contemplating perfection absolute,
And entertained as in a placid sleep.

  But not betrayed by tenderness of mind
That feared, or wholly overlooked the
    truth,
Did we come hither, with romantic hope
To find in midst of so much loveliness
Love, perfect love: of so much majesty
A like majestic frame of mind in those
Who here abide, the persons like the place.
Not from such hope, or aught of such
    belief,
Hath issued any portion of the joy
Which I have felt this day. An awful voice
'T is true hath in my walks been often
    heard,
Sent from the mountains or the sheltered
    fields,
Shout after shout — reiterated whoop,
In manner of a bird that takes delight
In answering to itself: or like a hound
Single at chase among the lonely woods,
His yell repeating; yet it was in truth
A human voice—a spirit of coming night;
How solemn when the sky is dark, and
    earth
Not dark, nor yet enlightened, but by snow
Made visible, amid a noise of winds
And bleatings manifold of mountain sheep,
Which in that iteration recognize
Their summons, and are gathering round
    for food,
Devoured with keenness, ere to grove or
    bank
Or rocky bield with patience they retire.
    That very voice, which, in some timid
    mood
Of superstitious fancy, might have seemed

Awful as ever stray demoniac uttered,
His steps to govern in the wilderness;
Or as the Norman Curfew's regular beat
To hearths when first they darkened at
    the knell:
That shepherd's voice, it may have
    reached mine ear
Debased and under profanation, made
The ready organ of articulate sounds
From ribaldry, impiety, or wrath,
Issuing when shame hath ceased to check
    the brawls
Of some abused Festivity — so be it.
I came not dreaming of unruffled life,
Untainted manners; born among the hills,
Bred also there, I wanted not a scale
To regulate my hopes; pleased with the
    good
I shrink not from the evil with disgust,
Or with immoderate pain. I look for Man,
The common creature of the brotherhood,
Differing but little from the Man else-
    where,
For selfishness and envy and revenge,
Ill neighborhood — pity that this should
    be —
Flattery and double-dealing, strife and
    wrong.

  Yet is it something gained, it is in truth
A mighty gain, that Labor here preserves
His rosy face, a servant only here
Of the fireside or of the open field,
A Freeman therefore sound and unim-
    paired:
That extreme penury is here unknown,
And cold and hunger's abject wretched-
    ness
Mortal to body and the heaven-born mind:
That they who want are not too great a
    weight
For those who can relieve; here may the
    heart
Breathe in the air of fellow-suffering
Dreadless, as in a kind of fresher breeze
Of her own native element, the hand
Be ready and unwearied without plea,
From tasks too frequent or beyond its
    power,
For languor or indifference or despair.
And as these lofty barriers break the force
Of winds, — this deep Vale, as it doth in
    part
Conceal us from the storm, so here abides

A power and a protection for the mind,
Dispensed indeed to other solitudes
Favored by noble privilege like this,
Where kindred independence of estate
Is prevalent, where he who tills the field,
He, happy man! is master of the field,
And treads the mountains which his
    Fathers trod.
    Not less than halfway up yon moun-
        tain's side,
Behold a dusky spot, a grove of Firs
That seems still smaller than it is; this
        grove
Is haunted — by what ghost? a gentle
        spirit
Of memory faithful to the call of love;
For, as reports the Dame, whose fire
        sends up
Yon curling smoke from the gray cot
        below,
The trees (her first-born child being then
        a babe)
Were planted by her husband and herself,
That ranging o'er the high and houseless
        ground
Their sheep might neither want from
        perilous storm
Of winter, nor from summer's sultry heat,
A friendly covert; "and they knew it
        well,"
Said she, "for thither as the trees grew up
We to the patient creatures carried food
In times of heavy snow." She then began
In fond obedience to her private thoughts
To speak of her dead husband; is there
        not
An art, a music, and a strain of words
That shall be life, the acknowledged
        voice of life,
Shall speak of what is done among the
        fields,
Done truly there, or felt, of solid good
And real evil, yet be sweet withal,
More grateful, more harmonious than the
        breath,
The idle breath of softest pipe attuned
To pastoral fancies? Is there such a stream
Pure and unsullied flowing from the heart
With motions of true dignity and grace?
Or must we seek that stream where Man
        is not?
Methinks I could repeat in tuneful verse,
Delicious as the gentlest breeze that sounds

Through that aërial fir-grove — could pre-
        serve
Some portion of its human history
As gathered from the Matron's lips, and
        tell
Of tears that have been shed at sight of
        it,
And moving dialogues between this Pair
Who in their prime of wedlock, with joint
        hands
Did plant the grove, now flourishing,
        while they
No longer flourish, he entirely gone,
She withering in her loneliness. Be this
A task above my skill — the silent mind
Has her own treasures, and I think of
        these,
Love what I see, and honor humankind.
    No, we are not alone, we do not stand,
My sister here misplaced and desolate,
Loving what no one cares for but our-
        selves.
We shall not scatter through the plains
        and rocks
Of this fair Vale, and o'er its spacious
        heights,
Unprofitable kindliness, bestowed
On objects unaccustomed to the gifts
Of feeling, which were cheerless and for-
        lorn
But few weeks past, and would be so again
Were we not here; we do not tend a lamp
Whose lustre we alone participate,
Which shines dependent upon us alone,
Mortal though bright, a dying, dying flame.
Look where we will, some human hand
        has been
Before us with its offering; not a tree
Sprinkles these little pastures, but the
        same
Hath furnished matter for a thought; per-
        chance
For some one serves as a familiar friend.
Joy spreads, and sorrow spreads; and this
        whole Vale,
Home of untutored shepherds as it is,
Swarms with sensation, as with gleams of
        sunshine,
Shadows or breezes, scents or sounds.
        Nor deem
These feelings, though subservient more
        than ours
To every day's demand for daily bread,

And borrowing more their spirit and their
    shape
From self-respecting interests; deem them
    not
Unworthy therefore, and unhallowed—no,
They lift the animal being, do themselves
By nature's kind and ever-present aid
Refine the selfishness from which they
    spring,
Redeem by love the individual sense
Of anxiousness, with which they are com-
    bined.
And thus it is that fitly they become
Associates in the joy of purest minds:
They blend therewith congenially: mean-
    while
Calmly they breathe their own undying life
Through this their mountain sanctuary;
    long
Oh long may it remain inviolate,
Diffusing health and sober cheerfulness,
And giving to the moments as they pass
Their little boons of animating thought
That sweeten labor, make it seen and felt
To be no arbitrary weight imposed,
But a glad function natural to man.

    Fair proof of this, newcomer though I be,
Already have I gained; the inward frame,
Though slowly opening, opens every day
With process not unlike to that which
    cheers
A pensive stranger journeying at his leisure
Through some Helvetian Dell; when low-
    hung mists
Break up and are beginning to recede;
How pleased he is where thin and thinner
    grows
The veil, or where it parts at once, to spy
The dark pines thrusting forth their spiky
    heads;
To watch the spreading lawns with cattle
    grazed;
Then to be greeted by the scattered huts
As they shine out; and *see* the streams
    whose murmur
Had soothed his ear while *they* were hid-
    den; how pleased
To have about him which way e'er he goes
Something on every side concealed from
    view,
In every quarter something visible
Half seen or wholly, lost and found again,
Alternate progress and impediment,

And yet a growing prospect in the main.
    Such pleasure now is mine, albeit forced,
Herein less happy than the Traveller,
To cast from time to time a painful look
Upon unwelcome things which unawares
Reveal themselves, not therefore is my
    heart
Depressed, nor does it fear what is to
    come;
But confident, enriched at every glance,
The more I see the more delight my mind
Receives, or by reflection can create:
Truth justifies herself, and as she dwells
With Hope, who would not follow where
    she leads?
    Nor let me pass unheeded other loves
Where no fear is, and humbler sympathies.
Already hath sprung up within my heart
A liking for the small gray horse that bears
The paralytic man, and for the brute
In Scripture sanctified — the patient brute
On which the cripple, in the quarry
    maimed,
Rides to and fro: I know them and their
    ways.
The famous sheep-dog, first in all the vale,
Though yet to me a stranger, will not be
A stranger long; nor will the blind man's
    guide,
Meek and neglected thing, of no renown!
Soon will peep forth the primrose, ere it
    fades
Friends shall I have at dawn, blackbird
    and thrush
To rouse me, and a hundred warblers
    more!
And if those Eagles to their ancient hold
Return, Helvellyn's Eagles! with the
    Pair
From my own door I shall be free to claim
Acquaintance, as they sweep from cloud
    to cloud.
The owl that gives the name to Owlet-
    Crag
Have I heard whooping, and he soon
    will be
A chosen one of my regards. See there
The heifer in yon little croft belongs
To one who holds it dear; with duteous
    care
She reared it, and in speaking of her
    charge
I heard her scatter some endearing words

Domestic, and in spirit motherly,
She being herself a mother; happy Beast,
If the caresses of a human voice
Can make it so, and care of human hands.
  And ye as happy under Nature's care,
Strangers to me and all men, or at least
Strangers to all particular amity,
All intercourse of knowledge or of love
That parts the individual from his kind.
Whether in large communities ye keep
From year to year, not shunning man's
    abode,
A settled residence, or be from far
Wild creatures, and of many homes, that
    come
The gift of winds, and whom the winds
    again
Take from us at your pleasure; yet shall ye
Not want for this your own subordinate
    place
In my affections. Witness the delight
With which erewhile I saw that multitude
Wheel through the sky, and see them now
    at rest,
Yet not at rest upon the glassy lake:
They *cannot* rest — they gambol like
    young whelps;
Active as lambs, and overcome with joy
They try all frolic motions; flutter, plunge,
And beat the passive water with their
    wings.
Too distant are they for plain view, but lo!
Those little fountains, sparkling in the
    sun,
Betray their occupation, rising up
First one and then another silver spout,
As one or other takes the fit of glee,
Fountains and spouts, yet somewhat in
    the guise
Of plaything fireworks, that on festal
    nights
Sparkle about the feet of wanton boys.
— How vast the compass of this theatre,
Yet nothing to be seen but lovely pomp
And silent majesty; the birch-tree woods
Are hung with thousand thousand dia-
    mond drops
Of melted hoar-frost, every tiny knot
In the bare twigs, each little budding-
    place
Cased with its several beads; what myr-
    iads these
Upon one tree, while all the distant grove,

That rises to the summit of the steep,
Shows like a mountain built of silver
    light:
See yonder the same pageant, and again
Behold the universal imagery
Inverted, all its sun-bright features
    touched
As with the varnish and the gloss of
    dreams.
Dreamlike the blending also of the whole
Harmonious landscape: all along the
    shore
The boundary lost — the line invisible
That parts the image from reality;
And the clear hills, as high as they ascend
Heavenward, so deep piercing the lake
    below.
Admonished of the days of love to come
The raven croaks, and fills the upper air
With a strange sound of genial harmony;
And in and all about that playful band,
Incapable although they be of rest,
And in their fashion very rioters,
There is a stillness; and they seem to
    make
Calm revelry in that their calm abode.
Them leaving to their joyous hours I pass,
Pass with a thought the life of the whole
    year
That is to come: the throng of woodland
    flowers
And lilies that will dance upon the waves.
  Say boldly then that solitude is not
Where these things are: he truly is alone,
He of the multitude whose eyes are
    doomed
To hold a vacant commerce day by day
With Objects wanting life — repelling
    love;
He by the vast metropolis immured,
Where pity shrinks from unremitting calls,
Where numbers overwhelm humanity,
And neighborhood serves rather to divide
Than to unite — what sighs more deep
    than his,
Whose nobler will hath long been sacri-
    ficed;
Who must inhabit under a black sky
A city, where, if indifference to disgust
Yield not to scorn or sorrow, living men
Are oft-times to their fellow-men no more
Than to the forest Hermit are the leaves
That hang aloft in myriads; nay, far less,

For they protect his walk from sun and
 shower,
Swell his devotion with their voice in
 storms,
And whisper while the stars twinkle
 among them
His lullaby.   From crowded streets re-
 mote,
Far from the living and dead Wilderness
Of the thronged world, Society is here
A true community — a genuine frame
Of many into one incorporate.
That must be looked for here: paternal
 sway,
One household, under God, for high and
 low,
One family and one mansion; to them-
 selves
Appropriate, and divided from the world,
As if it were a cave, a multitude
Human and brute, possessors undisturbed
Of this Recess — their legislative Hall,
Their Temple, and their glorious Dwell-
 ing-place.
   Dismissing therefore all Arcadian
 dreams,
All golden fancies of the golden age,
The bright array of shadowy thoughts
 from times
That were before all time, or are to be
Ere time expire, the pageantry that stirs
Or will be stirring, when our eyes are
 fixed
On lovely objects, and we wish to part
With all remembrance of a jarring world,
— Take we at once this one sufficient
 hope,
What need of more? that we shall neither
 droop
Nor pine for want of pleasure in the life
Scattered about us, nor through want of
 aught
That keeps in health the insatiable mind.
— That we shall have for knowledge and
 for love
Abundance, and that feeling as we do
How goodly, how exceeding fair, how
 pure
From all reproach is yon ethereal vault,
And this deep Vale, its earthly counter-
 part,
By which and under which we are en-
 closed

To breathe in peace; we shall moreover
 find
(If sound, and what we ought to be our-
 selves,
If rightly we observe and justly weigh)
The inmates not unworthy of their home,
The Dwellers of their Dwelling.
                                  And if this
Were otherwise, we have within ourselves
Enough to fill the present day with joy,
And overspread the future years with
 hope,
Our beautiful and quiet home, enriched
Already with a stranger whom we love
Deeply, a stranger of our Father's house,
A never-resting Pilgrim of the Sea,
Who finds at last an hour to his content
Beneath our roof.   And others whom we
 love
Will seek us also, Sisters of our hearts,
And one, like them, a Brother of our
 hearts,
Philosopher and Poet, in whose sight
These mountains will rejoice with open
 joy.
— Such is our wealth!   O Vale of Peace
 we are
And must be, with God's will, a happy
 Band.
   Yet 't is not to enjoy that we exist,
For that end only; something must be
 done:
I must not walk in unreproved delight
These narrow bounds, and think of noth-
 ing more,
No duty that looks further, and no care.
Each Being has his office, lowly some
And common, yet all worthy if fulfilled
With zeal, acknowledgment that with the
 gift
Keeps pace a harvest answering to the
 seed.
Of ill-advised Ambition and of Pride
I would stand clear, but yet to me I
 feel
That an internal brightness is vouchsafed
That must not die, that must not pass
 away.
Why does this inward lustre fondly seek
And gladly blend with outward fellow-
 ship?
Why do *they* shine around me whom I
 love?

Why do they teach me, whom I thus
    revere?
Strange question, yet it answers not itself.
That humble Roof embowered among
    the trees,
That calm fireside, it is not even in them,
Blest as they are, to furnish a reply
That satisfies and ends in perfect rest.
Possessions have I that are solely mine,
Something within which yet is shared by
    none,
Not even the nearest to me and most dear,
Something which power and effort may
    impart;
I would impart it, I would spread it wide:
Immortal in the world which is to come —
Forgive me if I add another claim —
And would not wholly perish even in this,
Lie down and be forgotten in the dust,
I and the modest Partners of my days
Making a silent company in death;
Love, knowledge, all my manifold de-
    lights,
All buried with me without monument
Or profit unto any but ourselves!
It must not be, if I, divinely taught,
Be privileged to speak as I have felt
Of what in man is human or divine.
    While yet an innocent little one, with
    a heart
That doubtless wanted not its tender
    moods,
I breathed (for this I better recollect)
Among wild appetites and blind desires,
Motions of savage instinct my delight
And exaltation. Nothing at that time
So welcome, no temptation half so dear
As that which urged me to a daring feat,
Deep pools, tall trees, black chasms, and
    dizzy crags,
And tottering towers: I loved to stand
    and read
Their looks forbidding, read and disobey,
Sometimes in act and evermore in thought.
With impulses, that scarcely were by
    these
Surpassed in strength, I heard of danger
    met
Or sought with courage; enterprise forlorn
By one, sole keeper of his own intent,
Or by a resolute few, who for the sake
Of glory fronted multitudes in arms.
Yea, to this hour I cannot read a Tale

Of two brave vessels matched in deadly
    fight,
And fighting to the death, but I am
    pleased
More than a wise man ought to be; I
    wish,
Fret, burn, and struggle, and in soul am
    there.
But me hath Nature tamed, and bade to
    seek
For other agitations, or be calm;
Hath dealt with me as with a turbulent
    stream,
Some nursling of the mountains which
    she leads
Through quiet meadows, after he has
    learnt
His strength, and had his triumph and
    his joy,
His desperate course of tumult and of
    glee.
That which in stealth by Nature was
    performed
Hath Reason sanctioned: her deliberate
    Voice
Hath said; be mild, and cleave to gentle
    things,
Thy glory and thy happiness be there.
Nor fear, though thou confide in me, a
    want
Of aspirations that have been — of foes
To wrestle with, and victory to complete,
Bounds to be leapt, darkness to be ex-
    plored;
All that inflamed thy infant heart, the
    love,
The longing, the contempt, the un-
    daunted quest,
All shall survive, though changed their
    office, all
Shall live, it is not in their power to die.
    Then farewell to the Warrior's
    Schemes, farewell
The forwardness of soul which looks
    that way
Upon a less incitement than the Cause
Of Liberty endangered, and farewell
That other hope, long mine, the hope to
    fill
The heroic trumpet with the Muse's
    breath!
Yet in this peaceful Vale we will not
    spend

Unheard-of days, though loving peaceful
    thought,
A voice shall speak, and what will be
   . the theme?
    On Man, on Nature, and on Human
      Life,
Musing in solitude, I oft perceive
Fair trains of imagery before me rise,
Accompanied by feelings of delight
Pure, or with no unpleasing sadness
    mixed;
And I am conscious of affecting thoughts
And dear remembrances, whose presence
    soothes
Or elevates the Mind, intent to weigh
The good and evil of our mortal state.
— To these emotions, whencesoe'er they
    come,
Whether from breath of outward circum-
    stance,
Or from the Soul — an impulse to her-
    self —
I would give utterance in numerous verse.
Of Truth, of Grandeur, Beauty, Love,
    and Hope,
And melancholy Fear subdued by Faith;
Of blessèd consolations in distress;
Of moral strength, and intellectual Power;
Of joy in widest commonalty spread;
Of the individual Mind that keeps her
    own
Inviolate retirement, subject there
To Conscience only, and the law supreme
Of that Intelligence which governs all —
I sing: — " fit audience let me find
    though few ! "
    So prayed, more gaining than he asked,
    the Bard —
In holiest mood. Urania, I shall need
Thy guidance, or a greater Muse, if such
Descend to earth or dwell in highest
    heaven !
For I must tread on shadowy ground,
    must sink
Deep — and, aloft ascending, breathe in
    worlds
To which the heaven of heavens is but a
    veil.
All strength — all terror, single or in
    bands,
That ever was put forth in personal
    form —
Jehovah — with his thunder, and the choir

Of shouting Angels, and the empyreal
    thrones —
I pass them unalarmed. Not Chaos, not
The darkest pit of lowest Erebus,
Nor aught of blinder vacancy, scooped out
By help of dreams — can breed such fear
    and awe
As fall upon us often when we look
Into our Minds, into the Mind of Man —
My haunt, and the main region of my
    song
— Beauty — a living Presence of the
    earth,
Surpassing the most fair ideal Forms
Which craft of delicate Spirits hath com-
    posed
From earth's materials — waits upon my
    steps;
Pitches her tents before me as I move,
An hourly neighbor. Paradise, and
    groves
Elysian, Fortunate Fields — like those
    of old
Sought in the Atlantic Main — why should
    they be
A history only of departed things,
Or a mere fiction of what never was?
For the discerning intellect of Man,
When wedded to this goodly universe
In love and holy passion, shall find these
A simple produce of the common day.
— I, long before the blissful hour arrives,
Would chant, in lonely peace, the spousal
    verse
Of this great consummation: — and, by
    words
Which speak of nothing more than what
    we are,
Would I arouse the sensual from their
    sleep
Of Death, and win the vacant and the vain
To noble raptures; while my voice pro-
    claims
How exquisitely the individual Mind
(And the progressive powers perhaps no
    less
Of the whole species) to the external
    World
Is fitted: — and how exquisitely, too —
Theme this but little heard of among
    men —
The external World is fitted to the Mind;
And the creation (by no lower name

Can it be called) which they with blended
might
Accomplish:— this is our high argument.
— Such grateful haunts foregoing, if I oft
Must turn elsewhere — to travel near the
tribes
And fellowships of men, and see ill sights
Of madding passions mutually inflamed;
Must hear Humanity in fields and groves
Pipe solitary anguish; or must hang
Brooding above the fierce confederate
storm
Of sorrow, barricadoed evermore
Within the walls of cities — may these
sounds
Have their authentic comment; that even
these
Hearing, I be not downcast or forlorn ! —
Descend, prophetic Spirit ! that inspir'st [1]
The human Soul of universal earth,
Dreaming on things to come; and dost
possess
A metropolitan temple in the hearts
Of mighty Poets; upon me bestow
A gift of genuine insight; that my Song
With star-like virtue in its place may
shine,
Shedding benignant influence, and secure
Itself from all malevolent effect
Of those mutations that extend their sway
Throughout the nether sphere ! — And if
with this
I mix more lowly matter; with the thing
Contemplated, describe the Mind and Man
Contemplating; and who, and what he
was —
The transitory Being that beheld
This Vision; — when and where, and how
he lived;
Be not this labor useless. If such theme
May sort with highest objects, then —
dread Power !
Whose gracious favor is the primal source
Of all illumination — may my Life
Express the image of a better time,
More wise desires, and simpler man-
ners; — nurse
My Heart in genuine freedom: — all pure
thoughts
Be with me; — so shall thy unfailing love
Guide, and support, and cheer me to the
end !

1805 ?   1888.

[1] See Note.

CHARACTER OF THE HAPPY WARRIOR.

The course of the great war with the French naturally fixed one's attention upon the military character, and, to the honor of our country, there were many illustrious instances of the qualities that constitute its highest excellence. Lord Nelson carried most of the virtues that the trials he was exposed to in his department of the service necessarily call forth and sustain, if they do not produce the contrary vices. But his public life was stained with one great crime, so that, though many passages of these lines were suggested by what was generally known as excellent in his conduct, I have not been able to connect his name with the poem as I could wish, or even to think of him with satisfaction in reference to the idea of what a warrior ought to be. For the sake of such of my friends as may happen to read this note I will add, that many elements of the character here portrayed were found in my brother John, who perished by shipwreck as mentioned elsewhere. His messmates used to call him the Philosopher, from which it must be inferred that the qualities and dispositions I allude to had not escaped their notice. He often expressed his regret, after the war had continued some time, that he had not chosen the Naval, instead of the East India Company's service, to which his family connection had led him. He greatly valued moral and religious instruction for youth, as tending to make good sailors. The best, he used to say, came from Scotland; the next to them, from the North of England, especially from Westmoreland and Cumberland, where, thanks to the piety and local attachments of our ancestors, endowed, or, as they are commonly called, free, schools abound.

Who is the happy Warrior? Who is he
That every man in arms should wish to be?
— It is the generous Spirit, who, when
brought
Among the tasks of real life, hath wrought
Upon the plan that pleased his boyish
thought;
Whose high endeavors are an inward light
That makes the path before him always
bright:
Who, with a natural instinct to discern
What knowledge can perform, is diligent
to learn;
Abides by this resolve, and stops not there,
But makes his moral being his prime care;

Who, doomed to go in company with Pain,
And Fear, and Bloodshed, miserable train!
Turns his necessity to glorious gain;
In face of these doth exercise a power
Which is our human nature's highest dower;
Controls them and subdues, transmutes, bereaves
Of their bad influence, and their good receives:
By objects, which might force the soul to abate
Her feeling, rendered more compassionate;
Is placable — because occasions rise
So often that demand such sacrifice;
More skilful in self-knowledge, even more pure,
As tempted more; more able to endure,
As more exposed to suffering and distress;
Thence, also, more alive to tenderness.
—'T is he whose law is reason; who depends
Upon that law as on the best of friends;
Whence, in a state where men are tempted still
To evil for a guard against worse ill,
And what in quality or act is best
Doth seldom on a right foundation rest,
He labors good on good to fix, and owes
To virtue every triumph that he knows:
— Who, if he rise to station of command,
Rises by open means; and there will stand
On honorable terms, or else retire,
And in himself possess his own desire;
Who comprehends his trust, and to the same
Keeps faithful with a singleness of aim;
And therefore does not stoop, nor lie in wait
For wealth, or honors, or for worldly state;
Whom they must follow; on whose head must fall,
Like showers of manna, if they come at all:
Whose powers shed round him in the common strife,
Or mild concerns of ordinary life,
A constant influence, a peculiar grace;
But who, if he be called upon to face

Some awful moment to which Heaven has joined
Great issues, good or bad for human kind,
Is happy as a Lover; and attired
With sudden brightness, like a Man inspired;
And, through the heat of conflict, keeps the law
In calmness made, and sees what he foresaw;
Or if an unexpected call succeed,
Come when it will, is equal to the need:
— He who, though thus endued as with a sense
And faculty for storm and turbulence,
Is yet a Soul whose master-bias leans
To homefelt pleasures and to gentle scenes;
Sweet images! which, wheresoe'er he be,
Are at his heart; and such fidelity
It is his darling passion to approve;
More brave for this, that he hath much to love: —
'T is, finally, the Man, who, lifted high,
Conspicuous object in a Nation's eye,
Or left unthought-of in obscurity, —
Who, with a toward or untoward lot,
Prosperous or adverse, to his wish or not —
Plays, in the many games of life, that one
Where what he most doth value must be won:
Whom neither shape of danger can dismay,
Nor thought of tender happiness betray;
Who, not content that former worth stand fast,
Looks forward, persevering to the last,
From well to better, daily self-surpast:
Who, whether praise of him must walk the earth
Forever, and to noble deeds give birth,
Or he must fall, to sleep without his fame,
And leave a dead unprofitable name —
Finds comfort in himself and in his cause;
And, while the mortal mist is gathering draws
His breath in confidence of Heaven's applause:
This is the happy Warrior; this is He
That every Man in arms should wish to be.

1806.   1807.

THE HORN OF EGREMONT CASTLE. [1]

A tradition transferred from the ancient mansion of Hutton John, the seat of the Huddlestons, to Egremont Castle.

ERE the Brothers through the gateway
Issued forth with old and young,
To the Horn Sir Eustace pointed
Which for ages there had hung.
Horn it was which none could sound,
No one upon living ground,
Save He who came as rightful Heir
To Egremont's Domains and Castle fair.

Heirs from times of earliest record
Had the House of Lucie born,
Who of right had held the Lordship
Claimed by proof upon the Horn:
Each at the appointed hour
Tried the Horn, — it owned his power;
He was acknowledged: and the blast
Which good Sir Eustace sounded was the last.

With his lance Sir Eustace pointed,
And to Hubert thus said he,
" What I speak this Horn shall witness
For thy better memory.
Hear, then, and neglect me not!
At this time, and on this spot,
The words are uttered from my heart,
As my last earnest prayer ere we depart.

" On good service we are going
Life to risk by sea and land,
In which course if Christ our Saviour
Do my sinful soul demand,
Hither come thou back straightway,
Hubert, if alive that day;
Return, and sound the Horn, that we
May have a living House still left in thee!"

" Fear not," quickly answered Hubert;
" As I am thy Father's son,
What thou askest, noble Brother,
With God's favor shall be done."
So were both right well content:
Forth they from the Castle went,
And at the head of their Array
To Palestine the Brothers took their way.

[1] See Note.

Side by side they fought (the Lucies
Were a line for valor famed),
And where'er their strokes alighted,
There the Saracens were tamed.
Whence, then, could it come — the thought —
By what evil spirit brought?
Oh! can a brave Man wish to take
His Brother's life, for Lands' and Castle's sake?

" Sir!" the Ruffians said to Hubert,
" Deep he lies in Jordan flood."
Stricken by this ill assurance,
Pale and trembling Hubert stood.
" Take your earnings." — Oh! that I
Could have *seen* my Brother die!
It was a pang that vexed him then;
And oft returned, again, and yet again.

Months passed on, and no Sir Eustace!
Nor of him were tidings heard;
Wherefore, bold as day, the Murderer
Back again to England steered.
To his Castle Hubert sped;
Nothing has he now to dread.
But silent and by stealth he came,
And at an hour which nobody could name.

None could tell if it were night-time,
Night or day, at even or morn;
No one's eye had seen him enter,
No one's ear had heard the Horn.
But bold Hubert lives in glee:
Months and years went smilingly;
With plenty was his table spread;
And bright the Lady is who shares his bed

Likewise he had sons and daughters;
And, as good men do, he sate
At his board by these surrounded,
Flourishing in fair estate.
And while thus in open day
Once he sate, as old books say,
A blast was uttered from the Horn,
Where by the Castle-gate it hung forlorn.

'T is the breath of good Sir Eustace!
He is come to claim his right:
Ancient castle, woods, and mountains
Hear the challenge with delight.
Hubert! though the blast be blown
He is helpless and alone:

Thou hast a dungeon, speak the word!
And there he may be lodged, and thou
    be Lord.

Speak! — astounded Hubert cannot;
And, if power to speak he had,
All are daunted, all the household
Smitten to the heart, and sad.
'T is Sir Eustace; if it be
Living man, it must be he!
Thus Hubert thought in his dismay,
And by a postern-gate he slunk away.

Long, and long was he unheard of:
To his Brother then he came,
Made confession, asked forgiveness,
Asked it by a brother's name,
And by all the saints in heaven;
And of Eustace was forgiven:
Then in a convent went to hide
His melancholy head, and there he died.

But Sir Eustace, whom good angels
Had preserved from murderers' hands,
And from Pagan chains had rescued,
Lived with honor on his lands.
Sons he had, saw sons of theirs:
And through ages, heirs of heirs,
A long posterity renowned,
Sounded the Horn which they alone
    could sound.
    1806.   1807.

A COMPLAINT.

Written at Town-End, Grasmere. Suggested by
  a change in the manner of a friend.

THERE is a change — and I am poor;
Your love hath been, not long ago,
A fountain at my fond heart's door,
Whose only business was to flow;
And flow it did: not taking heed
Of its own bounty, or my need.

What happy moments did I count!
Blest was I then all bliss above!
Now, for that consecrated fount
Of murmuring, sparkling, living love,
What have I? shall I dare to tell?
A comfortless and hidden well.

A well of love — it may be deep —
I trust it is, — and never dry:
What matter? if the waters sleep
In silence and obscurity.
— Such change, and at the very door
Of my fond heart, hath made me poor.
1806.   1807.

STRAY PLEASURES.

" Pleasure is spread through the earth
In stray gifts to be claimed by whoever shall find."

Suggested on the Thames by the sight of one
of those floating mills that used to be seen
there. This I noticed on the Surrey side between
Somerset House and Blackfriars Bridge. Charles
Lamb was with me at the time; and I thought it
remarkable that I should have to point out to
him, an idolatrous Londoner, a sight so interest-
ing as the happy group dancing on the platform.
Mills of this kind used to be, and perhaps still
are, not uncommon on the Continent. I noticed
several upon the river Saône in the year 1799,
particularly near the town of Châlons, where my
friend Jones and I halted a day when we crossed
France; so far on foot: there we embarked, and
floated down to Lyons.

BY their floating mill,
    That lies dead and still,
Behold yon Prisoners three,
The Miller with two Dames, on the
    breast of the Thames!
The platform is small, but gives room for
    them all;
And they 're dancing merrily.

From the shore come the notes
    To their mill where it floats,
To their house and their mill tethered
    fast:
To the small wooden isle where, their
    work to beguile,
They from morning to even take what-
    ever is given; —
And many a blithe day they have past.

In sight of the spires,
    All alive with the fires
Of the sun going down to his rest,
In the broad open eye of the solitary sky,
They dance, — there are three, as jocund
    as free,
While they dance on the calm river's
    breast.

Man and Maidens wheel,
They themselves make the reel,
And their music 's a prey which they seize;
It plays not for them, — what matter?
 't is theirs;
And if they had care, it has scattered
 their cares,
While they dance, crying, " Long as ye
 please ! "

They dance not for me,
 Yet mine is their glee !
Thus pleasure is spread through the earth
In stray gifts to be claimed by whoever
 shall find;
Thus a rich loving-kindness, redundantly
 kind,
Moves all nature to gladness and mirth.

The showers of the spring
 Rouse the birds, and they sing;
If the wind do but stir for his proper
 delight,
Each leaf, that and this, his neighbor will
 kiss;
Each wave, one and t' other, speeds
 after his brother:
They are happy, for that is their right !
1806   1807.

POWER OF MUSIC.

Taken from life.

An Orpheus ! an Orpheus ! yes, Faith
 may grow bold,
And take to herself all the wonders of
 old; —
Near the stately Pantheon you 'll meet
 with the same
In the street that from Oxford hath bor-
 rowed its name.

His station is there; and he works on the
 crowd,
He sways them with harmony merry and
 loud;
He fills with his power all their hearts to
 the brim —
Was aught ever heard like his fiddle and
 him?

What an eager assembly ! what an empire
 is this !
The weary have life, and the hungry have
 bliss;
The mourner is cheered, and the anxious
 have rest;
And the guilt-burthened soul is no longer
 opprest.

As the Moon brightens round her the
 clouds of the night,
So He, where he stands, is a centre of
 light;
It gleams on the face, there, of dusky-
 browed Jack,
And the pale-visaged Baker's, with basket
 on back.

That errand-bound 'Prentice was passing
 in haste —
What matter ! he 's caught — and his
 time runs to waste;
The Newsman is stopped, though he
 stops on the fret;
And the half-breathless Lamplighter —
 he 's in the net !

The Porter sits down on the weight which
 he bore;
The Lass with her barrow wheels hither
 her store; —
If a thief could be here he might pilfer
 at ease;
She sees the Musician, 't is all that she
 sees !

He stands, backed by the wall; — he
 abates not his din.
His hat gives him vigor, with boons drop-
 ping in,
From the old and the young, from the
 poorest; and there !
The one-pennied Boy has his penny to
 spare.

O blest are the hearers, and proud be the
 hand
Of the pleasure it spreads through so
 thankful a band;
I am glad for him, blind as he is ! — all
 the while
If they speak 't is to praise, and they
 praise with a smile.

That tall Man, a giant in bulk and in
    height,
Not an inch of his body is free from
    delight;
Can he keep himself still, if he would?
    oh, not he!
The music stirs in him like wind through
    a tree.

Mark that Cripple who leans on his
    crutch; like a tower
That long has leaned forward, leans hour
    after hour! —
That Mother, whose spirit in fetters is
    bound,
While she dandles the Babe in her arms
    to the sound.

Now, coaches and chariots! roar on like
    a stream;
Here are twenty souls happy as souls in
    a dream:
They are deaf to your murmurs — they
    care not for you,
Nor what ye are flying, nor what ye
    pursue!
1806.   1807.

STAR-GAZERS.

Observed by me in Leicester-square, as here
described.

WHAT crowd is this? what have we here!
    we must not pass it by;
A Telescope upon its frame, and pointed
    to the sky:
Long is it as a barber's pole, or mast of
    little boat,
Some little pleasure-skiff, that doth on
    Thames's waters float.

The Showman chooses well his place, 't is
    Leicester's busy Square;
And is as happy in his night, for the
    heavens are blue and fair;
Calm, though impatient, is the crowd;
    each stands ready with the fee,
And envies him that 's looking; — what
    an insight must it be!

Yet, Showman, where can lie the cause?
    Shall thy Implement have blame,

A boaster, that when he is tried, fails,
    and is put to shame?
Or is it good as others are, and be their
    eyes in fault?
Their eyes, or minds? or, finally, is yon
    resplendent vault?

Is nothing of that radiant pomp so good
    as we have here?
Or gives a thing but small delight that
    never can be dear?
The silver moon with all her vales, and
    hills of mightiest fame,
Doth she betray us when they 're seen?
    or are they but a name?

Or is it rather that Conceit rapacious is
    and strong,
And bounty never yields so much but it
    seems to do her wrong?
Or is it, that when human Souls a journey
    long have had
And are returned into themselves, they
    cannot but be sad?

Or must we be constrained to think that
    these Spectators rude,
Poor in estate, of manners base, men of
    the multitude,
Have souls which never yet have risen,
    and therefore prostrate lie?
No, no, this cannot be; — men thirst for
    power and majesty!

Does, then, a deep and earnest thought
    the blissful mind employ
Of him who gazes, or has gazed? a grave
    and steady joy,
That doth reject all show of pride, ad-
    mits no outward sign,
Because not of this noisy world, but
    silent and divine!

Whatever be the cause, 't is sure that they
    who pry and pore
Seem to meet with little gain, seem less
    happy than before:
One after One they take their turn, nor
    have I one espied
That doth not slackly go away, as if dis-
    satisfied.
1806.   1807

"YES, IT WAS THE MOUNTAIN ECHO."

Written at Town-end, Grasmere. The echo came from Nab-scar, when I was walking on the opposite side of Rydal Mere. I will here mention, for my dear Sister's sake, that, while she was sitting alone one day high up on this part of Loughrigg Fell, she was so affected by the voice of the Cuckoo heard from the crags at some distance that she could not suppress a wish to have a stone in-scribed with her name among the rocks from which the sound proceeded. On my return from my walk I recited these verses to Mrs. Wordsworth.

YES, it was the mountain Echo,
Solitary, clear, profound,
Answering to the shouting Cuckoo,
Giving to her sound for sound!

Unsolicited reply
To a babbling wanderer sent;
Like her ordinary cry,
Like — but oh, how different!

Hears not also mortal Life?
Hear not we, unthinking Creatures!
Slaves of folly, love, or strife —
Voices of two different natures?

Have not *we* too? — yes, we have
Answers, and we know not whence;
Echoes from beyond the grave,
Recognized intelligence!

Such rebounds our inward ear
Catches sometimes from afar —
Listen, ponder, hold them dear;
For of God, — of God they are.
　1806.　　　　　　　　　　　1807.

"NUNS FRET NOT AT THEIR CONVENT'S NARROW ROOM."

In the cottage, Town-end, Grasmere, one after-noon in 1801, my sister read to me the Sonnets of Milton. I had long been well acquainted with them, but I was particularly struck on that occa-sion with the dignified simplicity and majestic harmony that runs through most of them, — in character so totally different from the Italian, and still more so from Shakspeare's fine Sonnets.

I took fire, if I may be allowed to say so, and produced three Sonnets the same afternoon, the first I ever wrote except an irregular one at school. Of these three, the only one I distinctly remember is — " I grieved for Buonaparté." One was never written down: the third, which was, I believe, preserved, I cannot particularize.

NUNS fret not at their convent's narrow
　　room;
And hermits are contented with their
　　cells;
And students with their pensive citadels;
Maids at the wheel, the weaver at his
　　loom,
Sit blithe and happy; bees that soar for
　　bloom,
High as the highest Peak of Furness-fells,
Will murmur by the hour in foxglove bells:
In truth the prison, unto which we doom
Ourselves, no prison is: and hence for me,
In sundry moods, 't was pastime to be
　　bound
Within the Sonnet's scanty plot of
　　ground;
Pleased if some Souls (for such there
　　needs must be)
Who have felt the weight of too much
　　liberty,
Should find brief solace there, as I have
　　found.
　1806.　　　　　　　　　　　1807.

PERSONAL TALK.

Written at Town-end, Grasmere. The last line but two stood, at first, better and more character-istically thus: —

" By my half-kitchen and half-parlor fire."

My Sister and I were in the habit of having the tea-kettle in our little sitting-room; and we toasted the bread ourselves, which reminds me of a little circumstance not unworthy of being set down among these minutiæ. Happening both of us to be engaged a few minutes one morning when we had a young prig of a Scotch lawyer to breakfast with us, my dear Sister, with her usual simplicity, put the toasting-fork with a slice of bread into the hands of this Edinburgh genius. Our little book-case stood on one side of the fire. To prevent loss of time, he took down a book, and fell to reading, to the neglect of the toast, which was burnt to a cinder. Many a time have we laughed at this circumstance, and other cottage simplicities of that day. By the bye, I have a spite at one of this series of Sonnets (I will leave the reader to discover which) as having been the means of nearly putting off forever our acquaintance with dear Miss Fenwick, who has always stigmatized one line of it as vulgar, and worthy only of having been composed by a country squire.

I.

I AM not One who much or oft delight
To season my fireside with personal talk.—
Of friends, who live within an easy walk,
Or neighbors, daily, weekly, in my sight:
And, for my chance-acquaintance, ladies bright,
Sons, mothers, maidens withering on the stalk,
These all wear out of me, like Forms, with chalk
Painted on rich men's floors, for one feast-night.
Better than such discourse doth silence long,
Long, barren silence, square with my desire;
To sit without emotion, hope, or aim,
In the loved presence of my cottage-fire,
And listen to the flapping of the flame,
Or kettle whispering its faint undersong.

II.

"Yet life," you say, "is life; we have seen and see,
And with a living pleasure we describe;
And fits of sprightly malice do but bribe
The languid mind into activity.
Sound sense, and love itself, and mirth and glee
Are fostered by the comment and the gibe."
Even be it so; yet still among your tribe,
Our daily world's true Worldlings, rank not me!
Children are blest, and powerful; their world lies
More justly balanced; partly at their feet,
And part far from them: sweetest melodies
Are those that are by distance made more sweet;

Whose mind is but the mind of his own eyes,
He is a Slave; the meanest we can meet!

III.

Wings have we, — and as far as we can go,
We may find pleasure: wilderness and wood,
Blank ocean and mere sky, support that mood
Which with the lofty sanctifies the low. ·
Dreams, books, are each a world; and books, we know,
Are a substantial world, both pure and good:
Round these, with tendrils strong as flesh and blood,
Our pastime and our happiness will grow.
There find I personal themes, a plenteous store,
Matter wherein right voluble I am,
To which I listen with a ready ear;
Two shall be named, pre-eminently dear, —
The gentle Lady married to the Moor;
And heavenly Una with her milk-white Lamb.

IV.

Nor can I not believe but that hereby
Great gains are mine; for thus I live remote
From evil-speaking; rancour, never sought,
Comes to me not; malignant truth, or lie.
Hence have I genial seasons, hence have I
Smooth passions, smooth discourse, and joyous thought:
And thus from day to day my little boat
Rocks in its harbor, lodging peaceably.
Blessings be with them — and eternal praise,
Who gave us nobler loves, and nobler cares —
The Poets, who on earth have made us heirs
Of truth and pure delight by heavenly lays!
Oh! might my name be numbered among theirs,
Then gladly would I end my mortal days.

1806.   1807.

ADMONITION.

Intended more particularly for the perusal of those who may have happened to be enamoured of some beautiful Place of Retreat, in the Country of the Lakes.

WELL may'st thou halt — and gaze with
    brightening eye !
The lovely Cottage in the guardian nook
Hath stirred thee deeply; with its own
    dear brook,
Its own small pasture, almost its own sky !
But covet not the Abode; — forbear to
    sigh,
As many do, repining while they look;
Intruders — who would tear from Nature's
    book
This precious leaf, with harsh impiety.
Think what the home must be if it were
    thine,
Even thine, though few thy wants ! —
    Roof, window, door,
The very flowers are sacred to the Poor,
The roses to the porch which they en-
    twine :
Yea, all, that now enchants thee, from
    the day
On which it should be touched, would
    melt away.
1806.   1807.

"BELOVED VALE! I SAID, WHEN I SHALL CON."

" BELOVÈD Vale ! " I said, " when I
    shall con
Those many records of my childish years,
Remembrance of myself and of my peers
Will press me down : to think of what is
    gone
Will be an awful thought, if life have
    one."
But, when into the Vale I came, no fears
Distressed me; from mine eyes escaped no
    tears;
Deep thought, or dread remembrance,
    had I none.
By doubts and thousand petty fancies crost
I stood, of simple shame the blushing
    Thrall;

So narrow seemed the brooks, the fields
    so small !
A Juggler's balls old Time about him
    tossed;
I looked, I stared, I smiled, I laughed;
    and all
The weight of sadness was in wonder lost.
1806.   1807.

"HOW SWEET IT IS, WHEN MOTHER FANCY ROCKS."

How sweet it is, when mother Fancy
    rocks
The wayward brain, to saunter through a
    wood !
An old place, full of many a lovely brood,
Tall trees, green arbors, and ground-
    flowers in flocks;
And wild rose tip-toe upon hawthorn
    stocks,
Like a bold Girl, who plays her agile
    pranks
At Wakes and Fairs with wandering
    Mountebanks, —
When she stands cresting the Clown's
    head, and mocks
The crowd beneath her.   Verily I think,
Such place to me is sometimes like a dream
Or map of the whole world : thoughts,
    link by link,
Enter through ears and eyesight, with such
    gleam
Of all things, that at last in fear I shrink,
And leap at once from the delicious stream.
1806.   1807.

"THOSE WORDS WERE UTTERED AS IN PENSIVE MOOD."

— " they are of the sky,
And from our earthly memory fade away."

THOSE words were uttered as in pensive
    mood
We turned, departing from that solemn
    sight :
A contrast and reproach to gross delight,
And life's unspiritual pleasures daily
    wooed !
But now upon this thought I cannot brood;
It is unstable as a dream of night;

Nor will I praise a cloud, however bright,
Disparaging Man's gifts, and proper food.
Grove, isle, with every shape of sky-built
    dome,
Though clad in colors beautiful and pure,
Find in the heart of man no natural home:
The immortal Mind craves objects that
    endure:
These cleave to it; from these it cannot
    roam,
Nor they from it: their fellowship is secure.
1806.   1807.

COMPOSED BY THE SIDE OF GRASMERE LAKE.

1806.

CLOUDS, lingering yet, extend in solid
    bars
Through the gray west; and lo! these
    waters, steeled
By breezeless air to smoothest polish, yield
A vivid repetition of the stars;
Jove, Venus, and the ruddy crest of Mars
Amid his fellows beauteously revealed
At happy distance from earth's groaning
    field,
Where ruthless mortals wage incessant
    wars.
Is it a mirror? — or the nether Sphere
Opening to view the abyss in which she
    feeds
Her own calm fires?— But list! a voice is
    near;
Great Pan himself low-whispering through
    the reeds,
" Be thankful, thou; for, if unholy deeds
Ravage the world, tranquillity is here ! "
1806.   1820.

" WITH HOW SAD STEPS, O MOON, THOU CLIMB'ST THE SKY."

WITH how sad steps, O Moon, thou
    climb'st the sky,
" How silently, and with how wan a face ! "
Where art thou?   Thou so often seen on
    high
Running among the clouds a Wood-
    nymph's race !
Unhappy Nuns, whose common breath 's
    a sigh

Which they would stifle, move at such a
    pace !
The northern Wind, to call thee to the
    chase,
Must blow to-night his bugle horn. Had I
The power of Merlin, Goddess ! this should
    be :
And all the stars, fast as the clouds were
    riven,
Should sally forth, to keep thee company,
Hurrying and sparkling through the clear
    blue heaven.
But, Cynthia ! should to thee the palm be
    given,
Queen both for beauty and for majesty.
1806.   1807.

" THE WORLD IS TOO MUCH WITH US; LATE AND SOON."

THE world is too much with us; late and
    soon,
Getting and spending, we lay waste our
    powers :
Little we see in Nature that is ours;
We have given our hearts away, a sordid
    boon !
The Sea that bares her bosom to the moon;
The winds that will be howling at all
    hours,
And are up-gathered now like sleeping
    flowers;
For this, for everything, we are out of tune;
It moves us not.—Great God ! I 'd rather
    be
A Pagan suckled in a creed outworn;
So might I, standing on this pleasant lea,
Have glimpses that would make me less
    forlorn;
Have sight of Proteus rising from the sea;
Or hear old Triton blow his wreathèd
    horn.
1806.   1807.

" WITH SHIPS THE SEA WAS SPRINKLED FAR AND NIGH."

WITH Ships the sea was sprinkled far and
    nigh,
Like stars in heaven, and joyously it
    showed;
Some lying fast at anchor in the road,

Some veering up and down, one knew
   not·why.
A goodly Vessel did I then espy
Come like a giant from a haven broad;
And lustily along the bay she strode,
Her tackling rich, and of apparel high.
This Ship was naught to me, nor I to her,
Yet I pursued her with a Lover's look;
This Ship to all the rest did I prefer:
When will she turn, and whither? She
   will brook
No tarrying; where She comes the winds
   must stir:
On went she, and due north her journey
   took.
1806.   1807.

"WHERE LIES THE LAND TO WHICH YON SHIP MUST GO?"

WHERE lies the Land to which yon Ship
   must go?
Fresh as a lark mounting at break of day,
Festively she puts forth in trim array;
Is she for tropic suns, or polar snow?
What boots the inquiry? — Neither friend
   nor foe
She cares for; let her travel where she may,
She finds familiar names, a beaten way
Ever before her, and a wind to blow.
Yet still I ask, what haven is her mark?
And, almost as it was when ships were
   rare,
(From time to time, like Pilgrims, here
   and there
Crossing the waters) doubt, and something
   dark,
Of the old Sea some reverential fear,
Is with me at thy farewell, joyous Bark!
1806.   1807.

TO SLEEP.

O GENTLE SLEEP! do they belong to thee,
These twinklings of oblivion? Thou dost
   love
To sit in meekness, like the brooding Dove,
A captive never wishing to be free.
This tiresome night, O Sleep! thou art to
   me
A Fly, that up and down himself doth
   shove

Upon a fretful rivulet, now above
Now on the water vexed with mockery.
I have no pain that calls for patience, no;
Hence am I cross and peevish as a child:
Am pleased by fits to have thee for my
   foe,
Yet ever willing to be reconciled:
O gentle Creature! do not use me so,
But once and deeply let me be beguiled
1806.   1807.

TO SLEEP.

A FLOCK of sheep that leisurely pass by,
One after one; the sound of rain, and bees
Murmuring; the fall of rivers, winds and
   seas,
Smooth fields, white sheets of water, and
   pure sky;
I have thought of all by turns, and yet do lie
Sleepless! and soon the small birds'
   melodies
Must hear, first uttered from my orchard
   trees;
And the first cuckoo's melancholy cry.
Even this last night, and two nights more,
   I lay,
And could not win thee, Sleep! by any
   stealth:
So do not let me wear to-night away:
Without Thee what is all the morning's
   wealth?
Come, blessed barrier between day and
   day,
Dear mother of fresh thoughts and joyous
   health!
1806.   1807.

TO SLEEP.

FOND words have oft been spoken to thee,
   Sleep!
And thou hast had thy store of tenderest
   names;
The very sweetest, Fancy culls or frames,
When thankfulness of heart is strong and
   deep!
Dear Bosom-child we call thee, that dost
   steep
In rich reward all suffering; Balm that
   tames
All anguish; Saint that evil thoughts and
   aims

Takest away, and into souls dost creep,
Like to a breeze from heaven. Shall I
   alone,
I surely not a man ungently made,
Call thee worst Tyrant by which Flesh is
   crost?
Perverse, self-willed to own and to disown,
Mere slave of them who never for thee
   prayed,
Still last to come where thou art wanted
   most!
  1806.   1807.

TWO TRANSLATIONS FROM MICHAEL ANGELO, AND A TRANSLATION FROM THE LATIN OF THOMAS WARTON.

GRATEFUL is Sleep, my life in stone bound
   fast;
More grateful still: while wrong and
   shame shall last,
On me can Time no happier state bestow
Than to be left unconscious of the woe.
Ah then, lest you awaken me, speak low.

GRATEFUL is Sleep, more grateful still to
   be
Of marble; for while shameless wrong
   and woe
Prevail, 't is best to neither hear nor see.
Then wake me not, I pray you. Hush,
   speak low.

COME, gentle Sleep, Death's image tho'
   thou art,
Come share my couch, nor speedily de-
   part;
How sweet thus living without life to lie,
Thus without death how sweet it is to die.
  1806?   1882.

FROM THE ITALIAN OF MICHAEL ANGELO.

Translations from Michael Angelo, done at the request of Mr. Duppa, whose acquaintance I made through Mr. Southey. Mr. Duppa was engaged in writing the life of Michael Angelo, and applied to Mr. Southey and myself to furnish some specimens of his poetic genius.

I.

YES! hope may with my strong desire
   keep pace,
And I be undeluded, unbetrayed;
For if of our affections none finds grace
In sight of Heaven, then, wherefore hath
   God made
The world which we inhabit? Better plea
Love cannot have, than that in loving thee
Glory to that eternal Peace is paid,
Who such divinity to thee imparts
As hallows and makes pure all gentle
   hearts.
His hope is treacherous only whose love
   dies
With beauty, which is varying every hour;
But, in chaste hearts uninfluenced by the
   power
Of outward change, there blooms a death-
   less flower,
That breathes on earth the air of paradise.
  1806.   1807.

FROM THE SAME.

II.

No mortal object did these eyes behold
When first they met the placid light of
   thine,
And my Soul felt her destiny divine,
And hope of endless peace in me grew
   bold:
Heaven-born, the Soul a heavenward
   course must hold;
Beyond the visible world she soars to seek
(For what delights the sense is false and
   weak)
Ideal Form, the universal mould.
The wise man, I affirm, can find no rest
In that which perishes: nor will he lend
His heart to aught which doth on time
   depend.
'T is sense, unbridled will, and not true
   love,
That kills the soul: love betters what is
   best,
Even here below, but more in heaven
   above.
  1806.   1807.

TO THE MEMORY OF RAISLEY CALVERT.

This young man, Raisley Calvert, to whom I was so much indebted, died at Penrith, 1795.

CALVERT! it must not be unheard by them
Who may respect my name, that I to thee
Owed many years of early liberty.
This care was thine when sickness did
    condemn
Thy youth to hopeless wasting, root and
    stem —
That I, if frugal and severe, might stray
Where'er I liked; and finally array
My temples with the Muse's diadem.
Hence, if in freedom I have loved the
    truth;
If there be aught of pure, or good, or
    great,
In my past verse; or shall be, in the lays
Of higher mood, which now I meditate; —
It gladdens me, O worthy, short-lived,
    Youth!
To think how much of this will be thy
    praise.
  1806.   1807.

"METHOUGHT I SAW THE FOOT-STEPS OF A THRONE."

The latter part of this Sonnet was a great favorite with my sister S. H. When I saw her lying in death, I could not resist the impulse to compose the Sonnet that follows it.

I.

METHOUGHT I saw the footsteps of a
    throne
Which mists and vapors from mine eyes
    did shroud —
Nor view of who might sit thereon
    allowed;
But all the steps and ground about were
    strown
With sights the ruefullest that flesh and
    bone
Ever put on; a miserable crowd,
Sick, hale, old, young, who cried before
    that cloud,
"Thou art our king, O Death! to thee we
    groan."

Those steps I clomb; the mists before me
    gave
Smooth way; and I beheld the face of one
Sleeping alone within a mossy cave,
With her face up to heaven; that seemed
    to have
Pleasing remembrance of a thought fore-
    gone;
A lovely Beauty in a summer grave!
  1806.   1807.

LINES.

Composed at Grasmere, during a walk one Evening, after a stormy day, the Author having just read in a Newspaper that the dissolution of Mr. Fox was hourly expected.

LOUD is the Vale! the Voice is up
With which she speaks when storms are
    gone,
A mighty unison of streams!
Of all her Voices, One!

Loud is the Vale; — this inland Depth
In peace is roaring like the Sea
Yon star upon the mountain-top
Is listening quietly.

Sad was I, even to pain deprest,
Importunate and heavy load! [1]
The Comforter hath found me here,
Upon this lonely road;

And many thousands now are sad —
Wait the fulfilment of their fear;
For he must die who is their stay,
Their glory disappear.

A Power is passing from the earth
To breathless Nature's dark abyss;
But when the great and good depart
What is it more than this —

That Man, who is from God sent forth,
Doth yet again to God return? —
Such ebb and flow must ever be,
Then wherefore should we mourn?
  1806.   1807.

[1] Importuna e grave salma. — MICHAEL AN-GELO.

NOVEMBER, 1806.

ANOTHER year! — another deadly blow!
Another mighty Empire overthrown!
And We are left, or shall be left, alone;
The last that dare to struggle with the Foe.
'T is well! from this day forward we shall
    know
That in ourselves our safety must be
    sought;
That by our own right hands it must be
    wrought;
That we must stand unpropped, or be laid
    low.
O dastard whom such foretaste doth not
    cheer!
We shall exult, if they who rule the land
Be men who hold its many blessings dear,
Wise, upright, valiant; not a servile band,
Who are to judge of danger which they
    fear,
And honor which they do not understand.[1]
   1806.   1807.

ADDRESS TO A CHILD

DURING A BOISTEROUS WINTER EVENING.

BY MY SISTER.

Written at Town-end, Grasmere.

WHAT way does the wind come? What
    way does he go?
He rides over the water, and over the
    snow,
Through wood, and through vale; and,
    o'er rocky height
Which the goat cannot climb, takes his
    sounding flight;
He tosses about in every bare tree,
As, if you look up, you plainly may see;
But how he will come, and whither he
    goes,
There's never a scholar in England knows.

He will suddenly stop in a cunning nook
And ring a sharp 'larum; — but, if you
    should look,
There's nothing to see but a cushion of
    snow

           [1] See Note.

Round as a pillow, and whiter than milk,
And softer than if it were covered with
    silk.
Sometimes he 'll hide in the cave of a rock,
Then whistle as shrill as the buzzard cock;
— Yet seek him, — and what shall you
    find in the place?
Nothing but silence and empty space;
Save, in a corner, a heap of dry leaves,
That he 's left, for a bed, to beggars or
    thieves!
As soon as 't is daylight to-morrow, with
    me
You shall go to the orchard, and then
    you will see
That he has been there, and made a
    great rout,
And cracked the branches, and strewn
    them about;
Heaven grant that he spare but that one
    upright twig
That looked up at the sky so proud and big
All last summer, as well you know,
Studded with apples, a beautiful show!

Hark! over the roof he makes a pause,
And growls as if he would fix his claws
Right in the slates, and with a huge rattle
Drive them down, like men in a battle:
— But let him range round; he does us
    no harm,
We build up the fire, we 're snug and
    warm;
Untouched by his breath see the candle
    shines bright,
And burns with a clear and steady light;
Books have we to read, — but that half-
    stifled knell,
Alas! 't is the sound of the eight o'clock
    bell.
— Come now we 'll to bed! and when
    we are there
He may work his own will, and what
    shall we care?
He may knock at the door, — we 'll not
    let him in;
May drive at the windows, — we 'll
    laugh at his din;
Let him seek his own home wherever it
    be;
Here's a *cozie* warm house for Edward
    and me.

   1806.   1815.

ODE.

INTIMATIONS OF IMMORTALITY FROM RECOLLECTIONS OF EARLY CHILDHOOD.

This was composed during my residence at Town-end, Grasmere. Two years at least passed between the writing of the four first stanzas and the remaining part. To the attentive and competent reader the whole sufficiently explains itself; but there may be no harm in adverting here to particular feelings or *experiences* of my own mind on which the structure of the poem partly rests. Nothing was more difficult for me in childhood than to admit the notion of death as a state applicable to my own being. I have said elsewhere —

> " A simple child,
> That lightly draws its breath,   .
> And feels its life in every limb,
> What should it know of death ! " —

But it was not so much from feelings of animal vivacity that *my* difficulty came as from a sense of the indomitableness of the Spirit within me. I used to brood over the stories of Enoch and Elijah, and almost to persuade myself that, whatever might become of others, I should be translated, in something of the same way, to heaven. With a feeling congenial to this, I was often unable to think of external things as having external existence, and I communed with all that I saw as something not apart from, but inherent in, my own immaterial nature. Many times while going to school have I grasped at a wall or tree to recall myself from this abyss of idealism to the reality. At that time I was afraid of such processes. In later periods of life I have deplored, as we have all reason to do, a subjugation of an opposite character, and have rejoiced over the remembrances, as is expressed in the lines —

> " Obstinate questionings
> Of sense and outward things,
> Fallings from us, vanishings ; " etc.

To that dream-like vividness and splendor which invest objects of sight in childhood, every one, I believe, if he would look back, could bear testimony, and I need not dwell upon it here: but having in the poem regarded it as presumptive evidence of a prior state of existence, I think it right to protest against a conclusion, which has given pain to some good and pious persons, that I meant to inculcate such a belief. It is far too shadowy a notion to be recommended to faith, as more than an element in our instincts of immor-

tality. But let us bear in mind that, though the idea is not advanced in revelation, there is nothing there to contradict it, and the fall of Man presents an analogy in its favor. Accordingly, a pre-existent state has entered into the popular creeds of many nations ; and, among all persons acquainted with classic literature, is known as an ingredient in Platonic philosophy. Archimedes said that he could move the world if he had a point whereon to rest his machine. Who has not felt the same aspirations as regards the world of his own mind? Having to wield some of its elements when I was impelled to write this poem on the " Immortality of the Soul," I took hold of the notion of pre-existence as having sufficient foundation in humanity for authorizing me to make for my purpose the best use of it I could as a poet.

> " The Child is Father of the Man ;
> And I could wish my days to be
> Bound each to each by natural piety."
> See p. 200.

I.

THERE was a time when meadow, grove, and stream,
The earth, and every common sight,
To me did seem
Apparelled in celestial light,
The glory and the freshness of a dream.
It is not now as it hath been of yore ;—
Turn wheresoe'er I may,
By night or day,
The things which I have seen I now can see no more.

II.

The Rainbow comes and goes,
And lovely is the Rose,
The Moon doth with delight
Look round her when the heavens are bare,
Waters on a starry night
Are beautiful and fair ;
The sunshine is a glorious birth ;
But yet I know, where'er I go,
That there hath passed away a glory from the earth.

III.

Now, while the birds thus sing a joyous song,
And while the young lambs bound
As to the tabor's sound,

To me alone there came a thought of grief:
A timely utterance gave that thought relief,
    And I again am strong:
The cataracts blow their trumpets from the steep;
No more shall grief of mine the season wrong;
I hear the Echoes through the mountains throng,
The Winds come to me from the fields of sleep,
    And all the earth is gay;
        Land and sea
    Give themselves up to jollity,
    And with the heart of May
Doth every Beast keep holiday; —
    Thou Child of Joy,
Shout round me, let me hear thy shouts, thou happy
        Shepherd-boy!

IV.

Ye blessèd Creatures, I have heard the call
    Ye to each other make; I see
The heavens laugh with you in your jubilee;
    My heart is at your festival,
    My head hath its coronal,
The fulness of your bliss, I feel — I feel it all.
    Oh evil day! if I were sullen
    While Earth herself is adorning,
        This sweet May-morning,
    And the Children are culling
        On every side,
    In a thousand valleys far and wide,
    Fresh flowers; while the sun shines warm,
And the Babe leaps up on his Mother's arm:—
    I hear, I hear, with joy I hear!
    — But there 's a Tree, of many, one,
A single Field which I have looked upon,
Both of them speak of something that is gone:
        The Pansy at my feet
        Doth the same tale repeat:
Whither is fled the visionary gleam?
Where is it now, the glory and the dream?

V.

Our birth is but a sleep and a forgetting:
The Soul that rises with us, our life's Star,
    Hath had elsewhere its setting,
        And cometh from afar:
    Not in entire forgetfulness,
    And not in utter nakedness,
But trailing clouds of glory do we come
    From God, who is our home:
Heaven lies about us in our infancy!
Shades of the prison-house begin to close
    Upon the growing Boy,
But He beholds the light, and whence it flows,
        He sees it in his joy;
The Youth, who daily farther from the east
    Must travel, still is Nature's Priest,
    And by the vision splendid
    Is on his way attended;
At length the Man perceives it die away,
And fade into the light of common day.

VI.

Earth fills her lap with pleasures of her own;
Yearnings she hath in her own natural kind,
And, even with something of a Mother's mind,
    And no unworthy aim,
    The homely Nurse doth all she can
To make her Foster-child, her Inmate Man,
    Forget the glories he hath known,
And that imperial palace whence he came.

VII.

Behold the Child among his new-born blisses,
A six years' Darling of a pygmy size!
See, where 'mid work of his own hand he lies,
Fretted by sallies of his mother's kisses,
With light upon him from his father's eyes!
See, at his feet, some little plan or chart,
Some fragment from his dream of human life,
Shaped by himself with newly-learnèd art;
    A wedding or a festival,
    A mourning or a funeral;

And this hath now his heart,
And unto this he frames his song:
Then will he fit his tongue
To dialogues of business, love, or strife;
But it will not be long
Ere this be thrown aside,
And with new joy and pride
The little Actor cons another part;
Filling from time to time his " humorous
stage "
With all the Persons, down to palsied Age,
That Life brings with her in her equipage;
As if his whole vocation
Were endless imitation.

VIII.

Thou, whose exterior semblance doth belie
Thy Soul's immensity;
Thou best Philosopher, who yet dost keep
Thy heritage, thou Eye among the blind,
That, deaf and silent, read'st the eternal
deep,
Haunted forever by the eternal mind, —
Mighty Prophet! Seer blest!
On whom those truths do rest,
Which we are toiling all our lives to find,
In darkness lost, the darkness of the
grave;
Thou, over whom thy Immortality
Broods like the Day, a Master o'er a
Slave,
A Presence which is not to be put by;
Thou little Child, yet glorious in the might
Of heaven-born freedom on thy being's
height,
Why with such earnest pains dost thou
provoke
The years to bring the inevitable yoke,
Thus blindly with thy blessedness at strife?
Full soon thy Soul shall have her earthly
freight,
And custom lie upon thee with a weight,
Heavy as frost, and deep almost as life!

IX.

O joy! that in our embers
Is something that doth live,
That nature yet remembers
What was so fugitive!
The thought of our past years in me doth
breed
Perpetual benediction: not indeed
For that which is most worthy to be blest—

Delight and liberty, the simple creed
Of Childhood, whether busy or at rest,
With new-fledged hope still fluttering in
his breast: —
Not for these I raise
The song of thanks and praise;
But for those obstinate questionings
Of sense and outward things,
Fallings from us, vanishings;
Blank misgivings of a Creature
Moving about in worlds not realized,
High instincts before which our mortal
Nature
Did tremble like a guilty Thing surprised:
But for those first affections,
Those shadowy recollections,
Which, be they what they may,
Are yet the fountain light of all our day,
Are yet a master light of all our seeing;
Uphold us, cherish, and have power
to make
Our noisy years seem moments in the being
Of the eternal Silence: truths that wake,
To perish never;
Which neither listlessness, nor mad en-
deavor,
Nor Man nor Boy,
Nor all that is at enmity with joy,
Can utterly abolish or destroy!
Hence in a season of calm weather
Though inland far we be,
Our Souls have sight of that immortal sea
Which brought us hither,
Can in a moment travel thither,
And see the Children sport upon the shore,
And hear the mighty waters rolling ever-
more.

X.

Then sing, ye Birds, sing, sing a joyous
song!
And let the young Lambs bound
As to the tabor's sound!
We in thought will join your throng,
Ye that pipe and ye that play,
Ye that through your hearts to-day
Feel the gladness of the May!
What though the radiance which was
once so bright
Be now forever taken from my sight,
Though nothing can bring back the
hour

Of splendor in the grass, of glory in the
    flower;
        We will grieve not, rather find
        Strength in what remains behind;
        In the primal sympathy
        Which having been must ever be;
        In the soothing thoughts that spring
        Out of human suffering;
        In the faith that looks through death,
In years that bring the philosophic mind.

XI.

And O, ye Fountains, Meadows, Hills,
    and Groves,
Forebode not any severing of our loves!
Yet in my heart of hearts I feel your
    might;
I only have relinquished one delight
To live beneath your more habitual sway.
I love the Brooks which down their
    channels fret,
Even more than when I tripped lightly
    as they;
The innocent brightness of a new-born
    Day
        Is lovely yet;
The Clouds that gather round the setting
    sun
Do take a sober coloring from an eye
That hath kept watch o'er man's mor-
    tality;
Another race hath been, and other palms
    are won.
Thanks to the human heart by which we
    live,
Thanks to its tenderness, its joys, and
    fears,
To me the meanest flower that blows can
    give
Thoughts that do often lie too deep for
    tears.

1803-6.   1807.

A PROPHECY. FEBRUARY, 1807.

HIGH deeds, O Germans, are to come
    from you!
Thus in your books the record shall be
    found,
"A watchword was pronounced, a potent
    sound —
ARMINIUS! — all the people quaked like
    dew

Stirred by the breeze; they rose, a Nation,
    true,
True to herself — the mighty Germany,
She of the Danube and the Northern Sea,
She rose, and off at once the yoke she
    threw.
All power was given her in the dreadful .
    trance;
Those new-born Kings she withered like
    a flame."
— Woe to them all! but heaviest woe and
    shame
To that Bavarian who could first advance
His banner in accursed league with
    France,
First open traitor to the German name!
1807.   1807.

THOUGHT OF A BRITON ON THE SUBJUGATION OF SWITZERLAND.

This was composed while pacing to and fro
between the Hall of Coleorton, then rebuilding,
and the principal Farm-house of the Estate, in
which we lived for nine or ten months. I will
here mention that the Song of the Restoration of
Lord Clifford, as well as that on the feast of
Brougham Castle, were produced on the same
ground.

TWO Voices are there; one is of the sea,
One of the mountains; each a mighty
    Voice:
In both from age to age thou didst rejoice,
They were thy chosen music, Liberty!
There came a Tyrant, and with holy glee
Thou fought'st against him; but hast
    vainly striven:
Thou from thy Alpine holds at length art
    driven,
Where not a torrent murmurs heard by
    thee.
Of one deep bliss thine ear hath been
    bereft:
Then cleave, O cleave to that which stil!
    is left;
For, high-souled Maid, what sorrow would
    it be
That Mountain floods should thunder as
    before,
And Ocean bellow from his rocky shore,
And neither awful Voice be heard by thee!
1807.   1807.

TO THOMAS CLARKSON.

ON THE FINAL PASSING OF THE BILL FOR THE ABOLITION OF THE SLAVE TRADE.

MARCH, 1807.

CLARKSON! it was an obstinate hill to
   climb:
How toilsome — nay, how dire — it was,
   by thee
Is known; by none, perhaps, so feelingly:
But thou, who, starting in thy fervent
   prime,
Didst first lead forth that enterprise sub-
   lime,
Hast heard the constant Voice its charge
   repeat,
Which, out of thy young heart's oracular
   seat,
First roused thee. — O true yoke-fellow
   of Time,
Duty's intrepid liegeman, see, the palm
Is won, and by all Nations shall be worn!
The blood-stained Writing is forever torn;
And thou henceforth wilt have a good
   man's calm,
A great man's happiness; thy zeal shall
   find
Repose at length, firm friend of human-
   kind!
  1807.   1807.

THE MOTHER'S RETURN.[1]

BY MY SISTER.

Written at Town-end, Grasmere.

A MONTH, sweet Little-ones, is past
Since your dear Mother went away, —
And she to-morrow will return;
To-morrow is the happy day.

O blessèd tidings! thought of joy!
The eldest heard with steady glee;
Silent he stood; then laughed amain, —
And shouted, " Mother, come to me."

Louder and louder did he shout,
With witless hope to bring her near;
"Nay, patience! patience, little boy!
Your tender mother cannot hear."

[1] See Note.

I told of hills, and far-off towns,
And long, long vales to travel through; —
He listens, puzzled, sore perplexed,
But he submits; what can he do?

No strife disturbs his sister's breast;
She wars not with the mystery
Of time and distance, night and day;
The bonds of our humanity.

Her joy is like an instinct, joy
Of kitten, bird, or summer fly;
She dances, runs without an aim,
She chatters in her ecstasy.

Her brother now takes up the note,
And echoes back his sister's glee;
They hug the infant in my arms,
As if to force his sympathy.

Then, settling into fond discourse,
We rested in the garden bower;
While sweetly shone the evening sun
In his departing hour.

We told o'er all that we had done, —
Our rambles by the swift brook's side
Far as the willow-skirted pool,
Where two fair swans together glide.

We talked of change, of winter gone,
Of green leaves on the hawthorn spray,
Of birds that build their nests and sing,
And all "since Mother went away!"

To her these tales they will repeat,
To her our new-born tribes will show,
The goslings green, the ass's colt,
The lambs that in the meadow go.

— But, see, the evening star comes forth!
To bed the children must depart;
A moment's heaviness they feel,
A sadness at the heart:

'T is gone — and in a merry fit
They run up-stairs in gamesome race;
I, too, infected by their mood,
I could have joined the wanton chase.

Five minutes past — and, O the change!
Asleep upon their beds they lie;
Their busy limbs in perfect rest,
And closed the sparkling eye.

1807.   1815.

GIPSIES.

Composed at Coleorton. I had observed them,
as here described, near Castle Donnington, on
my way to and from Derby.

YET are they here the same.unbroken knot
Of human Beings, in the self-same spot!
     Men, women, children, yea the frame
     Of the whole spectacle the same!
Only their fire seems bolder, yielding light,
Now deep and red, the coloring of night;
     That on their Gipsy-faces falls,
     Their bed of straw and blanket-walls.
— Twelve hours, twelve bounteous hours
     are gone, while I
Have been a traveller under open sky,
     Much witnessing of change and cheer,
     Yet as I left I find them here!
The weary Sun betook himself to rest; —
Then issued Vesper from the fulgent west,
     Outshining like a visible God
     The glorious path in which he trod.
And now, ascending, after one dark hour
And one night's diminution of her power,
     Behold the mighty Moon! this way
     She looks as if at them — but they
Regard not her: — oh better wrong and
     strife
(By nature transient) than this torpid life;
     Life which the very stars reprove
     As on their silent tasks they move!
Yet, witness all that stirs in heaven or
     earth!
In scorn I speak not; — they are what
     their birth
     And breeding suffer them to be;
     Wild outcasts of society!

1807.   1807.

"O NIGHTINGALE! THOU SURELY ART."

Written at Town-end, Grasmere. (*Mrs. W. says
in a note* — "AT COLEORTON.")

O NIGHTINGALE! thou surely art
A creature of a "fiery heart:" —

These notes of thine — they pierce and
     pierce;
Tumultuous harmony and fierce!
Thou sing'st as if the God of wine
Had helped thee to a Valentine;
A song in mockery and despite
Of shades, and dews, and silent night;
And steady bliss, and all the loves
Now sleeping in these peaceful groves.
I heard a Stock-dove sing or say
His homely tale, this very day;
His voice was buried among trees,
Yet to be come at by the breeze:
He did not cease; but cooed — and cooed;
And somewhat pensively he wooed:
He sang of love, with quiet blending,
Slow to begin, and never ending;
Of serious faith, and inward glee;
That was the song — the song for me!

1807.   1807.

TO LADY BEAUMONT.

The winter garden of Coleorton, fashioned out
of an old quarry under the superintendence and
direction of Mrs. Wordsworth and my sister
Dorothy, during the winter and spring we resided
there.

LADY! the songs of Spring were in the
     grove
While I was shaping beds for winter
     flowers;
While I was planting green unfading
     bowers,
And shrubs — to hang upon the warm al-
     cove,
And sheltering wall; and still, as Fancy
     wove
The dream, to time and nature's blended
     powers
I gave this paradise for winter hours,
A labyrinth, Lady! which your feet shall
     rove.
Yes! when the sun of life more feebly
     shines,
Becoming thoughts, I trust, of solemn
     gloom
Or of high gladness you shall hither bring;
And these perennial bowers and murmur-
     ing pines
Be gracious as the music and the bloom
And all the mighty ravishment of spring.

1807.   1807.

"THOUGH NARROW BE THAT OLD MAN'S CARES."

"gives to airy nothing
A local habitation and a name."

Written at Coleorton. This old man's name was Mitchell. He was, in all his ways and conversation, a great curiosity, both individually and as a representative of past times. His chief employment was keeping watch at night by pacing round the house, at that time building, to keep off depredators. He has often told me gravely of having seen the Seven Whistlers and the Hounds as here described. Among the groves of Coleorton, where I became familiar with the habits and notions of old Mitchell, there was also a laborer of whom, I regret, I had no personal knowledge; for, more than forty years after, when he was become an old man, I learnt that while I was composing verses, which I usually did aloud, he took much pleasure, unknown to me, in following my steps that he might catch the words I uttered; and, what is not a little remarkable, several lines caught in this way kept their place in his memory. My volumes have lately been given to him by my informant, and surely he must have been gratified to meet in print his old acquaintance.

THOUGH narrow be that old Man's cares,
    and near,
The poor old Man is greater than he seems:
For he hath waking empire, wide as
    dreams;
An ample sovereignty of eye and ear.
Rich are his walks with supernatural
    cheer;
The region of his inner spirit teems
With vital sounds and monitory gleams
Of high astonishment and pleasing fear.
He the seven birds hath seen, that never
    part,
Seen the SEVEN WHISTLERS in their
    nightly rounds,
And counted them: and oftentimes will
    start —
For overhead are sweeping GABRIEL'S
    HOUNDS
Doomed, with their impious Lord, the
    flying Hart
To chase forever, on aërial grounds!

1807.

SONG AT THE FEAST OF BROUGHAM CASTLE.

UPON THE RESTORATION OF LORD CLIFFORD, THE SHEPHERD, TO THE ESTATES AND HONORS OF HIS ANCESTORS.

See the note. This poem was composed at Coleorton while I was walking to and fro along the path that led from Sir George Beaumont's Farm-house, where we resided, to the Hall which was building at that time.

HIGH in the breathless Hall the Minstrel
    sate,
And Emont's murmur mingled with the
    Song. —
The words of ancient time I thus translate,
A festal strain that hath been silent long:
" From town to town, from tower to tower,
The red rose is a gladsome flower.
Her thirty years of winter past,
The red rose is revived at last;
She lifts her head for endless spring,
For everlasting blossoming:
Both roses flourish, red and white:
In love and sisterly delight
The two that were at strife are blended,
And all old troubles now are ended. —
Joy! joy to both! but most to her
Who is the flower of Lancaster!
Behold her how She smiles to-day
On this great throng, this bright array!
Fair greeting doth she send to all
From every corner of the hall;
But chiefly from above the board
Where sits in state our rightful Lord,
A Clifford to his own restored!
    They came with banner, spear, and
    shield,
And it was proved in Bosworth-field.
Not long the Avenger was withstood —
Earth helped him with the cry of blood:[1]
St. George was for us, and the might
Of blessed Angels crowned the right.
Loud voice the Land has uttered forth,
We loudest in the faithful north:
Our fields rejoice, our mountains ring,
Our streams proclaim a welcoming;
Our strong-abodes and castles see
The glory of their loyalty.
    How glad is Skipton at this hour —

1807.

[1] See Note.

Though lonely, a deserted Tower;
Knight, squire, and yeoman, page and
    groom: .
We have them at the feast of Brough'm.
How glad Pendragon — though the sleep
Of years be on her! — She shall reap
A taste of this great pleasure, viewing
As in a dream her own renewing.
Rejoiced is Brough, right glad I deem
Beside her little humble stream;
And she that keepeth watch and ward
Her statelier Eden's course to guard;
They both are happy at this hour,
Though each is but a lonely Tower: —
But here is perfect joy and pride
For one fair House by Emont's side,
This day, distinguished without peer
To see her Master and to cheer —
Him, and his Lady-mother dear!

    Oh! it was a time forlorn
When the fatherless was born —
Give her wings that she may fly,
Or she sees her infant die!
Swords that are with slaughter wild
Hunt the Mother and the Child.
Who will take them from the light?
—Yonder is a man in sight —
Yonder is a house — but where?
No, they must not enter there.
To the caves, and to the brooks,
To the clouds of heaven she looks;
She is speechless, but her eyes
Pray in ghostly agonies.
Blissful Mary, Mother mild,
Maid and Mother undefiled,
Save a Mother and her Child!

    Now Who is he that bounds with joy
On Carrock's side, a Shepherd-boy?
No thoughts hath he but thoughts that pass
Light as the wind along the grass.
Can this be He who hither came
In secret, like a smothered flame?
O'er whom such thankful tears were shed
For shelter, and a poor man's bread!
God loves the Child; and God hath willed
That those dear words should be fulfilled,
The Lady's words, when forced away,
The last she to her Babe did say:
' My own, my own, thy Fellow-guest
I may not be; but rest thee, rest,
For lowly shepherd's life is best! '

    Alas! when evil men are strong
No life is good, no pleasure long.

The Boy must part from Mosedale's
    groves,
And leave Blencathara's rugged coves,
And quit the flowers that summer brings
To Glenderamakin's lofty springs;
Must vanish, and his careless cheer
Be turned to heaviness and fear.
— Give Sir Lancelot Threlkeld praise!
Hear it, good man, old in days!
Thou tree of covert and of rest
For this young Bird that is distrest;
Among thy branches safe he lay,
And he was free to sport and play,
When falcons were abroad for prey.

    A recreant harp, that sings of fear
And heaviness in Clifford's ear!
I said, when evil men are strong,
No life is good, no pleasure long,
A weak and cowardly untruth!
Our Clifford was a happy Youth,
And thankful through a weary time,
That brought him up to manhood's prime.
— Again he wanders forth at will,
And tends a flock from hill to hill:
His garb is humble; ne'er was seen
Such garb with such a noble mien;
Among the shepherd grooms no mate
Hath he, a Child of strength and state!
Yet lacks not friends for simple glee,
Nor yet for higher sympathy.
To his side the fallow-deer
Came, and rested without fear;
The eagle, lord of land and sea,
Stooped down to pay him fealty;
And both the undying fish that swim [1]
Through Bowscale-tarn did wait on him;
The pair were servants of his eye
In their immortality;
And glancing, gleaming, dark or bright,
Moved to and fro, for his delight.
He knew the rocks which Angels haunt
Upon the mountains visitant;
He hath kenned them taking wing:
And into caves where Faeries sing
He hath entered; and been told
By Voices how men lived of old.
Among the heavens his eye can see
The face of thing that is to be;
And, if that men report him right,
His tongue could whisper words of might.
— Now another day is come,
Fitter hope, and nobler doom;
        [1] See Note.

He hath thrown aside his crook,
And hath buried deep his book;
Armor rusting in his halls
On the blood of Clifford calls; [1] —
'Quell the Scot,' exclaims the Lance —
Bear me to the heart of France,
Is the longing of the Shield —
Tell thy name, thou trembling Field;
Field of death where'er thou be,
Groan thou with our victory!
Happy day, and mighty hour,
When our Shepherd, in his power,
Mailed and horsed, with lance and sword,
To his ancestors restored,
Like a re-appearing Star,
Like a glory from afar,
First shall head the flock of war!"

Alas! the impassioned minstrel did not
 know
How, by Heaven's grace, this Clifford's
 heart was framed,
How he, long forced in humble walks to
 go,
Was softened into feeling, soothed, and
 tamed.

Love had he found in huts where poor
 men lie;
His daily teachers had been woods and
 rills,
The silence that is in the starry sky,
The sleep that is among the lonely hills.

In him the savage virtue of the Race,
Revenge, and all ferocious thoughts were
 dead:
Nor did he change; but kept in lofty
 place
The wisdom which adversity had bred.

Glad were the vales, and every cottage
 hearth;
The Shepherd-lord was honored more
 and more;
And, ages after he was laid in earth,
"The good Lord Clifford" was the name
 he bore.

1807.   1807.

¹ See Note.

THE WHITE DOE OF RYLSTONE;

OR, THE FATE OF THE NORTONS.[1]

The earlier half of this Poem was composed at Stockton-upon-Tees, when Mrs. Wordsworth and I were on a visit to her eldest Brother, Mr. Hutchinson, at the close of the year 1807. The country is flat, and the weather was rough. I was accustomed every day to walk to and fro under the shelter of a row of stacks in a field at a small distance from the town, and there poured forth my verses aloud as freely as they would come. Mrs. Wordsworth reminds me that her brother stood upon the punctilio of not sitting down to dinner till I joined the party; and it frequently happened that I did not make my appearance till too late, so that she was made uncomfortable. I here beg her pardon for this and similar transgressions during the whole course of our wedded life. To my beloved Sister the same apology is due.

When, from the visit just mentioned, we returned to Town-end, Grasmere, I proceeded with the Poem; and it may be worth while to note, as a caution to others who may cast their eye on these memoranda, that the skin having been rubbed off my heel by my wearing too tight a shoe, though I desisted from walking I found that the irritation of the wounded part was kept up, by the act of composition, to a degree that made it necessary to give my constitution a holiday. A rapid cure was the consequence. Poetic excitement, when accompanied by protracted labor in composition, has throughout my life brought on more or less bodily derangement. Nevertheless, I am, at the close of my seventy-third year, in what may be called excellent health; so that intellectual labor is not necessarily unfavorable to longevity. But perhaps I ought here to add that mine has been generally carried on out of doors.

Let me here say a few words of this Poem in the way of criticism. The subject being taken from feudal times has led to its being compared to some of Walter Scott's poems that belong to the same age and state of society. The comparison is inconsiderate. Sir Walter pursued the customary and very natural course of conducting an action, presenting various turns of fortune, to some outstanding point on which the mind might rest as a termination or catastrophe. The course I attempted to pursue is entirely different. Everything that is attempted by the principal personages in "The White Doe" fails, so far as its object is external and substantial. So far as it is moral and spiritual it succeeds. The Heroine of the Poem knows that her duty is not to interfere with the current of events, either to forward or delay them, but

> "To abide
> The shock, and finally secure
> O'er pain and grief a triumph pure."

This she does in obedience to her brother's injunction, as most suitable to a mind and character that, under previous trials, had been proved to accord with his. She achieves this not without aid from the communication with the inferior Creature, which often leads her thoughts to revolve upon the past with a tender and humanizing influence that exalts rather than depresses her. The anticipated beatification, if I may so say, of her mind, and the apotheosis of the companion of her solitude, are the points at which the Poem aims, and constitute its legitimate catastrophe, far too spiritual a one for instant or widely-spread sympathy, but not therefore the less fitted to make a deep and permanent impression upon that class of minds who think and feel more independently, than the many do, of the surfaces of things and interests transitory because belonging more to the outward and social forms of life than to its internal spirit. How insignificant a thing, for example, does personal prowess appear compared with the fortitude of patience and heroic martyrdom; in other words, with struggles for the sake of principle, in preference to victory gloried in for its own sake.

ADVERTISEMENT.

During the Summer of 1807 I visited, for the first time, the beautiful country that surrounds Bolton Priory, in Yorkshire; and the Poem of "The White Doe," founded upon a Tradition connected with that place, was composed at the close of the same year.

DEDICATION.

In trellised shed with clustering roses gay,
And, MARY! oft beside our blazing fire,
When years of wedded life were as a day
Whose current answers to the heart's desire,
Did we together read in Spenser's Lay
How Una, sad of soul — in sad attire,
The gentle Una, of celestial birth,
To seek her Knight went wandering o'er the earth.

Ah, then, Belovèd! pleasing was the smart,
And the tear precious in compassion shed
For Her, who, pierced by sorrow's thrilling dart,
Did meekly bear the pang unmerited;
Meek as that emblem of her lowly heart
The milk-white Lamb which in a line she led, —

And faithful, loyal in her innocence,
Like the brave Lion slain in her defence.

Notes could we hear as of a faery shell
Attuned to words with sacred wisdom fraught;
Free Fancy prized each specious miracle,
And all its finer inspiration caught;
Till in the bosom of our rustic Cell,
We by a lamentable change were taught
That "bliss with mortal Man may not abide:"
How nearly joy and sorrow are allied!

For us the stream of fiction ceased to flow,
For us the voice of melody was mute.
—But, as soft gales dissolve the dreary snow,
And give the timid herbage leave to shoot,
Heaven's breathing influence failed not to bestow
A timely promise of unlooked-for fruit,
Fair fruit of pleasure and serene content
From blossoms wild of fancies innocent.

It soothed us — it beguiled us — then, to hear
Once more of troubles wrought by magic spell;
And griefs whose aery motion comes not near
The pangs that tempt the Spirit to rebel:
Then, with mild Una in her sober cheer,
High over hill and low adown the dell
Again we wandered, willing to partake
All that she suffered for her dear Lord's sake.

Then, too, this Song *of mine* once more could
    please,
Where anguish, strange as dreams of restless
    sleep,
Is tempered and allayed by sympathies
Aloft ascending, and descending deep,
Even to the inferior Kinds; whom forest-trees
Protect from beating sunbeams, and the sweep
Of the sharp winds; — fair Creatures! — to whom
    Heaven
A calm and sinless life, with love, hath given.

This tragic Story cheered us; for it speaks
Of female patience winning firm repose;
And, of the recompense that conscience seeks,
A bright, encouraging, example shows;
Needful when o'er wide realms the tempest
    breaks,
Needful amid life's ordinary woes; —
Hence, not for them unfitted who would bless
A happy hour with holier happiness.

He serves the Muses erringly and ill,
Whose aim is pleasure light and fugitive:
Oh, that my mind were equal to fulfil
The comprehensive mandate which they give —
Vain aspiration of an earnest will!
Yet in this moral Strain a power may live,

Belovèd Wife! such solace to impart
As it hath yielded to thy tender heart.

RYDAL MOUNT, WESTMORELAND,
April 20, 1815.

"Action is transitory — a step, a blow,
The motion of a muscle — this way or that —
'T is done; and in the after-vacancy
We wonder at ourselves like men betrayed:
Suffering is permanent, obscure and dark,
And has the nature of infinity.[1]
Yet through that darkness (infinite though it seem
And irremoveable) gracious openings lie,
By which the soul — with patient steps of thought
Now toiling, wafted now on wings of prayer —
May pass in hope, and, though from mortal bonds
Yet undelivered, rise with sure ascent
Even to the fountain-head of peace divine."

"They that deny a God, destroy Man's nobility:
for certainly Man is of kinn to the Beast by his
Body; and if he be not of kinn to God by his
Spirit, he is a base, ignoble Creature. It destroys
likewise Magnanimity, and the raising of humane
Nature: for take an example of a Dogg, and
mark what a generosity and courage he will put
on, when he finds himself maintained by a Man,
who to him is instead of a God, or Melior Natura.
Which courage is manifestly such, as that Crea-
ture without that confidence of a better Nature
than his own could never attain. So Man, when
he resteth and assureth himself upon Divine
protection and favor, gathereth a force and faith
which human Nature in itself could not obtain."

LORD BACON.

CANTO FIRST.

FROM Bolton's old monastic tower[1]
The bells ring loud with gladsome power;
The sun shines bright; the fields are gay
With people in their best array
Of stole and doublet, hood and scarf,
Along the banks of crystal Wharf,
Through the Vale retired and lowly,
Trooping to that summons holy.
And, up among the moorlands, see
What sprinklings of blithe company!
Of lasses and of shepherd grooms,
That down the steep hills force their way,
Like cattle through the budded brooms;
Path, or no path, what care they?
And thus in joyous mood they hie
To Bolton's mouldering Priory.
     What would they there? — Full fifty
          years

That sumptuous Pile, with all its peers,
Too harshly hath been doomed to taste
The bitterness of wrong and waste:
Its courts are ravaged; but the tower
Is standing with a voice of power,
That ancient voice which wont to call
To mass or some high festival;
And in the shattered fabric's heart
Remaineth one protected part;
A Chapel, like a wild-bird's nest,[1]
Closely embowered and trimly drest;
And thither young and old repair,
This Sabbath-day, for praise and prayer.
     Fast the churchyard fills; — anon
Look again, and they all are gone;
The cluster round the porch, and the folk
Who sate in the shade of the Prior's Oak![1]
And scarcely have they disappeared
Ere the prelusive hymn is heard: —
With one consent the people rejoice,
Filling the church with a lofty voice!
They sing a service which they feel:
For 't is the sunrise now of zeal;
Of a pure faith the vernal prime —
In great Eliza's golden time.
     A moment ends the fervent din,
And all is hushed, without and within;
For though the priest, more tranquilly,
Recites the holy liturgy,
The only voice which you can hear
Is the river murmuring near.
— When soft! — the dusky trees between,
And down the path through the open
          green,
Where is no living thing to be seen;
And through yon gateway, where is found,
Beneath the arch with ivy bound,
Free entrance to the churchyard ground —
Comes gliding in with lovely gleam,
Comes gliding in serene and slow,
Soft and silent as a dream,
A solitary Doe!
White she is as lily of June,
And beauteous as the silver moon
When out of sight the clouds are driven
And she is left alone in heaven;
Or like a ship some gentle day
In sunshine sailing far away,
A glittering ship, that hath the plain
Of ocean for her own domain.
     Lie silent in your graves, ye dead!
Lie quiet in your churchyard bed!
Ye living, tend your holy cares;

[1] See Note.

Ye multitude, pursue your prayers;
And blame not me if my heart and sight
Are occupied with one delight!
'T is a work for sabbath hours
If I with this bright Creature go:
Whether she be of forest bowers,
From the bowers of earth below;
Or a Spirit for one day given,
A pledge of grace from purest heaven.
What harmonious pensive changes
Wait upon her as she ranges
Round and through this Pile of state
Overthrown and desolate!
Now a step or two her way
Leads through space of open day,
Where the enamoured sunny light
Brightens her that was so bright;
Now doth a delicate shadow fall,
Falls upon her like a breath,
From some lofty arch or wall,
As she passes underneath:
Now some gloomy nook partakes
Of the glory that she makes, —
High-ribbed vault of stone, or cell,
With perfect cunning framed as well
Of stone, and ivy, and the spread
Of the elder's bushy head;
Some jealous and forbidding cell,
That doth the living stars repel,
And where no flower hath leave to dwell.
The presence of this wandering Doe
Fills many a damp obscure recess
With lustre of a saintly show;
And, reappearing, she no less
Sheds on the flowers that round her blow
A more than sunny liveliness.
But say, among these holy places,
Which thus assiduously she paces,
Comes she with a votary's task,
Rite to perform, or boon to ask?
Fair Pilgrim! harbors she a sense
Of sorrow, or of reverence?
Can she be grieved for quire or shrine,
Crushed as if by wrath divine?
For what survives of house where God
Was worshipped, or where Man abode;
For old magnificence undone;
Or for the gentler work begun
By Nature, softening and concealing,
And busy with a hand of healing?
Mourns she for lordly chamber's hearth
That to the sapling ash gives birth;
For dormitory's length laid bare

Where the wild rose blossoms fair;
Or altar, whence the cross was rent,
Now rich with mossy ornament?
— She sees a warrior carved in stone,
Among the thick weeds, stretched alone;
A warrior, with his shield of pride
Cleaving humbly to his side,
And hands in resignation prest,
Palm to palm, on his tranquil breast;
As little she regards the sight
As a common creature might:
If she be doomed to inward care,
Or service, it must lie elsewhere.
— But hers are eyes serenely bright,
And on she moves — with pace how light!
Nor spares to stoop her head, and taste
The dewy turf with flowers bestrown;
And thus she fares, until at last
Beside the ridge of a grassy grave
In quietness she lays her down;
Gentle as a weary wave
Sinks, when the summer breeze hath died,
Against an anchored vessel's side;
Even so, without distress, doth she
Lie down in peace, and lovingly.
The day is placid in its going,
To a lingering motion bound,
Like the crystal stream now flowing
With its softest summer sound:
So the balmy minutes pass,
While this radiant Creature lies
Couched upon the dewy grass,
Pensively with downcast eyes.
— But now again the people raise
With awful cheer a voice of praise;
It is the last, the parting song;
And from the temple forth they throng,
And quickly spread themselves abroad,
While each pursues his several road.
But some — a variegated band
Of middle-aged, and old, and young,
And little children by the hand
Upon their leading mothers hung —
With mute obeisance gladly paid
Turn towards the spot, where, full in view,
The white Doe, to her service true,
Her sabbath couch has made.
It was a solitary mound;
Which two spears' length of level ground
Did from all other graves divide:
As if in some respect of pride;
Or melancholy's sickly mood,
Still shy of human neighborhood;

Or guilt, that humbly would express
A penitential loneliness.
　　"Look, there she is, my Child! draw
　　　　near;
She fears not, wherefore should we fear?
She means no harm;"—but still the Boy,
To whom the words were softy said,
Hung back, and smiled, and blushed for
　　joy,
A shame-faced blush of glowing red!
Again the Mother whispered low,
"Now you have seen the famous Doe;
From Rylstone she hath found her way
Over the hills this sabbath day.
Her work, whate'er it be, is done,
And she will depart when we are gone;
Thus doth she keep, from year to year,
Her sabbath morning, foul or fair."
　　Bright was the Creature, as in dreams
The Boy had seen her, yea, more bright;
But is she truly what she seems?
He asks with insecure delight,
Asks of himself, and doubts,—and still
The doubt returns against his will:
Though he, and all the standers-by,
Could tell a tragic history
Of facts divulged, wherein appear
Substantial motive, reason clear,
Why thus the milk-white Doe is found
Couchant beside that lonely mound;
And why she duly loves to pace
The circuit of this hallowed place.
Nor to the Child's inquiring mind
Is such perplexity confined:
For, spite of sober Truth that sees
A world of fixed remembrances
Which to this mystery belong,
If, undeceived, my skill can trace
The characters of every face,
There lack not strange delusion here,
Conjecture vague, and idle fear,
And superstitious fancies strong,
Which do the gentle Creature wrong.
　　That bearded, staff-supported Sire—
Who in his boyhood often fed
Full cheerily on convent-bread,
And heard old tales by the convent-fire,
And to his grave will go with scars,
Relics of long and distant wars—
That Old Man, studious to expound
The spectacle, is mounting high
To days of dim antiquity;
When Lady Aäliza mourned [1]

Her Son, and felt in her despair
The pang of unavailing prayer;
Her Son in Wharf's abysses drowned,
The noble Boy of Egremound.
From which affliction—when the grace
Of God had in her heart found place—
A pious structure, fair to see,
Rose up, this stately Priory!
The Lady's work!—but now laid low;
To the grief of her soul that doth come
　　and go,
In the beautiful form of this innocent Doe:
Which, though seemingly doomed in its
　　breast to sustain
A softened remembrance of sorrow and
　　pain,
Is spotless, and holy, and gentle, and
　　bright;
And glides o'er the earth like an angel of
　　light.
　　Pass, pass who will, yon chantry door; [1]
And, through the chink in the fractured
　　floor
Look down, and see a griesly sight;
A vault where the bodies are buried up-
　　right!
There, face by face, and hand by hand,
The Claphams and Mauleverers stand;
And, in his place, among son and sire,
Is John de Clapham, that fierce Esquire,
A valiant man, and a name of dread
In the ruthless wars of the White and Red;
Who dragged Earl Pembroke from Ban-
　　bury church
And smote off his head on the stones of
　　the porch!
Look down among them, if you dare;
Oft does the White Doe loiter there,
Prying into the darksome rent;
Nor can it be with good intent:
So thinks that Dame of haughty air,
Who hath a Page her book to hold,
And wears a frontlet edged with gold.
Harsh thoughts with her high mood
　　agree—
Who counts among her ancestry
Earl Pembroke, slain so impiously!
　　That slender Youth, a scholar pale,
From Oxford came to his native vale,
He also hath his own conceit:
It is, thinks he, the gracious Fairy,
Who loved the Shepherd-lord to meet [1]
In his wanderings solitary:

[1] See Note.

Wild notes she in his hearing sang,
A song of Nature's hidden powers;
That whistled like the wind, and rang
Among the rocks and holly bowers.
'T was said that She all shapes could wear;
And oftentimes before him stood,
Amid the trees of some thick wood,
In semblance of a lady fair;
And taught him signs, and showed him
    sights,
In Craven's dens, on Cumbrian heights;
When under cloud of fear he lay,
A shepherd clad in homely gray;
Nor left him at his later day.
And hence, when he, with spear and
    shield,
Rode full of years to Flodden-field,
His eye could see the hidden spring,
And how the current was to flow;
The fatal end of Scotland's King,
And all that hopeless overthrow.
But not in wars did he delight,
This Clifford wished for worthier might;
Nor in broad pomp, or courtly state;
Him his own thoughts did elevate, —
Most happy in the shy recess
Of Barden's lowly quietness.
And choice of studious friends had he
Of Bolton's dear fraternity;
Who, standing on this old church tower,
In many a calm propitious hour,
Perused, with him, the starry sky;
Or, in their cells, with him did pry
For other lore, — by keen desire
Urged to close toil with chemic fire;
In quest belike of transmutations
Rich as the mine's most bright creations.
But they and their good works are fled,
And all is now disquieted —
And peace is none, for living or dead!
  Ah, pensive Scholar, think not so,
But look again at the radiant Doe!
What quiet watch she seems to keep,
Alone, beside that grassy heap!
Why mention other thoughts unmeet
For vision so composed and sweet?
While stand the people in a ring,
Gazing, doubting, questioning;
Yea, many overcome in spite
Of recollections clear and bright;
Which yet do unto some impart
An undisturbed repose of heart.
And all the assembly own a law

Of orderly respect and awe;
But see — they vanish one by one,
And last, the Doe herself is gone.
  Harp! we have been full long beguiled
By vague thoughts, lured by fancies wild;
To which, with no reluctant strings,
Thou hast attuned thy murmurings;
And now before this Pile we stand
In solitude, and utter peace:
But, Harp! thy murmurs may not cease —
A Spirit, with his angelic wings,
In soft and breeze-like visitings,
Has touched thee — and a Spirit's hand:
A voice is with us — a command
To chant, in strains of heavenly glory,
A tale of tears, a mortal story!

Canto Second.

THE Harp in lowliness obeyed;
And first we sang of the greenwood shade
And a solitary Maid;
Beginning, where the song must end,
With her, and with her sylvan Friend;
The Friend who stood before her sight,
Her only unextinguished light;
Her last companion in a dearth
Of love, upon a hopeless earth.
  For She it was — this Maid, who
    wrought
Meekly, with foreboding thought,
In vermeil colors and in gold
An unblest work; which, standing by,
Her Father did with joy behold, —
Exulting in its imagery;
A Banner, fashioned to fulfil
Too perfectly his headstrong will:
For on this Banner had her hand
Embroidered (such her Sire's command)
The sacred Cross; and figured there
The five dear wounds our Lord did bear;
Full soon to be uplifted high,
And float in rueful company!
  It was the time when England's Queen
Twelve years had reigned, a Sovereign
    dread;
Nor yet the restless crown had been
Disturbed upon her virgin head;
But now the inly-working North
Was ripe to send its thousands forth,
A potent vassalage, to fight
In Percy's and in Neville's right,
Two Earls fast leagued in discontent,

Who gave their wishes open vent;
And boldly urged a general plea,
The rites of ancient piety
To be triumphantly restored,
By the stern justice of the sword!
And that same Banner, on whose breas.
The blameless Lady had exprest
Memorials chosen to give life
And sunshine to a dangerous strife;
That Banner, waiting for the Call,
Stood quietly in Rylstone-hall.

It came; and Francis Norton said,
"O Father! rise not in this fray —
The hairs are white upon your head;
Dear Father, hear me when I say
It is for you too late a day!
Bethink you of your own good name:
A just and gracious Queen have we,
A pure religion, and the claim
Of peace on our humanity. —
'T is meet that I endure your scorn;
I am your son, your eldest born;
But not for lordship or for land,
My Father, do I clasp your knees;
The Banner touch not, stay your hand,
This multitude of men disband,
And live at home in blameless ease;
For these my brethren's sake, for me;
And, most of all, for Emily!"

Tumultuous noises filled the hall;
And scarcely could the Father hear
That name — pronounced with a dying
    fall —
The name of his only Daughter dear,
As on the banner which stood near
He glanced a look of holy pride,
And his moist eyes were glorified;
Then did he seize the staff, and say:
"Thou, Richard, bear'st thy father's
    name,
Keep thou this ensign till the day
When I of thee require the same:
Thy place be on my better hand; —
And seven as true as thou, I see,
Will cleave to this good cause and me."
He spake, and eight brave sons straight-
    way
All followed him, a gallant band!

Thus, with his sons, when forth he
    came
The sight was hailed with loud acclaim
And din of arms and minstrelsy,
From all his warlike tenantry,

All horsed and harnessed with him to
    ride, —
A voice to which the hills replied!
But Francis, in the vacant hall,
Stood silent under dreary weight, —
A phantasm, in which roof and wall
Shook, tottered, swam before his sight;
A phantasm like a dream of night!
Thus overwhelmed, and desolate,
He found his way to a postern-gate;
And, when he waked, his languid eye
Was on the calm and silent sky;
With air about him breathing sweet,
And earth's green grass beneath his feet;
Nor did he fail ere long to hear
A sound of military cheer,
Faint — but it reached that sheltered spot;
He heard, and it disturbed him not.

There stood he, leaning on a lance
Which he had grasped unknowingly,
Had blindly grasped in that strong trance,
That dimness of heart-agony;
There stood he, cleansed from the despair
And sorrow of his fruitless prayer.
The past he calmly hath reviewed:
But where will be the fortitude
Of this brave man, when he shall see
That Form beneath the spreading tree,
And know that it is Emily?

He saw her where in open view
She sate beneath the spreading yew —
Her head upon her lap, concealing
In solitude her bitter feeling:
"Might ever son *command* a sire,
The act were justified to-day."
This to himself — and to the Maid,
Whom now he had approached, he said —
"Gone are they, — they have their desire;
And I with thee one hour will stay,
To give thee comfort if I may."

She heard, but looked not up, nor
    spake;
And sorrow moved him to partake
Her silence; then his thoughts turned ,
    round,
And fervent words a passage found.

"Gone are they, bravely, though mis-
    led;
With a dear Father at their head!
The Sons obey a natural lord;
The Father had given solemn word
To noble Percy; and a force
Still stronger, bends him to his course.

This said, our tears to-day may fall
As at an innocent funeral.
In deep and awful channel runs
This sympathy of Sire and Sons;
Untried our Brothers have been loved
With heart by simple nature moved;
And now their faithfulness is proved:
For faithful we must call them, bearing
That soul of conscientious daring.
—There were they all in circle — there
Stood Richard, Ambrose, Christopher,
John with a sword that will not fail,
And Marmaduke in fearless mail,
And those bright Twins were side by side;
And there, by fresh hopes beautified,
Stood He, whose arm yet lacks the power
Of man, our youngest, fairest flower!
I, by the right of eldest born,
And in a second father's place,
Presumed to grapple with their scorn,
And meet their pity face to face;
Yea, trusting in God's holy aid,
I to my Father knelt and prayed;
And one, the pensive Marmaduke,
Methought, was yielding inwardly,
And would have laid his purpose by,
But for a glance of his Father's eye,
Which I myself could scarcely brook.

Then be we, each and all, forgiven!
Thou, chiefly thou, my Sister dear,
Whose pangs are registered in heaven —
The stifled sigh, the hidden tear,
And smiles, that dared to take their
    place,
Meek filial smiles, upon thy face,
As that unhallowed Banner grew
Beneath a loving old Man's view.
Thy part is done — thy painful part;
Be thou then satisfied in heart!
A further, though a easier, task
Than thine hath been, my duties ask;
With theirs my efforts cannot blend,
I cannot for such cause contend;
Their aims I utterly forswear;
But I in body will be there.
Unarmed and naked will I go,
Be at their side, come weal or woe:
On kind occasions I may wait,
See, hear, obstruct, or mitigate.
Bare breast I take and an empty hand." [1] —
Therewith he threw away the lance,

[1] See the Old Ballad, — "The Rising of the North."

Which he had grasped in that strong
    trance,
Spurned it, like something that would
    stand
Between him and the pure intent
Of love on which his soul was bent.
    "For thee, for thee, is left the sense
Of trial past without offence
To God or man; such innocence,
Such consolation, and the excess
Of an unmerited distress;
In that thy very strength must lie.
—O Sister, I could prophesy!
The time is come that rings the knell
Of all we loved, and loved so well:
Hope nothing, if I thus may speak
To thee, a woman, and thence weak:
Hope nothing, I repeat; for we
Are doomed to perish utterly:
'T is meet that thou with me divide
The thought while I am by thy side,
Acknowledging a grace in this,
A comfort in the dark abyss.
But look not for me when I am gone,
And be no farther wrought upon:
Farewell all wishes, all debate,
All prayers for this cause, or for that!
Weep, if that aid thee; but depend
Upon no help of outward friend;
Espouse thy doom at once, and cleave
To fortitude without reprieve.
For we must fall, both we and ours —
This Mansion and these pleasant bowers,
Walks, pools, and arbors, homestead,
    hall —
Our fate is theirs, will reach them all;
The young horse must forsake his manger,
And learn to glory in a Stranger;
The hawk forget his perch; the hound
Be parted from his ancient ground:
The blast will sweep us all away —
One desolation, one decay!
And even this Creature!" which words
    saying,
He pointed to a lovely Doe,
A few steps distant, feeding, straying;
Fair creature, and more white than snow!
"Even she will to her peaceful woods
Return, and to her murmuring floods,
And be in heart and soul the same
She was before she hither came;
Ere she had learned to love us all,
Herself beloved in Rylstone-hall.

— But thou, my Sister, doomed to be
The last leaf on a blasted tree;
If not in vain we breathed the breath
Together of a purer faith;
If hand in hand we have been led,
And thou, (O happy thought this day:)
Not seldom foremost in the way;
If on one thought our minds have fed,
And we have in one meaning read;
If, when at home our private weal
Hath suffered from the shock of zeal,
Together we have learned to prize
Forbearance and self-sacrifice;
If we like combatants have fared,
And for this issue been prepared;
If thou art beautiful, and youth
And thought endue thee with all truth —
Be strong;—be worthy of the grace
Of God, and fill thy destined place:
A Soul, by force of sorrows high,
Uplifted to the purest sky
Of undisturbed humanity!"
He ended, — or she heard no more;
He led her from the yew-tree shade,
And at the mansion's silent door,
He kissed the consecrated Maid;
And down the valley then pursued,
Alone, the armèd Multitude.

Canto Third.

Now joy for you who from the towers
Of Brancepeth look in doubt and fear,[1]
Telling melancholy hours!
Proclaim it, let your Masters hear
That Norton with his band is near!
The watchmen from their station high
Pronounced the word, — and the Earls
descry,
Well-pleased, the armèd Company
Marching down the banks of Were.
Said fearless Norton to the pair
Gone forth to greet him on the plain —
"This meeting, noble Lords! looks fair,
I bring with me a goodly train;
Their hearts are with you: hill and dale
Have helped us: Ure we crossed, and
Swale,
And horse and harness followed — see
The best part of their Yeomanry!
— Stand forth, my Sons! — these eight
are mine,

[1] See Note.

Whom to this service I commend;
Which way soe'er our fate incline,
These will be faithful to the end;
They are my all " — voice failed him
here —
" My all save one, a Daughter dear!
Whom I have left, Love's mildest birth,
The meekest Child on this blessed earth.
I had — but these are by my side,
These Eight, and this is a day of pride!
The time is ripe. With festive din
Lo! how the people are flocking in, —
Like hungry fowl to the feeder's hand
When snow lies heavy upon the land."
He spake bare truth; for far and near
From every side came noisy swarms
Of Peasants in their homely gear;
And, mixed with these, to Brancepeth
came
Grave Gentry of estate and name,
And Captains known for worth in arms
And prayed the Earls in self-defence
To rise, and prove their innocence. —
" Rise, noble Earls, put forth your might
For holy Church, and the People's right!"
The Norton fixed, at this demand,
His eye upon Northumberland,
And said: " The Minds of Men will own
No loyal rest while England's Crown
Remains without an Heir, the bait
Of strife and factions desperate;
Who, paying deadly hate in kind
Through all things else, in this can find
A mutual hope, a common mind;
And plot, and pant to overwhelm
All ancient honor in the realm.
— Brave Earls! to whose heroic veins
Our noblest blood is given in trust,
To you a suffering State complains,
And ye must raise her from the dust.
With wishes of still bolder scope
On you we look, with dearest hope;
Even for our Altars — for the prize,
In Heaven, of life that never dies;
For the old and holy Church we mourn,
And must in joy to her return.
Behold!"— and from his Son whose stand
Was on his right, from that guardian hand
He took the Banner, and unfurled
The precious folds —" behold," said he,
" The ransom of a sinful world;
Let this your preservation be;
The wounds of hands and feet and side,

And the sacred Cross on which Jesus died.
— This bring I from an ancient hearth,
These Records wrought in pledge of love
By hands of no ignoble birth,
A Maid o'er whom the blessed Dove
Vouchsafed in gentleness to brood
While she the holy work pursued."
" Uplift the Standard ! " was the cry
From all the listeners that stood round,
" Plant it, — by this we live or die."
The Norton ceased not for that sound,
But said; "The prayer which ye have
          heard,
Much-injured Earls ! by these preferred,
Is offered to the Saints, the sigh
Of tens of thousands, secretly."
" Uplift it ! " cried once more the Band,
And then a thoughtful pause ensued :
" Uplift it ! " said Northumberland —
Whereat, from all the multitude
Who saw the Banner reared on high
·In all its dread emblazonry,
A voice of uttermost joy brake out:
The transport was rolled down the river
          of Were,
And Durham, the time-honored Durham,
          did hear,
And the towers of Saint Cuthbert were
          stirred by the shout !
    Now was the North in arms :—they shine
In warlike trim from Tweed to Tyne,
At Percy's voice : and Neville sees
His Followers gathering in from Tees,
From Were, and all the little rills
Concealed among the forkèd hills —
Seven hundred Knights, Retainers all
Of Neville, at their Master's call
·Had sate together in Raby Hall !
Such strength that Earldom held of yore;
Nor wanted at this time rich store
Of well-appointed chivalry.
— Not loth the sleepy lance to wield,
And greet the old paternal shield,
They heard the summons;—and, further-
          more,
Horsemen and Foot of each degree,
Unbound by pledge of fealty,
Appeared, with free and open hate
Of novelties in Church and State;
Knight, burgher, yeoman, and esquire;
And Romish priest, in priest's attire.
And thus, in arms, a zealous Band
Proceeding under joint command,

To Durham first their course they bear;
And in Saint Cuthbert's ancient seat
Sang mass, — and tore the book of
          prayer, —
And trod the bible beneath their feet.
    Thence marching southward smooth
          and free
"They mustered their host at Wetherby,
Full sixteen thousand fair to see," [1]
The Choicest Warriors of the North !
But none for beauty and for worth
Like those eight Sons—who, in a ring,
(Ripe men, or blooming in life's spring)
Each with a lance, erect and tall,.
A falchion, and a buckler small,
Stood by their Sire, on Clifford-moor,
To guard the Standard which he bore.
On foot they girt their Father round;
And so will keep the appointed ground
Where'er their march : no steed will he
Henceforth bestride;—triumphantly,
He stands upon the grassy sod,
Trusting himself to the earth, and God.
Rare sight to embolden and inspire !
Proud was the field of Sons and Sire;
Of him the most; and, sooth to say,
No shape of man in all the array
So graced the sunshine of that day.
The monumental pomp of age
Was with this goodly Personage;
A stature undepressed in size,
Unbent, which rather seemed to rise,
In open victory o'er the weight
Of seventy years, to loftier height;
Magnificent limbs of withered state;
A face to fear and venerate;
Eyes dark and strong; and on his head
Bright locks of silver hair, thick spread,
Which a brown morion half-concealed,
Light as a hunter's of the field;
And thus, with girdle round his waist,
Whereon the Banner-staff might rest
At need, he stood, advancing high
The glittering, floating Pageantry.
    Who sees him ? — thousands see, and
          One
With unparticipated gaze;
Who, 'mong those thousands, friend hath
          none,
And treads in solitary ways.
He, following wheresoe'er he might,
Hath watched the Banner from afar,

    [1] From the old ballad.

As shepherds watch a lonely star,
Or mariners the distant light
That guides them through a stormy night.
And now, upon a chosen plot
Of rising ground, yon heathy spot!
He takes alone his far-off stand,
With breast unmailed, unweaponed hand.
Bold is his aspect; but his eye
Is pregnant with anxiety,
While, like a tutelary Power,
He there stands fixed from hour to hour:
Yet sometimes in more humble guise,
Upon the turf-clad height he lies
Stretched, herdsman-like, as if to bask
In sunshine were his only task,
Or by his mantle's help to find
A shelter from the nipping wind:
And thus, with short oblivion blest,
His weary spirits gather rest.
Again he lifts his eyes; and lo!
The pageant glancing to and fro;
And hope is wakened by the sight,
He thence may learn, ere fall of night,
Which way the tide is doomed to flow.

To London were the Chieftains bent;
But what avails the bold intent?
A Royal army is gone forth
To quell the RISING OF THE NORTH;
They march with Dudley at their head,
And, in seven days' space, will to York
    be led! —
Can such a mighty Host be raised
Thus suddenly, and brought so near?
The Earls upon each other gazed,
And Neville's cheek grew pale with fear;
For, with a high and valiant name,
He bore a heart of timid frame;
And bold if both had been, yet they
"Against so many may not stay."[1]
Back therefore will they hie to seize
A strong Hold on the banks of Tees
There wait a favorable hour,
Until Lord Dacre with his power
From Naworth come; and Howard's aid
Be with them openly displayed.

While through the Host, from man to
    man,
A rumor of this purpose ran,
The Standard trusting to the care
Of him who heretofore did bear
That charge, impatient Norton sought
The Chieftains to unfold his thought,

[1] From the old ballad.

And thus abruptly spake; — "We yield
(And can it be?) an unfought field! —
How oft has strength, the strength of
    heaven,
To few triumphantly been given!
Still do our very children boast
Of mitred Thurston — what a Host
He conquered![2] — Saw we not the Plain
(And flying shall behold again)
Where faith was proved? — while to
    battle moved
The Standard, on the Sacred Wain
That bore it, compassed round by a bold
Fraternity of Barons old;
And with those gray-haired champions
    stood,
Under the saintly ensigns three,
The infant Heir of Mowbray's blood —
All confident of victory!
Shall Percy blush, then, for his name?
Must Westmoreland be asked with shame
Whose were the numbers, where the loss,
In that other day of Neville's Cross?[2]
When the Prior of Durham with holy hand
Raised, as the Vision gave command,
Saint Cuthbert's Relic — far and near
Kenned on the point of a lofty spear;
While the Monks prayed in Maiden's
    Bower
To God descending in his power.
Less would not at our need be due
To us, who war against the Untrue; —
The delegates of Heaven we rise,
Convoked the impious to chastise:
We, we, the sanctities of old
Would re-establish and uphold:
Be warned" — His zeal the Chiefs con-
    founded,
But word was given, and the trumpet
    sounded:
Back through the melancholy Host
Went Norton, and resumed his post.
Alas! thought he, and have I borne
This Banner raised with joyful pride,
This hope of all posterity,
By those dread symbols sanctified;
Thus to become at once the scorn
Of babbling winds as they go by,
A spot of shame to the sun's bright eye,
To the light clouds a mockery!
— "Even these poor eight of mine would
    stem — "

[2] See Note.

Half to himself, and half to them
He spake — "would stem, or quell, a
  force
Ten times their number, man and horse:
This by their own unaided might,
Without their father in their sight,
Without the Cause for which they fight;
A Cause, which on a needful day
Would breed us thousands brave as they."
— So speaking, he his reverend head
Raised towards that Imagery once more:
But the familiar prospect shed
Despondency unfelt before:
A shock of intimations vain,
Dismay, and superstitious pain,
Fell on him, with the sudden thought
Of her by whom the work was wrought:—
Oh wherefore was her countenance bright
With love divine and gentle light?
She would not, could not, disobey,
But her Faith leaned another way.
Ill tears she wept; I saw them fall,
I overheard her as she spake
Sad words to that mute Animal,
The White Doe, in the hawthorn brake;
She steeped, but not for Jesu's sake,
This Cross in tears: by her, and One
Unworthier far we are undone —
Her recreant Brother — he prevailed
Over that tender Spirit — assailed
Too oft, alas! by her whose head
In the cold grave hath long been laid:
She first, in reason's dawn beguiled
Her docile, unsuspecting Child:
Far back — far back my mind must go
To reach the well-spring of this woe!

  While thus he brooded, music sweet
Of border tunes was played to cheer
The footsteps of a quick retreat;
But Norton lingered in the rear,
Stung with sharp thoughts; and ere the
  last
From his distracted brain was cast,
Before his father, Francis stood,
And spake in firm and earnest mood.
  "Though here I bend a suppliant knee
In reverence, and unarmed, I bear
In your indignant thoughts my share;
Am grieved this backward march to see
So careless and disorderly.
·I scorn your chiefs — men who would lead,
And yet want courage at their need:
Then look at them with open eyes!

Deserve they further sacrifice? —
If — when they shrink, nor dare oppose
In open field their gathering foes,
(And fast, from this decisive day,
Yon multitude must melt away;)
If now I ask a grace not claimed
While ground was left for hope; unblamed
Be an endeavor that can do
No injury to them or you.
My Father! I would help to find
A place of shelter, till the rage
Of cruel men do like the wind
Exhaust itself and sink to rest;
Be Brother now to Brother joined!
Admit me in the equipage
Of your misfortunes, that at least,
Whatever fate remain behind,
I may bear witness in my breast
To your nobility of mind!"
  "Thou Enemy, my bane and blight!
Oh! bold to fight the Coward's fight
Against all good" — but why declare,
At length, the issue of a prayer
Which love had prompted, yielding scope
Too free to one bright moment's hope?
Suffice it that the Son, who strove
With fruitless effort to allay
That passion, prudently gave way;
Nor did he turn aside to prove
His Brothers' wisdom or their love —
But calmly from the spot withdrew;
His best endeavors to renew,
Should e'er a kindlier time ensue.

CANTO FOURTH.

'T IS night: in silence looking down,
The Moon, from cloudless ether, sees
A Camp, and a beleaguered Town,
And Castle, like a stately crown
On the steep rocks of winding Tees; —
And southward far, with moor between,
Hill-top, and flood, and forest green,
The bright Moon sees that valley small
Where Rylstone's old sequestered Hall
A venerable image yields
Of quiet to the neighboring fields;
While from one pillared chimney breathes
The smoke, and mounts in silver wreaths.
— The courts are hushed; — for timely
  sleep
The greyhounds to their kennel creep;
The peacock in the broad ash tree

Aloft is roosted for the night,
He who in proud prosperity
Of colors manifold and bright
Walked round, affronting the daylight;
And higher still, above the bower
Where he is perched, from yon lone Tower
The hall-clock in the clear moonshine
With glittering finger points at nine.
  Ah! who could think that sadness here
Hath any sway? or pain, or fear?
A soft and lulling sound is heard
Of streams inaudible by day;
The garden pool's dark surface, stirred
By the night insects in their play,
Breaks into dimples small and bright;
A thousand, thousand rings of light
That shape themselves and disappear
Almost as soon as seen: — and lo!
Not distant far, the milk-white Doe —
The same who quietly was feeding
On the green herb, and nothing heeding,
When Francis, uttering to the Maid
His last words in the yew-tree shade,
Involved whate'er by love was brought
Out of his heart, or crossed his thought,
Or chance presented to his eye,
In one sad sweep of destiny —
The same fair Creature, who hath found
Her way into forbidden ground;
Where now — within this spacious plot
For pleasure made, a goodly spot,
With lawns and beds of flowers, and
    shades
Of trellis-work in long arcades,
And cirque and crescent framed by wall
Of close-clipt foliage green and tall,
Converging walks, and fountains gay,
And terraces in trim array—
Beneath yon cypress spiring high,
With pine and cedar spreading wide
Their darksome boughs on either side,
In open moonlight doth she lie;
Happy as others of her kind,
That, far from human neighborhood,
Range unrestricted as the wind,
Through park, or chase, or savage wood.
  But see the consecrated Maid
Emerging from a cedar shade
To open moonshine, where the Doe
Beneath the cypress-spire is laid;
Like a patch of April snow —
Upon a bed of herbage green,
Lingering in a woody glade

Or behind a rocky screen —
Lonely relic! which, if seen
By the shepherd, is passed by
With an inattentive eye.
Nor more regard doth She bestow
Upon the uncomplaining Doe
Now couched at ease, though oft this
    day
Not unperplexed nor free from pain,
When she had tried, and tried in vain,
Approaching in her gentle way,
To win some look of love, or gain
Encouragement to sport or play
Attempts which still the heart-sick Maid
Rejected, or with slight repaid.
  Yet Emily is soothed; — the breeze
Came fraught with kindly sympathies.
As she approached yon rustic Shed
Hung with late-flowering woodbine,
    spread
Along the walls and overhead,
The fragrance of the breathing flowers
Revived a memory of those hours
When here, in this remote alcove,
(While from the pendent woodbine came
Like odors, sweet as if the same)
A fondly-anxious Mother strove
To teach her salutary fears
And mysteries above her years.
Yes, she is soothed: an Image faint,
And yet not faint — a presence bright
Returns to her — that blessèd Saint
Who with mild looks and language mild
Instructed here her darling Child,
While yet a prattler on the knee,
To worship in simplicity
The invisible God, and take for guide
The faith reformed and purified.
  'T is flown — the Vision, and the sense
Of that beguiling influence,
" But oh! thou Angel from above,
Mute Spirit of maternal love,
That stood'st before my eyes, more clear
Than ghosts are fabled to appear
Sent upon embassies of fear;
As thou thy presence hast to me
Vouchsafed, in radiant ministry
Descend on Francis; nor forbear
To greet him with a voice, and say; —
' If hope be a rejected stay,
Do thou, my christian Son, beware
Of that most lamentable snare,
The self-reliance of despair!' "

Then from within the embowered
          retreat
Where she had found a grateful seat
Perturbed she issues.   She will go!
Herself will follow to the war,
And clasp her Father's knees;— ah, no!
She meets the insuperable bar,
The injunction by her Brother laid;
His parting charge — but ill obeyed —
That interdicted all debate,
All prayer for this cause or for that;
All efforts that would turn aside
The headstrong current of their fate:
Her duty is to stand and wait:
In resignation to abide
The shock, AND FINALLY SECURE
O'ER PAIN AND GRIEF A TRIUMPH PURE.
- ~She feels it, and her pangs are checked.
But now, as silently she paced
The turf, and thought by thought was
          chased,
Came One who, with sedate respect,
Approached, and, greeting her, thus
          spake;
"An old man's privilege I take:
Dark is the time — a woful day!
Dear daughter of affliction, say
How can I serve you? point the way."
    "Rights have you, and may well be
          bold;
You with my Father have grown old
In friendship—- strive — for his sake go —
Turn from us all the coming woe:
This would I beg; but on my mind
A passive stillness is enjoined.
On you, if room for mortal aid
Be left, is no restriction laid;
You not forbidden to recline
With hope upon the Will divine."
    "Hope," said the old Man, "must
          abide
With all of us, whate'er betide.
In Craven's Wilds is many a den,
To shelter persecuted men:
Far under ground is many a cave,
Where they might lie as in the grave,
Until this storm hath ceased to rave:
Or let them cross the River Tweed,
And be at once from peril freed!"
    "Ah tempt me not!" she faintly
          sighed,
"I will not counsel nor exhort,
With my condition satisfied;

But you, at least, may make report
Of what befalls;— be this your task —
This may be done; — 't is all I ask!"
    She spake — and from the Lady's sight
The Sire, unconscious of his age,
Departed promptly as a Page
Bound on some errand of delight.
— The noble Francis — wise as brave,
Thought he, may want not skill to save.
With hopes in tenderness concealed,
Unarmed he followed to the field;
Him will I seek: the insurgent Powers
Are now besieging Barnard's Towers, —
"Grant that the Moon which shines this
          night
May guide them in a prudent flight!"
    But quick the turns of chance and
          change,
And knowledge has a narrow range;
Whence idle fears, and needless pain,
And wishes blind, and effort vain. —
The Moon may shine, but cannot be
Their guide in flight — already she
Hath witnessed their captivity.
She saw the desperate assault
Upon that hostile castle made;
But dark and dismal is the vault
Where Norton and his sons are laid!
Disastrous issue! — he had said
"This night yon faithless Towers must
          yield,
Or we forever quit the field.
    Neville is utterly dismayed,
For promise fails of Howard's aid;
And Dacre to our call replies
That *he* is unprepared to rise.
My heart is sick; — this weary pause
Must needs be fatal to our cause.
The breach is open — on the wall,
This night, the Banner shall be planted!"
— 'T was done: his Sons were with him
          — all;
They belt him round with hearts un-
          daunted
And others follow; — Sire and Son
Leap down into the court; — "'T is
          won" —
They shout aloud — but Heaven decreed
That with their joyful shout should close
The triumph of a desperate deed
Which struck with terror friends and foes!
The friend shrinks back — the foe recoils
From Norton and his filial band;

But they, now caught within the toils,
Against a thousand cannot stand;—
The foe from numbers courage drew,
And overpowered that gallant few.
" A rescue for the Standard ! " cried
The Father from within the walls;
But, see, the sacred Standard falls ! —
Confusion through the Camp spread wide:
Some fled; and some their fears detained:
But ere, the Moon had sunk to rest
In her pale chambers of the west,
Of that rash levy nought remained.

CANTO FIFTH.

HIGH on a point of rugged ground
Among the wastes of Rylstone Fell
Above the loftiest ridge or mound
Where foresters or shepherds dwell,
An edifice of warlike frame
Stands single — Norton Tower its
    name [1] —
It fronts all quarters, and looks round
O'er path and road, and plain and dell,
Dark moor, and gleam of pool and stream,
Upon a prospect without bound.
  The summit of this bold ascent —
Though bleak and bare, and seldom free
As Pendle-hill or Pennygent
From wind, or frost, or vapors wet —
Had often heard the sound of glee
When there the youthful Nortons met,
To practise games and archery:
How proud and happy they ! the crowd
Of Lookers-on how pleased and proud !
And from the scorching noon-tide sun,
From showers, or when the prize was won,
They to the Tower withdrew, and there
Would mirth run round, with generous
    fare;
And the stern old Lord of Rylstone-hall
Was happiest, proudest, of them all !
  But now, his Child, with anguish pale,
Upon the height walks to and fro;
'T is well that she hath heard the tale,
Received the bitterness of woe:
For she *had* hoped, had hoped and feared,
Such rights did feeble nature claim;
And oft her steps had hither steered,
Though not unconscious of self-blame;
For she her brother's charge revered,
His farewell words; and by the same,

[1] See Note.

Yea by her brother's very name,
Had, in her solitude, been cheered.
  Beside the lonely watch-tower stood
That gray-haired Man of gentle blood,
Who with her Father had grown old
In friendship; rival hunters they,
And fellow warriors in their day;
To Rylstone he the tidings brought;
Then on this height the Maid had sought,
And, gently as he could, had told
The end of that dire Tragedy,
Which it had been his lot to see.
  To him the Lady turned; " You said
That Francis lives, *he* is not dead? "
" Your noble brother hath been spared;
To take his life they have not dared;
On him and on his high endeavor
The light of praise shall shine forever !
Nor did he (such Heaven's will) in vain
His solitary course maintain;
Not vainly struggled in the might
Of duty, seeing with clear sight;
He was their comfort to the last,
Their joy till every pang was past.
  I witnessed when to York they came —
What, Lady, if their feet were tied;
They might deserve a good Man's blame;
But marks of infamy and shame —
These were their triumph, these their
    pride;
Nor wanted 'mid the pressing crowd
Deep feeling, that found utterance loud,
' Lo, Francis comes,' there were who cried,
' A Prisoner once, but now set free !
'T is well, for he the worst defied
Through force of natural piety;
He rose not in this quarrel; he,
For concord's sake and England's good,
Suit to his Brothers often made
With tears, and of his Father prayed —
And when he had in vain withstood
Their purpose — then did he divide,
He parted from them; but at their side
Now walks in unanimity.
Then peace to cruelty and scorn,
While to the prison they are borne,
Peace, peace to all indignity ! '
  And so in Prison were they laid —
Oh hear me, hear me, gentle Maid,
For I am come with power to bless,
By scattering gleams, through your distress,
Of a redeeming happiness.
Me did a reverent pity move

And privilege of ancient love;
And, in your service, making bold,
Entrance I gained to that stronghold.
  Your Father gave me cordial greeting;
But to his purposes that burned
Within him, instantly returned:
He was commanding and entreating,
And said — ' We need not stop, my Son !
Thoughts press, and time is hurrying on' —
And so to Francis he renewed
His words, more calmly thus pursued.
  ' Might this our enterprise have sped,
Change wide and deep the Land had seen,
A renovation from the dead,
A spring-tide of immortal green:
The darksome altars would have blazed
Like stars when clouds are rolled away;
Salvation to all eyes that gazed,
Once more the Rood had been upraised
To spread its arms, and stand for aye.
Then, then — had I survived to see
New life in Bolton Priory;
The voice restored, the eye of Truth
Re-opened that inspired my youth;
To see her in her pomp arrayed —
This·Banner (for such vow I made)
Should on the consecrated breast
Of that same Temple have found rest:
I would myself have hung it high,
Fit offering of glad victory !
  A shadow of such thought remains
To cheer this sad and pensive time;
A solemn fancy yet sustains
One feeble Being — bids me climb
Even to the last — one effort more
To attest my Faith, if not restore.
  Hear then,' said he, ' while I impart,
My Son, the last wish of my heart.
The Banner strive thou to regain;
And, if the endeavor prove not vain,
Bear it — to whom if not to thee
Shall I this lonely thought consign? --
Bear it to Bolton Priory,
And lay it on Saint Mary's shrine;
To wither in the sun and breeze
'Mid those decaying sanctities.
There let at least the gift be laid,
The testimony there displayed;
Bold proof that with no selfish aim,
But for lost Faith and Christ's dear name,
I helmeted a brow though white,
And took a place in all men's sight;
Yea offered up this noble Brood,

This fair unrivalled Brotherhood,
And turned away from thee, my Son !
And left — but be the rest unsaid,
The name untouched, the tear unshed; —
My wish is known, and I have done:
Now promise, grant this one request,
This dying prayer, and be thou blest !'
  Then Francis answered — ' Trust thy Son,
For, with God's will, it shall be done !'
  The pledge obtained, the solemn word
Thus scarcely given, a noise was heard, —
And Officers appeared in state
To lead the prisoners to their fate.
They rose, oh ! wherefore should I fear
To tell, or, Lady, you to hear?
They rose—embraces none were given —
They stood like trees when earth and heaven
Are calm; they knew each other's worth,
And reverently the Band went forth.
They met, when they had reached the door,
One with profane and harsh intent
Placed there — that he might go before
And, with that rueful Banner borne
Aloft in sign of taunting scorn,
Conduct them to their punishment:
So cruel Sussex, unrestrained
By human feeling, had ordained.
The unhappy Banner Francis saw,
And, with a look of calm command
Inspiring universal awe,
He took it from the soldier's hand;
And all the people that stood round
Confirmed the deed in peace profound.
— High transport did the Father shed
Upon his Son — and they were led,
Led on, and yielded up their breath;
Together died, a happy death ! —
But Francis, soon as he had braved
That insult, and the Banner saved,
Athwart the unresisting tide
Of the spectators occupied
In admiration or dismay,
Bore instantly his Charge away."
  These things, which thus had in the sight
And hearing passed of Him who stood
With Emily, on the Watch-tower height,
In Rylstone's woful neighborhood,
He told; and oftentimes with voice
Of power to comfort or rejoice;
For deepest sorrows that aspire,
Go high, no transport ever higher.

"Yes — God is rich in mercy," said
The old Man to the silent Maid,
"Yet, Lady! shines, through this black
    night,
One star of aspect heavenly bright;
Your Brother lives — he lives — is come
Perhaps already to his home;
Then let us leave this dreary place."
She yielded, and with gentle pace,
Though' without one uplifted look,
To Rylstone-hall her way she took.

CANTO SIXTH.

WHY comes not Francis? — From the dole-
    ful City
He fled, — and, in his flight, could hear
The death-sounds of the Minster-bell:
That sullen stroke pronounced farewell
To Marmaduke, cut off from pity!
To Ambrose that! and then a knell
For him, the sweet half-opened Flower!
For all — all dying in one hour!
— Why comes not Francis? Thoughts of
    love
Should bear him to his Sister dear
With the fleet motion of a dove;
Yea, like a heavenly messenger
Of speediest wing, should he appear.
Why comes he not? — for westward fast
Along the plain of York he past;
Reckless of what impels or leads,
Unchecked he hurries on; — nor heeds
The sorrow, through the Villages,
Spread by triumphant cruelties
Of vengeful military force,
And punishment without remorse.
He marked not, heard not, as he fled
All but the suffering heart was dead
For him abandoned to blank awe,
To vacancy, and horror strong:
And the first object which he saw,
With conscious sight, as he swept along —
It was the Banner in his hand!
He felt — and made a sudden stand.

    He looked about like one betrayed:
What hath he done? what promise made?
Oh weak, weak moment! to what end
Can such a vain oblation tend,
And he the Bearer? — Can he go
Carrying this instrument of woe,
And find, find anywhere, a right
To excuse him in his Country's sight?

No; will not all men deem the change
A downward course, perverse and strange?
Here is it; — but how! when? must she,
The unoffending Emily,
Again this piteous object see?
    Such conflict long did he maintain,
Nor liberty nor rest could gain:
His own life into danger brought
By this sad burden — even that thought,
Exciting self-suspicion strong,
Swayed the brave man to his wrong.
And how — unless it were the sense
Of all-disposing Providence,
Its will unquestionably shown —
How has the Banner clung so fast
To a palsied, and unconscious hand;
Clung to the hand to which it passed
Without impediment? And why,
But that Heaven's purpose might be
    known,
Doth now no hindrance meet his eye,
No intervention, to withstand
Fulfilment of a Father's prayer
Breathed to a Son forgiven, and blest
When all resentments were at rest,
And life in death laid the heart bare? —
Then, like a spectre sweeping by,
Rushed through his mind the prophecy
Of utter desolation made
To Emily in the yew-tree shade:
He sighed, submitting will and power
To the stern embrace of that grasping hour.
"No choice is left, the deed is mine —
Dead are they, dead! — and I will go,
And, for their sakes, come weal or woe,
Will lay the Relic on the shrine."
    So forward with a steady will
He went, and traversed plain and hill;
And up the vale of Wharf his way
Pursued; — and, at the dawn of day,
Attained a summit whence his eyes
Could see the Tower of Bolton rise.
There Francis for a moment's space
Made halt — but hark! a noise behind
Of horsemen at an eager pace!
He heard, and with misgiving mind.
— 'T is Sir George Bowes who leads the
    Band:
They come, by cruel Sussex sent;
Who, when the Nortons from the hand
Of death had drunk their punishment,
Bethought him, angry and ashamed,
How Francis, with the Banner claimed

As his own charge, had disappeared,
By all the standers-by revered.
His whole bold carriage (which had
    quelled
Thus far the Opposer, and repelled
All censure, enterprise so bright
That even bad men had vainly striven
Against that overcoming light)
Was then reviewed, and prompt word
    given,
That to what place soever fled
He should be seized, alive or dead.
    The troop of horse have gained the
        height
Where Francis stood in open sight.
They hem him round — "Behold the
    proof,"
They cried, "the Ensign in his hand!
He did not arm, he walked aloof!
For why? — to save his Father's land; —
Worst Traitor of them all is he,
A Traitor dark and cowardly!"
    "I am no Traitor," Francis said,
"Though this unhappy freight I bear;
And must not part with.   But beware :—
Err not by hasty zeal misled,
Nor do a suffering Spirit wrong,
Whose self-reproaches are too strong!"
At this he from the beaten road
Retreated towards a brake of thorn,
That like a place of vantage showed;
And there stood bravely, though forlorn.
In self-defence with warlike brow
He stood, — nor weaponless was now;
He from a Soldier's hand had snatched
A spear, —and, so protected, watched
The Assailants, turning round and round,
But from behind with treacherous wound
A Spearman brought him to the ground.
The guardian lance, as Francis fell,
Dropped from him; but his other hand
The Banner clenched; till, from out the
    Band,
One, the most eager for the prize,
Rushed in; and — while, O grief to tell!
A glimmering sense still left, with eyes
Unclosed the noble Francis lay —
Seized it, as hunters seize their prey;
But not before the warm life-blood
Had tinged more deeply, as it flowed,
The wounds the broidered Banner showed,
Thy fatal work, O Maiden, innocent as
    good!

    Proudly the Horsemen bore away
The Standard; and where Francis lay
There was he left alone, unwept,
And for two days unnoticed slept.
For at that time bewildering fear
Possessed the country, far and near;
But, on the third day, passing by
One of the Norton Tenantry
Espied the uncovered Corse; the Man
Shrunk as he recognized the face,
And to the nearest homesteads ran
And called the people to the place.
— How desolate is Rylstone-hall!
This was the instant thought of all;
And if the lonely Lady there
Should be; to her they cannot bear
This weight of anguish and despair.
So, when upon sad thoughts had prest
Thoughts sadder still, they deemed it best
That, if the Priest should yield assent
And no one hinder their intent,
Then they, for Christian pity's sake,
In holy ground a grave would make;
And straightway buried he should be
In the Churchyard of the Priory.
    Apart, some little space, was made
The grave where Francis must be laid.
In no confusion or neglect
This did they, — but in pure respect
That he was born of gentle blood;
And that there was no neighborhood
Of kindred for him in that ground:
So to the Churchyard they are bound,
Bearing the body on a bier;
And psalms they sing — a holy sound
That hill and vale with sadness hear.
    But Emily hath raised her head,
And is again disquieted;
She must behold! — so many gone,
Where is the solitary One?
And forth from Rylstone-hall stepped
    she, —
To seek her Brother forth she went,
And tremblingly her course she bent
Toward Bolton's ruined Priory.
She comes, and in the vale hath heard
The funeral dirge; — she sees the knot
Of people, sees them in one spot —
And darting like a wounded bird
She reached the grave, and with her breast
Upon the ground received the rest, —
The consummation, the whole ruth
And sorrow of this final truth!

Canto Seventh.

" Powers there are
That touch each other to the quick — in modes
Which the gross world no sense hath to perceive,
No soul to dream of."

Thou Spirit, whose angelic hand
Was to the harp a strong command,
Called the submissive strings to wake
In glory for this Maiden's sake,
Say, Spirit! whither hath she fled
To hide her poor afflicted head?
What mighty forest in its gloom
Enfolds her? — is a rifted tomb
Within the wilderness her seat?
Some island which the wild waves beat —
Is that the Sufferer's last retreat?
Or some aspiring rock, that shrouds
Its perilous front in mists and clouds?
High-climbing rock, low sunless dale,
Sea, desert, what do these avail?
Oh take her anguish and her fears
Into a deep recess of years!
      'T is done; — despoil and desolation
O'er Rylstone's fair domain have blown![1]
Pools, terraces, and walks are sown
With weeds; the bowers are overthrown,
Or have given way to slow mutation,
While, in their ancient habitation
The Norton name hath been unknown.
The lordly Mansion of its pride
Is stripped; the ravage hath spread wide
Through park and field, a perishing
That mocks the gladness of the Spring!
And, with this silent gloom agreeing,
Appears a joyless human Being,
Of aspect such as if the waste
Were under her dominion placed.
Upon a primrose bank, her throne
Of quietness, she sits alone;
Among the ruins of a wood,
Erewhile a covert bright and green,
And where full many a brave tree stood,
That used to spread its boughs, and ring
With the sweet bird's carolling.
Behold her, like a virgin Queen,
Neglecting in imperial state
These outward images of fate,
And carrying inward a serene
And perfect sway, through many a thought
Of chance and change, that hath been
      brought

[1] See Note.

To the subjection of a holy,
Though stern and rigorous, melancholy!
The like authority, with grace
Of awfulness, is in her face, —
There hath she fixed it; yet it seems
To o'ershadow by no native right
That face, which cannot lose the gleams,
Lose utterly the tender gleams,
Of gentleness and meek delight,
And loving-kindness ever bright:
Such is her sovereign mien: — her dress
(A vest with woollen cincture tied,
A hood of mountain-wool undyed)
Is homely, — fashioned to express
A wandering Pilgrim's humbleness.
      And she *hath* wandered, long and far,
Beneath the light of sun and star;
Hath roamed in trouble and in grief,
Driven forward like a withered leaf,
Yea like a ship at random blown
To distant places and unknown.
But now she dares to seek a haven
Among her native wilds of Craven;
Hath seen again her Father's roof,
And put her fortitude to proof;
The mighty sorrow hath been borne,
And she is thoroughly forlorn:
Her soul doth in itself stand fast,
Sustained by memory of the past
And strength of Reason; held above
The infirmities of mortal love;
Undaunted, lofty, calm, and stable,
And awfully impenetrable.
      And so — beneath a mouldered tree,
A self-surviving leafless oak
By unregarded age from stroke
Of ravage saved — sate Emily.
There did she rest, with head reclined,
Herself most like a stately flower,
(Such have I seen) whom chance of birth
Hath separated from its kind,
To live and die in a shady bower,
Single on the gladsome earth.
      When, with a noise like distant thunder,
A troop of deer came sweeping by;
And, suddenly, behold a wonder!
For One, among those rushing deer,
A single One, in mid career
Hath stopped, and fixed her large full eye
Upon the Lady Emily;
A Doe most beautiful, clear-white,
A radiant creature, silver-bright!
      Thus checked, a little while it stayed;

A little thoughtful pause it made;
And then advanced with stealth-like pace,
Drew softly near her, and more near —
Looked round — but saw no cause for fear;
So to her feet the Creature came,
And laid its head upon her knee,
And looked into the Lady's face,
A look of pure benignity,
And fond unclouded memory.
It is, thought Emily, the same,
The very Doe of other years ! —
The pleading look the Lady viewed,
And, by her gushing thoughts subdued,
She melted into tears —
A flood of tears, that flowed apace,
Upon the happy Creature's face.
    Oh, moment ever blest ! O Pair
Beloved of Heaven, Heaven's chosen
        care,
This was for you a precious greeting;
And may it prove a fruitful meeting !
Joined are they, and the sylvan Doe
Can she depart? can she forego
The Lady, once her playful peer,
And now her sainted Mistress dear?
And will not Emily receive
This lovely chronicler of things
Long past, delights and sorrowings?
Lone Sufferer ! will not she believe
The promise in that speaking face;
And welcome, as a gift of grace,
The saddest thought the Creature brings?
    That day, the first of a re-union
Which was to teem with high communion,
That day of balmy April weather,
They tarried in the wood together.
And when, ere fall of evening dew,
She from her sylvan haunt withdrew,
The White Doe tracked with faithful pace
The Lady to her dwelling-place;
That nook where, on paternal ground,
A habitation she had found,
The Master of whose humble board
Once owned her Father for his Lord;
A hut, by tufted trees defended,
Where Rylstone brook with Wharf is
        blended.
    When Emily by morning light
Went forth, the Doe stood there in sight.
She shrunk : — with one frail shock of pain
Received and followed by a prayer,
She saw the Creature once again;
Shun will she not, she feels, will bear; —

But, wheresoever she looked round,
All now was trouble-haunted ground;
And therefore now she deems it good
Once more this restless neighborhood
To leave. — Unwooed, yet unforbidden,
The White Doe followed up the vale,
Up to another cottage, hidden
In the deep fork of Amerdale; [1]
And there may Emily restore
Herself, in spots unseen before.
— Why tell of mossy rock, or tree,
By lurking Dernbrook's pathless side,
Haunts of a strengthening amity
That calmed her, cheered, and fortified?
For she hath ventured now to read
Of time, and place, and thought, and
        deed —
Endless history that lies
In her silent Follower's eyes;
Who with a power like human reason
Discerns the favorable season,
Skilled to approach or to retire, —
From looks conceiving her desire;
From look, deportment, voice, or mien,
That vary to the heart within.
If she too passionately wreathed
Her arms, or over-deeply breathed,
Walked quick or slowly, every mood
In its degree was understood;
Then well may their accord be true,
And kindliest intercourse ensue.
— Oh ! surely 't was a gentle rousing
When she by sudden glimpse espied
The White Doe on the mountain browsing,
Or in the meadow wandered wide !
How pleased, when down the Straggler
        sank
Beside her, on some sunny bank !
How soothed, when in thick bower
        enclosed,
They, like a nested pair, reposed !
Fair vision ! when it crossed the Maid
Within some rocky cavern laid,
The dark cave's portal gliding by,
White as whitest cloud on high
Floating through the azure sky.
— What now is left for pain or fear?
That Presence, dearer and more dear,
While they, side by side, were straying,
And the shepherd's pipe was playing,
Did now a very gladness yield
At morning to the dewy field,

        [1] See Note.

And with a deeper peace endued
The hour of moonlight solitude.
  With her Companion, in such frame
Of mind, to Rylstone back she came;
And, ranging through the wasted groves,
Received the memory of old loves,
Undisturbed and undistrest,
Into a soul which now was blest
With a soft spring-day of holy,
Mild, and grateful, melancholy:
Not sunless gloom or unenlightened,
But by tender fancies brightened.
  When the bells of Rylstone played
Their sabbath music — "God us ayde!"
That was the sound they seemed to speak;
Inscriptive legend which I ween
May on those holy bells be seen,
That legend and her Grandsire's name;
And oftentimes the Lady meek
Had in her childhood read the same;
Words which she slighted at that day;
But now, when such sad change was
    wrought,
And of that lonely name she thought —
The bells of Rylstone seemed to say,
While she sate listening in the shade,
With vocal music, "God us ayde;"
And all the hills were glad to bear
Their part in this effectual prayer.
  Nor lacked she Reason's firmest power;
But with the White Doe at her side
Up would she climb to Norton Tower,
And thence look round her far and wide,
Her fate there measuring; — all is
    stilled, —
The weak One hath subdued her heart;
Behold the prophecy fulfilled,
Fulfilled, and she sustains her part!
But here her Brother's words have failed;
Here hath a milder doom prevailed;
That she, of him and all bereft,
Hath yet this faithful Partner left;
This one Associate, that disproves
His words, remains for her, and loves.
If tears are shed, they do not fall
For loss of him — for one, or all;
Yet, sometimes, sometimes doth she weep
Moved gently in her soul's soft sleep;
A few tears down her cheek descend
For this her last and living Friend.
  Bless, tender Hearts, their mutual lot,
And bless for both this savage spot;
Which Emily doth sacred hold

For reasons dear and manifold —
Here hath she, here before her sight,
Close to the summit of this height,
The grassy rock-encircled Pound [1]
In which the Creature first was found.
So beautiful the timid Thrall
(A spotless Youngling white as foam)
Her youngest Brother brought it home;
The youngest, then a lusty boy,
Bore it, or led, to Rylstone-hall
With heart brimful of pride and joy!
  But most to Bolton's sacred Pile,
On favoring nights, she loved to go;
There ranged through cloister, court, and
    aisle,
Attended by the soft-paced Doe;
Nor feared she in the still moonshine
To look upon Saint Mary's shrine;
Nor on the lonely turf that showed
Where Francis slept in his last abode.
For that she came; there oft she sate
Forlorn, but not disconsolate:
And, when she from the abyss returned
Of thought, she neither shrunk nor
    mourned;
Was happy that she lived to greet
Her mute Companion as it lay
In love and pity at her feet;
How happy in its turn to meet
The recognition! the mild glance
Beamed from that gracious countenance;
Communication, like the ray
Of a new morning, to the nature
And prospects of the inferior Creature!
  A mortal Song we sing, by dower
Encouraged of celestial power;
Power which the viewless Spirit shed
By whom we were first visited;
Whose voice we heard, whose hand and
    wings
Swept like a breeze the conscious strings,
When, left in solitude, erewhile
We stood before this ruined Pile,
And, quitting unsubstantial dreams,
Sang in this Presence kindred themes;
Distress and desolation spread
Through human hearts, and pleasure
    dead, —
Dead — but to live again on earth,
A second and yet nobler birth;
Dire overthrow, and yet how high
The re-ascent in sanctity!

[1] See Note.

From fair to fairer; day by day
A more divine and loftier way!
Even such this blessèd Pilgrim trod,
By sorrow lifted towards her God;
Uplifted to the purest sky
Of undisturbed mortality.
Her own thoughts loved she; and could
    bend
A dear look to her lowly Friend;
There stopped; her thirst was satisfied
With what this innocent spring supplied:
Her sanction inwardly she bore,
And stood apart from human cares:
But to the world returned no more,
Although with no unwilling mind
Help did she give at need, and joined
The Wharfdale peasants in their prayers.
At length, thus faintly, faintly tied
To earth, she was set free, and died.
Thy soul, exalted Emily,
Maid of the blasted family,
Rose to the God from whom it came!
— In Rylstone Church her mortal frame
Was buried by her Mother's side.

Most glorious sunset! and a ray
Survives — the twilight of this day —
In that fair Creature whom the fields
Support, and whom the forest shields;
Who, having filled a holy place,
Partakes, in her degree, Heaven's grace;
And bears a memory and a mind
Raised far above the law of kind;
Haunting the spots with lonely cheer
Which her dear Mistress once held dear:
Loves most what Emily loved most —
The enclosure of this churchyard ground;
Here wanders like a gliding ghost,
And every sabbath here is found;
Comes with the people when the bells
Are heard among the moorland dells,
Finds entrance through yon arch, where
    way
Lies open on the sabbath-day;
Here walks amid the mournful waste
Of prostrate altars, shrines defaced,
And floors encumbered with rich show
Of fret-work imagery laid low;
Paces softly, or makes halt,
By fractured cell, or tomb, or vault;
By plate of monumental brass
Dim-gleaming among weeds and grass,
And sculptured Forms of Warriors brave:
But chiefly by that single grave,

That one sequestered hillock green,
The pensive visitant is seen.
There doth the gentle Creature lie
With those adversities unmoved;
Calm spectacle, by earth and sky
In their benignity approved!
And aye, methinks, this hoary Pile,
Subdued by outrage and decay,
Looks down upon her with a smile,
'A gracious smile, that seems to say —
" Thou, thou art not a Child of Time,
But Daughter of the Eternal Prime!"
1807.   1815.

THE FORCE OF PRAYER; [1]

OR,

THE FOUNDING OF BOLTON PRIORY.

A TRADITION.

An Appendage to the "White Doe." My
friend, Mr. Rogers, has also written on the sub-
ject. The story is preserved in Dr. Whitaker's
History of Craven — a topographical writer of
first-rate merit in all that concerns the past; but
such was his aversion from the modern spirit, as
shown in the spread of manufactories in those
districts of which he treats, that his readers are
left entirely ignorant both of the progress of these
arts and their real bearing upon the comfort, vir-
tues, and happiness of the inhabitants. While
wandering on foot through the fertile valleys and
over the moorlands of the Apennine that divides
Yorkshire from Lancashire, I used to be delighted
with observing the number of substantial cottages
that had sprung up on every side, each having its
little plot of fertile ground won from the sur-
rounding waste. A bright and warm fire, if
needed, was always to be found in these dwell-
ings. The father was at his loom; the children
looked healthy and happy. Is it not to be feared
that the increase of mechanic power has done
away with many of these blessings, and substi-
tuted many evils? Alas! if these evils grow,
how are they to be checked, and where is the
remedy to be found? Political economy will not
supply it; that is certain, we must look to some-
thing deeper, purer, and higher.

" **What is good for a bootless bene?** "
With these dark words begins my Tale;
And their meaning is, whence can com-
    fort spring
When Prayer is of no avail?

[1] See the "White Doe of Rylstone."

" What is good for a bootless bene? "
The Falconer to the Lady said;
And she made answer " ENDLESS SOR-
ROW ! "
For she knew that her Son was dead.

She knew it by the Falconer's words,
And from the look of the Falconer's eye;
And from the love which was in her soul
For her youthful Romilly.

— Young Romilly through Barden woods
Is ranging high and low;
And holds a greyhound in a leash,
To let slip upon buck or doe.

The pair have reached that fearful chasm,
How tempting to bestride !
For lordly Wharf is there pent in
With rocks on either side.

This striding-place is called THE STRID,
A name which it took of yore :
A thousand years hath it borne that name,
And shall a thousand more.

And hither is young Romilly come,
And what may now forbid
That he, perhaps for the hundredth time,
Shall bound across THE STRID?

He sprang in glee, — for what cared he
That the river was strong, and the rocks
were steep ? —
But the greyhound in the leash hung back,
And checked him in his leap.

The Boy is in the arms of Wharf,
And strangled by a merciless force;
For never more was young Romilly seen
Till he rose a lifeless corse.

Now there is stillness in the vale,
And long, unspeaking sorrow :
Wharf shall be to pitying hearts
A name more sad than Yarrow.

If for a lover the Lady wept,
A solace she might borrow
From death, and from the passion of
death; —
Old Wharf might heal her sorrow.

She weeps not for the wedding-day
Which was to be to-morrow :
Her hope was a further-looking hope,
And hers is a mother's sorrow.

He was a tree that stood alone,
And proudly did its branches wave;
And the root of this delightful tree
Was in her husband's grave !

Long, long in darkness did she sit,
And her first words were, " Let there be
In Bolton, on the field of Wharf,
A stately Priory ! "

The stately Priory was reared;
And Wharf, as he moved along, -
To matins joined a mournful voice,
Nor failed at evensong.

And the Lady prayed in heaviness
That looked not for relief !
But slowly did her succor come,
And a patience to her grief.

Oh ! there is never sorrow of heart
That shall lack a timely end,
If but to God we turn, and ask
Of Him to be our friend !

SEPTEMBER, 1807.   1815.

COMPOSED WHILE THE AUTHOR WAS ENGAGED IN WRITING A TRACT OCCASIONED BY THE CONVENTION OF CINTRA.

NOT 'mid the world's vain objects that
enslave
The free-born Soul — that World whose
vaunted skill
In selfish interest perverts the will,
Whose factions lead astray the wise and
brave —
Not there; but in dark wood and rocky
cave,
And hollow vale which foaming torrents
fill
With omnipresent murmur as they rave
Down their steep beds, that never shall
be still :
Here, mighty Nature ! in this school
sublime

I weigh the hopes and fears of suffering
    Spain;
For her consult the auguries of time,
And through the human heart explore
    my way;
And look and listen — gathering, whence
    I may,
Triumph, and thoughts no bondage can
    restrain.
    1808.   1815.

COMPOSED AT THE SAME TIME AND ON THE SAME OCCASION.

I DROPPED my pen; and listened to the
    Wind
That sang of trees uptorn and vessels
    tost —
A midnight harmony; and wholly lost
To the general sense of men by chains
    confined
Of business, care, or pleasure; or resigned
To timely sleep. Thought I, the impas-
    sioned strain,
Which, without aid of numbers, I sustain,
Like acceptation from the World will find.
Yet some with apprehensive ear shall drink
A dirge devoutly breathed o'er sorrows
    past;
And to the attendant promise will give
    heed —
The prophecy, — like that of this wild
    blast,
Which, while it makes the heart with
    sadness shrink,
Tells also of bright calms that shall suc-
    ceed.
    1808.   1815.

GEORGE AND SARAH GREEN.

WHO weeps for strangers? Many wept
    For George and Sarah Green;
Wept for that pair's unhappy fate,
    Whose grave may here be seen.

By night, upon these stormy fells,
    Did wife and husband roam;
Six little ones at home had left,
    And could not find that home.

For *any* dwelling-place of man
    As vainly did they seek.
He perish'd; and a voice was heard —
    The widow's lonely shriek.

Not many steps, and she was left
    A body without life —
A few short steps were the chain that bound
    The husband to the wife.

Now do those sternly-featured hills
    Look gently on this grave;
And quiet now are the depths of air,
    As a sea without a wave.

But deeper lies the heart of peace
    In quiet more profound;
The heart of quietness is here
    Within this churchyard bound.

And from all agony of mind
    It keeps them safe, and far
From fear and grief, and from all need
    Of sun or guiding star.

O darkness of the grave! how deep,
    After that living night —
That last and dreary living one
    Of sorrow and affright?

O sacred marriage-bed of death,
    That keeps them side by side
In bond of peace, in bond of love,
    That may not be untied!
    1808.   1839.

HOFFER.

OF mortal parents is the Hero born
By whom the undaunted Tyrolese are led?
Or is it Tell's great Spirit, from the dead
Returned to animate an age forlorn?
He comes like Phœbus through the gates
    of morn
When dreary darkness is discomfited,
Yet mark his modest state! upon his
    head,
That simple crest, a heron's plume, is
    worn.
O Liberty! they stagger at the shock
From van to rear — and with one mind
    would flee,

But half their host is buried : — rock on
    rock
Descends : — beneath this godlike War-
    rior, see !
Hills, torrents, woods, embodied to
    bemock
The Tyrant, and confound his cruelty.
    1809.   1815.

"ADVANCE — COME FORTH FROM THY TYROLEAN GROUND."

ADVANCE—come forth from thy Tyrolean
    ground,
Dear Liberty ! stern Nymph of soul un-
    tamed;
Sweet Nymph, O rightly of the moun-
    tains named !
Through the long chain of Alps from
    mound to mound
And o'er the eternal snows, like Echo,
    bound;
Like Echo, when the hunter train at dawn
Have roused her from her sleep: and
    forest, lawn,
Cliffs, woods and caves, her viewless
    steps resound
And babble of her pastime ! -— On, dread
    Power !
With such invisible motion speed thy
    flight,
Through hanging clouds, from craggy
    height to height,
Through the green vales and through the
    herdsman's bower —
That all the Alps may gladden in thy
    might,
Here, there, and in all places at one hour.
    1809.   1815.

FEELINGS OF THE TYROLESE.

THE Land we from our fathers had in
    trust,
And to our children will transmit, or die:
This is our maxim, this our piety;
And God and Nature say that it is just.
That which we *would* perform in arms —
    we must !
We read the dictate in the infant's eye;
In the wife's smile; and in the placid sky;
And, at our feet, amid the silent dust

Of them that were before us. — Sing aloud
Old songs, the precious music of the heart !
Give, herds and flocks, your voices to the
    wind !
While we go forth, a self-devoted crowd,
With weapons grasped in fearless hands,
    to assert
Our virtue, and to vindicate mankind.
    1809.   1815.

" ALAS ! WHAT BOOTS THE LONG LABORIOUS QUEST."

ALAS ! what boots the long laborious
    quest
Of moral prudence, sought through good
    and ill;
Or pains abstruse — to elevate the will,
And lead us on to that transcendent rest
Where every passion shall the sway attest
Of Reason, seated on her sovereign hill;
What is it but a vain and curious skill,
If sapient Germany must lie deprest,
Beneath the brutal sword ? — Her haughty
    Schools
Shall blush; and may not we with sorrow
    say —
A few strong instincts and a few plain
    rules,
Among the herdsmen of the Alps, have
    wrought
More for mankind at this unhappy day
Than all the pride of intellect and thought ?
    1809.   1815.

"AND IS IT AMONG RUDE UNTUTORED DALES ? "

AND is it among rude untutored Dales,
There, and there only, that the heart is
    true ?
And, rising to repel or to subdue,
Is it by rocks and woods that man prevails ?
Ah no ! though Nature's dread protection
    fails,
There is a bulwark in the soul. This knew
Iberian Burghers when the sword they drew
In Zaragoza, naked to the gales
Of fiercely-breathing war. The truth was
    felt
By Palafox, and many a brave compeer,

Like him of noble birth and noble mind;
By ladies, meek-eyed women without fear;
And wanderers of the street, to whom is
dealt
The bread which without industry they find.

1809.   1815.

"O'ER THE WIDE EARTH, ON MOUNTAIN AND ON PLAIN."

O'ER the wide earth, on mountain and on
plain,
Dwells in the affections and the soul of man
A Godhead, like the universal PAN;
But more exalted, with a brighter train:
And shall his bounty be dispensed in vain,
Showered equally on city and on field,
And neither hope nor steadfast promise
yield
In these usurping times of fear and pain?
Such doom awaits us.   Nay, forbid it
Heaven!
We know the arduous strife, the eternal
laws
To which the triumph of all good is given,
High sacrifice, and labor without pause,
Even to the death:—else wherefore should
the eye
Of man converse with immortality?

1809.   1815.

ON THE FINAL SUBMISSION OF THE TYROLESE.

IT was a *moral* end for which they fought;
Else how, when mighty Thrones were
put to shame,
Could they, poor Shepherds, have pre-
served an aim,
A resolution, or enlivening thought?
Nor hath that moral good been *vainly*
sought;
For in their magnanimity and fame
Powers have they left, an impulse, and a
claim
Which neither can be overturned nor
bought.
Sleep, Warriors, sleep! among your hills
repose!
We know that ye, beneath the stern control

Of awful prudence, keep the unvanquished
soul:
And when, impatient of her guilt and woes,
Europe breaks forth; then, Shepherds!
shall ye rise
For perfect triumph o'er your Enemies.

1809.   1815.

"HAIL, ZARAGOZA! IF WITH UNWET EYE."[1]

HAIL, Zaragoza!   If with unwet eye
We can approach, thy sorrow to behold,
Yet is the heart not pitiless nor cold;
Such spectacle demands not tear or sigh.
These desolate remains are trophies high
Of more than martial courage in the breast
Of peaceful civic virtue: they attest
Thy matchless worth to all posterity.
Blood flowed before thy sight without
remorse;
Disease consumed thy vitals; War up-
heaved
The ground beneath thee with volcanic
force:
Dread trials! yet encountered and sus-
tained
Till not a wreck of help or hope remained,
And law was from necessity received.

1809.   1815.

"SAY, WHAT IS HONOR?—'T IS THE FINEST SENSE."

SAY, what is Honor?—'T is the finest
sense
Of *justice* which the human mind can
frame,
Intent each lurking frailty to disclaim,
And guard the way of life from all offence
Suffered or done.   When lawless violence
Invades a Realm, so pressed that in the
scale
Of perilous war her weightiest armies fail,
Honor is hopeful elevation,—whence
Glory, and triumph.   Yet with politic skill
Endangered States may yield to terms
unjust;
Stoop their proud heads, but not unto the
dust—

[1] See Note.

A Foe's most favorite purpose to fulfil:
Happy occasions oft by self-mistrust
Are forfeited; but infamy doth kill.
1809. 1815.

"THE MARTIAL COURAGE OF A DAY IS VAIN."

THE martial courage of a day is vain,
An empty noise of death the battle's roar,
If vital hope be wanting to restore,
Or fortitude be wanting to sustain,
Armies or kingdoms. We have heard a
 strain
Of triumph, how the laboring Danube
 bore
A weight of hostile corses; drenched with
 gore
Were the wide fields, the hamlets heaped
 with slain.
Yet see (the mighty tumult overpast)
Austria a daughter of her Throne hath
 sold!
And her Tyrolean Champion we behold
Murdered, like one ashore by shipwreck
 cast,
Murdered without relief. Oh! blind as
 bold,
To think that such assurance can stand
 fast!
1809. 1815.

"BRAVE SCHILL! BY DEATH DELIVERED."

BRAVE Schill! by death delivered, take
 thy flight
From Prussia's timid region. Go, and rest
With heroes, 'mid the islands of the Blest,
Or in the fields of empyrean light.
A meteor wert thou crossing a dark night:
Yet shall thy name, conspicuous and
 sublime,
Stand in the spacious firmament of time,
Fixed as a star: such glory is thy right.
Alas! it may not be: for earthly fame
Is Fortune's frail dependant; yet there
 lives
A Judge, who, as man claims by merit,
 gives;
To whose all-pondering mind a noble aim,
Faithfully kept, is as a noble deed;
In whose pure sight all virtue doth succeed.
1809. 1815.

"CALL NOT THE ROYAL SWEDE UNFORTUNATE."

CALL not the royal Swede unfortunate,
Who never did to Fortune bend the knee;
Who slighted fear; rejected steadfastly
Temptation; and whose kingly name and
 state
Have "perished by his choice, and not
 his fate!"
Hence lives He, to his inner self endeared;
And hence, wherever virtue is revered,
He sits a more exalted Potentate,
Throned in the hearts of men. Should
 Heaven ordain
That this great Servant of a righteous cause
Must still have sad or vexing thoughts to
 endure,
Yet may a sympathizing spirit pause,
Admonished by these truths, and quench
 all pain
In thankful joy and gratulation pure.[1]
1809. 1815.

"LOOK NOW ON THAT ADVENTURER WHO HATH PAID."

LOOK now on that Adventurer who hath
 paid
His vows to Fortune; who, in cruel slight
Of virtuous hope, of liberty, and right,
Hath followed wheresoe'er a way was
 made
By the blind Goddess, — ruthless, undis-
 mayed;
And so hath gained at length a prosperous
 height,
Round which the elements of worldly
 might
Beneath his haughty feet, like clouds, are
 laid.
O joyless power that stands by lawless
 force!
Curses are *his* dire portion, scorn, and hate,
Internal darkness and unquiet breath;
And, if old judgments keep their sacred
 course,
Him from that height shall Heaven pre-
 cipitate
By violent and ignominious death.
1809. 1815.

[1] See Note to "The King of Sweden," p. 209.

"IS THERE A POWER THAT CAN SUSTAIN AND CHEER?"

Is there a power that can sustain and cheer
The captive chieftain, by a tyrant's doom,
Forced to descend into his destined tomb—
A dungeon dark! where he must waste
      the year,
And lie cut off from all his heart holds
      dear;
What time his injured country is a stage
Whereon deliberate Valor and the rage
Of righteous Vengeance side by side
      appear,
Filling from morn to night the heroic scene
With deeds of hope and everlasting
      praise:—
Say can he think of this with mind serene
And silent fetters?   Yes, if visions bright
Shine on his soul, reflected from the days
When he himself was tried in open light.
   1809.   1815.

"AH! WHERE IS PALAFOX? NOR TONGUE NOR PEN."

AH! where is Palafox? Nor tongue nor pen
Reports of him, his dwelling or his grave!
Does yet the unheard-of vessel ride the
      wave?
Or is she swallowed up, remote from ken
Of pitying human nature?   Once again
Methinks that we shall hail thee, Cham-
      pion brave,
Redeemed to baffle that imperial Slave,
And through all Europe cheer desponding
      men
With new-born hope.   Unbounded is the
      might
Of martyrdom, and fortitude, and right.
Hark, how thy Country triumphs!—
      Smilingly
The Eternal looks upon her sword that
      gleams,
Like his own lightning, over mountains
      high,
On rampart, and the banks of all her
      streams.
   1810.   1815.

"IN DUE OBSERVANCE OF AN ANCIENT RITE."

IN due observance of an ancient rite,
The rude Biscayans, when their children lie
Dead in the sinless time of infancy,
Attire the peaceful corse in vestments
      white;
And, in like sign of cloudless triumph
      bright,
They bind the unoffending creature's
      brows
With happy garlands of the pure white
      rose:
Then do a festal company unite
In choral song; and, while the uplifted
      cross
Of Jesus goes before, the child is borne
Uncovered to his grave: 't is closed, — her
      loss
The Mother *then* mourns, as she needs
      must mourn;
But soon, through Christian faith, is grief
      subdued;
And joy returns, to brighten fortitude.
   1810.   1815.

FEELINGS OF A NOBLE BISCAYAN AT ONE OF THOSE FUNERALS.

YET, yet, Biscayans! we must meet our
      Foes
With firmer soul, yet labor to regain
Our ancient freedom; else 't were worse
      than vain
To gather round the bier these festal
      shows.
A garland fashioned of the pure white rose
Becomes not one whose father is a slave:
Oh, bear the infant covered to his grave!
These venerable mountains now enclose
A people sunk in apathy and fear.
If this endure, farewell, for us, all good!
The awful light of heavenly innocence
Will fail to illuminate the infant's bier;
And guilt and shame, from which is no
      defence,
Descend on all that issues from our blood.
   1810.   1815.

ON A CELEBRATED EVENT IN ANCIENT HISTORY.

A ROMAN Master stands on Grecian
    ground,
And to the people at the Isthmian Games
Assembled, 'He, by a herald's voice, pro-
    claims
THE LIBERTY OF GREECE:— the words
    rebound
Until all voices in one voice are drowned;
Glad acclamation by which the air was
    rent!
And birds, high-flying in the element,
Dropped to the earth, astonished at the
    sound!
Yet were the thoughtful grieved; and still
    that voice
Haunts, with sad echoes, musing Fancy's
    ear:
Ah! that a *Conqueror's* words should be so
    dear:
Ah! that a *boon* could shed such rapturous
    joys!
A gift of that which is not to be given
By all the blended powers of Earth and
    Heaven.
1810.   1815.

UPON THE SAME EVENT.

WHEN, far and wide, swift as the beams
    of morn
The tidings past of servitude repealed,
And of that joy which shook the Isthmian
    Field,
The rough Ætolians smiled with bitter
    scorn.
" 'T is known," cried they, " that he, who
    would adorn
His envied temples with the Isthmian
    crown,
Must either win, through effort of his own,
The prize, or be content to see it worn
By more deserving brows.—Yet so ye prop,
Sons of the brave who fought at Marathon,
Your feeble spirits! Greece her head hath
    bowed,
As if the wreath of liberty thereon
Would fix itself as smoothly as a cloud,
Which, at Jove's will, descends on Pelion's
    top."
1810.   1815.

THE OAK OF GUERNICA.

The ancient oak of Guernica, says Laborde in
his account of Biscay, is a most venerable natural
monument. Ferdinand and Isabella, in the year
1476, after hearing mass in the church of Santa
Maria de la Antigua, repaired to this tree, under
which they swore to the Biscayans to maintain
their *fueros* (privileges). What other interest
belongs to it in the minds of this people will
appear from the following.

SUPPOSED ADDRESS TO THE SAME.

OAK of Guernica! Tree of holier power
Than that which in Dodona did enshrine
(So faith too fondly deemed) a voice divine
Heard from the depths of its aërial bower—
How canst thou flourish at this blighting
    hour?
What hope, what joy can sunshine bring
    to thee,
Or the soft breezes from the Atlantic sea,
The dews of morn, or April's tender
    shower?
Stroke merciful and welcome would that be
Which should extend thy branches on the
    ground,
If never more within their shady round
Those lofty-minded Lawgivers shall meet,
Peasant and lord, in their appointed seat,
Guardians of Biscay's ancient liberty.
1810.   1815.

INDIGNATION OF A HIGH-MINDED SPANIARD.

WE can endure that He should waste our
    lands,
Despoil our temples, and by sword and
    flame
Return us to the dust from which we came;
Such food a Tyrant's appetite demands:
And we can brook the thought that by his
    hands
Spain may be overpowered, and he pos-
    sess,
For his delight, a solemn wilderness
Where all the brave lie dead. But, when
    of bands
Which he will break for us he dares to
    speak,
Of benefits, and of a future day

When our enlightened minds shall bless
    his sway;
Then, the strained heart of fortitude
    proves weak;
Our groans, our blushes, our pale cheeks
    declare
That he has power to inflict what we
    lack strength to bear.
1810.   1815.

"AVAUNT ALL SPECIOUS PLIANCY OF MIND."

AVAUNT all specious pliancy of mind
In men of low degree, all smooth pre-
    tence!
I better like a blunt indifference,
And self-respecting slowness, disinclined
To win me at first sight: and be there
    joined
Patience and temperance with this high
    reserve,
Honor that knows the path and will not
    swerve;
Affections, which, if put to proof, are
    kind;
And piety towards God. Such men of old
Were England's native growth; and,
    throughout Spain
(Thanks to high God) forests of such
    remain:
Then for that Country let our hopes be
    bold;
For matched with these shall policy
    prove vain,
Her arts, her strength, her iron, and her
    gold.
1810.   1815.

"O'ERWEENING STATESMEN HAVE FULL LONG RELIED."

O'ERWEENING Statesmen have full long
    relied
On fleets and armies, and external wealth:
But from *within* proceeds a Nation's
    health;
Which shall not fail, though poor men
    cleave with pride

To the paternal floor; or turn aside,
In the thronged city, from the walks of
    gain,
As being all unworthy to detain
A Soul by contemplation sanctified.
There are who cannot languish in this
    strife,
Spaniards of every rank, by whom the
    good
Of such high course was felt and under-
    stood;
Who to their Country's cause have bound
    a life
Erewhile, by solemn consecration, given
To labor and to prayer, to nature, and to
    heaven.[1]
1810.   1815.

THE FRENCH AND THE SPANISH GUERILLAS.

HUNGER, and sultry heat, and nipping
    blast
From bleak hill-top, and length of march
    by night
Through heavy swamp, or over snow-clad
    height —
These hardships ill-sustained, these dan-
    gers past,
The roving Spanish Bands are reached
    at last,
Charged, and dispersed like foam: but
    as a flight
Of scattered quails by signs do reunite,
So these, — and, heard of once again,
    are chased
With combinations of long-practised art
And newly-kindled hope; but they are
    fled —
Gone are they, viewless as the buried
    dead:
Where now? — Their sword is at the
    Foeman's heart;
And thus from year to year his walk they
    thwart,
And hang like dreams around his guilty
    bed.
1810.   1815.

[1] See Laborde's character of the Spanish peo-
ple; from him the sentiment of these last two
lines is taken.

EPITAPHS.

1810.

TRANSLATED FROM CHIABRERA.

Those from Chiabrera were chiefly translated when Mr. Coleridge was writing his *"Friend,"* in which periodical my *"* Essay on Epitaphs," written about that time, was first published. For further notice of Chiabrera, in connection with his Epitaphs, see " Musings at Aquapendente."

I.

WEEP not, belovèd Friends ! nor let the air
For me with sighs be troubled. Not from life
Have I been taken; this is genuine life
And this alone — the life which now I live
In peace eternal; where desire and joy
Together move in fellowship without end. —
Francesco Ceni willed that, after death,
His tombstone thus should speak for him. And surely
Small cause there is for that fond wish of ours
Long to continue in this world; a world
That keeps not faith, nor yet can point a hope
To good, whereof itself is destitute.
1810.   1837.

II.

PERHAPS some needful service of the State
Drew TITUS from the depth of studious bowers,
And doomed him to contend in faithless courts,
Where gold determines between right and wrong.
Yet did at length his loyalty of heart,
And his pure native genius, lead him back
To wait upon the bright and gracious Muses,
Whom he had early loved. And not in vain
Such course he held ! Bologna's learned schools
Were gladdened by the Sage's voice, and hung

With fondness on those sweet Nestorian strains.
There pleasure crowned his days; and all his thoughts
A roseate fragrance breathed.[1] — O human life,
That never art secure from dolorous change !
Behold a high injunction suddenly
To Arno's side hath brought him, and he charmed
A Tuscan audience: but full soon was called
To the perpetual silence of the grave.
Mourn, Italy, the loss of him who stood
A Champion steadfast and invincible,
To quell the rage of literary War !
1810.   1810.

III.

O THOU who movest onward with a mind
Intent upon thy way, pause, though in haste !
'T will be no fruitless moment. I was born
Within Savona's walls,. of gentle blood.
On Tiber's banks my youth was dedicate
To sacred studies; and the Roman Shepherd
Gave to my charge Urbino's numerous flock.
Well did I watch, much labored, nor had power
To escape from many and strange indignities;
Was smitten by the great ones of the world,
But did not fall; for Virtue braves all shocks,
Upon herself resting immovably.
Me did a kindlier fortune then invite
To serve the glorious Henry, King of France,
And in his hands I saw a high reward
Stretched out for my acceptance, — but Death came.
Now, Reader, learn from this my fate, how false,

[1] Ivi vivea giocondo e i suoi pensieri
    Erano tutti rose.
    The Translator had. not skill to come nearer to his original.

How treacherous to her promise, is the
    world;
And trust in God — to whose eternal
    doom
Must bend the sceptred Potentates of
    earth.
    1810.   1810.

IV.

THERE never breathed a man who, when
    his life
Was closing, might not of that life relate
Toils long and hard. — The warrior will
    report
Of wounds, and bright swords flashing
    in the field,
And blast of trumpets.   He who hath
    been doomed
To bow his forehead in the courts of
    kings,
Will tell of fraud and never-ceasing hate,
Envy and heart-inquietude, derived
From intricate cabals of treacherous
    friends.
I, who on shipboard lived from earliest
    youth,
Could represent the countenance horrible
Of the vexed waters, and the indignant
    rage
Of Auster and Boötes.   Fifty years
Over the well-steered galleys did I
    rule: —
From huge Pelorus to the Atlantic pillars,
Rises no mountain to mine eyes unknown;
And the broad gulfs I traversed oft and
    oft:
Of every cloud which in the heavens
    might stir
I knew the force; and hence the rough
    sea's pride
Availed not to my Vessel's overthrow.
What noble pomp and frequent have
    not I
On regal decks beheld! yet in the end
I learned that one poor moment can suffice
To equalize the lofty and the low.
We sail the sea of life — a *Calm* One finds,
And One a *Tempest* — and, the voyage
    o'er,
Death is the quiet haven of us all.
If more of my condition ye would know,
Savona was my birthplace, and I sprang

Of noble parents; seventy years and three
Lived I — then yielded to a slow disease.
    1810.   1815.

V.

TRUE is it that Ambrosio Salinero
With an untoward fate was long involved
In odious litigation; and full long,
Fate harder still! had he to endure assaults
Of racking malady.   And true it is
That not the less a frank courageous heart
And buoyant spirit triumphed over pain;
And he was strong to follow in the steps
Of the fair Muses.   Not a covert path
Leads to the dear Parnassian forest's
    shade,
That might from him be hidden; not a
    track
Mounts to pellucid Hippocrene, but he
Had traced its windings. — This Savona
    knows,
Yet no sepulchral honors to her Son
She paid, for in our age the heart is ruled
Only by gold.   And now a simple stone
Inscribed with this memorial here is raised
By his bereft, his lonely, Chiabrera.
Think not, O Passenger! who read'st the
    lines,
That an exceeding love hath dazzled me;
No — he was One whose memory ought to
    spread
Where'er Permessus bears an honored
    name,
And live as long as its pure stream shall
    flow.
    1810.   1837.

VI.

DESTINED to war from very infancy
Was I, Roberto Dati, and I took
In Malta the white symbol of the Cross:
Nor in life's vigorous season did I shun
Hazard or toil; among the sands was
    seen
Of Libya; and not seldom, on the banks
Of wide Hungarian Danube, 't was my lot
To hear the sanguinary trumpet sounded
So lived I, and repined not at such fate:
This only grieves me, for it seems a wrong,
That stripped of arms I to my end am
    brought
On the soft down of my paternal home.
Yet haply Arno shall be spared all cause

To blush for me. Thou, loiter not nor
halt
In thy appointed way, and bear in mind
How fleeting and how frail is human life !
1810.   1815.

VII.

O FLOWER of all that springs from gentle
blood,
And all that generous nurture breeds to
make
Youth amiable; O friend so true of soul
To fair Aglaia; by what envy moved,
Lelius! has death cut short thy brilliant
day
In its sweet opening? and what dire mis-
hap
Has from Savona torn her best delight?
For thee she mourns, nor e'er will cease to
mourn;
And, should the out-pourings of her eyes
suffice not
For her heart's grief, she will entreat
Sebeto
Not to withhold his bounteous aid, Sebeto
Who saw thee, on his margin, yield to
death,
In the chaste arms of thy belovèd Love!
What profit riches? what does youth avail?
Dust are our hopes; — I, weeping bitterly,
Penned these sad lines, nor can forbear to
pray
That every gentle Spirit hither led
May read them, not without some bitter
tears.
1810.   1837.

VIII.

NOT without heavy grief of heart did He
On whom the duty fell (for at that time
The father sojourned in a distant land)
Deposit in the hollow of this tomb
A brother's Child, most tenderly beloved!
FRANCESCO was the name the Youth had
borne,
POZZOBONNELLI his illustrious house;
And, when beneath this stone the Corse
was laid,
The eyes of all Savona streamed with tears.
Alas! the twentieth April of his life
Had scarcely flowered: and at this early
time,
By genuine virtue he inspired a hope

That greatly cheered his country: to his
kin
He promised comfort; and the flattering
thoughts
His friends had in their fondness enter-
tained,[1]
He suffered not to languish or decay.
Now is there not good reason to break
forth
Into a passionate lament? — O Soul!
Short while a Pilgrim in our nether world,
Do thou enjoy the calm empyreal air;
And round this earthly tomb let roses rise,
An everlasting spring! in memory
Of that delightful fragrance which was
once
From thy mild manners quietly exhaled.
1810   1815.

IX.

PAUSE, courteous Spirit! — Balbi suppli-
cates
That Thou, with no reluctant voice, for him
Here laid in mortal darkness, wouldst pre-
fer
A prayer to the Redeemer of the world.
This to the dead by sacred right belongs;
All else is nothing. — Did occasion suit
To tell his worth, the marble of this tomb
Would ill suffice : for Plato's lore sublime,
And all the wisdom of the Stagyrite,
Enriched and beautified his studious mind:
With Archimedes also he conversed
As with a chosen friend; nor did he leave
Those laureat wreaths ungathered which
the Nymphs
Twine near their beloved Permessus. —
Finally,
Himself above each lower thought uplift-
ing,
His ears he closed to listen to the songs
Which Sion's Kings did consecrate of
old;
And his Permessus found on Lebanon.
A blessèd Man! who of protracted days
Made not, as thousands do, a vulgar sleep;
But truly did *He* live his life. Urbino,
Take pride in him! — O Passenger, fare-
well!
1810.   1815.

[1] In justice to the Author, I subjoin the original :—
e degli amici
Non lasciava languire i bei pensieri.

MATERNAL GRIEF.

This was in part an overflow from the Solitary's description of his own and his wife's feelings upon the decease of their children. (See " Excursion," book III.)

DEPARTED Child ! I could forget thee once
Though at my bosom nursed; this woful gain
Thy dissolution brings, that in my soul
Is present and perpetually abides
A shadow, never, never to be displaced
By the returning substance, seen or touched,
Seen by mine eyes, or clasped in my embrace.
Absence and death how differ they ! and how
Shall I admit that nothing can restore
What one short sigh so easily removed ? —
Death, life, and sleep, reality and thought,
Assist me, God, their boundaries to know,
O teach me calm submission to thy Will !
    The Child she mourned had overstepped the pale
Of Infancy, but still did breathe the air
That sanctifies its confines, and partook
Reflected beams of that celestial light
To all the Little-ones on sinful earth
Not unvouchsafed — a light that warmed and cheered
Those several qualities of heart and mind
Which, in her own blest nature, rooted deep,
Daily before the Mother's watchful eye,
And not hers only, their peculiar charms
Unfolded, — beauty, for its present self,
And for its promises to future years,
With not unfrequent rapture fondly hailed.
    Have you espied upon a dewy lawn
A pair of Leverets each provoking each
To a continuance of their fearless sport,
Two separate Creatures in their several gifts
Abounding, but so fashioned that, in all
That Nature prompts them to display, their looks,
Their starts of motion and their fits of rest,
An undistinguishable style appears
And character of gladness, as if Spring

Lodged in their innocent bosoms, and the spirit
Of the rejoicing morning were their own?
    Such union, in the lovely Girl maintained
And her twin Brother, had the parent seen,
Ere, pouncing like a ravenous bird of prey,
Death in a moment parted them, and left
The Mother, in her turns of anguish, worse
Than desolate; for oft-times from the sound
Of the survivor's sweetest voice (dear child,
He knew it not) and from his happiest looks,
Did she extract the food of self-reproach,
As one that lived ungrateful for the stay
By Heaven afforded to uphold her maimed
And tottering spirit.   And full oft the Boy,
Now first acquainted with distress and grief,
Shrunk from his Mother's presence, shunned with fear
Her sad approach, and stole away to find,
In his known haunts of joy where'er he might,
A more congenial object.   But, as time
Softened her pangs and reconciled the child
To what he saw, he gradually returned,
Like a scared Bird encouraged to renew
A broken intercourse; and, while his eyes
Were yet with pensive fear and gentle awe
Turned upon her who bore him, she would stoop
To imprint a kiss that lacked not power to spread
Faint color over both their pallid cheeks,
And stilled his tremulous lip.   Thus they were calmed
And cheered; and now together breathe fresh air
In open fields; and when the glare of day
Is gone, and twilight to the Mother's wish
Befriends the observance, readily they join
In walks whose boundary is the lost One's grave,
Which he with flowers hath planted, finding there

Amusement, where the Mother does not miss
Dear consolation, kneeling on the turf
In prayer, yet blending with that solemn rite
Of pious faith the vanities of grief;
For such, by pitying Angels and by Spirits
Transferred to regions upon which the clouds
Of our weak nature rest not, must be deemed
Those willing tears, and unforbidden sighs,
And all those tokens of a cherished sorrow,
Which, soothed and sweetened by the grace of Heaven
As now it is, seems to her own fond heart,
Immortal as the love that gave it being.

1810.   1842.

CHARACTERISTICS OF A CHILD THREE YEARS OLD.

Written at Allanbank, Grasmere. Picture of my Daughter Catharine, who died the year after.

LOVING she is, and tractable, though wild;
And Innocence hath privilege in her
To dignify arch looks and laughing eyes;
And feats of cunning; and the pretty round
Of trespasses, affected to provoke
Mock-chastisement and partnership in play.
And, as a fagot sparkles on the hearth,
Not less if unattended and alone
Than when both young and old sit gathered round
And take delight in its activity;
Even so this happy Creature of herself
Is all-sufficient, solitude to her
Is blithe society, who fills the air
With gladness and involuntary songs.
Light are her sallies as the tripping fawn's
Forth-startled from the fern where she lay couched;
Unthought-of, unexpected, as the stir
Of the soft breeze ruffling the meadow-flowers,
Or from before it chasing wantonly
The many-colored images imprest
Upon the bosom of a placid lake.

1811.   1815.

SPANISH GUERILLAS.

THEY seek, are sought; to daily battle led,
Shrink not, though far outnumbered by their Foes,
For they have learnt to open and to close
The ridges of grim war; and at their head
Are captains such as erst their country bred
Or fostered, self-supported chiefs, — like those
Whom hardy Rome was fearful to oppose;
Whose desperate shock the Carthaginian fled.
In One who lived unknown a shepherd's life
Redoubted Viriatus breathes again;
And Mina, nourished in the studious shade,
With that great Leader [1] vies, who, sick of strife
And bloodshed, longed in quiet to be laid
In some green island of the western main.

1811.   1815.

"THE POWER OF ARMIES IS A VISIBLE THING."

THE power of Armies is a visible thing,
Formal, and circumscribed in time and space;
But who the limits of that power shall trace
Which a brave People into light can bring
Or hide, at will, — for freedom combating
By just revenge inflamed? No foot may chase,
No eye can follow, to a fatal place
That power, that spirit, whether on the wing
Like the strong wind, or sleeping like the wind
Within its awful caves. — From year to year
Springs this indigenous produce far and near;
No craft this subtle element can bind,
Rising like water from the soil, to find
In every nook a lip that it may cheer.

1811.   1815.

[1] Sertorius.

"HERE PAUSE: THE POET CLAIMS AT LEAST THIS PRAISE."

HERE pause: the poet claims at least
    this praise,
That virtuous Liberty hath been the scope
Of his pure song, which did not shrink
    from hope
In the worst moment of these evil days;
From hope, the paramount *duty* that
    Heaven lays,
For its own honor, on man's suffering
    heart.
Never may from our souls one truth de-
    part —
That an accursed thing it is to gaze
On prosperous tyrants with a dazzled eye;
Nor — touched with due abhorrence of
    their guilt
For whose dire ends tears flow, and blood
    is spilt,
And justice labors in extremity —
Forget thy weakness, upon which is built,
O wretched man, the throne of tyranny!

1811.   1815.

EPISTLE.

TO SIR GEORGE HOWLAND BEAUMONT, BART.

FROM THE SOUTH-WEST COAST OF CUMBERLAND, 1811.

This poem opened, when first written, with a paragraph that has been transferred as an intro-duction to the first series of my Scotch Memorials The journey, of which the first part is here de-scribed, was from Grasmere to Bootle on the south-west coast of Cumberland, the whole among mountain roads through a beautiful country; and we had fine weather. The verses end with our breakfast at the head of Yewdale in a yeoman's house, which, like all the other property in that sequestered vale, has passed or is passing into the hands of Mr. James Marshall of Monk Coniston, — in Mr. Knott's, the late owner's, time called Waterhead. Our hostess married a Mr. Oldfield, a lieutenant in the Navy: they lived together for some time at Hacket, where she still resides as his widow. It was in front of that house, on the mountain side, near which stood the peasant who, while we were passing at a distance, saluted us, waving a kerchief in her hand as described in the poem. (This matron and her husband were then residing at the Hacket. The house and its in-mates are referred to in the fifth book of the " Excursion," in the passage beginning —

> " You behold,
> High on the breast of yon dark mountain, dark
> With stony barrenness, a shining speck."—J. C.)

The dog which we met with soon after our start-ing belonged to Mr. Rowlandson, who for forty years was curate of Grasmere in place of the rector, who lived to extreme old age in a state of insanity. Of this Mr. R. much might be said both with reference to his character, and the way in which he was regarded by his parishioners. He was a man of a robust frame, had a firm voice and authoritative manner, of strong natural talents, of which he was himself conscious, for he has been heard to say (it grieves me to add) with an oath —" If I had been brought up at college I should have been a bishop." Two vices used to struggle in him for mastery, avarice and the love of strong drink : but avarice, as is common in like cases, always got the better of its opponent; for, though he was often intoxicated, it was never, I believe, at his own expense. As has been said of one in a more exalted station, he would take any *given* quantity. I have heard a story of him which is worth the telling. One summer's morn-ing, our Grasmere curate, after a night's carouse in the vale of Langdale, on his return home, hav-ing reached a point near which the whole of the vale of Grasmere might be seen with the lake immediately below him, stepped aside and sat down on the turf. After looking for some time at the landscape, then in the perfection of its morning beauty, he exclaimed — " Good God, that I should have led so long such a life in such a place ! "—This no doubt was deeply felt by him at the time, but I am not authorized to say that any noticeable amendment followed. Penurious-ness strengthened upon him as his body grew feebler with age. He had purchased property and kept some land in his own hands, but he could not find in his heart to lay out the neces-sary hire for laborers at the proper season, and consequently he has often been seen in half-dotage working his hay in the month of Novem-ber by moonlight, a melancholy sight which I myself have witnessed. Notwithstanding all that has been said, this man, on account of his talents and superior education, was looked up to by his parishioners, who, without a single exception, lived at that time (and most of them upon their own small inheritances) in a state of republican equality, a condition favorable to the growth of kindly feelings among them, and in a striking degree exclusive to temptations to gross vice and scandalous behavior. As a pastor their curate did little or nothing for them; but what could more strikingly set forth the efficacy of the Church of England through its Ordinances and Liturgy than that, in spite of the unworthiness of the minister, his church was regularly attended; and, though there was not much appearance in his flock of what might be called animated piety, intoxication was rare, and dissolute morals unknown? With the Bible they were for the most part well acquainted; and, as was strikingly shown when they were under affliction, must have been supported and comforted by habitual belief in those truths which it is the aim of the Church to inculcate. — *Loughrigg Tarn.* This beautiful pool and the surrounding scene are minutely described in my little Book on the Lakes. Sir G. H. Beaumont, in the earlier part of his life, was induced, by his love of nature and the art of painting, to take up his abode at Old Brathay, about three miles from this spot, so that he must have seen it under many aspects; and he was so much pleased with it that he purchased the Tarn with a view to build, near it, such a residence as is alluded to in this Epistle. Baronets and knights were not so common in that day as now, and Sir Michael le Fleming, not liking to have a rival in that kind of distinction so near him, claimed a sort of lordship over the territory, and showed dispositions little in unison with those of Sir G. Beaumont, who was eminently a lover of peace. The project of building was in consequence given up, Sir George retaining possession of the Tarn. Many years afterwards a Kendal tradesman born upon its banks applied to me for the purchase of it, and accordingly it was sold for the sum that had been given for it, and the money was laid out under my direction upon a substantial oak fence for a certain number of yew trees to be planted in Grasmere churchyard; two were planted in each enclosure, with a view to remove, after a certain time, the one which throve the least. After several years, the stouter plant being left, the others were taken up and placed in other parts of the same churchyard, and were adequately fenced at the expense and under the care of the late Mr. Barber, Mr. Greenwood, and myself: the whole eight are now thriving, and are already an ornament to a place which, during late years, has lost much of its rustic simplicity by the introduction of iron palisades to fence off family burying-grounds, and by numerous monuments, some of them in very bad taste; from which this place of burial was in my memory quite free. See the lines in the sixth book of the "Excursion" beginning —"Green is the churchyard, beautiful and green." The "Epistle" to which these notes refer, though written so far

back as 1804, was carefully revised so late as 1842, previous to its publication. I am loth to add, that it was never seen by the person to whom it is addressed. So sensible am I of the deficiencies in all that I write, and so far does everything that I attempt fall short of what I wish it to be, that even private publication, if such a term may be allowed, requires more resolution than I can command. I have written to give vent to my own mind, and not without hope that, some time or other, kindred minds might benefit by my labors: but I am inclined to believe I should never have ventured to send forth any verses of mine to the world if it had not been done on the pressure of personal occasions. Had I been a rich man, my productions, like this "Epistle," the tragedy of the "Borderers," etc., would most likely have been confined to manuscript.

FAR from our home by Grasmere's quiet
    Lake,
From the Vale's peace which all her fields
    partake,
Here on the bleakest point of Cumbria's
    shore
We sojourn stunned by Ocean's ceaseless
    roar;
While, day by day, grim neighbor! huge
    Black Comb
Frowns deepening visibly his native
    gloom,
Unless, perchance rejecting in despite
What on the Plain *we* have of warmth
    and light,
In his own storms he hides himself from
    sight.
Rough is the time; and thoughts, that
    would be free
From heaviness, oft fly, dear Friend, to
    thee;
Turn from a spot where neither sheltered
    road
Nor hedge-row screen invites my steps
    abroad;
Where one poor Plane-tree, having as it
    might
Attained a stature twice a tall man's
    height,
Hopeless of further growth, and brown
    and sere
Through half the summer, stands with
    top cut sheer,
Like an unshifting weathercock which
    proves

How cold the quarter that the wind best
    loves,
Or like a Centinel that, evermore
Darkening the window, ill defends the
    door
Of this unfinished house — a Fortress
    bare,
Where strength has been the Builder's
    only care;
Whose rugged walls may still for years
    demand
The final polish of the Plasterer's hand.
— This Dwelling's Inmate more than
    three weeks space
And oft a Prisoner in the cheerless place,
I — of whose touch the fiddle would com-
    plain,
Whose breath would labor at the flute in
    vain,
In music all unversed, nor blessed with
    skill
A bridge to copy, or to paint a mill,
Tired of my books, a scanty company!
And tired of listening to the boisterous
    sea —
Pace between door and window mutter-
    ing rhyme,
An old resource to cheat a froward time!
Though these dull hours (mine is it, or
    their shame?)
Would tempt me to renounce that humble
    aim.
— But if there be a Muse who, free to take
Her seat upon Olympus, doth forsake
Those heights (like Phœbus when his gol-
    den locks
He veiled, attendant on Thessalian flocks)
And, in disguise, a Milkmaid with her pail
Trips down the pathways of some wind-
    ing dale:
Or, like a Mermaid, warbles on the shores
To fishers mending nets beside their doors;
Or, Pilgrim-like, on forest moss reclined,
Gives plaintive ditties to the heedless
    wind,
Or listens to its play among the boughs
Above her head and so forgets her vows —
If such a Visitant of Earth there be
And she would deign this day to smile on
    me
And aid my verse, content with local
    bounds
Of natural beauty and life's daily rounds,

Thoughts, chances, sights, or doings,
    which we tell
Without reserve to those whom we love
    well —
Then haply, Beaumont! words in current
    clear
Will flow, and on a welcome page appear
Duly before thy sight, unless they perish
    here.
    What shall I treat of? News from
    Mona's Isle?
Such have we, but unvaried in its style;
No tales of Runagates fresh landed,
    whence
And wherefore fugitive or on what pre-
    tence;
Of feasts, or scandal, eddying like the
    wind
Most restlessly alive when most confined.
Ask not of me, whose tongue can best
    appease
The mighty tumults of the HOUSE OF
    KEYS;
The last year's cup whose Ram or Heifer
    gained,
What slopes are planted, or what mosses
    drained:
An eye of fancy only can I cast
On that proud pageant now at hand or
    past,
When full five hundred boats in trim array,
With nets and sails outspread and stream-
    ers gay,
And chanted hymns and stiller voice of
    prayer,
For the old Manx-harvest to the Deep re-
    pair,
Soon as the herring-shoals at distance
    shine
Like beds of moonlight shifting on the
    brine.
    Mona from our Abode is daily seen,
But with a wilderness of waves between;
And by conjecture only can we speak
Of aught transacted there in bay or creek;
No tidings reach us thence from town or
    field,
Only faint news her mountain sunbeams
    yield,
And some we gather from the misty air,
And some the hovering clouds, our tele-
    graph, declare.
But these poetic mysteries I withhold;

For Fancy hath her fits both hot and cold,
And should the colder fit with You be on
When You might read, my credit would
be gone.
Let more substantial themes the pen
engage,
And nearer interests culled from the open-
ing stage
Of our migration. — Ere the welcome
dawn
Had from the east her silver star with-
drawn,
The Wain stood ready, at our Cottage-
door,
Thoughtfully freighted with a various
store;
And long or ere the uprising of the Sun
O'er dew-damped dust our journey was
begun,
A needful journey, under favoring skies,
Through peopled Vales; yet something
in the guise
Of those old Patriarchs when from well
to well
They roamed through Wastes where now
the tented Arabs dwell.
Say first, to whom did we the charge
confide,
Who promptly undertook the Wain to
guide
Up many a sharply-twining road and
down,
And over many a wide hill's craggy crown,
Through the quick turns of many a hol-
low nook,
And the rough bed of many an un-
bridged brook?
A blooming Lass — who in her better
hand
Bore a light switch, her sceptre of com-
mand
When, yet a slender Girl, she often led,
Skilful and bold, the horse and burthened
sled [1]
From the peat-yielding Moss on Gowdar's
head.
What could go wrong with such a Chari-
oteer
For goods and chattels, or those Infants
dear,
A Pair who smilingly sate side by side,
Our hope confirming that the salt-sea tide

[1] A local word for sledge.

Whose free embraces we were bound to
seek,
Would their lost strength restore and
freshen the pale cheek?
Such hope did either Parent entertain
Pacing behind along the silent lane.
Blithe hopes and happy musings soon
took flight,
For lo! an uncouth melancholy sight —
On a green bank a creature stood forlorn
Just half protruded to the light of morn,
Its hinder part concealed by hedge-row
thorn.
The Figure called to mind a beast of prey
Stript of its frightful powers by slow decay,
And, though no longer upon rapine bent,
Dim memory keeping of its old intent.
We started, looked again with anxious
eyes,
And in that griesly object recognize
The Curate's Dog — his long-tried friend,
for they,
As well we knew, together had grown
gray.
The Master died, his drooping servant's
grief
Found at the Widow's feet some sad relief;
Yet still he lived in pining discontent,
Sadness which no indulgence could pre-
vent;
Hence whole day wanderings, broken
nightly sleeps
And lonesome watch that out of doors he
keeps;
Not oftentimes, I trust, as we, poor brute!
Espied him on his legs sustained, blank,
mute,
And of all visible motion destitute,
So that the very heaving of his breath
Seemed stopt, though by some other
power than death.
Long as we gazed upon the form and face,
A mild domestic pity kept its place,
Unscared by thronging fancies of strange
hue
That haunted us in spite of what we knew.
Even now I sometimes think of him as lost
In second-sight appearances, or crost
By spectral shapes of guilt, or to the
ground,
On which he stood, by spells unnatural
bound,
Like a gaunt shaggy Porter forced to wait

In days of old romance at Archimago's gate.

Advancing Summer, Nature's law fulfilled,
The choristers in every grove had stilled;
But we, we lacked not music of our own,
For lightsome Fanny had thus early thrown,
Mid the gay prattle of those infant tongues,
Some notes prelusive, from the round of songs
With which, more zealous than the liveliest bird
That in wild Arden's brakes was ever heard,
Her work and her work's partners she can cheer,
The whole day long, and all days of the year.

Thus gladdened from our own dear Vale we pass
And soon approach Diana's Looking-glass!
To Loughrigg-tarn, round clear and bright as heaven,
Such name Italian fancy would have given,
Ere on its banks the few gray cabins rose
That yet disturb not its concealed repose
More than the feeblest wind that idly blows.

Ah, Beaumont! when an opening in the road
Stopped me at once by charm of what it showed,
The encircling region vividly exprest
Within the mirror's depth, a world at rest —
Sky streaked with purple, grove and craggy *bield*,[1]
And the smooth green of many a pendent field,
And, quieted and soothed, a torrent small,
A little daring would-be waterfall,
One chimney smoking and its azure wreath,
Associate all in the calm Pool beneath,
With here and there a faint imperfect gleam
Of water-lilies veiled in misty steam —

[1] A word common in the country, signifying shelter, as in Scotland.

What wonder at this hour of stillness deep,
A shadowy link 'tween wakefulness and sleep,
When Nature's self, amid such blending, seems
To render visible her own soft dreams,
If, mixed with what appeared of rock, lawn, wood,
Fondly embosomed in the tranquil flood,
A glimpse I caught of that Abode, by Thee
Designed to rise in humble privacy,
A lowly Dwelling, here to be outspread,
Like a small Hamlet, with its bashful head
Half hid in native trees. Alas 't is not,
Nor ever was; I sighed, and left the spot
Unconscious of its own untoward lot,
And thought in silence, with regret too keen,
Of unexperienced joys that might have been;
Of neighborhood and intermingling arts,
And golden summer days uniting cheerful hearts.
But time, irrevocable time, is flown.
And let us utter thanks for blessings sown
And reaped — what hath been, and what is, our own.

Not far we travelled ere a shout of glee,
Startling us all, dispersed my reverie;
Such shout as many a sportive echo meeting
Oft-times from Alpine *chalets* sends a greeting.
Whence the blithe hail? behold a Peasant stand
On high, a kerchief waving in her hand!
Not unexpectant that by early day
Our little Band would thrid this mountain way,
Before her cottage on the bright hill-side
She hath advanced with hope to be descried.
Right gladly answering signals we displayed,
Moving along a tract of morning shade,
And vocal wishes sent of like good will
To our kind Friend high on the sunny hill —
Luminous region, fair as if the prime
Were tempting all astir to look aloft or climb;

Only the centre of the shining cot
With door left open makes a gloomy spot,
Emblem of those dark corners sometimes
    found
Within the happiest breast on earthly
    ground.
  Rich prospect left behind of stream
    and vale,
And mountain-tops, a barren ridge we
    scale;
Descend, and reach, in Yewdale's depths,
    a plain
With haycocks studded, striped with yel-
    lowing grain —
An area level as a Lake and spread
Under a rock too steep for man to tread,
Where sheltered from the north and bleak
    north-west
Aloft the Raven hangs a visible nest,
Fearless of all assaults that would her
    brood molest.
Hot sunbeams fill the steaming vale; but
    hark,
At our approach, a jealous watch-dog's
    bark,
Noise that brings forth no liveried Page
    of state,
But the whole household, that our com-
    ing wait.
With Young and Old warm greetings we
    exchange,
And jocund smiles, and toward the lowly
    Grange
Press forward by the teasing dogs un-
    scared.
Entering, we find the morning meal pre-
    pared:
So down we sit, though not till each had
    cast
Pleased looks around the delicate repast—
Rich cream, and snow-white eggs fresh
    from the nest,
With amber honey from the mountain's
    breast;
Strawberries from lane or woodland,
    offering wild
Of children's industry, in hillocks piled;
Cakes for the nonce, and butter fit to lie
Upon a lordly dish; frank hospitality
Where simple art with bounteous nature
    vied,
And cottage comfort shunned not seemly
    pride.

Kind Hostess! Handmaid also of the
    feast,
If thou be lovelier than the kindling East,
Words by thy presence unrestrained may
    speak
Of a perpetual dawn from brow and cheek
Instinct with light whose sweetest prom-
    ise lies,
Never retiring, in thy large dark eyes,
Dark but to every gentle feeling true,
As if their lustre flowed from ether's
    purest blue.
  Let me not ask what tears may have
    been wept
By those bright eyes, what weary vigils
    kept,
Beside that hearth what sighs may have
    been heaved
For wounds inflicted, nor what toil re-
    lieved
By fortitude and patience, and the grace
Of heaven in pity visiting the place.
Not unadvisedly those secret springs
I leave unsearched: enough that memory
    clings,
Here as elsewhere, to notices that make
Their own significance for hearts awake,
To rural incidents, whose genial powers
Filled with delight three summer morn-
    ing hours.
  More could my pen report of grave or
    gay
That through our gypsy travel cheered
    the way;
But, bursting forth above the waves, the
    Sun
Laughs at my pains, and seems to say,
    " Be done."
Yet, Beaumont, thou wilt not, I trust,
    reprove
This humble offering made by Truth to
    Love,
Nor chide the Muse that stooped to break
    a spell
Which might have else been on me yet:—
                              FAREWELL.
1811.   1842.

UPON PERUSING THE FOREGOING EPISTLE
THIRTY YEARS AFTER ITS COMPOSITION.

Soon did the Almighty Giver of all rest
Take those dear young Ones to a fearless
    nest;

And in Death's arms has long reposed
    the Friend
For whom this simple Register was
    penned.
Thanks to the moth that spared it for
    our eyes;
And Strangers even the slighted Scroll
    may prize,
Moved by the touch of kindred sympa-
    thies.
For — save the calm, repentance sheds
    o'er strife
Raised by remembrances of misused life,
The light from past endeavors purely
    willed
And by Heaven's favor happily fulfilled;
Save hope that we, yet bound to Earth,
    may share
The joys of the Departed — what so fair
As blameless pleasure, not without some
    tears,
Reviewed through Love's transparent
    veil of years?
    1841?   1842.

NOTE. — LOUGHRIGG TARN alluded to in the foregoing Epistle, resembles, though much smaller in compass, the Lake Nemi, or *Speculum Dianæ* as it is often called, not only in its clear waters and circular form, and the beauty immediately surrounding it, but also as being overlooked by the eminence of Langdale Pikes as Lake Nemi is by that of Monte Calvo. Since this Epistle was written Loughrigg Tarn has lost much of its beauty by the felling of many natural clumps of wood, relics of the old forest, particularly upon the farm called "The Oaks," so called from the abundance of that tree which grew there.

It is to be regretted, upon public grounds, that Sir George Beaumont did not carry into effect his intention of constructing here a Summer Retreat in the style I have described; as his taste would have set an example how buildings, with all the accommodations modern society requires, might be introduced even into the most secluded parts of this country without injuring their native character.

UPON THE SIGHT OF A BEAUTI-
FUL PICTURE.

PAINTED BY SIR G. H. BEAUMONT, BART.

This was written when we dwelt in the Parsonage at Grasmere. The principal features of the picture are Bredon Hill and Cloud Hill near Coleorton. I shall never forget the happy feeling with which my heart was filled when I was impelled to compose this Sonnet. We resided only two years in this house; and during the last half of the time, which was after this poem had been written, we lost our two children, Thomas and Catharine. Our sorrow upon these events often brought it to my mind, and cast me upon the support to which the last line of it gives expression —

  "The appropriate calm of blest eternity."

It is scarcely necessary to add that we still possess the Picture.

PRAISED be the Art whose subtle power
    could stay
Yon cloud, and fix it in that glorious
    shape;
Nor would permit the thin smoke to
    escape,
Nor those bright sunbeams to forsake
    the day;
Which stopped that band of travellers on
    their way,
Ere they were lost within the shady wood;
And showed the Bark upon the glassy
    flood
Forever anchored in her sheltering bay.
Soul-soothing Art! whom Morning,
    Noontide, Even,
Do serve with all their changeful pa-
    geantry;
Thou, with ambition modest yet sublime,
Here, for the sight of mortal man, hast
    given
To one brief moment caught from fleet-
    ing time
The appropriate calm of blest eternity.
    1811.   1815.

INSCRIPTIONS.

IN THE GROUNDS OF COLEORTON, THE SEAT OF SIR GEORGE BEAUMONT, BART., LEICESTERSHIRE.

In the grounds of Coleorton these verses are engraved on a stone placed near the Tree, which was thriving and spreading when I saw it in the summer of 1841.

THE embowering rose, the acacia, and
    the pine,
Will not unwillingly their place resign;

If but the Cedar thrive that near them
stands,
Planted by Beaumont's and by Words-
worth's hands.
One wooed the silent Art with studious
pains:
These groves have heard the Other's
pensive strains;
Devoted thus, their spirits did unite
By interchange of knowledge and delight.
May Nature's kindliest powers sustain
the Tree,
And Love protect it from all injury!
And when its potent branches, wide out-
thrown,
Darken the brow of this memorial Stone,
Here may some Painter sit in future days,
Some future Poet meditate his lays;
Not mindless of that distant age renowned
When Inspiration hovered o'er this
ground,
The haunt of him who sang how spear
and shield
In civil conflict met on Bosworth-field;
And of that famous Youth, full soon
removed
From earth, perhaps by Shakspeare's
self approved,
Fletcher's Associate, Jonson's Friend
beloved.

1808.   1815.

IN A GARDEN OF SIR GEORGE BEAUMONT, BART.

This Niche is in the sandstone-rock in the
winter-garden at Coleorton, which garden, as has
been elsewhere said, was made under our direction
out of an old unsightly quarry. While the
laborers were at work, Mrs. Wordsworth, my
Sister, and I used to amuse ourselves occasion-
ally in scooping this seat out of the soft stone.
It is of the size, with something of the appearance,
of a Stall in a Cathedral. This inscription is not
engraven, as the former and the two following
are, in the grounds.

OFT is the medal faithful to its trust
When temples, columns, towers, are laid
in dust;
And 't is a common ordinance of fate
That things obscure and small outlive the
great:

Hence, when yon mansion and the flowery
trim
Of this fair garden, and its alleys dim,
And all its stately trees, are passed away,
This little Niche, unconscious of decay,
Perchance may still survive.   And be it
known
That it was scooped within the living
stone, —
Not by the sluggish and ungrateful pains
Of laborer plodding for his daily gains,
But by an industry that wrought in love;
With help from female hands, that proudly
strove
To aid the work, what time these walks
and bowers
Were shaped to cheer dark winter's lonely
hours.

1811.   1815.

WRITTEN AT THE REQUEST OF SIR
GEORGE BEAUMONT, BART., AND IN
HIS NAME, FOR AN URN, PLACED BY
HIM AT THE TERMINATION OF A
NEWLY-PLANTED AVENUE, IN THE
SAME GROUNDS.

YE Lime-trees, ranged before this hal-
lowed Urn,
Shoot forth with lively power at Spring's
return;
And be not slow a stately growth to rear
Of pillars, branching off from year to
year,
Till they have learned to frame a dark-
some aisle; —
That may recall to mind that awful Pile
Where Reynolds, 'mid our country's
noblest dead,
In the last sanctity of fame is laid.
— There, though by right the excelling
Painter sleep
Where Death and Glory a joint sabbath
keep,
Yet not the less his Spirit would hold
dear
Self-hidden praise, and Friendship's pri-
vate tear:
Hence, on my patrimonial grounds, have I
Raised this frail tribute to his memory;
From youth a zealous follower of the Art
That he professed; attached to him in
heart;

Admiring, loving, and with grief and pride
Feeling what England lost when Reynolds died.

1808.   1815.

FOR A SEAT IN THE GROVES OF COLEORTON.

BENEATH yon eastern ridge, the craggy bound,
Rugged and high, of Charnwood's forest ground
Stand yet, but, Stranger! hidden from thy view,
The ivied Ruins of forlorn GRACE DIEU;
Erst a religious House, which day and night
With hymns resounded, and the chanted rite:
And when those rites had ceased, the Spot gave birth
To honorable Men of various worth:
There, on the margin of a streamlet wild,
Did Francis Beaumont sport, an eager child:
There, under shadow of the neighboring rocks,
Sang youthful tales of shepherds and their flocks;
Unconscious prelude to heroic themes,
Heart-breaking tears, and melancholy dreams
Of slighted love, and scorn, and jealous rage,
With which his genius shook the buskined stage.
Communities are lost, and Empires die,
And things of holy use unhallowed lie;
They perish; — but the Intellect can raise,
From airy words alone, a Pile that ne'er decays.

1811.   1815.

SONG FOR THE SPINNING WHEEL.

FOUNDED UPON A BELIEF PREVALENT AMONG THE PASTORAL VALES OF WESTMORELAND.

The belief on which this is founded I have often heard expressed by an old neighbor of Grasmere.

SWIFTLY turn the murmuring wheel!
Night has brought the welcome hour,
When the weary fingers feel
Help, as if from faery power;
Dewy night o'ershades the ground;
Turn the swift wheel round and round!

Now, beneath the starry sky,
Couch the widely-scattered sheep; —
Ply the pleasant labor, ply!
For the spindle, while they sleep,
Runs with speed more smooth and fine,
Gathering up a trustier line.

Short-lived likings may be bred
By a glance from fickle eyes;
But true love is like the thread
Which the kindly wool supplies,
When the flocks are all at rest
Sleeping on the mountain's breast.

1812.   1820.

COMPOSED ON THE EVE OF THE MARRIAGE OF A FRIEND IN THE VALE OF GRASMERE.

WHAT need of clamorous bells, or ribands gay,
These humble nuptials to proclaim or grace?
Angels of love, look down upon the place;
Shed on the chosen vale a sun-bright day!
Yet no proud gladness would the Bride display
Even for such promise: — serious is her face,
Modest her mien; and she, whose thoughts keep pace
With gentleness, in that becoming way
Will thank you.   Faultless does the Maid appear;
No disproportion in her soul, no strife:
But, when the closer view of wedded life
Hath shown that nothing human can be clear
From frailty, for that insight may the Wife
To her indulgent Lord become more dear.

1812.   1815.

WATER-FOWL.

OBSERVED FREQUENTLY OVER THE LAKES
OF RYDAL AND GRASMERE.

" Let me be allowed the aid of verse to describe
the evolutions which these visitants sometimes
perform, on a fine day towards the close of
winter." — *Extract from the Author's Book on
the Lakes.*

MARK how the feathered tenants of the
    flood,
With grace of motion that might scarcely
    seem
Inferior to angelical, prolong
Their curious pastime! shaping in mid air
(And sometimes with ambitious wing that
    soars
High as the level of the mountain-tops)
A circuit ampler than the lake beneath —
Their own domain; but ever, while intent
On tracing and retracing that large round,
Their jubilant activity evolves
Hundreds of curves and circlets, to and
    fro,
Upward and downward, progress intricate
Yet unperplexed, as if one spirit swayed
Their indefatigable flight.   'T is done —
Ten times, or more, I fancied it had
    ceased;
But lo! the vanished company again
Ascending; they approach — I hear their
    wings,
Faint, faint at first; and then an eager
    sound,
Past in a moment — and as faint again!
They tempt the sun to sport amid their
    plumes;
They tempt the water, or the gleaming ice,
To show them a fair image; 't is them-
    selves,
Their own fair forms, upon the glimmer-
    ing plain,
Painted more soft and fair as they descend
Almost to touch; — then up again aloft,
Up with a sally and a flash of speed,
As if they scorned both resting-place and
    rest!

1812.   1827.

VIEW FROM THE TOP OF BLACK COMB.[1]

Mrs. Wordsworth and I, as mentioned in the
"Epistle to Sir G. Beaumont," lived some time
under its shadow.

THIS Height a ministering Angel might
    select:
Far from the summit of BLACK COMB
    (dread name
Derived from clouds and storms!) the
    amplest range
Of unobstructed prospect may be seen
That British ground commands: — low
    dusky tracts;
Where Trent is nursed, far southward!
    Cambrian hills
To the south-west, a multitudinous show;
And, in a line of eye-sight linked with
    these,
The hoary peaks of Scotland that give
    birth
To Tiviot's stream, to Annan, Tweed, and
    Clyde:—
Crowding the quarter whence the sun
    comes forth
Gigantic mountains rough with crags;
    beneath,
Right at the imperial station's western base
Main ocean breaking audibly, and stretched
Far into silent regions blue and pale;—
And visibly engirding Mona's Isle
That, as we left the plain, before our sight
Stood like a lofty mount, uplifting slowly
(Above the convex of the watery globe)
Into clear view the cultured fields that
    streak
Her habitable shores, but now appears
A dwindled object, and submits to lie
At the spectator's feet.—Yon azure ridge,
Is it a perishable cloud?   Or there
Do we behold the line of Erin's coast?
Land sometimes by the roving shepherd-
    swain
(Like the bright confines of another world)

[1] Black Comb stands at the southern extremity
of Cumberland: its base covers a much greater
extent of ground than any other mountain in
those parts; and, from its situation, the summit
commands a more extensive view than any other
point in Britain.

Not doubtfully perceived.—Look home-
ward now !
In depth, in height, in circuit, how serene
The spectacle, how pure !—Of Nature's
works,
In earth, and air, and earth embracing sea,
A revelation infinite it seems;
Display august of man's inheritance,
Of Britain's calm felicity and power !
1813.   1815.

WRITTEN WITH A SLATE PENCIL ON A STONE, ON THE SIDE OF THE MOUNTAIN OF BLACK COMB.

The circumstance alluded to at the conclusion
of these verses was told me by Dr. Satterthwaite,
who was Incumbent of Bootle, a small town at
the foot of Black Comb. He had the particulars
from one of the engineers who was employed in
making trigonometrical surveys of that region.

STAY, bold Adventurer; rest awhile thy
limbs
On this commodious Seat ! for much re-
mains
Of hard ascent before thou reach the top
Of this huge Eminence,— from blackness
named;·
And, to far-travelled storms of sea and
land,
A favorite spot of tournament and war !
But thee may no such boisterous visitants
Molest; may gentle breezes fan thy brow;
And neither cloud conceal, nor misty air
Bedim, the grand terraqueous spectacle,
From centre to circumference, unveiled !
Know, if thou grudge not to prolong thy
rest,
That on the summit whither thou art
bound,
A geographic Laborer pitched his tent,
With books supplied and instruments of
art,

To measure height and distance; lonely
task,
Week after week pursued !— To him was
given
Full many a glimpse (but sparingly be-
stowed
On timid man) of Nature's processes
Upon the exalted hills. He made report
That once, while there he plied his studi-
ous work
Within that canvas Dwelling, colors, lines,
And the whole surface of the outspread
map,
Became invisible: for all around
Had darkness fallen — unthreatened, un-
proclaimed —
As if the golden day itself had been
Extinguished in a moment; total· gloom,
In which he sate alone, with unclosed eyes,
Upon the blinded mountain's silent top !
1813.   1835.

NOVEMBER, 1813.

Now that all hearts are glad, all faces
bright,
Our aged Sovereign sits, to the ebb and
flow
Of states and kingdoms, to their joy or woe,
Insensible. He sits deprived of sight,
And lamentably wrapt in twofold night,
Whom no weak hopes deceived; whose
mind ensued,
Through perilous war, with regal fortitude,
Peace that should claim respect from law-
less Might.
Dread King of Kings, vouchsafe a ray
divine
To his forlorn condition ! let thy grace
Upon his inner soul in mercy shine;
Permit his heart to kindle, and to embrace
(Though it were only for a moment's
space)
The triumphs of this hour; for they are
THINE !
1813.   1815.